TENTH EDITION

Reading Critically, Writing Well

A READER AND GUIDE

D1308412

Rise B. Axelrod
University of California, Riverside

Charles R. Cooper
University of California, San Diego

Alison M. Warriner
California State University, East Bay

Bedford / St. Martin's
Boston • New York

For Bedford/St. Martin's

Senior Developmental Editor: Jane Carter
Senior Production Editor: Jessica Gould
Senior Production Supervisor: Jennifer Peterson
Marketing Manager: Emily Rowin
Editorial Assistant: Leah Rang
Copy Editor: Diana P. George
Indexer: Melanie Belkin
Photo Researcher: Roman Barnes
Art Director: Lucy Krikorian
Text Design: Jerilyn Bockorick
Cover Design: Billy Boardman
Cover Photos: Natural History Museum, Los Angeles, California, view of bicycle sculpture outside, photographer/artist: Dan Bannister; close-up of traffic light, photographer/artist: Rainer Schimpf; Marking for bicycle lane, photographer/artist: Tobias Thomassetti; 1950s turquoise bicycle, photographer/artist: Vito Aluia. All images © Getty Images.
Composition: Graphic World, Inc.
Printing and Binding: RR Donnelley and Sons

President, Bedford/St. Martin's: Denise B. Wydra
Editorial Director, English and Music: Karen S. Henry
Director of Marketing: Karen R. Soeltz
Production Director: Susan W. Brown
Director of Rights and Permissions: Hilary Newman

Manufactured in the United States of America.

8   7   6   5   4   3
f   e   d   c   b   a

For information, write: Bedford/St. Martin's, 75 Arlington Street, Boston, MA 02116 (617-399-4000)

ISBN 978-1-4576-3894-7 (Student Edition)
ISBN 978-1-4576-6228-7 (Instructor's Edition)

Acknowledgments

Preface

Reading Critically, Writing Well helps students learn to read analytically and write effectively for diverse rhetorical situations. It offers an ample selection of contemporary readings on subjects sure to interest students. Hands-on activities give students practice in a range of reading and writing strategies — strategies that enhance comprehension, inspire thoughtful response, stimulate critical inquiry, and foster rhetorical analysis.

With this new edition, *Reading Critically, Writing Well* has been reimagined with today's students in mind, many of whom have limited close reading experience and often find dense academic texts especially challenging to read. For many of these students, there is a disconnect between reading and writing. Without extensive reading experience to develop critical reading skills and an intuitive sense of the rhetorical situation, students now, more than ever, need the kind of instruction and practice that *Reading Critically, Writing Well* offers.

This new edition has three goals:

1. **Less Is More.** Provide a more streamlined reader chock-full of engaging selections and doable activities from which instructors can create their own course.

2. **Show, Don't Tell.** Replace dense explanations with graphic examples and easy-to-use templates that model academic writing patterns.

3. **Learn by Doing.** Offer a variety of hands-on activities that are clear, concrete, and informative.

Here are the core features that scaffold students' learning, features that are either new to this edition or have been updated with these three goals in mind:

AN INSPIRING, YET PRACTICAL
INTRODUCTION

A radically revised Chapter 1 introduces the four essential Academic Habits of Mind that students need to succeed in college:

1. Intellectual curiosity (a questioning frame of mind)
2. Rhetorical sensitivity (understanding the purposes motivating writers and readers and how they work within the constraints of genre and medium)
3. Critical analysis (assessing evidence accurately)
4. Civility (fair-mindedness in the face of contradictory points of view)

These habits of mind, so crucial for success in college, are introduced by a sequence of brief reading selections on the topic of bullying, a topic students know and care about. Each reading selection is accompanied by thought-provoking reading, writing, and discussion activities that engage students in active learning from day one.

ACCESSIBLE, ENGAGING READINGS IN THE
BOOK AND ONLINE IN e-PAGES

Reading Critically, Writing Well includes a great variety of readings — by published as well as student authors — that give instructors flexibility in constructing a course to meet the needs and interests of their students. In addition to the readings in the print book, online e-Pages, a new feature, increase the variety, number, and type of reading selections without adding bulk to or increasing the cost of the book.

More than a third of the reading selections in the book — seventeen of forty-eight — are new. Online, there are eight multimodal professional readings, from Web sites and podcasts to videos and interactive graphics, plus eight more student essays, all available free to students who buy a new book. Selected for their writing quality and level of interest, the readings include pieces by award-winning writers such as Annie Dillard, Brent Staples, and Daniel J. Solove; social critics such as Jenée Desmond-Harris, Gabriel Thompson, Shankar Vedantam, and Malcolm Gladwell; and distinguished professors and researchers such as Deborah Tannen, Amitai Etzioni, Sherry Turkle, and Beth L. Bailey. The new readings engage students with current topics close to their daily lives, such as evaluations of the cult film *Scott Pilgrim vs. the World* and of the *U.S. News* annual "Best Colleges" guide, as well as arguments about digitally mediated communication versus face-to-face conversation, the importance of protecting privacy, and the regulation of energy drinks.

Although the reading selections are organized by genre, the flexibility of *Reading Critically, Writing Well* makes it easy for you to create your own sequence of readings. Chapters 2–9 present eight different kinds of writing familiar to us in our roles as students, citizens, and professionals. They include four expository genres (autobiography, observation, reflection, and explanation of concepts) and four argument genres (evaluation, position paper on a controversial issue, speculation about causes or effects, and proposal to solve a problem). Because every selection (in print and online) is introduced and followed by close reading activities that stimulate discussion and writing, instructors have the flexibility to create their own reading list from the resources in the print book as well as those online in e-Pages.

HANDS-ON ACTIVITIES FOR ACTIVE LEARNING

Throughout *Reading Critically, Writing Well*, students are invited to learn by doing. Because these activities are visually attractive and color-coded, clear and doable, they make it possible for even the most inexperienced readers to complete them and engage in a serious program of active learning.

Activities include the following:

- **New *Before* and *As You Read* questions.**   These questions preceding the reading selections excite interest and lead students to adopt a questioning attitude.
- *Reading for Meaning* **Prompts.**   Following each reading, these prompts provide students with three different kinds of activities to help in understanding and interpreting what they are reading:

   1. **Read to Summarize** activities enhance comprehension, giving students confidence that they can get the main idea of even hard-to-understand texts.
   2. **Read to Respond** activities inspire active engagement, leading students to explore the cultural contexts of the readings as well as their own responses to the readings.
   3. **Read to Analyze Assumptions** activities lead students to think more critically about the beliefs and values implicit in the text's word choices, examples, and assertions and also to examine the bases for their own assumptions as readers.

- *A Special Reading Strategy* **Boxes.**   These boxes demonstrate how to apply additional critical reading strategies that range from annotating, synthesizing, and comparing and contrasting to evaluating the logic of an argument and judging the writer's credibility. These strategies are explained and illustrated in Chapter 10, using an excerpt from Martin Luther King Jr.'s "Letter from Birmingham Jail."
- *Reading Like a Writer* **Activities.**   Following each reading, these activities show how texts work rhetorically in different writing situations to achieve

the writer's purpose by addressing audience expectations and concerns and by recognizing the constraints and possibilities of the genre and medium. Annotated and highlighted example passages are a new feature of this edition, along with templates that show students how to generate their own sentences using the patterns they have analyzed in the readings.

In the e-Pages, you will find additional activities:

- **An auto-graded, multiple-choice comprehension quiz** for every professional reading selection in the print text and in the e-Pages that you can use to check understanding or completion of the reading assignment
- **Summary practice with feedback** for each professional reading in the print text and in the e-Pages that you can use to reinforce the summary skills so many students struggle with
- **Vocabulary quizzes with feedback** for each textual professional reading selection that you can use to check understanding and help students acquire a college-level vocabulary

NEW EMPHASIS ON THE RHETORICAL SITUATION

Students are asked to think about the rhetorical situation as they read texts written by others and write texts of their own. One of the academic habits of mind, sensitivity to the rhetorical situation, is emphasized in this edition to help students understand how context affects reading as well as writing.

FOREGROUNDING THE READING-WRITING CONNECTION

Reading Critically, Writing Well teaches students how to analyze texts and to apply what they have learned to their own writing. Instructors may emphasize writing analytically about the readings or writing rhetorically in the genre they are reading, or they may have students do both kinds of writing. *Reading Critically, Writing Well* provides many opportunities for writing.

- **Writing Analytically.** The Reading for Meaning activities as well as the additional critical reading strategies offer numerous prompts for writing analytically about the readings. Students can begin by writing brief responses to these prompts, and later expand some of them into more fully developed essays. For example, using the Read to Summarize activity, they might compose brief summaries or "gist" statements. The Read to Respond and Read to Analyze Assumptions prompts can generate longer essays. Similarly, the

Chapter 10 reading strategies could be used to assign a written comparison of different readings or a synthesis essay, a reflective essay examining how a reading challenges the readers' beliefs or values, an evaluation of a reading's logic or its use of figurative language, an analysis or a position essay refuting a reading's argument. There are any number of possibilities.

- **Writing Rhetorically.** Students are also given many opportunities to write in the genre they have been reading. Chapters 2–9 each present a different genre or rhetorical situation. Each chapter is framed by two guides — beginning with a Guide to Reading and ending with a Guide to Writing. These guides promote genre awareness and sensitivity to different rhetorical situations, aiding the transfer of skills from one rhetorical situation to another, so that students can learn for themselves how to approach each new writing situation. Scaffolded through example and modeling, the guides teach students to employ in their own writing the genre features and rhetorical strategies they studied in their reading. These guides provide a set of flexible activities designed to help students learn to read a specific kind of writing with a critical eye and write in that genre with a clear purpose for their own readers.

For this new edition, the Guides to Writing have been redesigned to provide even greater flexibility, to reflect the realities of writing in the digital age, to overcome student resistance to invention and revision, and to support a fuller, more developed composing process. Commonsensical and easy to follow, these writing guides teach students to

- assess the rhetorical situation, focusing on their purpose and audience, with special attention to the genre and medium in which they are writing;
- ask probing analytical questions;
- practice finding answers through various kinds of research, including memory search, field research, and traditional source-based research;
- assess the effectiveness of their own writing and the writing of their classmates;
- troubleshoot ways to improve their draft.

In short, the guides to writing help students make their writing thoughtful, clear, organized, and compelling — in a word, effective for the rhetorical situation.

INTENSIVE COVERAGE OF FINDING, EVALUATING, AND CITING SOURCES

Chapters 2–9 highlight Working with Sources activities that illustrate how sources are typically used in the genre, such as integrating quotations from interviews in observational essays and citing statistics in proposals. The newly revised strategies for research and documentation in Chapter 11 provide students with clear, helpful guidelines for researching and evaluating sources, integrating them into their writing, and citing them using the most current MLA and APA styles. With eight different genres, students have an opportunity to practice the full gamut of research strategies, from memory search to the field research methods of observation and interview to library and Internet research.

ACTIVITIES THAT ASK STUDENTS TO REFLECT ON THEIR LEARNING

Research has shown that when students reflect on their learning, they clarify their understanding and remember what they have learned longer. Reflecting also enables students to think critically about what they have learned and how they have learned it. *Reading Critically, Writing Well* provides three opportunities in each chapter for students to reflect on their learning and also to discuss what they have learned with others: Thinking about the Genre, Reviewing What Makes [the Genre] Effective, and Reflecting on What You Have Learned. These activities are placed at important transitions in each chapter, at points when looking back at what they have learned will help students move forward more productively.

ACKNOWLEDGMENTS

We first want to thank our students and colleagues at the University of California, Riverside, and the University of California, San Diego; California State University, East Bay, and California State University, San Bernardino; and the University of Nevada, Reno, who have taught us so much about reading, writing, and teaching.

We also owe a debt of gratitude to the many reviewers who made suggestions for this revision. They include G. Travis Adams, Auburn University; Gary Bays, the University of Akron Wayne College; Siobhan Brownson, Winthrop University; Laurie Buchanan, Clark State Community College; Annalisa Buerke, Northwestern College; S. V. Buffamanti, Niagara County Community College; William Carr, Genesee Community College; Darren DeFrain, Wichita State University; Jacqueline Den Hartog, Northwestern College; Marie Eckstrom, Rio Hondo College; Sarah Gallup, Central Oregon Community College; Sondra Gates, Kirkwood Community College; Billie Hara, the University of Texas — Arlington; Debra Johanyak, the University of Akron Wayne College; Peggy Jolly, the University of Alabama at Birmingham; Daniel Keller, the Ohio State University at Newark; Cecilia Kennedy, Clark State Community College; Bridget Kozlow, North Carolina State University; Elizabeth Langenfeld, Crafton Hills College; Judy Lloyd, Southside Virginia Community College; James Lu, California Baptist University; Marie Mandiak, Genesee Community College; Deborah Miller-Zournas, the University of Akron Wayne College; Ervin Nieves, Kirkwood Community College; Stephen Nowka, Clark State Community College; Tom Pace, John Carroll University; Jessica Parker, Metropolitan State University of Denver; Gwendolynne Reid, North Carolina State University; Leanne Rowley, Central Oregon Community College; Tony Russell, Central Oregon Community College; Betty Spence, Memphis College of Art; Mary Thompson, Sussex County Community College; Chris Tonelli, North Carolina State University; Susan Waldman, Leeward Community College; Lois Williams, the University of Pittsburgh; Stephen Wolcott, Kirkwood Community College; and Georgie Ziff, California State University, East Bay.

We want especially to thank our developmental editor, Jane Carter. This book could not have been written without her insightful criticism, skillful editing, cheerful persistence, and good humor. We also want to thank Joan Feinberg, Karen Henry, Denise Wydra, and Erica Appel for their leadership and support. Our deepest appreciation goes out to Nancy Perry, who has been our mainstay at Bedford/St. Martin's lo these many years; thank you, Nancy, for your wise guidance and kind friendship. We are grateful for Jessica Gould's seamless coordination of the production process, Leah Rang's unstinting efforts throughout the editorial and production processes, Diana George's skillful copy editing, Judy Kiviat and Dorothy Hoffman's careful proofreading, Barbara Hernandez and Roman Barnes's work on permissions and art research, and Emily Rowin's help in marketing.

Rise dedicates this book to two young women whose writing she very much looks forward to reading: Amalia Serenity Axelrod-Delcampo and Sophie Amistad Axelrod-Delcampo.

Alison dedicates this book with love to her family, with special mention of her husband, Jeremiah Hallisey, and her daughter, Dawn Warriner, both of whom respected deadlines and gave daily support.

Rise B. Axelrod
Charles R. Cooper
Alison M. Warriner

YOU GET MORE CHOICES FOR *READING CRITICALLY, WRITING WELL*

Bedford/St. Martin's offers resources and format choices that help you and your students get even more out of the book and your course. To learn more about or order any of the following products, contact your Bedford/St. Martin's sales representative, e-mail sales support (sales_support@bfwpub.com), or visit the Web site at **bedfordstmartins.com/readingcritically/catalog**.

Let Students Choose Their Format

Bedford/St. Martin's offers a range of affordable formats, including the portable, downloadable *Bedford e-Book to Go for Reading Critically, Writing Well* at about half the price of the print book. To order access cards for the *Bedford e-Book to Go*, use ISBN 978-1-4576-4991-2. For details, visit **bedfordstmartins.com /readingcritically/catalog** and click on the formats and packages tab.

Choose the Flexible *Bedford e-Portfolio*

Students can collect, select, and reflect on their coursework and personalize and share their e-Portfolio for any audience. Instructors can provide as much or as little structure as they see fit. Rubrics and learning outcomes can be aligned to student work, so instructors and programs can gather reliable and useful assessment data. Every *Bedford e-Portfolio* comes preloaded with *Portfolio Keeping* and *Portfolio Teaching*, by Nedra Reynolds and Elizabeth Davis. *Bedford e-Portfolio* can be purchased separately or packaged with the print book at a significant discount. An activation code is required. To order *e-Portfolio* with the print book, use ISBN 978-1-4576-8046-5. Visit **bedfordstmartins.com/eportfolio**.

Watch Peer Review Work

Eli Review lets instructors scaffold their assignments in a clearer, more effective way for students — making peer review more visible and teachable. *Eli* can be purchased separately or packaged with the book at a significant discount. An activation code is required. To order *Eli Review* with the print book, use ISBN 978-1-4576-8045-8. Visit **bedfordstmartins.com/eli**.

Select Value Packages

Add value to your course by packaging one of the following resources with *Reading Critically, Writing Well*, Tenth Edition, at a significant discount. To learn more about package options, contact your Bedford/St. Martin's sales representative or visit **bedfordstmartins.com/readingcritically/catalog**.

LearningCurve for Readers and Writers, Bedford/St. Martin's adaptive quizzing program, quickly learns what students already know and helps them practice what they don't yet understand. Gamelike quizzing motivates students to engage with their course, and reporting tools help teachers discern their students' needs. An activation code is required. To order LearningCurve packaged with the print book, use ISBN 978-1-4576-8047-2. For details, visit **bedfordstmartins.com /englishlearningcurve**.

VideoCentral is a growing collection of videos for the writing class that captures real-world, academic, and student writers talking about how and why they write. Writer and teacher Peter Berkow interviewed hundreds of people — from Michael Moore to Cynthia Selfe — to produce more than 140 brief videos about topics such as revising and getting feedback. VideoCentral can be packaged with *Reading Critically, Writing Well*, Tenth Edition, at a significant discount. An activation code is required. To order VideoCentral packaged with the print book, use ISBN 978-1-4576-8050-2.

i-series presents multimedia tutorials in a flexible format—because there are things you can't do in a book.

- *ix visualizing composition 2.0* (available online) helps students put into practice key rhetorical and visual concepts. To order *ix visualizing composition* packaged with the print book, use ISBN 978-1-4576-8049-6.
- *i-claim: visualizing argument* (available online) offers a new way to see argument — with six multimedia tutorials, an illustrated glossary, and a wide array of multimedia arguments. To order *i-claim: visualizing argument* packaged with the print book, use ISBN 978-1-4576-8048-9.

***Portfolio Keeping*, Third Edition, by Nedra Reynolds and Elizabeth Davis** provides all the information students need to use the portfolio method successfully in a writing course. *Portfolio Teaching*, a companion guide for instructors, provides the practical information instructors and writing-program administrators need to use the portfolio method successfully in a writing course. To order *Portfolio Keeping* packaged with the print book, use ISBN 978-1-4576-8051-9.

Try *Re:Writing 2* for Fun

What's the fun of teaching writing if you can't try something new? The best collection of free writing resources on the Web, *Re:Writing 2* gives you and your students even more ways to think, watch, practice, and learn about writing concepts. Listen to Nancy Sommers on using a teacher's comments to revise. Try a logic puzzle. Consult our resources for writing centers. All free for the fun of trying it. Visit **bedfordstmartins.com/rewriting**.

Instructor Resources

bedfordstmartins.com/readingcritically/catalog
You have a lot to do in your course. Bedford/St. Martin's wants to make it easy for you to find the support you need — and to get it quickly.

***Instructor's Manual for Reading Critically, Writing Well*, Tenth Edition,** is available in PDF that can be downloaded from the Bedford/St. Martin's online catalog. The instructor's manual includes detailed plans for every chapter in the book; discussion of every reading, both in the print book and in the e-Pages; strategies for teaching with *Reading Critically, Writing Well*; and more.

TeachingCentral offers the entire list of Bedford/St. Martin's print and online professional resources in one place. You'll find landmark reference works, sourcebooks on pedagogical issues, award-winning collections, and practical advice for the classroom — all free for instructors.

Bits (**bedfordbits.com**) collects creative ideas for teaching a range of composition topics in an easily searchable blog format. A community of teachers — leading scholars, authors, and editors — discusses revision, research, grammar and style, technology, peer review, and much more. Take, use, adapt, and pass the ideas around. Then, come back to the site to comment or share your own suggestions.

Bedford Coursepacks (**bedfordstmartins.com/coursepacks**) for the most common course management systems — Blackboard, Angel, Desire2Learn, WebCT, Moodle, or Sakai — allow you to easily download digital materials from Bedford/ St. Martin's for your course.

Contents

Preface   iii

Using the Special Reading Strategies   xxix

1 ACADEMIC HABITS OF MIND: FROM READING CRITICALLY TO WRITING WELL   1

■ **ACTIVITY 1**   **2**

JOINING THE ACADEMIC CONVERSATION   2

■ **ACTIVITY 2**   **9**

■ **ACTIVITY 3**   **13**

FROM READING CRITICALLY TO WRITING WELL   13

THE WRITING PROCESS   14

■ **ACTIVITY 4**   **15**

■ **ACTIVITY 5**   **16**

■ **ACTIVITY 6**   **19**

2 AUTOBIOGRAPHY   20

Rhetorical Situations for Autobiographies   20

■ **THINKING ABOUT THE GENRE: Autobiography**   **21**

For readings and quizzes that go beyond the printed page, see
bedfordstmartins.com/readingcritically.

A GUIDE TO READING AUTOBIOGRAPHY   22

Annie Dillard, *An American Childhood*   22
A celebrated essayist remembers, with strange affection, a childhood prank and its scary consequences.

Reading for Meaning   26

Reading Like a Writer   27

READINGS   32

Tom Ruprecht, *In Too Deep*   32
An Emmy-nominated writer for his work on the Late Show with David Letterman, *Ruprecht uses humor to explore an ill-advised attempt to look good in the eyes of others.*

Saira Shah, *Longing to Belong*   37
An award-winning journalist and documentary filmmaker recounts how events forced her to recognize the naïveté of her fairy-tale vision of her homeland.

■ **A SPECIAL READING STRATEGY: Comparing and Contrasting Related Readings   41**

Jenée Desmond-Harris, *Tupac and My Non-Thug Life*   42
A prominent writer and Harvard Law graduate, Desmond-Harris reflects on the effect that the death of rapper Tupac Shakur had on her and the formation of her identity.

■ **ANALYZING VISUALS   48**

Brad Benioff, *Rick (Student Essay)*   49
A first-year composition student looks back at his complex relationship with a demanding, sometimes abusive, high-school coach.

Shannon Lewis, *We Were There (Student Essay)* :e:
A student writer recalls taking her children on a trip through historic Philadelphia that retraces a trip she took with her father as a teenager.

Kate Beaton, *Treasure* :e:
In this graphic memoir, a woman digs up a jar she buried in the backyard as a child, implying a newfound appreciation for her younger self's take on the world.

■ **REVIEWING WHAT MAKES AUTOBIOGRAPHY EFFECTIVE   54**

bedfordstmartins.com/readingcritically

A GUIDE TO WRITING AUTOBIOGRAPHY   55

■ THE WRITING ASSIGNMENT   55

Writing a Draft: Invention, Planning, and Composing   55

Evaluating the Draft: Getting a Constructive Critical Reading   62

Reading a Draft Critically   62

Improving the Draft: Revising, Editing, and Proofreading   63

■ REFLECTING ON WHAT YOU HAVE LEARNED: Autobiography   66

3 OBSERVATION   68

Rhetorical Situations for Observations   68

■ THINKING ABOUT THE GENRE: Observation   69

A GUIDE TO READING OBSERVATIONS   70

The *New Yorker, Soup*   71
A magazine writer profiles a restaurateur — a temperamental master of the art of soup making — along with his tiny storefront establishment.

Reading for Meaning   74

Reading Like a Writer   75

READINGS   80

John T. Edge, *I'm Not Leaving Until I Eat This Thing*   80
Daring himself to eat a food that makes him queasy, an expert on Southern food observes a factory that processes and bottles pig lips.

■ ANALYZING VISUALS   86

■ A SPECIAL READING STRATEGY: Comparing and Contrasting Related Readings   87

Gabriel Thompson, *A Gringo in the Lettuce Fields*   89
A prolific writer and community organizer, Thompson writes about the skill and endurance required of fieldwork that he experienced firsthand.

Peggy Orenstein, *The Daily Grind: Lessons in the Hidden Curriculum* **96**
An investigative reporter profiles an eighth-grade math class, revealing how gender affects students' interactions with one another and with their teacher.

■ **A SPECIAL READING STRATEGY: Looking for Patterns of Opposition   102**

Brian Cable, *The Last Stop (Student Essay)*   **104**
A first-year composition student observes the unfamiliar world of the mortuary, ending up in the embalming room, which he leaves only after placing his finger on the firm, cold skin of a dead body.

Brianne O'Leary, *Fatty's Custom Tattooz and Body Piercing (Student Essay)*   e
A first-year composition student observes a tattoo parlor, along with its customers and idiosyncratic owner and tattoo artist.

Sarah Kate Kramer/WNYC, *Niche Market: Fountain Pen Hospital*   e
For the Web site of a local public radio station, Kramer profiles a store in New York City that exists solely to repair and sell fountain pens.

■ **REVIEWING WHAT MAKES OBSERVATION EFFECTIVE   111**

A GUIDE TO WRITING OBSERVATIONAL ESSAYS   112

■ **THE WRITING ASSIGNMENT   112**

Writing a Draft: Invention, Planning, and Composing   112

■ **WORKING WITH SOURCES: Integrating Quotations from Interviews   116**

Evaluating the Draft: Getting a Constructive Critical Reading   123

Reading a Draft Critically   123

Improving the Draft: Revising, Editing, and Proofreading   125

■ **REFLECTING ON WHAT YOU HAVE LEARNED: Observation   128**

4 REFLECTION   129

Rhetorical Situations for Reflections   130

■ **THINKING ABOUT THE GENRE: Reflection   130**

e bedfordstmartins.com/readingcritically

A GUIDE TO READING REFLECTIVE ESSAYS　131

Brent Staples, *Black Men and Public Space*　132
An African American member of the New York Times *editorial board notes how his presence on a city street triggers defensive reactions in white passersby and addresses the "alienation that comes of being ever the suspect."*

Reading for Meaning　135

Reading Like a Writer　136

■ **A SPECIAL READING STRATEGY: Comparing and Contrasting Related Readings　140**

READINGS　143

Dana Jennings, *Our Scars Tell the Stories of Our Lives*　143
A newspaper columnist ponders the significance of his scars and the stories they tell.

■ **A SPECIAL READING STRATEGY: Exploring the Significance of Figurative Language　147**

Dan Zevin, *Father Shops Best*　149
An essayist known for his humor reflects on a shopping trip with his father and what it showed him about their relationship.

■ **ANALYZING VISUALS**　155

Rob Walker, *Replacement Therapy: Why Our Gadgets Can't Wear Out Fast Enough*　156
A prolific journalist speculates that we are secretly glad to have excuses to replace our quickly outdated technology — and this might be one of the reasons why technology becomes outdated so quickly.

Katherine Haines, *Whose Body Is This? (Student Essay)*　161
A first-year composition student considers society's obsession with the perfect body — especially the perfect female body — and the negative pressures this obsession creates.

Wendy Lee, *Peeling Bananas (Student Essay)*　　e
A Chinese American high-school student contemplates the positive and negative aspects of growing up as a "hybrid of two cultures."

Francine Wheeler, *Sandy Hook Victim's Mother Delivers
President Obama's Weekly Address, April 13, 2013* :e:
*The bereaved mother of a boy killed in the Sandy Hook school shooting
reflects on her loss and uses that reflection to persuade Americans to
push for tougher gun laws.*

■ **REVIEWING WHAT MAKES REFLECTION EFFECTIVE** **166**

A GUIDE TO WRITING REFLECTIVE ESSAYS **167**

■ **THE WRITING ASSIGNMENT** **167**

Writing a Draft: Invention, Planning, and Composing   **167**

Evaluating the Draft: Getting a Constructive Critical Reading   **172**

Reading a Draft Critically   **173**

Improving the Draft: Revising, Editing, and Proofreading   **174**

■ **REFLECTING ON WHAT YOU HAVE LEARNED: Reflection** **176**

5 EXPLAINING CONCEPTS   **178**

Rhetorical Situations for Concept Explanations   **178**

■ **THINKING ABOUT THE GENRE: Concept Explanation** **179**

A GUIDE TO READING CONCEPT EXPLANATIONS **180**

Susan Cain, *Shyness: Evolutionary Tactic?* *181*
*A prominent author and journalist explains that shyness, far from being
a debilitating social handicap, actually confers benefits like introspection
and attentiveness.*

Reading for Meaning   **186**

Reading Like a Writer   **187**

READINGS **192**

Deborah Tannen, *Marked Women* *192*
*A linguist explains the linguistic concept of marked forms: "Each of the
women at the conference had to make decisions about hair, clothing,
makeup and accessories, and each decision carried meaning. Every style
available to us was marked."*

:e: bedfordstmartins.com/readingcritically

Beth L. Bailey, *Dating* 201
A sociologist explains the concept of dating and shows how courtship rituals have changed over the years — to the disadvantage of poor men and strong-minded women.

■ **A SPECIAL READING STRATEGY: Synthesizing Information from Sources 209**

Dan Hurley, *Can You Make Yourself Smarter?* 212
A science writer explains fluid intelligence and shows how you just might be able to make yourself smarter.

■ **ANALYZING VISUALS 221**

Linh Kieu Ngo, *Cannibalism: It Still Exists (Student Essay)* 223
A first-year composition student explains the anthropological concept of cannibalism, delineating the three functional categories of survival, dietary, and ritual cannibalism.

Justin Ton, *Hip-Hop You Don't Stop (Student Essay)*
A college student explains the origins and "four pillars" of hip-hop music, detailing its evolution and arguing that it turns young people away from violence and toward positive expression.

Linda Stone, *Continuous Partial Attention*
A high-tech visionary describes continuous partial attention — a phenomenon fostered by the multitasking demanded by our fast-paced, digital culture — and anticipates a reaction against this phenomenon in a longing for engaged attention.

■ **REVIEWING WHAT MAKES CONCEPT EXPLANATIONS EFFECTIVE 229**

A GUIDE TO WRITING ESSAYS EXPLAINING CONCEPTS 230

■ **THE WRITING ASSIGNMENT 230**

Writing a Draft: Invention, Planning, and Composing 230

■ **Considering a Useful Sentence Strategy 238**

Evaluating the Draft: Getting a Constructive Critical Reading 240

Reading a Draft Critically 240

Improving the Draft: Revising, Editing, and Proofreading 241

■ **REFLECTING ON WHAT YOU HAVE LEARNED: Explaining Concepts 244**

bedfordstmartins.com/readingcritically

6 EVALUATION   246

Rhetorical Situations for Evaluations   246

■ THINKING ABOUT THE GENRE: Evaluation   247

A GUIDE TO READING EVALUATIONS   248

Amitai Etzioni, *Working at McDonald's*   249
A respected sociologist argues that after-school jobs at fast-food restaurants are bad for teenagers.

Reading for Meaning   252

Reading Like a Writer   254

READINGS   260

Malcolm Gladwell, *What College Rankings Really Tell Us*   260
An award-winning author explains why consumers aren't getting the full picture when they look to rankings for an assessment of a complicated institution like a college or a university.

■ A SPECIAL READING STRATEGY: Judging the Writer's Credibility   268

Christine Rosen, *The Myth of Multitasking*   270
A prominent writer and commentator on such subjects as bioethics, fundamentalism, feminism, and technology warns that "when people do their work . . . with crumbs of attention rationed out among many competing tasks, their culture may gain in information, but it will surely weaken in wisdom."

■ A SPECIAL READING STRATEGY: Looking for Patterns of Opposition   278

William Akana, Scott Pilgrim vs. the World: *A Hell of a Ride* (Student Essay)   279
A student reviews a favorite film — Scott Pilgrim vs. the World — concluding that it succeeds on the strength of its innovative approach and its humor.

■ ANALYZING VISUALS   286

Christine Romano, *Jessica Statsky's "Children Need to Play, Not Compete": An Evaluation (Student Essay)*   287
A first-year college student applies critical reading skills to another student's essay and comes up with an assertive but carefully balanced evaluation.

bedfordstmartins.com/readingcritically

Brittany Lemus, Requiem for a Dream: *Fantasy versus Reality (Student Essay)* e
A student writer argues that the film Requiem for a Dream *may be initially off-putting but that its memorable characters and central message prove powerful over time.*

Marlon Bishop, *Gig Alert: Bright Eyes* e
Written for the Web site of a local public radio station, this brief online review allows readers to decide for themselves whether the indie rock band Bright Eyes is worth seeing by providing a sound file of one of the band's songs.

■ **REVIEWING WHAT MAKES EVALUATIONS EFFECTIVE   294**

A GUIDE TO WRITING EVALUATIONS   295

■ **THE WRITING ASSIGNMENT   295**

Writing a Draft: Invention, Planning, and Composing   295

■ **WORKING WITH SOURCES: Using Summary to Support Your Evaluative Argument   303**

Evaluating the Draft: Getting a Constructive Critical Reading   305

Reading a Draft Critically   305

Improving the Draft: Revising, Editing, and Proofreading   307

■ **REFLECTING ON WHAT YOU HAVE LEARNED: Evaluation   310**

7 ARGUING FOR A POSITION   312

Rhetorical Situations for Position Arguments   312

■ **THINKING ABOUT THE GENRE: Position Arguments   313**

A GUIDE TO READING ESSAYS ARGUING FOR A POSITION   314

Brian Greene, *Put a Little Science in Your Life*   315
A scientist argues that science is "a way of life" and that to practice and understand it is to undergo a "transformation … that is … one of the most precious of human experiences."

Reading for Meaning   318

Reading Like a Writer   320

READINGS 325

Karen Stabiner, *Boys Here, Girls There: Sure, If Equality's the Goal* 325
A journalist defends the position that single-sex schools benefit girls, especially those in low-income families.

■ A SPECIAL READING STRATEGY: Comparing and Contrasting Related Readings 332

Sherry Turkle, *The Flight from Conversation* 334
An author and professor at MIT argues that our electronic tools are robbing us of opportunities for in-person communication, substituting instead superficial interactions that lack richness and depth.

■ A SPECIAL READING STRATEGY: Reflecting on Challenges to Your Beliefs and Values 340

Daniel J. Solove, *Why Privacy Matters Even If You Have "Nothing to Hide"* 341
A scholar and legal expert argues that invasions of privacy in the name of security harm all of us, even when we have "nothing to hide."

Jessica Statsky, *Children Need to Play, Not Compete* (Student Essay) 349
Documenting the excesses and dangers of competitive sports for children under the age of thirteen, a first-year college student argues for eliminating such programs in favor of programs that "emphasize fitness, cooperation, sportsmanship, and individual performance."

■ ANALYZING VISUALS 356

Tan-Li Hsu, *High on Caffeine: Regulating Energy Drinks* (Student Essay) [e]
Alarmed at the level of caffeine in popular energy drinks, a college student argues that drinks put young people at risk of serious damage to their health and urges marketers to label cans and issue warnings accordingly.

U.S. Department of Transportation/Ad Council, *The "It's Only Another Beer" Black and Tan* [e]
This public service announcement uses the recipe genre to offer good reasons to avoid drinking and driving.

■ REVIEWING WHAT MAKES POSITION ARGUMENTS EFFECTIVE 356

[e] bedfordstmartins.com/readingcritically

A GUIDE TO WRITING POSITION ARGUMENTS 358

■ **THE WRITING ASSIGNMENT** 358

   Writing a Draft: Invention, Planning, and Composing 358

   ■ **WORKING WITH SOURCES: Using Sources to Reinforce Your Credibility** 365

   Evaluating the Draft: Getting a Constructive Critical Reading 368

   Reading a Draft Critically 368

   Improving the Draft: Revising, Editing, and Proofreading 370

■ **REFLECTING ON WHAT YOU HAVE LEARNED: Arguing for a Position** 373

8 SPECULATING ABOUT CAUSES OR EFFECTS   375

   Rhetorical Situations for Speculating about Causes or Effects 375

■ **THINKING ABOUT THE GENRE: Speculations about Causes or Effects** 376

A GUIDE TO READING ESSAYS SPECULATING ABOUT CAUSES OR EFFECTS 377

   Stephen King, *Why We Crave Horror Movies* 378
   America's best-known writer of horror novels and film scripts speculates about why we continue "daring the nightmare."

   Reading for Meaning 380

   Reading Like a Writer 382

READINGS 385

   Claudia Wallis, *The Multitasking Generation* 385
   Questioning the idea that multitasking saves time, a writer and editor at Time *magazine presents evidence that, for "Generation M" at least, multitasking has possibly alarming consequences.*

   ■ **A SPECIAL READING STRATEGY: Comparing and Contrasting Related Readings** 399

Shankar Vedantam, *The Telescope Effect*   400
*An award-winning journalist speculates about why people were
generous to one lone dog but often ignore tragedy on a massive scale.*

Nicholas Carr, *Is Google Making Us Stupid?*   408
*An author and professional speaker wonders whether technology is
changing our brains and the way we think, impairing our ability to
concentrate, focus, and do research.*

■ **ANALYZING VISUALS   417**

**Sheila McClain, *Fitness Culture: A Growing Trend in America*
(Student Essay)   418**
*A first-year composition student speculates about the reasons for the
growing popularity of fitness clubs.*

Michelle Cox, *The Truth about Lying (Student Essay)*   [e]
*A student investigates the motivations for lying, backing up her
assertions with findings from psychologists and other observers.*

On the Media, *The Reel Sounds of Violence*   [e]
*A podcast from this National Public Radio show explores the trend of
"sound inflation" in violent movies.*

■ **A SPECIAL READING STRATEGY: Evaluating the Logic of an
Argument   424**

■ **REVIEWING WHAT MAKES SPECULATIVE ARGUMENTS EFFECTIVE   425**

**A GUIDE TO WRITING ESSAYS SPECULATING ABOUT
CAUSES OR EFFECTS   426**

■ **THE WRITING ASSIGNMENT   426**

Writing a Draft: Invention, Planning, and Composing   426

■ **WORKING WITH SOURCES: Citing a Variety of Sources   433**

■ **CONSIDERING A USEFUL SENTENCE STRATEGY   437**

Evaluating the Draft: Getting a Constructive Critical Reading   438

Reading a Draft Critically   438

Improving the Draft: Revising, Editing, and Proofreading   440

■ **REFLECTING ON WHAT YOU HAVE LEARNED: Speculating about Causes
or Effects   443**

[e] bedfordstmartins.com/readingcritically

9 PROPOSAL TO SOLVE A PROBLEM   445

Rhetorical Situations for Proposals   445

■ THINKING ABOUT THE GENRE: Proposals   446

A GUIDE TO READING PROPOSALS   447

David Bornstein, *Fighting Bullying with Babies*   447
An award-winning author and blogger proposes an effective way to get
children to stop bullying one another: spend time with a baby.

Reading for Meaning   452

Reading Like a Writer   454

■ A SPECIAL READING STRATEGY: Comparing and Contrasting
   Related Readings   457

■ ANALYZING VISUALS   458

READINGS   459

William F. Shughart II, *Why Not a Football Degree?*   459
Impatient with "half-measures" that have been adopted or proposed
to try to reform college sports, an economics professor recommends a
three-pronged solution that treats the issue as a business proposition.

**Kelly D. Brownell and Thomas R. Frieden, *Ounces of
Prevention — The Public Policy Case for Taxes on Sugared
Beverages*   466**
A professor of psychology and a physician argue that taxing sugared
beverages is one effective way to combat the national obesity epidemic.

Karen Kornbluh, *Win-Win Flexibility*   474
An economist and political activist proposes a solution to problems
faced by the new "juggler family" in which parents have trouble
balancing time between working and caring for their children and
elderly parents.

■ A SPECIAL READING STRATEGY: Recognizing Emotional
   Manipulation   482

**Patrick O'Malley, *More Testing, More Learning*
(Student Essay)   483**
In a strongly reasoned message to professors on his campus, a first-year
student advocates an increase in testing throughout the academic term.

bedfordstmartins.com/readingcritically

Molly Coleman, *Missing the Fun (Student Essay)* 🄴
A first-year student proposes blacking out dates for sporting events that conflict with major social occasions at school, so student-athletes don't have to miss out.

Phoebe Sweet and Zach Wise, *The Problem with Lawns: The Transforming Landscape of Las Vegas* 🄴
Two local journalists produced this video capturing the strategies the Las Vegas Water Department has used to keep this city in the desert alive.

■ REVIEWING WHAT MAKES PROPOSALS EFFECTIVE   490

A GUIDE TO WRITING PROPOSALS   491

■ THE WRITING ASSIGNMENT   491

Writing a Draft: Invention, Planning, and Composing   491

■ WORKING WITH SOURCES: Citing Statistics to Establish the Problem's Existence and Seriousness   498

■ CONSIDERING A USEFUL SENTENCE STRATEGY   501

Evaluating the Draft: Getting a Constructive Critical Reading   501

Reading a Draft Critically   502

Improving the Draft: Revising, Editing, and Proofreading   503

■ REFLECTING ON WHAT YOU HAVE LEARNED: Proposal to Solve a Problem   505

10 A CATALOG OF READING STRATEGIES   507

Annotating   508

Martin Luther King Jr., *An Annotated Sample from "Letter from Birmingham Jail"*   509

Taking Inventory   515

Outlining   515

Summarizing   518

Paraphrasing   519

🄴 bedfordstmartins.com/readingcritically

Synthesizing   520

Contextualizing   522

Exploring the Significance of Figurative Language   523

Looking for Patterns of Opposition   525

Reflecting on Challenges to Your Beliefs and Values   526

Comparing and Contrasting Related Readings   527

Lewis H. Van Dusen Jr., *Legitimate Pressures and Illegitimate Results*   **528**

Evaluating the Logic of an Argument   530

Recognizing Logical Fallacies   532

Recognizing Emotional Manipulation   536

Judging the Writer's Credibility   537

11 STRATEGIES FOR RESEARCH AND DOCUMENTATION   539

PLANNING A RESEARCH PROJECT   539

Analyzing Your Rhetorical Situation and Setting a Schedule   542

Choosing a Topic and Getting an Overview   542

Narrowing Your Topic and Drafting Research Questions   544

Establishing a Research Log   544

Creating a Working Bibliography   544

Annotating Your Working Bibliography   546

Taking Notes on Your Sources   547

FINDING SOURCES   548

Searching Library Catalogs and Databases   548

Searching for Government Documents and Statistical Information Online   551

Searching for Web Sites and Interactive Sources   551

CONDUCTING FIELD RESEARCH   555

Conducting Observational Studies   555

Conducting Interviews   557

Conducting Surveys   559

EVALUATING SOURCES   563

Choosing Relevant Sources   563

Choosing Reliable Sources   564

USING SOURCES TO SUPPORT YOUR IDEAS   569

Synthesizing Sources   569

Acknowledging Sources and Avoiding Plagiarism   570

Using Information from Sources to Support Your Claims   571

CITING AND DOCUMENTING SOURCES IN MLA STYLE   581

Using In-Text Citations to Show Where You Have Used Source Material   581

Creating a List of Works Cited   586

CITING AND DOCUMENTING SOURCES IN APA STYLE   599

Using In-Text Citations to Show Where You Have Used Source Material   599

Creating a List of References   601

12 STRATEGIES FOR ANALYZING VISUALS   609

Criteria for Analyzing Visuals   610

■ CRITERIA FOR ANALYZING VISUALS   611

A Sample Analysis   613

■ PAUL TAYLOR'S ANALYSIS OF *EMERGING MAN*   615

Paul Taylor, *The Rising (Student Essay)*   618

Index to Methods of Development   625

Index of Authors, Titles, and Terms   629

 bedfordstmartins.com/readingcritically

Using the Special Reading Strategies

Special Reading Strategy boxes throughout the text ask students to analyze one or more readings in the chapter using one of the reading strategies that appear in Chapter 10. Below, the page number in parentheses indicates the first page of the reading; the boldface number at the end indicates the first page of the activity. In addition, e-Page selections that work well with the reading strategy are listed in parentheses following the readings in the printed text.

Comparing and Contrasting Related Readings: Saira Shah's *Longing to Belong* (p. 37) and Jenée Desmond-Harris's *Tupac and My Non-Thug Life* (p. 42) (Kate Beaton, *Treasure*, e) **41**

Comparing and Contrasting Related Readings: The *New Yorker*'s *Soup* (p. 71) and John T. Edge's *I'm Not Leaving Until I Eat This Thing* (p. 80) **87**

Looking for Patterns of Opposition: Peggy Orenstein's *The Daily Grind: Lessons in the Hidden Curriculum* (p. 96) **102**

Comparing and Contrasting Related Readings: Brent Staples's *Black Men and Public Space* (p. 132) and an excerpt from Staples's autobiography, *Parallel Time* (p. 140) **140**

Exploring the Significance of Figurative Language: Dana Jennings's *Our Scars Tell the Stories of Our Lives* (p. 143) **147**

Synthesizing Information from Sources: Beth L. Bailey's *Dating* (p. 201) (Justin Ton, *Hip Hop You Don't Stop*, e) **209**

Judging the Writer's Credibility: Malcolm Gladwell's *What College Rankings Really Tell Us* (p. 260) (*On the Media*, *The Reel Sounds of Violence*, e) **268**

Looking for Patterns of Opposition: Christine Rosen's *The Myth of Multitasking* (p. 270)   **278**

Comparing and Contrasting Related Readings: Peggy Orenstein's *The Daily Grind: Lessons in the Hidden Curriculum* (p. 96) and Karen Stabiner's *Boys Here, Girls There: Sure, If Equality's the Goal* (p. 325)   **332**

Reflecting on Challenges to Your Beliefs and Values: Sherry Turkle's *The Flight from Conversation* (p. 334) (Phoebe Sweet and Zach Wise, *The Problem with Lawns: The Transforming Landscape of Las Vegas,* e)   **340**

Comparing and Contrasting Related Readings: Claudia Wallis's *The Multitasking Generation* (p. 385) and Sherry Turkle's *The Flight from Conversation* (p. 334) (Linda Stone, *Continuous Partial Attention,* e)   **399**

Evaluating the Logic of an Argument: Sheila McClain's *Fitness Culture: A Growing Trend in America* (p. 418) (U.S. Department of Transportation/ Ad Council, *The "It's Only Another Beer" Black and Tan,* e)   **424**

Comparing and Contrasting Related Readings: David Bornstein's *Fighting Bullying with Babies* (p. 477) and Excerpts on Bullying from Chapter 1 (pp. 3, 6, 7, 10, 11)   **457**

Recognizing Emotional Manipulation: Karen Kornbluh's *Win-Win Flexibility* (p. 474) (Francine Wheeler, *Sandy Hook Victim's Mother Delivers President Obama's Weekly Address, April 13, 2013,* e)   **482**

Academic Habits of Mind: From Reading Critically to Writing Well

Imagine yourself on a journey to a part of your country where you have never been. You already know the language and have some background in common with the people, but some of the traditions, customs, and laws are different from what you're accustomed to. When you arrive, you are immersed in a new job with people you haven't met before, but you are expected to know the lay of the land and the rules, including how to communicate, how to produce the products the job involves, and how to deal with difficulties.

This new place is college. Sure, you've been through high school, and you've been accepted into college, so you have what it takes to do well in your courses. But the world of college has its own special requirements and demands, and knowing what they are and how to respond to them will help you succeed.

Your professors will assume you already understand what college requires. In fact, a recent survey of college professors revealed that they expect students already to have what are often called *academic habits of mind* — ways of thinking and inquiring that people in college (and often in the world of work) use every day. As the word *habit* suggests, these skills can be acquired through practice. So what are these habits of mind? Here's a list of what we think are the most crucial habits:

- **Curiosity:** The desire to ask provocative questions, generate hypotheses, and respond to others' ideas thoughtfully and enthusiastically

- **Rhetorical sensitivity:** The understanding of the purposes motivating writers and readers, the expectations of the audience, and the constraints of the **genre** and **medium**, including the ability to recognize different genres, or types, of writing (such as laboratory reports and movie reviews) and mediums (print or digital, visual or audio) and know when to use them, as well as to recognize and use vocabulary, grammar, punctuation, and spelling that is appropriate to the purpose, audience, genre, and medium in which you are writing

- **Critical analysis:** The willingness to subject your ideas and those of others to critical analysis and to assess evidence — facts, events, texts — accurately and fairly, including sources that support both your own position and opposing positions

- **Civility:** The ability to treat the ideas of others fairly and respectfully, even when they challenge your own beliefs

Before reading further, consider which habits of mind you already have and which you will need to develop.

ACTIVITY **1**

Exploring Your Habits of Mind

What habits of mind do you already possess as you approach this course? To determine this, think about your high-school study habits or how you mastered a subject, hobby, or technology inside or outside of school. Then write down your answers to the following questions:

- What sparked your interest in the first place?

- What questions did you initially have?

- How did your questions evolve as you learned more?

- How did you go about finding out answers to your questions?

- How did the answers you found lead to further questioning or additional research?

Having looked back on your experience, which habits of mind did you form as you satisfied your curiosity and followed through on your interest? Write down the habits of mind you have acquired; you may see as you read on that you have a head start on the habits expected of college students. At the end of this chapter, you will revisit this activity.

JOINING THE ACADEMIC CONVERSATION

The academic habits of mind we have been discussing are essential to success in all academic areas and disciplines (and most career paths), but these alone are not enough. You may also need to develop skills that will allow you to join the *academic conversation* on issues and concepts important to individual disciplines such as economics or sociology. In your first year or two of college, you will enter a variety of academic conversations by reading textbooks and academic articles in different disciplines and by participating in discussions in class and with your instructor. You might join the conversation in some disciplines for a term or a year; you might join the conversation in your major permanently. As you read this text, you will find references to these conversations and your role in them. The habits of mind we discussed above — developing curiosity and thinking, reading, and writing critically — will allow you to develop the skills you need to join these conversations.

Thinking and Reading Critically: Developing Curiosity

Read the following four passages on bullying in schools.* All of these passages speculate about *causes and effects* (the genre, or type, of readings in Chapter 8). They also

- *assert* (or *claim*) that bullying is a problem,
- *define* bullying, and
- try to determine the *consequences* of bullying.

But each differs in how the authors define the term or what the authors believe the consequences of bullying may be.

As you read the excerpts, ask yourself these questions and write down the answers:

- What are the guiding questions the writers asked themselves as they researched and wrote these texts?
- What questions do you need to ask as a reader to clarify the meaning of each of these passages?

Asking and answering these questions will help you figure out the authors' *perspectives*, as well as what the authors state **explicitly** (or directly), and what they leave **implicit** (implied). Asking questions of the text and the topic, writing notes in the margins, researching answers when you have questions, and figuring out the **assumptions** (underlying beliefs and values) of the author will also help you understand your own perspectives.

We have annotated the first reading to get you started.

1. Ron Banks, "Bullying in Schools"

Writer's question: What does the research tell us about the incidence of bullying and its consequences for the bully?

As established by studies in Scandinavian countries, a strong correlation appears to exist between bullying other students during the school years and experiencing legal or

*A listing of the sources of texts 1–4 can be found at the end of the chapter.

Reader's questions: Is this research reliable—author credible, publication trustworthy, date current? Is Scandinavia comparable to the United States?

Reader's questions: 60 percent sounds like a lot, but is the "criminal conviction" serious? Is there any proof bullying leads to criminal behavior or just a correlation? Any shared causes underlying both bullying and criminal behavior—such as abuse?

Reader's questions: How can we tell who a bully is? How is bullying defined in this research?

Reader's questions: How do the authors know this? Is the situation in Scandinavia the same as in the United States? Why is bullying even allowed in schools? Isn't there something that can help prevent it?

Writer's questions: Are there consequences to being bullied that go beyond the bully and the bullied? Do these traits develop in other people besides those who have been bullied? Do these traits develop in all children who are bullied?

criminal troubles as adults. In one study, 60 percent of those characterized as bullies in grades 6–9 had at least one criminal conviction by age 24 (Olweus 1993). Chronic bullies seem to maintain their behaviors into adulthood, negatively influencing their ability to develop and maintain positive relationships (Oliver, Hoover, and Hazler 1994).

Victims often fear school and consider school to be an unsafe and unhappy place. As many as 7 percent of America's eighth-graders stay home at least once a month because of bullies. The act of being bullied tends to increase some students' isolation because their peers do not want to lose status by associating with them or because they do not want to increase the risks of being bullied themselves. Being bullied leads to depression and low self-esteem, problems that can carry into adulthood (Olweus 1993; Batsche and Knoff 1994).

Note how Banks relies on statistics as evidence to support his assertions. There are many additional strategies writers use to provide evidence, such as the following:

- Narrating a story
- Providing facts and statistics
- Describing
- Illustrating (providing examples)
- Classifying
- Comparing and contrasting
- Reporting causes or effects
- Summarizing or paraphrasing

(See Chapter 5, Explaining Concepts, and Chapter 10, A Catalog of Reading Strategies, for more information about writers' strategies for providing evidence.)

Now take a look at some of the evidence Banks offers and the questions prompted by it:

Is Scandinavia similar enough to the United States that American bullies will have the same rate of criminal conviction? Who is Olweus? Is this source reliable? What's the context of this statistic? Is 7 percent a lot? How many skip to have fun, to avoid a test, etc.?	[I]n Scandinavian countries, . . . 60 percent of those characterized as bullies in grades 6–9 had at least one criminal conviction by age 24 (Olweus 1993). . . . As many as 7 percent of America's eighth-graders stay home at least once a month because of bullies.

The *source* Banks cites — Olweus — is one you could look up and assess for yourself.* (See Chapter 11, Strategies for Research and Documentation.) When considering the statistics Banks provides, consider the context as well: Statistics have little meaning out of context. (See Contextualizing in Chapter 10, A Catalog of Reading Strategies.)

Now read the next excerpt, noting the following:

- The questions the author asks herself

- The assertions (or claims) she makes

- The evidence she supplies to support her assertions/claims

- The assumptions she makes

Keep in mind that the assumptions a writer makes — the ideas and attitudes that he or she takes for granted as commonly accepted truths — may be assumptions of the writer alone or they may reflect the *values* and *beliefs* of a community. They may also reflect the assumptions held by readers or sources cited by the writer. Sometimes the assumptions may be stated explicitly, but often they will only be implied, so you may have to search for the underlying assumptions by analyzing the *tone* or *connotation* of the words the writer chooses or by thinking critically about the examples the writer uses. Ask yourself whose assumption the writer is giving voice to — her or his own, the wider community's, a source's. Here are some additional questions you can ask to bring a writer's assumptions to the surface:

- What are the effects of the assumption, in the context of the essay specifically or in society more generally?

- What do I think about the assumption, and is there anything in the essay that raises doubts about it?

*Olweus, Dan. "A Profile of Bullying at School." *Educational Leadership.* Mar. 2003. *Academic Search Premier.* Web. 14 Feb. 2005.

- How does the assumption reinforce or critique commonly held views, and are there any *alternative ideas, beliefs, or values* that would challenge this assumption?

2. **Tara L. Kuther, "Understanding Bullying"**

   Bullying is not a normal part of growing up. Victims of bullying suffer psychological and sometimes physical scars that last a lifetime. Victims report greater fear and anxiety, feel less accepted, suffer from more health problems, and score lower on measures of academic achievement and self-esteem than students who are not bullied. Victims often turn their anger inward, which may lead to depression, anxiety, and even suicide. The experience of bullying is also linked with violence, as the fatal school shootings in Littleton, Colorado, and Jonesborough, Arkansas, have illustrated.

   However, it's not just victims who are hurt by bullying. Bullies fail to learn how to cope, manage their emotions, and communicate effectively — skills vital to success in the adult world. Without intervention, bullies suffer stunted emotional growth and fail to develop empathy. Since bullies are accustomed to achieving their immediate goals by pushing others around, they don't learn how to have genuine relationships with other people. Instead, they externalize and blame others for their problems, never taking responsibility, nor learning how to care for another's needs. Bullies who don't learn other ways of getting what they want develop into adult bullies who are more likely to experience criminal troubles, be abusive toward their spouses, and have more aggressive children, perhaps continuing the cycle of bullying into the next generation.

   Now read the next two excerpts, noting the implied and explicit questions the authors ask, the conclusions they draw, and whether those conclusions are reasonable given the *evidence* the authors provide.

3. **Colleen Newquist, "Bully-Proof Your School"**

   Recognized as more than just a problem between kids, schools are called upon to put forth a team effort to end bullies' longtime reign of terror.

   In *Arthur's April Fool*, Marc Brown's lovable aardvark gets the best of a school bully by playing a joke on him. Lucky for Arthur, the book ends there.

   As most children know, and many adults remember, struggles with real-life bullies rarely are resolved so easily. The enormity of those struggles are now recognized, and bullying in schools, once shrugged off with a kids-will-be-kids attitude, has come to be regarded as a serious problem around the world.

   The facts about bullying show that 10 to 15 percent of children are bullied regularly, and bullying most often takes place in school, frequently right in the classroom. The facts show, too, that bullying is an equal-opportunity torment — the size of a school, its setting (rural, urban or suburban) and racial composition seem to have no bearing on its occurrence.

Bullying takes a heavy toll on the victims. As many as 7 percent of eighth grade students in the United States stay home at least once a month because of bullies. Chronic fear can be the source of all-too-real stomachaches and head-aches and other stress-related illnesses. According to Norway's Dan Olweus, a leading authority on the subject, being bullied also leads to depression and low self-esteem, problems that can carry into adulthood.

The effects of such behavior are grim for the offender, too. One study by Olweus shows that 60 percent of kids characterized as bullies in sixth through ninth grades had at least one criminal conviction by age 24.

4. **Paul R. Smokowski and Kelly Holland Kopasz, "Bullying in School: An Overview of Types, Effects, Family Characteristics, and Intervention Strategies"**

Bullying is usually defined as a form of aggression in which one or more chil-dren intend to harm or disturb another child who is perceived as being unable to defend himself or herself (Glew, Rivara, & Feudtner, 2000). Typically, a power imbalance exists between the bully and the victim, with the bully being either physically or psychologically more powerful (Nansel et al., 2001). Often, the perpetrator uses bullying as a means to establish dominance or maintain status (Pellegrini, Bartini, & Brooks, 1999; Roberts, 2000). In addition, bullying behaviors tend to occur repeatedly (Nansel et al.). Such behaviors include name calling, physically assaulting, threatening, stealing, vandalizing, slandering, excluding, and taunting (Beale, 2001).

Short-Term Effects of Victimization

Victims may gradually see themselves as outcasts and failures. Studies suggest that victimization has a significant positive correlation with several internaliz-ing disorders, such as anxiety and depression (Brockenbrough et al., 2002; Kaltiala-Heino et al., 2000). This link between victimization and internalizing disorders is particularly strong for adolescent girls and may contribute to the development of eating disorders (Bond, Carlin, Thomas, Rubin, & Patton, 2001). One study found that attention-deficit disorder was common among victims (Kumpulainen et al., 2001). This connection with attention-deficit disorder is understandable considering that these children may feel the need to constantly monitor their environment, anxiously anticipating the next vic-timization episode. Victims of bullying often suffer from one or more of the following: chronic absenteeism, reduced academic performance, increased apprehension, loneliness, feelings of abandonment, and suicidal ideation (Beale, 2001; Roberts & Coursol, 1996).

You can see that even though the authors of the four excerpts above did not directly ask questions in their texts, all of them were curious about the long-term effects of bullying, especially on people who later committed crimes or who suffered from difficult psychological adjustments in adult life. The questions you asked as you read allowed you to engage with and think critically about the reading selections, necessary steps to take before you can write productively about a reading selection.

Throughout this book, readings are followed by a section called *Reading for Meaning*, which is divided into three activities based on the kinds of questions you asked of the texts you just read:

- *Read to summarize* involves asking yourself what the main point of the reading is.

- *Read to respond* asks you to explore your reactions to the text and bring to it your own knowledge and experience.

- *Read to analyze assumptions* asks you to uncover the authors' perspectives, values, and beliefs as well as to probe your own. Often, you will have to **infer** (or figure out) an author's assumptions because they are not stated explicitly.

Various approaches to thinking and reading critically are addressed in detail with illustrative examples in Chapter 10, A Catalog of Reading Strategies.

Thinking and Reading Critically: Developing Rhetorical Sensitivity

Rhetoric means the ways writers make their ideas understandable and seek to influence their readers. When you develop rhetorical sensitivity, you understand the writer's purpose, audience, context, and genre, and you recognize that the decisions the writer makes — including the types of evidence the writer includes, the kinds of vocabulary he or she chooses, and the *writing strategies* he or she uses — grow out of the rhetorical situation.

You probably already have a fairly sophisticated understanding of rhetorical situations: You wouldn't write a thank-you note to your great-aunt using the same tone or vocabulary that you would use when posting a Facebook update about a concert you attended, because you know your purpose, audience, context, and genre are very different in these two situations. Your ability to analyze the rhetorical situation — to identify the writer's purpose, audience, context, and genre — and to adapt your writing to your rhetorical situation is central to your success in college and beyond. Your teachers will expect you to analyze the rhetorical situation in each discipline, and by doing so, you will cultivate the skills necessary to join their academic conversation. We explore how to examine the rhetorical situation later in this chapter.

You may have noticed that the excerpts on bullying above were written in different styles. The texts that were written for an academic audience assumed their readers were familiar with the terminology (vocabulary) and concepts characteristic of the discipline — what we call the discipline's **discourse** — as well as its genre **conventions** (typical ways of organizing material and using sources). For example, readers familiar with scientific discourse (biology, for example) would expect a scientific report to include technical descriptions of the methods used and the results obtained and to be organized with separate sections for methods, results, discussion, and references. If the same experiment were discussed in an article for a general audience, however, readers would expect little, if any, technical detail. They would expect specialized concepts to be defined, they would not expect detailed descriptions of methods or results in separate sections with headings, and they would not expect a list of sources.

Readers also take note of the *tone* of a reading. Authors of academic discourse try to keep their tone objective and courteous, so they will be taken seriously and not provoke an emotional (and perhaps unreasonable) reaction in the reader. Less formal authors may allow passion into their writing, or they may write in a chatty tone, with informal language and direct addresses to the reader. (Note, for instance, how some of the authors refer to bullied people as "kids," while others refer to them as "children." Such words provide a key to the tone.)

ACTIVITY 2

Developing Your Rhetorical Sensitivity

To develop your rhetorical sensitivity for academic writing, look again at the excerpts on bullying above to identify one that you think was written for a general audience and one written for an academic audience. What characteristics can you identify for the two types of writing? List the characteristics of the two excerpts in facing columns:

Excerpt for more general audience	Excerpt for academic audience

Now write a paragraph or two explaining the features that led you to identify the different audiences for these two excerpts.

Thinking and Reading Critically: Analyzing Ideas with Critical Analysis and Civility

In college, you will deepen and extend your critical thinking and reading skills by reading a variety of texts that may expose you to wholly new ideas, make you question your own value system, and help you see different points of view. You will also often have opportunities to discuss what you read with your professors and classmates, and doing so will introduce you to additional critical reading strategies that can enhance your existing habits of mind. In order to get the most from texts and discussions, participants in the academic conversation examine all the ideas — their own and others' — critically but also with civility, whether they agree with them or not.

To see this process in action, read the two excerpts below, which include definitions of and discuss the prevalence of bullying in school. The first is from the *Journal of the American Medical Association* — an academic journal — and the second is from a 2004 book on bullying written for the general public and for people who work in schools. As you read, make notes about the following:

1. Any ideas that are new to you, especially those that challenge what you currently think about bullying

2. Any references to assumptions that are contrary to the writers' beliefs. Look especially for references by the authors to the beliefs other people might have that differ from their own, or to values that may be currently accepted but are open to question

3. How the writers handle assumptions that are contrary to their own

Tonja R. Nansel, Mary Overpeck, Ramani S. Pilla, W. June Ruan, Bruce Simons-Morton, and Peter Scheidt, "Bullying Behaviors among U.S. Youth: Prevalence and Association with Psychosocial Adjustment"

Bullying among school-aged youth is increasingly being recognized as an important problem affecting well-being and social functioning. While a certain amount of conflict and harassment is typical of youth peer relations, bullying presents a potentially more serious threat to healthy youth development. The definition of bullying is widely agreed on in literature on bullying.[1-4] Bullying is a specific type of aggression in which (1) the behavior is intended to harm or disturb, (2) the behavior occurs repeatedly over time, and (3) there is an imbalance of power, with a more powerful person or group attacking a less powerful one. This asymmetry of power may be physical or psychological, and the aggressive behavior may be verbal (e.g., name-calling, threats), physical (e.g., hitting), or psychological (e.g., rumors, shunning/exclusion). . . .

Bullying takes many forms, and findings about the types of bullying that occur are fairly similar across countries. A British study involving 23 schools found that direct verbal aggression was the most common form of bullying, occurring with similar frequency in both sexes.[13] Direct physical aggression was more common among boys, while indirect forms were more common among girls. Similarly, in a study of several middle schools in Rome, the most common types of bullying reported by boys were threats, physical harm, rejection, and name-calling.[14] The most common forms for girls were name-calling, teasing, rumors, rejection, and taking of personal belongings. . . .

Notes

1. Boulton MJ, Underwood K. Bully/victim problems among middle school children. *Br J Educ Psychol.* 1992;62:73–87.
2. Olweus D. *Aggression in the Schools: Bullies and Whipping Boys.* Washington, DC: Hemisphere Publishing Corp; 1978.
3. Salmivalli C, Kaukiainen A, Kaistaniemi L, Lagerspetz KM. Self-evaluated self-esteem, peer-evaluated self-esteem, and defensive egotism as predictors of adolescents' participation in bullying situations. *Pers Soc Psychol Bull.* 1999;25:1268–1278.
4. Slee PT. Bullying in the playground: The impact of inter-personal violence on Australian children's perceptions of their play environment. *Child Environ.* 1995;12:320–327.
13. Rivers I, Smith PK. Types of bullying behaviour and their correlates. *Aggressive Behav.* 1994;20:359–368.
14. Baldry AC. Bullying among Italian middle school students. *Sch Psychol Int.* 1998;19:361–374.

Barbara Coloroso, "The Bully, the Bullied, and the Bystander"

In a study conducted in 2001 by the Kaiser Foundation, a U.S. health care philanthropy organization, in conjunction with the Nickelodeon TV network and Children Now, a youth advocacy group, almost three-quarters of pre-teens interviewed said bullying is a regular occurrence at school and that it becomes even more pervasive as kids start high school; 86 percent of the children between the ages of twelve and fifteen said that they get teased or bullied at school — making bullying more prevalent than smoking, alcohol, drugs, or sex among the same age group. More than half of children between the ages of eight and eleven said that bullying is a "big problem" at school. "It's a big concern on kids' minds. It's something they're dealing with every day," reports Lauren Asher of the Kaiser Foundation . . . (p. 12).

Individual incidents of verbal, physical, or relational bullying can appear trivial or insignificant, nothing to be overly concerned about, part of the school culture. But it is the imbalance of power, the intent to harm, the threat of further aggression, and the creation of an atmosphere of terror that should raise red flags and signal a need for intervention. Sadly, even when the[se] four markers of bullying are clearly in evidence, adults have been known to minimize or dismiss the bullying, underestimate its seriousness, blame the bullied child, and/or heap on additional insult to injury (p. 22).

Considering the ideas that are new to you, think about what you expect from the authors after they have raised these ideas: Do you want more information about what *causes* bullying? About *where* it happens and *what to do about it*? Do you need more evidence of the *problem* before you can be convinced of its importance?

Reread these two excerpts to consider where and how the authors respond to the statements and assumptions of people with whom they disagree. (See Looking for Patterns of Opposition in Chapter 10, A Catalog of Reading Strategies.) For example, note that Nansel and her coauthors *acknowledge* the common idea that "boys must be boys" or that "all kids tease each other" when they write, but notice how they introduce this *concession* and then *refute* it.

Cue/*Concession*	While *a certain amount of conflict and harassment is typical*
Refutation	*of youth peer relations,* bullying presents a potentially more serious threat to healthy youth development.

The authors introduce the concession with a transition indicating contrast (like *although*, *but*, or *however*) to indicate that an exception, refinement, or contradiction is coming. The structure looks like this:

▶ While .... may be true, ... is more likely to contribute to

....

▶ Although ...., I think ....

▶ .... may be true in some circumstances, but not in others.

▶ Researchers X and Y provide some evidence that .... occurs in some settings; however, they don't offer sufficient evidence that it occurs in all settings.

As a reader, you can decide whether you need more evidence to convince you (see Evaluating the Logic of an Argument in Chapter 10, A Catalog of Reading Strategies). Review the excerpt from Coloroso to see if you find a similar concession-refutation structure.

Now consider the tone Nansel et al. use in the example above. Their sentence reflects careful word choices that will not offend the professional writers with whom they disagree or any members of their audience who might share their beliefs. They hedge their statement with *qualifying terms*, such as "a certain amount" and "potentially," to avoid making a stronger claim than they can prove given the evidence. A stronger claim may put off their readers. The hedges also demonstrate the writers' willingness to engage in conversation about this subject.

Barbara Coloroso's text, written for a popular audience, maintains a courteous tone but takes a firmer stance:

Terms that suggest the writer's point of view and undermine writer's neutrality. Hedging terms	Sadly, even when the[se] four markers of bullying are clearly in evidence, adults have been known to minimize or dismiss the bullying, underestimate its seriousness, blame the bullied child, and/or heap on additional insult to injury.

Writers, though — even those endeavoring to be courteous — find that sometimes the authors of alternative arguments use sources that are not convincing. It is then their job to question or challenge those questionable sources. For example, one of the authors cited in the Banks excerpt (pp. 3–4), Olweus, concludes in his own article that while girls suffer from bullying and bully others too, they do not do *more* bullying than boys: "Our research data . . . clearly contradict the view that girls are the most frequent and worst bullies, a view suggested by such recent books as *Queen Bees and Wannabes* (Wiseman 2002) and *Odd Girl Out* (Simmons 2002)."*

ACTIVITY 3

Honing Ideas through Discussion

Once you have analyzed the way Nansel and colleagues and Coloroso respond to others, try discussing bullying with your classmates, friends, or family to develop your own definition of bullying, as well as to develop your ideas about what causes it and what schools could do about it. Work hard to analyze these ideas carefully while retaining an objective and courteous tone. By discussing your reading and speculating about other ways of looking at the problem, you generate and test your *hypotheses*, improving them as you refine them.

FROM READING CRITICALLY TO WRITING WELL

As the successful novelist Stephen King says: "If you want to be a writer, you must do two things above all others: read a lot and write a lot. There's no way around these two things that I'm aware of, no shortcut." All college students have experience with reading and writing for school, and many of you have extensive experience with informal writing as well, especially in technology-based forums such as blogs, Twitter, and Facebook. This kind of online writing can make you more comfortable with the written word and help you become more aware of who your audience is, because your writing is directed to a variety of people other than your teachers. But for academic writing to be effective, it must grow out of the same habits of mind discussed so far in this chapter:

- Curiosity: The desire to explore ideas before writing and to revise your ideas as your thinking and writing on a topic evolve

- Rhetorical sensitivity: The ability to write and revise to make your writing the most effective it can be, given your purpose, genre, and *stance* (your perspective and attitude), your audience, and the medium you choose.

---

*Olweus, Dan. "A Profile of Bullying at School." *Educational Leadership* Mar. 2003. *Academic Search Premier.* Web. 14 Feb. 2005.

- Critical analysis: The willingness to think hard about a topic and to subject your ideas and the ideas of others to critical scrutiny, including both sources that support your position and sources that support opposing views

- Civility: The ability to treat those who disagree with you fairly and respectfully

To explore and revise ideas fully, to analyze critically, and to demonstrate courtesy and rhetorical sensitivity, academic writers can take advantage of the *writing process*, writing and revising multiple times. This process allows them to shape and hone their writing until it expresses their ideas clearly and effectively, and satisfies (and perhaps even surpasses) the expectations of their audience.

THE WRITING PROCESS

In Chapters 2 through 9 of *Reading Critically, Writing Well*, questions following the reading selections help you move from analyzing the selection to writing about it. Each chapter also includes a Guide to Writing to help you explore and develop the ideas you express in your *drafts* and then revise those drafts deeply in response to feedback from other readers.

In college, much of the writing you submit will be formal, academic discourse in specific genres (such as research reports and essay exams). The activities in the Guides to Writing will help you develop the ideas and language that you will use in those formal writing assignments, with example paragraphs and sentence strategies demonstrating effective methods for presenting your ideas and responding to evidence. As writers, we rarely if ever begin with a complete understanding of our subject or a clear, detailed plan for writing about it. Instead, we write to learn, using the questions and unexpected complexities that arise while writing to inspire more writing and, nearly always, generate further ideas and deeper insights.

As you write, remember that the writing process is *recursive:* it does not proceed smoothly in a straight line from beginning to end, but rather may be chaotic. The steps in the process may include the following:

- Generating and researching ideas

- Drafting your essay

- Getting feedback from others

- Revising deeply

- Editing and proofreading

You may find yourself rethinking, rearranging, and rewriting much of your original text, so you may revisit one or more of these stages several times for one essay.

Using Writing and Researching to Generate Ideas

There are many different ways to generate and research ideas, and the activities in the Guides to Writing will introduce you to some of them. For example, you can brainstorm on paper or with a friend or a group to get a firmer grasp of your ideas and where they might lead you. You can figure out what others have said and how that relates to your ideas. You can discover which genre would be best for presenting your ideas — or, if you have chosen your genre, you can examine its *basic features* to include those necessary for your writing. You can explore what you know about your audience so you can tailor your writing to their needs. And you can gather material for your writing so you can support your claim when you figure out what it is. While you are researching, you may need to *summarize, paraphrase,* or *synthesize* material to be able to use it in your essay. For guidance on doing these writing tasks well, refer to Chapters 10 and 11, where there are instructions and examples of these and other common academic tasks. The activities in Chapters 10, 11, and 12, A Catalog of Reading Strategies, Strategies for Research and Documentation, and Strategies for Analyzing Visuals, also suggest fruitful ways to generate ideas.

ACTIVITY 4

Freewriting to Develop Ideas

To understand how writing can help you generate ideas, try the following activity. For fifteen minutes, write nonstop — keep your pen on the paper or your fingers on the keyboard — in response to one of these two statements about your own experiences with bullying:

- I have had firsthand experience with bullying, and . . .

Or

- I haven't had firsthand experience with bullying, but . . .

Don't take time to make corrections or revisions — just keep writing as ideas occur to you, even if you write how stupid you think this exercise is. You will likely think you have nothing further to write after about seven or eight minutes, but it is the struggle to get through the blank minutes that usually yields the most interesting and helpful material.

Note that you need not share your response with anyone else, including your instructor or classmates, although you may choose to do so. You can write exactly what occurs to you — uncensored — because no one else will see it.

Now reread what you have written. Does anything surprise you — did you write anything that you hadn't planned to write, but that emerged from the experience of writing? If so, you've now seen how writing itself can help you generate ideas. If not, keep trying: the more you write, the more likely you will discover new ideas.

(continued)

Experienced writers have learned to trust this unstructured writing as a discovery process because they know that writing is an unparalleled way of thinking. Writing helps you discover, explore, develop, and refine your ideas in a way that cannot compare with just sitting around and thinking about a subject. Because writing leaves a record of your thinking, it reduces the burden of remembering and allows you to direct all your mental energy toward other tasks. By rereading what you have written, you can figure out where you became derailed, recall points that you forgot were important, or see new possibilities you did not notice before.

Exploring the Rhetorical Situation

Asking and answering the following questions when reading *and* when writing will help you explore the rhetorical situation:

- What is the author's purpose?

- Who is the audience?

- What is the author's stance — perspective and attitude toward the material?

- What is the genre?

- What is the best medium or design for this text?

Asking these questions while reading will help you develop a writer's eye, will help you notice the maneuvers and strategies that writers use to communicate their ideas. (Reread pp. 3–4 to recall the differences between reader's and writer's questions.) The Reading Like a Writer questions following each reading selection will help you learn how to ask the "writer's questions" that will help shape your writing. Asking these questions about your own writing will help you develop the objectivity you will need to revise effectively.

ACTIVITY 5

Asking Writer's Questions

Choose one of the readings from earlier in this chapter, and ask writer's questions of the excerpt. Consider the rhetorical situation and explore how you know the answers to these questions. For example, you quickly know that Nansel et al.'s essay is written for a specialist audience — but how do you know that? Is it the language? The evidence of research? The kinds of research? What are the indications that let you know your writer's questions are being answered?

Writing a Draft

Having devised a *main idea* (or **thesis**) and developed different kinds of reasons and evidence to support it, you have already begun writing a draft. You will develop the draft by drawing on the language and ideas you generated and researched earlier. (See p. 4 to refresh your mind about effective forms of evidence.) You should have a clear sense of who your readers are and what they need to know to be persuaded by your observations, and you should have some grasp of their values and beliefs, so you can appeal to *common ground* between them and you. You can always return to idea-generating activities as you determine what else you might need.

Getting Feedback from Others

Writers need feedback from others to determine the strengths and weaknesses of their early draft(s). You may turn to a friend, your classmates, a tutor in your writing center or online, or your instructor to get constructive criticism. Ask questions like those below so you get the feedback you need:

- Is my main idea /thesis clear?

- What evidence is most persuasive? Least?

- Are there places where you can't follow my reasoning, and can you explain why?

- Do I show evidence of having practiced the habits of mind expected of college students: curiosity, rhetorical sensitivity, critical analysis, and civility? Please point it out.

Ask your readers to review Reading a Draft Critically — found in each chapter's Guide to Writing — before they finish.

Revising Deeply

Many writers spend more time revising than writing their original draft, another indication that writing generates ideas. You may find that you have to revise your whole thesis in light of the feedback you receive from reviewers or expand on your ideas, sharpen your reasons, augment your evidence, answer possible objections or questions, reorganize in light of readers' confusion, trim bloated parts, or rework your ideas into a more reader-friendly form. You may have to augment your ideas; it's common for reviewers to ask questions that require answers you haven't yet considered, so you may have to do more research and more idea-generating.

Editing and Proofreading

What would your reaction be to reading material that was difficult to follow, had inconsistent references, and included misspellings and grammatical errors for no apparent reason — in short, writing that seemed to disregard the needs of a reader? All of the excerpts in this chapter are in final, polished form, with correct spelling, grammar, and punctuation, and with vocabulary appropriate to the audience for which they are written. In fact, this is true of every reading selection in this book, as well as the text supporting it. Academic and professional authors work hard to ensure that their written work is as perfect as they can make it when they submit it to publishers: Most authors revise several times until their writing satisfies them, and often they give it to a friend, family member, or colleague — sometimes to several people — for review. Their publishers also edit the work, carefully scrutinizing the writing before setting it before the public. This care and attention to detail yield writing that deserves the careful consideration of those reading it — whether they be specialists, members of the general public, or, in the case of student writing, professors.

When you reach the stage in your draft where you think you have

- properly expressed your purpose,

- considered the needs and ideas of your audience,

- supported your position on your subject with a clear thesis and substantial evidence,

- decided on the appropriate genre, and

- determined the most successful medium for publication,

you are ready to clean and polish it. This often means even further rewriting, though if you've been attentive to your habits of mind and revised your writing through several stages, you may have been making editing and polishing decisions all along.

To edit and proofread effectively, you need to read your essay through the eyes of your reader. This is no time to be lazy! Rigorously check sentences and paragraphs to make sure your writing includes the following:

- A clear thesis placed in a prominent place

- Transitions between sentences and between paragraphs to help your reader follow your line of thinking

- Vocabulary appropriate to the subject and audience's needs

- Correct grammar so you can communicate effectively and not confuse or annoy your reader

- Correct spelling so your reader knows exactly what word you mean

- Sentence construction that helps your reader understand your points (If you struggle with reading your own sentences, your reader will probably just give up and move on or, worse yet, stop reading altogether.)

- An appropriate tone given your approach to your subject and your audience

---

ACTIVITY 6

Pulling It All Together

Look back at what you wrote for Activity 1, where you speculated about the academic habits of mind you already practice. Think now about what you have learned about the habits of mind that lead to successful thinking, reading, and writing in college and beyond. To solidify your understanding, write a note to a person — a friend, a colleague, a sibling, your own child — who is preparing for college. In a page or two, describe the habits of mind you think this person should start (or continue) practicing to ensure his or her success in college and career. Feel free to use examples from this chapter, but try as well to draw on your own experience to support your assertions. As you write, bear in mind the writing process we've just described. By the time you finish this short essay, you should be ready to begin the next stage of your course, beginning with Chapter 2, Autobiography, or any other chapter your teacher chooses to work on first.

Sources for Texts on pp. 3–7 and 10–11

Banks, Ron. "Bullying in Schools." *ERIC Clearinghouse on Elementary and Early Childhood Education* 1997. *Infotrac.* Web. 15 Aug. 2003.

Coloroso, Barbara. *The Bully, the Bullied, and the Bystander.* New York: Harper / Quill, 2004. Print.

Kuther, Tara L. "Understanding Bullying." Parent Teacher Association, n.d. Web. 3 May 2010.

Nansel, Tonja R., Mary Overpeck, Ramani S. Pilla, W. June Ruan, Bruce Simons-Morton, and Peter Scheidt. "Bullying Behaviors among U.S. Youth: Prevalence and Association with Psychosocial Adjustment." *Journal of the American Medical Association* 25 (Apr. 2001): 2094–2100. Print.

Newquist, Colleen. "Bully-Proof Your School." *Education World* 8 Sept. 2004. Web. 21 Jan. 2005.

Smokowski, Paul R., and Kelly Holland Kopasz. "Bullying in School: An Overview of Types, Effects, Family Characteristics, and Intervention Strategies." *Children and Schools* Apr. 2005. *Academic Search Premier.* Web. 6 Feb. 2013.

Autobiography

Writing and reading about the memorable events and people in our lives can be exhilarating, leading us to think deeply about why certain experiences have meaning for us. They can also help us understand the cultural influences that helped shape who we are and what we value. Whether you are reading or writing, however, it is important to remember that, as a genre, autobiography is public, not private like a diary. Although it involves self-presentation and contributes to self-knowledge, autobiography does not require unwanted self-disclosure. Readers expect autobiographers to portray themselves purposely for their readers, in other words, to write with an awareness of the rhetorical situation. For example, writing about yourself for a college admissions essay, you undoubtedly want to impress readers with such qualities as your thoughtfulness, diligence, social responsibility, and ambition. Writing for friends and family about a dodgy experience, you may want to share your anxieties but also show how you handled the situation.

This chapter offers several brief autobiographical reading selections for you to enjoy, with exploratory activities that will help you learn to read critically and write well. The Reading for Meaning and Reading Like a Writer activities following each selection invite you to analyze and write about the reading's ideas and writing strategies. You can also use the brief Guide to Writing Autobiography toward the end of the chapter to help you write about an important event or a person who played a vital role in your life.

RHETORICAL SITUATIONS FOR AUTOBIOGRAPHIES

You may think that only politicians and celebrities write their autobiographies, but autobiographical writing is much more common, as the following examples suggest:

- As part of her college application, a high-school senior writes an autobiographical essay that shows what inspired her to want to become a biomedical researcher. She tells what happened when she did her first science experiment on the nutritional effects of different breakfast cereals. Because the mice eating Count Chocula and Froot Loops, and not eating anything else, were dying, she convinced her teacher to let her stop the experiment early. Writing as an eighteen-year-old, she wants her audience of college admissions officers to understand how this incident raised her awareness about the ethics of scientific research.

- Asked to post online a few paragraphs reflecting on a significant early childhood memory, a student in a psychology class writes about a fishing trip he took as a six-year-old. The trip was the first time he spent alone with his father, and he recalls that although he tried hard to win his father's approval, his father criticized everything he did. Looking back on that painful event — now that he knows what a bad relationship his dad had had with his own father — the student reflects on the importance of role models in teaching people how to be good parents.

- As part of a workshop on management skills, a business executive writes about a person who influenced his ideas about leadership. He gives a couple of examples to illustrate his mentor's methods, and then details what happened on one occasion. He tries to help his audience understand why that incident was a turning point that led him to realize that the management style he had admired and sought to emulate was actually counterproductive. He shows that his mentor's style was ultimately a kind of bullying. Instead of encouraging people to work creatively through collaboration, he got people to do as he wanted by belittling and intimidating them.

Thinking about the Genre

Autobiography

Before studying a type of writing, it is useful to spend some time thinking about what you already know about it. You have almost certainly heard friends or family tell stories about their lives. Just as surely, you have told stories about events in your life and described people you have known. When you tell such stories, you are composing autobiography.

Recall one occasion when you recounted an event or described a person who played a significant role in your life, or an occasion when you heard or read such a story. Your instructor may ask you to write about your storytelling experience or discuss it with others in class or online. Use the following questions to develop your thoughts.

- Who was the *audience*? How did communicating to this audience affect what was told, or how? For example, was the event's drama, dialogue, or autobiographical significance emphasized?

(continued)

- What was the *purpose*? Was the goal to make the audience think and feel a certain way; to make them laugh with, and perhaps also at, the speaker or writer; to recognize mistreatment or justify behavior; to appreciate why the memory is still so powerful? What was the audience's reaction? How do you account for this reaction?

- If the audience or purpose had been different, how might the narration have changed? For example, might dialogue have been included to show readers how the person was treated? Consider also whether including photos, videos, recorded conversation, or other media would have contributed to the story or portrait.

A GUIDE TO READING AUTOBIOGRAPHY

This guide introduces you to autobiography by inviting you to analyze a brief but powerful autobiographical selection by Annie Dillard, first by *reading for meaning* and then by *reading like a writer*.

- *Reading for meaning* will help you grasp the event's significance for Dillard — what the incident meant to her both at the time she experienced it and years later when she wrote about it. It may also help you explore broader cultural meanings in Dillard's story — for example, ideas about heroism and gender.

- *Reading like a writer* will help you learn how Dillard makes her story exciting and suspenseful, as well as meaningful, by examining how she employs some basic features and strategies typical of autobiographical writing, such as:

1. Narrating a story dramatically
2. Presenting people and places vividly
3. Conveying the significance powerfully

Annie Dillard

An American Childhood

Annie Dillard (b. 1945) is a prolific writer whose first book, Pilgrim at Tinker Creek *(1974), won the Pulitzer Prize for nonfiction writing. Since then, she has written eleven other books in a variety of genres. They include* Teaching a Stone to Talk *(1988),* The Writing Life *(1989),* Mornings Like

This *(1996), and* The Maytrees *(2007). Dillard has also written an auto-biography of her early years,* An American Childhood *(1987), from which the following selection comes.*

- **Before you read,** *notice that Dillard tells us in the opening paragraph that she liked learning to play football because "[y]our fate, and your team's score, depended on your concentration and courage." Think about the kinds of play you liked as a child and why.*

- **As you read,** *notice Dillard titled this selection and her full-length auto-biography "An American Childhood." The word* an *suggests that hers may not have been a typical American childhood. How, if at all, does your childhood experience enable you to understand or empathize with the young Dillard?*

Some boys taught me to play football. This was fine sport. You thought up a 1 new strategy for every play and whispered it to the others. You went out for a pass, fooling everyone. Best, you got to throw yourself mightily at someone's running legs. Either you brought him down or you hit the ground flat out on your chin, with your arms empty before you. It was all or nothing. If you hesitated in fear, you would miss and get hurt: you would take a hard fall while the kid got away, or you would get kicked in the face while the kid got away. But if you flung yourself wholeheartedly at the back of his knees—if you gathered and joined body and soul and pointed them diving fearlessly—then you likely wouldn't get hurt, and you'd stop the ball. Your fate, and your team's score, depended on your concentration and courage. Nothing girls did could compare with it.

Boys welcomed me at baseball, too, for I had, through enthusiastic 2 practice, what was weirdly known as a boy's arm. In winter, in the snow, there was neither baseball nor football, so the boys and I threw snowballs at passing cars. I got in trouble throwing snowballs, and have seldom been happier since.

On one weekday morning after Christmas, six inches of new snow had just 3 fallen. We were standing up to our boot tops in snow on a front yard on trafficked Reynolds Street, waiting for cars. The cars traveled Reynolds Street slowly and evenly; they were targets all but wrapped in red ribbons, cream puffs. We couldn't miss.

I was seven; the boys were eight, nine, and ten. The oldest two Fahey 4 boys were there—Mikey and Peter—polite blond boys who lived near me on Lloyd Street, and who already had four brothers and sisters. My parents approved Mikey and Peter Fahey. Chickie McBride was there, a tough kid, and Billy Paul and Mackie Kean too, from across Reynolds, where the boys

For a multimodal autobiographical selection, go to **bedfordstmartins.com/readingcritically**.

grew up dark and furious, grew up skinny, knowing, and skilled. We had all drifted from our houses that morning looking for action, and had found it here on Reynolds Street.

5   It was cloudy but cold. The cars' tires laid behind them on the snowy street a complex trail of beige chunks like crenellated castle walls. I had stepped on some earlier; they squeaked. We could not have wished for more traffic. When a car came, we all popped it one. In the intervals between cars we reverted to the natural solitude of children.

6   I started making an iceball—a perfect iceball, from perfectly white snow, perfectly spherical, and squeezed perfectly translucent so no snow remained all the way through. (The Fahey boys and I considered it unfair actually to throw an iceball at somebody, but it had been known to happen.)

7   I had just embarked on the iceball project when we heard tire chains come clanking from afar. A black Buick was moving toward us down the street. We all spread out, banged together some regular snowballs, took aim, and, when the Buick drew nigh, fired.

8   A soft snowball hit the driver's windshield right before the driver's face. It made a smashed star with a hump in the middle.

9   Often, of course, we hit our target, but this time, the only time in all of life, the car pulled over and stopped. Its wide black door opened; a man got out of it, running. He didn't even close the car door.

10   He ran after us, and we ran away from him, up the snowy Reynolds sidewalk. At the corner, I looked back; incredibly, he was still after us. He was in city clothes: a suit and tie, street shoes. Any normal adult would have quit, having sprung us into flight and made his point. This man was gaining on us. He was a thin man, all action. All of a sudden, we were running for our lives.

11   Wordless, we split up. We were on our turf; we could lose ourselves in the neighborhood backyards, everyone for himself. I paused and considered. Everyone had vanished except Mikey Fahey, who was just rounding the corner of a yellow brick house. Poor Mikey, I trailed him. The driver of the Buick sensibly picked the two of us to follow. The man apparently had all day.

12   He chased Mikey and me around the yellow house and up a backyard path we knew by heart: under a low tree, up a bank, through a hedge, down some snowy steps, and across the grocery store's delivery driveway. We smashed through a gap in another hedge, entered a scruffy backyard and ran around its back porch and tight between houses to Edgerton Avenue; we ran across Edgerton to an alley and up our own sliding woodpile to the Halls' front yard; he kept coming. We ran up Lloyd Street and wound through mazy backyards toward the steep hilltop at Willard and Lang.

13   He chased us silently, block after block. He chased us silently over picket fences, through thorny hedges, between houses, around garbage cans, and across streets. Every time I glanced back, choking for breath, I

expected he would have quit. He must have been as breathless as we were. His jacket strained over his body. It was an immense discovery, pounding into my hot head with every sliding, joyous step, that this ordinary adult evidently knew what I thought only children who trained at football knew: that you have to fling yourself at what you're doing, you have to point yourself, forget yourself, aim, dive.

Mikey and I had nowhere to go, in our own neighborhood or out of it, but away from this man who was chasing us. He impelled us forward; we compelled him to follow our route. The air was cold; every breath tore my throat. We kept running, block after block; we kept improvising, backyard after backyard, running a frantic course and choosing it simultaneously, failing always to find small places or hard places to slow him down, and discovering always, exhilarated, dismayed, that only bare speed could save us—for he would never give up, this man—and we were losing speed. 14

He chased us through the backyard labyrinths of ten blocks before he caught us by our jackets. He caught us and we all stopped. 15

We three stood staggering, half blinded, coughing, in an obscure hilltop backyard: a man in his twenties, a boy, a girl. He had released our jackets, our pursuer, our captor, our hero: he knew we weren't going anywhere. We all played by the rules. Mikey and I unzipped our jackets. I pulled off my sopping mittens. Our tracks multiplied in the backyard's new snow. We had been breaking new snow all morning. We didn't look at each other. I was cherishing my excitement. The man's lower pants legs were wet; his cuffs were full of snow, and there was a prow of snow beneath them on his shoes and socks. Some trees bordered the little flat backyard, some messy winter trees. There was no one around: a clearing in a grove, and we the only players. 16

It was a long time before he could speak. I had some difficulty at first recalling why we were there. My lips felt swollen; I couldn't see out of the sides of my eyes; I kept coughing. 17

"You stupid kids," he began perfunctorily. 18

We listened perfunctorily indeed, if we listened at all, for the chewing out was redundant, a mere formality, and beside the point. The point was that he had chased us passionately without giving up, and so he had caught us. Now he came down to earth. I wanted the glory to last forever. 19

But how could the glory have lasted forever? We could have run through every backyard in North America until we got to Panama. But when he trapped us at the lip of the Panama Canal, what precisely could he have done to prolong the drama of the chase and cap its glory? I brooded about this for the next few years. He could only have fried Mikey Fahey and me in boiling oil, say, or dismembered us piecemeal, or staked us to anthills. None of which I really wanted, and none of which any adult was likely to do, even in the spirit of fun. He could only chew us out there in the Panamanian jungle, after months or years of exalting pursuit. He could only 20 begin, "You stupid kids," and continue in his ordinary Pittsburgh accent with his normal righteous anger and the usual common sense.

21   If in that snowy backyard the driver of the black Buick had cut off our heads, Mikey's and mine, I would have died happy, for nothing has required so much of me since as being chased all over Pittsburgh in the middle of winter—running terrified, exhausted—by this sainted, skinny, furious redheaded man who wished to have a word with us. I don't know how he found his way back to his car.

READING FOR MEANING

This section presents three activities that will help you think about the meanings in Dillard's autobiographical story. Your instructor may ask you to do one or more of these activities in class or online.

For more help with summarizing, see Chapter 10, pp. 518–19.

1. **Read to Summarize.** Reading to summarize involves asking yourself what the main point of the reading is. To summarize the Dillard selection, write a sentence or two explaining what the story is about.

2. **Read to Respond.** Reading to respond asks you to explore your reactions to a text in light of your own knowledge or experience. To explore this autobiographical story, write a paragraph analyzing your initial reactions to Dillard's essay. Consider anything that resonates with your experience or that seems contradictory, surprising, or fascinating, such as:

You may also try contextualizing; see Chapter 10, pp. 522–23.

   - What a particular scene — such as the iceball scene (pars. 6–7) or the confrontation scene (pars. 15–21) — tells you about Dillard or why the event is so memorable for her;

   - The apparent contradiction between Dillard's description of the man who chased her as a "hero" (par. 16) and "sainted" (par. 21) and her dismissal of what he said as "redundant, a mere formality, and beside the point" (par. 19).

3. **Read to Analyze Assumptions. Assumptions** are ideas, beliefs, or values that are taken for granted, assumed to be commonly accepted truths. The assumptions in a text usually reflect the writer's own attitudes or cultural traditions, but they may also represent other people's views. Reading to analyze assumptions asks you to uncover these perspectives as well as to probe your own. Sometimes assumptions are stated explicitly, but often they are only implied or hinted at through the writer's choice of words or examples. Write a paragraph or two analyzing an assumption you find intriguing in Dillard's story. Here are some ideas:

Take a quiz to check your reading and vocabulary comprehension:
bedfordstmartins.com/readingcritically

Assumptions about the value of rules and fair play. Dillard asserts proudly that "[w]e all played by the rules" (par. 16) and that she and the Fahey boys "considered it unfair actually to throw an iceball at somebody" (par. 6). Words like *rules* and *unfair* suggest there are principles of conduct or ethics that determine what is considered fair or right. To think critically about the assumptions in this essay related to rules and fairness, consider questions like these:

- What unwritten rule do you think the man assumes the kids have broken? Who would agree (or disagree) that what the kids did was wrong? Why?

You may also try looking for patterns of opposition; see Chapter 10, pp. 525–26.

- Even though the young Dillard admires his persistence in chasing them, why might some readers question the man's decision to chase and reprimand the kids? How do you think he would defend his behavior? Do you think he was right? Why or why not?

Assumptions about the superiority of boys' play. Dillard describes the way the neighborhood boys taught her to play football, claiming that "[n]othing girls did could compare with it" (par. 1). To think critically about the assumptions in this essay related to the different ways boys and girls play, ask yourself questions like these:

- What does Dillard seem to be saying about social expectations regarding gender at the time (1950s) and place (Pittsburgh) that she is describing? To what extent do you share these expectations? Why?

- How have assumptions about girls and boys changed in American culture today, if at all?

READING LIKE A WRITER

This section presents four brief activities that will help you analyze Dillard's writing. Your instructor may ask you to do one or more of these activities in class or online.

Narrating the Story

Stories of all kinds, including autobiographical stories, try to arouse the reader's curiosity, often by structuring the story around a *conflict* that grows increasingly intense until it reaches a high point or **climax**. The structural elements can be visualized in the form of a **dramatic arc** (see Figure 2.1, p. 28) and can help us analyze narratives like the chase Dillard remembers from her childhood.

To intensify the rising action of the chase, Dillard constructs a dramatic *action sequence* by using *action verbs* (instead of static verbs like *is* and *was*). In passages, like the one below, the frantic activity signaled by the verbs is amplified by a series of *prepositional phrases* that show movement through space.

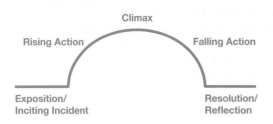

Exposition/Inciting Incident: Background information, scene set-ting, or an introduction to the characters or an initial conflict or problem that sets off the action, arousing curiosity and suspense

Rising Action: The developing crisis, possibly leading to other conflicts and complications

Climax: The emotional high point, often a turning point marking a change for good or ill

Falling Action: Resolution of tension and unraveling of conflicts; may include a final surprise

Resolution/Reflection: Conflicts come to an end but may not be fully resolved, and writer reflects on the event's meaning and importance—its significance

FIGURE 2.1 DRAMATIC ARC   The shape of the arc varies. Not all stories devote the same amount of space to each element, and some may omit elements.

Action verbs Prepositional phrases	He chased Mikey and me around the yellow house and up a backyard path . . . under a low tree, up a bank, through a hedge. . . . We smashed . . . entered . . . and ran. . . . (par. 12)

Other intensifying strategies include the repetition of key words and sentence patterns:

Repetition	He chased us silently, block after block. He chased us silently. . . . (par. 13) He impelled us forward; we compelled him to follow our route. (par. 14)

Whereas the exact repetitions in the first example suggest the experience of being chased relentlessly, the sentence pattern repetition in the second example (*He impelled us . . . we compelled him*) emphasizes the connection between the man (*He*) and the children (*we*).

To keep readers oriented, writers often provide pointers such as *transitional words and phrases, verb tense,* and *adverbs and prepositions marking location in time and space:*

Time and date	On one weekday morning after Christmas . . . (par. 3)
Adverbs/Prepositions of time Verb tenses showing simultaneous action	I had just embarked on the iceball project when we heard . . . (par. 7) At the corner, I looked back; incredibly, he was still after us . . . (par. 10)

Analyze & Write

Write a paragraph analyzing Dillard's construction of an action sequence.

1. Skim paragraphs 11–13, circling the action verbs, underlining adverbs and prepositions indicating movement in time and space, and highlighting any other words or phrases that contribute to the action and help orient readers. Note the verb tenses and use arrows to identify repetitions.

2. Read some of these sentences aloud to consider the effect these patterns have on the rhythm of Dillard's sentences. Also consider whether they help you visualize the action, as if it were a film.

3. Consider also how Dillard uses her point of view (*I* and *we*) in the middle of the action to dramatize the narrative. For example, think about how Dillard's story would be different if we saw the chase through the eyes of the man instead of one of the children, or if we saw it from an outsider's point of view watching from a distance.

Describing Places

Whether autobiography centers on an event or a person, it nearly always includes some *description* of places. As we have seen, because Dillard is describing a chase through her neighborhood, she uses a series of prepositional phrases, particularly prepositions that indicate direction or location in space. To provide specific information about the places and help readers visualize the scene, autobiographers rely on the describing strategies of **naming** objects and **detailing** their colors, shapes, and textures:

Prepositional phrase	. . . around the yellow house and up a backyard path we knew by heart; under a low tree, up a bank, through a hedge, down some snowy steps, and
Naming	across the grocery store's delivery driveway. (par. 12)
Detailing	

In addition to using these sensory images, writers may characterize and evaluate features of the scene ("perfect iceball" and "scruffy backyard" [pars. 6, 12]). Occasionally, they also use **comparisons** in the form of a **simile** or **metaphor** to add suggestive images that contribute to the overall or **dominant impression**:

Metaphor	The cars traveled Reynolds Street slowly and evenly; they were targets all but wrapped in red ribbons, cream puffs. (par. 3)
Simile	The cars' tires laid behind them on the snowy street a complex trail of beige chunks like crenellated castle walls. (par. 5)

Analyze & Write

Write a paragraph analyzing and evaluating Dillard's use of the describing strategies of naming, detailing, and comparing to make the scene come to life for you.

1. Find an example where Dillard uses naming and detailing to make her description especially vivid and informative. Consider whether the names she gives to the objects in the example you chose are *concrete* or *abstract* and what attri-

butes or sense impressions the details convey. What is the dominant impression you get from this description of the scene?

2. Choose a simile or metaphor that stands out for you. What ideas and associations does it add to the sensory description? How does it help you imagine what the place looked and felt like to Dillard? Also, how does the comparison you've analyzed (along with any other comparisons you notice) reinforce, extend, or complicate the dominant impression?

Presenting People

The describing strategies of naming and detailing are often also used to describe people, as in these brief descriptions of some of Dillard's playmates:

Naming   The oldest two Fahey boys were there — Mikey and Peter — polite blond
Detailing   boys ... (par. 4)

Writers not only depict what people look like, but they sometimes also characterize or evaluate their behavior and personality. Often, just a few well-chosen details about the way a person looks, dresses, talks, or acts will be sufficient to give readers a vivid impression of the person:

> ... Billy Paul and Mackie Kean too, from across Reynolds, where the boys grew up dark and furious, grew up skinny, knowing, and skilled. (par. 4)

In this example, one could read Dillard's choice of words like *dark* and *skinny* as metaphorical rather than literal. That is, they suggest character traits or attitudes. For example, the word *dark*, especially when associated with "furious," suggests that the boys were moody, possibly surly or sullen.

Analyze & Write

Write a paragraph exploring the dominant impression you get of the man who chased Dillard and Mikey.

1. Underline the words in paragraphs 10, 16, and 21 that describe the man physically, and circle those that characterize or evaluate him.

2. Skim paragraph 18 and the last sentence of paragraph 20, where Dillard presents the man through dialogue. Underline the details Dillard uses to describe how the man looks and sounds. What does Dillard's choice of words like "perfunctorily" (par. 18) and "normal" (par. 20) suggest about her evaluation of him? How does this evaluation affect the impression you get of the man?

Conveying the Autobiographical Significance

Autobiographers convey the significance of an event or a person in two ways:

1. by showing

2. by telling

Through your analysis of how Dillard narrates the story, presents people, and describes places, you have looked at some of the ways she *shows* the event's significance and creates a dominant impression. Now consider what Dillard *tells* readers. For example, when Dillard writes in the opening paragraphs about boys teaching her to play football and baseball, she is telling why these experiences were memorable and important.

Autobiographers usually tell both what they remember thinking and feeling *at the time* and what they think and feel now *as they write about the past*. Readers must infer from the ideas and the writer's choice of words whether the words convey the writer's *past* or *present perspective* — remembered feelings and thoughts or current ones. For example, consider whether you agree with this analysis, and why or why not.

Remembered feelings and thoughts	Some boys taught me to play football. This was fine sport. You thought up a new strategy for every play and whispered it to the others. (par. 1)
Present perspective	I got in trouble throwing snowballs, and have seldom been happier since. (par. 2)

Analyze & Write

Write a paragraph or two analyzing Dillard's use of showing and telling to create autobiographical significance.

1. Reread paragraphs 19–21, where Dillard comments on the chase and what happens at the end. Choose one or two examples that convey Dillard's present perspective as she looks back and reflects on her childhood experience. Also choose one or two examples that seem to be Dillard's remembered feelings and thoughts, how she felt at the time the event occurred. How can you tell the difference?

2. Compare Dillard's remembered and present perspectives. Has her thinking changed over time? If so, how? If you detect a note of self-irony in her tone, a suggestion that she is making fun of her younger self, where do you see it and what does it tell you about Dillard's adult perspective on her younger self?

READINGS

Tom Ruprecht

In Too Deep

Tom Ruprecht is the author of the book George W. Bush: An Unauthorized Oral History *(2007) and was an Emmy Award–nominated writer for the* Late Show with David Letterman. *With Craig Finn, from the band the Hold Steady, he co-wrote a film adaptation of* Fargo Rock City *based on the book by Chuck Klosterman. His writing has also appeared in periodicals, including the* Wall Street Journal *and the* New York Times Magazine, *where "In Too Deep" appeared in 2011.*

Throughout the reading selection, Ruprecht refers to various current events that readers of the New York Times Magazine *in 2011 would probably have been aware of: that Osama Bin Laden was assumed to have taken refuge in a cave following the U.S. invasion of Afghanistan in 2001; that Aron Ralston amputated his own arm to escape a half-ton boulder pinning him to a canyon wall (an event that was depicted in the 2010 film* 127 Hours, *starring James Franco); that the 2010 rescue of thirty-three Chilean miners trapped underground for six weeks was greeted with worldwide jubilation.*

- *Before you read, notice that Ruprecht expresses concern in the opening paragraph about not looking "cool." Reflect on occasions when you were concerned about how you appeared to others and what you did about it, if anything.*

- *As you read, consider Ruprecht's use of the current events mentioned above: What effect might the references to these events have had on his original audience? What effect do these same references have on readers, like you, who read the article years later?*

1   It's impossible to look cool when you're part of a tour group. Instead of bravely exploring on your own, you've chosen to be led around like a frightened kindergartner. My wife and I were on a tour bus while in Hawaii recently, and our guide made me feel even more uncool because he was very rugged and handsome. After a couple of hours, he announced we were stopping for what he called "snack break," as if we actually were kindergartners. He then mentioned that down a nearby path there was a cave we could check out. Not being a terrorist mastermind, I've never had

For a multimodal autobiographical selection, go to
bedfordstmartins.com/readingcritically.

a huge desire to hang out in a cave. But the opinion of absolute strangers means a lot to me, and I was desperate to differentiate myself from the other travelers in this cool, rugged guide's eyes.

"I'm going to the cave," I declared and marched down the path to check 2 out its mouth. The mouth. That's as far as I was willing to go.

When I arrived, I found another guy from the group standing there. 3

"Hey, I'm Ernie. I'm a spelunker." 4

Ernie said he was going to take a quick look in the cave and invited me 5 to come along. I politely declined. He insisted. I thought of my dad, who has encouraged me to say "yes!" to every opportunity while traveling. During a trip to Puerto Rico in the '70s, it was this *carpe diem* spirit that led my dad to play tennis all week long with the adult-film star Harry Reems—the same Harry Reems who was in *Deep Throat* (not that you recognized the name, dear reader), though true aficionados prefer his later work, in films like *For Your Thighs Only*. So I entered the mouth of the cave.

Thirty feet in, I began telling Ernie we should probably head back. But 6 he simply rushed ahead, and because he had the flashlight, I had no choice but to follow. I soon found myself slithering through tight spaces in order to get to slightly tighter places. I panicked. It was only a matter of time before I would be wedged between rocks. I began looking around for a knife, so I could pre-emptively chop off my arm like James Franco in that movie I was too scared to see.

Things Ernie did made me question his spelunking expertise. For in- 7 stance, there was a weird greenish-whitish substance on the cave's roof. "That's probably sodium," Ernie said, and he swabbed a finger on the slimy substance and stuck it in his mouth. He muttered, "That's not sodium." I believe it was Ernie's pride that kept him from adding, "I think it's bat guano."

We were a good mile inside the cave when Ernie looked at me, gave a 8 little laugh and then turned off the flashlight. A mile deep in the cave. "Scared?" he whispered. Then he chuckled, turned the flashlight back on and said, "Nah, the thing you should really be worried about is what would happen if there were an earthquake right now." Seeing my terrified expression, Ernie said, "Oh, hadn't you thought about that?" I had to get out of there. People were waiting for us. More important, my wife was above ground chatting with a ruggedly handsome tour guide. I implored Ernie to turn back. He reluctantly agreed. On the way, we came upon a fork in the cave. I asked if we should go to the right or the left. Ernie, the great spelunker, replied: "Oh, I have a terrible sense of direction." So Ernie had me choose. I, of course, picked the wrong way. We wandered aimlessly for 10 minutes, wondering if we were passing the same generic rocks we passed on the way in or if we were passing slightly different generic rocks. If only there had been a spelunker there, I would have asked him.

9   Eventually Ernie's spelunking expertise did kick in. He realized we were headed down the wrong path. We doubled back, took the other path and, finally, saw a sliver of sunlight. I popped out of the cave, expecting a welcome worthy of a Chilean miner. Instead I was greeted by 11 annoyed people whose trip Ernie and I had hindered. As my wife hugged me, she whispered, "People are kinda mad."

10   The guide reprimanded us for endangering our lives and delaying the others. But as we started back to the bus, he pulled Ernie and me aside and said in a low voice, "Don't tell anybody, but I think what you guys did was seriously kick-ass!" The rest of the day I walked around with a happy smile, like the proudest little kindergartner you've ever seen.

READING FOR MEANING

This section presents three activities that will help you think about the meanings in Ruprecht's autobiographical story. Your instructor may ask you to do one or more of these activities in class or online.

For more help with summarizing, see Chapter 10, pp. 518–19.

1. **Read to Summarize.** Write a sentence or two explaining what the story is about.

2. **Read to Respond.** Write a paragraph exploring your initial thoughts and feelings about Ruprecht's autobiographical story. For example, consider anything that resonates with your experience or that seems contradictory, surprising, or fascinating, such as:

   • Ruprecht's comment that "the opinion of absolute strangers means a lot to me" (par. 1);

   • The guide's contradictory reactions in the final paragraph.

3. **Read to Analyze Assumptions.** Write a paragraph or two analyzing an assumption you find intriguing in Ruprecht's essay. For example:

   Assumptions about the **carpe diem** *spirit.* Ruprecht explains that he agreed to enter the cave because he remembered his father's encouragement "to say 'yes!' to every opportunity" (par. 5). *Carpe diem*, Latin for "seize the day," assumes that you should take advantage of an opportunity when it arises because you may not have another chance like it. To think critically about the assumptions in this essay related to the *carpe diem* spirit, ask yourself questions like these:

   • How does Ruprecht's opportunity compare to the one his father did not pass up, of playing tennis with a porn star? Do you think the author is being ironic about his dad or serious? How can you tell?

Take a quiz to check your reading and vocabulary comprehension:
bedfordstmartins.com/readingcritically

- Ruprecht says that about thirty feet into the cave, he "had no choice but to follow" Ernie (par. 6). Why would he think this? How does this feeling that he has "no choice" contrast with his earlier decision to seize the day?

Assumptions about wanting to impress others. Ruprecht admits that "the opinion of absolute strangers means a lot" to him, but he emphasizes that the person he really wants to impress is the "cool," "very rugged and handsome" guide (par. 1). To think critically about the assumptions in this essay related to the desire to impress others, consider questions like these:

- Why do you think Ruprecht is so concerned about how he appears to others, particularly to the tour guide? What does Ruprecht's description of the guide suggest about his attitude (par. 1)?
- Ruprecht also points out that the guide's use of the phrase "snack break" makes him feel that the guide is talking to the tourists "as if we actually were kindergartners" (par. 1). How is his decision to go to the "mouth" of the cave and then to go into it with Ernie a reaction to what he sees as the guide's attitude toward the tourists? What does his behavior tell readers about Ruprecht?

READING LIKE A WRITER

NARRATING THE STORY

Like most autobiographers, Ruprecht employs elements of the dramatic arc to arouse readers' curiosity and build suspense (Figure 2.1, p. 28). When he tells us that he entered the cave with Ernie, readers naturally wonder what happened next. Dillard, as we've seen, uses several strategies to intensify the drama of the rising action: action verbs to mobilize the narrative, prepositional phrases to orient readers through space and time, and repetition of key words and phrases to enhance the conflict. All of these strategies are also used by Ruprecht:

Action verb	I began telling Ernie we should probably head back. But he simply rushed
Prepositional phrase	ahead. . . . I soon found myself slithering through tight spaces in order to
	get to slightly tighter places. I panicked. . . . I began looking around for a
Repetition	knife, so I could pre-emptively chop off my arm. . . . (par. 6)

Ruprecht adds several other strategies as well. For example, he uses *dialogue* to add immediacy and heighten the tension. The dialogue (most of it in the form of *quotation* rather than *summary*) emphasizes Ernie's peculiarities and their prickly relationship — for example, after turning off his flashlight: "'Scared?' he whispered" (par. 8). Another strategy Ruprecht uses to enhance the drama is exaggeration or **hyperbole** — for example, comparing his situation to that of Aron Ralston, who actually did "chop off" his arm to escape from a tight crevice.

Such an extreme comparison, however, may serve to weaken or undermine rather than bolster the drama. In effect, Ruprecht's self-deprecating humor could be said to turn his story from a heroic epic story into a mock epic.

| Analyze & Write |

Write a paragraph analyzing how Ruprecht constructs his narrative and about how his choices affect the reader:

1. Look back at the dramatic arc (Figure 2.1, p. 28) and skim the selection, noting in the margin where you find the *exposition, rising action, climax, falling action,* and *resolution.* (Don't be surprised if some of the elements are very brief or missing altogether.)

2. Consider Ruprecht's choices about how to plot his story: How effective were his strategies for dramatizing the rising action, for example? How would spending more (or less) time on exposition or resolution have changed your reaction?

3. Describe how useful the dramatic arc was for you in terms of understanding Ruprecht's narrative technique.

Saira Shah

Longing to Belong

Saira Shah (b. 1964) is a journalist and documentary filmmaker. The daughter of an Afghan father and Indian mother, she was born and educated in England. After graduating from the School of Oriental and African Studies at London University, Shah began her career as a freelance journalist and eventually became a war correspondent, receiving the Courage under Fire and Television Journalist of the Year awards for her risky reporting on conflicts in some of the world's most troubled areas. She is best known in the United States for her undercover documentary films about the Taliban rule in Afghanistan, Beneath the Veil *(2001) and* Unholy War *(2002).*

"Longing to Belong," originally published in the New York Times Magazine *in 2003, is adapted from Shah's autobiography,* The Storyteller's Daughter *(2003), which relates her search to understand her father's homeland of Afghanistan. In this essay, Shah tells what happened when, at the age of seventeen, she visited her father's Afghan relatives living in Pakistan. As she explained in an interview, "I wanted this kind of romantic vision. This is the exile's condition, though, isn't it? If you grow up outside the place that you think of as your home, you want it to be impossibly marvelous. There is also the question of how Afghan I am. When I was growing up, I had this secret doubt — which I couldn't even admit to myself — that I was not at all an Afghan because I was born in Britain to a mixed family."*

- ***Before you read,*** *think about any experiences you might have had as an outsider longing to belong, such as when you moved to a new school or joined a club.*

- ***As you read,*** *think about how Shah conveys her search for her ethnic identity and the sense of cultural dislocation she experiences.*

The day he disclosed his matrimonial ambitions for me, my uncle sat me at his right during lunch. This was a sign of special favor, as it allowed him to feed me choice tidbits from his own plate. It was by no means an unadulterated pleasure. He would often generously withdraw a half-chewed delicacy from his mouth and lovingly cram it into mine—an Afghan habit with which I have since tried to come to terms. It was his way of telling me that I was valued, part of the family.

My brother and sister, Tahir and Safia, and my elderly aunt Amina and I were all attending the wedding of my uncle's son. Although my uncle's home was closer than I'd ever been, I was not yet inside Afghanistan. This branch of my family lived in Peshawar, Pakistan. On seeing two unmarried daughters in the company of a female chaperone, my uncle obviously concluded that we had been sent to be married. I was taken aback by the visceral longing I felt to be part of this world. I had never realized that I had been starved of anything. Now, at 17, I discovered that like a princess in a fairy tale, I had been cut off from my origins. This was the point in the tale where, simply by walking through a magical door, I could recover my gardens and palaces. If I allowed my uncle to arrange a marriage for me, I would belong.

3   Over the next few days, the man my family wished me to marry was introduced into the inner sanctum. He was a distant cousin. His luxuriant black mustache was generally considered to compensate for his lack of height. I was told breathlessly that he was a fighter pilot in the Pakistani Air Force. As an outsider, he wouldn't have been permitted to meet an unmarried girl. But as a relative, he had free run of the house. Whenever I appeared, a female cousin would fling a child into his arms. He'd pose with it, whiskers twitching, while the women cooed their admiration.

4   A huge cast of relatives had assembled to see my uncle's son marry. The wedding lasted nearly 14 days and ended with a reception. The bride and groom sat on an elevated stage to receive greetings. While the groom was permitted to laugh and chat, the bride was required to sit perfectly still, her eyes demurely lowered. I didn't see her move for four hours.

5   Watching this *tableau vivant* of a submissive Afghan bride, I knew that marriage would never be my easy route to the East. I could live in my father's mythological homeland only through the eyes of the storyteller. In my desire to experience the fairy tale, I had overlooked the staggeringly obvious: the storyteller was a man. If I wanted freedom, I would have to cut my own path. I began to understand why my uncle's wife had resorted to using religion to regain some control—at least in her own home. Her piety gave her license to impose her will on others.

6   My putative fiancé returned to Quetta, from where he sent a constant flow of lavish gifts. I was busy examining my hoard when my uncle's wife announced that he was on the phone. My intended was a favorite of hers; she had taken it upon herself to promote the match. As she handed me the receiver, he delivered a line culled straight from a Hindi movie: "We shall have a love-match, *ach-cha*?" Enough was enough. I slammed down the phone and went to find Aunt Amina. When she had heard me out, she said: "I'm glad that finally you've stopped this silly wild goose chase for your roots. I'll have to extricate you from this mess. Wait here while I put on something more impressive." As a piece of Islamic one-upmanship, she returned wearing not one but three head scarves of different colors.

7   My uncle's wife was sitting on her prayer platform in the drawing room. Amina stormed in, scattering servants before her like chaff. "Your relative . . . ," was Amina's opening salvo, ". . . has been making obscene

remarks to my niece." Her mouth opened, but before she could find her voice, Amina fired her heaviest guns: "Over the *telephone*!"

"How dare you!" her rival began. 8

It gave Amina exactly the opportunity she needed to move in for the 9 kill. "What? Do you support this lewd conduct? Are we living in an American movie? Since when have young people of mixed sexes been permitted to speak to each other *on the telephone*? Let alone to talk—as I regret to inform you your nephew did—of love! Since when has love had anything to do with marriage? What a dangerous and absurd concept!"

My Peshawari aunt was not only outclassed; she was out-Islamed too. 10 "My niece is a rose that hasn't been plucked," Amina said. "It is my task as her chaperone to ensure that this happy state of affairs continues. A match under such circumstances is quite out of the question. The engagement is off." My uncle's wife lost her battle for moral supremacy and, it seemed, her battle for sanity as well. In a gruff, slack-jawed way that I found unappealing, she made a sharp, inhuman sound that sounded almost like a bark.

READING FOR MEANING

This section presents three activities that will help you think about the meanings in Shah's autobiographical story. Your instructor may ask you to do one or more of these activities in class or online.

1. **Read to Summarize.** Write a sentence or two explaining what the story is about.

   For more help with summarizing, see Chapter 10, pp. 518–19.

2. **Read to Respond.** Write a paragraph exploring your initial thoughts and feelings about Shah's autobiographical story. For example, consider anything that resonates with your experience or that seems contradictory, surprising, or fascinating, such as:

   - Her uncle's assumption that Shah and her sister were sent to Pakistan "to be married" (par. 2);
   - Shah's realization that "[i]f I wanted freedom, I would have to cut my own path" (par. 5).

3. **Read to Analyze Assumptions.** Write a paragraph or two analyzing an assumption you find intriguing in Shah's essay. For example:

   Assumptions about the values underlying cultural differences. Shah begins her story by describing how her uncle "would often generously withdraw a half-chewed delicacy from his mouth and lovingly cram it into mine" (par. 1). Shah seems ambivalent about this "Afghan habit" —

Take a quiz to check your reading and vocabulary comprehension:
bedfordstmartins.com/readingcritically

expressing distaste as well as gratitude. To think critically about the assumptions in this essay related to cultural differences, consider questions like these:

- What do you think are the beliefs or values underlying Shah's mixed feelings about her uncle's "Afghan habit"?
- Where in this essay do you find evidence of Shah's ambivalence about any other Afghan custom, and what underlies her attitude toward it?
- If you have experienced cultural difference, what was your attitude and what values affected your way of thinking?

Assumptions about the influence of fairy tales. Shah describes herself as "a princess in a fairy tale" (par. 2). She refers specifically to her father's stories about his "mythological homeland" (par. 5), but romantic stories about princesses such as *Cinderella*, *Sleeping Beauty*, and *The Little Mermaid* are also popular in America. To think critically about the assumptions in this essay regarding the influence of fairy tales, consider questions like these:

- What are girls — and perhaps also boys — taught by the fairy tales with which you are familiar?
- What attitudes or ideas do fairy tales seem to encourage?
- How does Shah achieve a critical perspective toward her own "desire to experience the fairy tale" (par. 5)?

READING LIKE A WRITER

PRESENTING PEOPLE

To present people, autobiographers often combine description with narration to show how the person looks, acts, and talks. These strategies give readers a memorable image of the person, creating a **dominant impression** that helps readers understand the autobiographical significance. In paragraph 3, for example, Shah describes the man chosen by the family to marry her:

Naming	His luxuriant black mustache was generally considered to compensate
Detailing	for his lack of height. I was told breathlessly that he was a fighter
Cues for recurring	pilot. . . . Whenever I appeared, a female cousin would fling a child
activities	into his arms. He'd pose with it, whiskers twitching, while the women
	cooed their admiration. (par. 3)

Shah uses the describing strategies of naming and detailing to give readers a vivid image of the man and to help us picture the scene. Her summarized dialogue ("I was told") lets us know *what* was said as well as *how* it was said ("breathlessly"). Shah also uses recurring activities to show readers how the man and the women in the family typically behaved. Notice how Shah uses cues (such as the transitions "whenever" and "while" together with the verb form "would") to let readers know that these kind of things were happening over and over again.

Analyze & Write

Write a paragraph explaining the dominant impression you get from Shah's description of the man chosen to be her husband.

1. Why do you think Shah focuses her physical description on the man's mustache? Why does she comment that his mustache was thought "to compensate for his lack of height"? What is Shah trying to say to readers about the man and his female admirers?

2. What do the recurring activities contribute to the dominant impression Shah creates?

3. Compare the description of Shah's intended fiancé in paragraph 3 to the "*tableau vivant*" (which literally means "living picture") of the bride and groom in paragraphs 4 and 5. How do these two images reinforce each other?

A Special Reading Strategy

Comparing and Contrasting Related Readings: Shah's "Longing to Belong" and Desmond-Harris's "Tupac and My Non-Thug Life"

Comparing and contrasting related readings is a critical reading strategy that is particularly applicable when writers present similar subjects, as is the case in the autobiographical narratives in this chapter by Saira Shah (p. 37) and Jenée Desmond-Harris (p. 42). To compare and contrast these two autobiographies, think about issues such as these:

- Both stories show teenagers in search of their cultural identity. They use the word *belong* or *belonging* to convey their need to find their place in a community. How are their efforts similar and different?

- Both authors explore what Desmond-Harris calls "the contradictory textures" of the alternative identity they are trying on (par. 9). Where in their writing do you see evidence of ambivalence or confusion? How do they resolve their contradictory feelings, if at all?

See Chapter 10, pp. 527–30, for detailed guidelines on comparing and contrasting related readings.

Jenée Desmond-Harris

Tupac and My Non-Thug Life

Jenée Desmond-Harris is a staff writer at the Root, *an online magazine dedicated to African American news and culture. She writes about the intersection of race, politics, and culture in a variety of genres. She has also contributed to* Time *magazine, MSNBC's* Powerwall, *and* xoJane *on topics ranging from her relationship with her grandmother, to the political significance of Michelle Obama's hair, to the stereotypes that hinder giving to black-teen mentoring programs. She has provided television commentary on CNN, MSNBC, and Current TV. Desmond-Harris is a graduate of Howard University and Harvard Law School. The selection below was published in the* Root *in 2011. It chronicles Desmond-Harris's reaction to the murder of gangsta rap icon Tupac Shakur in a Las Vegas drive-by shooting in 1996. She mentions Tupac's mother, Afeni, as well as the "East Coast–West Coast war"— the rivalry between Tupac and the Notorious B.I.G., who was suspected of being involved in Tupac's murder.*

- *Before you read, recall a public event that affected you. Reflect on why something that didn't affect you personally nevertheless had an emotional impact on you.*

- *As you read, consider how the photograph that appeared in the* Root *article and that is reproduced here contributes to readers' understanding of the young Desmond-Harris's reaction to the news of Tupac's death. What does the photo capture about the fifteen-year-old Desmond-Harris? How does it influence your understanding of the author's persona, or self-presentation?*

1   I learned about Tupac's death when I got home from cheerleading practice that Friday afternoon in September 1996. I was a sophomore in high school in Mill Valley, Calif. I remember trotting up my apartment building's stairs, physically tired but buzzing with the frenetic energy and possibilities for change that accompany fall and a new school year. I'd been cautiously allowing myself to think during the walk home about a topic that felt frighteningly taboo (at least in my world, where discussion of race was avoided as delicately as obesity or mental illness): what it meant to be biracial and on the school's mostly white cheerleading team instead of the mostly black dance team. I remember acknowledging, to the sound of an 8-count that still pounded in my head as I walked through the door, that I didn't really have a choice: I could memorize a series of stiff and precise motions but couldn't actually dance.

2   My private musings on identity and belonging—not original in the least, but novel to me—were interrupted when my mom heard me slam the front door and drop my bags: *"Your friend died!"* she called out from another room. Confused silence. *"You know, that rapper you and Thea love so much!"*

MOURNING A DEATH IN VEGAS

The news was turned on, with coverage of the deadly Vegas shooting.   3
Phone calls were made. Ultimately my best friend, Thea, and I were left to
our own 15-year-old devices to mourn that weekend. Her mother and
stepfather were out of town. Their expansive, million-dollar home was
perched on a hillside less than an hour from Tupac's former stomping
grounds in Oakland and Marin City. Of course, her home was also worlds
away from both places.

We couldn't "pour out" much alcohol undetected for a libation, so we   4
limited ourselves to doing somber shots of liqueur from a well-stocked
cabinet. One each. Tipsy, in a high-ceilinged kitchen surrounded by
hardwood floors and Zen flower arrangements, we baked cookies for his
mother. We packed them up to ship to Afeni with a handmade card. ("Did
we really do that?" I asked Thea this week. I wanted to ensure that this
story, which people who know me now find hilarious, hadn't morphed
into some sort of personal urban legend over the past 15 years. "Yes," she
said. "We put them in a lovely tin.")

On a sound system that echoed through speakers perched discreetly   5
throughout the airy house, we played "Life Goes On" on a loop and
sobbed. We analyzed lyrics for premonitions of the tragedy. We, of course,
cursed Biggie. Who knew that the East Coast–West Coast war had two earnest soldiers in flannel pajamas, lying on a king-size bed decorated with
pink toe shoes that dangled from one of its posts? There, we studied our
pictures of Tupac and re-created his tattoos on each other's body with a
Sharpie. I got "Thug Life" on my stomach. I gave Thea "Exodus 1811"
inside a giant cross. Both are flanked by "West Side."

A snapshot taken that Monday on our high school's front lawn (seen   6
here) shows the two of us lying side by side, shirts lifted to display the trib-
utes in black marker. Despite our best efforts, it's the innocent, bubbly let-
tering of notes passed in class and of poster boards made for social studies
presentations. My hair has recently been straightened with my first (and
last) relaxer and a Gold 'N Hot flatiron on too high a setting. Hers is slicked
back with the mixture of Herbal Essences and Blue Magic that we formulated in a bathroom laboratory.

My rainbow-striped tee and her white wifebeater capture a transition   7
between our skater-inspired Salvation Army shopping phase and the next
one, during which we'd wear the same jeans slung from our hip bones,
revealing peeks of flat stomach, but transforming ourselves from Alternative Nation to MTV Jams imitators. We would get bubble coats in primary
colors that Christmas and start using silver eyeliner, trying—and failing—
to look something like Aaliyah.[1]

---

[1]A hit rhythm-and-blues and hip-hop recording artist. Aaliyah Dana Haughton
died in a plane crash at age twenty-two. [Editor's note]

MIXED IDENTITIES: TUPAC AND ME

8   Did we take ourselves seriously? Did we feel a real stake in the life of this "hard-core" gangsta rapper, and a real loss in his death? We did, even though we were two mixed-race girls raised by our white moms in a privileged community where we could easily rattle off the names of the small handful of other kids in town who also had one black parent: Sienna. Rashea. Brandon. Aaron. Sudan. Akio. Lauren. Alicia. Even though the most subversive thing we did was make prank calls. Even though we hadn't yet met our first boyfriends, and Shock G's proclamations about putting satin on people's panties sent us into absolute giggling fits. And even though we'd been so delicately cared for, nurtured and protected from any of life's hard edges—with special efforts made to shield us from those involving race—that we sometimes felt ready to explode with boredom. Or maybe because of all that.

9   I mourned Tupac's death then, and continue to mourn him now, because his music represents the years when I was both forced and privileged to confront what it meant to be black. That time, like his music, was about exploring the contradictory textures of this identity: The ambience and indulgence of the fun side, as in "California Love" and "Picture Me Rollin'." But also the burdensome anxiety and outright anger—"Brenda's Got a Baby," "Changes" and "Hit 'Em Up."

10   For Thea and me, his songs were the musical score to our transition to high school, where there emerged a vague, lunchtime geography to race: White kids perched on a sloping green lawn and the benches above it.

The author (left) with her friend Thea

Below, black kids sat on a wall outside the gym. The bottom of the hill beckoned. Thea, more outgoing, with more admirers among the boys, stepped down boldly, and I followed timidly. Our formal invitations came in the form of unsolicited hall passes to go to Black Student Union meetings during free periods. We were assigned to recite Maya Angelou's "Phenomenal Woman" at the Black History Month assembly.

Tupac was the literal sound track when our school's basketball team would come charging onto the court, and our ragtag group of cheerleaders kicked furiously to "Toss It Up" in a humid gymnasium. Those were the games when we might breathlessly join the dance team after our cheer during time-outs if they did the single "African step" we'd mastered for BSU performances.   11

EVERYODY BLACK—AND COOL

. . . Blackness became something cool, something to which we had brand-new access. We flaunted it, buying Kwanzaa candles and insisting on celebrating privately (really, just lighting the candles and excluding our friends) at a sleepover. We memorized "I Get Around"[2] and took turns singing verses to each other as we drove through Marin County suburbs in Thea's green Toyota station wagon. Because he was with us through all of this, we were in love with Tupac and wanted to embody him. On Halloween, Thea donned a bald cap and a do-rag, penciled in her already-full eyebrows and was a dead ringer.   12

Tupac's music, while full of social commentary (and now even on the Vatican's playlist), probably wasn't made to be a treatise on racial identity. Surely it wasn't created to accompany two girls (*little* girls, really) as they embarked on a coming-of-age journey. But it was there for us when we desperately needed it.   13

READING FOR MEANING

This section presents three activities that will help you think about the meanings in Desmond-Harris's autobiographical story. Your instructor may ask you to do one or more of these activities in class or online.

1. **Read to Summarize.** Write a sentence or two explaining what the story is about.

   For more help with summarizing, see Chapter 10, pp. 518–19.

---

[2]Tupac Shakur's first top-twenty single, released in 1993 on *Strictly 4 My N.I.G.G.A.Z.*, Shakur's second studio album. [Editor's note]

 Take a quiz to check your reading and vocabulary comprehension: **bedfordstmartins.com/readingcritically**

2. **Read to Respond.** Write a paragraph exploring your initial thoughts and feelings about Desmond-Harris's autobiographical story. For example, consider anything that resonates with your experience or that seems contradictory, surprising, or fascinating, such as:

- Desmond-Harris's identification with Tupac, perhaps reflecting on why Desmond-Harris and Thea give themselves Sharpie tattoos and take a photograph showing them off (pars. 5–6);

- Desmond-Harris's claim that Tupac's music was the "sound track" for her youth (par. 11), possibly considering the impact of music during certain periods of your own life.

3. **Read to Analyze Assumptions.** Write a paragraph or two analyzing an assumption you find intriguing in Desmond-Harris's essay. For example:

Assumptions about celebrity. The fifteen-year-old Desmond-Harris apparently thought of Tupac as someone she knew personally, not as some distant star but as a family "friend" (par. 2). As she looks back, the author can hardly believe that she and Thea felt so close to Tupac that they even "baked cookies" and sent them with a "handmade" condolence card to Tupac's mother (par. 4). To think critically about assumptions regarding celebrity in this essay, consider questions like these:

- What is it about Tupac that made him so important to Desmond-Harris? Why do you think she took his death so personally?

- We often call celebrities by their first names. Consider whether there are any celebrities that you refer to by first name only, as if you knew them personally.

- How do the media contribute to the sense that we have a personal relationship with certain celebrities?

- Critics like Daniel Boorstin argue that celebrities often are admired not because of their special talents or achievements but simply because they are famous. Why do you think Desmond-Harris is so enamored of Tupac?

Assumptions about identity. Desmond-Harris tells us that as a teenager she began to explore what she calls "the contradictory textures" — "the fun side" as well as "the burdensome anxiety and outright anger" — of her biracial identity (par. 9). To think critically about assumptions regarding identity in this essay, consider questions like these:

- Desmond-Harris describes the social and racial divisions in her high school, what she calls "a vague, lunchtime geography" (par. 10). Given your own experience growing up at a different place and time, what kinds of divisions existed in your high school and how did they affect how you presented yourself to others?

- In the last paragraph, Desmond-Harris explains that during the period she is writing about, she and her friend had "embarked on a coming-of-age journey" (par. 13). What do you think she learned about herself from Tupac's life and from his death?

READING LIKE A WRITER

CONVEYING THE AUTOBIOGRAPHICAL SIGNIFICANCE

Events that have lasting significance nearly always involve mixed or ambivalent feelings. Therefore, readers expect and appreciate some degree of complexity. Multiple layers of meaning make autobiographical stories more, not less, interesting. Significance that seems simplistic or predictable makes stories less successful.

Analyze & Write

Write a paragraph or two analyzing Desmond-Harris's handling of the complex personal and cultural significance of Tupac's death:

1. Skim the last two sections (pars. 8–13), noting passages where Desmond-Harris tells readers her remembered feelings and thoughts at the time and her present perspective as an adult reflecting on the experience. Consider Desmond-Harris's dual perspective—that of the fifteen-year-old experiencing the event and the thirty-year-old writing about it. How does she use this dual perspective to convey complexity?

2. Look closely at paragraph 8, and highlight the following sentence strategies:
   - Rhetorical questions (questions writers answer themselves)
   - Repeated words and phrases
   - Stylistic sentence fragments (incomplete sentences used for special effect)

   What effect do these sentence strategies have on readers? How do they help convey the significance of the event for Desmond-Harris?

ANALYZING VISUALS

Write a paragraph analyzing the photograph included in Desmond-Harris's autobiographical essay and explaining what it contributes to the essay.

To do the analysis, you can use the Criteria for Analyzing Visuals chart in Chapter 12 on pp. 611–12. Don't feel you have to answer all of the questions in the chart; focus on those that seem most productive in helping you write a paragraph-length analysis. To help you get started, consider adding these questions that specifically refer to Desmond-Harris's photo:

- What is the photograph's purpose, and why did Desmond-Harris include it? What does the photograph contribute or show us that the text alone does not convey?

- Why does Desmond-Harris not only include a photograph but also describe the picture, pointing out features such as the hairstyles and outfits? Consider, especially, the references to particular styles and brand names (such as "our skater-inspired Salvation Army shopping phase" [par. 7]).

- What is the dominant impression you get of the young Desmond-Harris from this photo and how she describes it?

- How does the inclusion of this photograph contribute to the impression you get of the author as a teenager? How does the photograph help convey the adult writer's perspective?

Brad Benioff

Rick

Brad Benioff was a first-year college student when he wrote the following essay for an assignment in his composition class. Like Desmond-Harris in the preceding selection, Benioff focuses his essay on a memorable person, but unlike Desmond-Harris, Benioff focuses on someone he knew personally: his high-school water-polo coach, Rick Rezinas.

- *Before you read, reflect on your own experience of trying to impress someone. What did you do to win that person's approval? Why was it important to you to do so?*

- *As you read, consider the impression Benioff gives readers of himself as a high-school student in paragraph 7: "My reflection in his glasses stared back at me, accusing me of being too skinny, too young, too stupid, too weak to be on his team." What does this way of describing himself tell readers about Benioff?*

I walked through the dawn chill, shivering as much from nervousness as   1
from the cold. Steam curled up from the water in the pool and disappeared
in the ocher morning light. Athletes spread themselves about on the deck,
lazily stretching and whispering to each other as if the stillness were
sacred. It was to be my first practice with the high school water polo team.
I knew nothing about the game, but a friend had pushed me to play, arguing, "It's the most fun of any sport. Trust me." He had awakened me that
morning long before daylight, forced me into a bathing suit, and driven me
to the pool.

"Relax," he said. "Rick is the greatest of coaches. You'll like him. You'll   2
have fun."

The mythical Rick. I had heard of him many times before. All the older   3
players knew him by his first name and always spoke of him as a friend
rather than a coach. He was a math teacher at our school, and his classes
were very popular. Whenever class schedules came out, everyone hoped
to be placed in Mr. Rezinas's class. He had been known to throw parties
for the team or take them on weekend excursions skiing or backpacking.
To be Rick's friend was to be part of an exclusive club, and I was being
invited to join. And so I looked forward with nervous anticipation to meeting this man.

My friend walked me out to the pool deck and steered me toward a   4
man standing beside the pool.

"Rick," announced my friend, "I'd like you to meet your newest player."   5

Rick was not a friendly looking man. He wore only swim trunks, and his   6
short, powerful legs rose up to meet a bulging torso. His big belly was

solid. His shoulders, as if to offset his front-heaviness, were thrown back, creating a deep crease of excess muscle from his sides around the small of his back, a crease like a huge frown. His arms were crossed, two medieval maces placed carefully on their racks, ready to be swung at any moment. His round cheeks and chin were darkened by traces of black whiskers. His hair was sparse. Huge, black, mirrored sunglasses replaced his eyes. Below his prominent nose was a thin, sinister mustache. I couldn't believe this menacing-looking man was the legendary jovial Rick.

7   He said nothing at first. In those moments of silence, I felt more inade-quate than ever before in my life. My reflection in his glasses stared back at me, accusing me of being too skinny, too young, too stupid, too weak to be on his team. Where did I get the nerve to approach him with such a ridicu-lous body and ask to play water polo, a man's game? Finally, he broke the silence, having finished appraising my meager body. "We'll fatten him up," he growled.

8   Thus began a week of torture. For four hours a day, the coach stood beside the pool scowling down at me. I could do nothing right.

9   "No! No! No!" He shook his head in disgust. "Throw the damn ball with your whole arm! Get your goddamn elbow out of the water!"

10   Any failure on my part brought down his full wrath. He bellowed at my incompetence and punished me with push-ups and wind sprints. Even when I was close to utter exhaustion, I found no sympathy. "What the hell are you doing on the wall?" he would bellow. "Coach . . . my side, it's cramped."

11   "Swim on it! If you can't take a little pain, then you don't play!" With this, he would push me off the wall.

12   He seemed to enjoy playing me against the older, stronger players. "Goddamn it, Brad! If someone elbows or hits you, don't look out at me and cry, 'It's not fair.' Push back! Don't be so weak!" I got elbowed around until it seemed that none of my internal organs was unscathed. He worked me until my muscles wouldn't respond, and then he demanded more.

13   "You're not trying! Push it!"

14   "Would you move? You're too slow! Swim!"

15   "Damn it! Get out and give me twenty!"

16   It took little time for me to hate both the game and the man who ruled it.

17   I reacted by working as hard as I could. I decided to deprive him of the pleasure of finding fault with me. I learned quickly and started playing as flawlessly as possible. I dispensed with looking tired, showing pain, or complaining of cramps. I pushed, hit, and elbowed back at the biggest of players. No matter how flawless or aggressive my performance, though, he would find fault and let me know it. He was never critical of other players. He would laugh and joke with the other players; but whenever he saw me, he frowned.

I decided to quit.   18

After a particularly demanding practice, I walked up to this tyrant.   19
I tried to hold his gaze, but the black glasses forced me to look down.

"Coach Rezinas," I blurted, "I've decided that I don't want to play water   20
polo." His scowl deepened. Then after a moment he said, "You can't quit.
Not until after the first game." And he walked away. The dictator had issued
his command.

There was no rule to keep me from quitting. Anger flushed through me.   21
Somehow I would get revenge on this awful man. After the first game?
Okay. I would play. I would show him what a valuable player I was. He
would miss my talents when I quit. I worked myself up before the first
game by imagining the hated face: the black glasses, the thin mustache,
the open, snarling mouth. I was not surprised that he placed me in the
starting lineup because I was certain he would take me out soon. I played
furiously. The ball, the goal, the opposition, even the water seemed to be
extensions of Rick, his face glaring from every angle, his words echoing
loudly in my ears. Time and time again I would get the ball and, thinking of
his tortures, fire it toward the goal with a strength to kill. I forgot that he
might take me out. No defender could stand up to me. I would swim by
them or over them. Anger and the need for vengeance gave me energy.
I didn't notice the time slipping by, the quarters ending.

Then, the game ended. My teammates rushed out to me, congratulating   22
and cheering me. I had scored five goals, a school record for one game,
and shut out the other team with several key defensive plays. Now I could
get revenge. Now I could quit. I stepped out of the pool prepared with the
words I would spit into his face: "I QUIT!"

As I approached him, I stopped dead. He was smiling at me, his glasses   23
off. He reached out with his right hand and shook mine with exuberance.

"I knew you had it in you! I knew it!" he laughed.   24

Through his laughter, I gained a new understanding of the man. He had   25
pushed me to my fullest potential, tapping into the talent I may never have
found in myself. He was responsible for the way I played that day. My glory
was his. He never hated me. On the contrary, I was his apprentice, his
favored pupil. He had brought out my best. Could I really hate someone
who had done that much for me? He had done what he had promised: he
had fattened me up mentally as well as physically. All this hit me in a second and left me completely confused. I tried to speak, but only managed
to croak, "Coach . . . uh . . . I, uh. . . ." He cut me off with another burst of
laughter. He still shook my hand.

"Call me Rick," he said.   26

For an additional student reading, go to
bedfordstmartins.com/readingcritically.

READING FOR MEANING

This section presents three activities that will help you think about the meanings in Benioff's autobiographical essay. Your instructor may ask you to do one or more of these activities in class or online.

For more
help with
summarizing,
see Chapter 10,
pp. 518–19.

1. **Read to Summarize.** Write a sentence or two explaining what the story is about.

2. **Read to Respond.** Write a paragraph exploring your initial thoughts and feelings about Benioff's autobiographical essay. For example, consider anything that resonates with your experience or that seems contradictory, surprising, or fascinating, such as:

   - Rick's coaching style, perhaps comparing it with other styles of coaching or teaching with which you are familiar;

   - The high-school students' desire to be "Rick's friend" and thus "part of an exclusive club" (par. 3), perhaps in relation to your experience with exclusive groups in high school or college.

3. **Read to Analyze Assumptions.** Write a paragraph analyzing an assumption you find intriguing in Benioff's essay. For example:

   Assumptions about the good and bad qualities of coaching. Benioff's friend describes Rick as "the greatest of coaches" (par. 2), and Benioff writes that "the older players . . . always spoke of him as a friend rather than a coach" (par. 3). But Benioff calls Rick a "tyrant" (par. 19) and a "dictator" (par. 20). He complains that Rick demands too much of him and works him too hard, always finding fault and never giving him praise — at least, until Benioff proves himself to be worthy. To think critically about the assumptions in this essay related to coaching, consider questions like these:

   - What does Benioff assume are the good and the bad qualities of coaching? Why does his attitude change after the match?

   - In your experience, are coaches like Rick or other authority figures (such as parents, teachers, bosses) expected to be tough and critical rather than sympathetic and encouraging?

   - How do you think the historical or social context affects Rick's style of leadership or authority?

   Assumptions about the male body and masculinity. Benioff calls water polo "a man's game" and seems delighted that Rick "fattened [him] up mentally as well as physically" (par. 25). For example, Benioff describes his own body before undergoing Rick's makeover as "too skinny . . . too weak," "ridiculous," and "meager" (par. 7). These images are in sharp contrast to those he uses to describe Rick's "powerful," "bulging," "solid" muscular body (par. 6). To think critically about the assumptions in this essay related to the male body and masculinity, consider questions like these:

- What qualities of the male body does Benioff come to share with Rick? Where do you see evidence that our culture celebrates the same physical qualities that Benioff does?

- If you think of masculinity, or manliness, as a set of attitudes and behavior that may change over time and vary among different communities and cultural traditions, what does Benioff's admiration of Rick suggest about American ideas of manliness early in the twenty-first century?

- Where, if anywhere, does Benioff question the kind of masculinity Rick represents? What other qualities, if any, does our culture (or another culture of which you are aware) associate with masculinity?

READING LIKE A WRITER

PRESENTING PEOPLE

Description and dialogue can help create a vivid portrait and provide readers with insight into the writer's attitude toward and relationship with a person. Effective descriptions name the person and include a few well-chosen details that allow readers to visualize him or her. Descriptions may also compare the person to something else, often using *figures of speech* such as metaphor and simile. Dialogue can make readers feel as though they were overhearing what was said and how it was said. It usually includes **speaker tags** that identify the speaker ("he said" [par. 2]) and may also indicate the speaker's tone or attitude ("I blurted" [par. 20]).

> "Rick," announced my friend, "I'd like you to meet your newest player." (par. 5)

Speaker tag　"No! No! No!" He shook his head in disgust. "Throw the damn ball with your whole arm! Get your goddamn elbow out of the water!" (par. 9)

> "What the hell are you doing on the wall?" he would bellow. (par. 10)

In the third example, note that the word *would* indicates that the coach's typical tone of voice was bellowing (roaring like a bull).

Dialogue that is quoted can be especially expressive and vivid. But when the word choice is not particularly memorable, writers usually summarize dialogue to give readers the gist and move the story along more quickly.

Speaker tag   My teammates rushed out to me, congratulating and cheering me. (par. 22)
Summary

Analyze & Write

Write a paragraph or two analyzing Benioff's use of description and dialogue (whether quoted, paraphrased, or summarized) to portray Rick and help readers understand why he was such an important figure in Benioff's life.

1. Reread paragraph 6. Circle the parts of Rick's body Benioff names and under-line the visual details he uses to describe Rick's body. Also examine the two comparisons: a simile in sentence 4 and a metaphor in sentence 5. What do the naming, detailing, and comparing contribute to the dominant impression you get of Rick from Benioff's visual description?

2. Skim the dialogue between Rick and Benioff. Then pick two or three places where you think the dialogue is illuminating. What does each bit of dialogue tell you about the speaker or the relationship? What feelings or attitudes does it convey?

Reviewing What Makes Autobiography Effective

An effective autobiographical essay

- tells a story that is meaningful as well as engaging and dramatic;

- presents a vivid impression of people and places;

- helps readers understand why the event or person described in the story is important as well as memorable, bearing personal signifi-cance for the writer as well as cultural significance for readers.

Analyze & Write

Write a brief evaluation — positive, negative, or mixed — of one of the readings in this chapter, explaining why you think it succeeds or fails as an auto-biographical essay. Be sure to consider the characteristics that distinguish autobiographical writing, as well as how successful the writer has been in communicating her or his purpose to the intended audience. You may also want to consider the effect the medium of presentation had on decisions the writer made.

A GUIDE TO WRITING AUTOBIOGRAPHY

As you've read and discussed the reading selections in this chapter, you have probably done a good deal of analytical writing. Your instructor may assign a capstone project to write a brief autobiography of your own. Having learned how autobiographers invest their writing with drama, vividness, and significance and how readers interpret and respond to autobiographical writing, you can now approach autobiography confidently as a writer. This Guide to Writing offers detailed suggestions for writing autobiographical essays and resources to help you meet the special challenges this kind of writing presents.

THE WRITING ASSIGNMENT

Write an autobiographical essay about a significant event or person in your life.

- Choose an event or person that you feel comfortable writing about for this audience (your instructor and classmates), given your purpose (to present something meaningful).

- Consider how you can tell the story dramatically or describe the person vividly.

- Try to convey the meaning and importance in your life — what we call the **autobiographical significance** — of the event or person you've chosen to write about. Think about how you can lead readers to understand you better, to reflect on their own lives, to become aware of social and cultural influences, or to gain some other insights.

WRITING A DRAFT

INVENTION, PLANNING, AND COMPOSING

The following activities will help you choose a memorable event or an important person to write about, recall details about your subject, explore its significance in your life, and develop it into a well-told, vivid story.

Choosing a Subject

Rather than limiting yourself to the first subject that comes to mind, take a few minutes to consider your options and list as many subjects as you can. Below are some criteria that can help you choose a promising subject, followed by suggestions for the types of events and people you might consider writing about.

The subject should

- reveal something significant, possibly by centering on a conflict (within yourself or between you and another person or institution)

- express complex or ambivalent feelings (rather than superficial or sentimental ones that oversimplify the subject or make it predictable)

- lead readers to think about their own experience and about the cultural forces that shape their lives and yours

Appropriate events might include

- a difficult situation (for example, a time you had to make a tough choice or struggled to perform a challenging task)

- an incident that shaped you in a particular way or revealed a personality trait (independence, insecurity, ambition, jealousy, or heroism) that you had not recognized before

- an occasion when something did not turn out as you thought it would (for example, when you expected to be criticized but were praised or ignored instead, or when you were convinced you would succeed but failed)

- an encounter with another person that changed you (for example, altered how you see yourself, changed your ideas about other people, or led you to understand someone else's point of view)

An appropriate person might be

- someone who made you feel you were part of a larger community or had something worthwhile to contribute, or someone who made you feel alienated or like an outsider

- someone who helped you develop a previously unknown or undeveloped side of yourself or who led you to question assumptions or stereotypes you had about other people

- someone who surprised, pleased, or disappointed you (for example, someone you admired who let you down, or someone you did not appreciate who turned out to be admirable)

- someone in a position of power over you or someone over whom you had power

Shaping Your Story

Use the elements of the dramatic arc in Figure 2.1 (p. 28) to organize the story:

Sketching Out the Exposition, or Backstory. Your readers will need to understand what happened. Using the sentence strategies below as a starting point, sketch out the backstory of your event:

► In .... [year], while I was ....ing in .... [location], ...
► [Person's name] knew all about .... because s/he was a/an ...., an expert on ....
► In past years, I had previously .... Now I was starting ....

Drafting the "Inciting Incident." Sketch out the conflict that triggers the story. To dramatize it, try creating action sequences, using action verbs and prepositional phrases and dialogue, including speaker tags and quotation marks:

Action verb   A black Buick was moving toward us down the street. We all spread
Prepositional   out, banged together some regular snowballs, took aim, and, when the
phrase   Buick drew nigh, fired. (Dillard, par. 7)

                 "I'm going to the cave," I declared and marched down the path to check
                 out its mouth. (Ruprecht, par. 2)

Dramatizing the Rising Action and Climax. The moment of surprise, confrontation, crisis, or discovery — the climax of your story — can be dramatized by using action sequences and by repeating key words. Some writers also include dialogue to dramatize the climax:

He chased us through the backyard labyrinths of ten blocks before he caught us by our jackets. He caught us and we all stopped. [. . .] "You stupid kids," he began perfunctorily. (Dillard, pars. 15, 18)

Anger and the need for vengeance gave me energy. [. . .] Now I could get revenge. Now I could quit. [. . .] "I knew you had it in you! I knew it!" he laughed. (Benioff, pars. 21–22, 24)

Experimenting with Endings. Try out a variety of endings. For example, refer in the ending to something from the beginning — repetition with a difference.

Instead of bravely exploring on your own, you've chosen to be led around like a frightened kindergartner. (Ruprecht, par. 1)

The rest of the day I walked around with a happy smile, like the proudest little kindergartner you've ever seen. (Ruprecht, par. 10)

Presenting Important People and Places

Using Naming, Detailing, and Comparing. Describe the way important people look, dress, walk, or gesture; their tones of voice and mannerisms — anything that would help readers see the person as you remember her or him.

Naming   Rick was not a friendly looking man. [. . .] His shoulders, as if
Detailing   to offset his front-heaviness, were thrown back, creating a
Comparing (metaphor,   deep crease of excess muscle from his sides around the small
simile)   of his back, a crease like a huge frown. His arms were crossed,

two medieval maces placed carefully on their racks, ready to be swung at any moment. [. . .] Huge, black, mirrored sunglasses replaced his eyes. (Benioff, par. 6)

Using Dialogue. Reconstruct dialogue, using speaker tags to identify the speaker and possibly indicate the speaker's **tone** or attitude. Dialogue may be quoted to emphasize certain words or give readers a sense of the speaker's personality. It may also be summarized when the gist of what was said is most important, or paraphrased when the speaker's word choices are not important but the details are.

Summarized dialogue	The guide reprimanded us for endangering our lives and delaying the others. But as we started back to the bus, he pulled Ernie and
Speaker tag	me aside and said in a low voice, "Don't tell anybody, but I think
Quoted dialogue	what you guys did was seriously kick-ass!" (Ruprecht, par. 10)

Detailing Important Places. Incorporate descriptions of important places, identifying where the event happened or a place you associate with the person and including specific sensory details — size, shape, color, condition, and texture of the scene or memorable objects in it — that contribute to the dominant impression you want to create. Imagine the place from the front and from the side, from a distance and from up close. Try to keep a consistent point of view, describing the place as if you were walking through the scene or moving from right to left, or front to back.

Descriptive naming & detailing	. . . Ultimately my best friend, Thea, and I were left to our own 15-year-old devices to mourn that weekend. Her mother and
Comparing	stepfather were out of town. Their expansive, million-dollar
Location information	home was perched on a hillside less than an hour from Tupac's former stomping grounds in Oakland and Marin City. Of course, her home was also worlds away from both places.

  We couldn't "pour out" much alcohol undetected for a libation, so we limited ourselves to doing somber shots of liqueur from a well-stocked cabinet. One each. Tipsy, in a high-ceilinged kitchen surrounded by hardwood floors and Zen flower arrangements, we baked cookies for his mother. . . .

  On a sound system that echoed through speakers perched discreetly throughout the airy house, we played "Life Goes On" on a loop and sobbed. . . . (Desmond-Harris, pars. 3–5)

Including Visuals. Including visuals — photographs, postcards, ticket stubs — may strengthen your presentation of the event or person. If you submit your essay electronically or post it on a Web site, consider including snippets of video with sound as well as photographs or other memorabilia that might give readers a more vivid sense of the time, place, and people about which you are writing. If you want to use any photographs or recordings, though, be sure to request the permission of those depicted.

Reflecting on Your Subject

The following activities will help you think about the significance of your subject by reviewing the dominant impression made by your description and narration, recalling your remembered feelings and thoughts, and exploring your present perspective. The activities will also help you consider your purpose in writing about this subject and formulate a tentative thesis statement, even though the thesis in autobiography tends to be implied rather than stated explicitly.

Reviewing the Dominant Impression Your Description and Narration Create. Write for a few minutes about the kind of impression your writing now conveys and what you would like it to convey.

- Begin by rereading.

- Look back at the words you chose to describe places and people, as well as the way you dramatized the story.

- Consider the tone and connotations of your word choices. What meanings or feelings do they evoke?

- Note any contradictions or changes in tone or mood that could lead you to a deeper understanding.

Exploring How You Felt at the Time. Write for a few minutes, trying to recall your thoughts and feelings when the event was occurring or when you knew the person:

- What did you feel — in control or powerless, proud or embarrassed, vulnerable, detached, judgmental — and how did you show or express your feelings?

- What did you want others to think of you at the time, and what did you think of yourself?

- What were the immediate consequences for you personally?

These sentence strategies may help you put your feelings into words:

- ▶ As the event started [or during or right after the event], I felt .... and ....
- ▶ I showed or expressed these feelings by ....
- ▶ I hoped others would think of me as ....

Exploring Your Present Perspective. Write for a few minutes, trying to express your present thoughts and feelings as you look back on the event or person:

- How have your feelings changed, and what insights do you now have?

- What does your present perspective reveal about what you were like at the time?

- Try looking at the event or person in broad cultural or social terms. For example, consider whether you or anyone else upset gender expectations or felt out of place in some way.

These sentence strategies may help you put your feelings into words:

- My feelings since the event [have/have not] changed in the following ways: ....

- At the time, I had been going through ...., which may have affected my experience by ....

- Looking back at the event now, I realize I was probably trying to ...., though I didn't appreciate that fact at the time.

Considering Your Purpose and Audience.   Write for several minutes exploring what you want your readers to understand about the significance of the event or person. Use the following questions to help clarify your thoughts:

- What will writing about this event or person enable you to suggest about yourself as an individual?

- What will it let you suggest about the social and cultural forces that helped shape you — for example, how people exercise power over one another, how family and community values and attitudes affect individuals, or how economic and social conditions influence our sense of self?

- What about the event or relationship still puzzles you or seems contradictory? What do you feel ambivalent about?

- What about your subject do you expect will seem familiar to your readers? What do you think will surprise them, perhaps getting them to think in new ways or to question some of their assumptions and stereotypes?

Formulating a Working Thesis.   Write a few sentences trying to articulate a working thesis that explains the significance that you want your writing to convey. Even though readers do not expect autobiographical writing to include an explicit thesis statement, stating a thesis now may help you explore ambivalent feelings and lead you to a deeper understanding of your subject. It also may help you as you continue working on your draft, organizing the story, selecting descriptive details, and choosing words to relate your feelings and thoughts.

Drafting Your Story

By this point, you have done a lot of writing

- to develop a plan for telling a compelling story;

- to present people and places in vivid detail;

- to show or tell the autobiographical significance of your story in a way that will be meaningful for your readers.

Now stitch that material together to create a draft. The next two parts of this Guide to Writing will help you evaluate and improve your draft.

Considering a Useful Sentence Strategy

Participial phrases can be useful additions to autobiographical stories because they help make descriptions of people, places, and events more vivid and dramatic. **Participles** are verb forms ending in *-ing* (*being, longing, grasping, drinking*) or *-ed, -d, -en, -n,* or *-t* (*baked, found, driven, torn, sent*). (Participles ending in *-ing* are in the present tense and participles ending in *-ed, -d, -en, -n,* or *-t* are in the past tense.)

Participial phrases work as adjectives to modify the nouns that precede them, but because they are based on verbs, they express the energy inherent in action verbs. Here's an example:

Participial phrase   I remember trotting up my apartment building's stairs, physically
Participle   tired but buzzing with the frenetic energy and possibilities for
                      change that accompany fall and a new school year. (Desmond-
                      Harris, par. 1)

The participial phrase here colorfully describes how Desmond-Harris felt at that moment just before hearing of the death of her teen idol.

Here are a few ways you can use participial phrases in autobiographical writing:

To show simultaneous actions

Noun/pronoun   Every time I glanced back, choking for breath, . . . (Dillard, par. 13)
Participial phrase   He'd pose with it, whiskers twitching, while the women cooed their
                    admiration. (Shah, par. 3)

To make a previously mentioned action or image more specific and vivid

We flaunted it, buying Kwanzaa candles and insisting on celebrating privately (really, just lighting the candles and excluding our friends) at a sleepover. (Desmond-Harris, par. 12)

To relate what you or someone else was thinking or feeling at the time

I popped out of the cave, expecting a welcome worthy of a Chilean miner. (Ruprecht, par. 9)

I walked through the dawn chill, shivering as much from nervousness as from the cold. (Benioff, par. 1)

EVALUATING THE DRAFT

GETTING A CONSTRUCTIVE CRITICAL READING

Getting a critical reading of your draft will help you see how to improve it. Your instructor may schedule class time for reading drafts, or you may want to ask a classmate or a tutor in the writing center to read your draft. Ask your reader to use the following guidelines and to write out a response for you to consult during your revision.

READING A DRAFT CRITICALLY

Read for a First Impression

1. **Read the draft without stopping, and then write a few sentences giving your general impression.**

2. **Identify one aspect of the draft that seems especially effective.**

Read Again to Suggest Improvements

1. **Recommend ways to make the narrative more dramatic and telling.**

   - Note where the narrative seems especially effective in arousing curiosity, building suspense, revealing something important.

   - Point to any passages where the action seems to drag and suggest strategies to intensify the drama, such as adding action verbs, dialogue, prepositional phrases; repeating key words and phrases; using exaggeration.

   - Indicate any passages where quotations could be more effective than paraphrasing or summary.

2. **Suggest ways to make the description more vivid or to convey the dominant impression more effectively.**

   - Describe the dominant impression you get from the description of people and places.

   - Identify one or two passages where you think the description is especially vivid.

   - Point to any passages where the description could be made more vivid or where it seems to contradict the impression you get from other parts of the essay.

3. **Suggest how the autobiographical significance could be better developed.**

   - Briefly explain your understanding of the significance, indicating anything that puzzles or surprises you.

   - Note any word choice, contradiction, or irony — in the way people and places are described or in the way the story is told — that alerts you to a deeper meaning that the writer could develop.

   - Point to any passages where the writer needs to clarify the historical, social, or cultural dimensions of the experience or relationship.

4. **Suggest how the organization could be improved.**

   - Consider the overall plan, perhaps by making a scratch outline using the elements of the dramatic arc.

   - Note any passages where transitions could clarify time or space relationships.

5. **Evaluate the effectiveness of visuals.**

   - Point to any visuals that seem especially effective, and briefly explain why.

   - Identify any visuals that the writer could consider dropping or changing, and briefly explain why.

For coverage of scratch outlines, see Chapter 10, p. 517; for coverage of the dramatic arc, see pp. 27–28.

IMPROVING THE DRAFT

REVISING, EDITING, AND PROOFREADING

Start improving your draft by reflecting on what you have written thus far:

- Review critical reading comments from your classmates, instructor, or writing center tutor. What are your readers getting at?

- Take another look at your notes and ideas: What else should you consider?

- Review your draft: What else can you do to make your story compelling?

Revising Your Draft

Revising means reenvisioning your draft, trying to see it in a new way, given your purpose and audience, in order to develop a more engaging, more thoughtful autobiographical essay. Think imaginatively and boldly about cutting unconvincing material, adding new material, and moving material around. The suggestions in the chart below may help you solve problems and strengthen your essay.

TROUBLESHOOTING YOUR DRAFT

To Make the Narrative More Dramatic

Problem	Suggestions for Revising
The story meanders and seems to have no point.	• Cut unnecessary exposition and make the inciting incident more dramatic and suspenseful. • Tighten the inciting incident, rising and falling action by eliminating complications. • Connect the inciting incident directly to the climax, showing how they both stem from the central conflict.
The narrative drags or tension slackens.	• Add strategies to intensify the drama, such as action verbs, prepositional phrases, repetition of key words and phrases. • Use participial phrases to show simultaneous actions. • Dramatize the conflict with quoted dialogue. • Add transitions to propel the story through time and space.
Background information or descriptive detail interrupts the drama.	• Keep only the essential information and vivid detail. • Move the information or detail to the exposition or resolution, or cut it altogether.
The dialogue does not seem interesting or important.	• Paraphrase or summarize dialogue instead of quoting it. • Quote only memorable words or phrases. • Add vivid description to the speaker tags.

To Present People Vividly

Problem	Suggestions for Revising
The description of people is vague.	• Add sensory details showing what people look and sound like. • Use speaker tags to reveal the people's attitudes and personality.
Some of the detail seems contradictory.	• Consider whether the contradictions can be used to develop the significance or could be cut.

To Describe Places Vividly

Problem	Suggestions for Revising
The dominant impression is unclear or contradictory.	• Cut unnecessary details. • Consider whether contradictions may suggest ways to clarify or deepen the significance.
Readers cannot imagine the place.	• Add more specific nouns to name objects in the scene. • Add more sensory detail to evoke the sense of sight, touch, smell, taste, or hearing. • Use metaphor or simile to add suggestive comparisons.
The point of view is confusing.	• Make the point of view consistent.

To Convey the Autobiographical Significance

Problem	Suggestions for Revising
Readers may not understand the significance.	• Sharpen the dominant impression to show the significance. • Expand or add passages where you use telling to convey the significance directly. • Add remembered thoughts and feelings, using participial phrases to reveal what you were thinking or feeling at the time. • Articulate your present perspective.
The significance seems too pat or simplistic.	• Explore and develop contradictions and complexities in how you view the significance. • Express ambivalent feelings.
Readers may not understand the context.	• Give social, cultural, or historical background information to reveal important influences.

To Make the Organization More Effective

Problem	Suggestions for Revising
Readers may be confused about what happened when.	• Add or clarify transitions. • Make sure the verb tenses are not confusing.

Editing and Proofreading Your Draft

Check for errors in usage, punctuation, and mechanics, and consider matters of style. If you keep a list of errors you typically make, begin by checking your draft against this list. Ask someone else to proofread your essay before you submit it to your instructor.

Research on student writing shows that autobiographical writing often has sentence fragments, run-together sentences, and verb tense errors. Check a writer's handbook for help with these potential problems.

Reflecting on What You Have Learned

Autobiography

In this chapter, you have read critically several pieces of autobiography and have written one of your own. To better remember what you have learned, pause now to reflect on the reading and writing activities you completed in this chapter.

1. Write a page or so reflecting on what you have learned. Begin by describing what you are most pleased with in your essay. Then explain what you think contributed to your achievement. Be specific about this contribution.

   - If it was something you learned from the readings, indicate which readings and specifically what you learned from them.

   - If it came from the writing you did in response to prompts in this chapter, point out the section or sections that helped you most.

   - If you got good advice from a critical reader, explain exactly how the person helped you — perhaps by helping you understand a problem in your draft or by helping you add a new dimension to your writing.

   Try to write about your achievement in terms of what you have learned about the genre.

2. Reflect more generally on how you tend to interpret autobiographical writing, your own as well as other writers'. Consider some of the following questions:

   - In reading for meaning, do you tend to find yourself interpreting the significance of the event or person in terms of the writer's personal feelings, sense of self-esteem, or psychological well-being? Or do you more often think of significance in terms of larger social or economic influences — for example, in terms of the writer's gender, class, or ethnicity?

- Where do you think you learned to interpret the significance of people's stories about themselves and their relationships — from your family, friends, television, school?

Observation

Observational writing comprises analytical, informative, and thought-provoking portraits, or *profiles*, of a person or a place. These profiles may be cultural ethnographies, ranging from "a day-in-the-life" to an extended immersion study of a community or people at work or at play. They are intensively researched, centering on the field-research techniques of detailed observations and edifying interviews. As a result, observational profiles are generally entertaining to read, sometimes amusing, and often surprising and captivating. Whether written in a college course, for the broader community, or about the workplace, at its best, observational writing brings the subject to life, taking readers behind the scenes and giving them new insights.

This chapter offers several brief observational reading selections for you to enjoy, with exploratory activities that will help you learn to read critically and write well. The Reading for Meaning and Reading Like a Writer activities following each selection invite you to analyze and write about the reading's ideas and writing strategies. You can also use the brief Guide to Writing Observational Essays toward the end of the chapter to help you write about an important event or a person who played a vital role in your life.

RHETORICAL SITUATIONS FOR OBSERVATIONS

Many people — including bloggers, journalists, psychologists, and cultural anthropologists — write essays based on observations and interviews, as the following examples suggest:

- For an art history course, a student writes a paper about a local artist recently commissioned to paint an outdoor mural for the city. The student visits the artist's studio and talks with him about the process of painting murals, large pictures painted on walls or the sides of buildings. The artist invites the student to spend the following day as a part of a team of local art students and neighborhood volunteers working on the mural under the artist's direction. This firsthand experience helps the student profile the artist, present some of the students on his team, and give readers an intimate understanding of the process and collaboration involved in mural painting.

- For a company Web site, a public relations officer profiles the corporation's new chief executive officer (CEO). He begins by interviewing several lower-level managers and office personnel to learn about their expectations and first impressions of her. Then he follows the CEO from meeting to meeting, taking photographs and observing her interactions with colleagues. Between meetings, he interviews her about her management philosophy. He decides to contrast employees' preconceptions of her as hard-nosed with the collaborative management style she advocated in the interview and exhibited in the meetings he observed.

- For a blog, a student writes about a controversial urban renewal project to replace decaying houses with a library and park. To learn about the history of the project, she reads newspaper reports and interviews people who helped plan the project as well as some neighborhood residents and activists who oppose it. She also tours the site with the project manager to see what is actually being done. In addition to presenting different points of view about the project, her essay describes the library and park in detail, including pictures of the neighborhood before the project and drawings of what it will look like afterward.

Thinking about the Genre

Observation

Before studying a type of writing, it is useful to spend some time thinking about what you already know about it. You may have spoken or written about your firsthand observations, describing what you saw or heard, for a school assignment or during a trip. Alternatively, you may have heard friends or family recount their observations or have read the observations of others.

Recall one occasion when you reported your observations or heard or read the observations of others. Your instructor may ask you to write about your experience or discuss it with others in class or online. Use the following questions to develop your thoughts:

- Who was the audience? How did reporting observations to this audience affect the way the writer conveyed his or her perspective? How did communicating to this audience affect how the story was

(continued)

told? For example, would the readers have been intrigued by the people described and what they said or would they have been interested in the information you conveyed?

- What was the purpose? What did the writer want the audience to learn? For example, was the report primarily intended to teach them something, to show them what the writer had learned, to entertain them, or for some other reason? What did the writer choose to emphasize? Why?

- If the audience or purpose had been different, how might the observation have changed? For example, would the writer have acted as a spectator observing the subject from afar or would the writer have tried to become involved as a participant observer? Would the writer have chosen other people to interview or asked different questions? Also think about how changing the medium of presentation would affect what the writer chose to include and how he or she presented it. For example, if making a documentary film or a podcast based on observations and interviews, how would the film have begun and ended? How would the writer have introduced the people the film interviewed?

A GUIDE TO READING OBSERVATIONS

This guide introduces you to the strategies typical of observational writing by inviting you to analyze a brief but intriguing profile of Albert Yeganeh and his unique restaurant, Soup Kitchen International, first by *reading for meaning* and then by *reading like a writer*.

- *Reading for meaning* will help you understand what we call the writer's **perspective** — the main idea or cultural significance that the writer wants readers to take away from reading the observational profile.

- *Reading like a writer* will help you learn how the writer makes the essay interesting and informative, by examining how he or she uses some of the basic features and strategies typical of observational writing:

  1. Deciding whether to take the role of a spectator or a participant

  2. Determining what information to include and how to present it

  3. Organizing the information in a way that will be entertaining to readers

  4. Conveying a perspective on the subject

The *New Yorker*

Soup

"Soup" (1989) was published anonymously in the New Yorker, *a magazine known for its observational profiles of fascinating people and places. The subject of the article is Albert Yeganeh, the creative and demanding owner/chef of a small take-out restaurant (originally called Soup Kitchen International, now called Soup Man). Yeganeh's restaurant inspired an episode of the then-popular television sitcom* Seinfeld *called "The Soup Nazi." Apparently Yeganeh was so angry that when Jerry Seinfeld went to the restaurant after the episode aired, the chef demanded an apology and told Seinfeld to leave.*

- ● **Before you read,** *note the title and these quotations that open the essay: "Soup is my lifeblood" and "I am extremely hard to please." The title and first quote clearly refer to the kind of food served at the restaurant, but the second quote seems to have a different purpose. What does it lead you to expect from the essay?*

- ● **As you read,** *think about how the writer represented Yeganeh to the original* New Yorker *readers. If you have seen the "Soup Nazi" episode from* Seinfeld, *you might compare the way Yeganeh is portrayed in the sitcom to the way he is portrayed in the article. Consider also how Yeganeh is portrayed on his franchise Web site, originalsoupman.com: "His standing and reputation have nothing to do with his personality or any urban legends that swirl around him. Everything starts — and ends — in the soup bowl."*

Soup Man

1   When Albert Yeganeh says "Soup is my lifeblood," he means it. And when he says "I am extremely hard to please," he means that, too. Working like a demon alchemist in a tiny storefront kitchen at 259-A West Fifty-fifth Street, Mr. Yeganeh creates anywhere from eight to seventeen soups every weekday. His concoctions are so popular that a wait of half an hour at the lunchtime peak is not uncommon, although there are strict rules for conduct in line. But more on that later.

2   "I am psychologically kind of a health freak," Mr. Yeganeh said the other day, in a lisping staccato of Armenian origin. "And I know that soup is the greatest meal in the world. It's very good for your digestive system. And I use only the best, the freshest ingredients. I am a perfectionist. When I make a clam soup, I use three different kinds of clams. Every other place uses canned clams. I'm called crazy. I am not crazy. People don't realize why I get so upset. It's because if the soup is not perfect and I'm still selling it, it's a torture. It's *my* soup, and that's why I'm so upset. First you clean and then you cook. I don't believe that ninety-nine per cent of the restaurants in New York know how to clean a tomato. I tell my crew to wash the parsley *eight* times. If they wash it five or six times, I scare them. I tell them they'll go to jail if there is sand in the parsley. One time, I found a mushroom on the floor, and I fired that guy who left it there." He spread his arms and added, "This place is the only one like it in . . . in . . . the whole earth! One day, I hope to learn something from the other places, but so far I haven't. For example, the other day I went to a very fancy restaurant and had borscht. I had to send it back. It was *junk*. I could see all the chemicals in it. I never use chemicals. Last weekend, I had lobster bisque in Brooklyn, a very well-known place. It was *junk*. When I make a lobster bisque, I use a whole lobster. You know, I never advertise. I don't have to. All the big-shot chefs and the kings of the hotels come here to see what *I'm* doing."

3   As you approach Mr. Yeganeh's Soup Kitchen International from a distance, the first thing you notice about it is the awning, which proclaims "Homemade Hot, Cold, Diet Soups." The second thing you notice is an aroma so delicious that it makes you want to take a bite out of the air. The third thing you notice, in front of the kitchen, is an electric signboard that flashes, saying, "Today's Soups . . . Chicken Vegetable . . . Mexican Beef Chili . . . Cream of Watercress . . . Italian Sausage . . . Clam Bisque . . . Beef Barley . . . Due to Cold Weather . . . For Most Efficient and Fastest Service the Line Must . . . Be Kept Moving . . . Please . . . Have Your Money . . . Ready . . . Pick the Soup of Your Choice . . . Move to Your Extreme . . . Left After Ordering."

4   "I am not prejudiced against color or religion," Mr. Yeganeh told us, and he jabbed an index finger at the flashing sign. "Whoever follows that I treat very well. My regular customers don't say anything. They are very intelligent and well educated. They know I'm just trying to move the line. The

New York cop is very smart—he sees everything but says nothing. But the young girl who wants to stop and tell you how nice you look and hold everyone up—*yah*!" He made a guillotining motion with his hand. "I tell you, I hate to work with the public. They treat me like a slave. My philosophy is: The customer is always wrong and I'm always right. I raised my prices to try to get rid of some of these people, but it didn't work."

The other day, Mr. Yeganeh was dressed in chef's whites with orange   5 smears across his chest, which may have been some of the carrot soup cooking in a huge pot on a little stove in one corner. A three-foot-long handheld mixer from France sat on the sink, looking like an overgrown gardening tool. Mr. Yeganeh spoke to two young helpers in a twisted Armenian-Spanish barrage, then said to us, "I have no overhead, no trained waitresses, and I have the cashier here." He pointed to himself theatrically. Beside the doorway, a glass case with fresh green celery, red and yellow peppers, and purple eggplant was topped by five big gray soup urns. According to a piece of cardboard taped to the door, you can buy Mr. Yeganeh's soups in three sizes, costing from four to fifteen dollars. The order of any well-behaved customer is accompanied by little waxpaper packets of bread, fresh vegetables (such as scallions and radishes), fresh fruit (such as cherries or an orange), a chocolate mint, and a plastic spoon. No coffee, tea, or other drinks are served.

"I get my recipes from books and theories and my own taste," Mr.   6 Yeganeh said. "At home, I have several hundreds of books. When I do research, I find that I don't know anything. Like cabbage is a cancer fighter, and some fish is good for your heart but some is bad. Every day, I should have one sweet, one spicy, one cream, one vegetable soup—and they *must* change, they should always taste a little different." He added that he wasn't sure how extensive his repertoire was, but that it probably includes at least eighty soups, among them African peanut butter, Greek moussaka, hamburger, Reuben, B.L.T., asparagus and caviar, Japanese shrimp miso, chicken chili, Irish corned beef and cabbage, Swiss chocolate, French calf's brain, Korean beef ball, Italian shrimp and eggplant Parmesan, buffalo, ham and egg, short rib, Russian beef Stroganoff, turkey cacciatore, and Indian mulligatawny. "The chicken and the seafood are an addiction, and when I have French garlic soup I let people have only one small container each," he said. "The doctors and nurses love that one."

A lunch line of thirty people stretched down the block from Mr.   7 Yeganeh's doorway. Behind a construction worker was a man in expensive leather, who was in front of a woman in a fur hat. Few people spoke. Most had their money out and their orders ready.

At the front of the line, a woman in a brown coat couldn't decide which   8 soup to get and started to complain about the prices.

"You talk too much, dear," Mr. Yeganeh said, and motioned her to move   9 to the left. "Next!"

10   "Just don't talk. Do what he says," a man huddled in a blue parka warned.

11   "He's downright rude," said a blond woman in a blue coat. "Even abusive. But you can't deny it, his soup is the best."

READING FOR MEANING

This section presents three activities that will help you think about the meanings in "Soup." Your instructor may ask you to do one or more of these activities in class or online.

For more help with summarizing, see Chapter 10, pp. 518–19.

1. **Read to Summarize.** Write a sentence or two briefly explaining what you learned about Yeganeh and his views about running a restaurant.

2. **Read to Respond.** Write a paragraph or two exploring your initial thoughts and feelings about the observational essay "Soup." For example, consider anything that resonates with your experience or that seems contradictory, surprising, or fascinating, such as:

   • Yeganeh's ideas about food quality and health, perhaps in comparison to the quality at fast-food restaurants with which you are familiar;

   • Yeganeh's work ethic, perhaps in relation to your experience as an employee or a manager.

You may also try contextualizing; see Chapter 10, pp. 522–23.

3. **Read to Analyze Assumptions. Assumptions** are ideas, beliefs, or values that are taken for granted as commonly accepted truths. The assumptions in a text usually reflect the writer's own attitudes or cultural traditions, but they may also represent other people's views. Sometimes assumptions are stated explicitly, but they also may be only implied or hinted at through the writer's choice of words or examples. Write a paragraph or two analyzing an assumption you find intriguing in this essay. For example:

   Assumptions about authority. Yeganeh describes himself as "a perfectionist" (par. 2) and admits he's "extremely hard to please" (par. 1). He brags about scaring his employees and defends his right to deny service to anyone who does not follow his rules. To think critically about the assumptions in this essay related to power, ask yourself questions like these:

   • When Yeganeh talks about scaring and firing his employees (par. 2), does he seem to be holding them to an appropriately high standard or is he just being a bully? In telling the story, is he showing off for the writer, making a serious point, or both?

   Take a quiz to check your reading and vocabulary comprehension:
   bedfordstmartins.com/readingcritically

- When Yeganeh tells a customer she talks too much and then refuses to serve her (par. 9), is he being a tyrant or is he right to use his power in this way?
- What do you think are Yeganeh's reasons for acting as he does? Is his behavior justifiable? Why or why not?

You may also try reflecting on challenges to your beliefs and values; see Chapter 10, pp. 526–27.

Assumptions about customer service. When Yeganeh says, "The customer is always wrong and I'm always right" (par. 4), he is reversing the popular saying that the customer is always right. To think critically about assumptions in this essay related to customer service, ask yourself questions like these:

- What seem to be the assumptions of the writer and of Yeganeh's customers about service?
- What influences our assumptions about service—for example, the type of restaurant (take-out or sit-down, family style or formal), how much it costs, our attitudes toward service work and workers?

READING LIKE A WRITER

This section presents four brief activities that will help you analyze the writing in "Soup." Your instructor may ask you to do one or more of these activities in class or online.

Presenting Information about the Subject

Observational writing, like autobiography (Chapter 2), succeeds in large part by describing people and places vividly. The describing strategies of *naming* objects together with *detailing* their color, shape, size, texture, and other qualities enable readers to imagine what the people and places look, sound, feel, and smell like. Writers also may use *comparing* in the form of simile or metaphor to add a playful or suggestive image to the description:

Naming   The other day, Mr. Yeganeh was dressed in chef's whites with orange smears
Detailing   across his chest, which may have been some of the carrot soup cooking in a
Comparing   huge pot on a little stove in one corner. A three-foot-long handheld mixer
(simile)   from France sat on the sink, looking like an overgrown gardening tool.
               (par. 5)

Writers often use *speaker tags* along with dialogue to characterize people as they talk and interact with others. For example:

Speaker tag   "I am psychologically kind of a health freak," *Mr. Yeganeh said the other day,*
                 in a lisping staccato of Armenian origin. (par. 2)

The author of "Soup" uses dialogue extensively to give readers a vivid impression of the man, his business, and his ideas. Indeed, most of the information in this selection comes from long chunks of an extended interview with Yeganeh, and the profile concludes with a brief overheard exchange between Yeganeh and two people in line.

| Analyze & Write |

Write a paragraph analyzing the use of naming, detailing, and comparing to present Albert Yeganeh:

1. Find a few examples in paragraphs 1, 2, 4, 5, and 6 where you think the naming and detailing give an especially vivid description of Yegenah. What is the dominant impression you get from this description?

2. Also find an example of comparing, either a *simile* (a comparison using *like* or *as*) or a *metaphor* (a comparison that does not use this kind of signaling word). What ideas and associations does this comparison contribute to the impression you got from the other describing strategies? How does it reinforce, extend, change, or complicate the dominant impression?

3. Reflect on what, if anything, you learn from Yeganeh about making soup or operating a restaurant.

Organizing the Information

Writers of observational essays typically rely on three basic organizational plans: *topical*, *narrative*, and *spatial*. As the following examples show, an essay may use all of these ways of arranging information. Note also the kinds of organizational cues — such as transitional words and phrases, calendar and clock time, and prepositional phrases indicating time or location — writers use for each kind of organization.

Topic Organizational cue	"I am psychologically kind of a health freak." … "And I know that soup is … very good for your digestive system. And I use only the best, the freshest ingredients. I am a perfectionist." (par. 2)
Narrative cue	The other day, Mr. Yeganeh … Mr. Yeganeh spoke to two young helpers in a twisted Armenian-Spanish barrage, then said to us … (par. 5)
Spatial cue	As you approach Mr. Yeganeh's Soup Kitchen International from a distance, the first thing you notice about it is … The second thing you notice is … The third thing you notice, in front of the kitchen, is … (par. 3)

Analyze & Write

Write a paragraph analyzing the use of topical, narrative, and spatial organizing strategies in "Soup":

1. First, make a scratch outline of paragraphs 4, 5, and 6 of "Soup," listing the topics or kinds of information presented. (Some paragraphs include more than one topic. You do not have to list every topic, but try to identify the most important ones.)

2. Then reread paragraphs 7 to 11, where the writer presents a brief narrative. Consider what relation, if any, this concluding narrative has to the topics that were presented in earlier paragraphs. What, if anything, do you learn from the narrative that illuminates or adds to what you learned from the earlier paragraphs?

3. Finally, scan the essay looking for any other parts that, in addition to the passage quoted above from paragraph 3, organize the information spatially. What cues help you recognize the spatial arrangement?

Adopting an Authorial Role

In making observations and writing them up, writers have a choice of roles to perform: as a *detached spectator* or as a *participant observer*. In the **spectator** role, the writer acts as an independent reporter, watching and listening but remaining outside of the activity. In contrast, the **participant observer** becomes an insider, at least for a short time, joining in the activity with the people being interviewed and observed. We can see examples of both roles in this excerpt from the reading selection by John T. Edge (pp. 80–84):

Participant role   It's just past 4:00 on a Thursday afternoon in June at Jesse's Place . . . I sit alone at the bar, one empty bottle of Bud in front of me, a second in my hand. I drain the beer, order a third, and stare down at the pink juice spreading outward from a crumpled foil pouch and onto the bar.

     I'm not leaving until I eat this thing, I tell myself.

Spectator role   Half a mile down the road, behind a fence coiled with razor wire, Lionel Dufour, proprietor of Farm Fresh Food Supplier, is loading up the last truck of the day, wheeling case after case of pickled pork offal out of his cinder-block processing plant and into a semitrailer bound for Hattiesburg, Mississippi. (pars. 1–3)

| Analyze & Write |

Write a paragraph discussing the role the writer of "Soup" chose to adopt:

1. Find one or two signs indicating the role the writer has taken, such as the use of the first- or third-person perspective or places where the writer included insider knowledge derived from taking the role of participant observer.

2. What advantages or disadvantages do you see in the role the writer chose to take? What would have been gained (or lost) had the writer chosen a different role?

Conveying a Perspective on the Subject

Writers of observational essays, like autobiographers, convey their perspective on what is significant or intriguing about the subject in two ways:

- by showing
- by telling

One way writers show their perspective is through the dominant impression they create. (See Presenting Information about the Subject, p. 75.) Another way writers use showing is by selecting choice quotes that give readers insight into the speaker, as in this example of Yeganeh's comments about what makes his cooking special:

> Does he really want to learn from others?
>
> Do chefs really respect him or does he have delusions of grandeur?

"One day, I hope to learn something from the other places, but so far I haven't. For example, the other day I went to a very fancy restaurant and had borscht. I had to send it back. It was *junk*. I could see all the chemicals in it. I never use chemicals. Last weekend, I had lobster bisque in Brooklyn, a very well-known place. It was *junk*. . . . All the big-shot chefs and the kings of the hotels come here to see what *I'm* doing." (par. 2)

Observational writers occasionally also use telling to say explicitly what they think of the subject. More often, they imply their judgment of or attitude toward the subject through their word choices. For example, consider whether the writer is praising or criticizing Yeganeh in these opening sentences. Is the tone sarcastic, flattering, or something else?

> When Albert Yeganeh says "Soup is my lifeblood," he means it. And when he says "I am extremely hard to please," he means that, too. (par. 1)

| Analyze & Write |

Write a paragraph examining how the writer uses showing and/or telling to convey a perspective on Yeganeh and his Soup Kitchen International:

1. Skim paragraphs 3–11, looking for examples of showing in the descriptions and in the choice of quotations. Choose one or two examples and explain what they suggest about the writer's perspective on Yeganeh as a human being, cook, and businessman.

2. Look also for one or two examples of telling. What do they add to your understanding of the writer's perspective?

READINGS

John T. Edge

I'm Not Leaving Until I Eat This Thing

John T. Edge (b. 1962) earned an MFA in creative nonfiction from Goucher College as well as an MA in southern studies from the University of Mississippi, where he currently directs the Southern Foodways Alliance at the Center for the Study of Southern Culture. A food writer for outlets such as Oxford American, *the* New York Times, *and NPR's* All Things Considered, *Edge has also been published in many anthologies. He has coedited several cookbooks and travel guides, and he has written several books, including* Truck Food Cookbook *(2012), a study of American street food;* Southern Belly *(2007), a portrait of southern food told through profiles of people and places; and a series on iconic American foods, including* Hamburgers and Fries: An American Story *(2005) and* Donuts: An American Passion *(2006). This reading first appeared in 1999 in* Oxford American *magazine (where the illustration on p. 82 appeared) and was reprinted in the* Utne Reader.

- *Before you read, think about what the title leads you to expect from the essay. What rhetorical effect does this strategy have on readers?*

- *As you read, you will see that Edge moves between two different scenes — Jesse's Place and the Farm Fresh Food Supplier processing plant. Notice that whereas Edge uses a chronological narrative to relate what happened at Jesse's Place, he uses a topical organization to present the information he learned from his observations and interview at Farm Fresh. Why do you think he uses different methods for presenting these two scenes?*

How does Edge help readers visualize the scene?

It's just past 4:00 on a Thursday afternoon in June at Jesse's Place, a country juke 17 miles south of the Mississippi line and three miles west of Amite, Louisiana. The air conditioner hacks and spits forth torrents of Arctic air, but the heat of summer can't be kept at bay. It seeps around the splintered doorjambs and settles in, transforming the squat particleboard-plastered roadhouse into a sauna. Slowly, the dank barroom fills with grease-smeared mechanics from the truck stop up the road and farmers straight from the fields, the soles of their brogans thick with dirt clods. A few weary souls make their way over from the nearby sawmill. I sit alone at the bar, one empty bottle of Bud in front of me, a second in my hand. I drain the beer, order a third, and stare down at the pink juice spreading outward from a crumpled foil pouch and onto the bar.

1

2   *I'm not leaving until I eat this thing,* I tell myself.

3   Half a mile down the road, behind a fence coiled with razor wire, Lionel Dufour, proprietor of Farm Fresh Food Supplier, is loading up the last truck of the day, wheeling case after case of pickled pork offal out of his cinder-block processing plant and into a semi-trailer bound for Hattiesburg, Mississippi.

4   His crew packed lips today. Yesterday, it was pickled sausage; the day before that, pig feet. Tomorrow, it's pickled pig lips again. Lionel has been on the job since 2:45 in the morning, when he came in to light the boilers. Damon Landry, chief cook and maintenance man, came in at 4:30. By 7:30, the production line was at full tilt: six women in white smocks and blue bouffant caps, slicing ragged white fat from the lips, tossing the good parts in glass jars, the bad parts in barrels bound for the rendering plant. Across the aisle, filled jars clatter by on a conveyor belt as a worker tops them off with a Kool-Aid-red slurry of hot sauce, vinegar, salt, and food coloring. Around the corner, the jars are capped, affixed with a label, and stored in pasteboard boxes to await shipping.

5   Unlike most offal—euphemistically called "variety meats"—lips belie their provenance. Brains, milky white and globular, look like brains. Feet, the ghosts of their cloven hoofs protruding, look like feet. Testicles look like, well, testicles. But lips are different. Loosed from the snout, trimmed of their fat, and dyed a preternatural pink, they look more like candy than like carrion.

6   At Farm Fresh, no swine root in an adjacent feedlot. No viscera-strewn killing floor lurks just out of sight, down a darkened hallway. These pigs died long ago at some Midwestern abattoir. By the time the lips arrive in Amite, they are, in essence, pig Popsicles, 50-pound blocks of offal and ice.

7   "Lips are all meat," Lionel told me earlier in the day. "No gristle, no bone, no nothing. They're bar food, hot and vinegary, great with a beer. Used to be the lips ended up in sausages, headcheese, those sorts of things. A lot of them still do."

8   Lionel, a 50-year-old father of three with quick, intelligent eyes set deep in a face the color of cordovan, is a veteran of nearly 40 years in the pickled pig lips business. "I started out with my daddy when I

Which of the details in pars. 3–4 come from observations? Interviews? How do you know?

Why does Edge define offal *and contrast lips to other parts?*

What is the effect of comparing pig lips to "candy" and "Popsicles"?

What do these details contribute to your impression of Lionel?

wasn't much more than 10," Lionel told me, his shy smile framed by a coarse black mustache flecked with whispers of gray. "The meatpacking business he owned had gone broke back when I was 6, and he was peddling out of the back of his car, selling dried shrimp, napkins, straws, tubes of plastic cups, pig feet, pig lips, whatever the bar owners needed. He sold to black bars, white bars, sweet shops, snowball stands, you name it. We made the rounds together after I got out of school, sometimes staying out till two or three in the morning. I remember bringing my toy cars to this one joint and racing them around the floor with the bar owner's son while my daddy and his father did business."

For years after the demise of that first meatpacking company, the Dufour family sold someone else's product. "We used to buy lips from Dennis Di Salvo's company down in Belle Chasse," recalled Lionel. "As far as I can tell, his mother was the one who came up with the idea to pickle and pack lips back in the '50s, back when she was working for a company called Three Little Pigs over in Houma. But pretty soon, we were selling so many lips that we had to almost beg Di Salvo's for product. That's when we started cooking up our own," he told me, gesturing toward the cast-iron kettle that hangs from the rafters by the front door of the plant. "My daddy started cooking lips in that very pot." 9

10   Lionel now cooks lips in 11 retrofitted milk tanks, dull stainless-steel cauldrons shaped like oversized cradles. But little else has changed. Though Lionel's father has passed away, Farm Fresh remains a family-focused company. His wife, Kathy, keeps the books. His daughter, Dana, a button-cute college student who has won numerous beauty titles, takes to the road in the summer, selling lips to convenience stores and wholesalers. Soon, after he graduates from business school, Lionel's younger son, Matt, will take over operations at the plant. And his older son, a veterinarian, lent his name to one of Farm Fresh's top sellers, Jason's Pickled Pig Lips.

If Edge got this information from Lionel, why do you think he summarizes it instead of quoting it?

11   "We do our best to corner the market on lips," Lionel told me, his voice tinged with bravado. "Sometimes they're hard to get from the packing houses. You gotta kill a lot of pigs to get enough lips to keep us going. I've got new customers calling every day; it's all I can do to keep up with demand, but I bust my ass to keep up. I do what I can for my family—and for my customers.

12   "When my customers tell me something," he continued, "just like when my daddy told me something, I listen. If my customers wanted me to dye the lips green, I'd ask, 'What shade?' As it is, every few years we'll do some red and some blue for the Fourth of July. This year we did jars full of Mardi Gras lips—half purple, half gold," Lionel recalled with a chuckle. "I guess we'd had a few beers when we came up with that one."

13   Meanwhile, back at Jesse's Place, I finish my third Bud, order my fourth. *Now*, I tell myself, my courage bolstered by booze, *I'm ready to eat a lip.*

How does Edge help readers follow the change in time and location here?

14   They may have looked like candy in the plant, but in the barroom they're carrion once again. I poke and prod the six-inch arc of pink flesh, peering up from my reverie just in time to catch the barkeep's wife, Audrey, staring straight at me. She fixes me with a look just this side of pity and asks, "You gonna eat that thing or make love to it?"

15   Her nephew, Jerry, sidles up to a bar stool on my left. "A lot of people like 'em with chips," he says with a nod toward the pink juice pooling on the bar in front of me. I offer to buy him a lip, and Audrey fishes one from a jar behind the counter, wraps it in tinfoil,

and places the whole affair on a paper towel in front of him.

I take stock of my own cowardice, and, following 16 Jerry's lead, reach for a bag of potato chips, tear open the top with my teeth, and toss the quivering hunk of hog flesh into the shiny interior of the bag, slick with grease and dusted with salt. Vinegar vapors tickle my nostrils. I stifle a gag that rolls from the back of my throat, swallow hard, and pray that the urge to vomit passes.

With a smash of my hand, the potato chips are 17 reduced to a pulp, and I feel the cold lump of the lip beneath my fist. I clasp the bag shut and shake it hard in an effort to ensure chip coverage in all the nooks and crannies of the lip. The technique that Jerry uses— and I mimic—is not unlike that employed by home cooks mixing up a mess of Shake 'n Bake chicken.

I pull from the bag a coral crescent of meat now 18 crusted with blond bits of potato chips. When I chomp down, the soft flesh dissolves between my teeth. It tastes like a flaccid cracklin', unmistakably porcine, and not altogether bad. The chips help, providing texture where there was none. Slowly, my brow unfurrows, my stomach ceases its fluttering.

Sensing my relief, Jerry leans over and peers into 19 my bag. "Kind of look like Frosted Flakes, don't they?" he says, by way of describing the chips rapidly turning to mush in the pickling juice. I offer the bag to Jerry, order yet another beer, and turn to eye the pig feet floating in a murky jar by the cash register, their blunt tips bobbing up through a pasty white film.

> How does Edge's describing this process help you as a reader?

> Why do you think Edge concludes his profile of Lionel's Farm Fresh business by dramatizing his effort to eat a pig lip?

READING FOR MEANING

This section presents three activities that will help you think about the meanings in Edge's observational essay. Your instructor may ask you to do one or more of these activities in class or online.

For more help with summarizing, see Chapter 10, pp. 518–19.

1. **Read to Summarize.** Write a sentence or two explaining the main idea Edge wants his readers to understand about pickled pig lips and the Dufour family business.

 Take a quiz to check your reading and vocabulary comprehension:
bedfordstmartins.com/readingcritically

2. **Read to Respond.** Write a paragraph exploring your initial thoughts and feelings about Edge's observational essay. For example, consider anything that resonates with your experience or that seems contradictory, surprising, or fascinating, such as:

   - Edge's description of the production line at Farm Fresh Food Supplier (par. 4), perhaps in relation to your own work experience;

   You may also try contextualizing; see Chapter 10, pp. 522–23.

   - Lionel Dufour's story about how he "made the rounds" with his father after school (par. 8), perhaps in relation to your own experience learning from a relative or mentor;

   - Your reaction to Edge's attempt to eat the pig lip, possibly in relation to your own experience trying an unusual food.

3. **Read to Analyze Assumptions.** Write a paragraph or two analyzing an assumption you find intriguing in Edge's essay. For example:

   Assumptions about culture and food. For many people, foods that they did not eat as children seem strange and sometimes even repulsive. Even though he is a southerner, Edge is squeamish about eating a popular southern delicacy, pickled pig lips. To think critically about assumptions regarding culture and food, ask yourself questions like these:

   - Why do you suppose Edge uses the words *courage* (par. 13) and *cowardice* (par. 16) to describe his reluctance to try pickled pig lips?

   - What, if anything, did Edge learn from visiting the Farm Fresh Food Supplier factory that might make him reluctant to eat a pig lip?

   - What do you think causes food anxieties, your own as well as Edge's aversion to pickled pig lips?

   Assumptions about entrepreneurship. In interviewing Lionel Dufour and observing the Farm Fresh Food Supplier factory, Edge gives readers information about one small business and its hands-on proprietor. To think critically about the assumptions in this essay related to entrepreneurship, ask yourself questions like these:

   - Among the first things Edge tell readers about Farm Fresh is that Lionel is the "proprietor" (par. 3) but that he loads trucks and "has been on the job since 2:45 in the morning" (par. 4). What does Edge think his readers are likely to assume about the kinds of work small-business owners like Lionel do?

   - Why do you suppose Edge chooses to include so much information about the previous, current, and future generations of Dufours?

   - How might this essay have been different if Edge had also interviewed Farm Fresh employees?

- Although Americans usually celebrate a strong work ethic, we also tend to value entrepreneurship over manual labor. In what ways, if any, do you see these values reflected in this essay?

ANALYZING VISUALS

Write a paragraph analyzing the photograph included in Edge's essay and explaining what it contributes to the essay.

To do the analysis, you can use the Criteria for Analyzing Visuals chart in Chapter 12 on pp. 611–12. Don't feel you have to answer all of the questions in the chart; focus on those that seem most productive in helping you write a paragraph-length analysis. To help you get started, consider adding these questions that specifically refer to Edge's visual:

- Edge could have included a full-body photograph of a pig, a picture of pigs at play, or some other composition. Why do you think he chose a close-up of a pig's face taken from one particular angle?

- Given his purpose and audience, why do you think Edge chose a photograph of a pig instead of a photograph of pig lips in a jar or being eaten at a site like Jesse's Place? Or why didn't he choose a photograph of the Farm Fresh company or the Dufour family? What does the choice of visual suggest about the subject and the writer's perspective?

READING LIKE A WRITER

PRESENTING INFORMATION ABOUT THE SUBJECT

Like "Soup," much of the information in this profile comes from an extended interview. Edge uses three strategies for presenting what he learned from this interview:

Quotation   "Lips are all meat," Lionel told me earlier in the day. "No gristle, no bone, no nothing." (par. 7)

Paraphrase   By the time the lips arrive in Amite, they are, in essence, pig Popsicles, 50-pound blocks of offal and ice. (par. 6)

Summary   For years after the demise of that first meatpacking company, the Dufour family sold someone else's product. (par. 9)

Writers typically choose to **quote** language that is especially vivid or memorable, giving an impression of the speaker as well as providing important information. **Paraphrase** tends to be used when the writer needs to go into detail but can put the information in a more striking form than the speaker originally used. **Summary** is often used to condense lengthy information.

From his interview with Lionel, Edge gathered a lot of information about the Dufour family history and business as well as about the various products Farm Fresh sells and their production process. In addition, Edge presents information he derived from observations, particularly in paragraphs 3 through 6. Notice how he alternates information from the interview with descriptive details from his firsthand observations. Edge even tells us what he does *not* see — blood and guts on a slaughterhouse floor (par. 6). Letting readers know what he had expected, perhaps feared, appeals to readers who may share his anxieties. Moreover, it encourages readers to embrace Edge's point of view, a process of identification that begins in the opening scene in Jesse's Place and continues through the closing paragraphs.

Analyze & Write

Write a paragraph analyzing and evaluating Edge's use of quoting, paraphrasing, and summarizing information from an interview.

1. Find at least one other example of each of these strategies in paragraphs 3–12.

2. How effective are these ways of presenting information? For example, is there any quotation that could have been better presented as paraphrase or even as summary? What would have been gained or lost?

3. Locate a passage where Edge presents his observations. How do you recognize this part as coming from firsthand observations? How does the alternation of information from interviews and observations contribute to your engagement as a reader?

A Special Reading Strategy

Comparing and Contrasting Related Readings: "Soup" and Edge's "I'm Not Leaving Until I Eat This Thing"

Comparing and contrasting related readings is a special critical reading strategy that is useful both in reading for meaning and in reading like a writer. This strategy is particularly applicable when writers present similar subjects, as is the case in the observational essays in this chapter by the *New Yorker* writer (p. 71) and John T. Edge (p. 80). Both writers describe a business they observed and report on their interview with the business owner. In both instances, the business involves food products and their preparation; however, Edge adopts the role of participant observer to

(continued)

relate what he learned, whereas the author of "Soup" maintains a more objective distance. To compare and contrast these two observational essays, think about issues such as these:

- What are the cultural contexts of these two businesses (and the periodicals in which these articles appeared)? What seems most significant about the two business philosophies represented in these essays?

- How did the two writers organize the information derived from interviews and observation? Highlight the places in each essay where information from interviews is quoted or summarized and places where information from direct observation is presented.

- Edge alternates between the participant-observer and spectator roles, while the *New Yorker* writer consistently maintains a spectator role. Note any places in "Soup" where you get a sense of the writer's point of view or judgment. What do the participant observations add to Edge's essay?

See Chapter 10, pp. 527–30, for detailed guidelines on comparing and contrasting related readings.

Gabriel Thompson

A Gringo in the Lettuce Fields

Gabriel Thompson has worked as a community organizer and has written extensively about the lives of undocumented immigrants to the United States. He has published numerous articles in periodicals such as New York *magazine, the* New York Times, *and the* Nation. *His books include* There's No José Here: Following the Hidden Lives of Mexican Immigrants *(2006),* Calling All Radicals: How Grassroots Organizers Can Help Save Our Democracy *(2007), and* Working in the Shadows: A Year of Doing the Jobs (Most) Americans Won't Do *(2010), from which the selection below is taken. We added the photograph on p. 91 showing lettuce cutters at work. Thompson includes more photos at his blog,* Working in the Shadows.

- *Before you read, consider Thompson's choice of titles:* Working in the Shadows: A Year of Doing the Jobs (Most) Americans Won't Do *and* "A Gringo in the Lettuce Fields." *What do these titles lead you to expect will be the subject of the observations and the writer's perspective on the subject?*

- *As you read, notice how Thompson as an outsider uses participant observation to get an insider's view of the daily experience of farm workers. What does his outsider status enable him to understand — or prevent him from understanding — about the community he has entered?*

I wake up staring into the bluest blue I've ever seen. I must have fallen into a deep sleep because I need several seconds to realize that I'm looking at the Arizona sky, that the pillow beneath my head is a large clump of dirt, and that a near-stranger named Manuel is standing over me, smiling. I pull myself to a sitting position. To my left, in the distance, a Border Patrol helicopter is hovering. To my right is Mexico, separated by only a few fields of lettuce. "*Buenos días*," Manuel says.

I stand up gingerly. It's only my third day in the fields, but already my 30-year-old body is failing me. I feel like someone has dropped a log on my back. And then piled that log onto a truck with many other logs, and driven that truck over my thighs. "Let's go," I say, trying to sound energetic as I fall in line behind Manuel, stumbling across rows of lettuce and thinking about "the five-day rule." The five-day rule, according to Manuel, is simple: Survive the first five days and you'll be fine. He's been a farmworker for almost two decades, so he should know. I'm on day three of five — the goal is within sight. Of course, another way to look at my situation is that I'm on day three of what I promised myself would be a two-month immersion in the work life of the people who do a job that most Americans won't do. But thinking about the next seven weeks doesn't benefit anyone. *Day three of five.*

3   "Manuel! Gabriel! Let's go! *¡Vámonos!*" yells Pedro, our foreman. Our short break is over. Two dozen crew members standing near the lettuce machine are already putting on gloves and sharpening knives. Manuel and I hustle toward the machine, grab our own knives from a box of chlorinated water, and set up in neighboring rows, just as the machine starts moving slowly down another endless field.

4   Since the early 1980s, Yuma, Ariz., has been the "winter lettuce capital" of America. Each winter, when the weather turns cold in Salinas, California—the heart of the nation's lettuce industry—temperatures in sunny Yuma are still in the 70s and 80s. At the height of Yuma's growing season, the fields surrounding the city produce virtually all of the iceberg lettuce and 90 percent of the leafy green vegetables consumed in the United States and Canada.

5   America's lettuce industry actually needs people like me. Before applying for fieldwork at the local Dole headquarters, I came across several articles describing the causes of a farmworker shortage. The stories cited an aging workforce, immigration crackdowns, and long delays at the border that discourage workers with green cards who would otherwise commute to the fields from their Mexican homes.[1] Wages have been rising somewhat in response to the demand for laborers (one prominent member of the local growers association tells me average pay is now between $10 and $12 an hour), but it's widely assumed that most U.S. citizens wouldn't do the work at any price. Arizona's own Senator John McCain created a stir in 2006 when he issued a challenge to a group of union members in Washington, D.C. "I'll offer anybody here $50 an hour if you'll go pick lettuce in Yuma this season, and pick for the whole season," he said. Amid jeers, he didn't back down, telling the audience, "You can't do it, my friends."

6   On my first day I discover that even putting on a lettuce cutter's uniform is challenging (no fieldworkers, I learn, "pick" lettuce). First, I'm handed a pair of black galoshes to go over my shoes. Next comes the *gancho*, an S-shaped hook that slips over my belt to hold packets of plastic bags. A white glove goes on my right hand, a gray glove, supposedly designed to offer protection from cuts, goes on my left. Over the cloth gloves I pull on a pair of latex gloves. I put on a black hairnet, my baseball cap, and a pair of protective sunglasses. Adding to my belt a long leather sheath, I'm good to go. I feel ridiculous.

7   The crew is already working in the field when Pedro walks me out to them and introduces me to Manuel. Manuel is holding an 18-inch knife in his hand. "Manuel has been cutting for many years, so watch him to see how it's done," Pedro says. Then he walks away. Manuel resumes cutting,

---

[1]A green card is an immigration document that allows noncitizens to work legally in the United States, whether they live here or commute across the border. Undocumented workers (or illegal immigrants, depending on your position) lack green cards. [Editor's note]

following a machine that rolls along just ahead of the crew. Every several seconds Manuel bends down, grabs a head of iceberg lettuce with his left hand, and makes a quick cut with the knife in his right hand, separating the lettuce from its roots. Next, he lifts the lettuce to his stomach and makes a second cut, trimming the trunk. He shakes the lettuce, letting the outer leaves fall to the ground. With the blade still in his hand, he then brings the lettuce toward the *gancho* at his waist, and with a flick of the wrist the head is bagged and dropped onto one of the machine's extensions. Manuel does this over and over again, explaining each movement. "It's not so hard," he says. Five minutes later, Pedro reappears and tells me to grab a knife. Manuel points to a head of lettuce. "Try this one," he says.

I bend over, noticing that most of the crew has turned to watch. I take my knife and make a tentative sawing motion where I assume the trunk to be, though I'm really just guessing. Grabbing the head with my left hand, I straighten up, doing my best to imitate Manuel. Only my lettuce head doesn't move; it's still securely connected to the soil. Pedro steps in. "When you make the first cut, it is like you are stabbing the lettuce." He makes a quick jabbing action. "You want to aim for the center of the lettuce, where the trunk is," he says.

Ten minutes later, after a couple of other discouraging moments, I've cut maybe 20 heads of lettuce and am already feeling pretty accomplished. I'm not perfect: If I don't stoop far enough, my stab—instead of landing an inch above the ground—goes right through the head of lettuce, ruining it entirely. The greatest difficulty, though, is in the trimming. I had no idea that a head of lettuce was so humongous. In order to get it into a shape that can be bagged, I trim and trim and trim, but it's taking me upward of a minute to do what Manuel does in several seconds.

10   Pedro offers me a suggestion. "Act like the lettuce is a bomb," he says. "Imagine you've only got five seconds to get rid of it."

11   Surprisingly, that thought seems to work, and I'm able to greatly increase my speed. For a minute or two I feel euphoric. "Look at me!" I want to shout at Pedro; I'm in the zone. But the woman who is packing the lettuce into boxes soon swivels around to face me. "Look, this lettuce is no good." She's right: I've cut the trunk too high, breaking off dozens of good leaves, which will quickly turn brown because they're attached to nothing. With her left hand she holds the bag up, and with her right she smashes it violently, making a loud pop. She turns the bag over and the massacred lettuce falls to the ground. She does the same for the three other bags I've placed on the extension. "It's okay," Manuel tells me. "You shouldn't try to go too fast when you're beginning." Pedro seconds him. "That's right. Make sure the cuts are precise and that you don't rush."

12   So I am to be very careful and precise, while also treating the lettuce like a bomb that must be tossed aside after five seconds.

13   That first week on the job was one thing. By midway into week two, it isn't clear to me what more I can do to keep up with the rest of the crew. I know the techniques by this time and am moving as fast as my body will permit. Yet I need to somehow *double* my current output to hold my own. I'm able to cut only one row at a time while Manuel is cutting two. Our fastest cutter, Julio, meanwhile can handle three. But how someone could cut two rows for an hour—much less an entire day—is beyond me. "Oh, you will get it," Pedro tells me one day. "You will most definitely get it." Maybe he's trying to be hopeful or inspiring, but it comes across as a threat.

14   That feeling aside, what strikes me about our 31-member crew is how quickly they have welcomed me as one of their own. I encountered some suspicion at first, but it didn't last. Simply showing up on the second day seemed to be proof enough that I was there to work. When I faltered in the field and fell behind, hands would come across from adjacent rows to grab a head or two of my lettuce so I could catch up. People whose names I didn't yet know would ask me how I was holding up, reminding me that it would get easier as time went by. If I took a seat alone during a break, someone would call me into their group and offer a homemade taco or two.

15   Two months in, I make the mistake of calling in sick one Thursday. The day before, I put my left hand too low on a head of lettuce. When I punched my blade through the stem, the knife struck my middle finger. Thanks to the gloves, my skin wasn't even broken, but the finger instantly turned purple. I took two painkillers to get through the afternoon, but when I wake the next morning it is still throbbing. With one call to an answering machine that morning, and another the next day, I create my own four-day weekend.

16   The surprise is that when I return on Monday, feeling recuperated, I wind up having the hardest day of my brief career in lettuce. Within hours,

my hands feel weaker than ever. By quitting time—some 10 hours after our day started—I feel like I'm going to vomit from exhaustion. A theory forms in my mind. Early in the season—say, after the first week—a farmworker's body gets thoroughly broken down. Back, legs, and arms grow sore, hands and feet swell up. A tolerance for the pain is developed, though, and two-day weekends provide just enough time for the body to recover from the trauma. My four-day break had been too long; my body actually began to recuperate, and it wanted more time to continue. Instead, it was thrown right back into the mix and rebelled. Only on my second day back did my body recover that middle ground. "I don't think the soreness goes away," I say to Manuel and two other co-workers one day. "You just forget what it's like not to be sore." Manuel, who's 37, considers this. "That's true, that's true," he says. "It always takes a few weeks at the end of the year to get back to normal, to recover."

An older co-worker, Mateo, is the one who eventually guesses that I 17 have joined the crew because I want to write about it. "That is good," he says over coffee at his home one Sunday. "Americans should know the hard work that Mexicans do in this country."

Mateo is an unusual case. There aren't many other farmworkers who are 18 still in the fields when they reach their 50s. It's simply not possible to do this work for decades and not suffer a permanently hunched back, or crooked fingers, or hands so swollen that they look as if someone has attached a valve to a finger and pumped vigorously. The punishing nature of the work helps explain why farmworkers don't live very long; the National Migrant Resources Program puts their life expectancy at 49 years.

"Are you cutting two rows yet?" Mateo asks me. "Yes, more or less," I 19 say. "I thought I'd be better by now." Mateo shakes his head. "It takes a long time to learn how to really cut lettuce. It's not something that you learn after only one season. Three, maybe four seasons—then you start understanding how to really work with lettuce."

READING FOR MEANING

This section presents three activities that will help you think about the meanings in Thompson's observational essay. Your instructor may ask you to do one or more of these activities in class or online.

1. **Read to Summarize.** Write a sentence or two explaining the main idea Thompson wants his readers to understand about his observations.

For more help with summarizing, see Chapter 10, pp. 518–19.

 Take a quiz to check your reading and vocabulary comprehension:
bedfordstmartins.com/readingcritically

2. **Read to Respond.** Write a paragraph exploring your initial thoughts and feelings about Thompson's observational essay. For example, consider anything that resonates with your experience or that seems contradictory, surprising, or fascinating, such as:

   - Thompson's "euphoric" feeling and impulse to shout "Look at me!" only to discover he'd been doing a bad job (par. 11);

   - Thompson's surprise that the other members of the crew "welcomed [him] as one of their own" (par. 14);

   - Thompson's "theory" that farmworkers develop a "tolerance for the pain" and his comment that "[y]ou just forget what it's like not to be sore," perhaps in relation to your experience of doing intensive physical work or exercise (par. 16).

3. **Read to Analyze Assumptions.** Write a paragraph or two analyzing an assumption you find intriguing in Thompson's essay. For example:

   Assumptions about the ethics of undercover observation. Participant observation does not necessarily involve secrecy, but Thompson chose to keep secret his intention to write about his experience as a lettuce cutter. To think critically about assumptions regarding undercover observation, ask yourself questions like these:

   - Why do you think Thompson chose to keep his intentions secret? How do you think the other lettuce cutters or their bosses would have responded had they known his reasons for joining the crew?

   - What do you think of Mateo's comment after guessing Thompson's true purpose: "That is good. . . . Americans should know the hard work that Mexicans do in this country" (par. 17)?

   - How valuable are immersion experiences like Thompson's to the individual observing, to the group being observed, and to readers in general?

   - What ethical challenges, if any, do you see with this kind of observational writing?

   Assumptions about the kinds of work done by guest or immigrant workers. As the subtitle of his book indicates, Thompson assumes that cutting lettuce falls into the category of *Jobs (Most) Americans Won't Do.* The people who traditionally do these jobs are documented, many of whom are itinerant farm workers traveling seasonally from field to field (par. 5). To think critically about the assumptions about this kind of work and who will and will not do it, ask yourself questions like these:

   - Given that wages for farmworkers are "between $10 and $12 an hour," why do you think it is "widely assumed that most U.S. citizens wouldn't do the work at any price" (par. 5)?

- Thompson seems to be surprised not only by the physical demands of the work, but by the high level of skill required to do it well. What do you think most Americans assume about skilled labor versus the "unskilled" manual labor performed by guest and immigrant workers?
- What does Mateo assume about Americans' knowledge of the work done by Mexicans (and other guest workers and immigrants) in this country (par. 17)?

READING LIKE A WRITER

ADOPTING AN AUTHORIAL ROLE

Thompson assumes the role of participant observer: He does not watch lettuce cutters from the sidelines but rather works among them for two months. His informal interviews take place during work or on breaks or at the homes of his coworkers during the weekend. Nevertheless, there is a significant difference between a two-month experiment and a personal account written by a lettuce cutter like Mateo after a lifetime at the job. An observational writer may participate, but is always to some extent an outsider looking in.

Analyze & Write

Write a paragraph or two analyzing Thompson's use of the participant-observer role:

1. Skim the text, highlighting each time Thompson
   - reminds readers of his status as an outsider—for example, when he refers to a coworker as a "near-stranger" (par. 1)
   - tells readers about something he thinks will be unfamiliar to them—for example, when he explains people do not "'pick' lettuce" (par. 6)
   - calls attention to his own incompetence or failings—for example, when he describes his first attempt to cut lettuce (par. 8)
2. Why do you think Thompson tells us about his errors and reminds us that he is an outsider? What effect are these moves likely to have on his target audience? What are the advantages, if any, of adopting the participant-observer role (as Thompson does) instead of the spectator role (as Brian Cable, in the essay on pp. 104–109, and the author of "Soup" do, for example)?

Peggy Orenstein

The Daily Grind:
Lessons in the Hidden Curriculum

Peggy Orenstein (1961), a graduate of Oberlin College, has been a managing editor of Mother Jones, *a member of the editorial board of* Esquire, *and a contributing writer for the* New York Times Magazine. *Her writing has been featured in such outlets as the* New Yorker, Salon.com, *and NPR's* All Things Considered, *as well as* The Best American Science Writing *(2004). Among her books are the best-seller* Cinderella Ate My Daughter *(2011). Orenstein also was featured in the documentary films* Crumb *(1994) and* Searching for Asian America *(2003) and was the executive producer of the Oscar-nominated documentary* The Mushroom Club *(2006). "The Daily Grind" comes from the opening chapter of* School Girls: Young Women, Self-Esteem, and the Confidence Gap *(1994).*

- *Before you read, consider that Orenstein observed an eighth-grade classroom in the early 1990s to explore the so-called "gender gap" in math and science. Reflecting on your own school experience, do you think boys and girls were treated differently by teachers when you were in elementary or middle school? If so, how?*

  - *As you read, think about how Orenstein tries to engage readers' interest in Amy Wilkinson. What, if anything, makes you care about what happens to Amy in Mrs. Richter's classroom? How would you evaluate Mrs. Richter's handling of the class?*

1   Amy Wilkinson has looked forward to being an eighth grader forever—at least for the last two years, which, when you're thirteen, seems like the same thing. By the second week of September she's settled comfortably into her role as one of the school's reigning elite. Each morning before class, she lounges with a group of about twenty other eighth-grade girls and boys in the most visible spot on campus: at the base of the schoolyard, between one of the portable classrooms that was constructed in the late 1970s and the old oak tree in the overflow parking lot. The group trades gossip, flirts, or simply stands around, basking in its own importance and killing time before the morning bell.

2   At 8:15 on Tuesday the crowd has already convened, and Amy is standing among a knot of girls, laughing. She is fuller-figured than she'd like to be, wide-hipped and heavy-limbed with curly blond hair, cornflower-blue eyes, and a sharply upturned nose. With the help of her mother, who is a drama coach, she has become the school's star actress: last year she played

For a multimodal observational selection, go to
bedfordstmartins.com/readingcritically.

Eliza in Weston's production of *My Fair Lady*. Although she earns solid grades in all of her subjects—she'll make the honor roll this fall—drama is her passion, she says, because "I love entertaining people, and I love putting on characters."

Also, no doubt, because she loves the spotlight: this morning, when she mentions a boy I haven't met, Amy turns, puts her hands on her hips, anchors her feet shoulder width apart, and bellows across the schoolyard, "Greg! Get over here! You have to meet Peggy."

She smiles wryly as Greg, looking startled, begins to make his way across the schoolyard for an introduction. "I'm not exactly shy," she says, her hands still on her hips. "I'm bold."

Amy is bold. And brassy, and strong-willed. Like any teenager, she tries on and discards different selves as if they were so many pairs of Girbaud jeans, searching ruthlessly for a perfect fit. During a morning chat just before the school year began, she told me that her parents tried to coach her on how to respond to my questions. "They told me to tell you that they want me to be my own person," she complained. "My mother *told* me to tell you that. I do want to be my own person, but it's like, you're interviewing me about who I am and she's telling me what to say—that's not my own person, is it?"

When the morning bell rings, Amy and her friends cut off their conversations, scoop up their books, and jostle toward the school's entrance. Inside, Weston's hallways smell chalky, papery, and a little sweaty from gym class. The wood-railed staircases at either end of the two-story main building are worn thin in the middle from the scuffle of hundreds of pairs of sneakers pounding them at forty-eight-minute intervals for nearly seventy-five years. Amy's mother, Sharon, and her grandmother both attended this school. So will her two younger sisters. Her father, a mechanic who works on big rigs, is a more recent Weston recruit: he grew up in Georgia and came here after he and Sharon were married.

Amy grabs my hand, pulling me along like a small child or a slightly addled new student: within three minutes we have threaded our way through the dull-yellow hallways to her locker and then upstairs to room 238, Mrs. Richter's math class.

The twenty-two students that stream through the door with us run the gamut of physical maturity. Some of the boys are as small and compact as fourth graders, their legs sticking out of their shorts like pipe cleaners. A few are trapped in the agony of a growth spurt, and still others cultivate downy beards. The girls' physiques are less extreme: most are nearly their full height, and all but a few have already weathered the brunt of puberty. They wear topknots or ponytails, and their shirts are tucked neatly into their jeans.

Mrs. Richter, a ruddy, athletic woman with a powerful voice, has arranged the chairs in a three-sided square, two rows deep. Amy walks to the far side of the room and, as she takes her seat, falls into a typically feminine pose: she crosses her legs, folds her arms across her chest, and hunches forward toward her desk, seeming to shrink into herself. The sauciness of the playground disappears, and, in fact, she says hardly a word during class. Meanwhile, the boys, especially those who are more physically mature, sprawl in their chairs, stretching their legs long, expanding into the available space.

10   Nate, a gawky, sanguine boy who has shaved his head except for a small thatch that's hidden under an Oakland A's cap, leans his chair back on two legs and, although the bell has already rung, begins a noisy conversation with his friend, Kyle.

11   Mrs. Richter turns to him. "What's all the discussion about, Nate?" she asks.

12   "*He's* talking to *me*," Nate answers, pointing to Kyle. Mrs. Richter writes Nate's name on the chalkboard as a warning toward detention and he yells out in protest. They begin to quibble over the justice of her decision, their first—but certainly not their last—power struggle of the day. As they argue, Allison, a tall, angular girl who once told me, "My goal is to be the best wife and mother I can be," raises her hand to ask a question.

13   Mrs. Richter, finishing up with Nate, doesn't notice.

14   "Get your homework out, everyone!" the teacher booms, and walks among the students, checking to make sure no one has shirked on her or his assignment. Allison, who sits in the front row nearest both the blackboard and the teacher, waits patiently for another moment, then, realizing she's not getting results, puts her hand down. When Mrs. Richter walks toward her, Allison tries another tack, calling out her question. Still, she gets no response, so she gives up.

15   As a homework assignment, the students have divided their papers into one hundred squares, color-coding each square prime or composite—prime being those numbers which are divisible only by one and themselves, and composite being everything else. Mrs. Richter asks them to call out the prime numbers they've found, starting with the tens.

16   Nate is the first to shout, "Eleven!" The rest of the class chimes in a second later. As they move through the twenties and thirties, Nate, Kyle, and Kevin, who sit near one another at the back of the class, call out louder and louder, casually competing for both quickest response and the highest decibel level. Mrs. Richter lets the boys' behavior slide, although they are intimidating other students.

17   "Okay," Mrs. Richter says when they've reached one hundred. "Now, what do you think of one hundred and three? Prime or composite?"

18   Kyle, who is skinny and a little pop-eyed, yells out, "Prime!" but Mrs. Richter turns away from him to give someone else a turn. Unlike Allison, who gave up when she was ignored, Kyle isn't willing to cede his teacher's attention. He begins to bounce in his chair and chant, *"Prime! Prime! Prime!"* Then, when he turns out to be right, he rebukes the teacher, saying, "See, I told you."

When the girls in Mrs. Richter's class do speak, they follow the rules.   19
When Allison has another question, she raises her hand again and waits
her turn; this time, the teacher responds. When Amy volunteers her sole
answer of the period, she raises her hand, too. She gives the wrong answer
to an easy multiplication problem, turns crimson, and flips her head forward so her hair falls over her face.

Occasionally, the girls shout out answers, but generally they are to the   20
easiest, lowest-risk questions, such as the factors of four or six. And their
stabs at public recognition depend on the boys' largesse: when the girls venture responses to more complex questions, the boys quickly become ter-
ritorial, shouting them down with their own answers. Nate and Kyle are
particularly adept at overpowering Renee, who, I've been told by the teacher,
is the brightest girl in the class. (On a subsequent visit, I will see her lay her
head on her desk when Nate overwhelms her and mutter, "I hate this class.")

Mrs. Richter doesn't say anything to condone the boys' aggressiveness,   21
but she doesn't have to: they insist on — and receive — her attention even
when she consciously tries to shift it elsewhere in order to make the class
more equitable.

After the previous day's homework is corrected, Mrs. Richter begins a   22
new lesson, on the use of exponents.

"What does three to the third power mean?" she asks the class.   23

"*I know!*" shouts Kyle.   24

Instead of calling on Kyle, who has already answered more than his   25
share of questions, the teacher turns to Dawn, a somewhat more voluble
girl who has plucked her eyebrows down to a few hairs.

"Do you know, Dawn?"   26

Dawn hesitates, and begins "Well, you count the number of threes   27
and. . . ."

"*But I know!*" interrupts Kyle. "*I know!*"   28

Mrs. Richter deliberately ignores him, but Dawn is rattled: she never   29
finishes her sentence, she just stops.

"*I know! ME!*" Kyle shouts again, and then before Dawn recovers her-   30
self he blurts, "*It's three times three times three!*"

At this point, Mrs. Richter gives in. She turns away from Dawn, who is   31
staring blankly, and nods at Kyle. "Yes," she says. "Three times three times
three. Does everyone get it?"

"*YES!*" shouts Kyle; Dawn says nothing.   32

Mrs. Richter picks up the chalk. "Let's do some others," she says.   33

"Let me!" says Kyle.   34

"I'll pick on whoever raises their hand," she tells him.   35

Nate, Kyle, and two other boys immediately shoot up their hands, fin-   36
gers squeezed tight and straight in what looks like a salute.

"Don't you want to wait and hear the problem first?" she asks, laughing.   37

They drop their hands briefly. She writes "8^4" on the board. "Okay, what   38
would that look like written out?"

39   Although a third of the class raise their hands to answer, including a number of students who haven't yet said a word, she calls on Kyle anyway.

40   "Eight times eight times eight times eight," he says triumphantly, as the other students drop their hands.

41   When the bell rings, I ask Amy about the mistake she made in class and the embarrassment it caused her. She blushes again.

42   "Oh yeah," she says. "That's about the only time I ever talked in there. I'll never do that again."

READING FOR MEANING

This section presents three activities that will help you think about the meanings in Orenstein's observational essay. Your instructor may ask you to do one or more of these activities in class or online.

For more help with summarizing, see Chapter 10, pp. 518–19.

1. **Read to Summarize.** Write a sentence or two explaining the main idea Orenstein wants readers to understand about Amy's experience in Mrs. Richter's classroom.

2. **Read to Respond.** Write a paragraph exploring your initial thoughts and feelings about Orenstein's observational essay. For example, consider anything that resonates with your experience or that seems contradictory, surprising, or fascinating, such as:

   • Cliques like the one Amy belongs to and which Orenstein describes as "the school's reigning elite" (par. 1);

   • The contradictory images of Amy — the "bold," "brassy, and strong-willed" Amy (par. 5), who is an honor roll student and actress, in contrast to the Amy in math class, "seeming to shrink into herself" and "say[ing] hardly a word" (par. 9);

You may also want to try reflecting on challenges to your beliefs and values or judging the writer's credibility; see Chapter 10, pp. 526–27 or 537–38.

   • The ways that your own school experiences add to your understanding of and response to the essay.

3. **Read to Analyze Assumptions.** Write a paragraph or two analyzing an assumption you find intriguing in Orenstein's essay. For example:

   Assumptions about power struggles. Orenstein describes Mrs. Richter's math class as the site of power struggles — between some boys and girls and between the teacher and two boys, Nate and Kyle. Even though she is the only adult and teacher in the room and presumably possesses power (she sets the rules and can send students to detention), Mrs. Richter seems unable to exercise it effectively or fairly. To think critically about assumptions in this essay related to power struggles, ask yourself questions like these:

Take a quiz to check your reading and vocabulary comprehension:
bedfordstmartins.com/readingcritically

- In what ways do Mrs. Richter, Nate, Kyle, and even the girls assert power in the classroom? For example, how do you interpret the fact that the boys raise their hands most of the time or that Mrs. Richter is the one asking questions and presumably determining which answers are correct?

- How do the behaviors of Mrs. Richter and girls like Allison and Dawn create a space for Nate and Kyle to exercise power?

- What assumptions about power do you think Orenstein, Mrs. Richter, the boys, and the girls hold?

- What were your assumptions about power in the classroom before you read this essay? Did reading it affect those assumptions? If so, how?

Assumptions about gender differences. In Mrs. Richter's math class, the boys seem to know all the answers. In the 1980s, standardized test scores showed that (at least in the United States) girls were significantly behind boys in math, but in recent years the gap seems to be narrowing. Nevertheless, many people continue to assume that boys are better than girls at math and science. Several theories have been put forward to explain this apparent gender difference: (1) boys are naturally endowed with better spatial abilities and logical thinking skills than girls; (2) boys are more interested in math and science careers; (3) boys, unlike girls, typically play games such as baseball that help them develop math skills; and (4) parents and teachers tend to treat girls stereotypically as weaker in math and therefore create a self-fulfilling prophecy. To think critically about assumptions in this essay related to gender differences, ask yourself questions like these:

- What do Orenstein, Mrs. Richter, the boys, and the girls seem to assume about who will be able to answer Mrs. Richter's questions?

- When you were in elementary or middle school, how common was the assumption that boys would do better in math and science than girls?

- Which, if any, of the four theories listed above do you think you or your teachers would have accepted?

- What are your assumptions about this issue now?

You may also want to try contextualizing; see Chapter 10, pp. 522–23.

READING LIKE A WRITER

CONVEYING A PERSPECTIVE ON THE SUBJECT

Because writers of observational essays usually do not assert the main idea in an explicit thesis statement, readers have to read closely and critically to infer the writer's *perspective* on the subject. As you have seen, reading critically includes analyzing the assumptions you find in the essay, assumptions that are often implied by how people are described as well as by what they say and do.

Contrast is another strategy writers may use to convey their perspective. Orenstein contrasts the image of Amy with her friends with the image of Amy in Mrs. Richter's class. Juxtaposing, or putting side by side, two contrasting images can reveal contradictions in a person's self-image. Note, for example, the irony in this contrast:

> "I'm not exactly shy," she says, her hands still on her hips. "I'm bold." (par. 4)

> Amy walks to the far side of the room. . . . The sauciness of the playground disappears, and, in fact, she says hardly a word during class. (par. 9)

Juxtaposition can also reveal broader cultural patterns, such as the differences in how girls and boys behave in Mrs. Richter's class. In addition to dramatizing this contrast, note that Orenstein also comments on it:

> Unlike Allison, who gave up when she was ignored, Kyle isn't willing to cede his teacher's attention. (par. 18)

> [W]hen the girls venture responses to more complex questions, the boys quickly become territorial, shouting them down with their own answers. (par. 20)

Analyze & Write

Write a paragraph examining how Orenstein uses contrast to convey her perspective on Amy:

1. Reread paragraphs 1–5, noting any descriptions, dialogue, or comments that help readers understand Amy. What is the dominant impression you get of her from these paragraphs?

2. Compare the images of Amy in Mrs. Richter's class (par. 9) and after class (pars. 41–42). How do these passages affect the impression you have of Amy?

3. Consider how analyzing the assumptions in this essay about gender differences and power struggles helped you understand Orenstein's perspective.

A Special Reading Strategy

Looking for Patterns of Opposition

Looking for patterns of opposition can be an especially useful strategy for reading observational essays like Peggy Orenstein's "The Daily Grind: Lessons in the Hidden Curriculum" that teem with oppositions or binaries. Following the instructions in Chapter 10, pp. 525–26, you will see that the first thing you need to do is reread the essay and mark the oppositions you find. In many instances, two opposing terms are obvious,

(continued)

such as *girls* versus *boys*. A less obvious opposition is the contrasting description *feminine pose . . . seeming to shrink into herself* versus *boys . . . expanding into the available space* (par. 9). Sometimes, one of the opposing terms is not introduced until later in the essay. For example, Amy is described in paragraph 5 as *bold*, but later, in paragraph 9, she is described as *say*[*ing*] *hardly a word during class.* You may even find instances where only one of the terms appears in the essay and you need to supply the missing opposite term. For example, Amy is described in paragraph 3 as someone who *loves the spotlight*, but in Mrs. Richter's class it is clear from her behavior that she doesn't want to be noticed. So you could present the opposition as *loves the spotlight* versus *flips her head forward so her hair falls over her face* (par. 19).

Brian Cable

The Last Stop

Brian Cable wrote the following observational essay based on a visit to a mortuary, or funeral home, when he was a first-year college student. He records what he sees and interviews two key people, the funeral director and the embalmer. In reporting his observations, he seems equally concerned with the burial process — from the purchase of a casket to the display of the body — and the people who manage this process. Notice also that Cable introduces two pieces of information he got from background research rather than from his own observations and interviews: the photograph of the Promethean casket in paragraph 21 and the information in paragraph 22 about the amount of money spent on funerals. Both came from the Internet. Cable follows academic conventions to reference the photograph as "Fig. 1" with a caption that indicates the source of the photograph. For the statistics, he uses parenthetical citation keyed to a Works Cited list at the end of the essay.

- *Before you read, notice that Cable opens his essay with a quotation, or epigraph, from Mark Twain. What does this quotation lead you to expect?*

- *As you read, notice passages where Cable tries to use humor. Given his subject and the rhetorical situation of writing for a class, how effective is his choice of tone?*

Let us endeavor so to live that when we come to die even the undertaker will be sorry.

—MARK TWAIN, *PUDD'NHEAD WILSON*

1   Death is a subject largely ignored by the living. We don't discuss it much, not as children (when Grandpa dies, he is said to be "going away"), not as adults, not even as senior citizens. Throughout our lives, death remains intensely private. The death of a loved one can be very painful, partly because of the sense of loss, but also because someone else's mortality reminds us all too vividly of our own.

2   More than a few people avert their eyes as they walk past the dusty-pink building that houses the Goodbody Mortuary. It looks a bit like a church — tall, with gothic arches and stained glass — and somewhat like an apartment complex — low, with many windows stamped out of red brick.

3   It wasn't at all what I had expected. I thought it would be more like Forest Lawn, serene with lush green lawns and meticulously groomed gardens, a place set apart from the hustle of day-to-day life. Here instead was an odd pink structure set in the middle of a business district. On top of the

For an additional student reading, go to
bedfordstmartins.com/reading critically.

A recent photo of Goodbody Mortuary, the subject of Cable's profile. Does this photo match Cable's description? How would the addition of such a photo, or other photos of the mortuary, have strengthened Cable's profile?

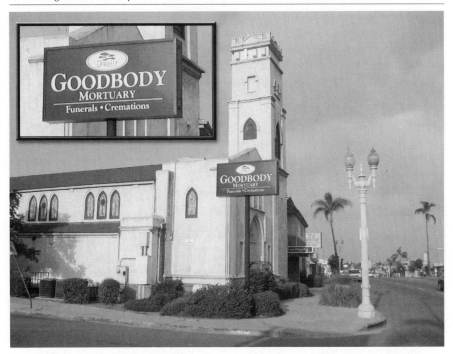

Goodbody Mortuary sign was a large electric clock. What the hell, I thought. Mortuaries are concerned with time, too.

I was apprehensive as I climbed the stone steps to the entrance. I feared 4 rejection or, worse, an invitation to come and stay. The door was massive, yet it swung open easily on well-oiled hinges. "Come in," said the sign. "We're always open." Inside was a cool and quiet reception room. Curtains were drawn against the outside glare, cutting the light down to a soft glow.

I found the funeral director in the main lobby, adjacent to the reception 5 room. Like most people, I had preconceptions about what an undertaker looked like. Mr. Deaver fulfilled my expectations entirely. Tall and thin, he even had beady eyes and a bony face. A low, slanted forehead gave way to a beaked nose. His skin, scrubbed of all color, contrasted sharply with his jet black hair. He was wearing a starched white shirt, gray pants, and black shoes. Indeed, he looked like death on two legs.

He proved an amiable sort, however, and was easy to talk to. As funeral 6 director, Mr. Deaver ("Call me Howard") was responsible for a wide range of services. Goodbody Mortuary, upon notification of someone's death, will remove the remains from the hospital or home. They then prepare the body for viewing, whereupon features distorted by illness or accident are restored to their natural condition. The body is embalmed and then placed in a casket selected by the family of the deceased. Services are held in one of three chapels at the mortuary, and afterward the casket is placed in a "visitation room," where family and friends can pay their last respects. Goodbody also makes arrangements for the purchase of a burial site and transports the body there for burial.

7   All this information Howard related in a well-practiced, professional manner. It was obvious he was used to explaining the specifics of his profession. We sat alone in the lobby. His desk was bone clean, no pencils or paper, nothing—just a telephone. He did all his paperwork at home; as it turned out, he and his wife lived right upstairs. The phone rang. As he listened, he bit his lips and squeezed his Adam's apple somewhat nervously.

8   "I think we'll be able to get him in by Friday. No, no, the family wants him cremated."

9   His tone was that of a broker conferring on the Dow Jones. Directly behind him was a sign announcing "Visa and Master Charge Welcome Here." It was tacked to the wall, right next to a crucifix.

10   "Some people have the idea that we are bereavement specialists, that we can handle emotional problems which follow a death: Only a trained therapist can do that. We provide services for the dead, not counseling for the living."

11   Physical comfort was the one thing they did provide for the living. The lobby was modestly but comfortably furnished. There were several couches, in colors ranging from earth brown to pastel blue, and a coffee table in front of each one. On one table lay some magazines and a vase of flowers. Another supported an aquarium. Paintings of pastoral scenes hung on every wall. The lobby looked more or less like that of an old hotel. Nothing seemed to match, but it had a homey, lived-in look.

12   "The last time the Goodbodies decorated was in '59, I believe. It still makes people feel welcome."

13   And so "Goodbody" was not a name made up to attract customers but the owner's family name. The Goodbody family started the business way back in 1915. Today, they do over five hundred services a year.

14   "We're in *Ripley's Believe It or Not*, along with another funeral home whose owners' names are Baggit and Sackit," Howard told me, without cracking a smile.

15   I followed him through an arched doorway into a chapel that smelled musty and old. The only illumination came from sunlight filtered through a stained glass ceiling. Ahead of us lay a casket. I could see that it contained a man dressed in a black suit. Wooden benches ran on either side of an aisle that led to the body. I got no closer. From the red roses across the dead man's chest, it was apparent that services had already been held.

"It was a large service," remarked Howard. "Look at that casket—a beautiful work of craftsmanship." 16

I guess it was. Death may be the great leveler, but one's coffin quickly reestablishes one's status. 17

We passed into a bright, fluorescent-lit "display room." Inside were thirty coffins, lids open, patiently awaiting inspection. Like new cars on the showroom floor, they gleamed with high-gloss finishes. 18

"We have models for every price range." 19

Indeed, there was a wide variety. They came in all colors and various materials. Some were little more than cloth-covered cardboard boxes, others were made of wood, and a few were made of steel, copper, or bronze. Howard told me prices started at $500 and averaged about $1,800. He motioned toward the center of the room: "The top of the line." 20

This was a solid bronze casket, its seams electronically welded to resist corrosion. Moisture-proof and air-tight, it could be hermetically sealed off from all outside elements. Its handles were plated with 14-karat gold. The Promethean casket made by the Batesville Casket Company is the choice of celebrities and the very wealthy. The price: a cool $25,000. (See Fig. 1.) 21

FIG. 1. "The top of the line." The Promethean casket that Michael Jackson was buried in.

22   A proper funeral remains a measure of respect for the deceased. But it is expensive. In the United States, the amount spent annually on funerals is around $12 billion (Grassley). Among ceremonial expenditures, funerals are second only to weddings. As a result, practices are changing. Howard has been in this business for forty years. He remembers a time when everyone was buried. Nowadays, with burials costing more than $7,000 a shot (Grassley), people often opt instead for cremation—as Howard put it, "a cheap, quick, and easy means of disposal." In some areas of the country, according to Howard, the cremation rate is now over 60 percent. Observing this trend, one might wonder whether burials are becoming obsolete. Do burials serve an important role in society?

23   For Tim, Goodbody's licensed mortician, the answer is very definitely yes. Burials will remain in common practice, according to the slender embalmer with the disarming smile, because they allow family and friends to view the deceased. Painful as it may be, such an experience brings home the finality of death. "Something deep within us demands a confrontation with death," Tim explained. "A last look assures us that the person we loved is, indeed, gone forever."

24   Apparently, we also need to be assured that the body will be laid to rest in comfort and peace. The average casket, with its innerspring mattress and pleated satin lining, is surprisingly roomy and luxurious. Perhaps such an air of comfort makes it easier for the family to give up their loved one. In addition, the burial site fixes the deceased in the survivors' memory, like a new address. Cremation provides none of these comforts.

25   Tim started out as a clerk in a funeral home but then studied to become a mortician. "It was a profession I could live with," he told me with a sly grin. Mortuary science might be described as a cross between pre-med and cosmetology, with courses in anatomy and embalming as well as in restorative art.

26   Tim let me see the preparation, or embalming, room, a white-walled chamber about the size of an operating room. Against the wall was a large sink with elbow taps and a draining board. In the center of the room stood a table with equipment for preparing the arterial embalming fluid, which consists primarily of formaldehyde, a preservative, and phenol, a disinfectant. This mixture sanitizes and also gives better color to the skin. Facial features can then be "set" to achieve a restful expression. Missing eyes, ears, and even noses can be replaced.

27   I asked Tim if his job ever depressed him. He bridled at the question: "No, it doesn't depress me at all. I do what I can for people and take satisfaction in enabling relatives to see their loved ones as they were in life." He said that he felt people were becoming more aware of the public service his profession provides. Grade-school classes now visit funeral homes as often as they do police stations and museums. The mortician is no longer regarded as a minister of death.

Before leaving, I wanted to see a body up close. I thought I could be   28
indifferent after all I had seen and heard, but I wasn't sure. Cautiously, I
reached out and touched the skin. It felt cold and firm, not unlike clay. As I
walked out, I felt glad to have satisfied my curiosity about dead bodies, but
all too happy to let someone else handle them.

Works Cited

Grassley, Chuck. "Opening Statement of Chairman Grassley." U.S. Senate
    Special Committee on Aging. 21 Sept. 2000. Web. 6 Jan. 2012.
Twain, Mark. *Pudd'nhead Wilson.* New York: Pocket Books, 2004. 45. Print.

READING FOR MEANING

This section presents three activities that will help you think about the meanings
in Cable's observational essay.

1. **Read to Summarize.** Write a sentence or two explaining the main idea
   Cable wants his readers to understand about the Goodbody Mortuary.   For more
                                                                           help with
2. **Read to Respond.** Write a paragraph exploring your initial thoughts and   summarizing,
   feelings about Cable's observational essay. For example, consider anything   see Chapter 10,
   that resonates with your experience or that seems contradictory, surpris-   pp. 518–19.
   ing, or fascinating, such as:

   - Cable's preconceptions about what an undertaker would look like
     (par. 5), perhaps in relation to fictional representations with which you
     are familiar;

   - The information that "[g]rade-school classes now visit funeral homes
     as often as they do police stations and museums" (par. 27), perhaps in   You may also
     relation to the field trips you took in grade school;   try reflecting
                                                               on challenges
   - Cable's "curiosity about dead bodies" and what one feels like (par. 28),   to your beliefs
     perhaps in relation to your own firsthand experience with death.   and values; see
                                                                           Chapter 10,
3. **Read to Analyze Assumptions.** Write a paragraph or two analyzing an   pp. 526–27.
   assumption you find intriguing in Cable's essay. For example:

   Assumptions about death. Cable begins his essay by suggesting that
   people tend not to talk directly and openly about death and that the
   painfulness of a loved one's death may be in part "because someone
   else's mortality reminds us all too vividly of our own" (par. 1). Later, he
   reports Tim's different idea that "[s]omething deep within us demands
   a confrontation with death" (par. 23). To think critically about the

 Take a quiz to check your reading and vocabulary comprehension:
bedfordstmartins.com/readingcritically

assumptions in this essay related to death, ask yourself questions like these:

- How are Cable's and Tim's beliefs reflected in their comments elsewhere in the essay?
- What cultural, family, and religious traditions affect your thinking about death?
- As you compare your assumptions with those of other students in your class, particularly students brought up with different traditions, what important differences do you see in the way people view death?

Assumptions about funerals as a status symbol. Comparing the coffin "display room" to a new car "showroom" (par. 18) and describing the top-of-the-line $25,000 "solid bronze casket" with "14-karat gold" handles (par. 21), Cable suggests that "[d]eath may be the great leveler, but one's coffin quickly reestablishes one's status" (par. 17). To think critically about the assumptions in this essay related to funerals as status symbols, ask yourself questions like these:

- It is fairly obvious why someone would want an expensive car (because of its luxury and performance, for example) or an expensive home (for its appearance and location, for example), but why do you suppose so many people buy expensive caskets, cemetery plots, and newspaper death notices and spend as much money on a funeral as they do on a wedding?
- What messages does an expensive funeral send to the people who attend? What other kinds of assumptions besides those about status might motivate people to spend a lot of money for this purpose?

READING LIKE A WRITER

ORGANIZING THE INFORMATION

Observations may be organized **topically**, with the writer bringing up a series of topics about the subject, as in "Soup"; they may be organized **narratively**, with the writer telling a story that extends over a period of time (as Thompson does); or they may be organized **spatially**, with the writer taking readers on a tour of a place, pointing out interesting sights and bringing up various topics about the subject as they move through the scene (as Cable does):

Begins on the sidewalk	More than a few people avert their eyes as they walk past the dusty-pink building that houses the Goodbody Mortuary. . . . It wasn't at all what
Prepositional phrases mark locations	I had expected. . . . I was apprehensive as I climbed the stone steps to the entrance. . . . Inside was a cool and quiet reception room. . . . I found the funeral director in the main lobby, adjacent to the reception room. (pars. 2–5)

Cable acts as a tour guide or as the camera in a documentary. He marks his progress with transitional words and phrases, "I followed him . . . into a chapel" (par. 15), for example. Cable uses each room he enters as a place to introduce a new topic. For example, in the display room, he talks about the commercialization of death. In the embalming room, where he interviews the mortician Tim, Cable discusses cultural attitudes toward death.

| Analyze & Write |

Write a paragraph analyzing how Cable orients readers as he takes them on a tour of the mortuary.

1. Skim the essay and find the passages where Cable takes readers from one room to another. How does he signal to readers the transition in space?
2. Find an example that shows how these spatial transitions also introduce new topics.
3. How effective or ineffective is a tour as a way of organizing information in a place like a mortuary?

Reviewing What Makes Observation Effective

An effective observational essay

- presents detailed information about the subject;
- organizes the information topically, narratively, or spatially to make it interesting and clear;
- takes a detached observer or participant-observer role, or alternates between the two;
- conveys the writer's perspective on what makes the subject intriguing and/or culturally significant.

| Analyze & Write |

Write a brief evaluation—positive, negative, or mixed—of one of the readings in this chapter, explaining why you think it succeeds or fails as an observational essay. Be sure to consider the characteristics that distinguish observational writing, as well as how successful the writer has been in communicating his or her purpose to the intended audience. You may also want to consider the effect the medium of presentation had on decisions the writer made.

A GUIDE TO WRITING OBSERVATIONAL ESSAYS

As you've read and discussed the reading selections in this chapter, you have probably done a good deal of analytical writing. Your instructor may assign a capstone project to write a brief observation of your own. Having learned how writers present information and organize it for readers, as well as how they decide on a role (spectator, participant, or some combination) and how to convey their perspective on the subject to their readers, you can now approach observation confidently as a writer. This Guide to Writing offers detailed suggestions for writing observations and resources to help you meet the special challenges this kind of writing presents.

THE WRITING ASSIGNMENT

Write an observational essay about an intriguing or unusual place, person, or activity.

- Choose a subject that is relatively unfamiliar to your audience or a familiar subject that you can present in a fresh and surprising way, perhaps focusing on a little-noticed or poorly understood aspect of the subject.

- Research the subject, gathering detailed information primarily from close observations and interviews, and present that information in a clear, logical way that is entertaining as well as informative.

- Analyze and interpret the subject so that you can take readers behind the scenes, giving them insight into the subject's cultural significance.

WRITING A DRAFT

INVENTION, PLANNING, AND COMPOSING

The following activities will help you choose a subject (an intriguing place, person, or activity) to write about, conduct research, and develop an essay that presents the subject in vivid detail that communicates your perspective on the subject to your readers.

Choosing a Subject

Rather than limiting yourself to the first subject that comes to mind, take a few minutes to consider your options and list as many subjects as you can. Below are some criteria that can help you choose a promising subject, followed by suggestions for the types of places, people, and activities you might consider writing about.

The subject should

- spark your — and your readers' — interest and curiosity
- be accessible, allowing you to make detailed observations and conduct in-depth interviews in the time allotted
- lead to ideas about its cultural significance and meanings

Note: Whenever you write an observational report or profile, consider carefully the ethics involved in such research. You will want to treat participants fairly and with respect in the way you both approach and depict them. You may need to obtain permission from your school's ethics review board. Discuss the ethical implications of your research with your instructor, and think carefully about the goals of your research and the effect your research will have on others.

An appropriate person might be

- someone doing work that you might want to do — a city council member, police officer, lab technician, computer programmer, attorney, salesperson
- someone with an unusual job or hobby — a dog trainer, private detective, ham radio operator, race car driver, novelist
- someone recently recognized for academic or community service or achievement

An appropriate place might be

- a place where people come together because they are of the same age, gender, sexual orientation, or ethnic group (for example, a foreign language–speaking residence hall or lesbian gay bisexual transgender club) or a place where people of different ages, genders, sexual orientations, or ethnic groups have formed a community (for example, a Sunday morning pickup basketball game in the park, political action headquarters, or barber shop)
- a place where people are trained for a certain kind of work (for example, a police academy, CSI program, or truck driving school)
- a place where a group of people are working together for a particular purpose (for example, a laboratory where scientists are collaborating on a research project)

An appropriate activity might be

- an unconventional sporting event — a dogs' Frisbee tournament, chess match, dog sledding, log sawing and splitting competition; an amateur wrestling or boxing meet, ice-fishing contest, or Olympics for people with disabilities

- a team practicing a sport or other activity (one you can observe as a curious outsider, not as an experienced participant)

- a community improvement project — graffiti cleaning, tree planting, house repairing, church painting, road or highway litter collecting

Researching Your Subject

Conducting observations and interviews takes time, so determine whether you can get permission before committing yourself too deeply, and plan your site visits carefully. The most common error students report making on this assignment is waiting too long to make that first call. Be aware, too, that the people and places you contact may not respond immediately (or at all); be sure to follow up if you have not gotten an answer to your request within a few days.

Making a Schedule.   Set up a tentative schedule for your observations and interviews. Backward planning is one of the best strategies for scheduling your time so everything gets done by your deadline:

1. Write on a calendar the date the project is due and any other interim due dates (such as the date that your first draft is due).

2. Move backward through the calendar, writing in due dates for other tasks you need to do. For example

   - Schedule interviews and observations.

   - Conduct initial interviews and observations.

   - Conduct follow-up observations or interviews.

   - Complete interviews, observations, and additional background research.

   - Complete interview and observation write-ups. (Writing up your notes involves filling in details, organizing your notes, and adding analysis and ideas.)

Setting Up, Preparing for, and Conducting Interviews and Observations.   The following activities will help you plan your research:

1. **Make a list of people you would like to interview or the places you would like to observe.** Include a number of possibilities in case your first choice turns you down.

2. **Write out your intentions and goals,** so you can explain them clearly to others. If you would like to take on the participant-observer role, ask permission to take part in a small way for a limited time.

For a detailed discussion of planning and conducting interviews and observations, see Chapter 11, pp. 555–59.

3. **Call or e-mail for an appointment** with your interview subject or to make arrangements to visit the site. Explain who you are and what you are doing. Student research projects are often embraced, but be prepared for your request to be rejected.

4. **Make notes about what you expect** to learn before you interview your subject or visit your site. The questions below might help:

   - How would I define or describe the subject?

   - What is the subject's purpose or function?

   - What typically takes place at this location?

   - Who will I likely observe?

   - Why do I assume it will interest me and my readers?

   - How will my presence affect those I am observing?

   - What do I hope or expect to learn about my subject?

5. Write some interview questions in advance, or consider how best to conduct the observation.

6. During the interview or observation, make a recording (audio or video) if allowed, but also take careful notes, including notes about what you see, hear, and smell, as well as notes about tone, gestures, mannerisms, or overheard conversations.

Reflecting on What You Learned. Immediately after your interview or observation, be sure to review your notes and write down your first impressions:

   ▶ My dominant impression of the subject is ....
   ▶ The most interesting aspect of .... is .... because ....
   ▶ Although my thoughts about .... were confirmed, I was surprised to learn ....

Focus on *sensory details* that could paint a vivid portrait of the person or people, place, or activity, and write down any questions or concerns you might like to consider for a follow-up interview or observation.

Working with Sources

Integrating Quotations from Interviews

As you write up your interviews and observations and begin drafting your essay, you need to choose quotations that will present information about the subject in an interesting way. To make quotations arresting, use speaker tags (*he shouts, she blurts*). Speaker tags play an important role in observational writing because they help readers visualize the speakers and imagine what they sound like.

To integrate quotations and speaker tags smoothly into your sentences, you may rely on an all-purpose verb, such as *said* or *remarked*:

> "Try this one," he <u>says</u>. (Thompson, par. 7)

> "I am not prejudiced against color or religion," Mr. Yeganeh <u>told</u> us. . . . ("Soup," par. 4)

To depict the speaker's tone or attitude more precisely and vividly, use speaker tags with descriptive verbs, such as *protested* or *yells out*:

> *"I know! ME!"* Kyle <u>shouts</u> again, and then before Dawn recovers herself he <u>blurts</u>, *"It's three times three times three!"* (Orenstein, par. 30)

> I asked Tim if his job ever depressed him. He <u>bridled</u> at the question: "No, it doesn't depress me at all." (Cable, par. 27)

You may also add a word or phrase to a speaker tag to reveal more about how, where, when, or why the speaker speaks:

> "We're in *Ripley's Believe It or Not*, along with another funeral home whose owners' names are Baggit and Sackit," Howard told me, <u>without cracking a smile</u>. (Cable, par. 14)

> "We do our best to corner the market on lips," Lionel told me, <u>his voice tinged with bravado</u>. (Edge, par. 11)

In addition to being carefully introduced, quotations must be precisely punctuated. Fortunately, there are only two general rules:

1. Enclose all quotations in quotation marks. These always come in pairs, one at the beginning and one at the end of the quotation.

2. Separate the quotation from the speaker tag with appropriate punctuation, usually a comma. But if you have more than one sentence (as in the Orenstein example above), be careful to punctuate the separate sentences properly.

Developing Your Perspective on the Subject

The following activities will help you deepen your analysis and think of ways to help your readers gain a better understanding of your subject's cultural significance. Complete them in any order that seems helpful to you, and use the sentence strategies to come up with ideas.

Exploring Your Perspective.   Write for five minutes exploring your perspective on the subject — what about the subject seems important and meaningful?

If you are focusing on a place, ask yourself what you find interesting about its culture: What rituals or habits are practiced there? Who visits it? What is its function in the community?

▶ [Name a particular feature of the place] seems to encourage [behavior or way of thinking] perhaps because of ....

▶ If the location were changed, it is likely that .... would be different.

If you are focusing on an activity, consider how it has changed over time, for good or ill; how outsiders are initiated into the activity; who benefits from it; and what its value is for the community.

▶ Although .... [activity] might seem .... , it's important to .... because .... , says [name interviewee]. .... , in particular, benefit from it in the following ways: .... , ... , and ....

▶ .... [name activity] today is [somewhat/very] different from .... [in the past/long ago/just a few years ago]: Instead of .... , a change brought on by .... , those interested in participating are likely to ....

If you are focusing on a person or group, ask yourself what sense of identity they have; what customs and ways of communicating they have; what their values and attitudes are; what they think about social hierarchies or gender differences; and how they see their role in the community.

▶ Despite common assumptions that .... , ... [subject] thinks of him/herself as .... , an identity that comes across [in/through] ....

▶ He/She cares less about .... than about .... , to the point of ....

Defining Your Purpose for Your Readers.   Write for five minutes exploring what you want your readers to learn about the subject. Use these sentence strategies to help clarify your thinking:

▶ In addition to my teacher and classmates, I envision my ideal readers as ....

▶ They probably know .... about my subject and are likely to believe ....

> ▶ They would be most surprised to learn .... and most interested in the following facets of the subject: .... , ... , and ....
>
> ▶ I can help change their opinions of the subject by .... and get them to think about the subject's social and cultural significance by ....
>
> ▶ What I've learned about .... implies .... about our shared values and concerns, and I can help readers understand this by ....

Considering Your Main Point. Review what you have written, and add a couple of sentences summarizing the main idea you want readers to take away from your observational essay. Readers don't expect an observational essay to have an explicit thesis statement, as they do for an argumentative essay, but the descriptive details and other information need to work together to convey the main idea.

Clarifying the Dominant Impression. Although you need to create a dominant impression, readers appreciate profiles that reveal the richness and complexity of a subject. Even as Cable shows that the Goodbody Mortuary is guided by commercialism, he also gets readers to think about cultural attitudes toward death, perhaps exemplified in his own complex feelings. To create a dominant impression, try reviewing your notes and write-ups, highlighting in one color the descriptive language that supports the dominant impression you want your essay to create. Then highlight in a second color any descriptions that seem to create a different impression. Finally, write for a few minutes exploring how these different impressions relate to one another. Consider whether they reveal complexity in the subject or ambivalence in your perspective that could be developed further in your essay. You might start with one of the following sentence strategies and elaborate from there.

> ▶ Although .... [subject] clearly seemed .... , I couldn't [shake the feeling that/ignore/stop thinking about] ....
>
> ▶ Although .... [subject] [tries to/pretends to/has made progress toward .... , [overall/for the most part/primarily] he/she ....

Adopting a Role

The writing and research activities that follow will enable you to gather information and ideas about your subject and begin shaping your observations for your readers.

Considering Your Role. Will you take a detached spectator or participant-observer role to research your subject, or will you alternate between these two roles?

- As a detached spectator, you maintain an outsider's point of view, visiting the place and interviewing people there to learn about the subject.

- As a participant observer, you take part in the activity, observing from an insider's point of view and conducting interviews with others involved in the activity.

- As a spectator *and* a participant observer, you may maintain an outsider's point of view about some aspects of your subject and participate in others.

Consider the advantages and disadvantages of the three roles and then try writing some sentences to put yourself in one role or the other before you decide which works best for your subject.

Advantages

Participant-observer role

. . . is a good way to profile physical activities readers won't be familiar with, helping readers imagine going through the same experience.

▶ As I tried to ...., I was surprised to find that .... [name first impressions]. I picked up the .... It felt like ...., and it [smelled/tasted/sounded] like ....

▶ After .... [hours/minutes/days] of ...., I felt like

....

. . . enables you to explore the effect of your actions on the scene.

▶ I interrupted .... as [he/she] was explaining .... to ask why.

▶ I can't be sure whether that interruption led to ...., but I think ....

Spectator role

. . . is a good way to focus your attention on your subject rather than on yourself and to depict the subject clearly.

▶ On the other side of ...., a .... [appeared/came into view/did something].

▶ .... [name person] talked as [he/she] ....-ed. "........................," [he/she] said. "........................."

. . . is a good way to give readers the feeling that they're looking over the shoulders of the people there.

▶ Looking at .... [name feature of place or activity], ... [name person] remarked that ....

. . . is a good way to build an aura of objectivity, of just reporting what you saw and heard.

▶ .... makes [name person] angry. [He/She] says it's because "........................."

Participant-spectator (alternating)	. . . is the best of both worlds, making activities come alive while portraying people and places without much interference.

> ▶ [Above/around/before] me, [activity happened]. I tried to .... [describe what you did] and found it .... "........................" [name person who was watching me] said. "........................"

Disadvantages

Participant-observer role	. . . can become distracting if it's overdone.
	. . . can begin to feel as if you're the subject (especially when profiling a person or place).
Spectator role	. . . can feel detached, especially if profiling a physical or difficult activity.
Participant-spectator (alternating)	. . . can be challenging to juggle.
	. . . can be confusing to readers when handled poorly.

Using Your Role. Whatever role you adopt, you need to think about how you can use your role to engage readers and present the information you've chosen to include. Either role can be used to help readers identify with you. For example:

- If you are entering a place most of us avoid (as Cable does when he enters the mortuary), you can take us with you as you learn about the place and look over other people's shoulders to see what they're doing.

- If you act as a participant trying to learn how to do what others routinely do (as Edge does when he tries to eat a pickled pig lip), readers can imagine themselves in your shoes.

Regardless of your role, also consider whether to refer to yourself in your draft. Here are some possibilities:

- Place yourself at the scene. (For example, "I followed him through an arched doorway into a chapel that smelled musty and old" [Cable, par. 15].)

- Refer to your own actions. (For example, "Amy grabs my hand, pulling me along like a small child or a slightly addled new student" [Orenstein, par. 7].)

- Share your thoughts and feelings. (For example, "The surprise is that when I return on Monday, feeling recuperated, I wind up having the hardest day of my brief career. . . . I feel like I'm going to vomit from exhaustion" [Thompson, par. 16].)

Formulating a Working Thesis Statement

Review what you have written and try out a few working thesis statements that articulate your insights into, interpretations of, or ideas about the person, place, or activity that you want readers to take away from reading the essay. Like autobiography, observational writing tends not to include an explicit thesis statement, but does include sentences that reinforce and extend the dominant impression you have created.

For example, "Soup" opens and ends with these quotations that capture the writer's two main ideas about the subject:

> When Albert Yeganeh says "Soup is my lifeblood," he means it. And when he says "I am extremely hard to please," he means that, too. (par. 1)

> "He's downright rude," said a blond woman in a blue coat. "Even abusive. But you can't deny it, his soup is the best." (par. 12)

Thompson uses a similar strategy, concluding his essay with two quotations that summarize his key points:

> "Americans should know the hard work that Mexicans do in this country." (par. 17)

> "It takes a long time to learn how to really cut lettuce." (par. 19)

Cable uses the opening paragraph to introduce his ideas about death:

> Death is a subject largely ignored by the living. We don't discuss it much, not as children (when Grandpa dies, he is said to be "going away"), not as adults, not even as senior citizens. Throughout our lives, death remains intensely private. The death of a loved one can be very painful, partly because of the sense of loss, but also because someone else's mortality reminds us all too vividly of our own. (par. 1)

But he also intersperses his insights throughout the essay. Here are two examples:

> Death may be the great leveler, but one's coffin quickly reestablishes one's status. (par. 17)

> Do burials serve an important role in society? . . . For Tim, Goodbody's licensed mortician, the answer is very definitely yes. Burials will remain in common practice . . . because they allow family and friends to view the deceased. Painful as it may be, such an experience brings home the finality of death. (pars. 22–23)

Considering Adding Visuals or Other Media

Think about whether visual or audio elements — photographs, a map of the layout, illustrative materials you picked up at the place or downloaded, still or moving visuals or audio clips — would strengthen your observational essay. If you can recall profiles you've seen in magazines, on Web pages, or on television shows, what visual or audio elements were used to create a strong sense of the subject? Profiles don't require such elements to be effective, but they can be helpful.

Note: Be sure to cite the source of visual or audio elements you didn't create, and get permission from the source if your essay is going to be published on a Web site that is not password-protected.

Consider also whether your readers might benefit from design features such as headings, bulleted or numbered lists, or other typographic elements that can make an essay easier to follow.

Organizing Your Draft

As you have seen, observational profiles often include more than one kind of organization: topical, narrative, spatial tour. For example, Edge begins and ends with a narrative of his effort to eat a pig lip, but he organizes the middle section of his essay — his observations at Farm Fresh — topically. Nevertheless, it is helpful to consider which plan should predominate:

- To organize topically, group your observations and information by topic.

- To organize narratively, make a timeline and note where the information from your observations and interviews fits.

- To organize spatially (like Cable), sketch the movement from one site to another, noting where you could integrate information from observations and interviews.

For more on outlining, see Chapter 10, pp. 515–17.

For briefer essays, a scratch outline may be sufficient; for longer, more complex essays, a formal outline may be helful.

Drafting Your Observational Essay

By this point, you have done a lot of writing

- to develop something interesting to say about a subject;

- to devise a plan for presenting that information;

- to identify a role for yourself in the essay;

- to explore your perspective on the subject.

Now stitch that material together to create a draft. The next two parts of this Guide to Writing will help you evaluate and improve your draft.

Considering a Useful Sentence Strategy

As you draft your observational essay, you will need to help your readers imagine actions, people, and objects. A sentence strategy called an *absolute phrase* enables writers to show simultaneous parts of a complex action or to detail observations of a person or object.

Here is an example from Orenstein:

Absolute phrase   Some of the boys are as small and compact as fourth graders, their legs sticking out of their shorts like pipe cleaners. (par. 8)

Orenstein could have presented her observation of the boys' skinny legs in a separate sentence, but the absolute phrase gives a visual image showing just how skinny they are. Here's another example, this one from Edge:

I offer the bag to Jerry, order yet another beer, and turn to eye the pig feet floating in a murky jar by the cash register, their blunt tips bobbing up through a pasty white film. (par. 19)

EVALUATING THE DRAFT

GETTING A CONSTRUCTIVE CRITICAL READING

Getting a critical reading of your draft will help you see how to improve it. Your instructor may schedule class time for reading drafts, or you may want to ask a classmate or a tutor in the writing center to read your draft. Ask your reader to use the following guidelines and to write out a response for you to consult during your revision.

READING A DRAFT CRITICALLY

Read for a First Impression

1. **Read the draft without stopping, and then write a few sentences giving your general impression.**

2. **Identify one aspect of the draft that seems particularly effective.**

(continued)

Read Again to Suggest Improvements

1. **Suggest ways of making the information more vivid and interesting.**

   - Find a description of a place, and suggest what details could be added to objects in the scene (location, size, color, and shape) or what sensory information (look, sound, smell, taste, and touch) could be included to help you picture the place.

   - Find a description of a person, and indicate what else you would like to know about the person's dress, facial expression, tone of voice, and gestures.

   - Find a place where an activity is described with a narration of the process, and tell the writer if there is too much or too little detail.

   - Note any topics that could use more explanation, as well as any places where there is too much information on a topic or where there are too many topics to follow.

2. **Recommend ways of making the organization clearer or more effective.**

   - For narratively organized sections, look for passages where the narrative seems to wander pointlessly or leaves out important information. Also suggest cues that could be added to indicate time sequence (*initially*, *then*, *afterward*).

   - For topically organized sections, mark topics that get too much or too little attention, transitions between topics that need to be added or clarified, and topics that should be placed elsewhere.

   - For spatially organized sections, note if any of the transitions or cues that orient readers in space could be clarified, or if any need to be added.

   - For essays that alternate organizational strategies, suggest where transitions could be made smoother or sequencing could be improved.

3. **Suggest how the essay could be made more engaging and informative.**

   - If the essay seems boring or you feel overwhelmed by too much information, suggest how the information could alternate with vivid description or lively narration. Also consider whether any of the information could be cut or simplified.

   - List any questions you still have about the subject.

4. **Suggest ways to make the perspective more focused and coherent.**

   - Tell the writer what dominant impression you get from the descriptions of people, places, and activities.

   - Consider the way people, places, and activities are described, and note any word choice, contradiction, or irony that alerts you to a deeper meaning that the writer could develop.

   - Point to any passages where the writer needs to clarify the historical, social, or cultural dimensions of the subject.

   - Point to any passages that illuminate the writer's perspective or that suggest how it could be clarified or expanded.

5. **Evaluate the effectiveness of visuals or other media.**

   - If any visuals or other media do not seem relevant, or if there seem to be too many visuals, identify the ones that the writer could consider dropping, explaining your thinking.

   - If a visual does not seem to be appropriately placed, suggest a better place for it.

IMPROVING THE DRAFT

REVISING, EDITING, AND PROOFREADING

Start improving your draft by reflecting on what you have written thus far:

- Review critical reading comments from your classmates, instructor, or writing center tutor. What are your readers getting at?

- Take another look at your notes and ideas: What else should you consider?

- Review your draft: What else can you do to make your observational essay clearer or more interesting to your readers?

Revising Your Draft

Revising means reenvisioning your draft, trying to see it in a new way, given your purpose and audience, in order to develop an informative and engaging observational essay. Think imaginatively and boldly about cutting unconvincing material, adding new material, and moving material around. The suggestions in the chart on page 126 may help you solve problems and strengthen your essay.

TROUBLESHOOTING YOUR DRAFT

To Present the Information More Clearly and Vividly	
Problem	**Suggestions for Revising**
People do not come alive.	• Show people interacting with each other by including dialogue and describing movements and gestures. • Add speaker tags that characterize how people talk. • Quote only the language that conveys personality or essential information, and paraphrase or summarize other parts.
The place is hard to visualize.	• Identify items in the place by name using specific nouns and descriptive adjectives. • Add sensory detail—describe sights, sounds, smells, tastes, textures. • Say what the place is like or unlike. • Consider adding a visual—a photograph or sketch, even a film clip if your observation will appear online.
Activities or processes are not clear.	• Make sure the tense of your verbs clearly indicates the sequence of the actions. • Clarify or add transitions showing what happened when.

To Organize the Observation More Clearly and Effectively	
Problem	**Suggestions for Revising**
A narratively arranged section drags or rambles.	• Try adding drama by including dialogue or more action. • Give the narrative shape—for example, by building suspense or tension, or by making process narratives easier to follow.
A topically arranged section seems disorganized or unbalanced, with too much about some topics and too little about others.	• Try rearranging topics to see whether another order makes more sense. • Add clearer, more explicit transitions. • Move, cut, or condense information to restore balance.
A spatially arranged section is confusing.	• Add clearer, more explicit transitions to orient readers. • Use prepositional phrases to show direction or movement through space.

To Make the Essay More Engaging and Informative

Problem	Suggestions for Revising
The opening fails to engage readers' attention.	• Consider alternatives. Think of questions you could open with, or look for an engaging image or dialogue later in the essay to move to the beginning. • Go back to your notes for other ideas. • Recall how the writers in this chapter open their essays.
The essay bores or overwhelms readers with too much information about the subject.	• Cut obvious or extraneous information. • Consider alternating blocks of information with descriptive or narrative materials. • Try presenting more of the information through lively dialogue.
Readers have questions about the subject.	• Look over your research notes to see if you can answer readers' questions. • If you have time, do follow-up research to find out answers to their questions.

To Strengthen the Writer's Perspective on the Subject

Problem	Suggestions for Revising
Readers get a dominant impression you did not expect.	• Look at what gave them this impression and consider whether it could be used to enrich the impression you intended. • Cut or revise the language that gave a wrong impression.
The perspective is unclear, simplistic, or contradicted by details.	• Add language or details that strengthen, extend, or clarify the writer's perspective. • Write an explicit thesis statement—and either include it or use quotations and descriptions to convey this idea. • Discuss more directly the contradictions or complexities you see in the subject.
Readers may not understand the importance of the social, cultural, or historical context.	• Add background information to reveal important influences on the subject. • Add quotations or citations.

Editing and Proofreading Your Draft

Check for errors in usage, punctuation, and mechanics, and consider matters of style. If you keep a list of errors you typically make, begin by checking your draft against this list. Ask someone else to proofread your essay before you submit it to your instructor.

From our research on student writing, we know that observational essays tend to have errors in the use of quotation marks, when writers quote the exact words of people they have interviewed. Check a writer's handbook for help with these potential problems.

Reflecting on What You Have Learned

Observation

In this chapter, you have read several observational essays critically and have written one of your own. To better remember what you have learned, pause now to reflect on the reading and writing activities you completed in this chapter.

1. Write a page or so reflecting on what you have learned. Begin by describing what you are most pleased with in your essay. Then explain what you think contributed to your achievement. Be specific about this contribution.

   - If it was something you learned from the readings, indicate which readings and specifically what you learned from them.

   - If it came from your research notes and write-ups, point out the parts that helped you most.

   - If you got good advice from a critical reader, explain exactly how the person helped you — perhaps by helping you recognize a problem in your draft or by helping you add a new dimension to your writing.

   Try to write about your achievement in terms of what you have learned about the genre.

2. Reflect more generally on how you tend to interpret observational writing, your own as well as other writers'. Consider some of the following questions:

   - In reading for meaning, do you find yourself paying attention to larger cultural or social contexts — for example, thinking of the subject in terms of gender, ethnicity, or class?

   - How do you think the writer's perspective influenced how you saw the subject?

Reflection

Like autobiographical and observational writing, *reflective writing* is based on the writer's personal experience. Reflective writers present something they did, saw, heard, or read in writing so vivid that the reader can imagine what they experienced. But unlike writers of autobiography and observation, reflective writers aim not only to help readers imagine the experience but also to explore its meanings. Reflective writers use events, people, and places as springboards for thinking about society — how people live and what people believe about social change with its many opportunities and challenges (such as changes in scientific knowledge, the environment, and ways to perfect the body); about customs in our culturally diverse society (such as those related to eating and dating); about traditional virtues and vices (pride, jealousy, and compassion); or about common hopes and fears (the desire for an ecologically balanced world). They do not attempt to exhaust their subjects, nor do they set themselves up as experts. Instead, writers use their reflective essays as exercises, experiments, and opportunities to explore ideas informally and tentatively. Reading a reflective essay can be as stimulating as having a lively conversation, often surprising us with insights and unlikely connections and encouraging us to look in new ways at even the most familiar things.

This chapter offers several reflective selections for you to enjoy, with exploratory activities that will help you learn to read critically and write well. The Reading for Meaning and Reading Like a Writer activities following each selection invite you to analyze and write about the reading's ideas and writing strategies. You can also use the brief Guide to Writing Reflective Essays toward the end of the chapter to help you write an essay reflecting on the meaning of something you have observed or experienced.

RHETORICAL SITUATIONS FOR REFLECTIONS

Writers use a wide range of occasions to reflect on some aspect of contemporary culture, as the following examples indicate:

- A former football player writes a reflective essay for his college alumni magazine about a game in which he sustained a serious injury but continued to play because playing with pain was regarded as a sign of manliness. He reflects on learning this custom from his father and later from coaches and other players, and he wonders why boys are taught not to show pain but encouraged to show aggression and competitiveness. Taking an anthropological view, he sees contemporary sports as equivalent to the kind of training Native American boys traditionally went through to become warriors, and he questions whether playing sports prepares boys (and girls, too) for the kinds of roles they will play in contemporary society.

- Writing a blog post for a political science course, a student reflects on her first experience voting in a presidential election. She contrasts her decision-making process—examining the candidate's experience and voting record and reading endorsements from trusted experts—with those of her acquaintances, one of whom said she chose a candidate because he reminded her of her grandfather, and another who based his choice on his dislike of the way one candidate dressed. The writer then reflects on the implications of such voting decisions.

- A first-year college student, in an essay for his composition course, reflects on a performance of his high-school chorus in a statewide competition: the members' unexpected feelings of confidence, their precision and control, and the exuberance of their performance. He considers factors that led to their success, such as fear of embarrassment, affection for their teacher, the excitement of a trip to the state capital, and the fact that they had rehearsed especially attentively for weeks because the music was so challenging and the competition so fierce. He concludes with some ideas about the special pleasures of success for which cooperation and individual creativity are essential.

Thinking about the Genre

Reflection

Before studying a type of writing, it is useful to spend some time thinking about what you already know about it. You have surely told others of your ideas and reactions to things you have seen, heard, or read, even if you have not written these reflections down. Just as surely, you have heard friends or family members reflect on their experiences or read selections in which writers reflect on their experiences.

Recall an occasion when you shared a reflection with others or others shared a reflection with you, either orally or in writing. Use the following questions to develop your thoughts. Your instructor may ask you to write about this occasion or discuss it with others in class or online.

- Who was the *audience*? How do you think addressing the reflections to this audience affected the way they were "hooked"? Did the writer (or speaker) attempt to grab audience members' attention by focusing on a shocking or humorous occasion, for example?

- What was the *purpose*? How did the writer (or speaker) want the audience to react to the observations or experiences that gave rise to the reflections? For example, was the goal to make the audience identify with the writer (or speaker) or to make an experience seem strange so that audience members could see it differently?

- How might the reflection have changed if the audience or purpose had been different? For example, would the tone (or mood) have been lighter or darker if the writer (or speaker) had a different purpose or audience? How would changing the medium have affected the way the reflection was presented? For example, if the reflection were published online, might the writer (or speaker) have used background music to help convey the mood? If so, how would that have changed the experience of audience members?

A GUIDE TO READING REFLECTIVE ESSAYS

This guide introduces you to the basic features and strategies typical of reflective writing by inviting you to analyze a powerful reflective essay by Brent Staples, first by *reading for meaning* and then by *reading like a writer*:

- *Reading for meaning* will help you think about the occasions that prompted Staples's reflections, about his attitudes and assumptions regarding racial profiling, and about the broader social implications of, for example, his musical choices.

- *Reading like a writer* will help you learn how Staples employs strategies typical of reflective essays, such as

  1. Presenting the occasion vividly and in a way that prepares readers for the reflections

  2. Developing the reflections fully, using appropriate writing strategies

  3. Maintaining coherence by providing cues for readers

  4. Engaging readers' interest

Brent Staples

Black Men and Public Space

Brent Staples (b. 1951) earned his PhD in psychology from the University of Chicago and went on to become a journalist, writing for several magazines and newspapers, including the Chicago Sun-Times. *In 1985, he became assistant metropolitan editor of the* New York Times, *where he is now a member of the editorial board. His autobiography,* Parallel Time: Growing Up in Black and White *(1994), won the Anisfield Wolff Book Award.*

The following essay originally appeared in Ms. *magazine under the title "Just Walk on By." Staples revised it slightly for publication in* Harper's *under the present title.*

- *Before you read, think about a time that you frightened others by your presence (by popping up unexpectedly in a doorway, for example) or that you have been frightened by others (walking home alone after dark, for example).*

- *As you read, think about why Staples changed the title of the essay from "Just Walk on By" to "Black Men and Public Space."*

1   My first victim was a woman—white, well dressed, probably in her early twenties. I came upon her late one evening on a deserted street in Hyde Park, a relatively affluent neighborhood in an otherwise mean, impoverished section of Chicago. As I swung onto the avenue behind her, there seemed to be a discreet, uninflammatory distance between us. Not so. She cast back a worried glance. To her, the youngish black man—a broad six feet two inches with a beard and billowing hair, both hands shoved into the pockets of a bulky military jacket—seemed menacingly close. After a few more quick glimpses, she picked up her pace and was soon running in earnest. Within seconds she disappeared into a cross street.

2   That was more than a decade ago, I was twenty-two years old, a graduate student newly arrived at the University of Chicago. It was in the echo of

that terrified woman's footfalls that I first began to know the unwieldy inheritance I'd come into—the ability to alter public space in ugly ways. It was clear that she thought herself the quarry of a mugger, a rapist, or worse. Suffering a bout of insomnia, however, I was stalking sleep, not defenseless wayfarers. As a softy who is scarcely able to take a knife to a raw chicken—let alone hold one to a person's throat—I was surprised, embarrassed, and dismayed all at once. Her flight made me feel like an accomplice in tyranny. It also made it clear that I was indistinguishable from the muggers who occasionally seeped into the area from the surrounding ghetto. That first encounter, and those that followed, signified that a vast, unnerving gulf lay between nighttime pedestrians—particularly women—and me. And I soon gathered that being perceived as dangerous is a hazard in itself. I only needed to turn a corner into a dicey situation, or crowd some frightened, armed person in a foyer somewhere, or make an errant move after being pulled over by a policeman. Where fear and weapons meet—and they often do in urban America—there is always the possibility of death.

In that first year, my first away from my hometown, I was to become 3 thoroughly familiar with the language of fear. At dark, shadowy intersections, I could cross in front of a car stopped at a traffic light and elicit the thunk, thunk, thunk of the driver—black, white, male, or female— hammering down the door locks. On less traveled streets after dark, I grew accustomed to but never comfortable with people crossing to the other side of the street rather than pass me. Then there were the standard unpleasantries with policemen, doormen, bouncers, cabdrivers, and others whose business it is to screen out troublesome individuals before there is any nastiness.

I moved to New York nearly two years ago and I have remained an avid 4 night walker. In central Manhattan, the near-constant crowd cover minimizes tense one-on-one street encounters. Elsewhere—in SoHo, for example, where sidewalks are narrow and tightly spaced buildings shut out the sky—things can get very taut indeed.

After dark, on the warrenlike streets of Brooklyn where I live, I often see 5 women who fear the worst from me. They seem to have set their faces on neutral, and with their purse straps strung across their chests bandolier-style, they forge ahead as though bracing themselves against being tackled. I understand, of course, that the danger they perceive is not a hallucination. Women are particularly vulnerable to street violence, and young black males are drastically overrepresented among the perpetrators of that violence. Yet these truths are no solace against the kind of alienation that comes of being ever the suspect, a fearsome entity with whom pedestrians avoid making eye contact.

It is not altogether clear to me how I reached the ripe old age of twenty- 6 two without being conscious of the lethality nighttime pedestrians attributed to me. Perhaps it was because in Chester, Pennsylvania, the small, angry industrial town where I came of age in the 1960s, I was scarcely noticeable against a backdrop of gang warfare, street knifings, and murders. I grew up one of the good boys, had perhaps a half-dozen fistfights. In retrospect, my shyness of combat has clear sources.

7   As a boy, I saw countless tough guys locked away; I have since buried several, too. They were babies, really—a teenage cousin, a brother of twenty-two, a childhood friend in his mid-twenties—all gone down in episodes of bravado played out in the streets. I came to doubt the virtues of intimidation early on. I chose, perhaps unconsciously, to remain a shadow—timid, but a survivor.

8   The fearsomeness mistakenly attributed to me in public places often has a perilous flavor. The most frightening of these confusions occurred in the late 1970s and early 1980s, when I worked as a journalist in Chicago. One day, rushing into the office of a magazine I was writing for with a deadline story in hand, I was mistaken for a burglar. The office manager called security and, with an ad hoc posse, pursued me through the labyrinthine halls, nearly to my editor's door. I had no way of proving who I was. I could only move briskly toward the company of someone who knew me.

9   Another time I was on assignment for a local paper and killing time before an interview. I entered a jewelry store on the city's affluent Near North Side. The proprietor excused herself and returned with an enormous red Doberman pinscher straining at the end of a leash. She stood, the dog extended toward me, silent to my questions, her eyes bulging nearly out of her head. I took a cursory look around, nodded, and bade her good night.

10   Relatively speaking, however, I never fared as badly as another black male journalist. He went to nearby Waukegan, Illinois, a couple of summers ago to work on a story about a murderer who was born there. Mistaking the reporter for the killer, police officers hauled him from his car at gunpoint and but for his press credentials would probably have tried to book him. Such episodes are not uncommon. Black men trade tales like this all the time.

11   Over the years, I learned to smother the rage I felt at so often being taken for a criminal. Not to do so would surely have led to madness. I now take precautions to make myself less threatening. I move about with care, particularly late in the evening. I give a wide berth to nervous people on subway platforms during the wee hours, particularly when I have exchanged business clothes for jeans. If I happen to be entering a building behind some people who appear skittish, I may walk by, letting them clear the lobby before I return, so as not to seem to be following them. I have been calm and extremely congenial on those rare occasions when I've been pulled over by the police.

12   And on late-evening constitutionals I employ what has proved to be an excellent tension-reducing measure: I whistle melodies from Beethoven

and Vivaldi and the more popular classical composers. Even steely New Yorkers hunching toward nighttime destinations seem to relax, and occasionally they even join in the tune. Virtually everybody seems to sense that a mugger wouldn't be warbling bright, sunny selections from Vivaldi's *Four Seasons*. It is my equivalent of the cow-bell that hikers wear when they know they are in bear country.

READING FOR MEANING

This section presents three activities that will help you think about the meanings in Staples's reflective essay. Your instructor may ask you to do one or more of these activities in class or online.

1. **Read to Summarize.** Write a sentence or two briefly explaining some of the occasions that prompted Staples's reflection and how Staples explores the actions he took to address these occasions.

For more help with summarizing, see Chapter 10, pp. 518–19.

2. **Read to Respond.** Reading to respond asks you to explore your reactions to a text in light of your own knowledge or experience. To explore this reflection, write a paragraph or two analyzing your initial reactions to Staples's essay. For example, consider anything that resonates with your experience or that seems contradictory, surprising, or fascinating, such as:

   • Staples's reactions to being seen as threatening, perhaps in relation to how you think you would react if you were in his position;

   • An experience you have had in which race, gender, age, or other differences caused tension, comparing your experience with that of Staples or one of the people he encountered.

You may also try reflecting on challenges to your beliefs and values; see Chapter 10, pp. 526–27.

3. **Read to Analyze Assumptions. Assumptions** are ideas, beliefs, or values that are taken for granted as commonly accepted truths. The assumptions in a text usually reflect the writer's own attitudes or cultural traditions, but they may also represent other people's views. Reading to analyze assumptions asks you to uncover these perspectives as well as to probe your own. Sometimes the assumptions are stated explicitly, but often you will have to infer them (or figure them out) because they are only implied or hinted at through the writer's choice of words or examples. Write a paragraph or two analyzing an assumption you find intriguing in Staples's essay. For example:

   Assumptions about the unfairness and danger of racial profiling. The example Staples uses to begin his reflection — the young woman who

 Take a quiz to check your reading and vocabulary comprehension:
bedfordstmartins.com/readingcritically

suddenly becomes frightened of him out late on a deserted street in Chicago (par. 1) — illustrates how often he and other black men assume they are the object of racial profiling. A "softy" (par. 2) according to himself, he realizes that another pedestrian could see him as a "mugger, a rapist, or worse." He sees that this faulty perception could be a danger to him and to all black men because frightened people can behave violently. To think critically about the assumptions in this essay related to racial profiling, ask yourself questions like these:

- How did Staples become aware of racial profiling and its consequences?

- Why does he acknowledge that "[w]omen are particularly vulnerable to street violence, and young black males are drastically overrepresented among the perpetrators of that violence" (par. 5) and then follow this acknowledgment with "[y]et these truths are no solace against the kind of alienation that comes of being ever the suspect. . . ." (par. 5)?

- To what extent, if any, are pedestrians aware of the effects their behavior has on black men? Is Staples right in his assumption that he has been racially profiled? Are there any other possible explanations? Is there any usefulness in racial profiling?

Assumptions about how musical choices affect others. Staples concludes by writing that to reduce tension on his late-night walks, he whistles Beethoven and Vivaldi along with works of other classical composers. "Virtually everybody seems to sense that a mugger wouldn't be warbling bright, sunny selections from Vivaldi's *Four Seasons*" (par. 12). To think critically about the assumptions in this essay related to the effects of one's musical choices, ask yourself questions like these:

- Why is a classical piece more effective at reducing fear than other kinds of music such as rock, country, or rap? Why is a "sunny selection" more effective than, say, blues?

- Do you share Staples's assumption that classical music calms fearful people, or do you think there could be another explanation for how they react to his whistling? For example, could it be that the music calms Staples himself and therefore he sends out a different message?

READING LIKE A WRITER

This section presents four brief activities that will help you analyze Staples's writing. Your instructor may ask you to do one or more of these activities in class or online.

Presenting the Occasion

Reflective writers present an occasion — something they experienced or observed — in a vivid and suggestive way that encourages readers to want to know more about the writer's thoughts. For example, Staples begins with an occasion when his mere presence on the street frightened a woman into running away from him. He uses this event to introduce the general subject, fear resulting from racial profiling: "It was in the echo of that terrified woman's footfalls that I first began to know the unwieldy inheritance I'd come into — the ability to alter public space in ugly ways" (par. 2). Throughout the rest of the essay, Staples reflects on this "inheritance" from various angles:

- He expresses his feelings at being misperceived as a threat.
- He gives examples of other occasions when people reacted to him with fear or hostility.
- He explains the effects of racial profiling, including the danger to himself, and the "precautions" he takes to make himself appear "less threatening" (par. 11).

Analyze & Write

Write a paragraph or two analyzing how Staples uses examples to illustrate and explain his reflections:

1. Reread the opening sentence of paragraph 3, where Staples introduces the idea that there is a "language of fear." Then skim the rest of paragraph 3 and paragraphs 5–6 and 8–10. What examples does Staples use to help readers understand how this fear is expressed?

2. Now skim paragraphs 11 and 12. What "precautions" does Staples take to seem "less threatening"?

3. What have you learned from Staples's essay about how examples can help readers understand or accept a writer's reflections? Choose one or two examples and explain why you think they work especially well to help readers understand what Staples means.

Developing the Reflections

While Staples uses an occasion to introduce his subject, his reflections explore the subject by developing his ideas. Consider, for example, the words he uses to present his "first victim" and the location where he encounters her:

Naming / Detailing   My first victim was a woman — white, well dressed, probably in her early twenties. I came upon her late one evening on a deserted street in Hyde Park, a relatively affluent neighborhood in an otherwise mean, impoverished section of Chicago. (par. 1)

Staples uses a combination of words — some neutral, some with strongly negative connotations — to create a vivid picture. He also uses the word *first* to suggest that this woman was not his only "victim."

Analyze & Write

Write a paragraph analyzing how else Staples makes this occasion vivid for his readers as well as how he prepares them for the reflections that follow.

1. Reread paragraphs 1–2. Underline the names Staples uses to identify himself, and circle the details he uses to describe himself physically and the actions he takes.

2. Now put brackets around words and phrases in these paragraphs that suggest the larger meanings Staples will develop in subsequent paragraphs.

3. Consider the tone of the words he uses in these paragraphs. How do the words Staples chooses affect you as a reader? How do they help you identify (or hinder you from identifying) with him and his "victims"? Use concrete details from the paragraphs to support your claims.

Maintaining Coherence

Reflective essays explore ideas on a subject by turning them this way and that, examining them first from one perspective and then from another, and sometimes piling up examples to illustrate the ideas. This apparently casual organization is deceptive, however, because in fact the reflective writer has used a number of strategies to create coherence. An important way of achieving coherence is to refer to the subject at various points in the essay by repeating certain key words or phrases associated with it. In the opening anecdote presenting the occasion, Staples dramatizes the woman's fear of him. He then repeats the word "fear," or synonyms for it, throughout the essay. Another way reflective writers achieve coherence is through carefully placed transitions. Staples uses transitions of time and place to introduce a series of examples illustrating the fear he engenders in others simply because of his race and gender. Consider paragraphs 2–4:

Synonym for key term

Transition of time/place

Key term

... It was in the echo of that terrified woman's footfalls that I first began to know the unwieldy inheritance I'd come into — the ability to alter public space in ugly ways. . . . I only needed to turn a corner into a dicey situation, or crowd some frightened, armed person in a foyer somewhere, or make an errant move after being pulled over by a policeman. Where fear and weapons meet — and they often do in urban America — there is always the possibility of death.

In that first year, my first away from my hometown, I was to become thoroughly familiar with the language of fear. . . . Elsewhere — in SoHo, for example, where sidewalks are narrow and tightly spaced buildings shut out the sky — things can get very taut indeed.

Write a paragraph or two analyzing how Staples uses these strategies of repetition and transitions to maintain coherence throughout the essay:

1. Skim paragraphs 3–12, highlighting the word *fear* each time Staples uses it and circling synonyms or near synonyms for it each time they appear.

2. Now go back through the essay underlining transitions of time and place.

3. Consider how effectively these strategies work to maintain coherence. Support your analysis with examples from the reading.

Engaging Readers

Readers of reflective essays, like readers of autobiographical and observational writing, expect writers to engage their interest. In fact, most readers have no pressing reason to read reflective writing. They choose to read an essay because something about it catches their eye—a familiar author's name, an intriguing title, an interesting graphic. Journalists typically begin feature articles, ones that do not deal with "hard" news, with a "hook" designed to catch readers' attention. The occasion that opens many reflective essays often serves this purpose. Staples's opening phrase, "My first victim," certainly grabs attention.

But once "caught," readers have to be kept reading. One of the ways reflective writers keep readers engaged is by projecting an image of themselves — sometimes called the writer's **persona** or **voice** — that readers can identify with or at least find interesting. Staples, for example, uses the first-person pronouns *my* and *I* to present himself in his writing and to speak directly to readers. In paragraph 2, he describes himself as "a softy" and explains how he felt when he realized that the woman was so frightened by him that she ran for her life. Like most reflective writers, Staples tries to make himself sympathetic to readers so that they will listen to what he has to say.

Write a paragraph or two describing the impression you have of Staples from reading this essay and exploring how these impressions affect your interest in his ideas.

1. Skim the essay, circling or highlighting words, phrases, or passages that give you a sense of Staples as a person.

2. Consider the impression you have: What would you add or change to make the essay more effective for you? What engages you or draws you into the essay?

A Special Reading Strategy

Comparing and Contrasting Related Readings: Brent Staples's "Black Men and Public Space" and an Excerpt from Staples's Autobiography, *Parallel Time*

Comparing and contrasting related readings is a critical reading strategy that is useful both in reading for meaning and in reading like a writer. This strategy is particularly applicable when writers present similar subjects, as is the case in the two reflective readings by Brent Staples that are compared here. The first, "Black Men and Public Space," the essay you have just read, was originally published eight years before the second, Staples's autobiography, *Parallel Time*. Both readings deal with the same occasion — when Staples encountered his "first victim" (par. 1 in both). But you will notice that the details of this first encounter, as well as Staples's reflections about it, differ significantly in the two readings. As you read, notice what Staples retains from the original and what he changes. To compare and contrast these two reflective readings, think about topics such as these:

- The way the occasion is described: What seems to you to be most significant about how these two descriptions differ? Note, for example, the details about the location and the woman's appearance as well as how Staples describes his immediate reaction.

- Staples's description of what he calls "the language of fear." Highlight the places in paragraph 3 of each reading where the language of fear is described. How are his descriptions similar and different? How does he explain its causes?

- Staples's thoughts and feelings about the situation and the actions he decides to take. What are the main differences in his reactions?

See Chapter 10, pp. 527–30, for detailed guidelines on comparing and contrasting related readings.

- His reasons for making so radical a revision of his earlier reflections: His autobiography was published nearly a decade after his original essay. What do you think might have changed (in Staples's feelings, in the broader cultural climate, or in some other way) during that period that led Staples to share with readers his angry response rather than leaving readers with the image of himself he projects at the end of the original version?

From *Parallel Time*

1   At night, I walked to the lakefront whenever the weather permitted. I was headed home from the lake when I took my first victim. It was late fall, and the wind was cutting. I was wearing my navy pea jacket, the collar turned up, my hands snug in the pockets. Dead leaves scuttled in shoals along the streets. I turned out of Blackstone

Avenue and headed west on 57th Street, and there she was, a few yards ahead of me, dressed in business clothes and carrying a briefcase. She looked back at me once, then again, and picked up her pace. She looked back again and started to run. I stopped where I was and looked up at the surrounding windows. What did this look like to people peeking out through their blinds? I was out walking. But what if someone had thought they'd seen something they hadn't and called the police. I held back the urge to run. Instead, I walked south to The Midway, plunged into its darkness, and remained on The Midway until I reached the foot of my street.

I'd been a fool. I'd been walking the streets grinning good evening at people who were frightened to death of me. I did violence to them by just being. How had I missed this? I kept walking at night, but from then on I paid attention.

I became expert in the language of fear. Couples locked arms or reached for each other's hand when they saw me. Some crossed to the other side of the street. People who were carrying on conversations went mute and stared straight ahead, as though avoiding my eyes would save them. This reminded me of an old wives' tale: that rabid dogs didn't bite if you avoided their eyes. The determination to avoid my eyes made me invisible to classmates and professors whom I passed on the street.

It occurred to me for the first time that I was big. I was 6 feet 1½ inches tall, and my long hair made me look bigger. I weighed only 170 pounds. But the navy pea jacket that Brian had given me was broad at the shoulders, high at the collar, making me look bigger and more fearsome than I was.

I tried to be innocuous but didn't know how. The more I thought about how I moved, the less my body belonged to me; I became a false character riding along inside it. I began to avoid people. I turned out of my way into side streets to spare them the sense that they were being stalked. I let them clear the lobbies of buildings before I entered, so they wouldn't feel trapped. Out of nervousness I began to whistle and discovered I was good at it. My whistle was pure and sweet—and also in tune. On the street at night I whistled popular tunes from the Beatles and Vivaldi's *Four Seasons*. The tension drained from people's bodies when they heard me. A few even smiled as they passed me in the dark.

Then I changed. I don't know why, but I remember when. I was walking west on 57th Street, after dark, coming home from the lake. The man and the woman walking toward me were laughing and talking but clammed up when they saw me. The man touched the woman's elbow, guiding her toward the curb. Normally I'd have given way and begun to whistle, but not this time. This time I veered

(continued)

toward them and aimed myself so that they'd have to part to avoid walking into me. The man stiffened, threw back his head and assumed the stare: eyes dead ahead, mouth open. His face took on a bluish hue under the sodium vapor streetlamps. I suppressed the urge to scream into his face. Instead I glided between them, my shoulder nearly brushing his. A few steps beyond them I stopped and howled with laughter. I called this game Scatter the Pigeons.

7   Fifty-seventh Street was too well lit for the game to be much fun; people didn't feel quite vulnerable enough. Along The Midway were heart-stopping strips of dark sidewalk, but these were so frightening that few people traveled them. The stretch of Blackstone between 57th and 55th provided better hunting. The block was long and lined with young trees that blocked out the streetlight and obscured the heads of people coming toward you.

8   One night I stooped beneath the branches and came up on the other side, just as a couple was stepping from their car into their town house. The woman pulled her purse close with one hand and reached for her husband with the other. The two of them stood frozen as I bore down on them. I felt a surge of power: these people were mine; I could do with them as I wished. If I'd been younger with less to lose, I'd have robbed them, and it would have been easy. All I'd have to do was stand silently before them until they surrendered their money. I thundered, "Good evening!" into their bleached-out faces and cruised away laughing.

9   I held a special contempt for people who cowered in their cars as they waited for the light to change at 57th and Woodlawn. The intersection was always deserted at night, except for a car or two stuck at the red. Thunk! Thunk! Thunk! They hammered down the door locks when I came into view. Once I had hustled across the street, head down, trying to seem harmless. Now I turned brazenly into the headlights and laughed. Once across, I paced the sidewalk, glaring until the light changed. They'd made me terrifying. Now I'd show them how terrifying I could be.

READINGS

Dana Jennings

Our Scars Tell the Stories of Our Lives

Dana Jennings (b. 1957), a journalist who has written for the Manchester Union Leader *and the* Wall Street Journal, *is now an editor at the* New York Times. *He is best known for his novel,* Lonesome Standard Time *(1996); his nonfiction,* Sing Me Back Home: Love, Death and Country Music *(2008); and his blog for the* New York Times *Well section in which he writes about prostate cancer, with which he was diagnosed in 2008. You can find his blog by typing his name into "search" at http://well.blogs.nytimes.com.*

The following essay appeared in the New York Times *on July 21, 2009. Pondering the scars on his own body, Jennings notes that scars tell stories. He develops his reflection by relating some of the stories prompted by his scars, and speculates about their larger meaning.*

- *Before you read, think about your own scars, what they mean to you, and whether you have memories associated with each scar.*

- *As you read, think about the differences between the scars Jennings first describes and the "heavy hitters, the stitched whips and serpents that make my other scars seem like dimples on a golf ball" (par. 7), to which he devotes the second half of his essay. What is the occasion (or two) that prompts Jennings to think about the meaning of scars?*

1 Our scars tell stories. Sometimes they're stark tales of life-threatening catastrophes, but more often they're just footnotes to the ordinary but bloody detours that befall us on the roadways of life. When I parse my body's motley parade of scars, I see them as personal runes and conversation starters. When I wear shorts, the footlong surgical scar on my right knee rarely fails to draw a comment. And in their railroad-track-like appearance, my scars remind me of the startling journeys that my body has taken—often enough to the hospital or the emergency room.

What is the particular occasion (or two) that prompts Jennings to think about the meaning of scars?

2 The ones that intrigue me most are those from childhood that I can't account for. The one on my right eyebrow, for example, and a couple of ancient pockmarks and starbursts on my knees. I'm not shocked by them. To be honest, I wonder why there aren't more.

How does this paragraph
help the reader identify
with Jennings?

I had a full and active boyhood, one that raged ₃ with scabs and scrapes, mashed and bloody knees, bumps and lumps, gashes and slashes, cats' claws and dogs' teeth, jagged glass, ragged steel, knots, knobs and shiners. Which raises this question: How do any of us get out of childhood alive?

My stubborn chin has sustained a fair bit of dam- ₄ age over the years. On close examination, there's a faint delta of scars that brings back memories of my teenage war on acne. Those frustrating days of tetra- cycline and gritty soaps left my face not clean and glowing but red and raw. The acne also ravaged my back, scoring the skin there so that it still looks scorched and lunar.

I further cratered my chin as an adult. First, I ₅ sprinted into a cast-iron lamppost while chasing a fly ball in a park in Washington; I actually saw a chorus line of stars dance before my eyes as I crumpled to the ground. Second, I hooked one of those old acne potholes with my razor and created an instant duel- ing scar.

How do these stories help
you see how scars have different effects on memory?

Scanning down from the jut of my chin to the tips ₆ of my toes, I've even managed to brand my feet. In high school and college I worked at Kingston Steel Drum, a factory in my New Hampshire hometown that scoured some of the 55-gallon steel drums it cleaned with acid and scalding water. The factory was eventually shut down by the federal government and became a Superfund hazardous waste site, but not before a spigot malfunctioned one day and soaked my feet in acid.

Why do you suppose
Jennings makes this para-
graph only one sentence
long?

Then there are the heavy hitters, the stitched whips ₇ and serpents that make my other scars seem like dim- ples on a golf ball.

There's that mighty scar on my right knee from ₈ when I was 12 years old and had a benign tumor cut out. Then there are the scars on my abdomen from when my colon (devoured by ulcerative colitis) was removed in 1984, and from my radical open prosta- tectomy last summer to take out my cancerous pros- tate. (If I ever front a heavy metal band, I think I'll call it Radical Open Prostatectomy.)

What kind of shift is indicated by this paragraph?
How does it affect you?

But for all the potential tales of woe that they sug- ₉ gest, scars are also signposts of optimism. If your body is game enough to knit itself back together after a hard physical lesson, to make scar tissue, that means you're still alive, means you're on the path toward healing.

10   Scars, perhaps, were the primal tattoos, marks of distinction that showed you had been tried and had survived the test. And like tattoos, they also fade, though the one from my surgery last summer is still a fierce and deep purple.

> What is the purpose of these more general descriptions of scars?

11   There's also something talismanic about them. I rub my scars the way other people fret a rabbit's foot or burnish a lucky penny. Scars feel smooth and dry, the same way the scales of a snake feel smooth and dry.

12   I find my abdominal scars to be the most profound. They vividly remind me that skilled surgeons unlocked me with their scalpels, took out what had to be taken, sewed me back up and saved my life. It's almost as if they left their life-giving signatures on my flawed flesh.

13   The scars remind me, too, that in this vain culture our vanity sometimes needs to be punctured and deflated—and that's not such a bad thing. To paraphrase Ecclesiastes, better to be a scarred and living dog than to be a dead lion.

> Here Jennings reminds us that scars are often seen as defacing. Where else does Jennings address this issue? Is Jennings being truthful when he says he's not proud of his scars? Could his reflection be interpreted in another way?

14   It's not that I'm proud of my scars—they are what they are, born of accident and necessity—but I'm not embarrassed by them, either. More than anything, I relish the stories they tell. Then again, I've always believed in the power of stories, and I certainly believe in the power of scars.

READING FOR MEANING

This section presents three activities that will help you think about the meanings in Jennings's reflective essay. Your instructor may ask you to do one or more of these activities in class or online.

1. **Read to Summarize.** Write a sentence or two briefly explaining some of the occasions that prompted Jennings's reflection and the history of the scars he observes.

For more help with summarizing, see Chapter 10, pp. 518–19.

2. **Read to Respond.** Write a paragraph or two analyzing your initial reactions to Jennings's essay. For example, consider anything that resonates

 Take a quiz to check your reading and vocabulary comprehension:
bedfordstmartins.com/readingcritically

with your experience or that seems contradictory, surprising, or fascinating, such as:

- Jennings's assertion that "[s]cars, perhaps, were the primal tattoos, marks of distinction that showed you had been tried and had survived the test" (par. 10);

- Jennings's concluding statement: "I've always believed in the power of stories, and I certainly believe in the power of scars" (par. 14);

- How you feel about any scars you might have, and what they might mean to other people.

You may also try recognizing emotional manipulation; see Chapter 10, pp. 536–37.

3. **Read to Analyze Assumptions.** Write a paragraph or two analyzing an assumption you find intriguing in Jennings's essay. For example:

Assumptions about the role of scars in memories. In the first eight paragraphs, Jennings details accidents and illnesses that led to many of his scars. Then he writes: "But for all the potential tales of woe that they suggest, scars are also signposts of optimism" (par. 9). Not only do scars mean healing, they are "primal tattoos, marks of distinction that showed you had been tried and had survived the test" (par. 10). These statements seem to contradict his assertion that he is not proud of his scars (par. 14). To think critically about the assumptions in this essay related to the role of scars in memories, ask yourself questions like these:

- How does the text support the idea that scars bring back memories of triumph and survival and also that they remind us of unhappy times?

- Is there a way to reconcile these two views? If so, what is it?

Assumptions about the power of stories. Clearly, Jennings values stories — the word *stories* is in his title and in his first sentence, and in his final paragraph, he says of his scars "I relish the stories they tell" and adds, "I've always believed in the power of stories" (par. 14). As Jennings scans the scars on his body, he tells brief stories to illustrate how he got many of them. To think critically about the assumptions in this essay related to the power of stories, ask yourself questions like these:

You may also consider reflecting on challenges to your beliefs and values; see Chapter 10, pp. 526–27.

- What effect does the story about each scar have on you as a reader?

- How do the stories differ from each other, and what difference does that make to your reading experience?

- How do the stories help you understand the kind of person Jennings is?

- Do the stories help you rethink your beliefs about scars?

A Special Reading Strategy

Exploring the Significance of Figurative Language

Figurative language adds color and richness to writing by taking words literally associated with one thing and applying them to something else, often in an unexpected or unconventional way, to create a vivid image or other sensory impression in readers' minds. For example, in "Our Scars Tell the Stories of Our Lives," Jennings refers to his scars as "footnotes to the ordinary but bloody detours that befall us on the roadways of life" (par. 1), and adds that his scars, in their "railroad-track-like appearance" remind him of the "journeys that [his] body has taken" (par. 1). To explore the significance of figurative language in this essay:

1. List and label all the figures of speech — metaphors, similes, and symbols — that you find.

2. Then, group the figures of speech according to similar feelings and attitudes, and label them. Look for patterns.

3. Write for ten minutes to explore the themes you discovered in step 2. What meanings emerge from the patterns and your writing?

See Chapter 10, pp. 523–24, for detailed guidelines on exploring the significance of figurative language.

READING LIKE A WRITER

PRESENTING THE OCCASION

Reflections are often triggered by an event that the writer presents as a story, including vivid details to help readers picture the scene. You have seen how Brent Staples narrates the event that started him thinking about his subject:

> Markers of a one-time event
>
> Details
>
> My first victim was a woman — white, well dressed, probably in her early twenties. I came upon her late one evening on a deserted street in Hyde Park, a relatively affluent neighborhood in an otherwise mean, impoverished section of Chicago. (par. 1)

Later, Staples refers to other occasions indicating that the event on that night was just the first of what became frequent occurrences.

A different tack is to begin with an observation, with the events that gave rise to it following the initial reflection. This is Jennings's approach. He begins with his observation: "Our scars tell stories" (par. 1). Then he narrates the story each scar prompts, grouping them according to their significance, making meaning out of his memories.

| Analyze & Write |

Write a paragraph or two about analyzing Jennings's use of vivid details and narratives to present the occasions that gave rise to his reflections:

1. Reread Jennings's narratives in paragraphs 4, 5, 6, and 8. Highlight or circle the words that mark each story as a one-time or ongoing event, and underline the details that help you picture what happened.

2. Now skim paragraphs 9–13. How does Jennings use the stories of his scars to draw conclusions about their meanings?

Dan Zevin

Father Shops Best

Dan Zevin (b. 1964) graduated with a journalism degree from New York University. He writes humorous books and essays, contributing to national publications such as Details, Glamour, Parents, *and* Rolling Stone, *and to regional publications such as* Boston Magazine *and the* Boston Phoenix. *His books are largely based on his own experiences with college, marriage, and parenthood:* Entry-Level Life: A Complete Guide to Masquerading as a Member of the Real World *(1994);* The Nearly-wed Handbook: How to Survive the Happiest Day of Your Life *(2001);* The Day I Turned Uncool: Confessions of a Reluctant Grownup; *and* Dan Gets a Minivan: Life at the Intersection of Dude and Dad *(2012), where you can find a longer version of the essay below, which was first published in the magazine* Real Simple.

- *Before you read, think about your relationship with your parents or other people who were in charge of raising you. Did you ever have a moment when you felt sudden insight into yourself by observing them? What were the conditions?*

- *As you read, note where you smile or laugh. What strategies does Zevin use to create humor? See if you can find three or four. Do you recognize any strategies you could use to help you write a humorous reflection?*

" 'A man should never stop learning, even on his last day,' " my father tells me. "Maimonides." The two of us are standing at the entrance to a Costco near his home in New Jersey. It is our first trip there together. He's about to demonstrate how to maximize the cargo space of the wide-load shopping carts he has selected for us. "Observe," he says. With a flick of the wrist, he expands the folding baby seat. 1

"But why?" I ask. "Why must we expand these baby seats when the kids are at home with my wife?" 2

" 'All in good time thou shalt see.' Cervantes." 3

As the glass doors slide open, I experience a fight-or-flight sensation. My vision is blurred by an onslaught of flashing flat-panel screens. A man exhorts me to eat free samples of crabmeat salad. A guard demands to see my membership card. Then she notices my father. "Dr. Zevin!" she exclaims. "I wondered when you were coming!" 4

"I tied her tubes three weeks ago," he says, as we walk away. (My dad is a gynecologist, FYI.) "Follow me," he adds. "Wait till you see all the bananas here. My treat." 5

Lately my friends are worried they're turning into their fathers. I'm worried that I'm not. My dad is calm and collected. I am clammy and confused. His interests range from numismatics to philosophy. As the father of two young kids and the husband of a working wife, I care little about any activity that's not preceded by the term "after-school." 6

7   Above all, my dad is generous. Which, I'm afraid, has made me a taker. Specifically, a taker of the toilet-paper 36-packs he gives me, the casks of dishwashing liquid he gives me, the tallboys of wood cleaner he gives me. Although I appreciate my father's kindness, I've grown uncomfortable about accepting his many gifts. It's hard to feel like a man when you're in your 40s and your dad is still buying you paper towels. In an effort to become a better provider, I asked my father to teach me all he knows—a journey that has led us here, to Costco.

8   This trip isn't easy for me. Unlike my father, who can zero in on a carton of nine-volt batteries the way a hunter senses his prey, I can barely walk into a supermarket without being paralyzed by all the peanut butter. No wonder I'm instantly spellbound by a tank of orange cheese balls. "Monosodium glutamate," Dad solemnly says. "Not healthy." Ashamed, I follow him to the produce section. "Ever seen bananas like these, Danny?" he inquires, holding his harvest high in the air. He places a bunch in my cart, along with a mile-long vine of red grapes and the gross national product of Nova Scotia in blueberries.

9   Minutes later we are in aisle 4,000, clutching a shrink-wrapped 250-pack of paper towels. After getting hugged by a staffer named Rosario, whom he has treated for fibroids, Dad announces that it's time to reveal the secrets of the expandable child seat.

10   As he instructs, I flip down the plastic red covering, thus blocking the leg holes. Words are not necessary as Dad presents me with the paper towels. He motions with his chin to put them where the child normally goes. It is uncanny: a precise fit.

11   " 'A new type of thinking is essential if mankind is to survive and move to higher levels,' " my father says. "Albert Einstein."

12   At first I am overwhelmed by the largeness of everything: by the Flintstones-size sirloin; by what must be the Guinness World Records holder for biggest piece of breaded, seasoned tilapia; by the miles of Brillo boxes (big enough for an Andy Warhol display).

13   I'm nervous about placing anything in my cart. *Where will I put all this?* I wonder. Our town house is already at overflow capacity with the stuff my father has given me. Under my daughter's bed is where we keep the Kleenex. Behind the pedestal sink is where we stack the vitamins. I can't recline in my reclining chair. The last time I tried, I smashed into a tower of diet-dog-food cans.

14   But resistance is futile, which I learn when I am overcome by a nearly primal pull toward a double-wide flat of Poland Spring mini bottles. It seemed to me we were running low the last time I looked in the fireplace. Yes. I distinctly remember writing down this reminder: "More Poland Spring mini bottles (tell Dad)."

15   Where is he now, anyway? Probably in the pharmacy department, dispensing advice about endometriosis. If I wish to replenish my family's water supply, it is up to me and me alone.

Seizing my conquest from the shelf, the wisdom of the elder echoes in   16
my mind: "Use the rack under your cart for oversize flats, Danny. Many
people don't even notice it."

With the water beneath my cart, I complete a critical step in my initia-   17
tion. I am on my way to becoming a true provider. By the time my cart is
three-quarters full, a sense of inner peace replaces my Shopper's ADD.
This is how my father must feel all the time, I reflect, thanks to his relationship with Costco. He is never preoccupied with the threat of carbon
monoxide in his home, since he knows where to get a two-pack of Night-
hawk carbon monoxide detectors. Safety pins, rubber bands, twist ties,
hangers—those things a person never buys but somehow still has? I finally
understand their significance. A man can't attain the enlightened state of
provider until he knows all that is possible to provide.

I feel increasingly focused. I stop bouncing like a pinball from floor   18
coverings to Q-tips, now aware that each purchase should lead logically to
the next. I hit my stride with the Little Giant MegaLite ladder. My thought
process is perfectly linear:

(a) Oh look, there is a case of lightbulbs that are the same brand as the
one that's burned out in the living-room ceiling.
(b) I left it burned out because it's a hassle to reach it on our crappy
little stepladder.
(c) In order to reach it, I must get that MegaLite ladder over there by the
fire extinguishers.
(d) Speaking of fire extinguishers, we should have some of those.
(e) And, yes, we need battery-operated smoke alarms. Our hard-wired
ones go off the second you light a candle.
(f) Which is why I am getting a new LED flashlight.

When I return to my father, he surveys the spoils of my well-stocked   19
cart. He is beaming. It is an expression I have rarely seen. When your
father is a lifelong provider, you get precious few chances to make him
proud. You might suspect that the real reason he's providing is that he feels
slightly sorry for you, believing on some level that you can't take care of
yourself. But now I relax—until I see the karaoke machine on display and
remember how my father likes to celebrate.

Asking me to sing karaoke with him is something my father has done at   20
joyful moments ever since my siblings and I gave a command performance of "Papa Was a Rollin' Stone" at his 70th-birthday bash. And,
frankly, singing karaoke once every 70 years seems like an ideal schedule
to me. Or, rather, it seemed that way to the old me—the inhibited, uptight
one who had not yet conquered Costco with his father. But here, today,
everything is different. Dad and I have become equals: not a father and a
son, but two fathers together. The result is an electrifying duet of "American Pie." When a man is a provider, you must understand, he wants to
break out into song.

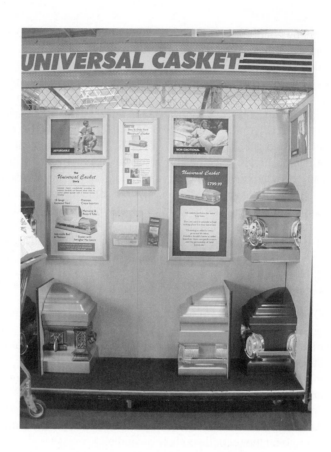

21   Outside the sun is setting. One last challenge awaits: the membership desk. Dad introduces me to Lucille (hormone disorder), who signs me up for an executive membership. My father pulls out his wallet.

22   "No, Dad," I insist. "Allow me."

23   Not long from now, our roles will reverse and I'll be providing for him. I'll bring him a deluxe rolling walker with a built-in cup holder, a 30-pack of hearing-aid batteries, and maybe even the final item we glimpse by the exit doors: the Costco coffin. My father quotes Woody Allen when he sees it. " 'I'm not afraid of dying,' " he says. " 'I just don't want to be there when it happens.' "

24   I shall bring my son Leo to Costco one day, and Leo shall bring his son, and the patriarchal cycle of Zevin providers shall continue. In the meantime, I've got to pay for a few thousand bananas. Handing my new ID to the cashier, it strikes me that you don't really know what you look like until you've seen your digitized face on a Costco card. On mine, I'm the spitting image of my dad.

READING FOR MEANING

This section presents three activities that will help you think about the meanings in Zevin's reflective essay. Your instructor may ask you to do one or more of these activities in class or online.

For more help with summarizing, see Chapter 10, pp. 518–19.

1. **Read to Summarize.** Write a sentence or two examining Zevin's reflection, briefly tracing the journey he takes through Costco and what he learns.

2. **Read to Respond.** Write a paragraph analyzing your initial reactions to Zevin's reflective essay. Consider anything that resonates with your experience or that seems contradictory, surprising, or fascinating. For example, you might consider the following:

   - Zevin's speculation that "[l]ately my friends are worried they're turning into their fathers. I'm worried that I'm not" (par. 6);

   You may also consider contextualizing; see Chapter 10, pp. 522–23.

   - Zevin's use of **hyperbole** (exaggerations not intended to be taken literally) and its effect on you.

3. **Read to Analyze Assumptions.** Write a paragraph or two analyzing an assumption you find intriguing in Zevin's essay. For example:

   Assumptions about heritage, and how cultural practices are passed from one generation to the next. Zevin relates that he asked his father "to teach me all he knows — a journey that has led us here, to Costco" (par. 7). To think critically about the assumptions in this essay related to cultural practices, ask yourself questions like these:

   - Why is Costco the example Zevin chooses to explore his heritage?
   - What do paragraphs 23–24 say about passing on cultural practices?
   - Does Zevin belittle the notion of "heritage" in his reflection, or is his purpose to illuminate certain cultural practices in the United States? How do you know?

   Assumptions about humor as a vehicle for reflection. Zevin uses humor as a strategy to help his readers think about serious subjects. For example, he uses hyperbole, or exaggeration, describing the bounty at Costco to highlight the inevitability of his father's death: "Not long from now, our roles will reverse and I'll be providing for him. I'll bring him a deluxe rolling walker with a built-in cup holder, a 30-pack of hearing-aid

Take a quiz to check your reading and vocabulary comprehension:
bedfordstmartins.com/readingcritically

batteries, and maybe even the final item we glimpse by the exit doors: the Costco coffin" (par. 23). He also quotes his father quoting humorist Woody Allen to lighten the tone. To think critically about the assumptions in this essay related to the place of humor in reflections on serious topics, ask yourself questions like these:

You may also consider annotating; see Chapter 10, p. 508.

- What effect do Zevin's attempts at humor have? Are some funnier than others? Why?

- How could humor backfire on Zevin?

- What is humor's role in relation to Zevin? Does it illuminate him or his father? What about their relationship?

READING LIKE A WRITER

ENGAGING READERS

In reflective essays, writers often tell **anecdotes** — brief, entertaining stories — about themselves and the people with whom they interact or the incidents they experience. These anecdotes help engage readers, and they may also convey the writer's reflection dramatically. To present firsthand the characters and their actions, writers sometimes also use dialogue — they *show* the scene rather than *tell* it, so readers can come to their own conclusions. Zevin's entire essay is an anecdote, about his first trip to Costco, but within it are several short anecdotes, a number of which include dialogue. Here's an example:

> First-person pronoun
> Present-tense verb
>
> As the glass doors slide open, I experience a fight-or-flight sensation. My vision is blurred by an onslaught of flashing flat-panel screens. A man exhorts me to eat free samples of crabmeat salad. A guard demands to see my membership card. Then she notices my father. "Dr. Zevin!" she exclaims. "I wondered when you were coming!" (par. 4)

The essay is written in the **first person** (the *I* voice) and the present tense to convey the experience with immediacy. Any reader who has been to Costco (or almost any "big-box" store) will recognize this scene and be drawn into the essay, and will also see instantly that Zevin's father is a favorite customer.

In this essay, Zevin includes two kinds of quotations from his father: **adages** (sayings expressing widely accepted truths) that his father quotes — "A man should never stop learning, even on his last day" (par. 1) — and bits of advice he offers when they're in Costco: "Monosodium glutamate . . . not healthy" (par. 8), referring to the orange cheese balls. Both help develop Zevin's reflections, but they also help develop the father as an amusing character.

| Analyze & Write |

Write several sentences analyzing Zevin's use of anecdotes and dialogue to engage his readers.

1. Reread the essay to identify the brief anecdotes Zevin includes. What commonalities do these anecdotes share? How do they illuminate Zevin and his father? What other roles do they play in the essay? If you find some of the anecdotes funny, try to figure out why.

2. Underline each adage Zevin's father quotes. Is each one appropriate to the occasion? What do they reveal about Zevin's father? What do they reveal about the larger issues Zevin explores in his reflection?

ANALYZING VISUALS

Write a paragraph analyzing the photograph included in Zevin's reflection (p. 152) and explaining what it contributes to the essay. To do the analysis, you can use the Criteria for Analyzing Visuals chart in Chapter 12 on pp. 611–12. Don't feel you have to answer all of the questions in the chart; focus on those that seem most productive in helping you write a paragraph-length analysis. To help you get started, consider adding these questions that specifically refer to Zevin's photo:

- How does this shot illustrate the final paragraphs of Zevin's reflection?

- What is the message of juxtaposing the caskets with the ATM machine?

- If you were to shoot a photo of a section of the local Costco or another big-box store, what would you choose? Why?

Rob Walker

Replacement Therapy: Why Our Gadgets Can't Wear Out Fast Enough

Rob Walker (b. 1968) graduated from the University of Texas at Austin. Author of the Consumed column in the New York Times Magazine *from 2004 to 2011, he often writes about consumer issues in publications such as* Slate.com, Money, *and the* American Lawyer. *He also writes a blog on* Design Observer. *His publications include* Letters from New Orleans *(2005) and* Buying In: The Secret Dialogue between What We Buy and Who We Are *(2008). The selection below appeared in the* Atlantic *in 2012.*

- *Before you read, think about your own electronic gadgets and whether you yearn for new ones to replace the old ones, or whether you have some other point of view toward them.*

- *As you read, think about Walker's question in paragraph 6: "Imagine . . . that tomorrow some company unveiled a cell phone guaranteed to last for 20 years. Who would genuinely want it?" How would you respond?*

1   An inexplicable line has appeared on the screen of my iPod, and I can't get rid of it. The battery life has been flagging lately, too. Plus, the thing won't sync properly with Last.fm anymore. Yet none of these problems—and the device mortality they portend—bother me. On the contrary, I'm practically cheering them on, because my iPod is a "classic" model from 2007, and for years I've coveted an iPod touch. Spending money to replace something that works would make me feel wasteful and guilty. So I poke at my iPod with the perverse hope that it won't respond. I have a gadget death wish.

2   Possibly you know the feeling. When I've confessed to others my enthusiasm for the breakdown of an expensive, enjoyable product, I've encountered surprising reinforcement. One friend said the debut of the white iPhone had her wishing a cruel fate upon her current smart phone. Another acquaintance, who blogs actively about cool new tech toys, confessed his constant yearning for one or another of his electronic possessions to require untimely replacement. A third described himself as "delighted" when his wife accidentally dunked his old iPhone in the Atlantic, "giving me the excuse I needed to get a 3G."

3   We're all familiar with the sinister idea of "planned obsolescence," a corporate strategy of supplying the market with products specifically built not to last. Consumer-culture critic Annie Leonard describes such items as

"designed for the dump"; she recounts reading industrial-design journals from the 1950s in which designers "actually discuss how fast can they make stuff break" and still leave consumers with "enough faith in the product to go out and buy another one." When that doesn't work, she says, the market suckers us with aesthetic tweaks that have no impact on functionality: the taller tail fins and shorter skirts of "perceived obsolescence."

But the emerging prevalence—anecdotally, at least—of the gadget death   4
wish suggests an intriguing possibility: where electronic gizmos are concerned, product obsolescence is becoming a demand-side phenomenon.

Consider that most ubiquitous gadget, the mobile phone. According to   5
J. D. Power and Associates, the typical American gets a new one every 18 months. This is not because of some time bomb in the design that renders a phone useless over that span. ReCellular, a big recycler and reseller of mobiles, collects millions of unwanted phones every year. Joe McKeown, the company's vice president of marketing and communications, told me that many are several years old—not because they've been in use all that time, but because, after being replaced, they were dumped in desk drawers and forgotten. But despite this, only 18 percent of the phones the company collects are "beyond economic repair," and thus broken down to recyclable parts. The rest either work fine or can easily be refurbished and put right back into the marketplace. The problem, if that's the right word for it, is that new devices perform more functions, faster—and people, as a result, want them.

This demand-side obsolescence does not extend to all products, of   6
course. I have no death wish, for example, for the three-year-old dishwasher now in terminal condition in my kitchen. But the light-speed innovations in consumer electronics have turned many of us into serial replacers. A dealer in vintage home-entertainment equipment recently convinced me that it used to be possible to buy a top-notch stereo system that really would function admirably for decades. Imagine, by contrast, that tomorrow some company unveiled a cell phone guaranteed to last for 20 years. Who would genuinely want it? It's not our devices that wear thin, it's our patience with them.

The very real problem of electronic waste makes people like me hesi-   7
tate to replace good-working-order possessions. Yet at the same time, we like to stay current with new technological innovations. So rather than provide evidence of some cynical corporate strategy, our gadgets' minor malfunctions or disappointing features or unacceptably slow speeds largely provide an excuse to replace them—with a lighter laptop, a slimmer tablet, a clearer e-book reader. Obsolescence isn't something companies are forcing on us. It's progress, and it's something we pretty much demand. As usual, the market gives us exactly what we want.

READING FOR MEANING

This section presents three activities that will help you think about the meanings in Walker's reflective essay. Your instructor may ask you to do one or more of these activities in class or online.

For more
help with
summarizing,
see Chapter 10,
pp. 518–19.

1. **Read to Summarize.** Write a sentence or two explaining what Walker's reflective essay is about.

2. **Read to Respond.** Write a paragraph analyzing your initial reactions to Walker's essay. For example, consider anything that resonates with your experience or that seems contradictory, surprising, or fascinating, such as:

   - "Planned obsolescence," the corporate strategy of building in the malfunction of a machine or gadget (par. 3). Do you believe that corporations intentionally build their machines to self-destruct after a few years? Why or why not?

You may also try
contextualizing;
see Chapter 10,
pp. 522–23.

   - Walker's attitude toward his gadgets. Do you share Walker's death wish for his electronic gadgets, or do you treasure them — or, perhaps, does your attitude differ depending on the gadget?

3. **Read to Analyze Assumptions.** Write a paragraph or two analyzing an assumption you find intriguing in Walker's essay. For example:

   The assumption that "new" is better. Walker points out that "the light-speed innovations in consumer electronics have turned many of us into serial replacers" (par. 6). But is new always better? To think critically about the assumptions in this essay that "new" is better, ask yourself questions like these:

   - What seem to be Walker's assumptions about newness? Is there a downside to the release of new computer software or the availability of the next-generation smartphone or tablet?

   - When Walker states that his desire for the demise of his gadgets does not apply to all machinery — "I have no death wish, for example, for the three-year-old dishwasher now in terminal condition in my kitchen" (par. 6) — do you agree? In your experience, what kinds of possessions (if any) are exempt from the wish for new ones? Is the desire for new things directed by a person's interests and preferences, by the amount of time or effort needed to select a new item, by the cost of replacement, or by something else?

Take a quiz to check your reading and vocabulary comprehension:
bedfordstmartins.com/readingcritically

The assumption that we should not be wasteful. Throughout his essay, Walker repeats that wastefulness should be avoided: "Spending money to replace something that works would make me feel wasteful and guilty" (par. 1), and "The very real problem of electronic waste makes people like me hesitate to replace good-working-order possessions" (par. 7). To think critically about the assumptions in this essay regarding wastefulness, ask yourself questions like these:

- What seem to be the author's assumptions about wastefulness? Why would *wastefulness* be seen as a problem to begin with? How might the essay have differed if Walker had talked about *splurging on* a new iPod instead of thinking himself wasteful for buying a new one when the old one still worked?

  You may also try reflecting on challenges to your beliefs and values; see Chapter 10, pp. 526–27.

- How do people justify being wasteful? What do their justifications say about their attitude toward wastefulness?

READING LIKE A WRITER

MAINTAINING COHERENCE

Writers maintain coherence by providing *cues* that help readers move from paragraph to paragraph and from section to section without losing the thread. The most familiar *cohesive device* is probably the transitional word or phrase. Some transitions (*however, because*) alert readers to the logical relationships among ideas, while others indicate relationships in time or space (*next, beyond*). A less familiar, but equally effective, strategy is to repeat key terms and their synonyms or to use pronouns (*it, they*) to refer to the key term. Notice how Walker introduces the idea of gadget death by introducing examples of his gadget's "illness" and using synonyms.

Transition
Key term/
synonym
An inexplicable line has appeared on the screen of my iPod, and I can't get rid of it. The battery life has been flagging lately, too. Plus, the thing won't sync properly with Last.fm anymore. Yet none of these problems — and the device mortality they portend — bother me. On the contrary, I'm practically cheering them on, because my iPod is a "classic" model from 2007, and for years I've coveted an iPod touch. Spending money to replace something that works would make me feel wasteful and guilty. So I poke at my iPod with the perverse hope that it won't respond. I have a gadget death wish. (par. 1)

Walker also uses transitions to convey the idea that, rather than the usual mournful response, he actually feels gleeful (par. 1).

Analyze & Write

Write a paragraph or two analyzing how Walker creates coherence in the rest of "Replacement Therapy: Why Our Gadgets Can't Wear Out Fast Enough":

1. Skim the rest of the essay, highlighting any words associated with *death*, such as "cruel fate" (par. 2), "untimely replacement" (par. 2), and "'obsolescence'" (par. 3). How do these words underscore the meaning of "gadget death"?

2. Now underline the transitions Walker uses, noting especially those that indicate a contrast and those that introduce examples showing that others share Walker's gadget death wish.

3. Finally, consider how effectively these strategies work to maintain coherence. Support your analysis with examples from the reading.

Katherine Haines

Whose Body Is This?

Katherine Haines wrote this essay for an assignment in her first-year college composition course. As the title suggests, the writer reflects on her dismay and anger about American society's obsession with the perfect body—especially the perfect female body.

- **Before you read,** *think about your own attitude toward the female body as it is portrayed in the media. Do you find anything disturbing about it?*

- **As you read,** *consider Haines's rhetorical situation; she is writing about a sensitive topic for many women: their bodies. What strategies does she use to develop her reflection and support her opinions?*

"Hey Rox, what's up? Do you wanna go down to the pool with me? It's a   1
gorgeous day."

"No thanks, you go ahead without me."   2

"What? Why don't you want to go? You've got the day off work, and   3
what else are you going to do?"

"Well, I've got a bunch of stuff to do around the house . . . pay the bills,   4
clean the bathroom, you know. Besides, I don't want to have to see myself
in a bathing suit — I'm so fat."

Why do so many women seem obsessed with their weight and body shape?   5
Are they really that unhappy and dissatisfied with themselves? Or are these
women continually hearing from other people that their bodies are not
acceptable?

In today's society, the expectations for women and their bodies are all   6
too evident. Fashion, magazines, talk shows, "lite" and fat-free food in
stores and restaurants, and diet centers are all daily reminders of these
expectations. For instance, the latest fashions for women reveal more and
more skin: shorts have become shorter, to the point of being scarcely larger
than a pair of underpants, and the bustier, which covers only a little more
skin than a bra, is making a comeback. These styles are flattering on only
the slimmest of bodies, and many women who were previously happy
with their bodies may emerge from the dressing room after a run-in with
these styles and decide that it must be diet time again. Instead of coming to
the realization that these clothes are unflattering for most women, how
many women will simply look for different and more flattering styles, and
how many women will end up heading for the gym to burn off some more
calories or to the bookstore to buy the latest diet book?

For an additional student reading, go to
bedfordstmartins.com/readingcritically.

7   When I was in junior high, about two-thirds of the girls I knew were on diets. Everyone was obsessed with fitting into the smallest-size miniskirt possible. One of my friends would eat a carrot stick, a celery stick, and two rice cakes for lunch. Junior high (and the onset of adolescence) seemed to be the beginning of the pressure for most women. It is at this age that appearance suddenly becomes important, especially for those girls who want to be "popular" and those who are cheerleaders or on the drill team. The pressure is intense; some girls believe no one will like them or accept them if they are "overweight," even by a pound or two. The measures these girls will take to attain the body that they think will make them acceptable are often debilitating and life threatening.

8   My sister was on the drill team in junior high. My sister wanted to fit in with the right crowd—and my sister drove herself to the edge of becoming anorexic. I watched as she came home from school, having eaten nothing for breakfast and at lunch only a bag of pretzels and an apple (and she didn't always finish that), and began pacing the Oriental carpet that was in our living room. Around and around and around, without a break, from four o'clock until dinnertime, which was usually at six or seven o'clock. And then at dinner, she would take minute portions and only pick at her food. After several months of this, she became much paler and thinner but not in any sort of attractive sense. Finally, after catching a cold and having to stay in bed for three days because she was so weak, she was forced to go to the doctor. The doctor said she was suffering from malnourishment and was to stay in bed until she regained some of her strength. He advised her to eat lots of fruits and vegetables until the bruises all over her body had healed (these were a result of vitamin deficiency). Although my sister did not develop anorexia, it was frightening to see what she had done to herself. She had little strength, and the bruises she had made her look like an abused child.

9   This mania to lose weight and have the "ideal" body is not easily avoided in our society. It is created by television and magazines as they flaunt their models and latest diet crazes in front of our faces. And then there are the Nutri-System and Jenny Craig commercials, which show hideous "before" pictures and glamorous "after" pictures and have smiling, happy people dancing around and talking about how their lives have been transformed simply because they have lost weight. This propaganda that happiness is in large part based on having the "perfect" body shape is a message that the media constantly sends to the public. No one seems to be able to escape it.

10   My mother and father were even sucked in by this idea. One evening, when I was in the fifth grade, I heard Mom and Dad calling me into the kitchen. Oh no, what had I done now? It was never good news when you got summoned into the kitchen alone. As I walked into the kitchen, Mom looked up at me with an anxious expression; Dad was sitting at the head of the table with a pen in hand and a yellow legal pad in front of him. They informed me that I was going on a diet. A diet!? I wanted to scream at

them, "I'm only ten years old, why do I have to be on a diet?" I was so embarrassed, and I felt so guilty. Was I really fat? I guess so, I thought, otherwise why would my parents do this to me?

It seems that this obsession with the perfect body and a woman's appearance has grown to monumental heights. It is ironic, however, that now many people feel that this problem is disappearing. People have begun to assume that women want to be thin because they just want to be "healthy." But what has happened is that the sickness slips in under the guise of wanting a "healthy" body. The demand for thin bodies is anything but "healthy." How many anorexics or bulimics have you seen that are healthy? 11

It is strange that women do not come out and object to society's pressure to become thin. Or maybe women feel that they really do want to be thin and so go on dieting endlessly (they call it "eating sensibly"), thinking this is what they really want. I think if these women carefully examined their reasons for wanting to lose weight—and were not allowed to include reasons that relate to society's demands, such as a weight chart, a questionnaire in a magazine, a certain size in a pair of shorts, or even a scale—they would find that they are being ruled by what society wants, not what they want. So why do women not break free from these standards? Why do they not demand an end to being judged in such a demeaning and senseless way? 12

Self-esteem plays a large part in determining whether women succumb to the will of society or whether they are independent and self-assured enough to make their own decisions. Lack of self-esteem is one of the things the women's movement has had to fight the hardest against. If women didn't think they were worthy, then how could they even begin to fight for their own rights? The same is true with the issue of body size. If women do not feel their body is worthy, then how can they believe that it is okay to just let it stay that way? Without self-esteem, women will be swayed by society and will continue to make themselves unhappy by trying to maintain whatever weight or body shape society is dictating for them. It is ironic that many of the popular women's magazines (*Cosmopolitan, Mademoiselle, Glamour*) often feature articles on self-esteem, how essential it is, and how to improve it—and then in the same issue give the latest diet tips. This mixed message will never give women the power they deserve over their bodies and will never enable them to make their own decisions about what type of body they want. 13

"Rox, why do you think you're fat? You work out all the time, and you just bought that new suit. Why don't you just come down to the pool for a little while?" 14

"No, I really don't want to. I feel so self-conscious with all those people around. It makes me want to run and put on a big, baggy dress so no one can tell what size I am!" 15

"Ah, Rox, that's really sad. You have to learn to believe in yourself and your own judgment, not other people's." 16

READING FOR MEANING

This section presents three activities that will help you think about the meanings in Haines's reflective essay. Your instructor may ask you to do one or more of these activities in class or online.

For more help with summarizing, see Chapter 10, pp. 518–19.

1. **Read to Summarize.** Write a sentence or two explaining what you think Haines wants readers to understand about the occasion she describes.

2. **Read to Respond.** Write a paragraph analyzing your initial reactions to the ideas Haines presents about the pressure women feel about measuring up to an unrealistic social idea, such as thinness or beauty. For example, consider anything that resonates with your experience or that seems contradictory, surprising, or fascinating, such as:

   - Haines's assertion that magazines and other media determine the kind of body most women desire;
   - Haines's discussion of her parents putting her on a diet when she was ten;
   - Haines' response to women who claim they maintain a thin body for "health" (pars. 11–12);

You may also try recognizing emotional manipulation; see Chapter 10, pp. 536–37.

   - Whether men have similar perfect-body issues that are not discussed here, but that are also worth considering.

3. **Read to Analyze Assumptions.** Write a paragraph or two analyzing an assumption you find intriguing in Haines's essay. For example:

   Assumptions about high self-esteem enabling women to make their own decisions. According to Haines, "[s]elf-esteem plays a large part in determining whether women succumb to the will of society or whether they are independent and self-assured enough to make their own decisions" (par. 13). To think critically about the assumptions in this essay regarding self-esteem, ask yourself questions like these:

   - How does a person acquire self-esteem?
   - What are the qualities of self-esteem that enable women to be independent and to make their own decisions?
   - Is a woman's being slim always an indication of a problem with self-esteem?

   Assumptions that media have a strong effect on human behavior. Haines writes that "[f]ashion, magazines, talk shows, 'lite' and fat-free food in

 Take a quiz to check your reading and vocabulary comprehension:
bedfordstmartins.com/readingcritically

stores and restaurants, and diet centers are all daily reminders of . . . expectations" (par. 6) for women to be thin. To think critically about the assumptions in this essay regarding the effect of the media on human behavior, ask yourself questions like these:

- Which examples in the essay rest on an assumption about the media's effect?
- Are fat-free foods and diet centers related to the media? Why or why not?
- If Haines's assumptions about media influence are true, and people wanted to change the media's effect, how could that be achieved?

READING LIKE A WRITER

DEVELOPING THE REFLECTIONS

In reflective writing, insights and ideas are central. Yet writers cannot merely list ideas, regardless of how fresh and daring their ideas might be. Instead, writers must work imaginatively to develop their ideas, to explain and elaborate on them, and to view them from one angle and then another. One way writers develop their reflections and make them compelling for readers is by drawing on examples from their personal experiences. For example, Haines uses current fashions in paragraph 6 and a junior-high-school friend's lunch ("a carrot stick, a celery stick, and two rice cakes") in paragraph 7 to make her point about the effects of fashion trends on self-esteem and the lengths women (and girls) will go to achieve the bodies society seems to be demanding.

| Analyze & Write |

Write a paragraph or two analyzing Haines's use of extended examples to convey her insights and ideas about the destructive power of unreasonable social ideals.

1. Skim paragraphs 1–4 and 14–16. How does Haines use dialogue to help readers understand the effects of unreasonable standards on women? What effect does presenting this example of one woman's struggle have on you as a reader?

2. Now reread paragraphs 8 and 10. How does Haines use examples from her own and her family's experience with worry regarding the "correct" image of women? How do these firsthand examples affect you? Does the use of personal examples strengthen or undermine Haines's message that our culture puts an unnatural emphasis on what women's bodies should look like?

Reviewing What Makes Reflection Effective

An effective reflective essay

- vividly presents the occasion that prompted the reflection;

- develops the reflections with varied strategies such as comparison-contrast, examples, anecdotes and stories, descriptive details, visuals, and figurative language;

- maintains coherence from paragraph to paragraph and within each paragraph with cohesive devices such as repetition and transitions;

- engages readers with varied strategies such as first-person narrative, dialogue, and anecdotes.

Analyze & Write

Write a brief evaluation—positive, negative, or mixed—of one of the readings in this chapter, explaining why you think it succeeds or fails as a reflective essay. Be sure to consider the characteristics that distinguish reflective writing, as well as how successful the writer has been in communicating his or her purpose to the intended audience. You may also want to consider the effect the medium of presentation had on decisions the writer made.

A GUIDE TO WRITING REFLECTIVE ESSAYS

As you've read and discussed the reading selections in this chapter, you have probably done a good deal of analytical writing. Your instructor may assign a capstone project to write a brief reflection of your own. Having learned how writers of reflections present the initial occasion, hook readers and keep them reading, explore their reflections with illustrations, and maintain coherence so readers don't get lost, you can now approach reflection confidently as a writer. This Guide to Writing offers detailed suggestions for writing reflective essays and resources to help you meet the special challenges this kind of writing presents.

THE WRITING ASSIGNMENT

Write a reflective essay that grows out of a specific occasion or event.

- Choose an occasion or event that you feel comfortable writing about for this audience (your instructor and classmates). You may want to select the general subject that you want to reflect on first, and then choose an event or occasion that effectively particularizes this subject.

- Consider how you can depict the occasion or event vividly so that readers can imagine what you experienced. Try to create a voice or persona that will appeal to your audience.

- Develop your reflections, including insights that interest, surprise, or enlighten your readers.

- Organize your reflection so that readers will be able to follow your train of thought.

WRITING A DRAFT

INVENTION, PLANNING, AND COMPOSING

The following activities will help you choose an occasion and develop a reflection on a subject worthy of your time and effort and your audience's attention.

Choosing an Occasion and General Subject

Writers of reflections often connect an occasion to a subject or a subject to an occasion. Sometimes writers choose a general subject (such as envy or friendship) and then search for the right occasion (an image or anecdote) with which to particularize it. Sometimes the occasion prompts the subject.

To get started, use a chart like the one below to list several possible occasions and the general subjects they suggest (or start with the "General Subjects" column and then list the occasions they suggest).

Particular Occasions	*General Subjects*
I had an experience on the train.	The social benefits of mass transit
I met someone (or am someone) with a disability.	Measures taken for people with disabilities
I had a great time skiing.	The importance of exercise or of time away from work

For occasions, consider the following:

* conversations you have had or overheard;
* memorable scenes you observed, read about, or saw in a movie or other media;
* incidents in your own or someone else's life that led you to reflect more generally.

Also consider the general subjects suggested by the occasions:

* human qualities such as compassion, vanity, jealousy, and faithfulness;
* social customs for dating, eating, and working;
* abstract notions such as fate, free will, and imagination.

In making your chart, you will find that a single occasion might suggest several subjects and that a subject might be particularized by a variety of occasions. A full and rich exploration of possible topics will give you confidence in the subject you finally choose and in your ability to write about it. As further occasions and subjects occur to you over the next two or three days, add them to your chart.

Shaping Your Reflection

Practice writing up the initial occasion that prompted your reflection. Use specific details and choose evocative words to make your description vivid; use active, specific verbs to make your writing lively; and use time markers to give immediacy and color to your narration of the occasion. The example paragraphs below demonstrate how two of the writers in this chapter used these strategies to shape their reflections:

Vivid description	My <u>first</u> victim was a woman — white, well dressed, probably in her
Active verb	early twenties. I came upon her late one evening on a deserted street
Time marker	in Hyde Park, a relatively affluent neighborhood in an otherwise mean, impoverished section of Chicago. As I swung onto the

avenue behind her, there seemed to be a discreet, uninflammatory distance between us. Not so. She cast back a worried glance. To her, the youngish black man — a broad six feet two inches with a beard and billowing hair, both hands shoved into the pockets of a bulky military jacket — seemed menacingly close. After a few more quick glimpses, she picked up her pace and was soon running in earnest. Within seconds she disappeared into a cross street. (Staples, par. 1)

An inexplicable line has appeared on the screen of my iPod, and I can't get rid of it. The battery life has been flagging lately, too. Plus, the thing won't sync properly with Last.fm anymore. Yet none of these problems — and the device mortality they portend — bother me. On the contrary, I'm practically cheering them on, because my iPod is a "classic" model from 2007, and for years I've coveted an iPod touch. Spending money to replace something that works would make me feel wasteful and guilty. So I poke at my iPod with the perverse hope that it won't respond. I have a gadget death wish. (Walker, par. 1)

Developing Your Reflection

The following activities will help you recall details about the occasion for your reflection.

Narrating an Event.   Write for five to ten minutes narrating what happened during the event. Try to make your story vivid so that readers can imagine what it was like. Describe the people involved in the event — what they looked like, how they acted, what they said — and the place where it occurred.

Describing What You Observed.   Write for five to ten minutes describing what you observed. Include as many details as you can recall so that your readers can imagine what you experienced.

Cubing.   To explore your ideas about the subject, try an invention strategy called *cubing*. Based on the six sides of a cube, this approach encourages you to examine your subject as you would turn over a cube, looking at it in six different ways. Below we list eight options for considering your subject. You can use some of these or come up with your own. Whichever six you choose, we recommend that you write about your subject for five minutes from each of the six perspectives to give yourself enough time to invent new ways of considering it.

- **Analyzing.** What is your subject composed of? How are the parts related to one another? Are they all of equal importance?

- **Applying.** How can you use your subject or act on it? What difference would it make to you and to others?

- **Comparing and Contrasting.** What subject could you compare with yours? What are the similarities and the differences between them?

- **Describing.** What details would you use to describe the people or places involved in the occasion that gave rise to your reflections?

- **Extending.** What are the implications of your subject? Where does it lead?

- **Generalizing.** What does the occasion suggest about people in general or about the society in which you live?

- **Giving Examples.** What examples would best characterize or help your readers understand your reflection?

- **Visualizing.** What would your occasion look like from the perspective of an outside observer?

Exploring How You Felt at the Time and What the Occasion Made You Realize Later. Write for a few minutes, trying to recall your thoughts and feelings when the occasion was occurring.

- What did you feel at the moment that the occasion was occurring — in control or powerless, proud or embarrassed, vulnerable, detached, judgmental? For example, Staples uses phrases like "swung onto the avenue" to indicate a light mood (par. 1) and "surprised, embarrassed, and dismayed all at once" (par. 2) to convey how the woman's sudden flight made him feel. Sentence strategies like these might help you describe your initial experience of the occasion:

  ▸ One day when I was ...., I found myself ....

  ▸ As soon as I [saw/did/imagined] ...., I felt ...., ..., and

        ....

  ▸ .... [describe occasion] made me feel as if ....

- What larger reflection was prompted by your occasion? Staples, for example, realizes "that being perceived as dangerous is a hazard in itself" (par. 2). Walker suggests "where electronic gizmos are concerned, product obsolescence is becoming a demand-side phenomenon" (par. 4). These sentence strategies may help you put your reflection into words:

  ▸ Since then, I realize ...., but also ....

  ▸ Now that I have seen ...., I know that .... and ....

Considering Your Purpose and Audience. Write for several minutes exploring what you want your readers to think about your reflection after reading your essay. Your answer may change as you write, but thinking about your goals may help you decide which of your ideas to include in the essay. Answering the following questions may help your clarify your purpose:

- Which of your ideas are most important to you? Why?

- How do your ideas relate to one another? If your ideas seem contradictory, consider how you could use the contradictions to convey to readers the complexity of your ideas and feelings on the subject.

- Which of your ideas do you think will most surprise your readers? Which are most likely to be familiar?

- Is the occasion for your reflection likely to resonate with your readers' experience and observation?

Formulating a Working Thesis. Review what you wrote for Considering Your Purpose and Audience and add another two or three sentences to bring your reflection into focus. What do they seem to be about? Try to write sentences that indicate what you think is most important or most interesting about the subject, what you want readers to understand from reading your essay. Readers may not expect reflective essays to begin with the kind of explicit thesis statement typical of the argumentative essays in Chapters 6–9 — none of the readings in this chapter begin with an explicit statement of the writer's main idea — but stating the main point of your reflective essay now may lead you to a deeper understanding of your occasion and the reflection it inspired, and it may guide your selection of ideas to develop, descriptive details to include, and words to express your feelings and thoughts.

Considering Visuals

Think about whether visuals — cartoons, photographs, drawings, charts — would help readers understand and appreciate your reflections. If you submit your essay electronically to other students and your instructor, or if you post it on a Web site, consider including photographs or even snippets of video or audio files. You could import your own photographs or drawings, or you could scan materials from books and magazines or download them from the Internet, but remember that you will need to cite any visuals you borrow from another source. See Chapter 11, pp. 594–96 and 606, to learn more about citing visuals.

Drafting Your Reflective Essay

By this point, you have done a lot of writing

- to present an occasion that prompts a reflection;

- to present the reflection and develop it using a variety of approaches;

- to relate the significance of your reflection in a way meaningful to your readers.

Now stitch that material together to create a draft. The next two parts of this Guide to Writing will help you evaluate and improve it.

Considering a Useful Sentence Strategy

In addition to planning the sequence of your ideas and repeating key words and phrases, you can enhance the coherence of your reflective essay by using parallel grammatical structures to connect related ideas or examples. For example, in the first paragraph of his essay, Jennings uses parallel structure:

Parallel structure   Sometimes they're stark tales of life-threatening catastrophes, but more often they're just footnotes . . . (sentence 2)

When I parse my body's . . . When I wear shorts . . . (sentences 3–4)

Notice that in sentence 2, he uses parallelism to emphasize contrast, using a structure that mimics "on the one hand, *this*, and on the other hand, *that*," while he begins the third and fourth sentences with *When I* plus a verb.

Now look at this sentence from paragraph 3:

I had a full and active boyhood, one that raged with scabs and scrapes, mashed and bloody knees, bumps and lumps, gashes and slashes, cats' claws and dogs' teeth, jagged glass, ragged steel, knots, knobs and shiners.

Here he uses parallel grammatical structure ("*X* and *Y*") as well as words that rhyme or that look and sound similar ("scabs and scrapes," "knots" and "knobs") to convey the wide range of his scars and the occasions that produced them.

Finally, in the last sentence of the essay, Jennings leaves readers with another powerful instance of parallel phrasing that sums up his reflection:

. . . I've always believed in the power of stories, and I certainly believe in the power of scars. (par. 14)

While there are many ways to signal that a group of ideas is related, writers of reflective essays tend to rely on parallel form because it is highly visible; readers notice it at a glance. Parallel form also creates a pleasant rhythm that engages readers and keeps them reading. Moreover, it is very flexible; the variations are endless. Clearly, parallelism is not required for a successful reflective essay, yet it provides you with an effective sentence option to try out in your own essay.

EVALUATING THE DRAFT

GETTING A CONSTRUCTIVE CRITICAL READING

Getting a critical reading of your draft will help you see how to improve it. Your instructor may schedule class time for reading drafts, or you may want to ask a classmate or a tutor in the writing center to read your draft. Ask your reader to use the following guidelines and to write out a response for you to consult during your revision.

READING A DRAFT CRITICALLY

Read for a First Impression

1. **Read the draft without stopping, and then write a few sentences giving your general impression.**

2. **Identify one aspect of the draft that seems especially effective.**

Read Again to Suggest Improvements

1. **Suggest ways of presenting the occasion more effectively.**

   - Tell the writer if the occasion that prompts the reflection dominates the essay, taking up an unjustified amount of space, or if it is scant and needs more development.

   - Note whether this occasion suggests the significance of the subject, and how well it prepares readers for the reflection by providing a context.

2. **Suggest ways the writer could develop the reflection.**

   - Look for two or three ideas that strike you as especially interesting, insightful, or surprising, and tell the writer what interests you about them. Then suggest ways these ideas might be developed further through examples, comparisons or contrasts, consideration of their social implications, connections to other ideas, and so on.

   - Identify any ideas you find uninteresting, explaining briefly why you find them so.

3. **Suggest ways to strengthen coherence.**

   - Skim the essay, marking gaps between sentences and paragraphs, those places where the meaning does not carry forward smoothly. Recommend a way to make the meaning clear.

   - Skim the essay again, marking irrelevant or unnecessary material that disrupts coherence and diverts the reader's attention. Explain your reasoning to the writer.

   - Consider the essay as a sequence of sections. Ask yourself whether time markers or other transitions could be added to make the connection between sections easier to follow. Mark any section that seems out of place, and suggest where it might be better located.

(continued)

4. **Suggest ways to engage readers further.**

- Point out parts of the essay that draw you in, hold your interest, inspire you to think, challenge your attitudes or values, or keep you wanting to read to the end.

- Suggest ways the writer might engage readers more fully. Consider the essay in light of what has been most engaging for you in the essays you have read in this chapter.

5. **Evaluate the effectiveness of visuals or other media.**

- Tell the writer what, if anything, the visuals contribute to the writer's reflection.

- If any visuals or other media do not seem relevant, or if there seem to be too many visuals, identify the ones that the writer could consider dropping, and explain your thinking.

- If a visual does not seem to be appropriately placed, suggest a better place for it.

IMPROVING THE DRAFT

REVISING, EDITING, AND PROOFREADING

Start improving your draft by reflecting on what you have written thus far:

- Review critical reading comments from your classmates, instructor, or writing center tutor. What are your readers getting at?

- Take another look at your notes and ideas: What else should you consider?

- Review your draft: What else can you do to make your reflective essay clearer or more interesting to your readers?

Revising Your Draft

Revising means reenvisioning your draft, trying to see it in a new way, given your purpose and audience, in order to develop a more engaging, more coherent reflective essay. Think imaginatively and boldly about cutting unconvincing material, adding new material, and moving material around. The suggestions in the following chart may help you solve problems and strengthen your essay.

TROUBLESHOOTING YOUR DRAFT

To Present the Particular Occasion More Effectively

Problem	Suggestions for Revising
The occasion seems uninteresting or too general and abstract.	• Add details to make it more dramatic or less predictable. • Make it into a story. • Try putting it into the first person. • Try the present tense, and make your verbs active.
The occasion is not clearly related to the reflection that follows.	• Revise it to be more relevant. • Choose another occasion that is more relevant.

To Develop the Reflection More Fully

Problem	Suggestions for Revising
Promising ideas are not fully developed.	• Provide further examples. • Develop your explanation of the ideas by comparing or contrasting them with other ideas.
Some ideas seem too predictable.	• Drop them. • Try to come up with more insightful ideas.
The reflection does not move beyond personal association.	• Extend it into the social realm. • Comment on its larger implications—what it might mean for people in general.

To Strengthen Coherence

Problem	Suggestions for Revising
There are distracting gaps between sentences or paragraphs.	• Try reordering the sequence of actions. • Add explicit transitions. • If there are pairs or series of related ideas or examples, revise into parallel form.
The reflection seems scattered and disorganized.	• Look for words and phrases whose repetition would help readers follow your reflections. • See if there is a timeline you could develop more clearly with time markers.

To Better Engage Readers	
Problem	Suggestions for Revising
The reflection doesn't encourage readers to reflect on their own lives.	• Expand beyond the personal with more generalized stories or anecdotes, by considering the broader social implications, or by considering what difference it would make to others. • Express the significance more directly.

Editing and Proofreading Your Draft

Check for errors in usage, punctuation, and mechanics, and consider matters of style. If you keep a list of errors you typically make, begin by checking your draft against this list. Ask someone else to proofread your essay before you submit it to your instructor.

From our research on student writing, we know that reflective essays have a high frequency of unnecessary shifts in verb tense and mood. Check a writer's handbook for help with these potential problems.

Reflecting on What You Have Learned

Reflection

In this chapter, you have read critically several reflective essays and have written one of your own. To better remember what you have learned, pause now to reflect on the reading and writing activities you completed in this chapter.

1. Write a page or so reflecting on what you have learned. Begin by describing what you are most pleased with in your essay. Then explain what you think contributed to your achievement. Be specific about this contribution.

   • If it was something you learned from the readings, indicate which readings and specifically what you learned from them.

   • If it came from the writing you did in response to prompts in this chapter, point out the section or sections that helped you most.

   • If you got good advice from a critical reader, explain exactly how the person helped you — perhaps by helping you understand a problem in your draft or by helping you add a new dimension to your writing.

Try to write about your achievement in terms of what you have learned about the genre.

2. Reflect more generally on how you tend to interpret reflective writing, your own as well as other writers'. Consider some of the following questions:

- How comfortable do you feel relying on your own experiences or observations as a basis for developing ideas about general subjects or for developing ideas about the ways people are and the ways they interact?

- Did you find rich enough material from your own personal ideas on a subject, or did you conduct research or interview people to collect their ideas?

- How might your gender, social class, or ethnic group have influenced the ideas you came up with for your essay?

- What contribution might reflective essays make to our society that other genres cannot make?

Explaining Concepts

A **concept** is a major idea. Concepts include abstract ideas, phenomena, and processes. We create concepts, name them, communicate them, and think with them in all areas of our lives. Every field of study has its concepts: Psychology, for example, has *schizophrenia* and *narcissism*; business has *micromanagement* and *direct marketing*; and nursing has *gerontology* and *whole-person caring*. *Explaining concepts* is a kind (or genre) of explanatory writing that is especially important for college students because it involves widely applicable strategies for critical reading and is frequently called for in essay exams and paper assignments. We learn new concepts by connecting them to what we have previously learned. Writing that explains concepts facilitates such connections through a range of writing strategies, including *definition, illustration, cause-effect*, and *comparison-contrast*, among others. To be effective, conceptual explanations must be pitched at the right level. They go wrong when the flow of information is too fast or too slow, too difficult or too simple for the intended audience.

This chapter offers several concept explanation selections for you to enjoy, with exploratory activities that will help you learn to read critically and write well. The Reading for Meaning and Reading Like a Writer activities following each selection invite you to analyze and write about the reading's ideas and writing strategies. You can also use the brief Guide to Writing toward the end of the chapter to help you write about a concept that intrigues you and that could enlighten your readers.

RHETORICAL SITUATIONS FOR CONCEPT EXPLANATIONS

Writing that explains concepts is familiar in college and professional life, as the following examples show:

- For a presentation at the annual convention of the American Medical Association, an anesthesiologist writes a report on the concept of *awareness during surgery*. He presents evidence that patients under anesthesia, as in hypnosis, can hear, and he reviews research demonstrating that they can perceive and carry out instructions that speed their recovery. He describes briefly how he applies the concept in his own work — how he prepares patients before surgery, what he tells them while they are under anesthesia, and what happens as they recover.

- A manager at a marketing research firm gives a presentation on *surveying*, an important research method, to fifth-grade science students. She begins by having students fill out a brief survey on their television-watching habits, and then asks them to speculate on what they expect their answers to show and how this data might be used by advertisers and programmers. Then, with the students' help, she selects the variables that seem significant: the respondents' gender, the number of hours they spend watching television, and the types of shows they watch. At the next class, she distributes graphs detailing her analysis and asks the students to see whether the results match their assumptions. She concludes by passing out a quiz to find out how much the students have learned about surveys.

- As part of a group assignment, a college student at a summer biology camp in the Sierra Nevada mountains reads about the condition of mammals at birth. She learns the distinction between infant mammals that are *altricial* (born nude and helpless within a protective nest) and those that are *precocial* (born well formed with eyes open and ears erect). In her part of a group report, she develops this contrast point by point, giving many examples of specific mammals but focusing in detail on altricial mice and precocial porcupines.

Thinking about the Genre

Concept Explanation

Before studying a type of writing, it is useful to spend some time thinking about what you already know about it. You have probably explained concepts on exams and in papers numerous times, and you likely have read concept explanations in textbooks and heard them in classes.

Recall an occasion when you explained a concept to others, or had a concept explained to you, either orally or in writing. Think about what made the explanation clear, focused, engaging, and authoritative. Use the following questions to develop your thoughts. Your instructor may

(continued)

ask you to write about this occasion or discuss it with others in class or online.

- Who was the *audience*? How do you think this audience affected how the concept was explained? For example, did the writer (or speaker) choose a particular example of the concept because it was in the news? Was the concept compared with something that would be familiar, given the age, level of expertise, and experience of audience members?

- What was the *purpose*? Why did the writer (or speaker) want the audience to understand the concept? For example, was it so that they could demonstrate their understanding on a test or understand the importance of the concept in their own lives?

- How might the explanation of the concept have changed if the audience or purpose had been different? For example, would the examples or comparisons have been changed or would more (or fewer) terms have been defined? How would changing the medium have affected the way the concept was explained? For example, if the concept explanation had been published online, might the writer (or speaker) have used animated graphics effectively to explain the concept?

A GUIDE TO READING CONCEPT EXPLANATIONS

This guide introduces you to the basic features and strategies typical of explanatory writing by inviting you to analyze an intriguing selection by Susan Cain that explains *introversion*, first by *reading for meaning* and then by *reading like a writer*:

- *Reading for meaning* will help you understand the topic and its significance for Cain. Why does Cain see our culture's attitude toward introversion as a long-term danger?

- *Reading like a writer* will help you learn how Cain employs strategies typical of concept explanations, such as

    1. using appropriate writing strategies: defining, illustrating, comparing and contrasting, and showing causes and effects

2. organizing the information clearly and logically

3. integrating sources smoothly

4. engaging readers' interest

Susan Cain

Shyness: Evolutionary Tactic?

Susan Cain (b. 1968) attended Princeton University and Harvard Law School, and worked for several years as an attorney and a negotiations consultant. She is the author of the book Quiet: The Power of Introverts in a World That Can't Stop Talking *(2012). She also writes a popular blog about introversion and has contributed articles on this topic to such journals and magazines as* Psychology Today *and* Time. *You can see her TED (Technology, Entertainment, and Design) talk on introversion online. The op-ed that appears below was published in the* New York Times *in 2011.*

- *Before you read, notice the title of this reading and the title of Cain's book (above). What do these titles lead you to expect? What kind of experience have you had with shyness?*

- *As you read, think about the rhetorical situation in which Cain is writing. Given that this selection was first published in a newspaper, consider how effective the opening paragraph is as a hook to catch readers' attention.*

A beautiful woman lowers her eyes demurely beneath a hat. In an earlier 1 era, her gaze might have signaled a mysterious allure. But this is a 2003 advertisement for Zoloft, a selective serotonin reuptake inhibitor (SSRI) approved by the FDA to treat social anxiety disorder. "Is she just shy? Or is it Social Anxiety Disorder?" reads the caption, suggesting that the young woman is not alluring at all. She is sick.

But is she? 2

It is possible that the lovely young woman has a life-wrecking form of 3 social anxiety. There are people too afraid of disapproval to venture out for a job interview, a date or even a meal in public. Despite the risk of serious side effects — nausea, loss of sex drive, seizures — drugs like Zoloft can be a godsend for this group.

But the ad's insinuation aside, it's also possible the young woman is 4 "just shy," or introverted — traits our society disfavors. One way we manifest

 For a multimodal reading that explains a concept, go to
bedfordstmartins.com/readingcritically.

this bias is by encouraging perfectly healthy shy people to see themselves as ill.

5   This does us all a grave disservice, because shyness and introversion — or more precisely, the careful, sensitive temperament from which both often spring — are not just normal. They are valuable. And they may be essential to the survival of our species.

6   Theoretically, shyness and social anxiety disorder are easily distinguishable. But a blurry line divides the two. Imagine that the woman in the ad enjoys a steady paycheck, a strong marriage and a small circle of close friends — a good life by most measures — except that she avoids a needed promotion because she's nervous about leading meetings. She often criticizes herself for feeling too shy to speak up.

7   What do you think now? Is she ill, or does she simply need public-speaking training?

8   Before 1980, this would have seemed a strange question. Social anxiety disorder did not officially exist until it appeared in that year's Diagnostic and Statistical Manual, the DSM-III, the psychiatrist's bible of mental disorders, under the name "social phobia." It was not widely known until the 1990s, when pharmaceutical companies received FDA approval to treat social anxiety with SSRI's and poured tens of millions of dollars into advertising its existence. The current version of the Diagnostic and Statistical Manual, the DSM-IV, acknowledges that stage fright (and shyness in social situations) is common and not necessarily a sign of illness. But it also says that diagnosis is warranted when anxiety "interferes significantly" with work performance or if the sufferer shows "marked distress" about it. According to this definition, the answer to our question is clear: the young woman in the ad is indeed sick.

9   The DSM inevitably reflects cultural attitudes; it used to identify homosexuality as a disease, too. Though the DSM did not set out to pathologize shyness, it risks doing so, and has twice come close to identifying introversion as a disorder, too. (Shyness and introversion are not the same thing. Shy people fear negative judgment; introverts simply prefer quiet, minimally stimulating environments.)

10   But shyness and introversion share an undervalued status in a world that prizes extroversion. Children's classroom desks are now often arranged in pods, because group participation supposedly leads to better learning; in one school I visited, a sign announcing "Rules for Group Work" included, "You can't ask a teacher for help unless everyone in your group has the same question." Many adults work for organizations that now assign work in teams, in offices without walls, for supervisors who value "people skills" above all. As a society, we prefer action to contemplation, risk-taking to heed-taking, certainty to doubt. Studies show that we rank fast and frequent talkers as more competent, likable and even smarter than slow ones. As the psychologists William Hart and Dolores

Albarracin point out, phrases like "get active," "get moving," "do something" and similar calls to action surface repeatedly in recent books.

Yet shy and introverted people have been part of our species for a very   11
long time, often in leadership positions. We find them in the Bible ("Who am I, that I should go unto Pharaoh?" asked Moses, whom the Book of Numbers describes as "very meek, above all the men which were upon the face of the earth.") We find them in recent history, in figures like Charles Darwin, Marcel Proust and Albert Einstein, and, in contemporary times: think of Google's Larry Page, or Harry Potter's creator, J. K. Rowling.

In the science journalist Winifred Gallagher's words: "The glory of the   12
disposition that stops to consider stimuli rather than rushing to engage with them is its long association with intellectual and artistic achievement. Neither $E = mc^2$ nor *Paradise Lost* was dashed off by a party animal."

We even find "introverts" in the animal kingdom, where 15 percent to   13
20 percent of many species are watchful, slow-to-warm-up types who stick to the sidelines (sometimes called "sitters") while the other 80 percent are "rovers" who sally forth without paying much attention to their surroundings. Sitters and rovers favor different survival strategies, which could be summed up as the sitter's "Look before you leap" versus the rover's inclination to "Just do it!" Each strategy reaps different rewards.

In an illustrative experiment, David Sloan Wilson, a Binghamton evolu-   14
tionary biologist, dropped metal traps into a pond of pumpkinseed sunfish. The "rover" fish couldn't help but investigate—and were immediately caught. But the "sitter" fish stayed back, making it impossible for Professor Wilson to capture them. Had Professor Wilson's traps posed a real threat, only the sitters would have survived. But had the sitters taken Zoloft and become more like bold rovers, the entire family of pumpkinseed sunfish would have been wiped out. "Anxiety" about the trap saved the fishes' lives.

Next, Professor Wilson used fishing nets to catch both types of fish;   15
when he carried them back to his lab, he noted that the rovers quickly acclimated to their new environment and started eating a full five days earlier than their sitter brethren. In this situation, the rovers were the likely survivors. "There is no single best . . . [animal] personality," Professor Wilson concludes in his book, *Evolution for Everyone,* "but rather a diversity of personalities maintained by natural selection."

The same might be said of humans, 15 percent to 20 percent of whom   16
are also born with sitter-like temperaments that predispose them to shyness and introversion. (The overall incidence of shyness and introversion is higher—40 percent of the population for shyness, according to the psychology professor Jonathan Cheek, and 50 percent for introversion. Conversely, some born sitters never become shy or introverted at all.)

Once you know about sitters and rovers, you see them everywhere,   17
especially among young children. Drop in on your local Mommy and Me

music class: there are the sitters, intently watching the action from their mothers' laps, while the rovers march around the room banging their drums and shaking their maracas.

18   Relaxed and exploratory, the rovers have fun, make friends and will take risks, both rewarding and dangerous ones, as they grow. According to Daniel Nettle, a Newcastle University evolutionary psychologist, extroverts are more likely than introverts to be hospitalized as a result of an injury, have affairs (men) and change relationships (women). One study of bus drivers even found that accidents are more likely to occur when extroverts are at the wheel.

19   In contrast, sitter children are careful and astute, and tend to learn by observing instead of by acting. They notice scary things more than other children do, but they also notice more things in general. Studies dating all the way back to the 1960s by the psychologists Jerome Kagan and Ellen Siegelman found that cautious, solitary children playing matching games spent more time considering all the alternatives than impulsive children did, actually using more eye movements to make decisions. Recent studies by a group of scientists at Stony Brook University and at Chinese universities using functional MRI technology echoed this research, finding that adults with sitter-like temperaments looked longer at pairs of photos with subtle differences and showed more activity in brain regions that make associations between the photos and other stored information in the brain.

20   Once they reach school age, many sitter children use such traits to great effect. Introverts, who tend to digest information thoroughly, stay on task, and work accurately, earn disproportionate numbers of National Merit Scholarship finalist positions and Phi Beta Kappa keys, according to the Center for Applications of Psychological Type, a research arm for the Myers-Briggs personality type indicator—even though their IQ scores are no higher than those of extroverts. Another study, by the psychologists Eric Rolfhus and Philip Ackerman, tested 141 college students' knowledge of 20 different subjects, from art to astronomy to statistics, and found that the introverts knew more than the extroverts about 19 subjects—presumably, the researchers concluded, because the more time people spend socializing, the less time they have for learning.

21   The psychologist Gregory Feist found that many of the most creative people in a range of fields are introverts who are comfortable working in solitary conditions in which they can focus attention inward. Steve Wozniak, the engineer who founded Apple with Steve Jobs, is a prime example: Mr. Wozniak describes his creative process as an exercise in solitude. "Most inventors and engineers I've met are like me," he writes in *iWoz*, his autobiography. "They're shy and they live in their heads. They're almost like artists. In fact, the very best of them are artists. And artists work best alone. . . . Not on a committee. Not on a team."

Sitters' temperaments also confer more subtle advantages. Anxiety, it 22 seems, can serve an important social purpose; for example, it plays a key role in the development of some children's consciences. When caregivers rebuke them for acting up, they become anxious, and since anxiety is unpleasant, they tend to develop pro-social behaviors. Shy children are often easier to socialize and more conscientious, according to the developmental psychologist Grazyna Kochanska. By six they're less likely than their peers to cheat or break rules, even when they think they can't be caught, according to one study. By seven they're more likely to be described by their parents as having high levels of moral traits such as empathy.

When I shared this information with the mother of a "sitter" daughter, 23 her reaction was mixed. "That is all very nice," she said, "but how will it help her in the tough real world?" But sensitivity, if it is not excessive and is properly nurtured, can be a catalyst for empathy and even leadership. Eleanor Roosevelt, for example, was a courageous leader who was very likely a sitter. Painfully shy and serious as a child, she grew up to be a woman who could not look away from other people's suffering—and who urged her husband, the constitutionally buoyant F.D.R., to do the same; the man who had nothing to fear but fear itself relied, paradoxically, on a woman deeply acquainted with it.

Another advantage sitters bring to leadership is a willingness to listen to 24 and implement other people's ideas. A groundbreaking study led by the Wharton management professor Adam Grant, to be published this month in *The Academy of Management Journal,* found that introverts outperform extroverts when leading teams of proactive workers—the kinds of employees who take initiative and are disposed to dream up better ways of doing things. Professor Grant notes that business self-help guides often suggest that introverted leaders practice their communication skills and smile more. But, he told me, it may be extrovert leaders who need to change, to listen more and say less.

What would the world look like if all our sitters chose to medicate 25 themselves? The day may come when we have pills that "cure" shyness and turn introverts into social butterflies—without the side effects and other drawbacks of today's medications. (A recent study suggests that today's SSRI's not only relieve social anxiety but also induce extroverted behavior.) The day may come—and might be here already—when people are as comfortable changing their psyches as the color of their hair. If we continue to confuse shyness with sickness, we may find ourselves in a world of all rovers and no sitters, of all yang and no yin.

As a sitter who enjoys an engaged, productive life, and a professional 26 speaking career, but still experiences the occasional knock-kneed moment, I can understand why caring physicians prescribe available medicine and encourage effective non-pharmaceutical treatments such as cognitive-behavioral therapy.

27   But even non-medical treatments emphasize what is wrong with the people who use them. They don't focus on what is right. Perhaps we need to rethink our approach to social anxiety: to address the pain, but to respect the temperament that underlies it. The act of treating shyness as an illness obscures the value of that temperament. Ridding people of social unease need not involve pathologizing their fundamental nature, but rather urging them to use its gifts.

28   It's time for the young woman in the Zoloft ad to rediscover her allure.

READING FOR MEANING

This section presents three activities that will help you think about the meanings in Cain's explanation of introversion. Your instructor may ask you to do one or more of these activities in class or online.

For more help with summarizing, see Chapter 10, pp. 518–19.

1. **Read to Summarize.** Reading to summarize involves asking yourself what the main point of the reading is. To explore Cain's concept explanation, write a sentence or two explaining what she means by *introversion*, and why she thinks it is important.

2. **Read to Respond.** Reading to respond asks you to explore your reactions to a text in light of your own knowledge or experience. To explore this concept explanation, write a paragraph or two analyzing your initial reactions to Cain's essay. For example, consider anything that resonates with your experience or that seems contradictory, surprising, or fascinating, such as:

   - Cain raises a question about the way psychiatrists and the pharmaceutical industry may be pathologizing shyness or introversion — in other words, "encouraging perfectly healthy shy people to see themselves as ill" (par. 4). What do you think about this issue?

   - After defining "sitters" and "rovers" (par. 13), Cain asserts that "[o]nce you know about sitters and rovers, you see them everywhere. . . ." (par. 17). Did you find this true after you finished the essay? Which of the characteristics of these two types seemed truest of your experience? Which surprised you the most? Why?

You may also try outlining; see Chapter 10, pp. 515–17.

3. **Read to Analyze Assumptions.** **Assumptions** are ideas, beliefs, or values that are taken for granted as commonly accepted truths. The assumptions

Take a quiz to check your reading and vocabulary comprehension:
bedfordstmartins.com/readingcritically

in a text usually reflect the writer's own attitudes or cultural traditions, but they may also represent other people's views. Reading to analyze assumptions asks you to uncover these perspectives as well as to probe your own. Sometimes the assumptions are stated explicitly, but often you will have to infer them (or figure them out) because they are only implied or hinted at through the writer's choice of words or examples. Write a paragraph or two analyzing an assumption you find intriguing in Cain's essay. For example:

Assumptions about medical conditions. Cain notes that "treatments emphasize what is wrong with the people who use them. They don't focus on what is right" (par. 27). She attempts to overturn that assumption by focusing on what is right about introverts. Examine two or three of the paragraphs that develop the idea that introverts are not sick but are instead assets to society (for example, pars. 11–13, 14, and 19–24).

- Do they alter your assumptions about medical conditions and how or whether to treat them?

- If they do, what assumptions made you believe the evidence should change your mind?

You may also try looking for patterns of opposition; see Chapter 10, pp. 525–26.

Assumptions that what is true of other animals is true of humans. Cain supports her title's assumption — that shyness is an evolutionary tactic — by demonstrating how different temperaments in animals are important to their survival (pars. 13–15). Evolution assumes that offspring who inherit beneficial traits are more likely to survive and reproduce than those who do not inherit such traits. For Cain, animal studies can be used as evidence because animals are similar enough to humans that what would be true of one would be true of both. To think critically about the assumptions in this essay related to traits shared by humans and other animals, ask yourself questions like these:

- What are some of the human traits Cain examines by drawing comparisons to animal behavior?

- Are there human traits that animal behavior would not illuminate? What are they?

READING LIKE A WRITER

This section presents four brief activities that will help you analyze Cain's writing. Your instructor may ask you to do one or more of these activities in class or online.

Using Appropriate Writing Strategies

When writers present information, they rely on explanatory strategies such as defining, illustrating, comparing and contrasting, and showing causes or effects. These are the building blocks of concept explanations. Writers narrow the focus on the concept, so readers are guided to a clear understanding of it. **Focus** means either eliminating qualities that the concept does not have, or defining and elaborating on the qualities the concept does have, with explanatory strategies. Comparing and contrasting, for example, allows the writer to show how the concept is similar to and different from other concepts that might be familiar to the reader.

Consider the passage below, in which Cain uses contrast to point out how shyness and introversion differ from social anxiety:

Repeated sentence pattern	It is possible that the lovely young woman has a life-wrecking form of social anxiety. . . .
Concept B	But the ad's insinuation aside, it's *also* possible the young
Transition	woman is "just shy," or introverted. . . . (pars. 3–4)
Concept A	

Analyze & Write

Write a paragraph or two analyzing how Cain uses contrast to explain her concept:

1. Find and highlight two or three of the sentence patterns she uses for cueing contrast in paragraphs 9, 10, 13, 18, and 19.

2. Analyze what is being contrasted and how each contrast works.

3. Explain why you think Cain uses contrast so often in this essay.

Organizing the Information Clearly and Logically

Experienced writers know that readers often have a hard time following explanations of unfamiliar concepts, so they make their explanations reader-friendly by providing road signs — forecasting statements, topic sentences, transitions, pronouns that refer to nouns that appear earlier in the sentence, synonyms, and summaries — to guide readers through the explanation. Consider how Cain guides readers in the paragraph below:

Transition and pronoun referent	But the ad's insinuation aside, it's also possible the young woman is "just shy," or introverted — traits our society disfavors.
Key term or synonym	One way we manifest this bias is by encouraging perfectly healthy shy people to see themselves as ill.
Summary	This does us all a grave disservice, because shyness and
Forecasting statement	introversion — or more precisely, the careful, sensitive temperament from which both often spring — *are not just normal. They are*

> *valuable. And they may be essential to the survival of our species.*
> (pars. 4–5)

Forecasting statements usually appear early in an essay, often in the thesis, to announce the main points the writer will address; they may also appear at the beginning of major sections. Topic sentences announce each main idea as it comes up, transitions (such as *in contrast* and *another*) and pronoun referents relate what is coming to what came before, and summaries remind readers of what has been explained already.

Analyze & Write

Write a paragraph or two analyzing the strategies Cain uses to make her concept explanation easy to follow:

1. Skim the rest of the essay (pars. 6–28), underlining other places Cain forecasts and summarizes main ideas or provides topic sentences, transitions, and pronoun referents. How do the strategies she uses make her concept explanation easier to follow?

2. Examine any places in the essay that you found hard to follow. How might Cain have used one or more of these strategies to make her concept explanation clearer? What would you suggest she add or change, and why?

Integrating Sources Smoothly

In addition to drawing on personal knowledge and fresh observations, writers often do additional research about the concepts they are trying to explain. Doing research in the library and on the Internet, writers immediately confront the ethical responsibility to their readers of locating relevant sources, evaluating them critically, and representing them without distortion. You will find advice on meeting this responsibility in Chapter 11 (pp. 563–68). Cain's essay first appeared in the *New York Times*. Like the authors of other articles published in popular periodicals, Cain names her sources and mentions their credentials, but she does not cite them formally as you must do when writing a paper for a college class. While you cannot use Cain's approach to citation as a model for your own academic writing, you can follow her lead by doing the following:

- Making a claim of your own and supporting it with appropriate, relevant evidence.
- Explaining how the evidence you provide supports your claim.
- Naming your source author(s) in a **signal phrase** (name plus an appropriate verb) and mentioning her (or his or their) credentials

Cain's idea

Research findings supporting Cain's idea

Author and credentials in signal phrase

Links Cain's idea and research findings

As a society, we prefer action to contemplation, risk-taking to heed-taking, certainty to doubt. Studies show that we rank fast and frequent talkers as more competent, likable and even smarter than slow ones. As the psychologists William Hart and Dolores Albarracin point out, phrases like "get active," "get moving," "do something" and similar calls to action surface repeatedly in recent books. (par. 10)

Analyze & Write

Write a paragraph analyzing another passage in which Cain integrates source material to support her explanation:

1. Review paragraphs 19, 20, or 21 to see how Cain uses a pattern similar to the one described above. Find and mark the following elements:

   • Cain's idea;

   • the name(s) and credentials of the source or sources;

   • what the source found;

   • text linking the source's findings to the original idea or extending the idea in some way.

2. Explain why writers, when using information from sources, often begin by stating their own idea (even if they got the idea from a source). What do you think would be the effect on readers if the opening sentence of paragraph 18 or 20 began with the source instead of with Cain's topic sentence?

Engaging Readers' Interest

Writers explaining concepts may engage readers' interest in a variety of ways. For example, they may

   • remind readers of what they already know about the concept;

   • show readers a new way of using a familiar concept;

   • dramatize that the concept has greater importance than readers had realized;

   • connect the concept, sometimes through *metaphor* or *analogy*, to common human experiences; or

   • present the concept in a humorous way to convince readers that learning about a concept can be pleasurable.

Analyze & Write

Write a paragraph analyzing how Cain engages her readers:

1. Reread three or four of the following paragraphs: 1, 4, 7, 8, 11–12, 21–22, 25, and 27. Note in the margin the strategies Cain uses.

2. Explain how Cain engages her readers' interest in the concept of introversion, using examples from your annotations to support your explanation.

READINGS

Deborah Tannen

Marked Women

Deborah Tannen (b. 1945), who is a university professor and professor of linguistics at Georgetown University, has written more than twenty books, over one hundred scholarly articles, and dozens of articles for a more general audience. She writes primarily on the ways that language reflects the society in which it develops. Her most recent book is You Were Always Mom's Favorite! Sisters in Conversation Throughout Their Lives *(2009). In addition, Tannen writes poetry, plays, and reflective essays and appears frequently on television and radio.*

In the following selection, originally published in the New York Times Magazine, *Tannen explains the concept of* markedness, *a "staple of linguistic theory"—the study of language as a system for making meaning—and applies it to the visual world (the marking of hairstyle and clothing).*

- *Before you read, think about how you approach daily dressing decisions, including hairstyle and other details of your appearance, and how these decisions result from your gender.*

- *As you read, think about the rhetorical situation in which Tannen is writing. What do you think her purpose is in this essay, whom is she addressing, and what kinds of evidence does she use to support her claims and appeal to this audience?*

How do these opening paragraphs engage the reader's interest?

In paragraphs 1–7, what are the main explanatory strategies Tannen employs? What is the effect of these strategies?

1 Some years ago I was at a small working conference of four women and eight men. Instead of concentrating on the discussion I found myself looking at the three other women at the table, thinking how each had a different style and how each style was coherent.

2 One woman had dark brown hair in a classic style, a cross between Cleopatra and Plain Jane. The severity of her straight hair was softened by wavy bangs and ends that turned under. Because she was beautiful, the effect was more Cleopatra than plain.

3 The second woman was older, full of dignity and composure. Her hair was cut in a fashionable style that left her with only one eye, thanks to a side part that let a curtain of hair fall across half her face. As she looked down to read her prepared paper, the hair

robbed her of bifocal vision and created a barrier between her and the listeners.

4   The third woman's hair was wild, a frosted blond avalanche falling over and beyond her shoulders. When she spoke she frequently tossed her head, calling attention to her hair and away from her lecture.

5   Then there was makeup. The first woman wore facial cover that made her skin smooth and pale, a black line under each eye and mascara that darkened already dark lashes. The second wore only a light gloss on her lips and a hint of shadow on her eyes. The third had blue bands under her eyes, dark blue shadow, mascara, bright red lipstick and rouge; her fingernails flashed red.

6   I considered the clothes each woman had worn during the three days of the conference: In the first case, man-tailored suits in primary colors with solid-color blouses. In the second, casual but stylish black T-shirts, a floppy collarless jacket and baggy slacks or a skirt in neutral colors. The third wore a sexy jump suit; tight sleeveless jersey and tight yellow slacks; a dress with gaping armholes and an indulged tendency to fall off one shoulder.

7   Shoes? No. 1 wore string sandals with medium heels; No. 2, sensible, comfortable walking shoes; No. 3, pumps with spike heels. You can fill in the jewelry, scarves, shawls, sweaters—or lack of them.

8   As I amused myself finding coherence in these styles, I suddenly wondered why I was scrutinizing only the women. I scanned the eight men at the table. And then I knew why I wasn't studying them. The men's styles were unmarked.

9   The term "marked" is a staple of linguistic theory. It refers to the way language alters the base meaning of a word by adding a linguistic particle that has no meaning on its own. The unmarked form of a word carries the meaning that goes without saying—what you think of when you're not thinking anything special.

Why does Tannen wait until now to introduce linguistic theory?

10   The unmarked tense of verbs in English is the present—for example, *visit*. To indicate past, you mark the verb by adding *ed* to yield *visited*. For future, you add a word: *will visit*. Nouns are presumed to be

singular until marked for plural, typically by adding *s* or *es*, so *visit* becomes *visits* and *dish* becomes *dishes*.

How does this paragraph prepare you for Tannen's assertion in paragraph 29 that she may be marked as a feminist?

The unmarked forms of most English words also 11 convey "male." Being male is the unmarked case. Endings like *ess* and *ette* mark words as "female." Unfortunately, they also tend to mark them for frivolousness. Would you feel safe entrusting your life to a doctorette? Alfre Woodard, who was an Oscar nominee for best supporting actress, says she identifies herself as an actor because "actresses worry about eyelashes and cellulite, and women who are actors worry about the characters we are playing." Gender markers pick up extra meanings that reflect common association with the female gender: not quite serious, often sexual.

What does this paragraph suggest about the organizational plan Tannen will follow in the rest of the essay?

Each of the women at the conference had to make 12 decisions about hair, clothing, makeup and accessories, and each decision carried meaning. Every style available to us was marked. The men in our group had made decisions, too, but the range from which they chose was incomparably narrower. Men can choose styles that are marked, but they don't have to, and in this group none did. Unlike the women, they had the option of being unmarked.

Take the men's hair styles. There was no marine 13 crew cut or oily longish hair falling into eyes, no asymmetrical, two-tiered construction to swirl over a bald top. One man was unabashedly bald; the others had hair of standard length, parted on one side, in natural shades of brown or gray or graying. Their hair obstructed no views, left little to toss or push back or run fingers through and, consequently, needed and attracted no attention. A few men had beards. In a business setting, beards might be marked. In this academic gathering, they weren't.

What is the purpose of pointing out the men's appearance in paragraphs 13–15? Together with the description of the women's appearance in paragraphs 2–7, what explanatory strategy does this represent?

There could have been a cowboy shirt with string 14 tie or a three-piece suit or a necklaced hippie in jeans. But there wasn't. All eight men wore brown or blue slacks and nondescript shirts of light colors. No man wore sandals or boots; their shoes were dark, closed, comfortable, and flat. In short, unmarked.

Although no man wore makeup, you couldn't say 15 the men didn't wear makeup in the sense that you could say a woman didn't wear makeup. For men, no makeup is unmarked.

16   I asked myself what style we women could have adopted that would have been unmarked, like the men's. The answer was none. There is no unmarked woman.

17   There is no woman's hair style that can be called standard, that says nothing about her. The range of women's hair styles is staggering, but a woman whose hair has no particular style is perceived as not caring about how she looks, which can disqualify her from many positions, and will subtly diminish her as a person in the eyes of some.

18   Women must choose between attractive shoes and comfortable shoes. When our group made an unexpected trek, the woman who wore flat, laced shoes arrived first. Last to arrive was the woman in spike heels, shoes in hand and a handful of men around her.

19   If a woman's clothing is tight or revealing (in other words, sexy), it sends a message—an intended one of wanting to be attractive, but also a possibly unintended one of availability. If her clothes are not sexy, that too sends a message, lent meaning by the knowledge that they could have been. There are thousands of cosmetic products from which women can choose and myriad ways of applying them. Yet no makeup at all is anything but unmarked. Some men see it as a hostile refusal to please them.

20   Women can't even fill out a form without telling stories about themselves. Most forms give four titles to choose from. "Mr." carries no meaning other than that the respondent is male. But a woman who checks "Mrs." or "Miss" communicates not only whether she has been married but also whether she has conservative tastes in forms of address—and probably other conservative values as well. Checking "Ms." declines to let on about marriage (checking "Mr." declines nothing since nothing was asked), but it also marks her as either liberated or rebellious, depending on the observer's attitudes and assumptions.

21   I sometimes try to duck these variously marked choices by giving my title as "Dr."—and in so doing risk marking myself as either uppity (hence sarcastic responses like "Excuse *me!*") or an over-achiever (hence reactions of congratulatory surprise like "Good for you!").

Why do you think Tannen does not describe her own appearance as part of this discussion?

What is the effect of piling up so many examples and illustrations of the ways women's appearance is marked?

Here Tannen does use herself as an example. Why here and not elsewhere?

All married women's surnames are marked. If a   22
woman takes her husband's name, she announces to
the world that she is married and has traditional values. To some it will indicate that she is less herself,
more identified by her husband's identity. If she does
not take her husband's name, this too is marked, seen
as worthy of comment: She has *done* something; she
has "kept her own name." A man is never said to have
"kept his own name" because it never occurs to anyone that he might have given it up. For him using his
own name is unmarked.

A married woman who wants to have her cake and   23
eat it too may use her surname plus his, with or without a hyphen. But this too announces her marital status and often results in a tongue-tying string. In a list
(Harvey O'Donovan, Jonathan Feldman, Stephanie
Woodbury McGillicutty), the woman's multiple name
stands out. It is marked.

Why does Tannen bring in a source here? What do you notice about the way she introduces it?

I have never been inclined toward biological expla-   24
nations of gender differences in language, but I was
intrigued to see Ralph Fasold bring biological phenomena to bear on the question of linguistic marking
in his book *The Sociolinguistics of Language*. Fasold
stresses that language and culture are particularly
unfair in treating women as the marked case because
biologically it is the male that is marked. While two
X chromosomes make a female, two Y chromosomes
make nothing. Like the linguistic markers *s*, *es*, or *ess*,
the Y chromosome doesn't "mean" anything unless it
is attached to a root form—an X chromosome.

Developing this idea elsewhere Fasold points out   25
that girls are born with full female bodies, while boys
are born with modified female bodies. He invites
men who doubt this to lift up their shirts and contemplate why they have nipples.

Tannen reminds readers that the female is the source of birth—and therefore life. Why bring that up here?

In his book, Fasold notes "a wide range of facts   26
which demonstrates that female is the unmarked sex."
For example, he observes that there are a few species
that produce only females, like the whiptail lizard.
Thanks to parthenogenesis, they have no trouble having as many daughters as they like. There are no species, however, that produce only males. This is no
surprise, since any such species would become
extinct in its first generation.

27   Fasold is also intrigued by species that produce individuals not involved in reproduction, like honeybees and leaf-cutter ants. Reproduction is handled by the queen and a relatively few males; the workers are sterile females. "Since they do not reproduce," Fasold said, "there is no reason for them to be one sex or the other, so they default, so to speak, to female."

28   Fasold ends his discussion of these matters by pointing out that if language reflected biology, grammar books would direct us to use "she" to include males and females and "he" only for specifically male referents. But they don't. They tell us that "he" means "he or she," and that "she" is used only if the referent is specifically female. This use of "he" as the sex-indefinite pronoun is an innovation introduced into English by grammarians in the eighteenth and nineteenth centuries, according to Peter Mühlhäusler and Rom Harré in *Pronouns and People*. From at least about 1500, the correct sex-indefinite pronoun was "they," as it still is in casual spoken English. In other words, the female was declared by grammarians to be the marked case.

29   Writing this article may mark me not as a writer, not as a linguist, not as an analyst of human behavior, but as a feminist—which will have positive or negative, but in any case powerful, connotations for readers. Yet I doubt that anyone reading Ralph Fasold's book would put that label on him.

30   I discovered the markedness inherent in the very topic of gender after writing a book on differences in conversational style based on geographical region, ethnicity, class, age, and gender. When I was interviewed, the vast majority of journalists wanted to talk about the differences between women and men. While I thought I was simply describing what I observed—something I had learned to do as a researcher—merely mentioning women and men marked me as a feminist for some.

31   When I wrote a book devoted to gender differences in ways of speaking, I sent the manuscript to five male colleagues, asking them to alert me to any interpretation, phrasing, or wording that might seem unfairly negative toward men. Even so, when the book came out, I encountered responses like that of

Is Tannen fully objective in this essay, or do you think that sometimes she is not? What evidence do you have for your answer?

the television talk show host who, after interviewing me, turned to the audience and asked if they thought I was male-bashing.

What explanatory strategy is Tannen using in paragraphs 31 and 32? How effective do you find it?

Leaping upon a poor fellow who affably nodded in agreement, she made him stand and asked, "Did what she said accurately describe you?" "Oh, yes," he answered. "That's me exactly." "And what she said about women—does that sound like your wife?" "Oh, yes," he responded. "That's her exactly." "Then why do you think she's male-bashing?" He answered, with disarming honesty, "Because she's a woman and she's saying things about men." 32

To say anything about women and men without marking oneself as either feminist or anti-feminist, male-basher or apologist for men seems as impossible for a woman as trying to get dressed in the morning without inviting interpretations of her character. 33

Do you agree with this conclusion? Why or why not?

Sitting at the conference table musing on these matters, I felt sad to think that we women didn't have the freedom to be unmarked that the men sitting next to us had. Some days you just want to get dressed and go about your business. But if you're a woman, you can't, because there is no unmarked woman. 34

READING FOR MEANING

This section presents three activities that will help you think about the meanings in Tannen's explanation of *marking*. Your instructor may ask you to do one or more of these activities in class or online.

For more help with summarizing, see Chapter 10, pp. 518–19.

1. **Read to Summarize.** Write a sentence or two explaining the concept of being "marked" as Deborah Tannen sees it.

2. **Read to Respond.** Write a paragraph or two analyzing your initial reactions to Tannen's essay. For example, consider anything that resonates with your experience or that seems contradictory, surprising, or fascinating, such as:

   - Tannen's assertion that how a choice like checking "Ms." on a form is understood depends on the interpreter's "attitudes and assumptions" (par. 20);

 Take a quiz to check your reading and vocabulary comprehension:
bedfordstmartins.com/readingcritically

- Tannen's assertion that "this article may mark me not as a writer, not as a linguist, not as an analyst of human behavior, but as a feminist — which will have positive or negative, but in any case powerful, connotations for readers" (par. 29).

You may also try recognizing emotional manipulation; see Chapter 10, pp. 536–37.

3. **Read to Analyze Assumptions.** Write a paragraph or two analyzing an assumption you find intriguing in Tannen's essay. For example:

Assumptions about the value of biologically based evidence. Tannen looks at "markers" through a linguist's eyes. For example, she provides a comparison to word forms that are "unmarked" and "marked" — such as the present and past forms of a verb and the singular and plural forms of a noun (par. 10). But near the end of her essay, she cites Ralph Fasold, who "bring[s] biological phenomena to bear on the question of linguistic marking" (par. 24), and she explains his evidence that the "unmarked" gender should really be female rather than male (par. 28). To think critically about the assumptions in this essay related to the value of biologically based evidence, ask yourself questions like these:

- Why does Tannen step out of her field of expertise to support her thesis that women in our culture are marked and men are not?

- Is biologically based evidence particularly convincing to readers in our culture, or is there perhaps another reason Tannen brings in Fasold's theories? If so, what might that reason be?

Assumptions about the effects of being "marked." In her final paragraph, Tannen says she feels "sad" that "women didn't have the freedom to be unmarked. . . . Some days you just want to get dressed and go about your business. But if you're a woman, you can't, because there is no unmarked woman" (par. 34). To think critically about the assumptions in this essay related to the effects of being "marked," ask yourself questions like these:

- Do you share Tannen's view that being marked is a burden?

- Can you think of ways in which being unmarked might be limiting or perhaps boring — or being marked could be liberating or creative?

READING LIKE A WRITER

ENGAGING READERS' INTEREST

Explanatory writing aimed at nonspecialist readers usually makes an effort to engage those readers' interest. Susan Cain, for example, writing for the *New York Times Magazine*, proves herself to be engaging, even entertaining, by starting with an example that might be familiar to her readers and asking questions to draw readers in. Also writing for a magazine read by an educated but nonspecialist audience, Tannen likewise attempts to engage and hold her readers' interest. Like Cain, she weaves these attempts into the flow of information. While they are not separate from the information — for information itself can interest readers — direct attempts to engage are a feature of Tannen's explanatory essay. For example, Tannen opens the essay with several intriguing descriptions, which later serve as examples of the concept. In addition, she adopts an informal **tone** (attitude or mood) by using the first-person pronoun *I* and commenting on her own thinking process.

| Analyze & Write |

Write a paragraph analyzing Tannen's tone and some of the strategies she uses to create it:

1. Reread paragraphs 1–8, and look for places where you are aware of Tannen's tone.

2. Skim the rest of the essay, annotating paragraphs 13–16, 21, 24, and 29–34, where Tannen uses the first-person *I* or other conversational devices, such as "Take the men's hair styles" as an opener for paragraph 13.

3. How did these devices affect you as a reader? Use examples from the reading to illustrate your analysis.

Beth L. Bailey

Dating

Beth L. Bailey (b. 1957) is professor of history at Temple University. She attended Northwestern University and the University of Chicago. Bailey has written several scholarly books on nineteenth- and twentieth-century American culture, including Sex in the Heartland *(1999), and co-written others, including* A People and a Nation *(2008). Her most recent book is* America's Army: Making the All-Volunteer Force *(2009). "Dating" comes from Bailey's first book,* From Front Porch to Back Seat: Courtship in Twentieth-Century America *(1988).*

Bailey first became interested in studying courtship attitudes and behavior when she appeared on a television talk show to defend coed dorms, which were then relatively new and controversial. She was surprised when many people in the audience objected to coed dorms, not on moral grounds, but out of fear that too much intimacy between young men and women would hasten "the dissolution of the dating system and the death of romance."

- ***Before you read** Bailey's historical explanation of dating, think about the attitudes and behavior of people your own age in regard to courtship and romance.*

- ***As you read,** note which of the features of explanatory writing Bailey employs, and to what effect on the reader. Consider whether she integrates sources smoothly and develops her explanation by using appropriate strategies, such as defining, comparing and contrasting, illustrating, and reporting causes or effects.*

One day, the 1920s story goes, a young man asked a city girl if he might call on her (Black, 1924, p. 340). We know nothing else about the man or the girl—only that, when he arrived, she had her hat on. Not much of a story to us, but any American born before 1910 would have gotten the punch line. "She had her hat on": those five words were rich in meaning to early twentieth-century Americans. The hat signaled that she expected to leave the house. He came on a "call," expecting to be received in her family's parlor, to talk, to meet her mother, perhaps to have some refreshments or to listen to her play the piano. She expected a "date," to be taken "out" somewhere and entertained. He ended up spending four weeks' savings fulfilling her expectations. 1

In the early twentieth century this new style of courtship, dating, had begun to supplant the old. Born primarily of the limits and opportunities of urban life, dating had almost completely replaced the old system of calling by the mid-1920s—and, in so doing, had transformed American courtship. Dating moved courtship into the public world, relocating it from family 2 parlors and community events to restaurants, theaters, and dance halls. At the same time, it removed couples from the implied supervision of the private sphere—from the watchful eyes of family and local community—to the anonymity of the public sphere. Courtship among strangers offered couples new freedom. But access to the public world of the city required money. One had to buy entertainment, or even access to a place to sit and talk. Money—men's money—became the basis of the dating system and, thus, of courtship. This new dating system, as it shifted courtship from the private to the public sphere and increasingly centered around money, fundamentally altered the balance of power between men and women in courtship.

3   The transition from calling to dating was as complete as it was fundamental. By the 1950s and 1960s, social scientists who studied American courtship found it necessary to remind the American public that dating was a "recent American innovation and not a traditional or universal custom" (Cavin, as cited in "Some," 1961, p. 125). Some of the many commentators who wrote about courtship believed dating was the best thing that had ever happened to relations between the sexes; others blamed the dating system for all the problems of American youth and American marriage. But virtually everyone portrayed the system dating replaced as infinitely simpler, sweeter, more innocent, and more graceful. Hardheaded social scientists waxed sentimental about the "horse-and-buggy days," when a young man's offer of a ride home from church was tantamount to a proposal and when young men came calling in the evenings and courtship took place safely within the warm bosom of the family. "The courtship which grew out of the sturdy social roots [of the nineteenth century]," one author wrote, "comes through to us for what it was—a gracious ritual, with clearly defined roles for man and woman, in which everyone knew the measured music and the steps" (Moss, 1963, p. 151).

4   Certainly a less idealized version of this model of courtship had existed in America, but it was not this model that dating was supplanting. Although only about 45 percent of Americans lived in urban areas by 1910, few of them were so untouched by the sweeping changes of the late nineteenth century that they could live that dream of rural simplicity. Conventions of courtship at that time were not set by simple yeoman farmers and their families but by the rising middle class, often in imitation of the ways of "society." . . .

5   The call itself was a complicated event. A myriad of rules governed everything: the proper amount of time between invitation and visit (a fortnight or less); whether or not refreshments should be served (not if one belonged to a fashionable or semi-fashionable circle, but outside of "smart" groups in cities like New York and Boston, girls *might* serve iced drinks with little cakes or tiny cups of coffee or hot chocolate and sandwiches); chaperonage (the first call must be made on daughter and mother,

but excessive chaperonage would indicate to the man that his attentions were unwelcome); appropriate topics of conversation (the man's interests, but never too personal); how leave should be taken (on no account should the woman "accompany [her caller] to the door nor stand talking while he struggles into his coat") ("Lady," 1904, p. 255).

Each of these "measured steps," as the mid-twentieth century author 6 nostalgically called them, was a test of suitability, breeding, and background. Advice columns and etiquette books emphasized that these were the manners of any "well-bred" person—and conversely implied that deviations revealed a lack of breeding. However, around the turn of the century, many people who did lack this narrow "breeding" aspired to politeness. Advice columns in women's magazines regularly printed questions from "Country Girl" and "Ignoramus" on the fine points of calling etiquette. Young men must have felt the pressure of girls' expectations, for they wrote to the same advisers with questions about calling. In 1907, *Harper's Bazaar* ran a major article titled "Etiquette for Men," explaining the ins and outs of the calling system (Hall, 1907, pp. 1095–97). In the first decade of the twentieth century, this rigid system of calling was the convention not only of the "respectable" but also of those who aspired to respectability.

At the same time, however, the new system of dating was emerging. By 7 the mid-1910s, the word *date* had entered the vocabulary of the middle-class public. In 1914, the *Ladies' Home Journal*, a bastion of middle-class respectability, used the term (safely enclosed in quotation marks but with no explanation of its meaning) several times. The word was always spoken by that exotica, the college sorority girl—a character marginal in her exoticness but nevertheless a solid product of the middle class. "One beautiful evening of the spring term," one such article begins, "when I was a college girl of eighteen, the boy whom, because of his popularity in every phase of college life, I had been proud gradually to allow the monopoly of my 'dates,' took me unexpectedly into his arms. As he kissed me impetuously I was glad, from the bottom of my heart, for the training of that mother who had taught me to hold myself aloof from all personal familiarities of boys and men" ("How," 1914, p. 9).

Sugarcoated with a tribute to motherhood and virtue, the dates—and 8 the kiss—were unmistakably presented for a middle-class audience. By 1924, ten years later, when the story of the unfortunate young man who went to call on the city girl was current, dating had essentially replaced calling in middle-class culture. The knowing smiles of the story's listeners had probably started with the word *call*—and not every hearer would have been sympathetic to the man's plight. By 1924, he really should have known better. . . .

Dating, which to the privileged and protected would seem a system of 9 increased freedom and possibility, stemmed originally from the lack of opportunities. Calling, or even just visiting, was not a practicable system for young people whose families lived crowded into one or two rooms. For even the more established or independent working-class girls, the parlor and the piano often simply didn't exist. Some "factory girls" struggled to find a way to receive callers. The *Ladies' Home Journal* approvingly reported the case of six girls, workers in a box factory, who had formed a club and pooled part of their wages to pay the "janitress of a tenement house" to let them use her front room two evenings a week. It had a piano. One of the girls explained their system: "We ask the boys to come when they like and spend the evening. We haven't any place at home to see them, and I hate seeing them on the street" (Preston, 1907, p. 31).

10   Many other working girls, however, couldn't have done this even had they wanted to. They had no extra wages to pool, or they had no notions of middle-class respectability. Some, especially girls of ethnic families, were kept secluded—chaperoned according to the customs of the old country. But many others fled the squalor, drabness, and crowdedness of their homes to seek amusement and intimacy elsewhere. And a "good time" increasingly became identified with public places and commercial amusements, making young women whose wages would not even cover the necessities of life dependent on men's "treats" (Peiss, 1986, pp. 51–52, 75). Still, many poor and working-class couples did not so much escape from the home as they were pushed from it.

11   These couples courted on the streets, sometimes at cheap dance halls or eventually at the movies. These were not respectable places, and women could enter them only so far as they, themselves, were not considered respectable. Respectable young women did, of course, enter the public world, but their excursions into the public were cushioned. Public courtship of middle-class and upper-class youth was at least *supposed* to be chaperoned; those with money and social position went to private dances with carefully controlled guest lists, to theater parties where they were a private group within the public. As rebels would soon complain, the supervision of society made the private parlor seem almost free by contrast. Women who were not respectable did have relative freedom of action—but the trade-off was not necessarily a happy one for them.

12   The negative factors were important, but dating rose equally from the possibilities offered by urban life. Privileged youth, as Lewis Erenberg shows in his study of New York nightlife, came to see the possibility of privacy in the anonymous public, in the excitement and freedom the city offered (1981, pp. 60–87, 139–42). They looked to lower-class models of freedom—to those beyond the constraints of respectability. As a society girl informed the readers of the *Ladies' Home Journal* in 1914: "Nowadays it is considered 'smart' to go to the low order of dance halls, and not only be a looker-on, but also to dance among all sorts and conditions of men and women. . . . Nowadays when we enter a restaurant and dance place it is

hard to know who is who" ("A Girl," 1914, p. 7). In 1907, the same maga- zine had warned unmarried women never to go alone to a "public restau- rant" with any man, even a relative. There was no impropriety in the act, the adviser had conceded, but it still "lays [women] open to misunderstanding and to being classed with women of undesirable reputation by the strangers present" (Kingsland, May 1907, p. 48). Rebellious and adventurous young people sought that confusion, and the gradual loosening of proprieties they engendered helped to change courtship. Young men and women went out into the world *together*, enjoying a new kind of companionship and the intimacy of a new kind of freedom from adult supervision.

The new freedom that led to dating came from other sources as well. 13 Many more serious (and certainly respectable) young women were taking advantage of opportunities to enter the public world—going to college, taking jobs, entering and creating new urban professions. Women who belonged to the public world by day began to demand fuller access to the public world in general. . . .

Between 1890 and 1925, dating—in practice and in name—had grad- 14 ually, almost imperceptibly, become a universal custom in America. By the 1930s it had transcended its origins: Middle America associated dating with neither upper-class rebellion nor the urban lower classes. The rise of dating was usually explained, quite simply, by the invention of the auto- mobile. Cars had given youth mobility and privacy, and so had brought about the system. This explanation—perhaps not consciously but defi- nitely not coincidentally—revised history. The automobile certainly con- tributed to the rise of dating as a *national* practice, especially in rural and suburban areas, but it was simply accelerating and extending a process already well under way. Once its origins were located firmly in Middle America, however, and not in the extremes of urban upper- and lower- class life, dating had become an American institution.

Dating not only transformed the outward modes and conventions of 15 American courtship, it also changed the distribution of control and power in courtship. One change was generational: the dating system lessened parental control and gave young men and women more freedom. The dat- ing system also shifted power from women to men. Calling, either as a sim- ple visit or as the elaborate late nineteenth-century ritual, gave women a large portion of control. First of all, courtship took place within the girl's home—in women's "sphere," as it was called in the nineteenth century— or at entertainments largely devised and presided over by women. Dating moved courtship out of the home and into man's sphere—the world out- side the home. Female controls and conventions lost much of their power outside women's sphere. And while many of the conventions of female pro- priety were restrictive and repressive, they had allowed women (young women and their mothers) a great deal of immediate control over court- ship. The transfer of spheres thoroughly undercut that control.

16   Second, in the calling system, the woman took the initiative. Etiquette books and columns were adamant on that point: it was the "girl's privilege" to ask a young man to call. Furthermore, it was highly improper for the man to take the initiative. In 1909 a young man wrote to the *Ladies' Home Journal* adviser asking, "May I call upon a young woman whom I greatly admire, although she had not given me the permission? Would she be flattered at my eagerness, even to the setting aside of conventions, or would she think me impertinent?" Mrs. Kingsland replied: "I think that you would risk her just displeasure and frustrate your object of finding favor with her." Softening the prohibition, she then suggested an invitation might be secured through a mutual friend (Kingsland, 1909, p. 58). . . .

17   Contrast these strictures with advice on dating etiquette from the 1940s and 1950s: An advice book for men and women warns that "girls who [try] to usurp the right of boys to choose their own dates" will "ruin a good dating career. . . . Fair or not, it is the way of life. From the Stone Age, when men chased and captured their women, comes the yen of a boy to do the pursuing. You will control your impatience, therefore, and respect the time-honored custom of boys to take the first step" (Richmond, 1958, p. 11). . . .

18   This absolute reversal of roles almost necessarily accompanied courtship's move from woman's sphere to man's sphere. Although the convention-setters commended the custom of woman's initiative because it allowed greater exclusivity (it might be "difficult for a girl to refuse the permission to call, no matter how unwelcome or unsuitable an acquaintance of the man might be"), the custom was based on a broader principle of etiquette (Hart and Brown, 1944, p. 89). The host or hostess issued any invitation; the guest did not invite himself or herself. An invitation to call was an invitation to visit in a woman's home.

19   An invitation to go out on a date, on the other hand, was an invitation into man's world—not simply because dating took place in the public sphere (commonly defined as belonging to men), though that was part of it, but because dating moved courtship into the world of the economy. Money—men's money—was at the center of the dating system. Thus, on two counts, men became the hosts and assumed the control that came with that position.

20   There was some confusion caused by this reversal of initiative, especially during the twenty years or so when going out and calling coexisted as systems. (The unfortunate young man in the apocryphal story, for example, had asked the city girl if he might call on her, so perhaps she was conventionally correct to assume he meant to play the host.) Confusions generally were sorted out around the issue of money. One young woman, "Henrietta L.," wrote to the *Ladies' Home Journal* to inquire whether a girl might "suggest to a friend going to any entertainment or place of amusement where there will be any expense to the young man." The reply:

"Never, under any circumstances." The adviser explained that the invitation to go out must "always" come from the man, for he was the one "responsible for the expense" (Kingsland, Oct. 1907, p. 60). This same adviser insisted that the woman must "always" invite the man to call; clearly she realized that money was the central issue.

The centrality of money in dating had serious implications for court- 21 ship. Not only did money shift control and initiative to men by making them the "hosts," it led contemporaries to see dating as a system of exchange best understood through economic analogies or as an economic system pure and simple. Of course, people did recognize in marriage a similar economic dimension—the man undertakes to support his wife in exchange for her filling various roles important to him—but marriage was a permanent relationship. Dating was situational, with no long-term commitments implied, and when a man, in a highly visible ritual, spent money on a woman in public, it seemed much more clearly an economic act.

In fact, the term *date* was associated with the direct economic exchange 22 of prostitution at an early time. A prostitute called "Maimie," in letters written to a middle-class benefactor/friend in the late nineteenth century, described how men made "dates" with her (Peiss, 1986, p. 54). And a former waitress turned prostitute described the process to the Illinois Senate Committee on Vice this way: "You wait on a man and he smiles at you. You see a chance to get a tip and you smile back. Next day he returns and you try harder than ever to please him. Then right away he wants to make a date, and offer you money and presents if you'll be a good fellow and go out with him" (Rosen, 1982, p. 151). These men, quite clearly, were buying sexual favors—but the occasion of the exchange was called a "date."

Courtship in America had always turned somewhat on money (or back- 23 ground). A poor clerk or stockyards worker would not have called upon the daughter of a well-off family, and men were expected to be economically secure before they married. But in the dating system money entered directly into the relationship between a man and a woman as the symbolic currency of exchange in even casual dating.

Dating, like prostitution, made access to women directly dependent on 24 money. . . . In dating, though, the exchange was less direct and less clear than in prostitution. One author, in 1924, made sense of it this way. In dating, he reasoned, a man is responsible for all expenses. The woman is responsible for nothing—she contributes only her company. Of course, the man contributes his company, too, but since he must "add money to balance the bargain" his company must be worth less than hers. Thus, according to this economic understanding, she is selling her company to him. In his eyes, dating didn't even involve an exchange; it was a direct purchase. The moral "subtleties" of a woman's position in dating, the author concluded, were complicated even further by the fact that young men, "discovering that she must be bought, [like] to buy her when [they happen] to have the money" (Black, 1924, p. 342).

25   Yet another young man, the same year, publicly called a halt to such "promiscuous buying." Writing anonymously (for good reason) in *American Magazine*, the author declared a "one-man buyer's strike." This man estimated that, as a "buyer of feminine companionship" for the previous five years, he had "invested" about $20 a week—a grand total of over $5,000. Finally, he wrote, he had realized that "there is a point at which any commodity—even such a delightful commodity as feminine companionship—costs more than it is worth" ("Too-high," 1924, pp. 27, 145–50). The commodity he had bought with his $5,000 had been priced beyond its "real value" and he had had enough. This man said "enough" not out of principle, not because he rejected the implications of the economic model of courtship, but because he felt he wasn't receiving value for money.

26   In . . . these economic analyses, the men are complaining about the new dating system, lamenting the passing of the mythic good old days when "a man without a quarter in his pocket could call on a girl and not be embarrassed," the days before a woman had to be "bought" ("Too-high," 1924, pp. 145–50). In recognizing so clearly the economic model on which dating operated, they also clearly saw that the model was a bad one—in purely economic terms. The exchange was not equitable; the commodity was overpriced. Men were operating at a loss.

27   Here, however, they didn't understand their model completely. True, the equation (male companionship plus money equals female companionship) was imbalanced. But what men were buying in the dating system was not just female companionship, not just entertainment—but power. Money purchased obligation; money purchased inequality; money purchased control.

28   The conventions that grew up to govern dating codified women's inequality and ratified men's power. Men asked women out; women were condemned as "aggressive" if they expressed interest in a man too directly. Men paid for everything, but often with the implication that women "owed" sexual favors in return. The dating system required men always to assume control, and women to act as men's dependents.

29   Yet women were not without power in the system, and they were willing to contest men with their "feminine" power. Much of the public discourse on courtship in twentieth-century America was concerned with this contestation. Thousands of sources chronicled the struggles of, and between, men and women—struggles mediated by the "experts" and arbiters of convention—to create a balance of power, to gain or retain control of the dating system. These struggles, played out most clearly in the fields of sex, science, and etiquette, made ever more explicit the complicated relations between men and women in a changing society.

References

Black, A. (1924, August). Is the young person coming back? *Harper's*, 340, 342.

Erenberg, L. (1981). *Steppin' out*. Westport, Conn.: Greenwood Press.

A Girl. (1914, July). Believe me. *Ladies' Home Journal*, 7.

Hall, F. H. (1907, November). Etiquette for men. *Harper's Bazaar*, 1095–97.

Hart, S., & Brown, L. (1944). *How to get your man and hold him*. New York: New Power Publications.

How may a girl know? (1914, January). *Ladies' Home Journal*, 9.

Kingsland. (1907, May). *Ladies' Home Journal*, 48.

————. (1907, October). *Ladies' Home Journal*, 60.

————. (1909, May). *Ladies' Home Journal*, 58.

Lady from Philadelphia. (1904, February). *Ladies' Home Journal*, 255.

Moss, A. (1963, April). Whatever happened to courtship? *Mademoiselle*, 151.

Peiss, K. (1986). *Cheap amusements: Working women and leisure in turn-of-the-century New York*. Philadelphia: Temple University Press.

Preston, A. (1907, February). After business hours—what? *Ladies' Home Journal*, 31.

Richmond, C. (1958). *Handbook of dating*. Philadelphia: Westminster Press.

Rosen, R. (1982). *The lost sisterhood: Prostitution in America, 1900–1918*. Baltimore: Johns Hopkins University Press, 1982.

Some expert opinions on dating. (1961, August). *McCall's*, 125.

Too-high cost of courting. (1924, September). *American Magazine*, 27, 145–50.

A Special Reading Strategy

Synthesizing Information from Sources

Synthesizing information is a strategy academic writers use regularly as they read sources to discover, support, challenge, or extend their ideas. It is also a skill writers use to support their ideas in research-based writing. Beth L. Bailey, for example, uses information from a variety of sources to chart the shift from "calling" to "dating."

To analyze how Bailey synthesizes information from sources to support her claims, skim paragraph 12, highlighting the sources she quotes, paraphrases, or summarizes. Look for signal phrases (made up of a reference to a speaker or source author and an appropriate verb such as "Lewis Erenberg shows" and "As a society girl informed") and parenthetical citations to sources such as "(Kingsland, May 1907, p. 48)". What is Bailey's central idea in this paragraph? How does she use information from the different sources she cites to support this central idea?

(continued)

For detailed guidelines on synthesizing information from sources, see pp. 520–21 and pp. 569–70; for guidance on using information to support your claims, see pp. 570–80; and for coverage of using signal phrases and parenthetical citations to cite sources, see pp. 189–90, 236–37, and 581–85.

READING FOR MEANING

This section presents three activities that will help you think about the meanings in Bailey's explanation of dating. Your instructor may ask you to do one or more of these activities in class or online.

For more help with summarizing, see Chapter 10, pp. 518–19.

1. **Read to Summarize.** Write a sentence or two explaining the concept of dating as Bailey explains it.

2. **Read to Respond.** Write a paragraph analyzing your initial reactions to Bailey's explanation of dating. For example, consider anything that resonates with your experience or that seems contradictory, surprising, or fascinating, such as:

You may also try reflecting on challenges to your beliefs and values; see Chapter 10, pp. 526–27.

   - Contrasts between the dating system in the early decades of the twentieth century (as described by Bailey) and the dating system you know today, contrasting aspects of your experience with specific features of the early system;
   - The "centrality of money in dating" (par. 21).

3. **Read to Analyze Assumptions.** Write a paragraph or two analyzing an assumption you find intriguing in Bailey's essay. For example:

   Assumptions about who has control in courtship. Bailey writes that the transformation from "calling" to "dating" in the twentieth century "changed the distribution of control and power in courtship" (par. 15). Under calling, she argues, women had control; under dating, men had control. To think critically about the assumptions in this reading related to who has control in courtship, ask yourself questions like these:

   - What assumptions about rules or rituals of courtship are observable in our current society, and where does the power lie now?
   - Are power and economics the only or even the main factors involved in courtship and intimacy between the sexes? For example, how do love, affection, physical chemistry, or even simple pleasure in companionship complicate the picture, either in the period Bailey is writing about or today?

Take a quiz to check your reading and vocabulary comprehension:
bedfordstmartins.com/readingcritically

Assumptions about the role of the media in courtship. Bailey uses examples from magazines, journals, and manuals to support her asser- tions about "calling" and "dating." She seems to assume that the informa- tion in these publications reflects accurately the customs of the time, but she also suggests that it may have helped to bring about changes in these customs. To think critically about the assumptions in this essay related to the role of the media in courtship, ask yourself questions like these:

- If someone were to write about the rituals of courtship in early-twenty- first-century America, what would be the best sources of information and how accurately would those sources represent what actually hap- pens in American culture?

- To what extent do media (such as magazine articles, television shows, or social networks like Facebook or Twitter) *create* cultural assumptions — about courtship or anything else — as well as reflect them?

READING LIKE A WRITER

USING COMPARISON AND CONTRAST

One of the best ways of explaining something new is to relate it, through compari- son or contrast, to something familiar. Sometimes writers of concept explanations use both comparison and contrast; sometimes they use only one or the other. Bailey uses comparison and contrast in her explanatory essay, but with a twist. Rather than explaining something new to readers by relating it to something already known to them, she is instead explaining something already known — *dating* — by relating it to something that most readers don't know about — *calling*, an earlier type of court- ship. Since she is studying dating from a historical perspective, she is able to con- sider the changing relationship between men and women and the things that it tells us about changing social and cultural expectations and practices.

> **Analyze & Write**

Write a paragraph or two analyzing how Bailey develops the contrast between calling and dating:

1. Reread paragraphs 15–19, and underline the sentences that assert the points of the contrast Bailey develops in these paragraphs. (Hint: To get started, underline the first and last sentences in paragraph 15. Except for paragraph 17, you will find one or two sentences in the other paragraphs that assert the points.)

2. Examine the other sentences to discover how Bailey develops or illustrates each of the points of the contrast between calling and dating.

3. What does Bailey suggest is the reason for the shift in power from women to men? Use examples from paragraphs 15–19 to support your explanation.

Dan Hurley

Can You Make Yourself Smarter?

Dan Hurley writes books and articles on science for both specialists and general readers. His books include Diabetes Rising: How a Rare Disease Became a Modern Pandemic and What to Do About It *(2010) and* Natural Causes: Death, Lies, and Politics in America's Vitamin and Herbal Supplement Industry *(2006). Among the medical newspapers he contributes to are* General Surgery News *and* Neurology Today. *In 1995, he won an award for investigative journalism for an article he published in* Psychology Today *on the violent mentally ill, and he is currently working on a book on intelligence. The article below was published in the* New York Times *in 2011. Although Hurley did not include references (as is customary when writing for popular periodicals like newspapers and magazines), we have added them so readers interested in this topic can explore it in greater depth.*

- *Before you read, think about your own views of intelligence and means of measuring it. Do you think IQ tests, or perhaps other kinds of tests such as the SAT or personality tests, accurately reflect the test-takers' abilities?*

- *As you read, think about Hurley's tone. Are there any passages where the tone seems conversational, stuffy, stiff, sarcastic, angry, amused, or anything else? How appropriate do you think Hurley's tone is given the audience for whom he is writing? How might he have modified his tone if the article were intended not for the general public, but for academic researchers or for students concerned about their test scores?*

1   Early on a drab afternoon in January, a dozen third graders from the working-class suburb of Chicago Heights, Ill., burst into the Mac Lab on the ground floor of Washington-McKinley School in a blur of blue pants, blue vests and white shirts. Minutes later, they were hunkered down in front of the Apple computers lining the room's perimeter, hoping to do what was, until recently, considered impossible: increase their intelligence through training.

2   "Can somebody raise their hand," asked Kate Wulfson, the instructor, "and explain to me how you get points?" On each of the children's monitors, there was a cartoon image of a haunted house, with bats and a crescent moon in a midnight blue sky. Every few seconds, a black cat appeared in one of the house's five windows, then vanished. The exercise was divided into levels. On Level 1, the children earned a point by remembering which window the cat was just in. Easy. But the game is progressive:

 For a multimodal reading that explains a concept, go to
bedfordstmartins.com/readingcritically.

the cats keep coming, and the kids have to keep watching and remembering. "And here's where it gets confusing," Wulfson continued. "If you get to Level 2, you have to remember where the cat was two windows ago. The time before last. For Level 3, you have to remember where it was three times ago. Level 4 is four times ago. That's hard. You have to keep track. O.K., ready? Once we start, anyone who talks loses a star."

So began 10 minutes of a remarkably demanding concentration game. At Level 2, even adults find the task somewhat taxing. Almost no one gets past Level 3 without training. But most people who stick with the game do get better with practice. This isn't surprising: practice improves performance on almost every task humans engage in, whether it's learning to read or playing horseshoes.

What is surprising is what else it improved. In a 2008 study, Susanne Jaeggi and Martin Buschkuehl, now of the University of Maryland, found that young adults who practiced a stripped-down, less cartoonish version of the game also showed improvement in a fundamental cognitive ability known as "fluid" intelligence: the capacity to solve novel problems, to learn, to reason, to see connections and to get to the bottom of things (Jaeggi et al.). The implication was that playing the game literally makes people smarter.

Psychologists have long regarded intelligence as coming in two flavors: crystallized intelligence, the treasure trove of stored-up information and how-to knowledge (the sort of thing tested on "Jeopardy!" or put to use when you ride a bicycle); and fluid intelligence. Crystallized intelligence grows as you age; fluid intelligence has long been known to peak in early adulthood, around college age, and then to decline gradually. And unlike physical conditioning, which can transform 98-pound weaklings into hunks, fluid intelligence has always been considered impervious to training. That, after all, is the premise of I.Q. tests, or at least the portion that measures fluid intelligence: we can test you now and predict all sorts of things in the future, because fluid intelligence supposedly sets in early and is fairly immutable. While parents, teachers and others play an essential role in establishing an environment in which a child's intellect can grow, even Tiger Mothers generally expect only higher grades will come from their children's diligence—not better brains.

How, then, could watching black cats in a haunted house possibly increase something as profound as fluid intelligence? Because the deceptively simple game, it turns out, targets the most elemental of cognitive skills: "working" memory. What long-term memory is to crystallized intelligence, working memory is to fluid intelligence. Working memory is more than just the ability to remember a telephone number long enough to dial it; it's the capacity to manipulate the information you're holding in your head—to add or subtract those numbers, place them in reverse order or sort them from high to low. Understanding a metaphor or an analogy is equally dependent on working memory; you can't follow even a simple statement like "See Jane run" if you can't put together how "see" and "Jane" connect with "run." Without it, you can't make sense of anything.

7   Over the past three decades, theorists and researchers alike have made significant headway in understanding how working memory functions. They have developed a variety of sensitive tests to measure it and deter-mine its relationship to fluid intelligence. Then, in 2008, Jaeggi turned one of these tests of working memory into a training task for building it up, in the same way that push-ups can be used both as a measure of physical fit-ness and as a strength-building task. "We see attention and working mem-ory as the cardiovascular function of the brain," Jaeggi says. "If you train your attention and working memory, you increase your basic cognitive skills that help you for many different complex tasks."

8   Jaeggi's study has been widely influential. Since its publication, others have achieved results similar to Jaeggi's not only in elementary-school children but also in preschoolers, college students and the elderly. The training tasks generally require only 15 to 25 minutes of work per day, five days a week, and have been found to improve scores on tests of fluid intel-ligence in as little as four weeks. Follow-up studies linking that improve-ment to real-world gains in schooling and job performance are just getting under way. But already, people with disorders including attention-deficit hyperactivity disorder (A.D.H.D.) and traumatic brain injury have seen benefits from training. Gains can persist for up to eight months after treatment.

9   In a town like Chicago Heights, where only 16 percent of high school-ers met the Illinois version of the No Child Left Behind standards in 2011, finding a clear way to increase cognitive abilities has obvious appeal. But it has other uses too, at all ages and aptitudes. Even high-level profession-als have begun training their working memory in hopes of boosting their fluid intelligence—and, with it, their job performance. If the effect is real—if fluid intelligence can be raised in just a few minutes a day, even by a bit, and not just on a test but in real life—then it would seem to offer, as Jaeggi's 2008 study concluded with Spock-like understatement, "a wide range of applications" (Jaeggi et al. 1).

10   Since the first reliable intelligence test was created just over a hundred years ago, researchers have searched for a way to increase scores mean-ingfully, with little success. The track record was so dismal that by 2002, when Jaeggi and her research partner (and now her husband), Martin Buschkuehl, came across a study claiming to have done so, they simply didn't believe it. The study, by a Swedish neuroscientist named Torkel Klingberg, involved just 14 children, all with A.D.H.D. (Klingberg). Half participated in computerized tasks designed to strengthen their working

memory, while the other half played less challenging computer games. After just five weeks, Klingberg found that those who played the working-memory games fidgeted less and moved about less. More remarkable, they also scored higher on one of the single best measures of fluid intelligence, the Raven's Progressive Matrices. Improvement in working memory, in other words, transferred to improvement on a task the children weren't training for. . . .

"At that time there was pretty much no evidence whatsoever that you can train on one particular task and get transfer to another task that was totally different," Jaeggi says. That is, while most skills improve with practice, the improvement is generally domain-specific: you don't get better at Sudoku by doing crosswords. And fluid intelligence was not just another skill; it was the ultimate cognitive ability underlying all mental skills, and supposedly immune from the usual benefits of practice. To find that training on a working-memory task could result in an increase in fluid intelligence would be cognitive psychology's equivalent of discovering particles traveling faster than light. 11

Together, Jaeggi and Buschkuehl decided to see if they could replicate the Klingberg transfer effect. To do so, they used the N-back test as the basis of a training regimen. As seen in the game played by the children at Washington-McKinley, N-back challenges users to remember something — the location of a cat or the sound of a particular letter — that is presented immediately before (1-back), the time before last (2-back), the time before that (3-back), and so on. If you do well at 2-back, the computer moves you up to 3-back. Do well at that, and you'll jump to 4-back. On the other hand, if you do poorly at any level, you're nudged down a level. The point is to keep the game just challenging enough that you stay fully engaged. 12

To make it harder, Jaeggi and Buschkuehl used what's called the dual N-back task. As a random sequence of letters is heard over earphones, a square appears on a computer screen moving, apparently at random, among eight possible spots on a grid. Your mission is to keep track of both the letters and the squares. (See figure 1 on p. 216.) So, for example, at the 3-back level, you would press one button on the keyboard if you recall that a spoken letter is the same one that was spoken three times ago, while simultaneously pressing another key if the square on the screen is in the same place as it was three times ago. The point of making the task more difficult is to overwhelm the usual task-specific strategies that people develop with games like chess and Scrabble. "We wanted to train underlying attention and working-memory skills," Jaeggi says. Jaeggi and Buschkuehl gave progressive matrix tests to students at Bern and then asked them to practice the dual N-back for 20 to 25 minutes a day. When they retested them at the end of a few weeks, they were surprised and delighted to find significant improvement. Jaeggi and Buschkuehl later expanded the study 13

FIG. 1.   Games based on N-back tests require players to remember the location of a symbol or the sound of a particular letter presented just before (1-back), the time before last (2-back), the time before that (3-back) and so on. Some researchers say that playing games like this may actually make us smarter. (To play a free, online version of the N-back game, go to http://www.soakyourhead.com/dual-n-back.aspx)

The N-Back Game

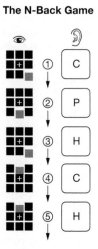

as postdoctoral fellows at the University of Michigan, in the laboratory of John Jonides, professor of psychology and neuroscience. "Those two things, working memory and cognitive control, I think, are at the heart of intellectual functioning," Jonides told me when I met with him, Jaeggi and Buschkuehl in their basement office. "They are part of what differentiates us from other species. They allow us to selectively process information from the environment, and to use that information to do all kinds of problem-solving and reasoning."

14   When they finally published their study, in a May 2008 issue of *Proceedings of the National Academy of Sciences*, the results were striking (Jaeggi et al., "Improving"). Before training, participants were able to correctly answer between 9 and 10 of the matrix questions. Afterward, the 34 young adults who participated in dual N-back training for 12 weeks correctly answered approximately one extra matrix item, while those who trained for 17 weeks were able to answer about three more correctly. After 19 weeks, the improvement was 4.4 additional matrix questions. "It's not just a little bit higher," Jaeggi says. "It's a large effect."

15   The study did have its shortcomings. "We used just one reasoning task to measure their performance," she says. "We showed improvements in this one fluid-reasoning task, which is usually highly correlated with other measures as well." Whether the improved scores on the Raven's would translate into school grades, job performance and real-world gains remained to be seen. Even so, accompanying the paper's publication in *Proceedings* was a commentary titled "Increasing Fluid Intelligence Is Possible After All," in which the senior psychologist Robert J. Sternberg (now provost at Oklahoma State University) called Jaeggi's and Buschkuehl's research "pioneer-

ing" (Sternberg 6792). The study, he wrote, "seems, in some measure, to resolve the debate over whether fluid intelligence is, in at least some meaningful measure, trainable."

For some, the debate is far from settled. Randall Engle, a leading intelligence researcher at the Georgia Tech School of Psychology, views the proposition that I.Q. can be increased through training with a skepticism verging on disdain. . . . The most prominent takedown of I.Q. training came in June 2010, when the neuroscientist Adrian Owen published the results of an experiment conducted in coordination with the BBC television show "Bang Goes the Theory." After inviting British viewers to participate, Owen recruited 11,430 of them to take a battery of I.Q. tests before and after a six-week online program designed to replicate commercially available "brain building" software. (The N-back was not among the tasks offered.) "Although improvements were observed in every one of the cognitive tasks that were trained," he concluded in the journal *Nature*, "no evidence was found for transfer effects to untrained tasks, even when those tasks were cognitively closely related" (775).   16

But even Owen, reached by telephone, told me that he respects Jaeggi's studies and looks forward to seeing others like it. If before Jaeggi's study, scientists' attempts to raise I.Q. were largely unsuccessful, other lines of evidence have long supported the view that intelligence is far from immutable. While studies of twins suggest that intelligence has a fixed genetic component, at least 20 to 50 percent of the variation in I.Q. is due to other factors, whether social, school or family-based. Even more telling, average I.Q.'s have been rising steadily for a century as access to schooling and technology expands, a phenomenon known as the Flynn Effect. As Jaeggi and others see it, the genetic component of intelligence is undeniable, but it functions less like the genes that control for eye color and more like the complex of interacting genes that affect weight and height (both of which have also been rising, on average, for decades). . . .   17

Torkel Klingberg, meanwhile, has continued studying the effects of training children with his own variety of working-memory tasks. In October 2010, a company he founded to offer those tasks as a package through psychologists and other training professionals, was bought by Pearson Education, the world's largest provider of educational assessment tools (*Cogmed*). Despite continuing academic debates, other commercial enterprises are rushing in to offer an array of "brain building" games that make bold promises to improve all kinds of cognitive abilities. Within a block of each other in downtown San Francisco are two of the best known. Posit Science, among the oldest in the field, remains relatively small, giving special attention to those with cognitive disorders. Lumosity began in 2007 and is now by far the biggest of the services, with more than 20 million   18 subscribers. Its games include a sleeker, more entertaining version of the N-back task.

19   In Chicago Heights, the magic was definitely not happening for one boy staring blankly at the black cats in the Mac Lab. Sipping from a juice box he held in one hand, jabbing at a computer key over and over with the other, he periodically sneaked a peek at his instructor, a look of abject boredom on his freckled face. "That's the biggest challenge we have as researchers in this field," Jaeggi told me, "to get people engaged and motivated to play our working-memory game and to really stick with it. Some people say it's hard and really frustrating and really challenging and tiring."

20   In a follow-up to their 2008 study in young adults, Jaeggi, Buschkuehl and their colleagues published a paper last year that described the effects of N-back training in 76 elementary- and middle-school children from a broad range of social and economic backgrounds (Jaeggi et al., "Short- and Long-Term"). Only those children who improved substantially on the N-back training had gains in fluid intelligence. But their improvement wasn't linked to how high they originally scored on Raven's; children at all levels of cognitive ability improved. And those gains persisted for three months after the training ended, a heartening sign of possible long-term benefits. Although it's unknown how much longer the improvement in fluid intelligence will last, Jaeggi doubts the effects will be permanent without continued practice. "Do we think they're now smarter for the rest of their lives by just four weeks of training?" she asks. "We probably don't think so. We think of it like physical training: if you go running for a month, you increase your fitness. But does it stay like that for the rest of your life? Probably not." . . .

21   Of course, in order to improve, you need to do the training. For some, whether brilliant or not so much, training may simply be too hard—or too boring. To increase motivation, the study in Chicago Heights offers third graders a chance to win a $10 prepaid Visa card each week. In collaboration with researchers from the University of Chicago's Initiative on Chicago Price Theory (directed by Steven D. Levitt, of "Freakonomics" fame), the study pits the kids against one another, sometimes one on one, sometimes in groups, to see if competition will spur them to try harder. Each week, whichever group receives more points on the N-back is rewarded with the Visa cards. To isolate the motivating effects of the cash prizes, a group of fourth graders is undergoing N-back training with the same black-cats-in-haunted-house program, but with no Visa cards, only inexpensive prizes—plastic sunglasses, inflatable globes—as a reward for not talking and staying in their seats.

22   The boy tapping randomly at his computer without even paying attention to the game? He was in the fourth-grade class. Although the study is not yet complete, perhaps it will show that the opportunity to increase intelligence is not motivation enough. Just like physical exercise, cognitive

exercises may prove to be up against something even more resistant to training than fluid intelligence: human nature.

Works Cited

Cogmed Working Memory Training. Torkel Klingberg, Pearson Assessments. 2011. Web. 14 Aug. 2012.

Engle, Randall. Personal interview. N.d.

Jaeggi, Susanne M. Personal interview. N.d.

Jaeggi, Susanne M., Martin Buschkuehl, John Jonides, and Walter J Perrig. "Improving Fluid Intelligence with Training on Working Memory." *Proceedings of the National Academy of Sciences of the United States of America* 105.19 (2008): 6829–33. Web. 14 Aug. 2012.

Jaeggi, Susanne M., Martin Buschkuehl, John Jonides, and Priti Shah. "Short- and Long-Term Benefits of Cognitive Training." *Proceedings of the National Academy of Sciences of the United States of America* 108.25 (2011): 10081–86. Web. 14 Aug. 2012.

Klingberg, Torkel, Hans Forssberg, and Helena Westerberg. "Training of Working Memory in Children with ADHD." *Journal of Clinical and Experimental Neuropsychology* 24.6 (2002): 781–91. *Academic Search Complete.* Web. 14 Aug. 2012.

READING FOR MEANING

This section presents three activities that will help you think about the meanings in Hurley's explanation of fluid intelligence. Your instructor may ask you to do one or more of these activities in class or online.

1. **Read to Summarize.** Write a sentence or two explaining the concept of *fluid intelligence* as Hurley defines it in this essay.

   For more help with summarizing, see Chapter 10, pp. 518–19.

2. **Read to Respond.** Write a paragraph analyzing your initial reactions to Hurley's explanation of fluid intelligence. For example, consider anything that resonates with your experience or that seems contradictory, surprising, or fascinating, such as:

   - The comparison Hurley makes to help define fluid intelligence — "What long-term memory is to crystallized intelligence, working memory is to fluid intelligence" (par. 6) — and his subsequent explanation of the relationship between working memory and fluid intelligence. Is fluid intelligence like working memory? In what ways?

     You may also try evaluating the logic of an argument; see Chapter 10, pp. 530–32.

   - The relationship between motivation and payment that Hurley decribes in paragraph 21.

 Take a quiz to check your reading and vocabulary comprehension:
bedfordstmartins.com/readingcritically

3. **Read to Analyze Assumptions.** Write a paragraph or two analyzing an assumption you find intriguing in Hurley's essay. For example:

Assumptions about the value of social-science-based evidence. Hurley supports his assertions with studies from social scientists who conduct experiments on human beings to support a *hypothesis* or confirm conclusions presumed to be likely. To think critically about the assumptions in this essay related to the value of social-scientific evidence, ask yourself questions like these:

- Hurley asserts that "[s]ince the first reliable intelligence test was created just over a hundred years ago, researchers have searched for a way to increase scores meaningfully, with little success" (par. 10). He goes on to cite several studies showing that intelligence test scores can be increased. What effect does citing these studies have on Hurley's readers? Does citing scientific research help convince readers that researchers may now have found a way to increase scores?

- Hurley quotes researchers Jaeggi and Buschkuehl as saying that the point of making the N-back test difficult "is to overwhelm the usual task-specific strategies that people develop. . . ." (par. 13). In other words, Jaeggi and Buschkuehl assume that test-takers who are able to solve new problems are more intelligent than those who can't. Is it possible that the ability to solve new problems may not be a reliable measure of intelligence?

Assumptions about the validity of analogies. Writers often use **analogies**, comparisons that encourage readers to understand one thing in terms of another. But in order for the comparison to be helpful, the two things being compared must share some underlying quality. To think critically about the value of the analogies Hurley uses, consider carefully the relationship among the items being compared:

- Hurley compares working memory to fluid intelligence (par. 6). Working memory is memory that is retained only briefly, such as a telephone number that someone needs to know only long enough to make the call. Fluid intelligence is the ability to solve novel problems. So is Hurley's comparison fair? Is fluid intelligence really like working memory? In what ways?

- In paragraph 20, one of the researchers that Hurley interviews compares the increase in fluid intelligence that some people develop after spending time playing the N-back game with physical fitness developed after exercise. Is this a fair comparison? In what ways are the development of fluid intelligence and the development of stronger biceps the same? How are they different?

READING LIKE A WRITER

INTEGRATING SOURCES SMOOTHLY

Writers of concept explanations nearly always conduct research, incorporate information (summaries, paraphrases, and quotations) from sources into their writing, and contextualize their sources so that readers recognize them as relevant and reliable. For example, when describing a study to support her claim that "[w]e even find 'introverts' in the animal kingdom" (par. 13), Cain names the researcher and identifies his academic specialty: "In an illustrative experiment, David Sloan Wilson, a Binghamton evolutionary biologist, dropped metal traps into a pond of pumpkinseed sunfish" (par. 14). Bailey, explaining the dating system of "calling," cites sources from the period (early-twentieth-century editions of *Harper's Bazaar* and the *Ladies' Home Journal*), assuming readers will recognize popular magazines of the period as relevant sources for a description of courtship rituals.

Analyze & Write

Write a paragraph or two analyzing the kinds of material Dan Hurley incorporates from sources, and how he identifies his sources so that his readers know that they are relevant and *credible* (reliable and believable).

1. Skim the essay, highlighting places where Hurley quotes, paraphrases, or summarizes information from sources. How does Hurley identify those sources? What information does he provide, and how does this information help readers know the source is relevant and reliable?

2. Now reread the quotations in paragraphs 2, 7, 9, 11, 13–16, and 19–20. Why do you think Hurley decided to use quotations, rather than summaries, in these places?

3. Why is simply identifying sources with a word or two in the text generally sufficient for nonacademic situations but not for academic ones? Given your experience reading online, do you think hyperlinks serve a purpose similar to that of formal citations? Why or why not?

ANALYZING VISUALS

Write a paragraph analyzing the illustration in Hurley's concept (figure 1) and explaining what it contributes to the essay. To do the analysis, you can use the Criteria for Analyzing Visuals chart in Chapter 12, on pp. 611–12. Don't feel you have to answer all of the questions on the chart: focus on

(continued)

those that seem most productive in helping you write a paragraph-length analysis. To help you get started, consider adding these questions that specifically refer to Hurley's visual:

- Does this illustration clarify the N-back game for you? If so, how, and if not, can you think of a better way to present it — some other kind of visual, an explanation dedicated just to understanding the game, or something else?

- Describe the symbols in this game: can you recognize and decode them easily, or are some of them difficult to follow?

- How would you use this illustration to engage in the N-back game — is there enough information in it for you to create the game on your own?

Linh Kieu Ngo

Cannibalism: It Still Exists

Linh Kieu Ngo wrote this essay when he was a first-year college student. In it, he explains a concept of importance in anthropology and of wide general interest — cannibalism, the eating of human flesh by other humans. Most Americans may have heard about survival cannibalism, but few may know about dietary and ritual cannibalism and their historical importance. Ngo explains all of these concepts in his essay.

- *Before you read, think about any examples of survival cannibalism you may know about (the people in the book* Alive, *the members of the Donner Party, etc.). Under what conditions has survival cannibalism been practiced?*

- *As you read, pay attention to any cues Ngo gives to keep readers on track. Consider his rhetorical situation: writing about what could be a repulsive practice for some members of his audience. What strategies does he use to keep his audience engaged?*

Fifty-five Vietnamese refugees fled to Malaysia on a small fishing boat to escape communist rule in their country following the Vietnam War. During their escape attempt, the captain was shot by the coast guard. The boat and its passengers managed to outrun the coast guard to the open sea, but they had lost the only person who knew the way to Malaysia, the captain. 1

The men onboard tried to navigate the boat, but after a week fuel ran out and they drifted farther out to sea. Their supply of food and water was gone; people were starving, and some of the elderly were near death. The men managed to produce a small amount of drinking water by boiling salt water, using dispensable wood from the boat to create a small fire near the stern. They also tried to fish, but had little success. 2

A month went by, and the old and weak died. At first, the crew threw the dead overboard, but later, out of desperation, the crew turned to human flesh as a source of food. Some people vomited as they attempted to eat it, while others refused to resort to cannibalism and see the bodies of their loved ones sacrificed for food. Those who did not eat died of starvation, and their bodies in turn became food for others. Human flesh was cut out, washed in salt water, and hung to dry for preservation. The liquids inside the cranium were eaten to quench thirst. The livers, kidneys, heart, stomach, and intestines were boiled and eaten. 3

Five months passed before a whaling vessel discovered the drifting boat, looking like a graveyard of bones. There was only one survivor. 4

 For an additional student reading, go to **bedfordstmartins.com/readingcritically**.

5　　　Cannibalism, the act of human beings eating human flesh (Sagan 2), has a long history and continues to hold interest and create controversy. Many books and research reports offer examples of cannibalism, but a few scholars have questioned whether cannibalism was ever practiced anywhere, except in cases of ensuring survival in times of famine or isolation (Askenasy 43–54). Recently, some scholars have tried to understand why people in the West have been so eager to attribute cannibalism to non-Westerners (Barker, Hulme, and Iversen). Cannibalism has long been a part of American popular culture. For example, Mark Twain's "Cannibalism in the Cars" tells a humorous story about cannibalism by well-to-do travelers on a train stranded in a snowstorm, and cannibalism is still a popular subject for jokes ("Cannibals").

6　　　If we assume there is some reality to the reports about cannibalism, how can we best understand this concept? Cannibalism can be broken down into two main categories: exocannibalism, the eating of outsiders or foreigners, and endocannibalism, the eating of members of one's own social group (Shipman 70). Within these categories are several functional types of cannibalism, three of the most common being survival cannibalism, dietary cannibalism, and religious and ritual cannibalism.

7　　　Survival cannibalism occurs when people trapped without food have to decide "whether to starve or eat fellow humans" (Shipman 70). In the case of the Vietnamese refugees, the crew and passengers on the boat ate human flesh to stay alive. They did not kill people to get human flesh for nourishment, but instead waited until the people had died. Even after human carcasses were sacrificed as food, the boat people ate only enough to survive. Another case of survival cannibalism occurred in 1945, when General Douglas MacArthur's forces cut supply lines to Japanese troops stationed in the Pacific Islands. In one incident, Japanese troops were reported to have sacrificed the Arapesh people of northeastern New Guinea for food in order to avoid death by starvation (Tuzin 63). The most famous example of survival cannibalism in American history comes from the diaries, letters, and interviews of survivors of the California-bound Donner Party, who in the winter of 1846 were snowbound in the Sierra Nevada Mountains for five months. Thirty-five of eighty-seven adults and children died, and some of them were eaten (Hart 116–17; Johnson).

8　　　Unlike survival cannibalism, in which human flesh is eaten as a last resort after a person has died, in dietary cannibalism, humans are purchased or trapped for food and then eaten as a part of a culture's traditions. In addition, survival cannibalism often involves people eating other people of the same origins, whereas dietary cannibalism usually involves people eating foreigners.

9　　　In the Miyanmin society of the west Sepik interior of Papua New Guinea, villagers do not value human flesh over that of pigs or marsupials because human flesh is part of their diet (Poole 17). The Miyanmin people observe no differences in "gender, kinship, ritual status, and bodily substance"; they eat anyone, even their own dead. In this respect, then, they practice both endocannibalism and exocannibalism; and to ensure a constant supply of human flesh for food, they raid neighboring tribes and drag their victims back to their village to be eaten (Poole 11). Perhaps, in the history of this society, there was at one time a shortage of wild game to be hunted for food, and because people were more plentiful than fish, deer, rabbits, pigs, or cows, survival cannibalism was adopted as a last resort. Then, as their culture developed, the Miyanmin may have retained the practice of dietary cannibalism, which has endured as a part of their culture.

Similar to the Miyanmin, the people of the Leopard and Alligator socie-   10
ties in South America eat human flesh as part of their cultural tradition. Practicing dietary exocannibalism, the Leopard people hunt in groups, with one member wearing the skin of a leopard to conceal the face. They ambush their victims in the forest and carry their victims back to their village to be eaten. The Alligator people also hunt in groups, but they hide themselves under a canoelike submarine that resembles an alligator, then swim close to a fisherman's or trader's canoe to overturn it and catch their victims (MacCormack 54).

Religious or ritual cannibalism is different from survival and dietary   11
cannibalism in that it has a ceremonial purpose rather than one of nourishment. Sometimes only a single victim is sacrificed in a ritual, while at other times many are sacrificed. For example, the Bangala tribe of the Congo River in central Africa honors a deceased chief or leader by purchasing, sacrificing, and feasting on slaves (Sagan 53). The number of slaves sacrificed is determined by how highly the tribe members revered the deceased leader.

Ritual cannibalism among South American Indians often serves as   12
revenge for the dead. Like the Bangalas, some South American tribes kill their victims to be served as part of funeral rituals, with human sacrifices denoting that the deceased was held in high honor. Also like the Bangalas, these tribes use outsiders as victims. Unlike the Bangalas, however, the Indians sacrifice only one victim instead of many in a single ritual. For example, when a warrior of a tribe is killed in battle, the family of the warrior forces a victim to take the identity of the warrior. The family adorns the victim with the deceased warrior's belongings and may even force him to marry the deceased warrior's wives. But once the family believes the victim has assumed the spiritual identity of the deceased warrior, the family kills him. The children in the tribe soak their hands in the victim's blood to symbolize their revenge of the warrior's death. Elderly women from the tribe drink the victim's blood and then cut up his body for roasting and eating (Sagan 53–54). By sacrificing a victim, the people of the tribe believe that the death of the warrior has been avenged and the soul of the deceased can rest in peace.

13   In the villages of certain African tribes, only a small part of a dead body is used in ritual cannibalism. In these tribes, where the childbearing capacity of women is highly valued, women are obligated to eat small, raw fragments of genital parts during fertility rites. Elders of the tribe supervise this ritual to ensure that the women will be fertile. In the Bimin-Kuskusmin tribe, for instance, a widow eats a small, raw fragment of flesh from the penis of her deceased husband in order to enhance her future fertility and reproductive capacity. Similarly, a widower may eat a raw fragment of flesh from his deceased wife's vagina along with a piece of her bone marrow; by eating her flesh, he hopes to strengthen the fertility capacity of his daughters borne by his dead wife, and by eating her bone marrow, he honors her reproductive capacity. Also, when an elder woman of the village who has shown great reproductive capacity dies, her uterus and the interior parts of her vagina are eaten by other women who hope to further benefit from her reproductive power (Poole 16–17).

14   Members of developed societies in general practice none of these forms of cannibalism, with the occasional exception of survival cannibalism when the only alternative is starvation. It is possible, however, that our distant-past ancestors were cannibals who through the eons turned away from the practice. We are, after all, descended from the same ancestors as the Miyanmin, the Alligator, and the Leopard people, and survival cannibalism shows that people are capable of eating human flesh when they have no other choice.

Works Cited

Askenasy, Hans. *Cannibalism: From Sacrifice to Survival.* Amherst: Prometheus, 1994. Print.

Barker, Francis, Peter Hulme, and Margaret Iversen, eds. *Cannibalism and the New World.* Cambridge: Cambridge UP, 1998. Print.

Brown, Paula, and Donald Tuzin, eds. *The Ethnography of Cannibalism.* Washington: Society for Psychological Anthropology, 1983. Print.

"Cannibals." *Jokes and Funny Stories.* N.p. 2006. Web. 4 Apr. 2009.

Hart, James D. *A Companion to California.* Berkeley: U of California P, 1987. Print.

Johnson, Kristin. "New Light on the Donner Party." Kristin Johnson, 31 Jan. 2006. Web. 4 Apr. 2009.

MacCormack, Carol. "Human Leopard and Crocodile." Brown and Tuzin 54–55.

Poole, Fitz John Porter. "Cannibals, Tricksters, and Witches." Brown and Tuzin 11, 16–17.

Sagan, Eli. *Cannibalism.* New York: Harper, 1976. Print.

Shipman, Pat. "The Myths and Perturbing Realities of Cannibalism." *Discover* Mar. 1987: 70+. Print.

Tuzin, Donald. "Cannibalism and Arapesh Cosmology." Brown and Tuzin 61–63.

Twain, Mark. "Cannibalism in the Cars." *The Complete Short Stories of Mark Twain.* Ed. Charles Neider. New York: Doubleday, 1957. 9–16. Print.

READING FOR MEANING

This section presents three activities that will help you think about the meanings in Ngo's concept explanation. Your instructor may ask you to do one or more of these activities in class or online.

1. **Read to Summarize.** Write a sentence or two explaining the concept of cannibalism.

For more help with summarizing, see Chapter 10, pp. 518–19.

2. **Read to Respond.** Write a paragraph analyzing your initial reactions to Ngo's essay. For example, consider writing anything that seems contradictory, surprising, or fascinating, such as:

   - The anecdotes about the Vietnamese refugees (pars. 1–4) and the Donner Party in California (par. 7).

You may also try reflecting on challenges to your beliefs and values; see Chapter 10, pp. 526–27.

   - The idea that cannibalism may be performed for ceremonial or ritual purposes (par. 11).

3. **Read to Analyze Assumptions.** Write a paragraph or two analyzing an assumption you find intriguing in Ngo's essay. For example:

   Assumptions about how to deal with the dead. Ngo discusses several tribes that practice cannibalism in some form to honor the dead or to take on the good traits of the dead (pars. 11–13). The people in these tribes believe that even a small portion of a human being can carry the meaning of the whole person. Many cultures and religions of the world practice a form of this belief, although they may substitute another substance to represent the human. Yet as Ngo reports, the practice of cannibalism, even of people who are already dead, is controversial (par. 5). To think critically about assumptions in this essay related to how people deal with their dead, ask yourself questions like these:

   - What beliefs and values come into play among those who find cannibalism disgusting?

   - How do people comfort themselves with portions of the bodies of the dead?

   Assumptions about what constitutes "developed societies." Ngo does not define "developed societies" (par. 14), so he must assume that readers know what he means. Many of the tribes he describes, though, might think our society is anything but "developed." To think critically about assumptions in this essay related to "development," ask yourself questions like these:

   - What might people in Western industrialized societies do that would make people in "undeveloped societies" uncomfortable?

   - How do you feel about the assumptions behind the idea of some societies' being "developed" while others are not?

Take a quiz to check your reading and vocabulary comprehension:
bedfordstmartins.com/readingcritically

READING LIKE A WRITER

ORGANIZING THE INFORMATION CLEARLY AND LOGICALLY

Think of an essay explaining a concept as a logical, interrelated sequence of topics. Each topic or main idea follows the preceding topic in a way that makes sense to readers and is cued by one or more of the following:

- a forecasting statement
- a topic sentence
- a brief summary of what came before
- one or more transitions

We see all of these *cueing devices* in Ngo's essay. Note how in the first several paragraphs Ngo cues readers by using time markers:

> . . . following the Vietnam War. During their escape attempt . . . (par. 1)
>
> . . . after a week . . . (par. 2)
>
> A month went by . . . At first . . . (par. 3)
>
> Five months passed . . . (par. 4)

He also guides readers with strong transitions in the first sentence of every paragraph. These transitions refer to the content of the previous paragraph, often including brief summaries, and forecast the content of the upcoming paragraph. Usually, the first sentence in the paragraph is also the **topic sentence**, a sentence announcing the idea the paragraph (or a series of paragraphs) will develop. For example, look at the last sentence of paragraph 6 and the first sentence of paragraph 7:

Forecast   Within these categories are several functional types of cannibalism, three
¶ topic   of the most common being survival cannibalism, dietary cannibalism, and
Topic   religious and ritual cannibalism.
sentence   Survival cannibalism occurs when people trapped without food have
          to decide "whether to starve or eat fellow humans" (Shipman 70). . . .

Analyze & Write

Write a paragraph or two analyzing how Ngo uses these strategies elsewhere to guide readers through his explanation of cannibalism:

1. Skim paragraphs 8–14, underlining or highlighting transitions, forecasting statements, and topic sentences.

2. Make an outline of the transitions. How do they help readers follow the logic of the essay?

3. Examine the way the transitions are constructed. Have you noticed similar constructions in any of the other reading selections in this book or elsewhere?

Reviewing What Makes Concept Explanations Effective

An effective concept explanation

- uses appropriate explanatory strategies;
- organizes the information clearly and logically;
- integrates sources smoothly into the writing;
- engages readers' interest.

Analyze & Write

Write a brief evaluation—positive, negative, or mixed—of one of the readings in this chapter, explaining why you think it succeeds or fails as an explanation of a concept. Be sure to consider the characteristics that distinguish concept explanations, as well as how successful the author has been in communicating her or his purpose to the intended audience. You may also want to consider the effect the medium of presentation had on decisions the writer made.

A GUIDE TO WRITING ESSAYS EXPLAINING CONCEPTS

As you've read and discussed the reading selections in this chapter, you have probably done a good deal of analytical writing. Your instructor may assign a capstone project to explain a concept of your own. Having learned how writers help their readers by organizing the explanation clearly and logically, integrating sources, using appropriate explanatory strategies, and making their writing engaging to their audience, you can now approach explaining a concept confidently as a writer. This Guide to Writing offers detailed suggestions for writing concept explanations and resources to help you meet the special challenges this kind of writing presents.

THE WRITING ASSIGNMENT

Write an explanation of a concept that interests you enough to study further.

- Choose a concept that you know a good deal about or about which you'd like to learn.
- Consider what your readers already know about the concept and how your explanation can add to their knowledge.
- Research material that helps clarify or provides examples of your concept.
- Consider the most effective writing strategies to convey your concept.
- Think about how to engage your readers' interest in your concept and guide them through your explanation.

WRITING A DRAFT

INVENTION, PLANNING, AND COMPOSING

The following activities will help you choose a concept, consider what you and your readers need to know, determine how best to explain your concept, and gather and sort through the information you need to explain your concept clearly and logically.

Choosing a Concept

Rather than limiting yourself to the first concept that comes to mind, take a few minutes to consider your options. Below are some criteria that can help you choose a promising concept to explain, followed by suggestions for the types of concepts you might consider writing about.

Choose a concept that

- you understand well or feel eager to learn more about;

- you think is important and will interest your readers;

- you can research sufficiently in the allotted time;

- is focused narrowly enough for you to explain fully in the length prescribed by your instructor;

- provides you with a clear purpose, such as to inform readers about an important idea or theory, to show how the concept has promoted original thinking and research, to help readers better understand the concept, or to demonstrate knowledge of the concept and the ability to apply it.

Below are some concepts from various fields of study:

- *Literature, philosophy, and art:* figurative language, postcolonialism, modernism, postmodernism, irony, epic; causality, syllogism, existentialism, nihilism, logical positivism, determinism, cubism, iconography, pop art, conceptual art, performance art, graffiti, Dadaism, surrealism, expressionism

- *Business management:* autonomous work group, quality circle, management by objectives, zero-based budgeting, benchmarking, focus group, pods, strike, minimum wage

- *Psychology:* phobia, narcissism, fetish, emotional intelligence, divergent and convergent thinking, behaviorism, Jungian archetype, Ringelmann effect, leadership, anxiety management, aggression, visualization

- *Government and law:* one person/one vote, federalism, socialism, theocracy, separation of church and state, exclusionary rule, political machine, political action committee, Astroturfing, Electoral College; arbitration, liability, reasonable doubt, sexual harassment, nondisclosure agreement, assumption of evidence

- *Biology and environmental studies:* photosynthesis, ecosystem, plasmolysis, phagocytosis, DNA, species, punctuated evolution, homozygosity, diffusion; acid rain, recycling, ozone depletion, toxic waste, endangered species, greenhouse effect, global warming, hydrologic cycle, El Niño, tsunami, superstorm, xeriscape

- *Nutrition and public health:* vegetarianism, bulimia, diabetes, food allergy, aerobic exercise, obesity, Maillard reaction, sustainability, locavore, epidemic, vaccination, drug abuse, contraception, AIDS education, disability, autism

- *Physical sciences and math:* gravity, mass, weight, energy, quantum theory, law of definite proportions, osmotic pressure, first law of thermodynamics, entropy, free energy, fusion, boundedness; complex numbers, exponent, polynomial, factoring, Pythagorean theorem, continuity, derivative, infinity

Analyzing Your Readers

Write for a few minutes, analyzing your potential readers:

- What might my potential readers already know about the concept or the field of study to which it applies? (Even if you are writing only for your instructor, you should consider what he or she knows about your concept.)

- What kinds of examples or information could I provide that readers will find new, useful, interesting, or amusing? How might I clarify misconceptions or faulty assumptions?

- Will a more or less formal writing style be appropriate for my readers?

- What kinds of sources will my readers find credible?

- What questions might they ask? What might they be interested in learning more about?

Researching the Concept

You will probably need to research your concept in three stages:

1. Gain an overview of the concept by considering what you already know and what you need to learn, and conducting some preliminary research.

2. Choose an aspect of your concept to focus on, an aspect that you can explore thoroughly in the space and time you have.

3. Conduct enough research to learn about this aspect of the concept.

Determining What You Know (and What You Don't Know).   You can determine what you already know about your concept by explaining it briefly, using one or more of the strategies below as a starting point:

▶ My concept can be divided into .... types or categories: ...., ..., ..., and ....

▶ Examples of my concept include ...., ..., and ....

- My concept is a .... [member of a larger category] that is/does/has .... [defining characteristics].
- My concept is [similar to/different from] .... in these ways: ...., ..., and ....

Hint: You may want to review your lecture notes, textbook, or other course materials to see how others have explained your concept.

Try to answer the questions you think your readers will have.

Conducting Background Research. If you had trouble writing a brief explanation, consider talking to experts, such as a professor or teaching assistant for an academic topic, or your boss or supervisor for a work-related topic. You could also post a question on a blog or in a chat room devoted to this subject.

Alternatively, you may want to consult some general reference sources or a reference database, such as the Gale Virtual Reference Library, Sage Reference Online, or Web of Science, to conduct a preliminary search on your concept. (Check with a librarian to find out which reference databases your school subscribes to.) After reading articles in several relevant reference sources, list the following:

- names of scholars, experts, or respected authors on your subject;
- terms, phrases, or synonyms that you might use as search terms later;
- interesting aspects of the concept that you might want to focus on.

To conduct an Internet search on your concept, start by entering the word *overview* or *definition* with the name of your concept, and then skim the top ten search results to get a general sense of your topic. You can bookmark useful links or save a copy using a free online tool like Zotero. Check with your instructor for special requirements, such as submitting photocopies or printouts of your sources or using a particular documentation style. See Chapter 11, pp. 555–68, to learn more about conducting research and assessing reliability.

Hint: Sites with the *.edu, .gov,* or *.org* domain are more likely to be reliable than sites with the *.com* domain.

Choosing an Aspect of Your Concept to Focus On. List two or three aspects of your concept that interest you and then answer these questions:

- Why does this aspect of the concept interest me? What aspect of my concept do I think my readers would be interested in learning about?
- How is it relevant to my life, family, community, work, or studies? How can I make it relevant to my readers' lives?
- What are my readers likely to know about the concept? How can I build on what they already know?

Conducting Additional Research on Your Focused Concept.   Your instructor may expect you to do in-depth research or may limit the number and type of sources you can use. Readers will want to be sure that your sources are reliable and relevant, and may want to read your sources for themselves, so be sure to include enough information in your notes to put your sources in context and to cite them accurately.

Formulating a Working Thesis Statement

A working thesis will help you begin drafting your essay purposefully. Your thesis should announce the concept and focus of the explanation, and may also forecast the main topics. (Forecasts, though not required, can be helpful to readers, especially when the concept is unfamiliar or the explanation is complicated.) Here are two example thesis statements from the readings.

Concept
Focus
Forecast

This does us all a grave disservice, because shyness and introversion — or more precisely, the careful, sensitive temperament from which both often spring — are not just normal. They are valuable. And they may be essential to the survival of our species. (Cain, par. 5)

Cannibalism can be broken down into two main categories: exocannibalism, the eating of outsiders or foreigners, and endocannibalism, the eating of members of one's own social group (Shipman 70). Within these categories are several functional types of cannibalism, three of the most common being survival cannibalism, dietary cannibalism, and religious and ritual cannibalism. (Ngo, par. 6)

Using Appropriate Explanatory Strategies

To explain your concept effectively, consider how you would define it, what examples you can provide, how similar or different it is from other concepts, how it happens or gets done, and what its causes or effects are. Your goal is not only to inform but also to engage. The following sentence strategies may help you find the best ways to explain your concept.

- What are the concept's defining characteristics? What broader class does it belong to, and how does it differ from other members of its class? (*definition*)

  ▸ .... [Concept] is a .... in which .... [list defining characteristics].

- What examples or anecdotes can make the concept less abstract, more focused, and more understandable? (*example*)

  ▸ [Experts/scientists/etc.] first became aware of [concept] in [year], when .... (citation).

▶ Interest in .... [concept] has been [rising/declining/steady] [because of/ in spite of] [recent examples/a shortage of recent examples] like .... , ... , and ....

- How is this concept like or unlike related concepts with which your readers may be more familiar? (*comparison and contrast*)

  ▶ Many people think the term .... [concept] means .... , but it might be more accurate to say it means ....

  ▶ .... [concept] is similar in some ways to .... [similar concept]: .... , ... , and .... [list areas of similarity]. However, unlike .... [similar concept], it .... , ... , and .... [list areas of difference].

  ▶ .... [concept], a kind of [grown-up, children's, bigger, smaller, local, international, or other adjective] version of .... [similar concept], [is/does/has] ....

- How can an explanation of this concept be divided into parts to make it easier for readers to understand? (*classification*)

  ▶ Experts like .... [name of expert] say there are .... [number] [categories, types, subtypes, versions] of .... [concept], ranging from .... to .... (citations).

- How does this concept happen, or how does one go about doing it? (*process narration*)

  ▶ To perform .... [concept or task related to concept], a [person, performer, participant, etc.] starts by .... Then [he/she/it] must .... [verb], ... [verb], and .... [verb]. [Insert or remove sections as necessary.] The process ends when [he/she/it] .... [verb].

- What are this concept's known causes or effects? (*cause and effect*)

  ▶ .... [concept or concept-related result] happens because ....

  ▶ Before .... [concept or concept-related result] can [happen/take place/ occur], ... [identify a condition that has to be met first]. However, ... [that condition] isn't enough by itself: .... [second condition] must also [happen/take place/be established].

  ▶ Experts disagree over the causes of .... [concept]. Some, like .... [name 1], believe .... (citation). Others, like .... [name 2], contend that .... (citation).

Including Visuals

Think about whether visuals — tables, graphs, drawings, photographs — would make your explanation clearer. You could construct your own visuals, download materials from the Internet, or scan and import visuals from books and magazines. Visuals are not a requirement of an essay explaining a concept, as you can tell from the readings in this chapter (only one of which includes a visual), but they sometimes add a new dimension to your writing. If you include visuals you did not create yourself, be sure to cite the source(s) from which you borrow them.

Integrating Information from Sources

Summaries, paraphrases, and quotations from sources are frequently used to explain concepts or reinforce an explanation:

- Use a summary to give the gist of a research report or other information.

- Use a paraphrase to provide specific details or examples when the language of the source is not especially memorable.

- Use a quotation to emphasize source material that is particularly vivid or clear, to convey an expert's voice, or to discuss the source's choice of words.

Your readers will want you to explain how the ideas from the sources you cite reinforce the points you are making. So make sure you comment on your sources, making the relationship between your own ideas and the supporting information from sources absolutely clear.

When introducing quotations, paraphrases, or summaries, writers often use a signal phrase — the source author's name plus an appropriate verb — to alert readers to the fact that they are borrowing someone else's words or ideas. Often the verb is neutral, as with the following two examples:

> Credentials of source author
>
> Signal phrase (name + verb)
>
> The psychologist Gregory Feist found that many of the most creative people in a range of fields are introverts who are comfortable working in solitary conditions in which they can focus attention inward. (Cain, par. 21)

(Notice in the example above that the writer also mentions the source's credentials, which is often an option when introducing sources with a signal phrase.)

> "The courtship which grew out of the sturdy social roots [of the nineteenth century]," one author wrote, "comes through to us for what it was — a gracious ritual, with clearly defined roles for man and woman, in which everyone knew the measured music and the steps" (Moss, 1963, p. 151). (Bailey, par. 3)

Sometimes, however, writers choose a descriptive verb to introduce a source:

> Fasold stresses that language and culture are particularly unfair in treating women as the marked case because biologically it is the male that is marked. (Tannen, par. 24)

> The *Ladies' Home Journal* approvingly reported the case of six girls, workers in a box factory, who had formed a club and pooled part of their wages to pay the "janitress of a tenement house" to let them use her front room two evenings a week. (Bailey, par. 9)

By choosing carefully among a wide variety of precise verbs, you can convey the attitude or approach of the source as you integrate supporting information.

Notice that Linh Kieu Ngo does not use signal phrases to introduce his sources in the body of "Cannibalism: It Still Exists." Instead, he simply integrates the information from them into his sentences and uses parenthetical citations and entries in the Works Cited list to show readers where the information he borrows comes from. Here is an example from paragraph 9, in which Ngo includes a quotation together with information he paraphrases from his source:

Parenthetical citation (name & page number)
> The Miyanmin people observe no differences in "gender, kinship, ritual status, and bodily substance"; they eat anyone, even their own dead. In this respect, then, they practice both endocannibalism and exocannibalism; and to ensure a constant supply of human flesh for food, they raid neighboring tribes and drag their victims back to their village to be eaten (Poole, 11).

This strategy of integrating source material without using a signal phrase is useful when you want to emphasize the information and play down the source.

Organizing Your Concept Explanation Effectively for Your Readers

The forecasting statement from your thesis can act as an informal outline when writing about simpler concepts, but for more complex concepts a tentative formal outline may be more useful for organizing your concept explanation effectively for your readers. You might even want to make two or three different outlines before choosing the organization that looks most promising. For more help with outlining, see Chapter 10, pp. 515–17.

Try to introduce new material in stages, so that readers' understanding of the concept builds slowly but steadily. Including a topic sentence for each paragraph or group of paragraphs on a single topic may help readers follow your explanation.

Keep in mind that an essay explaining a concept is made up of four basic parts:

1. an attempt to engage readers' interest in the explanation

2. the thesis statement, announcing the concept and perhaps also forecasting the sequence of topics

3. a description or definition of the concept

4. the information about the concept, organized around a series of topics that reflect how the information has been divided up

An initial attempt to gain your readers' interest — by starting with an intriguing question or surprising example, for instance — could take as little space as two or three sentences or as much as four or five paragraphs, but you will certainly want to maintain your readers' interest throughout the essay by providing examples or information that readers will find new, useful, interesting, or amusing. (Reviewing your analysis of your readers, p. 232, can help you determine the most effective approach to gaining your readers' interest.)

The thesis statement is quite brief, usually only one or two sentences. One topic may require one or several paragraphs, and there can be few or many topics, depending on how the information has been organized.

Consider any outline you create tentative before you begin drafting. As you draft, you will usually see ways to improve on your original plan. Be ready to revise your outline, shift parts around, or drop or add parts as you draft.

Drafting Your Concept Explanation

By this point, you have done a lot of writing

- to focus your explanation and develop a working thesis statement;

- to organize your explanation clearly for your readers;

- to try out writing strategies that can help you explain your concept;

- to integrate information into your explanation smoothly and in a way that supports your own ideas.

Now stitch that material together to create a draft. The next two parts of this Guide to Writing will help you evaluate and improve it.

Considering a Useful Sentence Strategy

As you draft your essay, you will need to identify people, introduce terms, and present details to help readers understand the concept you are explaining. One way to accomplish these goals efficiently is to use appositives. An **appositive** is a word or group of words, usually based on a noun or a pronoun, that identifies or gives more information about another noun or pronoun just preceding it. Appositives that are not essential to the meaning of the sentence may be set off by a pair of commas, dashes, or parentheses, or introduced by a colon:

. . . this new style of courtship, dating, . . . (Bailey, par. 2)

Preceding noun(s)
Appositive

. . . shyness and introversion — or more precisely, the careful, sensitive temperament from which both often spring — . . . (Cain, par. 5)

True, the equation (male companionship plus money equals female companionship) was imbalanced. (Bailey, par. 27)

When the appositive is essential to understanding, then no punctuation is needed:

> . . . the term *date* was associated with the direct economic exchange of prostitution. . . . (Bailey, par. 22)

Appositives serve many different purposes, including the following:

- To identify and characterize a source

> In 1914, the *Ladies' Home Journal*, **a bastion of middle-class respectability**, used the term. . . . (Bailey, par. 7)

- To provide examples or more specific information

> The third woman's hair was wild, **a frosted blond avalanche falling over and beyond her shoulders**. (Tannen, par. 4)

- To introduce and define a new term

> Cannibalism, **the act of human beings eating human flesh** (Sagan 2), has a long history and continues to hold interest and create controversy. (Ngo, par. 5)

Appositives accomplish these and other purposes efficiently by enabling the writer to put related bits of information next to each other in the same sentence, thereby merging two potential sentences into one or shrinking a potential clause to a phrase. For example, compare the example from Ngo above with the sentences that follow:

> Cannibalism can be defined as the act of human beings eating human flesh. It has a long history and continues to hold interest and create controversy.

> Cannibalism, which can be defined as the act of human beings eating human flesh, has a long history and continues to hold interest and create controversy.

Both of these versions are readable and clear, but the version with the appositive saves four or five words, subordinates the definition of cannibalism to Ngo's main idea about history and controversy, and locates the definition exactly where readers need to see it, right after the word being defined.

In addition to using appositives, you can strengthen your concept explanation with other kinds of sentence strategies. For example, you may want to review the information earlier in this chapter and consult the Considering a Useful Sentence Strategy section on comparison-contrast in Chapter 6 (pp. 304–5).

EVALUATING THE DRAFT

GETTING A CONSTRUCTIVE CRITICAL READING

Getting a critical reading of your draft will help you see how to improve it. Your instructor may schedule class time for reading drafts, or you may want to ask a classmate or a tutor in the writing center to read your draft. Ask your reader to use the following guidelines and to write out a response for you to consult during your revision.

READING A DRAFT CRITICALLY

Read for a First Impression

1. **Read the draft without stopping, and then write a few sentences giving your general impression.**

2. **Identify one aspect of the draft that seems particularly effective.**

Read Again to Suggest Improvements

1. **Consider whether the concept is focused and explained clearly and fully.**

   - Restate briefly what you understand the concept to mean, indicating if you have any uncertainty or confusion about its meaning.

   - Identify the focus of the explanation and assess whether the focus seems appropriate, too broad, or too narrow for the intended readers.

   - If you can, suggest another, possibly more interesting, way to focus the explanation.

2. **Suggest ways of making the organization clearer or more effective.**

   - Indicate whether a thesis is needed or whether it could be improved; consider whether a forecasting statement is needed.

   - Consider whether the topics are logically organized and clearly presented. Point to any place where more than one topic seems to be discussed, and suggest places where topic sentences could be added or revised.

   - Comment on whether stronger transitions are needed, and point to any place where you do not know how something relates to what went before.

   - Comment on whether the topics are addressed in a logical order, and whether the conclusion gives you a sense of closure or leaves you hanging.

3. **Assess whether information from sources is integrated smoothly and acknowledged properly.**

   - Point to any place where a summary, paraphrase, or quotation is not smoothly integrated into the writer's sentence, and suggest ways the writer could use a signal phrase or provide context to integrate the source information more effectively.

   - Indicate any quotations that would have been just as effective if put in the writer's own words.

   - If sources are not acknowledged correctly, remind the writer to consult Chapter 11.

4. **Consider whether the information provided is likely to engage readers' interest.**

   - Point to any place where the information might seem obvious to readers or too elementary for them.

   - Think of unanswered questions readers might have about the concept. Try to suggest where additional information is needed.

   - Recommend new strategies the writer could usefully adopt to engage or inform readers. For example:

     1. defining the concept by indicating the broader category into which the concept falls and listing the characteristics that distinguish the concept

     2. giving examples to illustrate the meaning of the concept

     3. comparing the concept to a more familiar concept

     4. reporting known causes or effects of the concept

5. **Evaluate the effectiveness of visuals.**

   - Look at any visuals in the essay, and tell the writer what, if anything, they contribute to your understanding of the concept.

   - If any visuals do not seem relevant, explain your thinking.

IMPROVING THE DRAFT

REVISING, EDITING, AND PROOFREADING

Start improving your draft by reflecting on what you have written thus far:

- Review critical reading comments from your classmates, instructor, or writing center tutor. What are your readers getting at?

- Take another look at your notes and ideas: What else should you consider?

- Review your draft: What else can you do to make your concept explanation clearer or more interesting to your readers?

Revising Your Draft

Revising means reenvisioning your draft, trying to see it in a new way, given your purpose and audience, in order to develop a clearer, more compelling concept explanation. Think imaginatively and boldly about cutting unconvincing or tangential material, adding new material, and moving material around. The suggestions in the chart below may help you solve problems and strengthen your essay.

TROUBLESHOOTING YOUR DRAFT

To Focus the Concept and Explain It Clearly and Fully	
Problem	**Suggestions for Revising**
The concept is confusing, unclear, or vague.	• Define the concept more precisely. • Give examples. • Use an appositive to introduce and define new terms or give specific details. • Compare the concept to something familiar. • Apply the concept to a real-world experience.
The focus seems too broad or too narrow.	• Concentrate on one aspect of the concept. • Review your invention and research notes for a larger or more significant aspect of the concept to focus on.
The content seems thin.	• Consider adding other explanatory strategies. • Consider developing your strategies more fully.
Some words are new to most readers.	• Define them; consider using appositives. • Explain how they relate to more familiar terms. • Add analogies and examples to make them less abstract.

To Improve the Organization

Problem	Suggestions for Revising
The essay as a whole is difficult to follow.	• At the beginning of the essay, forecast the topics you will cover in the order in which they will appear. • Rearrange your topics for logic or clarity. • Revise or add topic sentences to make it clear that you are moving on to a new topic. • Outline your essay to see if the connections between parts are clear and reorganize as needed.
The information is categorized in an unusual or unclear way.	• Add a sentence or two making your categories explicit.
Connections from one sentence or paragraph to the next are vague or unclear.	• Make the connections clearer by improving or adding transitions. • Revise or add topic sentences to make connections between paragraphs clear.

To Integrate Information from Sources Smoothly

Problem	Suggestions for Revising
Quotations, paraphrases, or summaries are not smoothly integrated into the text.	• Add appropriate signal phrases, using verbs that clarify the writer's position, approach, or attitude. • Explain how the quotation supports your point. • Use an appositive to identify the source and establish its credentials. • Contextualize the source to show its relevance and to establish its reliability.
Some quotations could just as effectively be expressed in your own words.	• Try paraphrasing the quotation. • Try summarizing the quotation.
Sources are not acknowledged properly.	• Include a signal phrase to identify the source. • Include the author's last name and a page number in parentheses following the borrowed material, and cite the source in a list at the end of the essay. (Check Chapter 11 for the correct citation form.) • Use an appositive to identify the source and establish its authority.

To Engage Readers	
Problem	Suggestions for Revising
Readers are not interested in the concept or focus.	• Select examples that readers are already familiar with or that may be relevant to readers' lives. • Dramatize the concept to show its importance or relevance. • Show readers a new way of using or understanding a familiar concept. • Draw readers in by addressing them directly or asking them questions.

Editing and Proofreading Your Draft

Check for errors in usage, punctuation, and mechanics, and consider matters of style. If you keep a list of errors you typically make, begin by checking your draft against this list. Ask someone else to proofread your essay before you submit it to your instructor.

From our research on student writing, we know that essays explaining concepts tend to have errors in essential or nonessential clauses beginning with *who*, *which*, or *that*. They also have errors in the use of commas to set off appositives. Check a writer's handbook for help with these potential problems.

Reflecting on What You Have Learned
Explaining Concepts

In this chapter, you have read critically several pieces explaining a concept and have written one of your own. To better remember what you have learned, pause now to reflect on the reading and writing activities you completed in this chapter.

1. Write a page or so reflecting on what you have learned. Begin by describing what you are most pleased with in your essay. Then explain what you think contributed to your achievement. Be specific about this contribution.

   • If it was something you learned from the readings, indicate which readings and specifically what you learned from them.

   • If it came from your research notes and the writing you did in response to prompts in this chapter, point out the parts that helped you most.

- If you got good advice from a critical reader, explain exactly how the person helped you — perhaps by helping you understand a particular problem in your draft or by helping you add a new dimension to your writing.

Try to write about your achievement in terms of what you have learned about the genre.

2. Reflect more generally on explaining concepts, a genre of writing important in education and in society. Consider some of the following questions:

   - When doing research, did you discover that some of the information on concepts was challenged by experts? What were the grounds for the challenge? Did you think your readers might question your information? How did you decide what information might seem new or surprising to readers?

   - Did you feel comfortable in your roles as the selector and giver of knowledge? Describe how you felt in these roles.

Evaluation

B efore you buy a computer, phone, or video game, do you take a look at the reviews? Brief reviews, written by consumers, are easy to find, but some are more helpful than others. The best reviewers know what they're talking about. They don't just say what they like, but they also justify *why* they like it, giving examples or other evidence. Moreover, their judgment is based not on individual taste alone but on commonly held standards or **criteria**. For example, no one would consider it appropriate to judge an action film by its poetic dialogue or its subtle characterizations; people judge such films by whether they deliver an exciting roller-coaster ride. The usefulness of an *evaluation*—be it a brief consumer comment or an expert's detailed review—depends on readers sharing, or at least respecting, the writer's criteria.

This chapter offers several brief evaluations for you to enjoy and analyze, with exploratory activities that will help you learn to read critically and write well. The Reading for Meaning and Reading Like a Writer activities following each selection invite you to analyze and write about the reading's ideas and writing strategies. You can also use the brief Guide to Writing Evaluations toward the end of the chapter to help you write a clear and convincing review.

RHETORICAL SITUATIONS FOR EVALUATIONS

Many people—including managers, reviewers, bloggers, and ordinary consumers—write evaluations, as the following examples suggest:

- For a conference on innovation in education, an elementary-school teacher evaluates *Schoolhouse Rock*, an animated television series developed in the 1970s and reinvented as CD-ROM learning games, interactive YouTube videos, and DVDs. She praises the original series as an entertaining way of presenting information, giving two reasons the series remains an effective teaching tool: Witty lyrics and catchy tunes make the information memorable, and cartoonlike visuals make the lessons pleasurable. She supports each reason by showing and discussing examples of popular *Schoolhouse Rock* segments, such as "Conjunction Junction," "We the People," and "Three Is a Magic Number." She ends by expressing her hope that teachers and developers of educational multimedia will learn from the example of *Schoolhouse Rock*.

- A supervisor reviews the work of a probationary employee. She judges the employee's performance as being adequate overall but still needing improvement in several key areas, particularly completing projects on time and communicating clearly with others. To support her judgment, she describes several problems that the employee has had over the six-month probationary period.

- An older brother, a college junior, sends an e-mail message to his younger brother, a high-school senior, who is trying to decide which college to attend. Because the older brother attends one of the colleges being considered and has friends at another, he feels competent to offer advice. He centers his message on the question of what standards to use in evaluating colleges. He argues that if playing football is the primary goal, then college number one is the clear choice. But if having the opportunity to work in an award-winning scientist's genetics lab is more important, then the second college is the better choice.

Thinking about the Genre

Evaluation

Before studying a type of writing, it is useful to spend some time thinking about what you already know about it. You may have discussed with friends or family members a fabulous new app or a disappointing quarterback, or composed evaluations for school assignments, posted reviews online, or given or received evaluations at work. Or you may have read evaluations before choosing a film to see.

Recall a time when you evaluated something you had seen, heard, read, or tried (such as a film, live performance, novel, sports team, restaurant, television show, game, computer, or cell phone) or a time that you read or heard an evaluation someone else had made. Your instructor may ask you to write about this experience or discuss it with others in class or online.

- Who was the *audience*? How do you think presenting the evaluation to this audience affected the writer's (or speaker's) judgment or the way the evaluation was supported? For example, did the audience's
  (continued)

knowledge of the subject, or of subjects like it, influence the reasons or examples given?

- What was the *purpose*? What did the writer (or speaker) want the audience to learn? For example, did he or she want to influence the actions of audience members, get them to think differently about the criteria or standards they should use when judging subjects of this kind, get them to look at the subject in a new way, or accomplish some other purpose? What did the writer (or speaker) choose to emphasize as a result? Why?

- How would the way the evaluation was presented have changed if the audience or purpose had been different? For example, if the audience knew a lot about the subject or if the writer (or speaker) wanted audience members to reconsider the criteria they usually use to evaluate subjects like this, would the subject have been compared with something surprising or unfamiliar? Also, how would changing the medium of presentation have affected the way the evaluation was presented? For example, how might film clips or other audiovisual material have helped?

A GUIDE TO READING EVALUATIONS

This guide introduces you to the basic features and strategies typical of evaluative writing by inviting you to analyze an intriguing selection by Amitai Etzioni that evaluates McDonald's–type fast-food jobs for high-school students, first by *reading for meaning* and then by *reading like a writer*.

- *Reading for meaning* will help you understand Etzioni's judgment and his reasoning.

- *Reading like a writer* will help you learn how Etzioni employs strategies typical of evaluative writing, such as

  1. presenting the subject in enough detail so that readers know what is being judged

  2. supporting an overall judgment based on appropriate criteria with credible evidence

  3. responding to objections and alternative judgments readers might prefer

  4. organizing the evaluation in a way that will be clear and logical to readers

Amitai Etzioni

Working at McDonald's

Amitai Etzioni (b. 1929) earned his PhD in sociology from the University of California at Berkeley and has taught at Berkeley, Columbia, Harvard, and George Washington universities. A respected scholar, he served as president of the American Sociological Association, and has written more than two dozen books, including Hot Spots: American Foreign Policy in a Post Human-Rights World *(2012) and* The Limits of Privacy *(2004). A highly visible public intellectual, Etzioni often appears in the media, writes op-eds, and blogs at amitaietzioni.org and the* Huffington Post. *Among his many awards is the Simon Wiesenthal Center's 1997 Tolerance Book Award. "Working at McDonald's" was originally published in 1986 in the* Miami Herald *with a headnote explaining that Etzioni's son Dari helped him write the essay.*

- *Before you read, think about any jobs you have had during high school or college (voluntary or for pay). Consider what you learned that might have made you a better student and prepared you for the kind of work you hope to do in the future.*

- *As you read, think about how the standards or criteria that Etzioni uses to evaluate jobs at fast-food restaurants would apply to the kinds of jobs you have held, and whether they are criteria you would apply.*

McDonald's is bad for your kids. I do not mean the flat patties and the white-flour buns; I refer to the jobs teen-agers undertake, mass-producing these choice items.   1

As many as two-thirds of America's high school juniors and seniors now hold down part-time paying jobs, according to studies. Many of these are in fast-food chains, of which McDonald's is the pioneer, trend-setter, and symbol.   2

At first, such jobs may seem right out of the Founding Fathers' educational manual for how to bring up self-reliant, work-ethic-driven, productive youngsters. But in fact, these jobs undermine school attendance and involvement, impart few skills that will be useful in later life, and simultaneously skew the values of teen-agers—especially their ideas about the worth of a dollar.   3

It has been a longstanding American tradition that youngsters ought to get paying jobs. In folklore, few pursuits are more deeply revered than the newspaper route and the sidewalk lemonade stand. Here the youngsters are to learn how sweet are the fruits of labor and self-discipline (papers are delivered early in the morning, rain or shine), and the ways of trade (if you price your lemonade too high or too low . . .).   4

5   Roy Rogers, Baskin Robbins, Kentucky Fried Chicken, et al. may at first seem nothing but a vast extension of the lemonade stand. They provide very large numbers of teen jobs, provide regular employment, pay quite well compared to many other teen jobs, and, in the modern equivalent of toiling over a hot stove, test one's stamina.

6   Closer examination, however, finds the McDonald's kind of job highly uneducational in several ways. Far from providing opportunities for entre-preneurship (the lemonade stand) or self-discipline, self-supervision, and self-scheduling (the paper route), most teen jobs these days are highly structured—what social scientists call "highly routinized."

7   True, you still have to have the gumption to get yourself over to the hamburger stand, but once you don the prescribed uniform, your task is spelled out in minute detail. The franchise prescribes the shape of the cof-fee cups; the weight, size, shape, and color of the patties; and the texture of the napkins (if any). Fresh coffee is to be made every eight minutes. And so on. There is no room for initiative, creativity, or even elementary re-arrangements. These are breeding grounds for robots working for yester-day's assembly lines, not tomorrow's high-tech posts.

8   There are very few studies of the matter. One of the few is a 1984 study by Ivan Charper and Bryan Shore Fraser. The study relies mainly on what teen-agers write in response to questionnaires rather than actual observa-tions of fast-food jobs. The authors argue that the employees develop many skills such as how to operate a food-preparation machine and a cash regis-ter. However, little attention is paid to how long it takes to acquire such a skill, or what its significance is.

9   What does it matter if you spend 20 minutes to learn to use a cash regis-ter, and then—"operate" it? What skill have you acquired? It is a long way from learning to work with a lathe or carpenter tools in the olden days or to program computers in the modern age.

10   A 1980 study by A. V. Harrell and P. W. Wirtz found that, among those students who worked at least 25 hours per week while in school, their unemployment rate four years later was half of that of seniors who did not work. This is an impressive statistic. It must be seen, though, together with the finding that many who begin as part-time employees in fast-food chains drop out of high school and are gobbled up in the world of low-skill jobs.

11   Some say that while these jobs are rather unsuited for college-bound, white, middle-class youngsters, they are "ideal" for lower-class, "non-academic," minority youngsters. Indeed, minorities are "over-represented" in these jobs (21 percent of fast-food employees). While it is true that these places provide income, work, and even some training to such youngsters, they also tend to perpetuate their disadvantaged status. They provide no career ladders, few marketable skills, and undermine school attendance and involvement.

The hours are often long. Among those 14 to 17, a third of fast-food   12
employees (including some school dropouts) labor more than 30 hours
per week, according to the Charper-Fraser study. Only 20 percent work
15 hours or less. The rest: between 15 and 30 hours.

Often the stores close late, and after closing one must clean up and tally   13
up. In affluent Montgomery County, Md., where child labor would not
seem to be a widespread economic necessity, 24 percent of the seniors at
one high school in 1985 worked as much as five to seven days a week;
27 percent, three to five. There is just no way such amounts of work will not
interfere with school work, especially homework. In an informal survey
published in the most recent yearbook of the high school, 58 percent of the
seniors acknowledged that their jobs interfere with their school work.

The Charper-Fraser study sees merit in learning teamwork and working   14
under supervision. The authors have a point here. However, it must be
noted that such learning is not automatically educational or wholesome.
For example, much of the supervision in fast-food places leans toward
teaching one the wrong kinds of compliance: blind obedience, or shared
alienation with the "boss."

Supervision is often both tight and woefully inappropriate. Today, fast-   15
food chains and other such places of work (record shops, bowling alleys)
keep costs down by having teens supervise teens with often no adult on
the premises.

There is no father or mother figure with which to identify, to emulate, to   16
provide a role model and guidance. The work-culture varies from one
place to another: Sometimes it is a tightly run shop (must keep the cash
registers ringing); sometimes a rather loose pot party interrupted by customers. However, only rarely is there a master to learn from, or much
worth learning. Indeed, far from being places where solid adult work values are being transmitted, these are places where all too often delinquent
teen values dominate. Typically, when my son Oren was dishing out ice
cream for Baskin Robbins in upper Manhattan, his fellow teen-workers
considered him a sucker for not helping himself to the till. Most youngsters
felt they were entitled to $50 severance "pay" on their last day on the job.

The pay, oddly, is the part of the teen work-world that is most difficult to   17
evaluate. The lemonade stand or paper route money was for your allowance. In the old days, apprentices learning a trade from a master contributed most, if not all, of their income to their parents' household. Today, the
teen pay may be low by adult standards, but it is often, especially in the
middle class, spent largely or wholly by the teens. That is, the youngsters
live free at home ("after all, they are high school kids") and are left with
very substantial sums of money.

Where this money goes is not quite clear. Some use it to support them-   18
selves, especially among the poor. More middle-class kids set some money
aside to help pay for college, or save it for a major purchase—often a car.

But large amounts seem to flow to pay for an early introduction into the most trite aspects of American consumerism: flimsy punk clothes, trinkets, and whatever else is the last fast-moving teen craze.

19 One may say that this is only fair and square; they are being good American consumers and spend their money on what turns them on. At least, a cynic might add, these funds do not go into illicit drugs and booze. On the other hand, an educator might bemoan that these young, yet unformed individuals, so early in life driven to buy objects of no intrinsic educational, cultural, or social merit, learn so quickly the dubious merit of keeping up with the Joneses in ever-changing fads, promoted by mass merchandising.

20 Many teens find the instant reward of money, and the youth status symbols it buys, much more alluring than credits in calculus courses, European history, or foreign languages. No wonder quite a few would rather skip school—and certainly homework—and instead work longer at a Burger King. Thus, most teen work these days is not providing early lessons in work ethic; it fosters escape from school and responsibilities, quick gratification, and a short cut to the consumeristic aspects of adult life.

21 Thus, parents should look at teen employment not as automatically educational. It is an activity—like sports—that can be turned into an educational opportunity. But it can also easily be abused. Youngsters must learn to balance the quest for income with the needs to keep growing and pursue other endeavors that do not pay off instantly—above all education.

22 Go back to school.

READING FOR MEANING

This section presents three activities that will help you think about the meanings in Etzioni's evaluative essay. Your instructor may ask you to do one or more of these activities in class or online.

1. **Read to Summarize.** Write a sentence or two briefly stating Etzioni's main point about the value of part-time jobs for teenagers.

2. **Read to Respond.** Write a paragraph or two analyzing your initial reactions to Etzioni's essay. For example, consider anything that resonates with your experience or that seems contradictory, surprising, or fascinating, such as:

   • The "longstanding American tradition that youngsters ought to get paying jobs" (par. 4), thinking about whether it is a tradition that most

Take a quiz to check your reading and vocabulary comprehension:
bedfordstmartins.com/readingcritically

Americans still follow or whether it is shared by other cultures with which you are familiar;

- Etzioni's argument that working while attending school interferes with schoolwork (par. 13), perhaps in relation to your own work and school experience.

You may also try contextualizing; see Chapter 10, pp. 522–23.

3. **Read to Analyze Assumptions. Assumptions** are ideas, beliefs, or values that are taken for granted as commonly accepted truths. The assumptions in a text usually reflect the writer's own attitudes or cultural traditions, but they may also represent other people's views. Reading to analyze assumptions asks you to uncover these perspectives as well as to probe your own. Sometimes the assumptions are stated explicitly, but often you will have to infer them (or figure them out) because they are only implied or hinted at through the writer's choice of words or examples. Write a paragraph or two analyzing an assumption you find intriguing in Etzioni's essay. For example:

Assumptions about the usefulness of certain skills. Etzioni asserts that fast-food jobs "impart few skills that will be useful in later life" (par. 3). For example, he claims they do not provide "opportunities for entrepreneurship . . . or self-discipline, self-supervision, and self-scheduling" (par. 6) and "[t]here is no room for initiative, creativity" (par. 7). To think critically about the assumptions in this essay related to what skills are learned at fast-food jobs and how useful they are, ask yourself questions like these:

- How different, really, is delivering newspapers from working at McDonald's in terms of the skills learned about discipline, scheduling, and so on?

- Similarly, what more is a young person likely to learn about entrepreneurship by operating a lemonade stand than by working in a fast-food restaurant (par. 4)?

- What other kinds of skills do teens learn when working at fast-food restaurants, and what potential use do you think these skills have in future life?

You may also try reflecting on challenges to your beliefs and values; see Chapter 10, pp. 526–27.

Assumptions about the culture of consumerism. Toward the end of the essay, Etzioni complains that the things teenagers choose to buy with the money they earn from fast-food jobs represent "the most trite aspects of American consumerism: flimsy punk clothes, trinkets, and whatever else is the last fast-moving teen craze" (par. 18). By referring to consumerism — enthusiastic spending on material possessions such as clothes, entertainment, and other consumer goods — as "American," Etzioni makes clear he is referring to something that is not limited to teenagers. Nevertheless, his focus on what teens buy and why they buy it reveals Etzioni's ideas about teenagers' indoctrination into a consumerist culture. To think critically about the assumptions in this essay related to American consumerism, ask yourself questions like these:

- Etzioni uses the words *trite*, *flimsy*, and *trinkets* to criticize the things teens buy, but if teens purchased items that were original, well-made, and valuable, do you think he would still object? What might he be criticizing other than teenagers' taste?

- In referring to "fads" and "mass merchandising," he seems to assume teens are especially vulnerable to the influence of advertising (par. 19). To what extent, if any, do you agree?

READING LIKE A WRITER

This section presents four brief activities that will help you analyze Etzioni's writing. Your instructor may ask you to do one or more of these activities in class or online.

Presenting the Subject

Writers must present the subject so readers know what is being judged and so that they can decide whether the criteria for evaluation they offer are appropriate. Writers often name the subject in the title and then describe it in some detail. A film reviewer, for example, might name the film in the title and then, in the review, indicate the category, or genre, of film he or she is critiquing as well as identify the actors, describe the characters they play, and tell some of the plot.

Similarly, Etzioni identifies the subject of his evaluation in his title: "Working at McDonald's"; he then specifies the type of work that concerns him, and explains why he focuses his attention on this company:

Subject	As many as two-thirds of America's high school juniors and seniors
Reasons why he uses McDonald's	now hold down part-time paying jobs, according to studies. Many of these are in fast-food chains, of which McDonald's is the pioneer, trend-setter, and symbol. (par. 2)

Although the fact that many teenagers hold fast-food jobs is common knowledge, Etzioni cites statistics to establish how widespread it is: "As many as two-thirds of America's high school juniors and seniors. . . ." (par. 2). Notice that he refers generally to "studies" without providing any detail that would help readers follow up on his sources. Later, however, he uses researchers' names and the publication dates — for example, "A 1980 study by A. V. Harrell and P. W. Wirtz"

See Chapter 11, pp. 581–608, for information on documenting sources in MLA and APA styles.

(par. 10) — to cite his sources more specifically, although still informally. Etzioni's original newspaper readersy would have been used to such informal references, but if he were writing for an academic audience, he would be expected to use a conventional documentation style. Citing sources specifically also helps convince readers of the statistics' reliability, especially if the statistics do not correspond to readers' experience.

Etzioni also names several other "fast-food chains" — "Roy Rogers, Baskin Robbins, Kentuck Fried Chicken" (par. 5) — to make the point that he is not singling out McDonald's but using it as an example and "symbol." He spends a good portion of the rest of his evaluation describing the kind of job he objects to.

| Analyze & Write |

Write a paragraph analyzing how Etzioni describes McDonald's-type jobs:

1. First, underline the factual details in paragraphs 5–7, 9, 12, 15, and 16 that describe the people who work at fast-food restaurants and what they do.

2. How do the details Etzioni provides in these paragraphs help you understand the subject of his essay as important or worth reading about?

3. Which of the details in these paragraphs do you accept as valid, inaccurate, or only partially true? How fair does Etzioni's description seem to you?

Supporting the Judgment

Evaluations analyze the subject, but they also present an argument designed to convince readers that the writer's judgment is trustworthy because the reasons are

- based on criteria, such as shared values, that are appropriate to the subject
- backed by reliable evidence

Writers usually declare their overall judgment early in the essay and may repeat it in the essay's conclusion. This judgment is the main idea or thesis, asserting that the subject is good or bad, or better or worse than something comparable. For example, Etzioni opens with the straightforward judgment:

Judgment   McDonald's is bad for your kids. (par. 1)

Although readers expect a definitive judgment, they also appreciate a balanced one that acknowledges good as well as bad qualities, so Etzioni acknowledges the benefits of fast-food jobs for teenagers:

Good qualities of   They provide very large numbers of teen jobs, provide regular
fast-food job   employment, pay quite well compared to many other teen jobs,
                     and, in the modern equivalent of toiling over a hot stove, test one's
                     stamina. (par. 5)

Etzioni makes two additional moves typical of strong reviews:

1. He reaches out to readers to establish shared values.

2. He gives reasons backed by evidence to support his judgment:

> *Shared value* At first, such jobs may seem right out of the Founding Fathers' educa-
> *Reason* tional manual for how to bring up self-reliant, work-ethic-driven, productive youngsters. But in fact, these jobs undermine school atten-dance and involvement, impart few skills that will be useful in later life, and simultaneously skew the values of teen-agers — especially their ideas about the worth of a dollar. (par. 3)

By referring to "the Founding Fathers" and using familiar phrases (such as "self-reliant" and "work-ethic") that connote traditional values, Etzioni builds his argument on values he expects his audience will share. Notice also that his rea-sons are framed in negative terms indicating that McDonald's jobs do not fulfill expectations: They "*undermine* school attendance," "impart *few* skills," "*skew . . .* values." But to be convincing, the reasons also must be supported by **evidence** such as facts, statistics, expert testimony, research studies, relevant examples, or personal anecdotes.

Analyze & Write

Write a paragraph analyzing how Etzioni supports one of his reasons:

1. First, choose *one* of the reasons Etzioni introduces in paragraph 3 and find the passage later in the essay where you think he supports that part of the argument.

2. Then analyze Etzioni's argument. For example, what kinds of evidence does he provide? Is the evidence appropriate and believable? Why or why not?

For more on evaluating the logic of an argument, see Chapter 10, pp. 530–32.

3. Would Etzioni's original *Miami Herald* readers have found this part of the argu-ment convincing? Explain why.

Responding to Objections or Alternative Judgments

Writers of evaluations often respond to possible objections and alternative judg-ments their readers may be likely to raise. They may **refute** (argue against) objec-tions or alternative judgments they believe are weak or flawed, or they may **concede** (accept) objections and judgments they think are valid. To alert readers that a response is coming, reviewers may provide a transition or other cue. Here's an example of a refutation from Etzioni:

Alternative judgment	The authors argue that the employees develop many skills such as how to
Cue	operate a food-preparation machine and a cash register. However, <u>little</u>
Refutation	<u>attention is paid to how long it takes to acquire such a skill, or what its</u>
	<u>significance is.</u>

> <u>What does it matter if you spend 20 minutes to learn to use a cash register, and then — "operate" it? What skill have you acquired? It is a long way from learning to work with a lathe or carpenter tools in the olden days or to program computers in the modern age.</u> (pars. 8–9)

Notice the basic structure of a refutation. (The cues signaling refutation are highlighted.)

- ► Although ...., I think ....
- ► X says ...., but I think .... because ....

Here's an example of conceding valid concerns or objections:

> [Fast-food jobs] provide very large numbers of teen jobs, provide regular employment, pay quite well compared to many other teen jobs, and, in the modern equivalent of toiling over a hot stove, test one's stamina. (par. 5)

Below are some typical sentence strategies for conceding, with cues signaling concession highlighted:

- ► Of course, ... is an important factor.
- ► Granted, ... must be taken into consideration.

Frequently, though, reviewers reach out to those who hold an opposing position by first conceding a portion of that position but then going on to indicate where they differ:

Cue signaling concession	True, you still have to have the gumption to get yourself over to the
	hamburger stand, but once you don the prescribed uniform, your task
Cue signaling refutation	is spelled out in minute detail. (par. 7)

Etzioni often uses this strategy of concession followed by refutation when citing research that initially appears to undermine his claim. For example, he begins by conceding when he cites a study by Harrell and Wirtz (par. 10) that links work as a student with greater likelihood of employment later on. However, he then refutes the significance of this finding, reinterpreting the data to suggest that the high likelihood of future employment could be an indication that workers in fast-food restaurants are more likely to drop out of school than an indication that workers are learning important employment skills. This strategy of conceding and then refuting by reinterpreting evidence can be especially effective in college writing, as Etzioni (a professor) well knows.

| Analyze & Write |

Write a paragraph analyzing how Etzioni responds to objections or alternative judgments.

1. First, find and highlight the alternative judgment or objection in paragraphs 8–11, 14, and 19.

2. Then choose *one* of these objections or alternative judgments and determine whether Etzioni responds by refuting or conceding or both.

3. Finally, evaluate the effectiveness of Etzioni's response. What made his response convincing (or unconvincing) for his original readers? How about for you reading today?

Organizing the Evaluation

Writers of evaluation usually try to make their writing clear, logical, and easy for readers to follow by providing **cues** or road signs. For example, they may

- forecast their reasons early in the essay and repeat key terms (or synonyms) from these reasons later in the evaluation

- use topic sentences to announce the subject of each paragraph or group of paragraphs

- use transitions (such as *but, however, on the other hand, thus*) to guide readers from one point to another

These strategies are all helpful and are often expected in college writing.

As we've seen, Etzioni forecasts his reasons in paragraph 3:

Forecasting statement   . . . these jobs undermine school attendance and involvement, impart few skills that will be useful in later life, and simultaneously skew the values of teen-agers — especially their ideas about the worth of a dollar.

He develops the argument supporting each of these reasons in subsequent paragraphs. His essay would be easier to follow if he addressed the reasons in the order he first introduced them in paragraph 3. Nevertheless, he helps readers find the reasons by repeating key terms, as when he uses the phrase "marketable *skills*" (par. 11) to refer to "few skills" from his forecasting statement; or he uses a close substitute, as when he uses the phrase "drop out of *high school*" (par. 10) to refer to "*undermine school attendance*" in paragraph 3.

Topic sentences are also used to orient readers. Often placed at the beginning of a paragraph or related sequence of paragraphs, they announce the topic that will be developed in the subsequent sentences. For example:

Topic sentence	It has been a longstanding American tradition that youngsters
Examples of traditional kids' jobs	ought to get paying jobs. In folklore, few pursuits are more deeply revered than the <u>newspaper route</u> and the <u>sidewalk lemonade</u>
What these jobs teach	stand. Here the youngsters are to learn how sweet are the fruits of labor and self-discipline (papers are delivered early in the morning, rain or shine), and the ways of trade (if you price your lemonade too high or too low . . .). (par. 4)

Notice that Etzioni focuses this paragraph on the topic of useful skills he introduced in the preceding forecasting statement. The next two paragraphs use topic sentences to make the argument that fast-food jobs "seem" like traditional jobs, but they do not teach the really valuable skills. Skimming the sequence of topic sentences in paragraphs 5 and 6, you can get an idea of the outline of Etzioni's argument:

| Transitions | Roy Rogers, Baskin Robbins, Kentucky Fried Chicken, et al. may at first seem nothing but a vast extension of the lemonade stand. . . . |
| | Closer examination, however, finds the McDonald's kind of job highly uneducational in several ways. . . . |

As the two topic sentences above suggest, transitions (and other cues) also play an important role in clarifying the logic of a sequence. For example, *at first* suggests that what follows is only a tentative conclusion, especially when combined with the hedging words *may* and *seem*; *however* firmly establishes a contrast or contradiction to that provisional conclusion.

Analyze & Write

Write a paragraph analyzing how Etzioni helps readers track his argument and how effective the cues he uses are.

1. Look at the way Etzioni uses topic sentences in the rest of his essay to announce the subject of individual paragraphs or groups of paragraphs.

2. Find a couple of examples that you think work well. What makes these topic sentences effective?

READINGS

Malcolm Gladwell

What College Rankings Really Tell Us

Malcolm Gladwell (b. 1963) has a BA in history from the University of Toronto. He is a staff writer for the New Yorker *magazine and has written a number of best-selling books, including* Outliers: The Story of Success *(2008) and* Blink: The Power of Thinking without Thinking *(2005). He received the American Sociological Association Award for Excellence in the Reporting of Social Issues and was named one of the hundred most influential people by* Time *magazine. "What College Rankings Really Tell Us" (2011) evaluates the popular U.S. News "Best Colleges" annual guide. You may be familiar with this guide and may have even consulted it when selecting a college. Excerpted from a longer* New Yorker *article, Gladwell's evaluation focuses on the* U.S. News *ranking system.*

- *Before you read, think about the criteria for choosing a college that are important to you.*

- *As you read Gladwell's review, consider who, besides prospective college students, would be likely to think the criteria* U.S. News *uses to rank colleges are important, and why.*

Car and Driver conducted a comparison test of three 1
sports cars, the Lotus Evora, the Chevrolet Corvette
Grand Sport, and the Porsche Cayman S. . . . Yet when
you inspect the magazine's tabulations it is hard to
figure out why *Car and Driver* was so sure that the
Cayman is better than the Corvette and the Evora. The
trouble starts with the fact that the ranking methodology *Car and Driver* used was essentially the same one
it uses for all the vehicles it tests—from S.U.V.s to
economy sedans. It's not set up for sports cars. Exterior
styling, for example, counts for four per cent of the
total score. Has anyone buying a sports car ever placed
so little value on how it looks? Similarly, the categories
of "fun to drive" and "chassis"—which cover the subjective experience of driving the car—count for only
eighty-five points out of the total of two hundred and
thirty-five. That may make sense for S.U.V. buyers. But,
for people interested in Porsches and Corvettes and
Lotuses, the subjective experience of driving is surely
what matters most. In other words, in trying to come

up with a ranking that is heterogeneous—a methodology that is broad enough to cover all vehicles—*Car
and Driver* ended up with a system that is absurdly ill-
suited to some vehicles. . . .

Why open with *Car &
Driver*, not *U.S. News?*

2   A heterogeneous ranking system works if it focuses
just on, say, how much fun a car is to drive, or how
good-looking it is, or how beautifully it handles. The
magazine's ambition to create a comprehensive ranking system—one that considered cars along twenty-
one variables, each weighted according to a secret
sauce cooked up by the editors—would also be fine,
as long as the cars being compared were truly similar.
It's only when one car is thirteen thousand dollars
more than another that juggling twenty-one variables
starts to break down, because you're faced with the
impossible task of deciding how much a difference of
that degree ought to matter. A ranking can be heterogeneous, in other words, as long as it doesn't try to be
too comprehensive. And it can be comprehensive as
long as it doesn't try to measure things that are heterogeneous. But it's an act of real audacity when a
ranking system tries to be comprehensive and heterogeneous—which is the first thing to keep in mind in
any consideration of *U.S. News & World Report*'s
annual "Best Colleges" guide.

Why use these criteria to
judge ranking systems?

3   The *U.S. News* rankings . . . relies on seven
weighted variables:

1. Undergraduate academic reputation, 22.5 per
   cent
2. Graduation and freshman retention rates, 20 per
   cent
3. Faculty resources, 20 per cent
4. Student selectivity, 15 per cent
5. Financial resources, 10 per cent
6. Graduation rate performance, 7.5 per cent
7. Alumni giving, 5 per cent

From these variables, *U.S. News* generates a score for
each institution on a scale of 1 to 100. . . . This ranking
system looks a great deal like the *Car and Driver* methodology. It is heterogeneous. It doesn't just compare
U.C. Irvine, the University of Washington, the University of Texas–Austin, the University of Wisconsin–
Madison, Penn State, and the University of Illinois,

How do these examples
help readers?

Urbana–Champaign—all public institutions of roughly the same size. It aims to compare Penn State—a very large, public, land-grant university with a low tuition and an economically diverse student body, set in a rural valley in central Pennsylvania and famous for its football team—with Yeshiva University, a small, expensive, private Jewish university whose undergraduate program is set on two campuses in Manhattan (one in midtown, for the women, and one far uptown, for the men) and is definitely not famous for its football team.

The system is also comprehensive. It doesn't simply compare schools along one dimension—the test scores of incoming freshmen, say, or academic reputation. An algorithm takes a slate of statistics on each college and transforms them into a single score: it tells us that Penn State is a better school than Yeshiva by one point. It is easy to see why the *U.S. News* rankings are so popular. A single score allows us to judge between entities (like Yeshiva and Penn State) that otherwise would be impossible to compare. . . .   4

A comprehensive, heterogeneous ranking system was a stretch for *Car and Driver*—and all it did was rank inanimate objects operated by a single person. The Penn State campus at University Park is a complex institution with dozens of schools and departments, four thousand faculty members, and forty-five thousand students. How on earth does anyone propose to assign a number to something like that?   5

The first difficulty with rankings is that it can be surprisingly hard to measure the variable you want to rank—even in cases where that variable seems perfectly objective. . . . There's no direct way to measure the quality of an institution—how well a college manages to inform, inspire, and challenge its students. So the *U.S. News* algorithm relies instead on proxies for quality—and the proxies for educational quality turn out to be flimsy at best.   6

Take the category of "faculty resources," which counts for twenty per cent of an institution's score (number 3 on the chart above). "Research shows that the more satisfied students are about their contact with professors," the College Guide's explanation of the category begins, "the more they will learn and   7 the more likely it is they will graduate." That's true. According to educational researchers, arguably the most important variable in a successful college education is a vague but crucial concept called student "engagement"—that is, the extent to which students immerse themselves in the intellectual and social life of their college—and a major component of engagement is the quality of a student's contacts with faculty. . . . So what proxies does *U.S. News* use to measure this elusive dimension of engagement? The explanation goes on:

> We use six factors from the 2009–10 academic year to assess a school's commitment to instruction. Class size has two components, the proportion of classes with fewer than 20 students (30 percent of the faculty resources score) and the proportion with 50 or more students (10 percent of the score). Faculty salary (35 percent) is the average faculty pay, plus benefits, during the 2008–09 and 2009–10 academic years, adjusted for regional differences in the cost of living. . . . We also weigh the proportion of professors with the highest degree in their fields (15 percent), the student-faculty ratio (5 percent), and the proportion of faculty who are full time (5 percent).

8   This is a puzzling list. Do professors who get paid more money really take their teaching roles more seriously? And why does it matter whether a professor has the highest degree in his or her field? Salaries and degree attainment are known to be predictors of research productivity. But studies show that being oriented toward research has very little to do with being good at teaching. Almost none of the *U.S. News* variables, in fact, seem to be particularly effective proxies for engagement. As the educational researchers Patrick Terenzini and Ernest Pascarella concluded after analyzing twenty-six hundred reports on the effects of college on students:

How does this research support Gladwell's evaluation?

> After taking into account the characteristics, abilities, and backgrounds students bring with them to college, we found that how much students grow or change has only inconsistent and, perhaps in a practical sense, trivial relationships with such traditional measures of institutional "quality" as educational

expenditures per student, student/faculty ratios, faculty salaries, percentage of faculty with the highest degree in their field, faculty research productivity, size of the library, [or] admissions selectivity. . . .

There's something missing from that list of variables, of course: it doesn't include price. That is one of the most distinctive features of the *U.S. News* methodology. Both its college rankings and its law-school rankings reward schools for devoting lots of financial resources to educating their students, but not for being affordable. Why? [Director of Data Research Robert] Morse admitted that there was no formal reason for that position. It was just a feeling. "We're not saying that we're measuring educational outcomes," he explained. "We're not saying we're social scientists, or we're subjecting our rankings to some peer-review process. We're just saying we've made this judgment. We're saying we've interviewed a lot of experts, we've developed these academic indicators, and we think these measures measure quality schools." 9

As answers go, that's up there with the parental "Because I said so." But Morse is simply being honest. If we don't understand what the right proxies for college quality are, let alone how to represent those proxies in a comprehensive, heterogeneous grading system, then our rankings are inherently arbitrary. . . . *U.S. News* thinks that schools that spend a lot of money on their students are nicer than those that don't, and that this niceness ought to be factored into the equation of desirability. Plenty of Americans agree: the campus of Vanderbilt University or Williams College is filled with students whose families are largely indifferent to the price their school charges but keenly interested in the flower beds and the spacious suites and the architecturally distinguished lecture halls those high prices make possible. Of course, given that the rising cost of college has become a significant social problem in the United States in recent years, you can make a strong case that a school ought to be rewarded for being affordable. . . . 10

The *U.S. News* rankings turn out to be full of these kinds of implicit ideological choices. One common 11

How effective is Gladwell's refutation?

statistic used to evaluate colleges, for example, is called "graduation rate performance," which compares a school's actual graduation rate with its predicted graduation rate given the socioeconomic status and the test scores of its incoming freshman class. It is a measure of the school's efficacy: it quantifies the impact of a school's culture and teachers and institutional support mechanisms. Tulane, given the qualifications of the students that it admits, ought to have a graduation rate of eighty-seven per cent; its actual 2009 graduation rate was seventy-three per cent. That shortfall suggests that something is amiss at Tulane. Another common statistic for measuring college quality is "student selectivity." This reflects variables such as how many of a college's freshmen were in the top ten per cent of their high-school class, how high their S.A.T. scores were, and what percentage of applicants a college admits. Selectivity quantifies how accomplished students are when they first arrive on campus.

12   Each of these statistics matters, but for very different reasons. As a society, we probably care more about efficacy: America's future depends on colleges that make sure the students they admit leave with an education and a degree. If you are a bright high-school senior and you're thinking about your own future, though, you may well care more about selectivity, because that relates to the prestige of your degree. . . .

13   There is no right answer to how much weight a ranking system should give to these two competing values. It's a matter of which educational model you value more—and here, once again, *U.S. News* makes its position clear. It gives twice as much weight to selectivity as it does to efficacy. . . .

Why conclude with these competing criteria?

14   Rankings are not benign. They enshrine very particular ideologies, and, at a time when American higher education is facing a crisis of accessibility and affordability, we have adopted a de facto standard of college quality that is uninterested in both of those factors. And why? Because a group of magazine analysts in an office building in Washington, D.C., decided twenty years ago to value selectivity over efficacy.

READING FOR MEANING

This section presents three activities that will help you think about the meanings in Gladwell's evaluative essay. Your instructor may ask you to do one or more of these activities in class or online.

For more help with summarizing, see Chapter 10, pp. 518–19.

1. **Read to Summarize.** Write a sentence or two identifying Gladwell's overall judgment and his main reasons.

2. **Read to Respond.** Write a paragraph analyzing your initial reactions to Gladwell's essay. For example, consider anything that resonates with your experience or that seems contradictory, surprising, or fascinating, such as:

   - The research finding that "student 'engagement' — that is, the extent to which students immerse themselves in the intellectual and social life of their college" may be "the most important variable in a successful" educational experience (par. 7) — perhaps in relation to your own high-school or college experience;

   - The fact that "price" was not included as a variable in the *U.S. News* college rankings — perhaps in relation to your own or your family's consideration of affordability in choosing a college.

3. **Read to Analyze Assumptions.** Write a paragraph or two analyzing an assumption you find intriguing in Gladwell's essay. For example:

You may also try reflecting on challenges to your beliefs and values; see Chapter 10, pp. 526–27.

   Assumptions about ideology. **Ideology** means the ideas, beliefs, values, and concerns of an individual or a group. Ideology often centers on issues concerning power and equality. In "What College Rankings Really Tell Us," Gladwell asserts that "The *U.S. News* rankings turn out to be full of . . . implicit ideological choices" (par. 11), such as not including affordability, and valuing "selectivity over efficacy" in its ranking formula (par. 14). Consequently, he claims: "Rankings are not benign" or harmless. To think critically about the ideology underlying a ranking system, ask yourself questions like these:

   - Gladwell criticizes rankings in general and the *U.S. News* ranking system in particular for having harmful effects. Who does a ranking system like that of the *U.S. News* benefit? Who does it potentially harm?

   - In paragraph 14, Gladwell specifies "affordability" as an important factor or criterion. In light of "the rising cost of college," he calls affordability "a significant social problem" (par. 10). What does the omission

Take a quiz to check your reading and vocabulary comprehension:
bedfordstmartins.com/readingcritically

of price indicate about the ideology behind the *U.S. News* ranking system? Who should care that some highly qualified students cannot afford to attend the best colleges? Why?

Assumptions about efficacy and selectivity. Gladwell explains that judging a school's efficacy is often at odds with judging its selectivity. Efficacy refers to the effectiveness in graduating the students the school accepted: in other words, the graduation rate. Selectivity refers to who is accepted in the first place, and therefore "quantifies how accomplished students are when they first arrive on campus" (par. 11). To think critically about the criteria used to rank colleges, ask yourself questions like these:

- Why do you think Gladwell claims that "[a]s a society, we probably care more about efficacy" . . . but "a bright high-school senior . . . may well care more about selectivity" (par. 12)? What added benefits are there to attending a highly selective, prestigious college?

- What assumptions do we make about the value of a college education? What is its value to you personally and to society in general?

READING LIKE A WRITER

RESPONDING TO OBJECTIONS AND ALTERNATIVE JUDGMENTS

Because it is a negative evaluation, one could say that Gladwell's entire essay is an implied refutation of those who think well of the *U.S. News* college rankings. However, Gladwell also responds specifically to comments made by Robert Morse, the director of data research for *U.S. News & World Report*. Gladwell cues his refutation with the rhetorical question "Why?" and he goes on to answer by quoting Morse:

Cue	Why? [Director of Data Research Robert] Morse admitted that
Words conveying tone	there was no formal reason for that position. It was just a feeling. "We're not saying that we're measuring educational outcomes," he explained. (par. 9)

Not only does he present his reasons for disagreeing with Morse, but Gladwell also expresses his attitude toward Morse's explanation through his choice of words. He continues in this *tone* when he comments at the beginning of the next paragraph: "As answers go, that's up there with the parental 'Because I said so'" (par. 10).

A writer's tone, especially when sarcastic or mocking, can have a strong effect on readers. Those who agree may appreciate it, but those who disagree or are uncertain may be put off by it.

Analyze & Write

Write a paragraph analyzing Morse's response to Gladwell and Gladwell's response to Morse:

1. Reread paragraph 9. How would you describe Morse's response to Gladwell's criticism: Which of Gladwell's points does Morse concede or refute?

2. Now reread paragraphs 10–12. How does Gladwell respond to Morse? How does he concede or refute Morse's response? How would you describe the tone, or emotional resonance, of Gladwell's response? Is he fair, mean, sarcastic, something else?

3. Given Gladwell's purpose and audience, how do you imagine readers would react to Morse's response to criticism as well as to Gladwell's handling of Morse's response? How did you respond?

A Special Reading Strategy

Judging the Writer's Credibility

Encountering an evaluation like Malcolm Gladwell's "What College Rankings Really Tell Us," readers typically consider the writer's credibility in order to determine whether what we are being told is worth taking seriously. We often take into account what we know—for example, the writer's academic and professional credentials as well as whether the text appeared in a reputable publication. But we also need to think about how the writer comes across in the text itself. In an evaluative argument, we especially want to see whether the writer is knowledgeable about the subject and fair in handling objections and alternative judgments, and also whether the writer shares our values or criteria for evaluating this kind of subject.

Follow the instructions in Chapter 10, pp. 537–38, for Judging the Writer's Credibility. As you reread Gladwell's essay, consider the questions below to help you analyze whether he comes across as a trustworthy judge of the *U.S. News & World Report* college ranking system. Then write a paragraph or two about your analysis and evaluation of Gladwell's credibility in this essay.

- If you already worked on the Reading Like a Writer activity, you've analyzed Gladwell's response to Robert Morse, the person responsible for the *U.S. News* ranking system. Now consider whether his tone makes Gladwell more or less credible. Does he seem fair or not, and why?

- Consider also how authoritative and knowledgeable Gladwell seems about ranking systems in general and the *U.S. News* system in particular. Point to any place in the essay that either instills confidence in his knowledge or makes you wonder whether he knows enough to make a judgment.

- Finally, review Gladwell's criteria. For example, do you agree or disagree that price or affordability ought to be a consideration in evaluating colleges? Do you agree with Gladwell that a college cannot be both selective and concerned with efficacy or helping students to graduate?

Christine Rosen

The Myth of Multitasking

Christine Rosen holds a PhD in history from Emory University and has been a scholar at the New America Foundation and the American Enterprise Institute. She has written several books, including The Extinction of Experience *(forthcoming 2013),* My Fundamentalist Education *(2005), and* The Feminist Dilemma *(2001). She also coedited* Acculturated: 23 Savvy Writers Find Hidden Virtue in Reality TV, Chic Lit, Video Games, and Other Pillars of Pop Culture *(2011). A commentator on bioethics and the social effects of technology, she frequently appears on National Public Radio, CNN, and Fox News and in other venues. Rosen's essays have appeared in such prestigious publications as the* New York Times Magazine, Washington Post, Wall Street Journal, National Review, *and* New Atlantis: A Journal of Technology & Society, *where she is a senior editor and where this essay originally appeared in 2008.*

- *Before you read, think about what Rosen might mean by her title, "The Myth of Multitasking." What does the word "myth" lead you to expect her judgment to be?*

- *As you read, think about your own experience with multitasking and what you think are its advantages and disadvantages. How well does Rosen's essay resonate with your experience?*

1   In one of the many letters he wrote to his son in the 1740s, Lord Chesterfield offered the following advice: "There is time enough for everything in the course of the day, if you do but one thing at once, but there is not time enough in the year, if you will do two things at a time." To Chesterfield, singular focus was not merely a practical way to structure one's time; it was a mark of intelligence. "This steady and undissipated attention to one object, is a sure mark of a superior genius; as hurry, bustle, and agitation, are the never-failing symptoms of a weak and frivolous mind."

2   In modern times, hurry, bustle, and agitation have become a regular way of life for many people—so much so that we have embraced a word to describe our efforts to respond to the many pressing demands on our time: *multitasking*. Used for decades to describe the parallel processing abilities of computers, multitasking is now shorthand for the human attempt to do simultaneously as many things as possible, as quickly as possible, preferably marshaling the power of as many technologies as possible.

3   In the late 1990s and early 2000s, one sensed a kind of exuberance about the possibilities of multitasking. Advertisements for new electronic gadgets—particularly the first generation of handheld digital devices—celebrated the notion of using technology to accomplish several things at once. The word *multitasking* began appearing in the "skills" sections

of résumés, as office workers restyled themselves as high-tech, high-performing team players. "We have always multitasked—inability to walk and chew gum is a time-honored cause for derision—but never so intensely or self-consciously as now," James Gleick wrote in his 1999 book *Faster*. "We are multitasking connoisseurs—experts in crowding, pressing, packing, and overlapping distinct activities in our all-too-finite moments." An article in the *New York Times Magazine* in 2001 asked, "Who can remember life before multitasking? These days we all do it." The article offered advice on "How to Multitask" with suggestions about giving your brain's "multitasking hot spot" an appropriate workout.

But more recently, challenges to the ethos of multitasking have begun to emerge. Numerous studies have shown the sometimes-fatal danger of using cell phones and other electronic devices while driving, for example, and several states have now made that particular form of multitasking illegal. In the business world, where concerns about time-management are perennial, warnings about workplace distractions spawned by a multitasking culture are on the rise. In 2005, the BBC reported on a research study, funded by Hewlett-Packard and conducted by the Institute of Psychiatry at the University of London, that found, "Workers distracted by e-mail and phone calls suffer a fall in IQ more than twice that found in marijuana smokers." The psychologist who led the study called this new "infomania" a serious threat to workplace productivity. One of the *Harvard Business Review*'s "Breakthrough Ideas" for 2007 was Linda Stone's notion of "continuous partial attention," which might be understood as a subspecies of multitasking: using mobile computing power and the Internet, we are "constantly scanning for opportunities and staying on top of contacts, events, and activities in an effort to miss nothing."

Dr. Edward Hallowell, a Massachusetts-based psychiatrist who specializes in the treatment of attention deficit/hyperactivity disorder and has written a book with the self-explanatory title *CrazyBusy*, has been offering therapies to combat extreme multitasking for years; in his book he calls multitasking a "mythical activity in which people believe they can perform two or more tasks simultaneously." In a 2005 article, he described a new condition, "Attention Deficit Trait," which he claims is rampant in the business world. ADT is "purely a response to the hyperkinetic environment in which we live," writes Hallowell, and its hallmark symptoms mimic those of ADD. "Never in history has the human brain been asked to track so many data points," Hallowell argues, and this challenge "can be controlled only by creatively engineering one's environment and one's emotional and physical health." Limiting multitasking is essential. Best-selling business advice author Timothy Ferriss also extols the virtues of "single-tasking" in his book, *The 4-Hour Workweek*.

Multitasking might also be taking a toll on the economy. One study by researchers at the University of California at Irvine monitored interruptions among office workers; they found that workers took an average of twenty-five minutes to recover from interruptions such as phone calls or answering e-mail and return to their original task. Discussing multitasking with the *New York Times* in 2007, Jonathan B. Spira, an analyst at the business research firm Basex, estimated that extreme multitasking—information overload—costs the U.S. economy $650 billion a year in lost productivity.

CHANGING OUR BRAINS

7   To better understand the multitasking phenomenon, neurologists and psychologists have studied the workings of the brain. In 1999, Jordan Grafman, chief of cognitive neuroscience at the National Institute of Neurological Disorders and Stroke (part of the National Institutes of Health), used functional magnetic resonance imaging (fMRI) scans to determine that when people engage in "task-switching"—that is, multitasking behavior—the flow of blood increases to a region of the frontal cortex called Brodmann area 10. (The flow of blood to particular regions of the brain is taken as a proxy indication of activity in those regions.) "This is presumably the last part of the brain to evolve, the most mysterious and exciting part," Grafman told the *New York Times* in 2001—adding, with a touch of hyperbole, "It's what makes us most human."

8   It is also what makes multitasking a poor long-term strategy for learning. Other studies, such as those performed by psychologist René Marois of Vanderbilt University, have used fMRI to demonstrate the brain's response to handling multiple tasks. Marois found evidence of a "response selection bottleneck" that occurs when the brain is forced to respond to several stimuli at once. As a result, task-switching leads to time lost as the brain determines which task to perform. Psychologist David Meyer at the University of Michigan believes that rather than a bottleneck in the brain, a process of "adaptive executive control" takes place, which "schedules task processes appropriately to obey instructions about their relative priorities and serial order," as he described to the *New Scientist*. Unlike many other researchers who study multitasking, Meyer is optimistic that, with training, the brain can learn to task-switch more effectively, and there is some evidence that certain simple tasks are amenable to such practice. But his research has also found that multitasking contributes to the release of stress hormones and adrenaline, which can cause long-term health problems if not controlled, and contributes to the loss of short-term memory.

9   In one recent study, Russell Poldrack, a psychology professor at the University of California, Los Angeles, found that "multitasking adversely affects how you learn. Even if you learn while multitasking, that learning is less flexible and more specialized, so you cannot retrieve the information as easily." His research demonstrates that people use different areas of the brain for learning and storing new information when they are distracted:

brain scans of people who are distracted or multitasking show activity in the striatum, a region of the brain involved in learning new skills; brain scans of people who are not distracted show activity in the hippocampus, a region involved in storing and recalling information. Discussing his research on National Public Radio recently, Poldrack warned, "We have to be aware that there is a cost to the way that our society is changing, that humans are not built to work this way. We're really built to focus. And when we sort of force ourselves to multitask, we're driving ourselves to perhaps be less efficient in the long run even though it sometimes feels like we're being more efficient."

If, as Poldrack concluded, "multitasking changes the way people learn," 10 what might this mean for today's children and teens, raised with an excess of new entertainment and educational technology, and avidly multitasking at a young age? Poldrack calls this the "million-dollar question." Media multitasking—that is, the simultaneous use of several different media, such as television, the Internet, video games, text messages, telephones, and e-mail—is clearly on the rise, as a 2006 report from the Kaiser Family Foundation showed: in 1999, only 16 percent of the time people spent using any of those media was spent on multiple media at once; by 2005, 26 percent of media time was spent multitasking. "I multitask every single second I am online," confessed one study participant. "At this very moment I am watching TV, checking my e-mail every two minutes, reading a news-group about who shot JFK, burning some music to a CD, and writing this message."

The Kaiser report noted several factors that increase the likelihood of 11 media multitasking, including "having a computer and being able to see a television from it." Also, "sensation-seeking" personality types are more likely to multitask, as are those living in "a highly TV-oriented household." The picture that emerges of these pubescent multitasking mavens is of a generation of great technical facility and intelligence but of extreme impatience, unsatisfied with slowness and uncomfortable with silence: "I get bored if it's not all going at once, because everything has gaps—waiting for a website to come up, commercials on TV, etc.," one participant said. The report concludes on a very peculiar note, perhaps intended to be optimistic: "In this media-heavy world, it is likely that brains that are more adept at media multitasking will be passed along and these changes will be naturally selected," the report states. "After all, information is power, and if one can process more information all at once, perhaps one can be more powerful." This is techno-social Darwinism, nature red in pixel and claw.

Other experts aren't so sure. As neurologist Jordan Grafman told *Time* 12 magazine: "Kids that are instant messaging while doing homework, playing games online and watching TV, I predict, aren't going to do well in the long run." "I think this generation of kids is guinea pigs," educational psychologist Jane Healy told the *San Francisco Chronicle*; she worries that they might become adults who engage in "very quick but very shallow thinking." Or, as the novelist Walter Kirn suggests in a deft essay in *The Atlantic*, we might be headed for an "Attention-Deficit Recession."

PAYING ATTENTION

13   When we talk about multitasking, we are really talking about attention: the art of paying attention, the ability to shift our attention, and, more broadly, to exercise judgment about what objects are worthy of our attention. People who have achieved great things often credit for their success a finely honed skill for paying attention. When asked about his particular genius, Isaac Newton responded that if he had made any discoveries, it was "owing more to patient attention than to any other talent."

14   William James, the great psychologist, wrote at length about the varieties of human attention. In *The Principles of Psychology* (1890), he outlined the differences among "sensorial attention," "intellectual attention," "passive attention," and the like, and noted the "gray chaotic indiscriminateness" of the minds of people who were incapable of paying attention. James compared our stream of thought to a river, and his observations presaged the cognitive "bottlenecks" described later by neurologists: "On the whole easy simple flowing predominates in it, the drift of things is with the pull of gravity, and effortless attention is the rule," he wrote. "But at intervals an obstruction, a set-back, a log-jam occurs, stops the current, creates an eddy, and makes things temporarily move the other way."

15   To James, steady attention was thus the default condition of a mature mind, an ordinary state undone only by perturbation. To readers a century later, that placid portrayal may seem alien—as though depicting a bygone world. Instead, today's multitasking adult may find something more familiar in James's description of the youthful mind: an "extreme mobility of the attention" that "makes the child seem to belong less to himself than to every object which happens to catch his notice." For some people, James noted, this challenge is never overcome; such people only get their work done "in the interstices of their mind-wandering." Like Chesterfield, James believed that the transition from youthful distraction to mature attention was in large part the result of personal mastery and discipline—and so was illustrative of character. "The faculty of voluntarily bringing back a wandering attention, over and over again," he wrote, "is the very root of judgment, character, and will."

16   Today, our collective will to pay attention seems fairly weak. We require advice books to teach us how to avoid distraction. In the not-too-distant future we may even employ new devices to help us overcome the unintended attention deficits created by today's gadgets. As one *New York Times* article recently suggested, "Further research could help create clever technology, like sensors or smart software that workers could

instruct with their preferences and priorities to serve as a high tech 'time nanny' to ease the modern multitasker's plight." Perhaps we will all accept as a matter of course a computer governor—like the devices placed on engines so that people can't drive cars beyond a certain speed. Our technological governors might prompt us with reminders to set mental limits when we try to do too much, too quickly, all at once.

Then again, perhaps we will simply adjust and come to accept what   17
James called "acquired inattention." E-mails pouring in, cell phones ringing, televisions blaring, podcasts streaming—all this may become background noise, like the "din of a foundry or factory" that James observed workers could scarcely avoid at first, but which eventually became just another part of their daily routine. For the younger generation of multitaskers, the great electronic din is an expected part of everyday life. And given what neuroscience and anecdotal evidence have shown us, this state of constant intentional self-distraction could well be of profound detriment to individual and cultural well-being. When people do their work only in the "interstices of their mind-wandering," with crumbs of attention rationed out among many competing tasks, their culture may gain in information, but it will surely weaken in wisdom.

READING FOR MEANING

This section presents three activities that will help you think about the meanings in Rosen's evaluative essay. Your instructor may ask you to do one or more of these activities in class or online.

1. **Read to Summarize.** Write a sentence or two summarizing Rosen's reasons for critiquing multitasking.

For more help with summarizing, see Chapter 10, pp. 518–19.

2. **Read to Respond**. Write a paragraph analyzing your initial reactions to Rosen's essay. For example, consider anything that resonates with your own experience or that seems contradictory, surprising, or fascinating, such as:

   - Your experience multitasking compared to "single-tasking" — and what the advantages or disadvantages are of focusing your attention on one task at a time (par. 5);

   - The idea that with practice people can get better at learning while multitasking, but that such learning is less effective than focused learning (pars. 8–9);

   - The suggestions that multitaskers are impatient and "uncomfortable with silence," and that they quickly get bored (par. 11).

Take a quiz to check your reading and vocabulary comprehension:
bedfordstmartins.com/readingcritically

3. **Read to Analyze Assumptions.** Write a paragraph or two analyzing an assumption you find intriguing in Rosen's essay. For example:

Assumptions about the causes of not focusing attention. Quoting Lord Chesterfield's writing from the eighteenth century and William James's from the nineteenth, Rosen suggests that not focusing one's attention may indicate "a weak and frivolous mind" (par. 1) or the lack of "a mature mind" or of "judgment, character, and will" (par. 15). Such language makes a moral judgment about a person's lack of seriousness or self-discipline. In contrast, quoting Edward Hallowell, Rosen suggests that not focusing attention may be a sign of illness akin to attention deficit/hyperactivity disorder (par. 5). To think critically about the assumptions in this essay about the causes of not focusing attention, ask yourself questions like these:

- Why might people, particularly young people, who do not focus their attention be labeled as lacking in character or intelligence or as suffering from a medical malady?

- Are critics less likely today than in the past to make judgments about intelligence or character, and perhaps more likely to make medical diagnoses about the same kinds of behavior? Why or why not?

Assumptions about the role of media in multitasking. According to Rosen, the Kaiser Family Foundation has reported a substantial increase in multitasking on media. She cites the foundation's finding that, in 1999, 16 percent of media time (for example, watching television, surfing the Internet, or texting friends) was spent doing two or more of such tasks simultaneously. By 2005, the time spent multitasking had increased to 26 percent. To think critically about the assumptions in this essay regarding media multitasking, ask yourself questions like these:

- When you are multitasking, is some kind of electronic medium always involved, or do you ever multitask without using media?

- One Kaiser survey participant stated, "I get bored if it's not all going at once, because everything has gaps — waiting for a website to come up, commercials on TV, etc." (par. 11). Do you primarily use media multitasking to fill or kill time, or for some other reason?

You may also want to try reflecting on challenges to your beliefs and values; see Chapter 10, pp. 526–27.

READING LIKE A WRITER

SUPPORTING THE JUDGMENT

Rosen relies primarily on authorities and research studies to support her argument about the value of multitasking. Because she is not writing for an academic audience, however, she does not have to include formal citations, as you will be expected to do in your college writing. Nevertheless, note that Rosen does provide many of the same kinds of information about her sources that formal citations offer — the source author or lead researcher's name, the title of the publication in which the borrowed material appeared, and the year of publication of the source — so that readers can locate and read the source themselves. Notice in the following examples how Rosen presents this information.

Bibliographical information

In one of the many letters he wrote to his son in the 1740s, Lord Chesterfield offered the following advice: "There is time enough for everything. . . ." (par. 1)

An article in the *New York Times Magazine* in 2001 asked, "Who can remember life before multitasking? These days we all do it." (par. 3)

"We have always multitasked . . . but never so intensely or self-consciously as now," James Gleick wrote in his 1999 book *Faster*. "We are multitasking connoisseurs. . . ." (par. 3)

Writers often begin with the source's name to provide context and establish credibility. In the third example, Rosen places the source information in the middle of the quotation, possibly because she wants to emphasize the opening phrases of both sentences.

Not all sources are quoted, of course. Writers sometimes summarize the main idea or paraphrase what the source has said:

Summary

One study by researchers at the University of California at Irvine monitored interruptions among office workers; they found that workers took an average of twenty-five minutes to recover from interruptions. . . . (par. 6)

Paraphrase

The psychologist who led the study called this new "infomania" a serious threat to workplace productivity. (par. 4)

Analyze & Write

Write a paragraph analyzing and evaluating how Rosen uses material from other authorities and research studies to support her argument:

1. First, skim paragraphs 4–9 and highlight the names of authorities and the research studies Rosen cites.
2. Then choose two sources, and determine how Rosen uses them to support her judgment about the value of multitasking. Also notice how she integrates these sources into her text.
3. Finally, consider why these sources might or might not be convincing for Rosen's readers. How convincing are they for you, and why?

A Special Reading Strategy

Looking for Patterns of Opposition

To refute a favorable judgment she expects readers to have made about multitasking, Rosen tries to reframe the argument about its value. Reframing is a common strategy writers use to help readers see the subject in a new way. Rosen tries to set up an opposition between focused attention and multitasking that makes multitasking seem less preferable. She uses Lord Chesterfield's letter advising his son and William James's ideas about psychology to associate focused attention with maturity and intelligence, and multitasking with immaturity and a lack of intelligence, or at least the inability to think properly. To see how Rosen reframes the subject, use the critical reading strategy looking for patterns of opposition (see Chapter 10, pp. 525–26).

- Reread paragraphs 1–3 and 13–16, highlighting the words Rosen uses to develop this opposition.

- Analyze the system of oppositions Rosen sets up by making a two-column chart and placing the words Rosen associates with focused attention in one column and the words she associates with multitasking in the other column. Then put an asterisk next to the word that Rosen values more highly — for example, *maturity* as opposed to *immaturity*.

- Write a couple of sentences describing the way that Rosen uses this system of oppositions to reframe readers' ideas about multitasking.

William Akana

Scott Pilgrim vs. the World:
A Hell of a Ride

William Akana wrote this review for his composition course. The assignment prompt asked students to choose a film and write a review that includes a close analysis of the cinematic techniques used in at least one important scene. Akana's instructor illustrated various cinematic techniques, such as camera angles and movements, and demonstrated how to take screen shots, explaining that students could use visuals for a class project without asking permission, but that to publish them they would have to get permission, as we have done.

- *Before you read,* think about what the title leads you to expect about Akana's evaluation. Why do you think he calls the film a "ride"?
- *As you read,* notice the screen shots and consider what purpose they serve. Would the evaluation be more or less clear and convincing without the screen shots?

As I leaned back in the movie theater seat, accompanied by my friends on a typical Saturday night, I knew I was in for something special. I was reassured; not only had my friends and I reached a unanimous vote to watch *Scott Pilgrim vs. the World*, but two of my friends had already seen the film and were eager to see it again. As soon as *Scott Pilgrim vs. the World* began, with its presentation of the classic Universal Studios introduction in old-timer eight-bit music and pixilated format, I knew I was in for one hell of a ride. From start to finish, *Scott Pilgrim vs. the World* delivers intense action in a hilarious slacker movie that also somehow reimagines romantic comedy.

Scott Pilgrim vs. the World, released in 2010 by Universal Studios, came into production as a comic book adaptation film under the direction of Edgar Wright (best known for the zombie movie masterpiece *Shaun of the Dead*). Scott Pilgrim (Michael Cera) is a twenty-two-year-old Canadian who plays bass for his indie band, Sex Bob-ombs, located in Toronto, Canada. Pilgrim's life takes a dramatic turn when he falls in love with Ramona Flowers (Mary Elizabeth Winstead), who is, quite literally, the girl of his dreams. However, he soon discovers that Ramona's former lovers have formed a league of evil exes to destroy him, and he is forced to fight to the death to prove his love. Although the film is especially targeted for old-school gamers, anime fans, and comic book fanatics, *Scott Pilgrim vs. the*

For an additional student reading, go to
bedfordstmartins.com/readingcritically.

FIG. 1. Screen shot showing gamertags

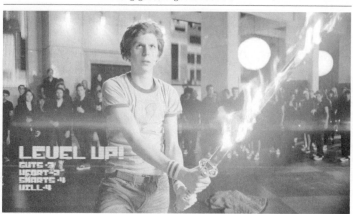

World can be appreciated and enjoyed by all audiences because of its inventive special effects, clever dialogue, and artistic cinematography and editing.

3   *Scott Pilgrim vs. the World* shines bright with superb special effects that serve to reinforce the ideas, themes, and style of the film. Special effects are plentiful throughout the entire film, ranging from superimposed annotations echoing classic gaming features to artful backgrounds and action sequences modeled on colorful comic book pages. For example, each of the main characters is described for the first time with "gamertags," short-timed boxes of information that include name, age, and rating (see fig. 1).

4   *Scott Pilgrim vs. the World* contains numerous amounts of other fun video-game-like gimmicks that were made possible through special effects. One humorous scene presents a pee bar that depletes as Pilgrim relieves himself. Another scene presents a bass battle between Pilgrim and one of the evil exes in the format of PlayStation's popular Guitar Hero (see fig. 2). It goes without saying that anyone who has ever dabbled in video games will greatly appreciate the gaming-culture inside jokes. As the reviewer for the Web site *Cinema Sight* wrote, this film is intended for "the video game generation" ("Rev.").

5   Comic book references are also installed using special effects. In almost every battle between Pilgrim and his enemies, comic-book-like backgrounds, added through CGI, enhance the eye-popping fight sequences as characters fly into the air to deliver devastating punches accompanied with traditional onomatopoeic "POWs" and "KAPOWs" (see fig. 3). However, comic book annotations are not reserved merely for fight scenes. Annotations range from even the simplest "RIIINGs" of a telephone to trails of shouting "AAAAHs" of Pilgrim as he is thrown into the air in battle. To make the film even more visually appealing, *Scott Pilgrim vs. the World*

FIG. 2.   Guitar face-off

portrays flashbacks using white and black comic strips similar to the original Scott Pilgrim comic books. Special effects play a truly vital part in enlivening the style of the film.

Another strong point of *Scott Pilgrim vs. the World* is its clever and humorous dialogue. One memorable scene in the film involves Knives Chau (Ellen Wong) and Scott Pilgrim in an awkward situation where Knives states sheepishly: "I've never even kissed a guy." In a supposedly intimate gesture of affection, Pilgrim moves closer only to pause shortly before saying "Hey . . . me neither." Additionally, *Scott Pilgrim vs. the World* is rich in cultural satire that pokes fun at adolescent and young adult behaviors. One scene contains Pilgrim telling Ramona Flowers: "I feel like I'm on drugs when I'm with you, not that I do drugs, unless you

6

FIG. 3.   Comic-book-style annotations

do—in which case, I do drugs all the time." Dialogue like this gives the film a raw yet rich sense of humor that is one of the many inventive risks of the film that pay off.

7   The best attribute by far is the film's creative cinematography and editing, which can be illustrated in the ultimate fight scene of the movie. Pilgrim finally confronts his former band members, who are playing in an underground lair for Ramona's seventh evil ex, Gideon (Jason Schwartzman). As Pilgrim admits his faults and proceeds to apologize to the band for former wrongs, the shot assumes a point of view from Pilgrim's perspective looking up to the band on stage. Shortly before Pilgrim is finished, Gideon, sitting on his throne atop a miniature pyramid, interrupts him. The shot quickly cuts to a close-up of Gideon's eyes, emphasizing his anger at Pilgrim. From this point, soft focusing is utilized to blur the background as a tracking shot follows Pilgrim in a medium close-up as he marches to the base of the pyramid. Then, shot reverse shots are used between high- and low-angled frames to illustrate Pilgrim's challenge to Gideon for a final duel.

8   Gideon, in response to the challenge, asks Pilgrim if he is fighting for Ramona, which leads to a climactic epiphany for Pilgrim as he realizes his true motive, admitting in a tight close-up: "No. I want to fight you for me." As Pilgrim finishes this confession, a deep narrating voice announces that "Scott Pilgrim has earned the power of self-respect," and in turn, he is awarded a magical sword with which he can defeat Gideon. Subsequently, the camera pans from left to right in a subjective shot to illustrate Gideon's goons closing in on Pilgrim. Pilgrim, in a series of fast-paced jump cuts, quickly dispatches the bad guys before charging up the pyramid. After an extended battle, deep focusing is used with a long shot to establish that the hierarchy has changed between hero and villain: Pilgrim is seen standing atop the pyramid, looking down at the kneeling Gideon before Pilgrim kicks him to smithereens.

9   This brilliantly executed scene illustrates the artful cinematography of *Scott Pilgrim vs. the World*. More importantly, it delivers the film's thematic message, which undercuts the cliché "love conquers all" and instead focuses on the fresh concept that, in the grand scheme of things, the only person you are fighting for is yourself. Some reviewers have criticized the film because they think that in the end it fails as a romantic comedy. For example, *Miami Herald* film reviewer Rene Rodriguez argues that the film ultimately fails because of the lack of "chemistry" or "emotional involvement" in the romance between Pilgrim and Ramona. But I agree with *New York Times* reviewer A. O. Scott, who argues that "the movie comes home to the well-known territory of the coming-of-age story, with an account of lessons learned and conflicts resolved." Fighting Ramona's exes forces Pilgrim to wake up out of his slacker stupor. Before he can begin a grown-up relationship with Ramona, he has to come to terms with his own fail-

FIG. 4.   Threshold of a new beginning?

ures, especially in relation to his own exes. The film ends, as director Edgar Wright explained in an interview, on the threshold of a new beginning: "Scott and Ramona might not make it past the end credits, or it might be the start of a beautiful relationship" (Cozzalio). (See fig. 4.)

Works Cited

Cozzalio, Dennis. "Scott Pilgrim's Dreamscape and the Glories of the Wright Stuff II: An interview with director Edgar Wright." *Sergio Leone and the Infield Fly Rule*. SergioLeoneIFR.blogspot.com, 15 Jan. 2011. Web. 30 Mar. 2011.

Rodriguez, Rene. Rev. of *Scott Pilgrim vs. the World*. *Miami Herald*. Miami .com, 11 Aug. 2010. Web. 28 Mar. 2011.

Scott, A. O. "This Girl Has a Lot of Baggage, and He Must Shoulder the Load." *New York Times*. New York Times, 12 Aug. 2010. Web. 29 Mar. 2011.

Rev. of *Scott Pilgrim vs. The World*. *Cinema Sight*. CinemaSight.com, 13 Sept. 2010. Web. 30 Mar. 2011.

READING FOR MEANING

This section presents three activities that will help you think about the meanings in Akana's evaluative essay. Your instructor may ask you to do one or more of these activities in class or online.

   1. **Read to Summarize.** Write a sentence or two identifying Akana's overall judgment and his main reasons.

   For more help with summarizing, see Chapter 10, pp. 518–19.

 Take a quiz to check your reading and vocabulary comprehension:
bedfordstmartins.com/readingcritically

2. **Read to Respond.** Write a paragraph analyzing your initial reaction to Akana's essay. For example, consider anything that resonates with your experience or that seems contradictory, surprising, or fascinating, such as:

- Akana's judgment that "*Scott Pilgrim vs. the World* can be appreciated and enjoyed by all audiences," even though it is "targeted for old-school gamers, anime fans, and comic book fanatics" (par. 2) — perhaps in relation to your own evaluation of the film, if you have seen it;

- Akana's close analysis of the cinematography in paragraphs 7–9, considering how clear and vivid his analysis is, whether or not you have seen the film.

You may also try judging the writer's credibility; see Chapter 10, pp. 537–38.

3. **Read to Analyze Assumptions.** Write a paragraph or two analyzing an assumption you find intriguing in Akana's essay. For example:

Assumptions about the value of special effects. Akana claims that even though "the film is especially targeted for old-school gamers, anime fans, and comic book fanatics," its "inventive special effects" "can be appreciated and enjoyed by all audiences" (par. 2). He then goes on to describe some of the special effects, which he also illustrates with screen shots. To think critically about the assumptions in this essay related to the value of special effects in the experience of watching a film, ask yourself questions like these:

- Whether or not you have seen this particular film, how convincing is Akana's argument that the film's special effects "can be appreciated and enjoyed by all audiences" (par. 2)?

- Akana claims that what makes the special effects in *Scott Pilgrim vs. the World* so effective is that they "reinforce the ideas, themes, and style of the film" (par. 3). Why do you think it is important to Akana for the special effects to play this reinforcing role? What other purposes could special effects serve?

- Think of another film you have seen that uses special effects. What do they contribute?

Assumptions about self-respect. Akana appears to accept the idea that it is crucial for Scott Pilgrim to recognize "his true motive": that he wants to fight for himself, not for Ramona's love (par. 8). In fact, Akana calls Pilgrim's "confession" the film's "climactic epiphany" or discovery. To think critically about the assumptions in this essay regarding self-respect, ask yourself questions like these:

- Why do you think Pilgrim's recognition of his true motive in fighting Gideon gives him a sense of self-respect?

- Akana points out that upon confessing his true motive, Gideon is awarded the "power of self-respect," in this case "a magical sword with which he can defeat Gideon" (par. 8). Why might gaining self-respect give one power?
- Do you agree with Akana that the film has a "fresh concept" — namely, that in place of the "cliché 'love conquers all,'" the film posits the idea that "the only person you are fighting for is yourself" (par. 9)? Is this a new or original idea, or does it really just reinforce the self-centeredness of Pilgrim's slacker persona?

READING LIKE A WRITER

PRESENTING THE SUBJECT

Writers of evaluative essays usually begin by naming and describing their subject, but often they provide only enough information to give readers a context for the judgment. However, certain kinds of evaluations — such as those looking at a book, app, game, musical performance, television, or film — may require more information because their readers will be trying to decide whether to buy the book or app, attend the performance, watch the show, or see the film. Reviewers of these kinds of subjects carefully choose details that help readers make a decision.

Plot/setting
Director and what he's known for
Actors in key roles

Scott Pilgrim vs. the World, released in 2010 by Universal Studios, came into production as a comic book adaptation film under the direction of Edgar Wright (best known for the zombie movie masterpiece *Shaun of the Dead*). Scott Pilgrim (Michael Cera) is a twenty-two-year-old Canadian who plays bass for his indie band, Sex Bob-ombs, located in Toronto, Canada. Pilgrim's life takes a dramatic turn when he falls in love with Ramona Flowers (Mary Elizabeth Winstead), who is, quite literally, the girl of his dreams. However, he soon discovers that Ramona's former lovers have formed a league of evil exes to destroy him, and he is forced to fight to the death to prove his love. (par. 2)

Film reviews, for example, typically identify the actors and director, describe the setting, tell a little about the plot without giving too much away, and identify the film by **genre** or type. Informing readers about the genre is especially important because different genres have different criteria to meet. All films may be evaluated on the basis of the acting, directing, screenwriting, and so on. But comedies have to be funny, and action films have to be exciting. Therefore, as a critical reader, you will want to think about how Akana classifies *Scott Pilgrim vs. the World*.

> ## Analyze & Write
>
> Write a paragraph analyzing how Akana classifies *Scott Pilgrim vs. the World*.
>
> 1. First, find and underline the words in paragraph 1 that Akana uses to classify the genres or kinds of films to which *Scott Pilgrim vs. the World* could be compared. Then skim the essay noting where he refers again to these genres. How do you think this information would help readers of his review?
>
> 2. Given the way he classifies the film, does he reveal too much of the plot, too little, or enough for readers to make a decision about whether or not to see the film
>
> 3. How appropriate are his criteria for judging the film, in light of his genre classification of the film?

ANALYZING VISUALS

Write a paragraph analyzing the still shots Akana includes in his essay and explaining what they contribute to his review. To do the analysis, you can use the Criteria for Analyzing Visuals chart in Chapter 12, on pp. 611–12. Don't feel you have to answer all of the questions in the chart; focus on those that seem most productive in helping you write a paragraph-length analysis. To help you get started, consider adding these questions that specifically refer to Akana's use of screen shots from the movie:

- What do the screen shots reveal about the story? About the characters and their relationships? About the tone, or mood, of the film overall?

- How does Akana use the visuals to support his claims about the film? Are the selected screen shots effective at illustrating his points?

- Given that his evaluation of *Scott Pilgrim vs. the World* is based on his claim that "its inventive special effects . . . and artistic cinematography and editing" (par. 2) make the film enjoyable, it is logical for Akana to include screen shots from the film as evidence. But do these screen shots play any other role? For example, do they help make the organization of the essay clear? Do they help persuade readers that the film is entertaining?

Christine Romano

Jessica Statsky's "Children Need to Play, Not Compete": An Evaluation

Christine Romano wrote the following essay when she was a first-year college student. In it, she evaluates a position paper written by another student, Jessica Statsky's "Children Need to Play, Not Compete," which appears in Chapter 7 of this book (pp. 349–54). Romano focuses not on the writing strategies Statsky uses but rather on her logic — that is, on whether Statsky's argument is likely to convince her intended readers. She evaluates the logic of the argument according to the criteria or standards presented in Chapter 10 (pp. 530–32).

- *Before you read Romano's evaluation, you might want to read Statsky's essay, thinking about what seems most and least convincing to you about her argument that competitive sports can be harmful to young children.*

- *As you read, think about Romano's criteria. How important is it that the supporting evidence for an argument be "appropriate, believable, consistent, and complete" (par. 1)?*

Parents of young children have a lot to worry about and to hope for. In "Children Need to Play, Not Compete," Jessica Statsky appeals to their worries and hopes in order to convince them that organized competitive sports may harm their children physically and psychologically. Statsky states her thesis clearly and fully forecasts the reasons she will offer to justify her position: Besides causing physical and psychological harm, competitive sports discourage young people from becoming players and fans when they are older and inevitably put parents' needs and fantasies ahead of children's welfare. Statsky also carefully defines her key terms. By *sports*, for example, she means to include both contact and noncontact sports that emphasize competition. The sports may be organized locally at schools or summer sports camps or nationally, as in the examples of Peewee Football and Little League Baseball. She is concerned only with children six to twelve years of age. 1

In this essay, I will evaluate the logic of Statsky's argument, considering whether the support for her thesis is appropriate, believable, consistent, and complete. While her logic *is* appropriate, believable, and consistent, her argument also has weaknesses. It seems incomplete because it neglects to anticipate parents' predictable questions and objections and because it fails to support certain parts fully. 2

 For an additional student reading, go to
bedfordstmartins.com/readingcritically.

3   Statsky provides appropriate support for her thesis. Throughout her essay, she relies for support on different kinds of information (she cites thirteen separate sources, including books, newspapers, and Web sites). Her quotations, examples, and statistics all support the reasons she believes competitive sports are bad for children. For example, in paragraph 3, Statsky offers the reason that competitive sports may damage children's bodies and that contact sports may be especially injurious. She supports this reason by paraphrasing Koppett's statement that muscle strain or even permanent injury may result when a twelve-year-old throws curve balls. She then quotes Tutko on the dangers of tackle football. The opinions of both experts are obviously appropriate. They are relevant to her reason, and we can easily imagine that they would worry many parents.

4   Not only is Statsky's support appropriate but it is also believable. Statsky quotes or summarizes authorities to support her argument in nearly every paragraph. The question is whether readers would find these authorities believable or credible. Since Statsky relies almost entirely on authorities to support her argument, readers must believe these authorities for her argument to succeed. I have not read Statsky's sources, but I think there are good reasons to consider them authoritative. First of all, the newspaper writers she quotes write for two of America's most respected newspapers, the *New York Times* and the *Los Angeles Times*. Both of these newspapers have sports reporters who not only report on sports events but also take a critical look at sports issues. In addition, both newspapers have reporters who specialize in children's health and education. Second, Statsky gives background information about the authorities she quotes, information intended to increase the person's believability in the eyes of parents of young children. In paragraph 3, she tells readers that Thomas Tutko is "a psychology professor at San Jose State University and coauthor of the book *Winning Is Everything and Other American Myths*." In paragraph 5, she announces that Martin Rablovsky is "a former sports editor for the *New York Times*," and she notes that he has watched children play organized sports for many years. Third, Statsky quotes from a number of Web sites, including the official Little League site and the American Orthopaedic Society for Sports Medicine. Parents are likely to accept the authority of these sites.

5   In addition to quoting authorities, Statsky relies on examples and anecdotes to support the reasons for her position. If examples and anecdotes are to be believable, they must seem representative to readers, not bizarre or highly unusual or completely unpredictable. Readers can imagine a similar event happening elsewhere. For anecdotes to be believable, they should, in addition, be specific and true to life. All of Statsky's examples and anecdotes fulfill these requirements, and her readers would likely find them believable. For example, early in her argument, in paragraph 4, Statsky reasons that fear of being hurt greatly reduces children's enjoyment

of contact sports. The anecdote comes from Tosches's investigative report on Peewee Football, as does the quotation by the mother of an eight-year-old player who says that the children become frightened and pretend to be injured in order to stay out of the game. In the anecdote, a seven-year-old makes himself vomit to avoid playing. Because these echo the familiar "I feel bad" or "I'm sick" excuse children give when they do not want to go somewhere (especially school) or do something, most parents would find them believable. They could easily imagine their own children pretending to be hurt or ill if they were fearful or depressed. The anecdote is also specific. Tosches reports what the boy said and did and what the coach said and did.

Other examples provide support for all the major reasons Statsky gives   6
for her position:

- That competitive sports pose psychological dangers—children becoming serious and unplayful when the game starts (par. 5)

- That adults' desire to win puts children at risk—parents fighting each other at a Peewee Football game and a baseball coach setting fire to an opposing team's jersey (par. 8)

- That organized sports should emphasize cooperation and individual performance instead of winning—a coach wishing to ban scoring but finding that parents would not support him and a New York City basketball league in which all children play an equal amount of time and scoring is easier (pars. 10–11)

All of these examples are appropriate to the reasons they support. They are also believable. Together, they help Statsky achieve her purpose of convincing parents that organized, competitive sports may be bad for their children and that there are alternatives.

If readers are to find an argument logical and convincing, it must be   7
consistent and complete. While there are no inconsistencies or contradictions in Statsky's argument, it is seriously incomplete because it neglects to support fully one of its reasons, it fails to anticipate many predictable questions parents would have, and it pays too little attention to noncontact competitive team sports. The most obvious example of thin support comes in paragraphs 10–11, where Statsky asserts that many parents are ready for children's team sports that emphasize cooperation and individual performance. Yet the example of a Little League official who failed to win parents' approval to ban scores raises serious questions about just how many parents are ready to embrace noncompetitive sports teams. The other support, a brief description of City Sports for Kids in New York City, is very convincing but will only be logically compelling to those parents who are already inclined to agree with Statsky's position. Parents inclined to disagree with Statsky would need additional evidence. Most parents know that big cities

receive special federal funding for evening, weekend, and summer recreation. Brief descriptions of six or eight noncompetitive teams in a variety of
sports in cities, rural areas, suburban neighborhoods—some funded publicly, some funded privately—would be more likely to convince skeptics.
Statsky is guilty here of failing to accept the burden of proof, a logical
fallacy.

8   Statsky's argument is also incomplete in that it fails to anticipate certain
objections and questions that some parents, especially those she most
wants to convince, are almost sure to raise. In the first sentences of paragraphs 10 and 12, Statsky does show that she is thinking about her readers'
questions. She does not go nearly far enough, however, to have a chance
of influencing two types of readers: those who themselves are or were fans
of and participants in competitive sports and those who want their six- to
twelve-year-old children involved in mainstream sports programs despite
the risks, especially the national programs that have a certain prestige.
Such parents might feel that competitive team sports for young children
create a sense of community with a shared purpose, build character
through self-sacrifice and commitment to the group, teach children to face
their fears early and learn how to deal with them through the support of
coaches and team members, and introduce children to the principles of
social cooperation and collaboration. Some parents are likely to believe
and to know from personal experience that coaches who burn opposing
teams' jerseys on the pitching mound before the game starts are the exception, not the rule. Some young children idolize teachers and coaches, and
team practice and games are the brightest moments in their lives. Statsky
seems not to have considered these reasonable possibilities, and as a result
her argument lacks a compelling logic it might have had. By acknowledging that she was aware of many of these objections—and perhaps even
accommodating more of them in her own argument, as she does in paragraph 12, while refuting other objections—she would have strengthened
her argument.

9   Finally, Statsky's argument is incomplete because she overlooks examples of noncontact team sports. Track, swimming, and tennis are good
examples that some readers would certainly think of. Some elementary
schools compete in track meets. Public and private clubs and recreational
programs organize competitive swimming and tennis competitions. In
these sports, individual performance is the focus. No one gets trampled.
Children exert themselves only as much as they are able to. Yet individual
performances are scored, and a team score is derived. Because Statsky fails
to mention any of these obvious possibilities, her argument is weakened.

10   The logic of Statsky's argument, then, has both strengths and weaknesses. The support she offers is appropriate, believable, and consistent.
The major weakness is incompleteness—she fails to anticipate more fully
the likely objections of a wide range of readers. Her logic would prevent

parents who enjoy and advocate competitive sports from taking her argument seriously. Such parents and their children have probably had positive
experiences with team sports, and these experiences would lead them to
believe that the gains are worth whatever risks may be involved. Many
probably think that the risks Statsky points out can be avoided by careful
monitoring. For those parents inclined to agree with her, Statsky's logic is
likely to seem sound and complete. An argument that successfully confirms readers' beliefs is certainly valid, and Statsky succeeds admirably
at this kind of argument. Because she does not offer compelling counterarguments to the legitimate objections of those inclined not to agree with
her, however, her success is limited.

READING FOR MEANING

This section presents three activities that will help you think about the meanings
in Romano's evaluative essay. Your instructor may ask you to do one or more of
these activities in class or online.

1. **Read to Summarize.** Write a sentence or two briefly summarizing the
   strengths and weaknesses of Statsky's argument, according to Romano.

   For more help with summarizing, see Chapter 10, pp. 518–19.

2. **Read to Respond.** Write a paragraph analyzing your initial thoughts and
   feelings about Romano's essay. For example, consider anything that resonates with your own experience or that seems contradictory, surprising,
   or fascinating, such as:

   - Reasons that Romano finds Statsky's argument believable (pars. 4–6);

   - Further reasons that parents of six- to twelve-year-old children might
     find Statsky's argument incomplete;

   - Your own experience as a member of an organized sports team for chil-
     dren of the same age group, comparing or contrasting it with what
     Romano finds believable or incomplete in Statsky's argument.

3. **Read to Analyze Assumptions.** Write a paragraph or two analyzing an
   assumption you find intriguing in Romano's essay. For example:

   You may also try evaluating the logic of an argument; see Chapter 10, pp. 530–32.

   Assumptions about the relative value of competition or cooperation.
   Romano gives an example supporting Statsky's argument that team
   sports for young children "should emphasize cooperation and individual
   performance instead of winning" (par. 6). In paragraph 8, however,
   Romano suggests that some parents believe that team sports may teach

Take a quiz to check your reading and vocabulary comprehension:
bedfordstmartins.com/readingcritically

cooperation together with competition and that the two skills and attitudes may be more closely related than Statsky acknowledges. To think critically about the assumptions in this essay related to competition and cooperation, ask yourself questions like these:

- What do you think leads Romano to suggest that children learn both competition and cooperation when they participate in team sports?
- Do you think that competition is highly valued in our society and, if so, why?
- Do you think that cooperation is valued as highly as competition? How is learning to cooperate and collaborate beneficial for us as individuals and as a society?

Assumptions about the importance of facing fear. As Romano notes in paragraph 5, "Statsky reasons that fear of being hurt greatly reduces children's enjoyment of contact sports," and as support she cites Tosches's anecdote about the child who "makes himself vomit to avoid playing." Nevertheless, Romano suggests that some parents think facing fear is a good thing — that "competitive team sports for young children . . . teach children to face their fears early and learn how to deal with them" (par. 8). To think critically about the assumptions in this essay related to facing fear, ask yourself questions like these:

- In what contexts, other than sports, do people typically experience physical or psychological fear?
- Why might some people think that learning how to deal with fear (presumably by doing something even though it causes us to be fearful) is a good thing?
- How do the stories we read and watch on television and film reinforce this assumption that fear should be faced and dealt with, if not overcome?

READING LIKE A WRITER

ORGANIZING THE EVALUATION

Transitions or cues play an important role in helping readers follow the logic of the argument. Logical transitions serve a variety of specific purposes, such as:

To list items consecutively

> . . . there are good reasons to consider them authoritative. First of all, the newspaper writers. . . . Second, Statsky gives. . . . Third, Statsky quotes. . . . (par. 4)

To call attention to additional points

>> In addition to quoting authorities, Statsky . . . (par. 5)

>> Statsky's argument is also incomplete in that . . . (par. 8)

>> Other examples provide support for all the major reasons Statsky gives for her position:

Note that items in bulleted list are parallel.

- That competitive sports pose . . .
- That adults' desire to win puts . . .
- That organized sports should emphasize . . . (par. 6)

To introduce a contrast or an opposing point

>> I have not read Statsky's sources, *but* I think . . . (par. 4)

>> She does not go nearly far enough, *however*, to . . . (par. 8)

To signal a cause or effect

Transition indicating a cause

>> It seems incomplete because it . . . (par. 2)

Transition indicating an effect

>> Statsky seems . . . , and as a result her argument lacks . . . (par. 8)

To introduce an example

>> For example, in paragraph 3, Statsky offers . . . (par. 3)

>> Finally, Statsky's argument is . . . (par. 9)

>> The logic of Statsky's argument, then, has . . . (par. 10)

| Analyze & Write |

Write a paragraph analyzing and evaluating the effectiveness of Romano's cueing strategies.

1. First, find Romano's thesis and forecasting statement, underlining the reasons supporting her argument.
2. Then skim the essay, noting where each of her reasons is brought up again, underlining topic sentences and any cues she uses to help readers follow her argument.
3. How effectively does Romano use these devices to orient readers? Where, if anywhere, would you appreciate more cueing?

Reviewing What Makes Evaluations Effective

An effective evaluation

- presents the subject in a way that is appropriate for the purpose and audience;

- supports the judgment with reasons and evidence based on shared criteria;

- responds sensitively to possible objections and alternative judgments;

- organizes the review clearly and logically, helping readers follow the argument.

Analyze & Write

Write a brief evaluation—positive, negative, or mixed—of one of the readings in this chapter, explaining why you think it succeeds or fails as an evaluation. Be sure to consider the characteristics that distinguish evaluative writing, as well as how successful the writer has been in communicating his or her purpose to the intended audience. You may also want to consider the effect the medium of presentation had on decisions the writer made.

A GUIDE TO WRITING EVALUATIONS

As you've read and discussed the reading selections in this chapter, you have probably done a good deal of analytical writing. Your instructor may assign a capstone project to write a brief evaluation of your own. Having learned how writers present the subject appropriately, support their judgment and respond effectively to other views, and help readers follow their argument, you can confidently turn to writing an evaluation of a subject that interests you. This Guide to Writing offers detailed suggestions for writing evaluative essays and resources to help you meet the special challenges this kind of writing presents.

THE WRITING ASSIGNMENT

Write an evaluation supporting your judgment.

- Choose a subject that you can analyze in detail.

- Base your judgment on widely recognized criteria for evaluating a subject like yours.

- Marshal evidence to support your judgment.

- Consider possible objections your readers might raise as well as alternative judgments they might prefer.

- Organize your evaluation clearly and logically.

WRITING A DRAFT

INVENTION, PLANNING, AND COMPOSING

The following activities will help you choose a subject, analyze it, and develop an essay that presents the subject and your judgment of it, with support based on shared criteria, sound reasoning, and solid evidence.

Choosing a Subject to Evaluate

Rather than limiting yourself to the first subject that comes to mind, take a few minutes to consider your options and list as many subjects as you can. Below are some criteria that can help you choose a promising subject, followed by suggestions for the types of subjects you might consider writing about.

Choose a subject that

- you can view and review (for example, a location you can visit; a printed text; or a Web site or digital recording from which you can capture stills or video clips to use as examples);

- is typically evaluated according to criteria or standards of judgment that you understand and share with your readers;

- has strengths and/or weaknesses you could illustrate.

Below are some categories and ideas for possible subjects:

- *Culture:* a film or group of films, a television show or series, a computer game, a song, a live or recorded performance, an art museum or individual work of art, a park

- *Written work:* an essay in this book or another your instructor approves, a short story, Web site, magazine, campus publication, textbook in a course you've taken

- *Education:* your high school, a course you have taken, a laboratory you have worked in, a library or campus support service, a teacher or program

- *Government:* an elected official or candidate for public office, a proposed or existing law, an agency or program

- *Social:* a club or organized activity such as a camping trip, sports team, debate group

Assessing Your Subject and Considering How to Present It to Your Readers

Once you have made a preliminary choice of a subject, consider how you can frame or reframe it so that readers will be open to your evaluation. To do this, consider first how you regard the subject and what your readers are likely to think. Use the following questions and sentence strategies as a jumping-off point. You can make the sentences you generate your own later, as you revise.

What Do I Think?

List those qualities of your subject that you like and dislike, or list its strengths and weaknesses or advantages and disadvantages.

- What makes .... [good/bad] is ...., ..., and ....
- Although .... is stellar in [these ways], it falls short in [these other ways].

What genre or kind of subject is it?

- The .... is a [name genre or category of subject, such as romantic comedy or horror movie].

► It is an innovative [name category in which the subject belongs] that combines elements of .... and ....

► [Subject] is rather unconventional for a [name category in which your subject belongs].

What criteria or standards of judgment do you usually use to evaluate things of this kind?

► I expect .... to be .... or ....

► I dislike it when .... are ....

How does your subject compare to other examples of the genre?

► Compared to [other subjects], ... has the [best or worst] .... [name trait].

► The .... is like [a comparable subject] in that both [are/do/make] .... , but this subject is [more/less] ....

► Whereas other [comparable subjects] can be [faulted/praised for] .... , this subject ....

What Do My Readers Think?

Who are your readers, and why will they be reading your evaluation? Is the subject new or familiar to them?

► My readers are .... and are probably reading my review [to learn about the subject or to decide whether to see it, play it, or buy it].

► My readers will probably be familiar with the subject [and may have heard or read others' evaluations of it]. They may be curious to know what I think because ....

How might factors such as the readers' age, gender, cultural background, or work experience affect their judgment of the subject?

► [Older/Younger] readers are [less/more] likely to ....

► People who work in .... or who are familiar with .... may be [more/less critical, or apply different standards] to a subject like this one.

What criteria or standards of judgment do you expect your readers to use when evaluating subjects of this kind? What other examples of the genre would they be familiar with?

► I expect readers to share my criteria.

► If they [like/dislike] [comparable subject], they are sure to [like/dislike] ....

► Judging [this kind of subject] on the basis of .... is likely to surprise readers because they probably are more familiar with .... and ....

Considering Your Purpose for Your Audience

Write for a few minutes exploring your purpose in writing to your particular audience. Ask yourself questions like these:

- What do I want my readers to believe or do after they read my essay?

- How can I connect to their experience with my subject (or subjects like it)? How can I interest them in a subject that is outside their experience?

- Can I assume that readers will share my standards for judging the subject, or must I explain and justify the standards?

- How can I offer a balanced evaluation that will enhance my credibility with readers?

Formulating a Working Thesis Statement

A working thesis will help you begin drafting your essay purposefully. Your thesis should announce your subject and make your overall judgment clear: stating whether your subject is good or bad, or better or worse than something else in the same genre or category.

Remember that evaluations can be mixed — you can concede shortcomings in a generally favorable review or concede admirable qualities in a mostly negative assessment. If you feel comfortable drafting a working thesis statement now, do so. You may use the sentence strategies below as a jumping-off point — you can always revise them later — or use language of your own. (Alternatively, if you prefer to develop your argument before trying to formulate a thesis, skip this activity now and return to it later.)

A good strategy is to begin by naming the subject and identifying the kind of subject it is, and then using value terms to state your judgment of the subject's strengths and weaknesses:

- .... is a brilliant embodiment of [the genre/category], especially notable for its superb .... and thorough ....
- Because I admire [name artist]'s other work, I expected .... to be .... But I was [disappointed/surprised] by ....
- .... has many good qualities, including .... and .... ; however, the pluses do not outweigh its one major drawback, namely that ....

As you develop your argument, you may want to rework your thesis to make it more compelling by sharpening the language and perhaps also by forecasting your reasons. You may also need to *qualify* your judgment with words like *generally*, *may*, or *in part*.

Here are two sample thesis statements from the readings:

McDonald's is bad for your kids. . . . [T]hese jobs undermine school attendance and involvement, impart few skills that will be useful in later life, and simultaneously skew the values of teen-agers — especially their ideas about the worth of a dollar. (Etzioni, pars. 1, 3)

While her logic *is* appropriate, believable, and consistent, her argument also has weaknesses. It seems incomplete because it neglects to anticipate parents' predictable questions and objections and because it fails to support certain parts fully. (Romano, par. 2)

Both of these thesis statements assert the writer's judgment clearly and also forecast the reasons that will support the argument. But whereas Etzioni's thesis is unmistakably negative in its overall judgment, Romano's is mixed.

Developing the Reasons and Evidence Supporting Your Judgment

The following activities will help you find reasons and evidence to support your evaluation. Begin by writing down what you already know. You can do some focused research later to fill in the details.

List the good and bad qualities of the subject. Begin by reviewing the criteria and the value terms you have already used to describe the good and bad qualities of the subject. These are the potential reasons for your judgment. Try restating them using this basic sentence strategy, which is also illustrated by an example from student William Akana's film review:

▶ .... is [your overall judgment] because ...., ..., and ....

Example:

... *Scott Pilgrim vs. the World* can be appreciated and enjoyed by all audiences because of its inventive special effects, clever dialogue, and artistic cinematography and editing. (par. 2)

Write steadily for at least five minutes, developing your reasons. Ask yourself questions like these:

▶ Why are the characteristics I'm pointing out for praise or criticism so important in judging my subject?

Example:

Akana singles out special effects, dialogue, cinematography and editing because of the particular kind of film *Scott Pilgrim vs. the World* is—"a hilarious slacker movie that also somehow reimagines romantic comedy" (par. 1).

▶ How can I prove to readers that the value terms I'm using to evaluate these characteristics are fair and accurate?

Example:

Akana analyzes the film's special effects and gives readers specific examples, including screen shots, to demonstrate that they are indeed "inventive."

Make notes of the evidence you will use to support your judgment. Evidence you might use to support each reason may include the following:

- examples

- quotations from authorities

- textual evidence (quotations, paraphrases, or summaries)

- illustrations, such as screen shots, video clips, or photographs

- statistics

- comparisons or contrasts

You may already have some evidence you could use. If you lack evidence for any of your reasons, make a *Research to Do* note for later.

Researching Your Evaluation

Consult your notes to determine what you need to find out. If you are evaluating a subject that others have written about, try searching for articles or books on your topic. Enter keywords or phrases related to the subject, genre, or category into the search box of

- an all-purpose database — such as *Academic OneFile* (InfoTrac) or *Academic Search Complete* (EBSCOHost) — to find relevant articles in magazines and journals;

- the database *Lexis/Nexis* to find newspaper reviews;

- a search engine like *Google* or *Yahoo!* (Akana used *Movie Review Query Engine* [mrqe.com] and *Rotten Tomatoes* to find film reviews of *Scott Pilgrim vs. the World*);

- your library's catalog to locate books on your topic.

For more about searching a database or catalog, see Chapter 11, pp. 548–51. Turn to databases and search engines for information on recent items, like films and popular novels; use books, databases, and search engines to find information on classic topics. (Books are more likely to provide in-depth information, but articles in print or online are more likely to be current.)

Responding to a Likely Objection or Alternative Judgment

Start by identifying an objection or an alternative judgment you expect some readers to raise. To come up with likely objections or alternative judgments, you might try the following:

- *Brainstorm* a list on your own or with fellow students.

- *Freewrite* for ten minutes on this topic.

- Conduct research to learn what others have said about your subject.
- Conduct interviews with experts.
- Distribute a survey to a group of people similar to your intended readers.

Then figure out whether to concede or refute a likely objection or alternative judgment. You may be able simply to acknowledge an objection or alternative judgment. But if the criticism is serious, consider conceding the point and qualifying your judgment. You might also try to refute an objection or alternative judgment by arguing that the standards you are using are appropriate and important. Use the following strategies for generating ideas and sentences as a jumping-off point, and revise them later to make them your own.

1. Start by listing objections you expect readers to have as well as their preferred alternative judgments. You have already considered your readers and the criteria they are likely to favor (p. 297). If their criteria differ from yours, you may need to explain or defend your criteria.

2. Analyze your list of objections and alternative judgments to determine which are likely to be most powerful for your readers.

3. Draft refutations and concession statements:

To refute

▶ Some people think .... [alternative judgment] because of .... , ... , and .... [reasons]. Although one can see why they might make this argument, the evidence does not back it up because ....

▶ Reviewers have remarked that .... [subject] is a pale imitation of [comparable subject]. I disagree. Whereas [comparable subject] is .... , ... [subject] is ....

▶ This .... has generated criticism for its supposed .... But .... is not .... Instead, it is ....

To concede

▶ Indeed, the more hard-core enthusiasts may carp that .... is not sufficiently .... [shortcomings].

▶ The one justifiable criticism that could be made against .... is ....

▶ As some critics have pointed out, ... follows the tried-and-true formula of ....

To concede and refute

Frequently, writers concede a point only to come back with a refutation. To make this move, follow concessions like those above with sentences that begin with a transition emphasizing contrast, like *but*, *however*, *yet*, or *nevertheless*, and then explain why you believe that your judgment is more powerful or compelling.

▶ As some critics have pointed out, ... follows the tried-and-true formula of .... In this case, however, the [director/writer/artist] is using the formula effectively to ....

Research Note: You may want to return to this activity after conducting further research. (For example, when he researched published reviews of *Scott Pilgrim*, student William Akana found objections to his argument as well as alternative judgments he could quote and refute.)

Including Visuals or Other Media

If appropriate to your rhetorical situation, consider whether visual or audio illustrations — screen shots, photographs, film clips, background music, or sound bites — would help you present your subject more effectively to readers or strengthen your evaluation of it. Visual and audio materials are not at all a requirement of an effective evaluation, but they could provide strong support to your argument.

Note: Be sure to cite the source of visual or audio elements you did not create, and get permission from the source if your essay is going to be published on a Web site that is not password-protected.

Organizing Your Evaluation Effectively for Your Readers

The forecasting statement from your thesis can act as a rough outline when you are writing a simpler evaluation, but for complex evaluations, a scratch outline of your argument may be more useful for organizing your evaluation effectively for your readers. You might even want to make two or three different outlines before choosing the organization that looks most promising.

An evaluative essay contains as many as four basic parts:

1. Presentation of the subject

2. Judgment of the subject

3. Presentation of reasons and support

4. Consideration of readers' objections and alternative judgments

These parts can be organized in various ways: If you are writing primarily for readers who disagree with your judgment, you could start by showing them what you think they have overlooked or misjudged about the subject. Then you could anticipate and refute their likely objections before presenting your own reasons. If you expect some readers to disagree with your judgment even though they share your standards, you could begin by restating these standards and then demonstrate how the subject fails to meet them. Then you could present your reasons and support before responding to alternative judgments.

Whether you choose either of these approaches or an approach of your own, never be a slave to an outline: As you draft, you may see ways to improve your original plan, and you should be ready to revise your outline, shift parts around, or drop or add parts as needed. If you use the outlining function of your word processing program, changing your outline will be easy, and you may be able to write the essay simply by expanding that outline.

Working with Sources

Using Summary to Support Your Evaluative Argument

Writers of evaluation often use summary to support their argument. For example, evaluations may summarize an expert source (as Etzioni and Rosen do), the plot of a film (as Akana does), or an aspect of a written text (as Romano and Gladwell do). Let's look closely at how Romano uses summary.

Romano's summary

Quotes	For example, in paragraph 3, Statsky offers the reason that competi-
Paraphrases	tive sports may damage children's bodies and that contact sports may
Describes	be especially injurious. She supports this reason by paraphrasing
Statsky's moves	Koppett's statement that muscle strain or even permanent injury may
	result when a twelve-year-old throws curve balls. She then quotes
	Tutko on the dangers of tackle football. (Romano, par. 3)

Statsky's original (see p. 350, par. 3)

Language	One readily understandable danger of overly competitive sports is that
paraphrased	they entice children into physical actions that are bad for growing
&/or quoted	bodies. "There is a growing epidemic of preventable youth sports inju-
	ries," according to the STOP Sports Injuries campaign. "Among athletes
	ages 5 to 14, 28 percent of football players, 25 percent of baseball
	players, 22 percent of soccer players, 15 percent of basketball players,
	and 12 percent of softball players were injured while playing their
	respective sports." Although the official Little League Web site acknowl-
	edges that children do risk injury playing baseball, it insists that "severe
	injuries . . . are infrequent," the risk "far less than the risk of riding a
	skateboard, a bicycle, or even the school bus" ("What about My
	Child?"). Nevertheless, Leonard Koppett in *Sports Illusion, Sports
	Reality* claims that a twelve-year-old trying to throw a curve ball, for

example, may put abnormal strain on developing arm and shoulder muscles, sometimes resulting in lifelong injuries (294). Contact sports like football can be even more hazardous. Thomas Tutko . . . writes:

> I am strongly opposed to young kids playing tackle football. . . .

Romano's summarizing strategies

- Repeats Statsky's main ideas in a condensed form, summarizing the gist.

- Paraphrases central ideas using her own words and sentence structures. Note that because some words are basic or not readily replaceable (words such as *curve ball*, *football*, and *muscle strain*), Romano's vocabulary does overlap with Statsky's, but this is to be expected. (If you are unsure about whether you need quotation marks around words that appear in your source, consult your instructor.)

- Provides a play-by-play description of Statsky's strategic moves to show readers exactly how she uses paraphrase and quotation to support her argument.

Drafting Your Evaluation

By this point, you have done a lot of writing

- to devise a well-presented subject and make a judgment about it;

- to support your judgment with reasons and evidence that your readers will find persuasive;

- to refute or concede objections and alternative judgments;

- to organize your ideas to make them clear, logical, and effective for readers.

Now stitch that material together to create a draft. The next two parts of this Guide to Writing will help you evaluate and improve it.

Considering a Useful Sentence Strategy

As you draft your evaluative essay, you may want to compare or contrast your subject with similar subjects to establish your authority with readers. In addition, you are likely to want to balance your evaluation by criticizing one or more aspects of the subject if you generally praise it, or by praising one or more aspects of it if you generally criticize it. To do so, you will need to use sentences that express comparisons or contrasts, including ones that contrast criticism with praise and vice versa.

Sentences comparing or contrasting your subject with similar subjects often make use of key comparative terms, such as *more*, *less*, *most*, *least*, *as*, *than*, *like*, *unlike*, *similar*, and *dissimilar*, as the readings in this chapter illustrate.

| Comparative terms | "Workers distracted by e-mail and phone calls suffer a fall in IQ more than twice that found in marijuana smokers." (Rosen [quoting a BBC report], par. 4) |

"Even if you learn while multitasking, that learning is less flexible and more specialized, so you cannot retrieve the information as easily." (Rosen [quoting Russell Poldrack], par. 9)

. . . it is hard to figure out why *Car and Driver* was so sure that the Cayman is better than the Corvette and the Evora. (Gladwell, par. 1)

The best attribute by far is the film's creative cinematography and editing. . . . (Akana, par. 7)

Sometimes writers do not use comparative terms but simply put compared or contrasted information side by side, as in these examples:

| Items being compared | Roy Rogers, Baskin Robbins, Kentucky Fried Chicken, et al. may at first seem nothing but a vast extension of the lemonade stand. (Etzioni, par. 5) |

A comprehensive, heterogeneous ranking system was a stretch for *Car and Driver* — and all it did was rank inanimate objects operated by a single person. The Penn State campus . . . is a complex institution. . . . (Gladwell, par. 5)

EVALUATING THE DRAFT

GETTING A CONSTRUCTIVE CRITICAL READING

Getting a critical reading of your draft will help you see how to improve it. Your instructor may schedule class time for reading drafts, or you may want to ask a classmate or a tutor in the writing center to read your draft. Ask your reader to use the following guidelines and to write out a response for you to consult during your revision.

READING A DRAFT CRITICALLY

Read for a First Impression

1. **Read the draft without stopping, and then write two or three sentences giving your general impression.**

2. **Identify one aspect of the draft that seems especially effective.**

(continued)

Read Again to Suggest Improvements

1. **Recommend ways to strengthen the presentation of the subject.**

   - Tell the writer if the subject is identified clearly, pointing out where there is not enough or too much information about it and whether any information seems unclear, inaccurate, or only partly true.

   - Suggest how the writer could better explain the kind of subject it is, either by identifying the genre or giving examples of familiar subjects of the same type.

   - If you are surprised by the way the writer has presented the subject, briefly explain what surprised you and what you expect in an evaluation of this kind of subject.

2. **Suggest ways to clarify the overall judgment and strengthen the supporting argument.**

   - Find and underline the writer's overall judgment, the essay's thesis statement. Let the writer know if you can't find a clearly stated thesis, one that asserts the subject's good and/or bad qualities. If you find several restatements of the thesis, examine them for consistency.

   - Note in the margins where the reasons and evidence supporting the overall judgment are introduced.

   - Point to any support that is not based on criteria generally accepted as appropriate for judging this kind of subject, or that is based on unclear or unconvincing criteria.

   - Indicate where more support is needed or where the support is not convincing.

3. **Suggest ways to improve the response to likely objections and/or alternative judgments.**

   - Suggest how the response to possible objections and/or alternative judgments could be strengthened through concession, refutation, or a combination of the two.

   - Let the writer know if other objections and/or alternative judgments should be responded to as well, and suggest how best to deal with them given the writer's audience and purpose.

4. **Suggest how the organization might be improved.**

- Look for a forecasting statement early in the essay to see how well it lays out the argument. If there is no forecast, let the writer know whether adding one would make the essay easier to follow. If the forecast is incorrect, point out what's wrong with it.

- Let the writer know if you see ways to improve the essay by rearranging the order of material or by inserting new or better transitions.

- Indicate if the conclusion seems abrupt or less than helpful.

5. **Evaluate the effectiveness of illustrations (visual or other media).**

- If illustrations are included in the draft, indicate what you think they add to it, if anything. If illustrations are not included, indicate whether they would be helpful — and, if so, what kind of illustration and where it could be inserted.

- If any illustrations do not seem relevant, or if there seem to be too many illustrations, identify the ones that the writer could consider dropping, and explain your thinking.

IMPROVING THE DRAFT

REVISING, EDITING, AND PROOFREADING

Start improving your draft by reflecting on what you have written thus far:

- Review critical reading comments from your classmates, instructor, or writing center tutor. How can you respond to your readers' concerns?

- Take another look at your notes and ideas: What else should you consider?

- Review your draft: What else can you do to make your evaluation clearer and more convincing to your readers?

Revising Your Draft

Revising means reenvisioning your draft, trying to see it in a new way, given your purpose and audience, in order to develop a better-argued evaluation. Think imaginatively and boldly about cutting unconvincing material, adding new material, and moving material around. The suggestions in the chart below may help you solve problems and strengthen your essay.

TROUBLESHOOTING YOUR DRAFT

To Present the Subject More Effectively

Problem	Suggestions for Revising
The subject is not identified clearly.	• Identify the subject (such as by naming the director and main actors of a film). • Describe the subject by summarizing it and giving examples. • Establish the subject's importance by citing statistics or quoting authorities. • Consider adding illustrations—photographs, graphs, tables, or charts—to help clarify the subject. • Consider what your readers need to know and what they don't need or want to know (such as how a film or novel ends).
It's not clear what kind of subject it is.	• Classify the subject into a genre or category. • Compare your subject to other, better-known examples of the genre. • Refer to other reviews or reviewers of subjects of this kind.

To Clarify and Strengthen the Argument

Problem	Suggestions for Revising
The overall judgment is not clear.	• Assert your overall judgment early in the essay, making clear if your judgment is mixed. • Qualify your judgment if it seems overstated or is not supported by your argument. • Make sure that your judgment is consistent throughout, even when you point out good as well as bad qualities.
The argument is not based on what readers consider appropriate criteria.	• Explain the criteria you are using and why they are appropriate for the kind of subject you are reviewing. • Justify your criteria—for example, by making comparisons or citing authorities.

Support is not provided, not convincing, or not clear.	• Add support by quoting or summarizing experts or research studies, providing facts or statistics, or giving specific examples. • To make the support convincing, cite your sources and indicate why they can be depended on. • Explain more fully why the evidence supports your judgment.
Illustrations don't help.	• Refer to the illustrations, and explain what they represent. • Find or create new visuals to support your argument.

To Improve the Response to Objections and/or Alternative Judgments

Problem	Suggestions for Revising
A likely objection has not been responded to adequately.	• If the objection undermines your argument, refute it—for example, by showing that it is not based on widely held or appropriate criteria, or that it misunderstands your argument or the subject itself. • If the objection cannot be refuted, concede the point but try to show it is only a minor concern that does not invalidate your evaluation. Try using sentence strategies like *It is true that . . . , but my point is. . . .*
A likely alternative judgment has not been responded to adequately.	• Mention good or bad qualities of the subject that others emphasize, even if your overall judgment is different. • If an alternative judgment is based on criteria you do not consider appropriate, consider citing authorities to justify your criteria or give reasons why the alternative criteria are inappropriate.

To Make the Organization Clearer

Problem	Suggestions for Revising
The thesis and forecast statements are missing, inaccurate, or unclear.	• Add or revise the thesis and forecasting statements. • Make sure your thesis and forecast are placed early in the essay to guide readers. • Repeat key terms in your topic sentences.

The essay seems disorganized or is hard to follow.	• Review the overall organization by outlining the essay. If necessary, move, add, or delete sections to strengthen coherence. Make sure your reasons follow a logical sequence. • Add appropriate transitions or improve the existing ones.
The conclusion seems abrupt or awkward.	• Add a transition to signal the conclusion. • Try restating your judgment or summarizing your argument. • Consider whether you can frame the essay by echoing something from the opening.

Editing and Proofreading Your Draft

Check for errors in usage, punctuation, and mechanics, and consider matters of style. If you keep a list of errors you typically make, begin by checking your draft against this list. Ask someone else to proofread your essay before you submit it to your instructor.

From our research on student writing, we know that evaluative essays have frequent problems in sentences that set up comparisons. The comparisons can be incomplete, illogical, or unclear. Check a writer's handbook for help with these potential problems.

Reflecting on What You Have Learned

Evaluation

In this chapter, you have read critically several evaluative essays and have written one of your own. To better remember what you have learned, pause now to reflect on the reading and writing activities you completed in this chapter.

1. Write a page or so reflecting on what you have learned. Begin by describing what you are most pleased with in your essay. Then explain what you think contributed to your achievement. Be specific about this contribution.

   • If it was something you learned from the readings, indicate which readings and specifically what you learned from them.

- If it came from your explorations of alternative points of view, point out the strategies that helped you most.

- If you got good advice from a critical reader, explain exactly how the person helped you — perhaps by identifying a problem in your draft or by helping you add a new dimension to your writing.

Try to write about your achievement in terms of what you have learned about the genre.

2. Reflect more generally on evaluative essays, a genre of writing important in education and in society. Consider some of the following questions:

- How confident do you feel about asserting a judgment and supporting it?

- How comfortable are you playing the role of judge and jury on the subject?

- How do your personal preferences and values influence your judgment?

- How might your gender, ethnicity, religious beliefs, age, or social class influence your ideas about the subject?

- What contribution might evaluative essays make to our society that other genres cannot make?

Arguing for a Position

P osition arguments take a position on controversial issues that have no obvious "right" answer, no truth everyone accepts, no single authority everyone trusts. Consequently, simply gathering information — finding the facts or learning from experts — will not settle these disputes because ultimately they are matters of opinion and judgment for which writers must argue.

You may associate arguing with quarreling or with the in-your-face debating we often hear on radio and television talk shows. These ways of arguing may let us vent strong feelings, but they seldom lead us to consider seriously other points of view, let alone to look critically at our own thinking or learn anything new. This chapter presents a more deliberative way of arguing that we call *reasoned argument* because it depends on giving reasons rather than raising voices. Although it is not possible to prove that a position on a controversial issue is right or wrong, it is possible to convince others to consider a particular position seriously or to accept or reject a position. A **position essay** must argue for its position by giving readers strong reasons and solid support. It also must anticipate opposing arguments.

This chapter offers several brief position arguments for you to enjoy and analyze, with exploratory activities that will help you learn to read critically and write well. The Reading for Meaning and Reading Like a Writer activities following each selection invite you to analyze and write about the reading's ideas and writing strategies. You can also use the brief Guide to Writing Position Arguments toward the end of the chapter to help you write about a controversial issue on which you take a strong position.

RHETORICAL SITUATIONS FOR POSITION ARGUMENTS

Writing that takes a position on a controversial issue plays a significant role in college work and professional life, as the following examples indicate:

- A committee made up of business and community leaders investigates the issue of regulating urban growth. After reviewing the arguments for and against government regulation, committee members argue against it on the grounds that supply and demand alone will regulate development, that landowners should be permitted to sell their property to the highest bidder, and that developers are guided by the needs of the market and thus serve the people.

- For an economics class, a student writes a term paper on the controversies surrounding the rising cost of public education. Online and in the library, she finds several blogs, newspaper and magazine articles, and contemporary books that help her understand the debate over the issues. She presents the strongest arguments on the different sides and takes the position that, to be economically viable, public education needs more financial support from various sectors, including business, government, and nonprofit organizations.

- For a political science class, a student writes an essay on public employees' right to strike. Having no well-defined position herself, she discusses the issue with her mother, who is a nurse in a county hospital, and her uncle, a firefighter. Her mother believes that public employees like hospital workers and teachers should have the right to strike but that police officers and firefighters should not because public safety would be endangered. The uncle disagrees, arguing that allowing hospital workers to strike would jeopardize public safety as much as allowing firefighters to strike. He insists that the central issue is not public safety but workers' rights. In her essay, the student supports the right of public employees to strike but argues for arbitration whenever a strike might jeopardize public safety.

Thinking about the Genre

Position Arguments

Before studying a type of writing, it is useful to spend some time thinking about what you already know about it. You may have heard friends or family argue about their positions on an issue or read articles in which writers argue for positions on controversial issues. You may also have argued for a position with friends or written essays that take up a position on a controversial issue for classes.

Recall a time when you argued for a position. Use the following questions to develop your thoughts. Your instructor may ask you to write about your experience or discuss it with others in class or online.

(continued)

- Who was your *audience*? Why were you arguing to this particular audience? What did you already know about the issue when you took your position? How do you think arguing to this audience affected how you presented your position?

- What was your *purpose*? What did you want your audience to learn or do? Did you want them to adopt your point of view, or be persuaded to think critically about their own? Did you choose certain pieces of evidence that would be more successful with this audience? Did you anticipate their objections and respond to them?

- How might your perspective on the subject have changed if you were writing for a different audience or had a different purpose in mind? Would you have investigated different sources, or chosen other people to interview? Think about how writing in a different medium would affect what you chose to include and how you presented it. For example, if you made a documentary film or a podcast or a chart, how do you think you would begin and end your position argument?

A GUIDE TO READING ESSAYS ARGUING FOR A POSITION

This guide introduces you to writing that takes a position by inviting you to analyze a brief but impassioned essay about science by Brian Greene, first by *reading for meaning* and then by *reading like a writer*.

- *Reading for meaning* will help you understand the scope of the issue as well as understand and respond to Greene's argument — for example, your own feelings about science and the way it is taught.

- *Reading like a writer* will help you learn how Greene makes the essay interesting, informative, and compelling by examining how the basic features and strategies typical of position writing are employed, such as

  1. presenting the controversial issue *fairly* and *credibly*

  2. asserting a *clear position*

  3. arguing directly for it with reasonable *evidence*

  4. *responding to objections and alternative positions* fairly

Brian Greene

Put a Little Science in Your Life

Brian Greene (b. 1963) earned his BS from Harvard and his PhD from Oxford University as a Rhodes Scholar. He is currently a professor of mathematics and physics at Columbia University, where he is also codirector of the Institute for Strings, Cosmology, and Astroparticle Physics (ISCAP). Greene is the author of numerous professional and popular essays, as well as four books about physics for a general audience: The Elegant Universe: Superstrings, Hidden Dimensions, and the Quest for the Ultimate Theory *(1999);* The Fabric of the Cosmos: Space, Time, and the Texture of Reality *(2004);* Icarus at the Edge of Time *(2008); and* The Elegant Universe: Parallel Universes and the Deep Laws of the Cosmos *(2011).*

Greene is a contributing editor for the New York Times, *where the essay below was published. He believes science should be placed alongside music, art, and literature as fields that give life meaning.*

- *Before you read, think about your own experiences with science, either in school or out of it. Do you understand science easily, or only with difficulty? What kind of educational experience have you had with it?*

- *As you read, think about Greene's assertion that "[l]ike a life without music, art or literature, a life without science is bereft of something that gives experience a rich and otherwise inaccessible dimension" (par. 11). Does Greene persuade you of the truth of this statement? If so, where and how?*

A couple of years ago I received a letter from an American soldier in Iraq. The letter began by saying that, as we've all become painfully aware, serving on the front lines is physically exhausting and emotionally debilitating. But the reason for his writing was to tell me that in that hostile and lonely environment, a book I'd written had become a kind of lifeline. As the book is about science—one that traces physicists' search for nature's deepest laws—the soldier's letter might strike you as, well, odd. 1

But it's not. Rather, it speaks to the powerful role science can play in giving life context and meaning. At the same time, the soldier's letter emphasized something I've increasingly come to believe: our educational system fails to teach science in a way that allows students to integrate it into their lives. 2

Allow me a moment to explain. 3

When we consider the ubiquity of cellphones, iPods, personal computers and the Internet, it's easy to see how science (and the technology to which it leads) is woven into the fabric of our day-to-day activities. When we benefit from CT scanners, M.R.I. devices, pacemakers and arterial stents, we can immediately appreciate how science affects the quality of our 4 lives. When we assess the state of the world, and identify looming challenges like climate change, global pandemics, security threats and diminishing resources, we don't hesitate in turning to science to gauge the problems and find solutions.

5   And when we look at the wealth of opportunities hovering on the horizon—stem cells, genomic sequencing, personalized medicine, longevity research, nanoscience, brain-machine interface, quantum computers, space technology—we realize how crucial it is to cultivate a general public that can engage with scientific issues; there's simply no other way that as a society we will be prepared to make informed decisions on a range of issues that will shape the future.

6   These are the standard—and enormously important—reasons many would give in explaining why science matters.

7   But here's the thing. The reason science really matters runs deeper still. Science is a way of life. Science is a perspective. Science is the process that takes us from confusion to understanding in a manner that's precise, predictive and reliable—a transformation, for those lucky enough to experience it, that is empowering and emotional. To be able to think through and grasp explanations—for everything from why the sky is blue to how life formed on earth—not because they are declared dogma but rather because they reveal patterns confirmed by experiment and observation, is one of the most precious of human experiences.

8   As a practicing scientist, I know this from my own work and study. But I also know that you don't have to be a scientist for science to be transformative. I've seen children's eyes light up as I've told them about black holes and the Big Bang. I've spoken with high school dropouts who've stumbled on popular science books about the human genome project, and then returned to school with newfound purpose. And in that letter from Iraq, the soldier told me how learning about relativity and quantum physics in the dusty and dangerous environs of greater Baghdad kept him going because it revealed a deeper reality of which we're all a part.

9   It's striking that science is still widely viewed as merely a subject one studies in the classroom or an isolated body of largely esoteric knowledge that sometimes shows up in the "real" world in the form of technological or medical advances. In reality, science is a language of hope and inspiration, providing discoveries that fire the imagination and instill a sense of connection to our lives and our world.

10   If science isn't your strong suit—and for many it's not—this side of science is something you may have rarely if ever experienced. I've spoken with so many people over the years whose encounters with science in school left them thinking of it as cold, distant and intimidating. They happily use the innovations that science makes possible, but feel that the science itself is just not relevant to their lives. What a shame.

Like a life without music, art or literature, a life without science is bereft   11
of something that gives experience a rich and otherwise inaccessible
dimension.

It's one thing to go outside on a crisp, clear night and marvel at a sky full   12
of stars. It's another to marvel not only at the spectacle but to recognize that
those stars are the result of exceedingly ordered conditions 13.7 billion
years ago at the moment of the Big Bang. It's another still to understand how
those stars act as nuclear furnaces that supply the universe with carbon,
oxygen and nitrogen, the raw material of life as we know it.

And it's yet another level of experience to realize that those stars   13
account for less than 4 percent of what's out there—the rest being of an
unknown composition, so-called dark matter and energy, which researchers are now vigorously trying to divine.

As every parent knows, children begin life as uninhibited, unabashed   14
explorers of the unknown. From the time we can walk and talk, we want to
know what things are and how they work—we begin life as little scientists. But most of us quickly lose our intrinsic scientific passion. And it's a
profound loss.

A great many studies have focused on this problem, identifying impor-   15
tant opportunities for improving science education. Recommendations
have ranged from increasing the level of training for science teachers to
curriculum reforms.

But most of these studies (and their suggestions) avoid an overarching   16
systemic issue: in teaching our students, we continually fail to activate rich
opportunities for revealing the breathtaking vistas opened up by science,
and instead focus on the need to gain competency with science's underlying technical details.

In fact, many students I've spoken to have little sense of the big ques-   17
tions those technical details collectively try to answer: Where did the universe come from? How did life originate? How does the brain give rise
to consciousness? Like a music curriculum that requires its students to
practice scales while rarely if ever inspiring them by playing the great
masterpieces, this way of teaching science squanders the chance to make
students sit up in their chairs and say, "Wow, that's science?"

In physics, just to give a sense of the raw material that's available to be   18
leveraged, the most revolutionary of advances have happened in the last
100 years—special relativity, general relativity, quantum mechanics—a
symphony of discoveries that changed our conception of reality. More
recently, the last 10 years have witnessed an upheaval in our understanding of the universe's composition, yielding a wholly new prediction for
what the cosmos will be like in the far future.

These are paradigm-shaking developments. But rare is the high school   19
class, and rarer still is the middle school class, in which these breakthroughs

are introduced. It's much the same story in classes for biology, chemistry and mathematics.

20 At the root of this pedagogical approach is a firm belief in the vertical nature of science: you must master *A* before moving on to *B*. When *A* happened a few hundred years ago, it's a long climb to the modern era. Certainly, when it comes to teaching the technicalities—solving this equation, balancing that reaction, grasping the discrete parts of the cell—the verticality of science is unassailable.

21 But science is so much more than its technical details. And with careful attention to presentation, cutting-edge insights and discoveries can be clearly and faithfully communicated to students independent of those details; in fact, those insights and discoveries are precisely the ones that can drive a young student to want to learn the details. We rob science education of life when we focus solely on results and seek to train students to solve problems and recite facts without a commensurate emphasis on transporting them out beyond the stars.

22 Science is the greatest of all adventure stories, one that's been unfolding for thousands of years as we have sought to understand ourselves and our surroundings. Science needs to be taught to the young and communicated to the mature in a manner that captures this drama. We must embark on a cultural shift that places science in its rightful place alongside music, art and literature as an indispensable part of what makes life worth living.

23 It's the birthright of every child, it's a necessity for every adult, to look out on the world, as the soldier in Iraq did, and see that the wonder of the cosmos transcends everything that divides us.

READING FOR MEANING

This section presents three activities that will help you think about the meanings in Greene's position argument. Your instructor may ask you to do one or more of these activities in class or online.

For more help with summarizing, see Chapter 10, pp. 518–19.

1. **Read to Summarize.** Reading to summarize involves asking yourself what the main point of the reading is. To summarize Greene's position argument, write a sentence or two explaining the author's position on science education.

2. **Read to Respond.** Reading to respond asks you to explore your reactions to a text in light of your own knowledge or experience. To explore this position argument, write a paragraph analyzing your initial reactions to

Take a quiz to check your reading and vocabulary comprehension:
bedfordstmartins.com/readingcritically

Greene's essay. For example, consider anything that resonates with your experience or that seems contradictory, surprising, or fascinating, such as:

You may also try recognizing emotional manipulation; see Chapter 10, pp. 536–37.

- Greene's assertion that "in teaching our students, we continually fail to activate rich opportunities for revealing the breathtaking vistas opened up by science, and instead focus on the need to gain competency with science's underlying technical details" (par. 16);
- Why you think Greene chooses to begin his essay with a letter from a soldier in Iraq (par. 1).

3. **Read to Analyze Assumptions. Assumptions** are ideas, beliefs, or values that are taken for granted as commonly accepted truths. The assumptions in a text usually reflect the writer's own attitudes or cultural traditions, but they may also represent other people's views. Reading to analyze assumptions asks you to uncover these perspectives as well as to probe your own. Sometimes the assumptions are stated explicitly, but often you will have to infer them (or figure them out) because they are only implied or hinted at through the writer's choice of words or examples. Write a paragraph or two analyzing an assumption you find intriguing in Greene's essay. For example:

Assumptions about the intrinsic excitement and pleasure of discovery. Greene asserts the idea not only that science matters, but also that it creates a "transformation . . . that is empowering and emotional" (par. 7) and is "a language of hope and inspiration, providing discoveries that fire the imagination and instill a sense of connection to our lives and our world" (par. 9). To think critically about the assumptions in this essay related to the excitement and pleasure of discovery, ask yourself questions like these:

- What kinds of discoveries does Greene mention, and what do they mean to you? Does discovery play a part in your own existence? Are your discoveries (if you have made them) scientific, or are they in other fields? How do you feel when you've made a discovery? How do you think others feel?
- Why does Greene group science with music, art, and literature? Does this suggest parallels among them, or underscore qualities they have in common?

Assumptions about the transforming role of education. Greene uses language like "transformation" (par. 7) and "transporting them out beyond the stars" (par. 21) to describe the effect he thinks science should have on children. He points out that children "begin life as little scientists" (par. 14) but that most of them lose their "intrinsic scientific passion" (par. 14) because schools "fail to activate rich opportunities for revealing the breathtaking vistas opened up by science, and instead focus on the need to gain competency with science's underlying technical details" (par. 16). To think critically about the assumptions in this essay related to the transforming role of education, ask yourself questions like these:

- What view of education is held by those who teach science as a "vertical" (par. 20) subject? Do you think Greene's view of science as "the greatest of all adventure stories" (par. 22) is held by most people? Is it the duty of education to be transforming — "to make students sit up in their chairs and say, 'Wow . . .'" (par. 17) or to make them recognize "the wonder of the cosmos" (par. 23)? If so, what is the best way to go about transforming students' perspectives? What value, if any, is there to gaining "competency with science's underlying technical details" (par. 16)?

- Greene criticizes schooling that doesn't teach the "big questions" (par. 17): "But rare is the high school class, and rarer still is the middle school class, in which these breakthroughs are introduced. It's much the same story in classes for biology, chemistry and mathematics" (par. 19). Greene seems to assume that exposure to contemporary scientific discoveries would benefit education. Do you share his assumption? What evidence does he offer that persuades you?

You may also try evaluating the logic of an argument; see Chapter 10, pp. 530–32.

READING LIKE A WRITER

This section presents four brief activities that will help you analyze Greene's writing. Your instructor may ask you to do one or more of these activities in class or online.

Presenting the Controversial Issue Fairly and Credibly

For position papers published during an ongoing public debate, writers may need only to mention the issue. In most cases, however, writers need to explain the issue to readers. They may, for example, place the issue in its historical or cultural context, cite specific instances to make the issue seem less abstract, show their personal interest in the debate, or establish or redefine the terms of the debate. Greene uses a common sentence pattern for redefining the terms of the debate. First he presents the issue as he believes it is commonly perceived, and then he contrasts this common perception with his own view:

▶ When .... [issue/event] happens, most people think .... , but I think
....

Here's an example from the reading selection:

▶ These are the standard—and enormously important—reasons many would give in explaining why science matters.
  But here's the thing. The reason science really matters runs deeper still. (pars. 6–7)

Note how civil Greene is in the first sentence; he respects those who have the standard reasons for explaining why science matters. Then in the second sentence he proposes that science matters for even "deeper" reasons.

Analyze & Write

1. Reread paragraphs 1–7, where Greene introduces the issue, and underline phrases that connect you to the issue. For example, in paragraph 1, Greene notes that "as we've all become painfully aware, serving on the front lines is physically exhausting and emotionally debilitating." How does using the first-person plural (*we*) help readers make a link to their own experience? Does Greene use other strategies in these paragraphs to present the issue in a way readers will find engaging?

2. Reread paragraphs 4–5. Look at Greene's lists of everything connected to science. For example, "the ubiquity of cellphones, iPods, personal computers and the Internet" (par. 4). How does his listing allow him to present the issue? How does it demonstrate the importance of the issue? What other strategies does he use here or elsewhere in the essay to demonstrate the importance of science education?

3. Now reread paragraph 8 to see how Greene establishes his credibility as a writer on the issue of science education. His last line in paragraph 7 heralds the scientific method as a way of enabling us to "think through and grasp explanations . . . not because they are declared dogma but rather because they reveal patterns confirmed by experiment and observation," and asserts that this is "one of the most precious of human experiences." What words and phrases in paragraph 8 establish Greene not only as a scientist but also as a teacher? What words and phrases remind the reader of important discoveries with which Greene is clearly familiar?

You might also try recognizing emotional manipulation; see Chapter 10, pp. 536–37.

Asserting a Clear Position

Writers of position papers take sides. Their primary purposes are to assert a position of their own and to influence readers' thinking. The assertion is the main point of the essay — its **thesis**. Presented simply and directly, the thesis statement often forecasts the stages of the argument as well, identifying the main reason or reasons that will be developed and supported in the essay.

Many writers place the thesis early in the essay to let readers know right away where they stand. But if they need to present the issue at length or define the terms of the debate, writers can postpone introducing their own position. Restating the thesis in different words at various points in the body of the essay and at the end can help keep readers oriented.

Analyze & Write

Write a paragraph analyzing how and why Greene states and restates his position:

1. Underline the sentence in which Greene explicitly asserts his position (at the end of par. 2). Note any key words he uses there.

2. Skim paragraphs 7–9, 11, 14, 16–17, 19, and 21–22, and put brackets around the sentences in these paragraphs that restate the thesis in various ways.

3. Now examine *how* Greene restates his thesis. Look closely at the language he uses to see whether he repeats key words, uses synonyms for them, or adds new phrasing. What do you learn from Greene's repetition and his variations? How do his strategies affect his credibility in your eyes?

Arguing Directly for the Position, and Supporting the Position with Reasonable Evidence

Not only do writers of position papers explicitly assert their positions, but they also give reasons for them. They usually support their reasons with facts, statistics, examples, anecdotes, expert opinions, and analogies:

- **Facts** are statements that can be proven objectively to be true, but readers may need to be reassured that the facts come from trustworthy sources.

- **Statistics** may be mistaken for facts, but they are only interpretations or compilations of numerical data. Their reliability depends on how and by whom the information was collected and interpreted.

- **Examples** are not usually claimed to be proof of the writer's position or to be evidence that the position applies in every case. Examples help a reader understand the situations in which the position is valid. Powerful examples are often the reason readers change their minds or at least grant that the position is true in the case of a particular example.

- **Anecdotes** tell stories and recall vivid images to help readers imagine themselves in the position of the writer. Anecdotes are also memorable, as many stories are, so readers remember why the author has taken a certain position.

- Expert opinions and analogies are also useful for support. Readers must decide whether to regard quotations from experts as credible and authoritative. They must also decide how much weight to give analogies — comparisons that encourage readers to assume that what is true about one thing is also true about something to which it is compared.

Position arguments are most convincing when writers are able to appeal to readers on three levels:

- **logos:** Appeals to readers' intellect, presenting them with logical reasoning and reliable evidence
- **ethos:** Appeals to readers' perception of the writer's credibility and fairness
- **pathos:** Appeals to readers' values and feelings

Analyze & Write

Write a paragraph or two analyzing Greene's strategy of arguing by example:

1. Reread paragraph 7 and paragraphs 17–18, where Greene develops his argument that the study of science should include the big questions as well as the technical details, and put brackets around the sentence or sentences in each paragraph that state this part of his argument.

2. Look closely at the examples in paragraphs 17–18, where Greene supports this reason with appropriate questions to ask and the scientific theories developed in the last one hundred years. Underline these questions and theories throughout both paragraphs, and then compare them to each other. Which examples are most effective for you? Why? Do you think that some readers would find the argument in this part of the essay compelling and other readers would not? If so, why or why not?

Responding to Objections and Alternative Positions Fairly and Credibly

Writers of position papers often try to anticipate the likely objections, questions, and alternative positions that readers might raise. Writers may concede points with which they agree and may even modify a thesis to accommodate valid objections. A typical way of conceding is to use sentence strategies like these:

▶ I agree that .... is certainly an important factor.

But when they think that the criticism is groundless or opposing arguments are flawed, writers respond assertively. They refute the challenges to their argument by pointing out the flaws in their opponents' reasoning and support. A typical refutation states the problem with the opposing view and then explains why the view is problematic, using sentence strategies like these:

▸ One problem with .... [opposing view] is that ....

▸ Some claim .... [opposing view], but in reality ....

Notice that writers often introduce the refutation with a transition that indicates contrast, such as *but, although, nevertheless,* or *however*. When writers deal with alternative viewpoints, they enhance their own fairness and credibility by treating those who hold these views with civility and respect.

Frequently, writers reach out to readers by making a concession, but then go on to point out where they differ. Writers conceding and then refuting often use sentence strategies like these:

▸ .... may be true for .... , *but* not for ....

▸ *Although* .... , I think ....

▸ .... insists that .... *Nevertheless,* in spite of her good intentions, ...

Not all writers use transition words to signal a response to alternative views, however. Consider, for example, the way Greene concedes and then refutes the existing approach to science education:

Cues signaling concession	These are the standard — and enormously important — reasons many would give in explaining why science matters.
Cues signaling refutation	But here's the thing. The reason science really matters runs deeper still. (pars. 6–7)

Analyze & Write

Write a paragraph or two analyzing how Greene responds to alternative views and evaluating Greene's credibility and likely success with his readers:

1. Reread paragraphs 9–10, 15–16, and 20–21, where Greene introduces alternative arguments to his position. Underline the sentence in each paragraph that best states the alternative position.

2. Now highlight the sentences in which Greene responds to these opposing arguments. Where does he concede and where does he refute these alternatives? What seems to be his attitude toward those who disagree with him or who object to parts of his argument? How effective are his strategies in persuading readers to accept his position? How effective were they in winning you over? Readers usually appreciate a tone that acknowledges legitimate differences of opinion, yet seeks to establish common ground where possible.

READINGS

Karen Stabiner

Boys Here, Girls There: Sure, If Equality's the Goal

Karen Stabiner is a journalist who is a regular contributor to the Huffington Post *and the* Los Angeles Times *Opinion section, a contributing editor for* Mother Jones, *a columnist for* New West, *and an adjunct professor at the Columbia University School of Journalism. A graduate of the University of Michigan, Stabiner has written several books on relationships and single-sex education. Her most recent are* My Girl: Adventures with a Teen in Training *(2005) and* The Empty Nest: Thirty-one Parents Tell the Truth about Relationships, Love, and Freedom after the Kids Fly the Coop *(2007). In her novel* Getting In *(2010), Stabiner writes about the challenge of getting a child into the perfect college.*

"Boys Here, Girls There: Sure, If Equality's the Goal" was first published in the Washington Post *Sunday Outlook section in 2002. The occasion was the George W. Bush administration's endorsement of single-sex schools as part of the No Child Left Behind Act of 2001.*

- *Before you read, think about the role that gender played in your high-school education. Do you feel that boys and girls were treated differently, and if so, how? If they were treated the same, do you think it would have been better if they had been treated differently? Why? If you went to a single-sex school, was there a point made about the absence of members of the opposite sex and why going to a single-sex school might be an advantage for you?*

- *As you read, pay special attention to Stabiner's strategies for acknowledging and responding to those who disagree with her.*

1 Many parents may be wondering what the fuss was about this past week, when the Bush administration endorsed single-sex public schools and classes. Separating the sexes was something we did in the days of auto shop and home ec, before Betty Friedan, Gloria Steinem and Title IX.[1] How, then, did an apparent

[1]Betty Friedan (1921–2006) and Gloria Steinem (b. 1934) were pioneers in the Second Wave feminist movement that began in the 1960s. Title IX of the Education Amendments of 1972 is the federal legislation that bans sexual discrimination in public schools, whether in academics or athletics.

return to the Fifties come to symbolize educational reform?

Here's how: By creating an alternate, parallel universe where smart matters more than anything, good looks hold little currency and a strong sense of self trumps a date on Saturday night—a place where "class clown" is a label that young boys dread and "math whiz" is a term of endearment for young girls.

I have just spent three years working on a book about two all-girls schools, the private Marlborough School in Los Angeles, and The Young Women's Leadership School of East Harlem (TYWLS), a six-year-old public school in New York City. I went to class, I went home with the girls, I went to dances and basketball games and faculty meetings, and what I learned is this: Single-sex education matters, and it matters most to the students who historically have been denied access to it.

Having said that, I do not intend to proselytize. Single-sex education is not the answer to everyone's prayers. Some children want no part of it and some parents question its relevance. The rest of us should not stop wondering what to do with our coeducational public schools just because of this one new option.

But single-sex education can be a valuable tool— if we target those students who stand to benefit most. For years, in the name of upholding gender equity, we have practiced a kind of harsh economic discrimination. Sociologist Cornelius Riordan says that poor students, minorities and girls stand to profit most from a single-sex environment. Until now, though, the only students who could attend a single-sex school were the wealthy ones who could afford private tuition, the relatively few lucky students who received financial aid or those in less-expensive parochial schools. We denied access to the almost 90 percent of American students who attend public schools.

For the fortunate ones—like the girls at Marlborough—the difference is one of attitude, more than any quantifiable measure; their grades and scores may be similar to the graduates of coed prep schools, but they perceive themselves as more competent, more willing to pursue advanced work in fields such as math and science.

Why does Stabiner list these "parallel" possibilities for what matters at school?

How does this paragraph enhance Stabiner's credibility?

Why would Stabiner mention how single-sex education might not "matter" to some people?

What is the effect of Stabiner's bringing in another source and statistics to buttress her contention that gender equity in schools has resulted in economic discrimination? Why does she include herself (see highlighted "we") among those she blames for this situation?

7   At TYWLS, though, the difference is more profound. Students there are predominantly Latina and African American, survivors of a hostile public system. Half of New York's high school students fail to graduate on time, and almost a third never graduate. Throughout the nation, one in six Latina and one in five African American teens become pregnant every year. But most of the members of TYWLS's two graduating classes have gone on to four-year colleges, often the first members of their families to do so, and pregnancy is the stark exception.

8   There are now 11 single-sex public schools in the United States, all of which serve urban students, many of them in lower-income neighborhoods. Most are side-by-side schools that offer comparable programs for boys and girls in the same facility. The stand-alone girls' schools say that they are compensating for years of gender discrimination; several attempts at similar schools for boys have failed, however, casualties of legal challenges.

9   Now, thanks to a bipartisan amendment to President Bush's education reform bill, sponsored by Sens. Kay Bailey Hutchison (R-Tex.) and Hillary Rodham Clinton (D-N.Y.), the administration is about to revise the way it enforces Title IX, to allow for single-sex schools and classes.

Compare this paragraph to paragraph 1. How have the intervening paragraphs educated you about single-sex schools?

10   The first objections last week came from the National Organization for Women and the New York Civil Liberties Union, both of which opposed the opening of TYWLS in the fall of 1996. The two groups continue to insist—as though it were 1896 and they were arguing *Plessy v. Ferguson*[2]—that separate can never be equal. I appreciate NOW's wariness of the Bush administration's endorsement of single-sex public schools, since I am of the generation that still considers the label "feminist" to be a compliment—and many feminists still fear that any public acknowledgment of differences between the sexes will hinder their fight for equality.

Why does Stabiner mention her appreciation of NOW's wariness and of feminism?

[2]In *Plessy v. Ferguson* (1896), the U.S. Supreme Court upheld racial segregation by stating that separate facilities for blacks and whites in public accommodations were constitutional as long as they were equal. The ruling was reversed by the Supreme Court in *Brown v. Board of Education* (1954).

Why does Stabiner make
the point that boys and
girls develop differently?

But brain research has shown us that girls and boys 11
develop and process information in different ways;
they do not even use the same region of the brain to
do their math homework. We cannot pretend that
such information does not exist just because it conflicts with our ideology. If we hang on to old, quantifiable measurements of equality, we will fail our
children. If we take what we learn and use it, we have
the chance to do better.

Why does Stabiner make
this paragraph so short?

Educators at single-sex schools already get it: 12
Equality is the goal, not the process. There may be
more than one path to the destination—but it is the
arrival, not the itinerary, that counts.

Again, Stabiner introduces
the arguments her oppo-
nents might use; how does
she follow up on these?

Some researchers complain that we lack definitive 13
evidence that single-sex education works. There are
so many intertwined variables; the students at TYWLS
might do well because of smaller class size, passionate teachers and an aggressively supportive atmosphere. Given that, the absence of boys might be
beside the point.

The American Association of University Women 14
called for more research even after publishing a 1998
report that showed some girls continued to suffer in
the coed classroom. But it is probably impossible to
design a study that would retire the question permanently, and, as TYWLS's first principal, Celenia Che-
vere, liked to say, "What am I supposed to do with
these girls in the meantime?"

Does giving the history of
girls' attendance in public
schools seem a surprising
way for Stabiner to present
her issue? What difference
could this information
make to her argument?

What is this misplaced reverence for the coed 15
school? Do not think that it was designed with the best
interests of all children at heart. As education professors David and Myra Sadker explained in their 1994
book, *Failing at Fairness: How America's Schools Cheat
Girls*, our schools were originally created to educate
boys. In the late 1700s, girls went to class early in the
morning and late in the day—and unlike the boys,
they had to pay for the privilege. When families
demanded that the public schools do more for their
girls, school districts grudgingly allowed the girls into
existing classrooms—not because it was the best way
to teach children but because no one had the money to
build new schools just for girls. Coed classrooms are
not necessarily better. They just are.

16   For those who like hard data, here is a number: 1,200 girls on the waiting list for a handful of spaces in the ninth grade at TYWLS. There is a growing desire for public school alternatives, for an answer more meaningful than a vague if optimistic call for system-wide reform. The demand for single-sex education exists—and now the Bush administration must figure out how to supply it.

17   Implementation will not be easy. Girls may learn better without boys, but research and experience show that some boys seem to need the socializing influence of girls: Will there be a group of educational handmaidens, girls who are consigned to coed schools to keep the boys from acting out? Who will select the chosen few who get to go to single-sex schools, and how will they make that choice? Will they take students who already show promise or those who most need help? Or perhaps the philosophy of a new pair of boys' and girls' schools in Albany, N.Y., provides the answer: Take the poorest kids first.

How do these questions that Stabiner poses add to her argument?

18   Whatever the approach, no one is calling for a wholesale shift to segregation by gender, and that means someone will be left out. Single-sex public schools perpetuate the kind of two-tiered system that used to be based solely on family income, even if they widen the net. But that has always been true of innovative public schools, and it is no reason to hesitate.

19   The most troubling question about single-sex public education—Why now?—has nothing to do with school. When support comes so readily from opposite ends of the political spectrum, it is reasonable to ask why everyone is so excited, particularly given the political debate about vouchers and school choice.

20   If the intention is to strengthen the public school system by responding to new information about how our children learn, then these classes can serve as a model of innovative teaching techniques, some of which can be transported back into existing coed classrooms. Single-sex public schools and classes, as odd as it may sound, are about inclusion; any school district that wants one can have one and everyone can learn from the experience.

If single-sex schools could benefit coed schools, who might still object to single-sex education?

In this final paragraph, Stabiner calls into question the motivation of those who support single-sex schools for the best and brightest. Why would she end her essay on this note?

But if this is about siphoning off the best and 21 potentially brightest, and ignoring the rest, then it is a cruel joke, a warm and fuzzy set-up for measures like vouchers. If single-sex becomes a satisfying distraction from existing schools that desperately need help, then it only serves to further erode the system. The new educational reform law is called the No Child Left Behind Act, an irresistible sentiment with a chilling edge to it—did we ever actually intend to leave certain children behind? The challenge, in developing these new schools and programs, is to make them part of a dynamic, ongoing reform, and not an escape hatch from a troubled system.

READING FOR MEANING

This section presents three activities that will help you think about the meanings in Stabiner's position argument. Your instructor may ask you to do one or more of these activities in class or online.

For more help with summarizing, see Chapter 10, pp. 518–19.

1. **Read to Summarize.** Write a sentence or two explaining why Stabiner favors single-sex public schools for girls.

2. **Read to Respond.** Write a paragraph analyzing your initial reactions to Stabiner's essay. For example, consider anything that resonates with your own experience or that seems contradictory, surprising, or fascinating, such as:

   - Any experience you have had with single-sex schools;

You may also try reflecting on challenges to your beliefs and values; see Chapter 10, pp. 526–27.

   - Stabiner's assertion that "[f]or years, in the name of upholding gender equity, we have practiced a kind of harsh economic discrimination" (par. 5);

   - Whether a difference in "attitude" (par. 6) can make the kind of difference Stabiner explores in her essay.

3. **Read to Analyze Assumptions.** Write a paragraph or two analyzing an assumption you find intriguing in Stabiner's essay. For example:

   Assumptions about the effects of innovations in education. In paragraph 20, speaking about single-sex classrooms, Stabiner notes that "[i]f the intention is to strengthen the public school system by responding to new information about how our children learn, then these classes can serve as a model of innovative teaching. . . ." What kinds of innovative

e Take a quiz to check your reading and vocabulary comprehension: **bedfordstmartins.com/readingcritically**

teaching might Stabiner mean? To think critically about the assumptions in this essay related to the effects of innovations in education, ask yourself questions like these:

- What the principal of TYWLS means when, referring to the American Association of University Women's call for more research on coed versus single-sex schools, she asks, "What am I supposed to do with these girls in the meantime?" (par. 14).

- What would happen to schools if innovations were encouraged (rather than being seen as a threat to the status quo) or if students — both boys and girls — were treated as "experiments" to see how they would turn out under single-sex circumstances? What kinds of circumstances could lead to disastrous innovations? To wondrous innovations? Would teaching innovations for girls necessarily be transferable to boys and vice versa?

Assumptions about how poverty affects learning. Stabiner asks a series of questions about how girls would be chosen for single-sex schools, and at the end of the paragraph she opts for an answer given by single-sex schools in Albany, N.Y.: "Take the poorest kids first" (par. 17). Earlier, she asserts that "[s]ingle-sex education . . . matters most to the students who historically have been denied access to it" (par. 3), by whom she means "poor students, minorities and girls" (par. 5). To think critically about the assumptions in this essay related to poverty and learning, ask yourself questions like these:

- What would be the consequences if single-sex public schools took "the poorest kids first"?

- Why does a difference in "attitude" (par. 6) among girls in single-sex schools lead them to pursue advanced degrees? How are attitude and economics linked?

> You may also try recognizing logical fallacies; see Chapter 10, pp. 532–36.

READING LIKE A WRITER

RESPONDING TO OBJECTIONS AND ALTERNATIVE POSITIONS FAIRLY

An effective argument concedes valid objections, concerns, or reasons and refutes opposing views that are weak or flawed, sometimes both. Consider the passage below:

Concession   . . . Single-sex education is not the answer to everyone's prayers. Some children want no part of it and some parents question its relevance. The rest of us should not stop wondering what to do with our coeducational public schools just because of this one new option.

Refutation   But single-sex education can be a valuable tool — if we target those students who stand to benefit most. . . . (pars. 4–5)

For more on responding to objections and alternative positions fairly, turn to the Reading Like a Writer section on pp. 323–24 and to Considering a Useful Sentence Strategy on pp. 367–68.

Stabiner responds to other points of view extensively. In fact, she organizes her argument around particular objections she anticipates her readers will raise. Notice also how she treats alternative views with civility and respect, enhancing her credibility, or **ethos**.

Analyze & Write

Write a paragraph or two analyzing other passages in which Stabiner responds to alternative points of view:

1. Reread paragraphs 10 and 13 and the first sentences of paragraphs 15 and 21, highlighting the words that signal Stabiner's acknowledgement of objections to single-sex schools.

2. Now reread paragraphs 11, 12, and 14 and the rest of paragraphs 15 and 21, highlighting the words that cue Stabiner's concession and refutation.

3. What seems to be Stabiner's attitude toward those who oppose single-sex schools? Does she come across as fair? How can you tell?

A Special Reading Strategy

Comparing and Contrasting Related Readings: Orenstein's "The Daily Grind: Lessons in the Hidden Curriculum" and Stabiner's "Boys Here, Girls There: Sure, If Equality's the Goal"

Comparing and contrasting related readings is a critical reading strategy that is useful both in reading for meaning and in reading like a writer. This strategy is particularly applicable when writers present similar subjects, as in the observational essay in Chapter 3 by Peggy Orenstein (pp. 96–100) and the position argument in this chapter by Karen Stabiner (pp. 325–30). Both essays focus on gender in the classroom. To compare and contrast these two essays, think about topics such as these:

- What are their cultural contexts? How do you think Orenstein or her subject, Amy Wilkinson, would react to Stabiner's argument in favor of single-sex education? If Wilkinson's school were single-sex instead of coed, what do you think she would gain and what do you think she would lose?

- What are their purposes and genres? Orenstein's essay describing her observations of a coed classroom may lead readers to question coed education, but Orenstein does not argue, at least not directly, either for or against it. Stabiner, on the other hand, makes an explicit argument in favor of giving public-school students the opportunity to attend single-sex schools. Compare the way these two authors try to influence readers.

See Chapter 10, pp. 527–30, for detailed guidelines on comparing and contrasting related readings.

Sherry Turkle

The Flight from Conversation

Sherry Turkle (b. 1948), professor of the social studies of science and technology at the Massachusetts Institute of Technology, earned her BA and PhD from Harvard University. She is the author of Psychoanalytic Politics: Jacques Lacan and Freud's French Revolution *(1978);* Second Self: Computers and the Human Spirit *(1984);* Life on the Screen: Identity in the Age of the Internet *(1995); and* Simulation and Its Discontents *(2009). Turkle's most recent book is* Alone Together: Why We Expect More from Technology and Less from Each Other *(2011). Turkle writes extensively about people's relationships with technology, especially computers. She is an expert on mobile technology, social networking, and sociable robotics, and is a media commentator on the social and psychological effects of technology. The article below was published in the Sunday Review section of the* New York Times *in 2012. You can see Turkle speak on the subject on the TED (Technology, Entertainment, Design) Web site: http://www.ted.com.*

- **Before you read,** *think about how much time you spend communicating with friends and family via "texting and e-mail and posting" (par. 10) versus how much time you spend talking with friends and family over the phone or face-to-face.*

- **As you read,** *pay attention to the kinds of evidence Turkle provides to support her assertions, such as quotations from interviews and written sources, examples, statistics, illustrations, and so on.*

1   We live in a technological universe in which we are always communicating. And yet we have sacrificed conversation for mere connection.

2   At home, families sit together, texting and reading e-mail. At work executives text during board meetings. We text (and shop and go on Facebook) during classes and when we're on dates. My students tell me about an important new skill: it involves maintaining eye contact with someone while you text someone else; it's hard, but it can be done.

3   Over the past 15 years, I've studied technologies of mobile connection and talked to hundreds of people of all ages and circumstances about their plugged-in lives. I've learned that the little devices most of us carry around are so powerful that they change not only what we do, but also who we are.

4   We've become accustomed to a new way of being "alone together." Technology-enabled, we are able to be with one another, and also elsewhere, connected to wherever we want to be. We want to customize our lives. We want to move in and out of where we are because the thing we value most is control over where we focus our attention. We have gotten used to the idea of being in a tribe of one, loyal to our own party.

Our colleagues want to go to that board meeting but pay attention only   5
to what interests them. To some this seems like a good idea, but we can
end up hiding from one another, even as we are constantly connected to
one another.

A businessman laments that he no longer has colleagues at work. He   6
doesn't stop by to talk; he doesn't call. He says that he doesn't want to
interrupt them. He says they're "too busy on their e-mail." But then he
pauses and corrects himself. "I'm not telling the truth. I'm the one who
doesn't want to be interrupted. I think I should. But I'd rather just do things
on my BlackBerry."

A 16-year-old boy who relies on texting for almost everything says   7
almost wistfully, "Someday, someday, but certainly not now, I'd like to
learn how to have a conversation."

In today's workplace, young people who have grown up fearing conver-   8
sation show up on the job wearing earphones. Walking through a college
library or the campus of a high-tech start-up, one sees the same thing: we
are together, but each of us is in our own bubble, furiously connected to
keyboards and tiny touch screens. A senior partner at a Boston law firm
describes a scene in his office. Young associates lay out their suite of technologies: laptops, iPods and multiple phones. And then they put their earphones on. "Big ones. Like pilots. They turn their desks into cockpits."
With the young lawyers in their cockpits, the office is quiet, a quiet that
does not ask to be broken.

In the silence of connection, people are comforted by being in touch   9
with a lot of people—carefully kept at bay. We can't get enough of one
another if we can use technology to keep one another at distances we can
control: not too close, not too far, just right. I think of it as a Goldilocks
effect.

Texting and e-mail and posting let us present the self we want to be.   10
This means we can edit. And if we wish to, we can delete. Or retouch: the
voice, the flesh, the face, the body. Not too much, not too little—just right.

Human relationships are rich; they're messy and demanding. We have   11
learned the habit of cleaning them up with technology. And the move from
conversation to connection is part of this. But it's a process in which we
shortchange ourselves. Worse, it seems that over time we stop caring, we
forget that there is a difference.

We are tempted to think that our little "sips" of online connection add   12
up to a big gulp of real conversation. But they don't. E-mail, Twitter,
Facebook, all of these have their places—in politics, commerce, romance
and friendship. But no matter how valuable, they do not substitute for
conversation.

Connecting in sips may work for gathering discrete bits of information or   13
for saying, "I am thinking about you." Or even for saying, "I love you."
But connecting in sips doesn't work as well when it comes to understanding

and knowing one another. In conversation we tend to one another. (The word itself is kinetic; it's derived from words that mean to move, together.) We can attend to tone and nuance. In conversation, we are called upon to see things from another's point of view.

14   Face-to-face conversation unfolds slowly. It teaches patience. When we communicate on our digital devices, we learn different habits. As we ramp up the volume and velocity of online connections, we start to expect faster answers. To get these, we ask one another simpler questions; we dumb down our communications, even on the most important matters. It is as though we have all put ourselves on cable news. Shakespeare might have said, "We are consum'd with that which we were nourish'd by."

15   And we use conversation with others to learn to converse with ourselves. So our flight from conversation can mean diminished chances to learn skills of self-reflection. These days, social media continually asks us what's "on our mind," but we have little motivation to say something truly self-reflective. Self-reflection in conversation requires trust. It's hard to do anything with 3,000 Facebook friends except connect.

16   As we get used to being shortchanged on conversation and to getting by with less, we seem almost willing to dispense with people altogether. Serious people muse about the future of computer programs as psychiatrists. A high school sophomore confides to me that he wishes he could talk to an artificial intelligence program instead of his dad about dating; he says the A.I. would have so much more in its database. Indeed, many people tell me they hope that as Siri, the digital assistant on Apple's iPhone, becomes more advanced, "she" will be more and more like a best friend—one who will listen when others won't.

17   During the years I have spent researching people and their relationships with technology, I have often heard the sentiment "No one is listening to me." I believe this feeling helps explain why it is so appealing to have a Facebook page or a Twitter feed—each provides so many automatic listeners. And it helps explain why—against all reason—so many of us are willing to talk to machines that seem to care about us. Researchers around the world are busy inventing sociable robots, designed to be companions to the elderly, to children, to all of us.

18   One of the most haunting experiences during my research came when I brought one of these robots, designed in the shape of a baby seal, to an elder-care facility, and an older woman began to talk to it about the loss of her child. The robot seemed to be looking into her eyes. It seemed to be following the conversation. The woman was comforted.

19   And so many people found this amazing. Like the sophomore who wants advice about dating from artificial intelligence and those who look forward to computer psychiatry, this enthusiasm speaks to how much we have confused conversation with connection and collectively seem to have embraced a new kind of delusion that accepts the simulation of com-

passion as sufficient unto the day. And why would we want to talk about love and loss with a machine that has no experience of the arc of human life? Have we so lost confidence that we will be there for one another?

We expect more from technology and less from one another and seem   20
increasingly drawn to technologies that provide the illusion of companionship without the demands of relationship. Always-on/always-on-you devices provide three powerful fantasies: that we will always be heard; that we can put our attention wherever we want it to be; and that we never have to be alone. Indeed our new devices have turned being alone into a problem that can be solved.

When people are alone, even for a few moments, they fidget and reach   21
for a device. Here connection works like a symptom, not a cure, and our constant, reflexive impulse to connect shapes a new way of being.

Think of it as "I share, therefore I am." We use technology to define our-   22
selves by sharing our thoughts and feelings as we're having them. We used to think, "I have a feeling; I want to make a call." Now our impulse is, "I want to have a feeling; I need to send a text."

So, in order to feel more, and to feel more like ourselves, we connect.   23
But in our rush to connect, we flee from solitude, our ability to be separate and gather ourselves. Lacking the capacity for solitude, we turn to other people but don't experience them as they are. It is as though we use them, need them as spare parts to support our increasingly fragile selves.

We think constant connection will make us feel less lonely. The oppo-   24
site is true. If we are unable to be alone, we are far more likely to be lonely. If we don't teach our children to be alone, they will know only how to be lonely.

I am a partisan for conversation. To make room for it, I see some first,   25
deliberate steps. At home, we can create sacred spaces: the kitchen, the dining room. We can make our cars "device-free zones." We can demonstrate the value of conversation to our children. And we can do the same thing at work. There we are so busy communicating that we often don't have time to talk to one another about what really matters. Employees asked for casual Fridays; perhaps managers should introduce conversational Thursdays. Most of all, we need to remember—in between texts and e-mails and Facebook posts—to listen to one another, even to the boring bits, because it is often in unedited moments, moments in which we hesitate and stutter and go silent, that we reveal ourselves to one another.

I spend the summers at a cottage on Cape Cod, and for decades I   26
walked the same dunes that Thoreau once walked. Not too long ago, people walked with their heads up, looking at the water, the sky, the sand and at one another, talking. Now they often walk with their heads down, typing. Even when they are with friends, partners, children, everyone is on their own devices.

So I say, look up, look at one another, and let's start the conversation.   27

READING FOR MEANING

This section presents three activities that will help you think about the meanings in Turkle's position argument. Your instructor may ask you to do one or more of these activities in class or online.

For more help with summarizing, see Chapter 10, pp. 518–19.

1. **Read to Summarize.** Write a sentence or two explaining Turkle's position on digitally mediated communication (texting, e-mailing, and posting) versus conversation.

2. **Read to Respond.** Write a paragraph analyzing your initial reactions to Turkle's essay. For example, consider anything that resonates with your experience or that seems contradictory, surprising, or fascinating, such as:

   - Turkle's claim about the messiness (par. 11) of relationships conducted face-to-face or via telephone conversations versus via texting, posting, and e-mailing;

You may also try looking for patterns of opposition; see Chapter 10, pp. 525–26.

   - Turkle's denial that "our little 'sips' of online connection add up to a big gulp of real conversation" (par. 12).

3. **Read to Analyze Assumptions.** Write a paragraph or two analyzing an assumption you find intriguing in Turkle's essay. For example:

   Assumptions about the role of conversation in our well-being and our lives. Turkle writes that "conversation unfolds slowly. It teaches patience. . . . [W]e use conversation with others to learn to converse with ourselves" (pars. 14–15). To think critically about the assumptions in this essay regarding the benefits of conversation, ask yourself questions like these:

   - What examples does Turkle offer when arguing in favor of the benefits of conversation and how conversation affects our thinking and our emotions? Is there a pattern in her examples? If so, what is it, and what does it reveal?

   - According to Turkle, conversation helps a person be alone, but not lonely, a seeming paradox (pars. 20–24). What is your experience? Does texting friends and family regularly enhance closeness? Does being someplace where you can't communicate by texting make you anxious or lonely?

   Assumptions about control of our selves. Turkle believes we (perhaps unconsciously) use technology to keep ourselves separate, at a distance

---

Take a quiz to check your reading and vocabulary comprehension:
bedfordstmartins.com/readingcritically

from others, and that we have come to value the way we can edit ourselves in our interactions with others through technology. To think
critically about the assumptions in this essay regarding our ability to
control the way we present ourselves, ask yourself questions like
these:

- Turkle writes that "people are comforted by being in touch with a lot of
  people — carefully kept at bay" (par. 9). Does texting, posting updates
  on Facebook, and e-mailing help you keep friends and family "at bay"?
  What are the advantages and disadvantages of keeping each other "at
  bay"? How does your communication style vary from that of close
  friends to acquaintances?
- What does Turkle think we lose when we allow technology to dictate
  the way our relationships are conducted? What do you think we lose —
  and gain?

READING LIKE A WRITER

ARGUING DIRECTLY FOR THE POSITION, AND SUPPORTING THE POSITION WITH REASONABLE EVIDENCE

A strong argument needs to present reasons and support for the writer's position
on an issue. Writers may use facts, statistics, examples, anecdotes, expert opinion,
or analogies to make their case. Turkle uses several of these types of evidence to
support her reasons, and she also includes quotations (presumably gleaned from
interviews) to support her assertion that by using modern technologies, we have
"sacrificed conversation for mere connection" (par. 1).

Analyze & Write

Write a paragraph or two analyzing how Turkle uses quotations to support her claims:

1. Reread paragraphs 6–8, highlighting the words she uses to introduce and contextualize quotations and underlining the quotations themselves. What do the
   quotations add? Does quoting her sources add something compelling that the
   use of other strategies would not provide? If so, what is it?

2. Now skim the rest of her essay, noting where Turkle quotes sources elsewhere in
   her position argument. What kind of pattern does she follow for introducing
   these quotations? How effective is it for you as a reader?

A Special Reading Strategy

Reflecting on Challenges to Your Beliefs and Values

Often when we read critically, we find ourselves uneasy, disturbed, or upset about something the author is writing about. It may be the way the author presents information, or the ideas he or she is exploring, or the examples that buttress a position. Usually when we are upset by a reading, it's because our fundamental values and beliefs are being challenged. Sometimes we don't even know we *have* these beliefs until we pay attention to our uneasiness. When we do, we may find that probing them helps us understand ourselves and the reading better. We can grow from this process.

Follow the instructions in Chapter 10, pp. 526–27, to reflect on challenges to your values and beliefs. As you reread Turkle's essay, think about your initial response to the essay and consider whether any of the three passages below make you feel resistant. Then write a paragraph or two about your feelings, not defending them but instead analyzing their source.

- "I've learned that the little devices most of us carry around are so powerful that they change not only what we do, but also who we are" (par. 3).

- "In the silence of connection, people are comforted by being in touch with a lot of people — carefully kept at bay. We can't get enough of one another if we can use technology to keep one another at distances we can control: not too close, not too far, just right. I think of it as a Goldilocks effect" (par. 9).

- "We think constant connection will make us feel less lonely. The opposite is true. If we are unable to be alone, we are far more likely to be lonely. If we don't teach our children to be alone, they will know only how to be lonely" (par. 24).

Daniel J. Solove

Why Privacy Matters
Even If You Have "Nothing to Hide"

Daniel J. Solove, currently John Marshall Harlan research professor of law at the George Washington University Law School, earned his BA at Washington University and his JD at Yale Law School. In addition to writing numerous books and articles on issues of privacy and the Internet, Solove is the founder of a company that provides privacy and data security training to corporations and universities. Among his books are The Future of Reputation: Gossip, Rumor, and Privacy on the Internet *(2007), and* Nothing to Hide: The False Tradeoff Between Privacy and Security *(2011). An earlier and longer version of this essay in a law review journal included citations that had to be eliminated for publication in the* Chronicle of Higher Education *in 2011, but we have restored them so that you can see how Solove uses a variety of sources to support his position.*

- *Before you read, think about how (or whether) you make an effort to protect your privacy on social networking and other Web sites (for example, by using privacy settings).*

- *As you read, notice the sources cited in the opening paragraphs, and consider how they contribute to your understanding of why many people think privacy is not something they should be concerned about.*

When the government gathers or analyzes personal information, many people say they're not worried. "I've got nothing to hide," they declare. "Only if you're doing something wrong should you worry, and then you don't deserve to keep it private." The nothing-to-hide argument pervades discussions about privacy. The data-security expert Bruce Schneier calls it the "most common retort against privacy advocates." The legal scholar Geoffrey Stone refers to it as an "all-too-common refrain." In its most compelling form, it is an argument that the privacy interest is generally minimal, thus making the contest with security concerns a foreordained victory for security. 1

The nothing-to-hide argument is everywhere. In Britain, for example, the government has installed millions of public-surveillance cameras in cities and towns, which are watched by officials via closed-circuit television. In a campaign slogan for the program, the government declares: "If you've got nothing to hide, you've got nothing to fear" (Rosen 36). Variations of nothing-to-hide arguments frequently appear in blogs, letters to the editor, television news interviews, and other forums. One blogger in the United States, in reference to profiling people for national-security purposes, declares: "I don't mind people wanting to find out things about me, 2

I've got nothing to hide! Which is why I support [the government's] efforts to find terrorists by monitoring our phone calls!" (greatcarrieoakey).

3   On the surface, it seems easy to dismiss the nothing-to-hide argument. Everybody probably has something to hide from somebody. As Aleksandr Solzhenitsyn declared, "Everyone is guilty of something or has something to conceal. All one has to do is look hard enough to find what it is" (192). . . . One can usually think of something that even the most open person would want to hide. As a commenter to my blog post noted, "If you have nothing to hide, then that quite literally means you are willing to let me photograph you naked? And I get full rights to that photograph—so I can show it to your neighbors?" (Andrew) . . .

4   But such responses attack the nothing-to-hide argument only in its most extreme form, which isn't particularly strong. In a less extreme form, the nothing-to-hide argument refers not to all personal information but only to the type of data the government is likely to collect. Retorts to the nothing-to-hide argument about exposing people's naked bodies or their deepest secrets are relevant only if the government is likely to gather this kind of information. In many instances, hardly anyone will see the information, and it won't be disclosed to the public. Thus, some might argue, the privacy interest is minimal, and the security interest in preventing terrorism is much more important. In this less extreme form, the nothing-to-hide argument is a formidable one. However, it stems from certain faulty assumptions about privacy and its value. . . .

5   Most attempts to understand privacy do so by attempting to locate its essence—its core characteristics or the common denominator that links together the various things we classify under the rubric of "privacy." Privacy, however, is too complex a concept to be reduced to a singular essence. It is a plurality of different things that do not share any one element but nevertheless bear a resemblance to one another. For example, privacy can be invaded by the disclosure of your deepest secrets. It might also be invaded if you're watched by a peeping Tom, even if no secrets are ever revealed. With the disclosure of secrets, the harm is that your concealed information is spread to others. With the peeping Tom, the harm is that you're being watched. You'd probably find that creepy regardless of whether the peeper finds out anything sensitive or discloses any information to others. There are many other forms of invasion of privacy, such as blackmail and the improper use of your personal data. Your privacy can also be invaded if the government compiles an extensive dossier about you. Privacy, in other words, involves so many things that it is impossible to reduce them all to one simple idea. And we need not do so. . . .

6   To describe the problems created by the collection and use of personal data, many commentators use a metaphor based on George Orwell's *Nineteen Eighty-Four*. Orwell depicted a harrowing totalitarian society ruled by a government called Big Brother that watches its citizens obsessively and

demands strict discipline. The Orwell metaphor, which focuses on the harms of surveillance (such as inhibition and social control), might be apt to describe government monitoring of citizens. But much of the data gathered in computer databases, such as one's race, birth date, gender, address, or marital status, isn't particularly sensitive. Many people don't care about concealing the hotels they stay at, the cars they own, or the kind of beverages they drink. Frequently, though not always, people wouldn't be inhibited or embarrassed if others knew this information.

Another metaphor better captures the problems: Franz Kafka's *The Trial.*   7
Kafka's novel centers around a man who is arrested but not informed why. He desperately tries to find out what triggered his arrest and what's in store for him. He finds out that a mysterious court system has a dossier on him and is investigating him, but he's unable to learn much more. *The Trial* depicts a bureaucracy with inscrutable purposes that uses people's information to make important decisions about them, yet denies the people the ability to participate in how their information is used.

The problems portrayed by the Kafkaesque metaphor are of a different   8
sort than the problems caused by surveillance. They often do not result in inhibition. Instead they are problems of information processing—the storage, use, or analysis of data—rather than of information collection. They affect the power relationships between people and the institutions of the modern state. They not only frustrate the individual by creating a sense of helplessness and powerlessness, but also affect social structure by altering the kind of relationships people have with the institutions that make important decisions about their lives.

Legal and policy solutions focus too much on the problems under   9
the Orwellian metaphor—those of surveillance—and aren't adequately addressing the Kafkaesque problems—those of information processing. The difficulty is that commentators are trying to conceive of the problems caused by databases in terms of surveillance when, in fact, those problems are different. Commentators often attempt to refute the nothing-to-hide argument by pointing to things people want to hide. But the problem with the nothing-to-hide argument is the underlying assumption that privacy is about hiding bad things. By accepting this assumption, we concede far too much ground and invite an unproductive discussion about information that people would very likely want to hide. As the computer-security specialist Schneier aptly notes, the nothing-to-hide argument stems from a faulty "premise that privacy is about hiding a wrong." Surveillance, for example, can inhibit such lawful activities as free speech, free association, and other First Amendment rights essential for democracy.

The deeper problem with the nothing-to-hide argument is that it   10
myopically views privacy as a form of secrecy. In contrast, understanding privacy as a plurality of related issues demonstrates that the disclosure of bad things is just one among many difficulties caused by government

security measures. To return to my discussion of literary metaphors, the problems are not just Orwellian but Kafkaesque. Government information-gathering programs are problematic even if no information that people want to hide is uncovered. In *The Trial*, the problem is not inhibited behavior but rather a suffocating powerlessness and vulnerability created by the court system's use of personal data and its denial to the protagonist of any knowledge of or participation in the process. The harms are bureaucratic ones—indifference, error, abuse, frustration, and lack of transparency and accountability.

11   One such harm, for example, which I call aggregation, emerges from the fusion of small bits of seemingly innocuous data. When combined, the information becomes much more telling. By joining pieces of information we might not take pains to guard, the government can glean information about us that we might indeed wish to conceal. For example, suppose you bought a book about cancer. This purchase isn't very revealing on its own, for it indicates just an interest in the disease. Suppose you bought a wig. The purchase of a wig, by itself, could be for a number of reasons. But combine those two pieces of information, and now the inference can be made that you have cancer and are undergoing chemotherapy. That might be a fact you wouldn't mind sharing, but you'd certainly want to have the choice.

12   Another potential problem with the government's harvest of personal data is one I call exclusion. Exclusion occurs when people are prevented from having knowledge about how information about them is being used, and when they are barred from accessing and correcting errors in that data. Many government national-security measures involve maintaining a huge database of information that individuals cannot access. Indeed, because they involve national security, the very existence of these programs is often kept secret. This kind of information processing, which blocks subjects' knowledge and involvement, is a kind of due-process problem. It is a structural problem, involving the way people are treated by government institutions and creating a power imbalance between people and the government. To what extent should government officials have such a significant power over citizens? This issue isn't about what information people want to hide but about the power and the structure of government.

13   A related problem involves secondary use. Secondary use is the exploitation of data obtained for one purpose for an unrelated purpose without the subject's consent. How long will personal data be stored? How will the information be used? What could it be used for in the future? The potential uses of any piece of personal information are vast. Without limits on or accountability for how that information is used, it is hard for people to assess the dangers of the data's being in the government's control.

14   Yet another problem with government gathering and use of personal data is distortion. Although personal information can reveal quite a lot

about people's personalities and activities, it often fails to reflect the whole person. It can paint a distorted picture, especially since records are reductive—they often capture information in a standardized format with many details omitted. For example, suppose government officials learn that a person has bought a number of books on how to manufacture methamphetamine. That information makes them suspect that he's building a meth lab. What is missing from the records is the full story: The person is writing a novel about a character who makes meth. When he bought the books, he didn't consider how suspicious the purchase might appear to government officials, and his records didn't reveal the reason for the purchases. Should he have to worry about government scrutiny of all his purchases and actions? Should he have to be concerned that he'll wind up on a suspicious-persons list? Even if he isn't doing anything wrong, he may want to keep his records away from government officials who might make faulty inferences from them. He might not want to have to worry about how everything he does will be perceived by officials nervously monitoring for criminal activity. He might not want to have a computer flag him as suspicious because he has an unusual pattern of behavior. . . .

Privacy is rarely lost in one fell swoop. It is usually eroded over time, little   15
bits dissolving almost imperceptibly until we finally begin to notice how much is gone. When the government starts monitoring the phone numbers people call, many may shrug their shoulders and say, "Ah, it's just numbers, that's all." Then the government might start monitoring some phone calls. "It's just a few phone calls, nothing more." The government might install more video cameras in public places. "So what? Some more cameras watching in a few more places. No big deal." The increase in cameras might lead to a more elaborate network of video surveillance. Satellite surveillance might be added to help track people's movements. The government might start analyzing people's bank records. "It's just my deposits and some of the bills I pay—no problem." The government may then start combing through credit-card records, then expand to Internet-service providers' records, health records, employment records, and more. Each step may seem incremental, but after a while, the government will be watching and knowing everything about us.

"My life's an open book," people might say. "I've got nothing to hide."   16
But now the government has large dossiers of everyone's activities, interests, reading habits, finances, and health. What if the government leaks the information to the public? What if the government mistakenly determines that based on your pattern of activities, you're likely to engage in a criminal act? What if it denies you the right to fly? What if the government thinks your financial transactions look odd—even if you've done nothing wrong—and freezes your accounts? What if the government doesn't

protect your information with adequate security, and an identity thief obtains it and uses it to defraud you? Even if you have nothing to hide, the government can cause you a lot of harm. . . .

Works Cited

Andrew. Weblog comment. *Concurring Opinions*. 16 Oct. 2006. Web. 24 May 2012.

greatcarrieoakey. "Reach for The Stars!" *Blogspot.com*. 14 May 2006. Web. 24 May 2012.

Rosen, Jeffrey. *The Naked Crowd: Reclaiming Security and Freedom in an Anxious Age*. New York: Random House, 2004. Print.

Schneier, Bruce. "The Eternal Value of Privacy." *Wired*. 18 May 2006. Web. 24 May 2012.

Solzhenitsyn, Aleksandr. *Cancer Ward*. Trans. Nicholas Bethell and David Burg. New York: Farrar, Straus and Giroux, 1969. Print.

Stone, Geoffrey R. "Freedom and Public Responsibility." *Chicago Tribune* 21 May 2006: 11. Print.

READING FOR MEANING

This section presents three activities that will help you think about the meanings in Solove's position argument. Your instructor may ask you to do one or more of these activities in class or online.

For more help with summarizing, see Chapter 10, pp. 518–19.

1. **Read to Summarize.** Write a sentence or two explaining Solove's position on privacy and information-gathering.

2. **Read to Respond.** Write a paragraph analyzing your initial reactions to Solove's essay. For example, consider anything that resonates with your experience or that seems contradictory, surprising, or fascinating, such as:

   • Solove's division of violations of privacy into two types: Orwellian, "which focuses on the harms of surveillance (such as inhibition and social control)" (par. 6) and Kafkaesque "problems of information processing — the storage, use, or analysis of data — rather than that of information collection" (par. 8). In your own words, what is the distinction between these two violations, and why does either of them matter?

   • Solove's argument that the loss of privacy is usually incremental, "eroded over time" (par. 15), and the examples Solove gives to support that assertion. Do the stages seem logical to you, and are they valid stepping-stones to more alarming consequences?

Take a quiz to check your reading and vocabulary comprehension:
bedfordstmartins.com/readingcritically

3. **Read to Analyze Assumptions.** Write a paragraph or two analyzing an assumption in Solove's essay. For example:

Assumptions that "privacy is about hiding bad things" (par. 9). Solove quotes "data-security expert" (par. 1) Bruce Schneier to make explicit a commonly held assumption, that privacy is "'about hiding a wrong'" (par. 9). To think critically about the assumptions in this essay related to the nature of privacy, ask yourself questions like these:

- Does the assumption that privacy is "a form of secrecy" (par. 10) — a way to hide bad behavior — drive any of the antiterrorist actions our government takes?

- Are "one's race, birth date, gender, address, or marital status [not] particularly sensitive," as Solove asserts (par. 6)? Can you think of situations in which this kind of information could be used to injure someone?

- Solove counters the assumption that privacy is about bad things by stating that this assumption is not the only way to think about privacy. What alternative does he offer? Is it convincing to you?

Assumptions that people would take steps to curb violations of privacy if they knew how the information could be used. Solove brings two kinds of privacy violation to our attention because he believes that doing so will change our point of view that we have "nothing to hide." To think critically about assumptions in this essay related to violations of privacy, ask yourself questions like these:

- Solove compares privacy violations to Franz Kafka's *The Trial*, in which information is withheld from a man who is arrested but not told why (par. 7). He adds that the problems are not from surveillance, but "are problems of information processing — the storage, use, or analysis of data — rather than of information collection" (par. 8). Why does Solove think this is a much bigger problem?

- In his final paragraph (par. 16), Solove speculates about the consequences to invasions of privacy that may not have occurred to readers. What is he assuming readers will value, now that he has opened their eyes? Do his examples reflect consequences that could make people change their behavior?

- After explaining how information can be gathered by the government and kept inaccessible, Solove notes that a "power imbalance between people and the government" results (par. 12). To what extent should government officials have such a significant power over citizens? Do you agree with Solove's assumption that a power differential is reason to be concerned, or do you look at the situation differently? For example, might hacking reestablish balance?

READING LIKE A WRITER

PRESENTING THE CONTROVERSIAL ISSUE FAIRLY AND CREDIBLY

Writers sometimes have to remind their readers why an issue is controversial. Beginning with the title, Solove works to undermine the widely held assumption that the erosion of privacy should not be a concern. He does this primarily by contrasting two different ways of thinking about threats to privacy, which he calls Orwellian and Kafkaesque. To present this contrast, Solove uses sentence patterns like these:

> ▶ Not _____, but _____.

> ▶ _____ focus on _____, which is characterized by _____, and they don't even notice _____, which is characterized by _____.

Here are a couple of examples from Solove's position argument:

> . . . the problems are not just Orwellian but Kafkaesque. (par. 10)

> Legal and policy solutions focus too much on the problems under the Orwellian metaphor — those of surveillance — and aren't adequately addressing the Kafka-esque problems — those of information processing. (par. 9)

| Analyze & Write |

Write a few paragraphs analyzing and evaluating the effectiveness of Solove's use of contrast to *reframe* the issue for readers:

1. Notice how Solove uses sources in his first three paragraphs. Given his purpose to reframe a commonly held view of privacy, why do you think he begins this way?

2. Reread paragraphs 6–7 to see how Solove explains the two contrasting metaphors. Then skim paragraphs 8–10, highlighting any sentence patterns he uses to mark the contrast.

3. Has Solove's reframing of the discussion affected your understanding of privacy and your concerns about its loss? Why or why not?

Jessica Statsky

Children Need to Play, Not Compete

Jessica Statsky was a college student when she wrote this position paper, in which she argues that organized sports are not good for children between the ages of six and twelve. Annotate the text, paying special attention to the features of a position paper — presenting the issue fairly and credibly, asserting a clear position, arguing directly for the position with reasonable evidence, and responding to objections and alternative positions fairly.

- *Before you read, recall your own experiences as an elementary-school student playing competitive sports, either in or out of school. If you were not actively involved yourself, did you know anyone who was? Was winning emphasized? What about having a good time? Getting along with others? Developing athletic skills and confidence?*

- *As you read, notice how Statsky sets forth her position clearly, supports the reasons for her position, and handles readers' likely objections. Also note the visible cues that Statsky provides to guide you through her argument step-by-step.*

"Organized sports for young people have become an institution in North America," reports sports journalist Steve Silverman, attracting more than 44 million youngsters according to a recent survey by the National Council of Youth Sports ("History"). Though many adults regard Little League Baseball and Peewee Football as a basic part of childhood, the games are not always joyous ones. When overzealous parents and coaches impose adult standards on children's sports, the result can be activities that are neither satisfying nor beneficial to children. 1

I am concerned about all organized sports activities for children between the ages of six and twelve. The damage I see results from noncontact as well as contact sports, from sports organized locally as well as those organized nationally. Highly organized competitive sports such as Peewee Football and Little League Baseball are too often played to adult standards, which are developmentally inappropriate for children and can be both physically and psychologically harmful. Furthermore, because they eliminate many children from organized sports before they are ready to compete, they are actually counterproductive for developing either future players or fans. Finally, because they emphasize competition and winning, they unfortunately provide occasions for some parents and coaches to place their own fantasies and needs ahead of children's welfare. 2

For an additional student reading, go to **bedfordstmartins.com/readingcritically**.

3   One readily understandable danger of overly competitive sports is that they entice children into physical actions that are bad for growing bodies. "There is a growing epidemic of preventable youth sports injuries," according to the STOP Sports Injuries campaign. "Among athletes ages 5 to 14, 28 percent of football players, 25 percent of baseball players, 22 percent of soccer players, 15 percent of basketball players, and 12 percent of softball players were injured while playing their respective sports." Although the official Little League Web site acknowledges that children do risk injury playing baseball, it insists that "severe injuries . . . are infrequent," the risk "far less than the risk of riding a skateboard, a bicycle, or even the school bus" ("What about My Child?"). Nevertheless, Leonard Koppett in *Sports Illusion, Sports Reality* claims that a twelve-year-old trying to throw a curve ball, for example, may put abnormal strain on developing arm and shoulder muscles, sometimes resulting in lifelong injuries (294). Contact sports like football can be even more hazardous. Thomas Tutko, a psychology professor at San Jose State University and coauthor of the book *Winning Is Everything and Other American Myths*, writes:

> I am strongly opposed to young kids playing tackle football. It is not the right stage of development for them to be taught to crash into other kids. Kids under the age of fourteen are not by nature physical. Their main concern is self-preservation. They don't want to meet head on and slam into each other. But tackle football absolutely requires that they try to hit each other as hard as they can. And it is too traumatic for young kids. (qtd. in Tosches A1)

4   As Tutko indicates, even when children are not injured, fear of being hurt detracts from their enjoyment of the sport. The Little League Web site ranks fear of injury as the seventh of seven reasons children quit ("What about My Child?"). One mother of an eight-year-old Peewee Football player explained, "The kids get so scared. They get hit once and they don't want anything to do with football anymore. They'll sit on the bench and pretend their leg hurts . . ." (qtd. in Tosches A1). Some children are driven to even more desperate measures. For example, in one Peewee Football game, a reporter watched the following scene as a player took himself out of the game:

> "Coach, my tummy hurts. I can't play," he said. The coach told the player to get back onto the field. "There's nothing wrong with your stomach," he said. When the coach turned his head the seven-year-old stuck a finger down his throat and made himself vomit. When the coach turned back, the boy pointed to the ground and told him, "Yes there is, coach. See?" (Tosches A33)

5   Besides physical hazards and anxieties, competitive sports pose psychological dangers for children. Martin Rablovsky, a former sports editor

for the *New York Times,* says that in all his years of watching young children play organized sports, he has noticed very few of them smiling. "I've seen children enjoying a spontaneous pre-practice scrimmage become somber and serious when the coach's whistle blows," Rablovsky says. "The spirit of play suddenly disappears, and sport becomes joblike" (qtd. in Coakley 94). The primary goal of a professional athlete—winning—is not appropriate for children. Their goals should be having fun, learning, and being with friends. Although winning does add to the fun, too many adults lose sight of what matters and make winning the most important goal. Several studies have shown that when children are asked whether they would rather be warming the bench on a winning team or playing regularly on a losing team, about 90 percent choose the latter (Smith, Smith, and Smoll 11).

Winning and losing may be an inevitable part of adult life, but they   6 should not be part of childhood. Too much competition too early in life can affect a child's development. Children are easily influenced, and when they sense that their competence and worth are based on their ability to live up to their parents' and coaches' high expectations—and on their ability to win—they can become discouraged and depressed. Little League advises parents to "keep winning in perspective" ("Your Role"), noting that the most common reasons children give for quitting, aside from change in interest, are lack of playing time, failure and fear of failure, disapproval by significant others, and psychological stress ("What about My Child?"). According to Dr. Glyn C. Roberts, a professor of kinesiology at the Institute of Child Behavior and Development at the University of Illinois, 80 to 90 percent of children who play competitive sports at a young age drop out by sixteen (Kutner).

This statistic illustrates another reason I oppose competitive sports for   7 children: because they are so highly selective, very few children get to participate. Far too soon, a few children are singled out for their athletic promise, while many others, who may be on the verge of developing the necessary strength and ability, are screened out and discouraged from trying out again. Like adults, children fear failure, and so even those with good physical skills may stay away because they lack self-confidence. Consequently, teams lose many promising players who with some encouragement and experience might have become stars. The problem is that many parent-sponsored, out-of-school programs give more importance to having a winning team than to developing children's physical skills and self-esteem.

Indeed, it is no secret that too often scorekeeping, league standings,   8 and the drive to win bring out the worst in adults who are more absorbed in living out their own fantasies than in enhancing the quality of the experience for children (Smith, Smith, and Smoll 9). Recent newspaper articles on children's sports contain plenty of horror stories. *Los Angeles Times*

FIG. 1.   Too many parents use their children's sports programs as a way to live out their own fantasies, as shown in this cartoon by James Mulligan from the *New Yorker*.

"Please, Mrs. Enright, if I let you pinch-hit for Tommy, all the mothers will want to pinch-hit."

reporter Rich Tosches, for example, tells the story of a brawl among seventy-five parents following a Peewee Football game (A33). As a result of the brawl, which began when a parent from one team confronted a player from the other team, the teams are now thinking of hiring security guards for future games. Another example is provided by a *Los Angeles Times* editorial about a Little League manager who intimidated the opposing team by setting fire to one of their team's jerseys on the pitcher's mound before the game began. As the editorial writer commented, the manager showed his young team that "intimidation could substitute for playing well" ("The Bad News").

9   Although not all parents or coaches behave so inappropriately, the seriousness of the problem is illustrated by the fact that Adelphi University in Garden City, New York, offers a sports psychology workshop for Little League coaches, designed to balance their "animal instincts" with "educational theory" in hopes of reducing the "screaming and hollering," in the words of Harold Weisman, manager of sixteen Little Leagues in New York City (Schmitt). In a three-and-one-half-hour Sunday morning workshop, coaches learn how to make practices more fun, treat injuries, deal with irate parents, and be "more sensitive to their young players' fears, emotional frailties, and need for recognition." Little League is to be credited with recognizing the need for such workshops.

Some parents would no doubt argue that children cannot start too soon   10
preparing to live in a competitive free-market economy. After all, secondary schools and colleges require students to compete for grades, and college admission is extremely competitive. And it is perfectly obvious how
important competitive skills are in finding a job. Yet the ability to cooperate is also important for success in life. Before children are psychologically
ready for competition, maybe we should emphasize cooperation and individual performance in team sports rather than winning.

Many people are ready for such an emphasis. In 1988, one New York   11
Little League official who had attended the Adelphi workshop tried to ban
scoring from six- to eight-year-olds' games—but parents wouldn't support
him (Schmitt). An innovative children's sports program in New York City,
City Sports for Kids, emphasizes fitness, self-esteem, and sportsmanship. In
this program's basketball games, every member on a team plays at least
two of six eight-minute periods. The basket is seven feet from the floor,
rather than ten feet, and a player can score a point just by hitting the rim
(Bloch). I believe this kind of local program should replace overly competitive programs like Peewee Football and Little League Baseball. As one
coach explains, significant improvements can result from a few simple rule
changes, such as including every player in the batting order and giving
every player, regardless of age or ability, the opportunity to play at least
four innings a game (Frank).

Some children *want* to play competitive sports; they are not being   12
forced to play. These children are eager to learn skills, to enjoy the camara-
derie of the team, and earn self-respect by trying hard to benefit their team.
I acknowledge that some children may benefit from playing competitive
sports. While some children do benefit from these programs, however,
many more would benefit from programs that avoid the excesses and dangers of many competitive sports programs and instead emphasize fitness,
cooperation, sportsmanship, and individual performance.

Works Cited

"The Bad News Pyromaniacs?" Editorial. *Los Angeles Times* 16 June 1990:
    B6. *LexisNexis*. Web. 16 May 2008.

Bloch, Gordon B. "Thrill of Victory Is Secondary to Fun." *New York Times*
    2 Apr. 1990, late ed.: C12. *LexisNexis*. Web. 14 May 2008.

Coakley, Jay J. *Sport in Society: Issues and Controversies*. St. Louis: Mosby,
    1982. Print.

Frank, L. "Contributions from Parents and Coaches." *CYB Message Board*.
    AOL, 8 July 1997. Web. 14 May 2008.

Koppett, Leonard. *Sports Illusion, Sports Reality*. Boston: Houghton, 1981.
    Print.

Kutner, Lawrence. "Athletics, through a Child's Eyes." *New York Times*
    23 Mar. 1989, late ed.: C8. *LexisNexis*. Web. 15 May 2008.

Schmitt, Eric. "Psychologists Take Seat on Little League Bench." *New York Times* 14 Mar. 1988, late ed.: B2. *LexisNexis*. Web. 14 May 2008.

Silverman, Steve. "The History of Youth Sports." Livestrong.com. Demand Media, Inc., 26 May 2011. Web. 10 Dec. 2011.

Smith, Nathan, Ronald Smith, and Frank Smoll. *Kidsports: A Survival Guide for Parents*. Reading: Addison, 1983. Print.

STOPSportsInjuries.org. American Orthopaedic Society for Sports Medicine, n.d. Web. 10 Dec. 2011.

Tosches, Rich. "Peewee Football: Is It Time to Blow the Whistle?" *Los Angeles Times* 3 Dec. 1988: A1+. *LexisNexis*. Web. 22 May 2008.

"What about My Child?" *Little League Online*. Little League Baseball, Incorporated, 1999. Web. 30 May 2008.

"Your Role as a Little League Parent." *Little League Online*. Little League Baseball, Incorporated, 1999. Web. 30 May 2008.

READING FOR MEANING

This section presents three activities that will help you think about the meanings in Statsky's position argument.

For more help with summarizing, see Chapter 10, pp. 518–19.

1. **Read to Summarize.** Write a sentence or two explaining what you learned about children and sports from Statsky's argument.

2. **Read to Respond.** Write a paragraph analyzing your initial reactions to Statsky's essay. For example, consider anything that resonates with your experience or that seems contradictory, surprising, or fascinating, such as:

   - Statsky's claim that children can become discouraged and depressed "when they sense that their competence and worth are based on their ability to live up to their parents' and coaches' high expectations — and on their ability to win" (par. 6). Was this true of your experience or that of your friends? Can you think of ways in which playing organized sports might help children develop a sense of "competence and worth" based on something beyond their parents' expectations, such as their willingness to work for the good of the team?

   You may also try looking for patterns of opposition; see Chapter 10, pp. 525–26.

   - Statsky's assertion that "it is no secret that too often scorekeeping, league standings, and the drive to win bring out the worst in adults . . ." (par. 8). What kinds of values do overzealous parents demonstrate? Are there any that are positive?

3. **Read to Analyze Assumptions.** Write a paragraph or two analyzing an assumption you find intriguing in Statsky's essay. For example:

   Assumptions that cooperation is as important a skill to develop as competition. Statsky explicitly states this assumption when she writes that the ability to cooperate is as important as competitive skills for success (par. 10). To think critically about assumptions regarding competition and cooperation, ask yourself questions like these:

- Statsky asserts in her first paragraph that "overzealous parents and coaches impose adult standards on children's sports, [leading to] activities that are neither satisfying nor beneficial to children." Do you agree that coaches and parents impose the desire to win on children? Do you agree that children's sports should have different standards?

- Later in her paper, Statsky acknowledges how important competitive skills are for getting into college and finding a job, but immediately follows with a response: "Yet the ability to cooperate is also important for success in life. Before children are psychologically ready for competition, maybe we should emphasize cooperation and individual performance in team sports rather than winning" (par. 10). Do you think Statsky provides enough evidence that most children are not psychologically ready for competition? If so, which kinds of evidence are most compelling for you? Why?

Assumptions that children's sports should be inclusive. Statsky argues that children's competitive sports should be reformed because they favor the most coordinated and strongest children (par. 7) to the exclusion of children who are weaker or less skilled.

- What evidence does Statsky offer to support this claim, especially for the youngest participants in PeeWee Football and Little League? Is it possible that the stronger and better-coordinated children might be drawn to organized sports because they enjoy playing more? Might children who enjoy physical activity have developed the skills needed to succeed on the playing field through practice rather than through the process of development?

- Should those who organize children's sports have an obligation to include all children who want to participate? Why or why not?

READING LIKE A WRITER

ASSERTING A CLEAR POSITION

Writers usually (but not always) assert their positions early in an essay and, to help readers focus, may reassert the position later in the essay. (They nearly always restate it in the conclusion.) The position must be stated clearly, but not necessarily without qualification. In fact, in order for it to be defensible, writers frequently must **qualify**, or limit, their position. Statsky, for example, limits her thesis, contending not that she's concerned about organized sports for all children, but only for those between the ages of six and twelve (par. 2).

Analyze & Write

Write a paragraph or two analyzing how effectively Statsky asserts her position:

1. Skim Statsky's essay, underlining her thesis statement and her restatement(s) of the thesis.

2. Now underline or highlight any sentences that assert a reason in support of Statsky's thesis. (Hint: Look for the word *because*.) How do the reasons Statsky supplies support her thesis statement? Does she include any reasons that undermine her position or make her position unclear? If so, what are they?

ANALYZING VISUALS

Write a paragraph analyzing the cartoon included in Statsky's position argument (fig. 1) and explaining what it contributes to the essay. To do the analysis, you can use the Criteria for Analyzing Visuals chart in Chapter 12, on pp. 611–12. Don't feel you have to answer all of the questions in the chart; focus on those that seem most productive in helping you write a paragraph-length analysis. To help you get started, consider adding these questions that specifically refer to Statsky's use of this cartoon:

- How does the cartoon illustrate Statsky's concerns about parents' involvement in their children's competitive sports?

- What does the cartoon's caption — what the coach is saying to Mrs. Enright — say about parents as role models for their children?

- Two schools of thought about how to raise children are (1) to show them what to do and (2) to allow them to learn on their own, including making mistakes. Clearly this cartoon illustrates the first school, taken to an extreme. How might you illustrate the second school?

Reviewing What Makes Position Arguments Effective

An effective position argument

- presents a controversial issue fairly and credibly;

- asserts a clear position on the issue;

- argues directly for the position, providing reasonable supporting evidence;

- responds to objections and alternative positions fairly.

Analyze & Write

Write a brief evaluation—positive, negative, or mixed—of one of the readings in this chapter, explaining why you think it succeeds or fails as a position argument. Be sure to consider the characteristics that distinguish essays arguing for a position, as well how successful the writer has been in communicating his or her purpose to the intended audience. You may also want to consider the effect the medium of presentation had on decisions the writer made.

A GUIDE TO WRITING
POSITION ARGUMENTS

As you've read and discussed the reading selections in this chapter, you have probably done a good deal of analytical writing. Your instructor may assign a capstone project to write a brief position argument of your own. Having learned how writers present a controversial issue fairly and credibly, assert and defend a clear position on that issue, and respond effectively and fairly to other views, you can now approach position arguments confidently as a writer. This Guide to Writing offers detailed suggestions for writing position arguments and resources to help you meet the special challenges this kind of writing presents.

THE WRITING ASSIGNMENT

Write an essay arguing a position on a controversial issue.

- Choose an issue on which you either have a position or that you'd like to investigate further.

- Consider what your readers might know about the issue, and what stance they might take toward it.

- Conduct research on the issue so you can support and clarify your own argument, and also so that you can address the objections your readers might raise as well as the alternative positions they might prefer.

- Adopt a reasonable tone, one that will lend credibility to your position.

WRITING A DRAFT

INVENTION, PLANNING, AND COMPOSING

The following activities will help you choose a controversial issue, consider what you and your readers need to know, determine your position on the issue, and gather and sort through the information you need to present your position clearly, logically, and fairly.

Choosing a Controversial Issue

Rather than limiting yourself to the first subject that comes to mind, take a few minutes to consider your options. When choosing an issue, keep in mind that the issue must be

- controversial — an issue that people disagree about;
- arguable — a matter of opinion on which there is no absolute proof or authority;
- one that you can research, as necessary, in the time you have;
- one that you care about but for which you can be fair and reasonable.

Choosing an issue about which you have special interest or knowledge usually works best, and it's important to focus the issue so that you can write a brief paper on it. For example, if you are thinking of addressing an issue of national concern, focus on a local or a specific aspect of it: Instead of addressing censorship in general, write about a recent lawmaker's effort to propose a law censoring the Internet, a city council attempt to block access to Internet sites at a public library, or a school board's ban on certain textbooks.

You may already have an issue in mind. If you do not, the topics that follow may suggest one you can make your own. Note that they are in the form of questions, the answers to which could be positions.

- Should particular courses, community service, or an internship be a graduation requirement at your high school or college?
- Should children raised in this country whose parents entered illegally be given an opportunity to become citizens upon finishing college or serving in the military?
- Should you look primarily for a job that is well paid, or for a job that is personally fulfilling or socially responsible?
- Should students attending public colleges be required to pay higher tuition fees if they have been full-time students but have not graduated within four years?
- Should the racial, ethnic, or gender makeup of the police force resemble the makeup of the community it serves?
- Should public employees be allowed to unionize and to bargain collectively for improved working conditions, pay, or pensions?
- Should your large lecture or online courses have frequent (weekly or biweekly) exams instead of only a midterm and final?

- Should the football conference your school (or another school in the area) participates in be allowed to expand?

- Should the state or federal government provide job training for those who are unemployed but able to work?

Before making a final decision about the issue on which you will take a position, try writing nonstop about it for a few minutes. Doing so will help stimulate your memory, letting you see what you already know about the issue and helping you decide how much research you will need to do. If your instructor expects you to conduct extensive research, choose an issue that has been written about extensively — such as whether weapons searches should be conducted on high-school campuses or affirmative action should be continued in college admissions. Other issues — such as whether students should be required to perform community service or be discouraged from taking part-time jobs that interfere with their studies — may be confidently based mainly on personal experience.

Developing Your Argument

The writing and research activities that follow will enable you to test your choice and discover good ways to argue for your position on the issue.

Presenting the Issue.   The following questions and sentence strategies can help you explore the issue and consider how best to present it to your readers.

How can I explore the issue?

What groups or notable individuals have shaped the debate on this issue? What positions have they taken?

- ▶ It may surprise you that .... is a controversial issue. Although many people take .... for granted, ... [list individuals/groups] oppose it on the grounds that ....
- ▶ Whereas supporters of .... , such as .... , ... , and .... , have argued that .... , opponents such as .... [list individuals/groups] contend that ....

How has the issue, or people's opinions about the issue, changed? What makes the issue important now?

- ▶ [Recent research/incidents reported in the news] have changed some people's minds on this issue. Instead of assuming .... , many people now think ....
- ▶ The debate over whether .... should .... was initially concerned that .... , but the main concern now seems to be that ....

What do my readers think?

What values and concerns do you and your readers share regarding the issue?

▶ Concern about .... leads many of us to oppose .... We worry that .... will happen if ....

▶ .... is a basic human right that needs to be protected. But what does it mean in everyday practice when ....?

What fundamental differences in worldview or experience might keep you and your readers from agreeing?

▶ Those who disagree about .... often see it as a choice between .... and .... But both are important. We don't have to choose between them because ....

▶ While others may view it as a matter of ...., for me, the issue hinges on ....

▶ According to ...., what's at stake in this issue is .... For me, however, what is most important is ....

How can I present the issue effectively?

What is the issue and why should your readers be concerned about it?

▶ I'm concerned about .... because ....

Example: I'm concerned about the high cost of tuition at state colleges like ours because students need to borrow more money to pay for their education than they will be able to repay.

Why are popular approaches or attitudes inappropriate or inadequate?

▶ Although some argue ...., I think .... because ....

Example: Although some argue that college football players should be paid, I think the current system should be maintained because it is only the money earned from football that enables our school to fund other, less lucrative sports programs.

Drafting a Working Thesis. You may already have a position on the issue; if so, try drafting a working thesis statement now. (If you have not yet taken a position on the issue, you may want to skip ahead to the section on researching an issue below. Researching the positions others have taken and their reasons may help you decide on your own position.) Begin by describing the issue, possibly indicating where others stand on it or what's at stake, and then saying what you think. These sentence strategies may help you get started:

▶ On this issue, ... and .... [list individuals/groups] say .... Although I understand and to some degree sympathize with their point of view, this is ultimately a question of .... What's at stake is not ...., but .... Therefore, we must ....

> ► This issue is dividing our community. Some people argue .... Others contend .... And still others believe .... It is in all of our interests to .... , however, because ....

> ► Conventional wisdom is that .... But I take a different view: ....

Here are four examples from the readings:

- "... our educational system fails to teach science in a way that allows students to integrate it into their lives." (Greene, par. 2)

- "Single-sex education matters, and it matters most to the students who historically have been denied access to it." (Stabiner, par. 3)

- "The deeper problem with the nothing-to-hide argument is that it myopically views privacy as a form of secrecy. In contrast, understanding privacy as a plurality of related issues demonstrates that the disclosure of bad things is just one among many difficulties caused by government security measures." (Solove, par. 10)

- "When overzealous parents and coaches impose adult standards on children's sports, the result can be activities that are neither satisfying nor beneficial to children. (Statsky, par. 1)

Developing the Reasons Supporting Your Position. The following activities will help you find plausible reasons and evidence for your position. Begin by writing down what you already know. (If you did this when choosing your issue, look back at what you wrote.) You can do some focused research later to fill in the details or skip ahead to conduct research now. At this point, don't worry about the exact language you will use in your final draft. Instead, just write the reasons you hold your position and the evidence (such as anecdotes, examples, statistics, expert testimony) that supports it. Keep your readers in mind — what will they find most convincing?

Writers sometimes prefer to brainstorm a list of reasons. If you are one of them, try this:

- Start by writing your position at the top of the page.

- List as many possible reasons as you can think of to support your position. (Don't be judgmental at this point.) If you think of a bit of supporting evidence such as a good example or a research study but you're not sure how to formulate the reason, simply list the support so you can work on it later.

- Once you have a list of reasons, try organizing them into related groups. For example, which reasons make an argument based on moral values, political ideology, or self-interest, and which are realistic or idealistic? Which would be most and least convincing for your readers? You may be able to use these lists as a starting point for drafting and organizing your writing project.

Once you have listed several reasons in support of your position, write steadily for at least five minutes exploring how best to present them. Ask yourself questions like these:

- How can I show readers that my reasons lead logically to my position?

- In addition to appealing to readers' intellect (logos), how could I appeal to my readers' sense of fairness (ethos) and their values or feelings (pathos)?

Where you need supporting evidence, make a note to remind yourself to fill in the gaps with research.

Researching the Issue. Research can help you look critically at your own thinking and help you anticipate your readers' arguments and possible objections to your argument.

- Enter keywords or phrases related to the issue or your position in the search box of an all-purpose database such as *Academic OneFile* (InfoTrac) or *Academic Search Complete* (EBSCOHost) to find relevant articles in magazines and journals, or a database like *LexisNexis* to find articles in newspapers. For example, Statsky could have tried a combination of keywords such as *children's competitive sports* or variations on her terms (such as *youth team sports*) to find relevant articles. A similar search could also be conducted in your library's catalog to locate books and other resources on your topic.

- If you think your issue has been dealt with by a government agency, explore the state, local, or tribal sections of usa.gov, the U.S. government's official Web portal, or visit the Library of Congress page on State Government Information, www.loc.gov/rr/news/stategov/stategov.html, and follow the links.

- Bookmark or keep a record of the URLs of promising sites. You may want to download or copy information you could use in your essay. When available, download PDF files rather than HTML files, because PDFs are likely to include visuals.

Remember to record source information and to cite and document any sources, including visuals, that you use in your essay.

To learn more about finding and documenting sources, see Chapter 11, Strategies for Research and Documentation.

Including Visuals. Consider whether visuals — drawings, photographs, tables, or graphs — would strengthen your argument. You could construct your own visuals, scan materials from books and magazines, or download them from the Internet. If you submit your essay electronically to other students and your instructor or if you post it on a Web site, consider including snippets of film or sound as well. Visual and auditory materials are not at all a requirement of a successful position argument, as you can tell from the readings in this chapter, but they could add a new dimension to your writing. If you want to use photographs or recordings of people, though, be sure to obtain permission.

Responding Fairly to Objections Your Readers Are Likely to Raise.   The activity below will help you anticipate alternative positions your readers may hold or objections they may have. You may want to return to this activity as you do additional research and learn more about the issue and the arguments people make. Use the research strategies above (p. 363) or consult Chapter 11.

1. Start by listing the positions you expect your readers will hold and the objections you expect them to raise. To think of readers' concerns, consider how you differ on values, beliefs, and priorities. (You may want to return to this step after conducting research into how others have argued for alternative positions.)

2. Analyze your list of objections. Which can you refute? Which may you need to concede? Again, you may want to return to this step after conducting research.

   Turn to Considering a Useful Sentence Strategy (on p. 367) to learn more about conceding and refuting those views.

Considering Your Purpose.   Write for several minutes about your purpose for writing this position paper. The following questions will help you think about your purpose:

- What do I hope to accomplish with my readers? How do I want to influence their thinking? What one big idea do I want them to grasp and remember?

- How much resistance to my argument should I expect from my readers? Will they be largely receptive? Skeptical but convincible? Resistant and perhaps even antagonistic?

- How can I interest my readers in the issue? How can I help my readers see its significance — both to society at large and to them personally?

- How can I present myself as fair and ethical?

Organizing Your Position Argument Effectively for Your Readers

For more on outlining, see Chapter 10, pp. 515–17.

Whether you have rough notes or a complete draft, making an outline of what you have written can help you organize your essay effectively for your audience. You may want to draft a sentence that forecasts the elements of your argument to alert your readers to your main points (and give yourself a tentative outline). Putting your points in a logical order (from least to most effective, for example) will make it easier for you to guide your readers from point to point.

   Keep in mind that a position argument has five basic parts:

- presentation of the issue

- thesis statement

- your most plausible reasons and evidence
- concessions or refutation of opposing reasons or objections to your argument
- a conclusion that reaffirms your position

These parts can be organized in various ways: If your readers are not likely to agree with your position, you may want to anticipate and respond to their possible objections right before you present the evidence in favor of your own position. If you expect readers *are* likely to favor your position, you may want to concede or refute alternatives after offering your own reasons. Either way, you may want to emphasize the common ground you share and conclude by emphasizing that your position takes into account your shared values. You might want to make two or three different outlines before choosing the organization that looks most promising.

Never be a slave to an outline. As you draft, you may see ways to improve your original plan, and you should be ready to revise your outline, shift parts around, or drop or add parts as needed. If you use the outlining function of your word processing program, changing your outline will be easy, and you may be able to write the essay simply by expanding that outline.

Drafting Your Position Argument

By this point, you have done a lot of writing

- to choose an arguable issue and draft a working thesis that asserts your position on it;
- to support your position with reasons and evidence;
- to respond to your readers' likely objections and alternative positions;
- to establish your credibility as thoughtful and fair.

Now stitch that material together to create a draft. The next two parts of this Guide to Writing will help you evaluate and improve it.

Working with Sources
Using Sources to Reinforce Your Credibility

How you represent your sources can quickly establish your credibility (ethos) — or the reverse. For example, by briefly describing the author's credentials the first time you summarize, paraphrase, or quote from a

(continued)

source, you establish the source's authority and demonstrate that you have selected sources appropriately. (Make sure the author's credentials are relevant to the topic you are discussing.) For example, in paragraph 5 of "Children Need to Play, Not Compete," Statsky writes:

> Martin Rablovsky, a former sports editor for the *New York Times*, says that in all his years of watching young children play organized sports, he has noticed very few of them smiling. "I've seen children enjoying a spontaneous pre-practice scrimmage become somber and serious when the coach's whistle blows," Rablovsky says . . . (qtd in Coakley 94).

Notice how Statsky integrates Rablovsky's credentials (underlined in green) and a summary of his main idea (black) into her own sentence. By doing so, she not only demonstrates her credibility but also provides context for the quotation and demonstrates its relevance to her claim.

In the example below, from her third paragraph, Statsky demonstrates her fairness by quoting from the Web site of Little League, a well-known organization, and establishes her credibility by illustrating that even those who disagree with her recognize that injuries occur:

> Although the official Little League Web site acknowledges that children do risk injury playing baseball, it insists that "severe injuries . . . are infrequent . . . far less than the risk of riding a skateboard, a bicycle, or even the school bus" ("What about My Child?").

In both examples, Statsky also introduces the source to her readers, demonstrating the relevance of the source material for readers rather than leaving readers to figure out its relevance for themselves.

Whenever you borrow information from sources, be sure to double-check that you are summarizing, paraphrasing, and quoting accurately and fairly. Compare Statsky's sentences with the source passage, shown below. (The portions she uses are underlined.) Notice that she has inserted an ellipsis to indicate that she has left out words from her source's second sentence.

Source

Injuries seem to be inevitable in any rigorous activity, especially if players are new to the sport and unfamiliar with its demands. But because of the safety precautions taken in Little League, severe injuries such as bone fractures are infrequent. Most injuries are sprains and strains, abrasions and cuts and bruises. The risk of serious injury in Little League Baseball is far less than the risk of riding a skateboard, a bicycle, or even the school bus.

In both examples above, Statsky uses quotation marks to indicate that she is borrowing the words of a source, and she provides an in-text citation so readers can locate her sources in her list of works cited. Both are essential to avoid plagiarism; doing one or the other is not enough.

For more on integrating language from sources into your own sentences and avoiding plagiarism, see Using Sources to Support Your Ideas in Chapter 11, pp. 569–80.

Considering a Useful Sentence Strategy

As you draft your essay, you will need to move back and forth smoothly between direct arguments for your position and your responses to your readers' likely objections and opposing positions. One useful strategy for making this move is to concede some value in a likely criticism but then immediately refute the idea that it weakens your larger point. The refutation may appear either in the same sentence or in the next one. The basic structure of the **concession-refutation move** is:

▶ I agree that .... is important, but so is ....

Notice that the refutation is signaled by a transition signaling that a contrast is coming, such as *but*, *however*, *although*, or *even though*.

Here are two examples from Statsky's essay and two examples from other essays in this chapter showing the concession-refutation move in action:

Concession   . . . The primary goal of a professional athlete — winning — is not appro-
Refutation   priate for children. Their goals should be having fun, learning, and
               being with friends. Although winning does add to the fun, too many
               adults lose sight of what matters and make winning the most important
               goal. . . . (Statsky, par. 5)

. . . And it is perfectly obvious how important competitive skills are in finding a job. Yet the ability to cooperate is also important for success in life. . . . (Statsky, par. 10)

These are the standard — and enormously important — reasons many would give in explaining why science matters.

But here's the thing. The reason science really matters runs deeper still. Science is a way of life. Science is a perspective. Science is the process that takes us from confusion to understanding in a manner that's precise, predictive and reliable — a transformation, for those lucky enough to experience it, that is empowering and emotional. . . . (Greene, pars. 6–7)

> Educators at single-sex schools already get it: Equality is the goal, not the process. There may be more than one path to the destination — but it is the arrival, not the itinerary, that counts. (Stabiner, par. 12)

(Because these illustrations are in each instance woven into an extended argument, you may better appreciate them if you look at them in context by turning to the paragraphs where they appear.)

Of course, not all writers concede before responding. Instead, writers sometimes begin not with a concession but with an acknowledgment; that is, the writer simply restates part of an opponent's argument fairly without conceding the wisdom of it. Here are some examples from the readings in this chapter:

> It's striking that science is still widely viewed as merely a subject one studies in the classroom or an isolated body of largely esoteric knowledge that sometimes shows up in the "real" world in the form of technological or medical advances. In reality, science is a language of hope and inspiration, providing discoveries that fire the imagination and instill a sense of connection to our lives and our world. (Greene, par. 9)

> What is this misplaced reverence for the coed school? Do not think that it was designed with the best interests of all children at heart. . . . (Stabiner, par. 15)

This approach, sometimes called the *"yes-but" strategy*, is important in most arguments. The activity below will help you anticipate alternative positions your readers may hold or objections they may have.

EVALUATING THE DRAFT

GETTING A CONSTRUCTIVE CRITICAL READING

Getting a critical reading of your draft will help you see how to improve it. Your instructor may schedule class time for reading drafts, or you may want to ask a classmate or a tutor in the writing center to read your draft. Ask your reader to use the following guidelines and to write out a response for you to consult during your revision.

READING A DRAFT CRITICALLY

Read for a First Impression

1. **Read the draft without stopping, and then write a few sentences giving your general impression.**

2. **Identify one aspect of the draft that seems particularly effective.**

Read Again to Suggest Improvements

1. **Suggest ways of presenting the issue more effectively.**

   - Read the paragraphs that present the issue, and tell the writer if you have trouble understanding what it is or what the controversy about it is.

   - Point to any key terms used to present the issue that seem surprising or confusing, or may be antagonizing to readers who disagree with the writer's position.

   - If you think a visual such as a photograph or chart would help readers understand the issue better, tell the writer so.

2. **Recommend ways of asserting the position more clearly and unequivocally.**

   - Find the writer's thesis, or position statement, and underline it. If you cannot find a clear thesis, let the writer know.

   - If you find several restatements of the thesis, examine them closely for consistency.

   - If the position seems extreme or overstated, suggest how it might be qualified and made more reasonable.

3. **Help the writer strengthen the argument for the position.**

   - Look at the reasons the writer gives for the position. Indicate any that seem unconvincing, and explain briefly why you think so.

   - Look at the support the writer provides for each reason. If you find any of it ineffective, explain why you think so and how it could be strengthened. If no support for a reason is provided, suggest what kinds (facts, statistics, quotations, anecdotes, examples, analogies, visuals) the writer might consider adding — and why.

4. **Suggest ways of improving the response to alternative points of view.**

   - If a likely objection or opposing position has not been addressed, tell the writer what it is. If possible, suggest how and where it could be addressed.

   - If any refutation seems weak, suggest what the writer could add or change.

   - If only the weakest criticisms have been addressed, remind the writer of stronger ones that should be taken into account.

5. **Suggest how the writer's credibility can be enhanced.**

   - Tell the writer whether the intended readers are likely to find the essay authoritative and trustworthy. Point to places where the argument seems most and least trustworthy.

(continued)

• Identify places where the writer seeks to establish a common ground of shared values, beliefs, and attitudes with readers. Suggest other ways the writer might do so.

6. **Suggest ways of improving readability.**

   • Consider whether the beginning adequately engages readers' interest and sets the stage for the argument, perhaps by establishing the tone or forecasting the argument.

   • If the organization does not seem to follow a logical plan, suggest how it might be rearranged or where transitions could be inserted to clarify logical connections.

   • Note whether the ending gives the argument a satisfactory sense of closure.

IMPROVING THE DRAFT

REVISING, EDITING, AND PROOFREADING

Start improving your draft by reflecting on what you have written thus far:

• Review critical reading comments from your classmates, instructor, or writing center tutor. What are your readers getting at?

• Take another look at your notes and ideas: What else should you consider?

• Review your draft: What else can you do to make your position argument clearer or more interesting to your readers?

Revising Your Draft

Revising means reenvisioning your draft, trying to see it in a new way, given your purpose and audience, to develop a well-argued position paper. Think imaginatively and boldly about cutting unconvincing or tangential material, adding new material, and moving material around. The suggestions in the chart on the next page may help you solve problems and strengthen your essay.

TROUBLESHOOTING YOUR DRAFT

To Present the Issue More Effectively

Problem	Suggestions for Revising
Readers don't understand what is at stake with the issue.	• Add anecdotes, examples, facts, quotations, or visuals to make the issue more specific and vivid. • Explain systematically why you see the issue as you do.
Your terms are surprising or are antagonistic to readers who disagree with your position.	• Use terms that are more familiar. • Use terms that are more neutral.

To Assert the Position More Clearly

Problem	Suggestions for Revising
Your position on the issue is unclear.	• Rephrase it or spell it out in more detail.
The thesis statement is hard to find.	• State it more directly or position it more boldly. • Repeat it in different words throughout your essay
The thesis is not qualified to account for valid opposing arguments or objections.	• Limit the scope of your thesis. • Use qualifying terms, such as *many*, *often*, or *in some cases*.

To Strengthen the Argument for the Position

Problem	Suggestions for Revising
A reason given for the position seems unconvincing.	• Clarify its relevance to the argument. • Add support for your reasoning.
The support for a reason is inadequate.	• Review your invention notes or do more research to find facts, statistics, quotations, examples, or other types of support to add.

To Improve the Response to Alternative Arguments

Problem	Suggestions for Revising
Your argument ignores a strong opposing position or reasonable objection.	• Address the criticism directly, perhaps using the sentence strategy of concession and refutation. • If necessary, modify your position to accommodate the criticism.
Your refutation of a criticism is unconvincing or attacks opponents on a personal level.	• Provide more or better support (such as facts and statistics from reputable sources). • Revise to eliminate personal attacks.

To Enhance Credibility

Problem	Suggestions for Revising
Readers consider some of your sources questionable.	• Establish the sources' credibility by providing background information about them. • Choose more reputable sources.
You ignore likely objections or opposing arguments.	• Demonstrate to readers that you know and understand, even if you do not accept, the criticisms of those who hold alternative views. • Use the sentence strategy of concession and refutation or acknowledgment and refutation.
Your tone is harsh or offensive.	• Look for ways to show respect for and establish common ground with readers. • Revise your word choices to create a more civil tone. • Consider the concession-refutation strategy.

To Improve Readability

Problem	Suggestions for Revising
The beginning is dull or unfocused.	• Rewrite it, perhaps by adding a surprising or vivid anecdote.
Your argument is disorganized or hard to follow.	• Add a brief forecast of your main points at the beginning of the essay. • Reorder your points in a logical arrangement, such as least to most important. • Announce each reason explicitly in a topic sentence. • Add transitions to make the connections between points clearer.
The end is weak or trails off.	• Search your invention and research notes for a memorable quotation or a vivid example to end with. • Explain the consequences if your position is adopted. • Reiterate the shared values that underlie your position.

Editing and Proofreading Your Draft

Check for errors in usage, punctuation, and mechanics, and consider matters of style. If you keep a list of errors you typically make, begin by checking your draft against this list. Ask someone else to proofread your essay before you submit it to your instructor.

From our research on student writing, we know that essays arguing positions have a high percentage of sentence fragment errors involving *subordinating conjunctions* as well as punctuation errors involving *conjunctive adverbs*. Because arguing a position often requires you to use subordinating conjunctions (such as *because, although,* and *since*) and conjunctive adverbs (such as *therefore, however,* and *thus*), be sure you know the conventions for punctuating sentences that include these types of words. Check a writer's handbook for help with avoiding sentence fragments and using punctuation correctly in sentences with these potential problems.

Reflecting on What You Have Learned

Arguing for a Position

In this chapter, you have read critically several position arguments and have written one of your own. To better remember what you have learned, pause now to reflect on the reading and writing activities you completed in this chapter.

1. Write a page or so reflecting on what you have learned. Begin by describing what you are most pleased with in your essay. Then explain what you think contributed to your achievement. Be specific about this contribution.

    - If it was something you learned from the readings, indicate which readings and specifically what you learned from them.

    - If it came from your invention writing, point out the section or sections that helped you most.

    - If it came from your research notes and write-ups, point out the parts that helped you most.

    - If you got good advice from a critical reader, explain exactly how the person helped you — perhaps by helping you understand a problem in your draft or by helping you add a new dimension to your writing.

    Try to write about your achievement in terms of what you have learned about the genre.

    (continued)

2. Reflect more generally on position arguments, a genre of writing that plays an important role in our society. Consider some of the following questions:

   • How important are reasons and supporting evidence? When people argue positions on television, on radio talk shows, and in online discussion forums like blogs, do they tend to emphasize reasons and support? If not, what do they emphasize?

   • How does the purpose of television, radio, and online position arguments differ from the purpose of the writers you read in this chapter and from your own purpose in writing a position argument?

   • What contribution might position arguments make to our society that other genres of writing cannot make?

Speculating about Causes or Effects

When a surprising event occurs, we ask, "Why did that happen?" Whether we want to understand the event, prevent its recurrence, or make it happen again, we need to speculate about what caused it. Sometimes our focus may shift from "Why did that happen?" to "What is going to happen?" so that we can plan or make decisions. In many cases, the connections between causes and effects can be answered by experimentation. For example, through experimentation, scientists have discovered that the HIV virus causes AIDS. In some cases, however, we cannot be certain of causes or effects; the best we can do is **speculate**, or make educated guesses. For example, at this point we cannot be certain what causes the HIV virus to develop into AIDS or what long-term effects AIDS will have on society.

This chapter offers several brief, intriguing arguments speculating about causes or effects for you to enjoy and analyze, with exploratory activities that will help you learn to read critically and write well. The Reading for Meaning and Reading Like a Writer activities following each selection invite you to analyze and write about the reading's ideas and writing strategies. You can also use the brief Guide to Writing Essays Speculating about Causes or Effects toward the end of the chapter to help you argue clearly and convincingly for your proposed causes or effects.

RHETORICAL SITUATIONS FOR SPECULATING ABOUT CAUSES OR EFFECTS

Many people, including political analysts, economists, sportswriters, and college students, write essays speculating about causes or effects, as the following examples suggest:

- For an introductory psychology class, a student speculates about the effects — positive and negative — of extensive video-game playing among preteens. Based on his own experience and observation, he hypothesizes that video games may improve children's hand-eye coordination and their ability to concentrate on a single task but also that some children may spend too much time playing video games, to the detriment of their physical fitness, the development of their social skills, and their performance in school.

- After an incident in which her twelve-year-old son is disciplined in school, a science reporter comes up with an idea for an article speculating on the reasons for intolerance of "boyish behavior" in school. After getting the go-ahead from her editor, she reviews recent research in sociological and medical journals, where she reads that boys are being diagnosed with various behavioral disorders at a far higher rate than girls. She conjectures that adults attempt to stamp out shouting, roughhousing, and other signs of aggression in boys for several reasons: because of concern about bullying; because boys' behavior is perceived as disruptive, especially in group-oriented classrooms; and because boys' fidgeting at their desks is seen as a threat to their eventual success in an economy that increasingly values sitting still and concentrating for seven or more hours a day.

- For a seminar on the environment, a first-year student writes a research project speculating about what is causing coral reefs to die off. She includes photographs and cites a 2011 study showing that six hundred square miles of reef have disappeared every year since the late 1960s. She argues that overfishing, runoff from agriculture, and damage from shipping are all contributing factors. But she also supplies evidence to support her argument that two other causes play the most significant role — rising ocean temperatures and increasing carbon dioxide in the atmosphere — and that both are caused by climate change. She concedes that some scientists question whether climate change is severe enough to have been responsible for these changes.

Thinking about the Genre

Speculations about Causes or Effects

Before studying a type of writing, it is useful to spend some time thinking about what you already know about it. You may have speculated with friends or family about the causes or effects of a phenomenon, event, or trend, or composed speculations for science or history exams. Or you may have read speculations for college classes — or even in the sports pages after a stunning upset.

　Recall a time when you speculated about a cause or effect or read or heard others doing so. Think about how you (or another writer or speaker) engaged readers in the subject, presented a credible case for the preferred cause or effect, and ruled out alternative explanations. Use the following questions to develop your thoughts. Your instructor may ask you to write about your experience or discuss it with others in class or online.

- Who was the *audience*? How do you think addressing this audience affected the choice of phenomenon, event, or trend, or the type of evidence presented? For example, did you (or the other writer or speaker) choose to explain the causes or effects of a meteor shower because one had just occurred or was predicted? Was the evidence presented in scientific detail (for an audience of astrophysicists, say) or in everyday language (for high-school science students)?

- What was the *purpose*? Why did you (or the other writer or speaker) want the audience to understand these causes or effects? For example, was it so that they could demonstrate their own understanding on a test or take action in the future?

- How might the argument have changed if the audience or purpose had been different? Would different sources have been investigated, or different alternative causes or effects have been explored? How would changing the medium have changed the way the phenomenon, trend, or event was presented? For example, how would presenting the phenomenon, trend, or event in a documentary film, a podcast, or a chart have changed the speculation?

A GUIDE TO READING ESSAYS SPECULATING ABOUT CAUSES OR EFFECTS

This guide introduces you to cause-and-effect writing by inviting you to analyze a brief but powerful causal argument by Stephen King, first by *reading for meaning*, and then by *reading like a writer*.

- *Reading for meaning* will help you think about the subject that prompted King's essay, as well as understand and respond to King's speculations about why horror movies are so popular.

- *Reading like a writer* will help you learn how King employs strategies typical of speculations about causes or effects, such as

  1. presenting the subject fairly

  2. making a logical, well-supported cause or effect argument

  3. responding to objections or alternative speculations

  4. establishing credibility to present the writer as thoughtful and fair

Stephen King

Why We Crave Horror Movies

Stephen King (b. 1947) is America's best-known writer of horror fiction. He received his BA from the University of Maine in 1970 and sold his first story in 1967. In 2003, he won a Lifetime Achievement Award from the Horror Writers Association, and he has also won many other awards, including the 2003 National Book Foundation Medal for Distinguished Contribution to American Letters. A prolific writer in many genres and media, King has recently published The Wind through the Keyhole *(2012), the latest in his* Dark Tower *graphic novel series;* Road Rage *(2012), a comic-book series co-written with his son Joe Hill;* 11/22/63 *(2012), a time-travel novel about the assassination of President John F. Kennedy; and* Stephen King Goes to the Movies *(2009), a short-story collection. Many films and television movies have been based on King's work, including the classics* The Shawshank Redemption *(1994),* Stand by Me *(1986), and* Carrie *(1976).*

The following selection is a classic essay that attempts to explain the causes for a common phenomenon: many people's liking — even craving — for horror movies.

- *Before you read, think about the horror movie that you remember best and consider why it appeals to you (or doesn't).*

- *As you read, test King's argument about the appeal of horror movies against your own experience. On first reading, how convincing are his causal speculations?*

1   I think that we're all mentally ill; those of us outside the asylums only hide it a little better — and maybe not all that much better, after all. We've all known people who talk to themselves, people who sometimes squinch their faces into horrible grimaces when they believe no one is watching, people who have some hysterical fear — of snakes, the dark, the tight place, the long drop . . . and, of course, those final worms and grubs that are waiting so patiently underground.

2   When we pay our four or five bucks and seat ourselves at tenth-row center in a theater showing a horror movie, we are daring the nightmare.

3   Why? Some of the reasons are simple and obvious. To show that we can, that we are not afraid, that we can ride this roller coaster. Which is not to say that a really good horror movie may not surprise a scream out of us at some point, the way we may scream when the roller coaster twists through a complete 360 or plows through a lake at the bottom of the drop. And horror movies, like roller coasters, have always been the special prov-

ince of the young; by the time one turns 40 or 50, one's appetite for double twists or 360-degree loops may be considerably depleted.

We also go to re-establish our feelings of essential normality; the horror movie is innately conservative, even reactionary. Freda Jackson as the horrible melting woman in *Die, Monster, Die!* confirms for us that no matter how far we may be removed from the beauty of a Robert Redford or a Diana Ross, we are still light-years from true ugliness. 4

And we go to have fun. 5

Ah, but this is where the ground starts to slope away, isn't it? Because this is a very peculiar sort of fun, indeed. The fun comes from seeing others menaced—sometimes killed. One critic has suggested that if pro football has become the voyeur's version of combat, then the horror film has become the modern version of the public lynching. 6

It is true that the mythic, "fairy tale" horror film intends to take away the shades of gray. . . . It urges us to put away our more civilized and adult penchant for analysis and to become children again, seeing things in pure blacks and whites. It may be that horror movies provide psychic relief on this level because this invitation to lapse into simplicity, irrationality, and even outright madness is extended so rarely. We are told we may allow our emotions a free rein . . . or no rein at all. 7

If we are all insane, then sanity becomes a matter of degree. If your insanity leads you to carve up women like Jack the Ripper or the Cleveland Torso Murderer, we clap you away in the funny farm (but neither of those two amateur-night surgeons was ever caught, heh-heh-heh); if, on the other hand, your insanity leads you only to talk to yourself when you're under stress or to pick your nose on your morning bus, then you are left alone to go about your business . . . though it is doubtful that you will ever be invited to the best parties. 8

The potential lyncher is in almost all of us (excluding saints, past and present; but then, most saints have been crazy in their own ways), and every now and then, he has to be let loose to scream and roll around in the grass. Our emotions and our fears form their own body, and we recognize that it demands its own exercise to maintain proper muscle tone. Certain of these emotional muscles are accepted—even exalted—in civilized society; they are, of course, the emotions that tend to maintain the status quo of civilization itself. Love, friendship, loyalty, kindness—these are all the emotions that we applaud, emotions that have been immortalized in the couplets of Hallmark cards and in the verses (I don't dare call it poetry) of Leonard Nimoy. 9

When we exhibit these emotions, society showers us with positive reinforcement; we learn this even before we get out of diapers. When, as children, we hug our rotten little puke of a sister and give her a kiss, all the aunts and uncles smile and twit and cry, "Isn't he the sweetest little thing?" Such coveted treats as chocolate-covered graham crackers often follow. 10

But if we deliberately slam the rotten little puke of a sister's fingers in the door, sanctions follow—angry remonstrance from parents, aunts, and uncles; instead of a chocolate-covered graham cracker, a spanking.

11 But anticivilization emotions don't go away, and they demand periodic exercise. We have such "sick" jokes as "What's the difference between a truckload of bowling balls and a truckload of dead babies?" (You can't unload a truckload of bowling balls with a pitchfork . . . a joke, by the way, that I heard originally from a ten-year-old.) Such a joke may surprise a laugh or a grin out of us even as we recoil, a possibility that confirms the thesis: If we share a brotherhood of man, then we also share an insanity of man. None of which is intended as a defense of either the sick joke or insanity but merely as an explanation of why the best horror films, like the best fairy tales, manage to be reactionary, anarchistic, and revolutionary all at the same time.

12 The mythic horror movie, like the sick joke, has a dirty job to do. It deliberately appeals to all that is worst in us. It is morbidity unchained, our most base instincts let free, our nastiest fantasies realized . . . and it all happens, fittingly enough, in the dark. For those reasons, good liberals often shy away from horror films. For myself, I like to see the most aggressive of them—*Dawn of the Dead*, for instance—as lifting a trap door in the civilized forebrain and throwing a basket of raw meat to the hungry alligators swimming around in that subterranean river beneath.

13 Why bother? Because it keeps them from getting out, man. It keeps them down there and me up here. It was Lennon and McCartney who said that all you need is love, and I would agree with that.

14 As long as you keep the gators fed.

READING FOR MEANING

This section presents three activities that will help you think about the meanings in King's causal argument. Your instructor may ask you to do one or more of these activities in class or online.

For more help with summarizing, see Chapter 10, pp. 518–19.

1. **Read to Summarize.** Reading to summarize involves asking yourself what the main point of the reading is. To summarize King's causal argument, write a sentence or two explaining why King thinks we crave horror movies.

2. **Read to Respond.** Reading to respond asks you to explore your reactions to a text in light of your own knowledge or experience. To explore this argument speculating about causes, write a paragraph analyzing your initial reactions to King's essay. For example, consider anything that

Take a quiz to check your reading and vocabulary comprehension:
bedfordstmartins.com/readingcritically

resonates with your experience or that seems contradictory, surprising, or fascinating, such as:

- King's assertion that "[i]f we are all insane, then sanity becomes a matter of degree" (par. 8);
- The difference between procivilization and "anticivilization" emotions as King presents them in paragraphs 10–13, indicating what you think about his distinction between these two kinds of emotions.

You may also try contextualizing; see Chapter 10, pp. 522–23.

3. **Read to Analyze Assumptions. Assumptions** are ideas, beliefs, or values that are taken for granted as commonly accepted truths. The assumptions in a text usually reflect the writer's own attitudes or cultural traditions, but they may also represent other people's views. Reading to analyze assumptions asks you to uncover these perspectives as well as to probe your own. Sometimes the assumptions are stated explicitly, but often you will have to infer them (or figure them out) because they are only implied or hinted at through the writer's choice of words or examples. Write a paragraph or two analyzing an assumption you find intriguing in King's essay. For example:

Assumptions about the universality and range of human emotions. King asserts that "[t]he mythic horror movie . . . has a dirty job to do. It deliberately appeals to all that is worst in us" (par. 12). He adds, "It is morbidity unchained, our most base instincts let free, our nastiest fantasies realized . . ." (par. 12). To think critically about the assumptions in this essay related to human emotions, ask yourself questions like these:

- What if we don't watch horror movies, don't like them, or don't believe they represent our "nastiest fantasies"? If you don't share King's assumption about universal human nastiness, how do you respond to his essay?
- What alternatives to King's thinking occur to you? In a culture that has a different view of the human mind, what other causes of horror movies' popularity might be just as believable?

Assumptions about differences between younger and older people. King asserts that "horror movies . . . have always been the special province of the young" (par. 3) and that we go to see them "to put away our more civilized and adult penchant for analysis and to become children again" (par. 7). To think critically about assumptions in this essay related to the differences between people of various ages, ask yourself questions like these:

- What viewpoints do children have that adults do not have or have outgrown?
- What does King assume distinguishes children and adults in their attitude toward scary situations (par. 3) or complex ones (par. 7)? Why would adults want to become children again?

You may also try recognizing emotional manipulation; see Chapter 10, pp. 536–37.

READING LIKE A WRITER

This section presents four brief activities that will help you analyze King's writing. Your instructor may ask you to do one or more of these activities in class or online.

Presenting the Subject Fairly

In writing an essay speculating about causes or effects, writers try to present their subject in an intriguing way that makes readers wonder about it. Writers also must judge whether or not they need to explain the subject for their audience before examining causes or effects. When writers decide they need to prove that the event, trend, or phenomenon they are writing about exists, they may describe it in detail, give examples, offer factual evidence, cite statistics, or quote statements by authorities. They may frame or reframe their subjects: **Framing** (or **reframing**) is like cropping and resizing a photograph to focus the viewer's eye on one part of the picture. Writers typically frame or reframe a subject in a way that sets the stage for their argument and promotes their point of view.

Analyze & Write

Write a couple of paragraphs analyzing and evaluating how King reframes his subject:

1. The subject of this essay is horror movies, but the key term in the title is the word "crave." Look up "crave" and "craving" to see what they mean. Then highlight some of the other words and phrases King associates with the appeal of horror movies, such as "mentally ill" and "hysterical fear" (par. 1). How do the words you highlighted relate to the word *crave?*

2. Given these key terms, how would you describe the way King reframes the subject for readers? How do these key terms enable him to plant the seed of his main idea at the beginning of the essay?

Making a Logical, Well-Supported Cause or Effect Argument

At the heart of an essay speculating about causes or effects is an argument with two essential elements:

1. the logical analysis of the proposed causes or effects

2. the reasoning and support offered for each cause or effect

Writers of essays speculating about causes or effects sometimes rely on certain sentence strategies to present these cause-effect relationships:

▶ When .... happens, ... is the result.
▶ If [I/he/she/we/they do/say/act] ...., then [others do/say/act] ....

These two types of sentences can be seen in King's essay:

Causes	When we exhibit these emotions, society showers us with positive reinforce-
Effects	ment; we learn this even before we get out of diapers. When, as children, we hug our rotten little puke of a sister and give her a kiss, all the aunts and uncles smile and twit and cry, "Isn't he the sweetest little thing?" Such coveted treats as chocolate-covered graham crackers often follow. But if we deliberately slam the rotten little puke of a sister's fingers in the door, sanctions follow — angry remonstrance from parents, aunts, and uncles; instead of a chocolate-covered graham cracker, a spanking. (par. 10)

Both of these sentence patterns establish a **chronological relationship** — one thing happens and then another thing happens. They also establish a **causal relationship**. (Chronology and causality do not always go together, however; see Recognizing Logical Fallacies, pp. 532–36.)

Analyze & Write

Write a paragraph or two analyzing and evaluating how King uses these sentence patterns elsewhere in this reading selection:

1. Skim paragraphs 1–9 and 11–14 to find and mark the sentences that use these strategies. Does each present a cause-effect relationship as well as a chronological sequence? How do you know?

2. Why do you think King repeats these sentence strategies so often in this essay? Is this repetition an effective or ineffective strategy?

Responding to Objections and Alternative Speculations

When causes or effects cannot be known for certain, there is bound to be disagreement. Consequently, writers may consider an array of possibilities before focusing on one or two serious probabilities. They may concede that certain possible causes play some role; they may refute them by providing reasons and supporting evidence for why they play no role (or only a minor role); or they may simply dismiss them as trivial or irrelevant, as King does. "Some of the reasons," King explicitly declares, "are simple and obvious" (par. 3).

| Analyze & Write |

Write a couple of paragraphs analyzing and evaluating how effectively King concedes or refutes alternative causes for the popularity of horror movies:

1. Look at the causes King considers in the opening paragraphs to determine how he responds to them. For example, how does he support the assertion that some of them are "simple and obvious" (par. 3)? What other arguments, if any, does he use to refute these causes?

2. Given his purpose and audience, why do you think King chooses to begin by presenting reasons he regards as "simple and obvious"? (par. 3)

Establishing Credibility to Present the Writer as Thoughtful and Fair

Because cause or effect writing is highly speculative, its effectiveness depends in large part on whether readers trust the writer. Writers seek to establish their credibility with readers by making their reasoning clear and logical, their evidence relevant and trustworthy, and their handling of objections fair and balanced. They try to be **authoritative** (knowledgeable) without appearing **authoritarian** (opinionated and dogmatic).

| Analyze & Write |

Write a paragraph or two analyzing King's **persona** (the personality he wants readers to infer) and assessing how it helps him establish credibility with his readers:

1. Reread the headnote that precedes King's essay, and reflect on what else his readers might already know about him.

2. Skim the essay to decide whether the reasoning is clear and logical and the examples and analogies relevant and trustworthy. Because King's reasoning is psychological (he argues that mental and emotional needs explain why some people crave horror films) you can evaluate King's credibility in light of your own personal experience—that is, your understanding of the role horror movies (and novels) play in your own life.

3. Describe the impression readers might get from King from reading both the headnote and his essay. What details in the headnote might make them trust or distrust what he says about his subject? Would most readers consider King a credible writer on the subject of horror movies? What word choices or other details in the essay might make him a credible authority on the subject?

READINGS

Claudia Wallis

The Multitasking Generation

Claudia Wallis graduated from Yale and from Columbia University's Graduate School of Journalism. Currently she is associate dean of strategic communications at Columbia University's Mailman School of Public Health. For many years she was editor-at-large and senior editor for Time *magazine, where as both a writer and an editor she specialized in stories about science and health, medicine, education, family, and social issues. Her writing has won citations from the Newspaper Guild of New York, the National Mental Health Association, and the Susan G. Komen Breast Cancer Foundation, among other organizations. Her most recent work is on autism, for which she maintains a Web site:* http://claudiawallis.com/autism. *She is also a conference speaker and panel leader.*

"The Multitasking Generation" was published online by Time / CNN *in 2006. In it, Wallis describes the relationship between multitasking and Generation "M," and she questions the notion that multitaskers get more done.*

- *Before you read, think about your own habits: Do you multitask often, or are you someone who focuses attention on one thing at a time? Have your habits changed with changes in technology during your lifetime?*

- *As you read, add your own notes to the annotations, especially where Wallis surprises you or supports her causal argument with evidence — facts, statistics, personal anecdotes, testimony of authorities, examples, or analogies. Consider also how plausible you find Wallis's argument about the effects of multitasking.*

1   It's 9:30 p.m., and Stephen and Georgina Cox know exactly where their children are. Well, their bodies, at least. Piers, 14, is holed up in his bedroom — eyes fixed on his computer screen — where he has been logged onto a MySpace chat room and AOL Instant Messenger (IM) for the past three hours. His twin sister Bronte is planted in the living room, having commandeered her dad's iMac — as usual. She, too, is busily IMing, while chatting on her cell phone and chipping away at homework.

2   By all standard space-time calculations, the four members of the family occupy the same three-bedroom home in Van Nuys, Calif., but psychologically each

exists in his or her own little universe. Georgina, 51, who works for a display-cabinet maker, is tidying up the living room as Bronte works, not that her daughter notices. Stephen, 49, who juggles jobs as a squash coach, fitness trainer, event planner and head of a cancer charity he founded, has wolfed down his dinner alone in the kitchen, having missed supper with the kids. He, too, typically spends the evening on his cell phone and returning e-mails—when he can nudge Bronte off the computer. "One gets obsessed with one's gadgets," he concedes.

Zooming in on Piers' screen gives a pretty good   3
indication of what's on his hyperkinetic mind. O.K., there's a Google Images window open, where he's chasing down pictures of Keira Knightley. Good ones get added to a snazzy Windows Media Player slide show that serves as his personal e-shrine to the actress. Several IM windows are also open, revealing such penetrating conversations as this one with a MySpace pal:

> MySpacer: suuuuuup!!! (Translation: What's up?)   4
> Piers: wat up dude   5
> MySpacer: nmu (Not much. You?)   6
> Piers: same   7

Naturally, iTunes is open, and Piers is blasting a   8
mix of Queen, AC/DC, classic rock and hip-hop. Somewhere on the screen there's a Word file, in which Piers is writing an essay for English class. "I usually finish my homework at school," he explains to a visitor, "but if not, I pop a book open on my lap in my room, and while the computer is loading, I'll do a problem or write a sentence. Then, while mail is loading, I do more. I get it done a little bit at a time."

Bronte has the same strategy. "You just multitask,"   9
she explains. "My parents always tell me I can't do homework while listening to music, but they don't understand that it helps me concentrate." The twins also multitask when hanging with friends, which has its own etiquette. "When I talk to my best friend Eloy," says Piers, "he'll have one earpiece [of his iPod] in and one out." Says Bronte: "If a friend thinks she's not getting my full attention, I just make it very clear that she is, even though I'm also listening to music."

Why do you think Wallis introduces her essay with nine paragraphs of anecdote, followed by two paragraphs about academic research? What is the effect on you?

10   The Coxes are one of 32 families in the Los Angeles area participating in an intensive, four-year study of modern family life, led by anthropologist Elinor Ochs, director of UCLA's Center on Everyday Lives of Families. While the impact of multitasking gadgets was not her original focus, Ochs found it to be one of the most dramatic areas of change since she conducted a similar study 20 years ago. "I'm not certain how the children can monitor all those things at the same time, but I think it is pretty consequential for the structure of the family relationship," says Ochs, whose work on language, interaction and culture earned her a MacArthur "genius" grant.

When a researcher shifts focus because of her findings (highlighted), does it add to or detract from her credibility?

11   One of the things Ochs' team of observers looks at is what happens at the end of the workday when parents and kids reunite—and what doesn't happen, as in the case of the Coxes. "We saw that when the working parent comes through the door, the other spouse and the kids are so absorbed by what they're doing that they don't give the arriving parent the time of day," says Ochs. The returning parent, generally the father, was greeted only about a third of the time, usually with a perfunctory "Hi." "About half the time the kids ignored him or didn't stop what they were doing, multitasking and monitoring their various electronic gadgets," she says. "We also saw how difficult it was for parents to penetrate the child's universe. We have so many videotapes of parents actually backing away, retreating from kids who are absorbed by whatever they're doing."

Is this homecoming scenario familiar to you? Does it happen in your own household?

12   Human beings have always had a capacity to attend to several things at once. Mothers have done it since the hunter-gatherer era—picking berries while suckling an infant, stirring the pot with one eye on the toddler. Nor is electronic multitasking entirely new: we've been driving while listening to car radios since they became popular in the 1930s. But there is no doubt that the phenomenon has reached a kind of warp speed in the era of Web-enabled computers, when it has become routine to conduct six IM conversations, watch *American Idol* on TV and Google the names of last season's finalists all at once.

13   That level of multiprocessing and interpersonal connectivity is now so commonplace that it's easy to

forget how quickly it came about. Fifteen years ago, most home computers weren't even linked to the Internet. In 1990 the majority of adolescents responding to a survey done by Donald Roberts, a professor of communication at Stanford, said the one medium they couldn't live without was a radio/CD player. How quaint. In a 2004 follow-up, the computer won hands down.

Today 82% of kids are online by the seventh grade, 14 according to the Pew Internet and American Life Project. And what they love about the computer, of course, is that it offers the radio/CD thing and so much more—games, movies, e-mail, IM, Google, MySpace. The big finding of a 2005 survey of Americans ages 8 to 18 by the Kaiser Family Foundation, co-authored by Roberts, is not that kids were spending a larger chunk of time using electronic media—that was holding steady at 6.5 hours a day (could it possibly get any bigger?)—but that they were packing more media exposure into that time: 8.5 hours' worth, thanks to "media multitasking"—listening to iTunes, watching a DVD and IMing friends all at the same time. Increasingly, the media-hungry members of Generation M, as Kaiser dubbed them, don't just sit down to watch a TV show with their friends or family. From a quarter to a third of them, according to the survey, say they simultaneously absorb some other medium "most of the time" while watching TV, listening to music, using the computer or even while reading.

Parents have watched this phenomenon unfold 15 with a mixture of awe and concern. The Coxes, for instance, are bowled over by their children's technical prowess. Piers repairs the family computers and DVD player. Bronte uses digital technology to compose elaborate photo collages and create a documentary of her father's ongoing treatment for cancer. And, says Georgina, "they both make these fancy PowerPoint presentations about what they want for Christmas." But both parents worry about the ways that kids' compulsive screen time is affecting their schoolwork and squeezing out family life. "We rarely have dinner together anymore," frets Stephen. "Everyone is in their own little world, and we don't get out together to have a social life."

How does this brief history of "media multitasking," along with current statistics from authorities, help you understand the issue Wallis is addressing?

How does Wallis shift here from presenting the subject to making her effects argument?

16   Every generation of adults sees new technology—
and the social changes it stirs—as a threat to the rightful order of things: Plato warned (correctly) that reading
would be the downfall of oral tradition and memory.
And every generation of teenagers embraces the free-
doms and possibilities wrought by technology in ways
that shock the elders: just think about what the automobile did for dating.

How does this paragraph
on the history of new technologies help to put the
effects of multitasking in
perspective?

17   As for multitasking devices, social scientists and
educators are just beginning to assess their impact,
but the researchers already have some strong opinions. The mental habit of dividing one's attention into
many small slices has significant implications for
the way young people learn, reason, socialize, do
creative work and understand the world. Although
such habits may prepare kids for today's frenzied
workplace, many cognitive scientists are positively
alarmed by the trend. "Kids that are instant messaging
while doing homework, playing games online and
watching TV, I predict, aren't going to do well in the
long run," says Jordan Grafman, chief of the cognitive
neuroscience section at the National Institute of Neurological Disorders and Stroke (NINDS). Decades
of research (not to mention common sense) indicate
that the quality of one's output and depth of thought
deteriorate as one attends to ever more tasks. Some
are concerned about the disappearance of mental
downtime to relax and reflect. Roberts notes Stanford
students "can't go the few minutes between their
10 o'clock and 11 o'clock classes without talking on
their cell phones. It seems to me that there's almost a
discomfort with not being stimulated—a kind of 'I
can't stand the silence.'"

What is the effect on you
of Wallis's acknowledg-
ment of the counterargu-
ment that multitasking may
prepare kids for work?
How do you respond to
her assertion that many
cognitive scientists find the
trend alarming?

18   Gen M's multitasking habits have social and psychological implications as well. If you're IMing four friends
while watching *That '70s Show*, it's not the same as sitting on the couch with your buddies or your sisters and
watching the show together. Or sharing a family meal
across a table. Thousands of years of evolution created
human physical communication—facial expressions,
body language—that puts broadband to shame in its
ability to convey meaning and create bonds. What happens, wonders UCLA's Ochs, as we replace side-by-
side and eye-to-eye human connections with quick,

Look at the highlighted
words. What do you think
Wallis is trying to communicate in this paragraph?
What might be lost by
multitasking?

disembodied e-exchanges? Those are critical issues not just for social scientists but for parents and teachers trying to understand—and do right by—Generation M.

YOUR BRAIN WHEN IT MULTITASKS

Wallis continues to present her effects argument, this time in several paragraphs on the physical processes the brain undergoes while multitasking. Why do you suppose she chooses to include the brain in her presentation?

Although many aspects of the networked life remain scientifically uncharted, there's substantial literature on how the brain handles multitasking. And basically, it doesn't. It may seem that a teenage girl is writing an instant message, burning a CD and telling her mother that she's doing homework—all at the same time—but what's really going on is a rapid toggling among tasks rather than simultaneous processing. "You're doing more than one thing, but you're ordering them and deciding which one to do at any one time," explains neuroscientist Grafman. 19

Then why can we so easily walk down the street while engrossed in a deep conversation? Why can we chop onions while watching *Jeopardy*? "We, along with quite a few others, have been focused on exactly this question," says Hal Pashler, psychology professor at the University of California at San Diego. It turns out that very automatic actions or what researchers call "highly practiced skills," like walking or chopping an onion, can be easily done while thinking about other things, although the decision to add an extra onion to a recipe or change the direction in which you're walking is another matter. "It seems that action planning—figuring out what I want to say in response to a person's question or which way I want to steer the car—is usually, perhaps invariably, performed sequentially" or one task at a time, says Pashler. On the other hand, producing the actions you've decided on—moving your hand on the steering wheel, speaking the words you've formulated—can be performed "in parallel with planning some other action." Similarly, many aspects of perception—looking, listening, touching—can be performed in parallel with action planning and with movement. 20

The switching of attention from one task to another, the toggling action, occurs in a region right behind the forehead called Brodmann's Area 10 in the brain's anterior prefrontal cortex, according to a 21 functional magnetic resonance imaging (fMRI) study by Grafman's team. Brodmann's Area 10 is part of the frontal lobes, which "are important for maintaining long-term goals and achieving them," Grafman explains. "The most anterior part allows you to leave something when it's incomplete and return to the same place and continue from there." This gives us a "form of multitasking," he says, though it's actually sequential processing. Because the prefrontal cortex is one of the last regions of the brain to mature and one of the first to decline with aging, young children do not multitask well, and neither do most adults over 60. New fMRI studies at Toronto's Rotman Research Institute suggest that as we get older, we have more trouble "turning down background thoughts when turning to a new task," says Rotman senior scientist and assistant director Cheryl Grady. "Younger adults are better at tuning out stuff when they want to," says Grady. "I'm in my 50s, and I know that I can't work and listen to music with lyrics; it was easier when I was younger."

22   But the ability to multiprocess has its limits, even among young adults. When people try to perform two or more related tasks either at the same time or alternating rapidly between them, errors go way up, and it takes far longer—often double the time or more—to get the jobs done than if they were done sequentially, says David E. Meyer, director of the Brain, Cognition and Action Laboratory at the University of Michigan: "The toll in terms of slowdown is extremely large— amazingly so." Meyer frequently tests Gen M students in his lab, and he sees no exception for them, despite their "mystique" as master multitaskers. "The bottom line is that you can't simultaneously be thinking about your tax return and reading an essay, just as you can't talk to yourself about two things at once," he says. "If a teenager is trying to have a conversation on an e-mail chat line while doing algebra, she'll suffer a decrease in efficiency, compared to if she just thought about algebra until she was done. People may think otherwise, but it's a myth. With such complicated tasks [you] will never, ever be able to overcome the inherent limitations in the brain for processing information during multitasking. It just can't be, any more than the best

of all humans will ever be able to run a one-minute mile."

Other research shows the relationship between stimulation and performance forms a bell curve: a little stimulation—whether it's coffee or a blaring soundtrack—can boost performance, but too much is stressful and causes a fall-off. In addition, the brain needs rest and recovery time to consolidate thoughts and memories. Teenagers who fill every quiet moment with a phone call or some kind of e-stimulation may not be getting that needed reprieve. Habitual multitasking may condition their brain to an overexcited state, making it difficult to focus even when they want to. "People lose the skill and the will to maintain concentration, and they get mental antsyness," says Meyer. 23

IS THIS ANY WAY TO LEARN?

Longtime professors at universities around the U.S. have noticed that Gen M kids arrive on campus with a different set of cognitive skills and habits than past generations. In lecture halls with wireless Internet access—now more than 40% of college classrooms, according to the Campus Computing Project—the compulsion to multitask can get out of hand. "People are going to lectures by some of the greatest minds, and they are doing their mail," says Sherry Turkle, professor of the social studies of science and technology at M.I.T. In her class, says Turkle, "I tell them this is not a place for e-mail, it's not a place to do online searches and not a place to set up IRC [Internet relay chat] channels in which to comment on the class. It's not going to help if there are parallel discussions about how boring it is. You've got to get people to participate in the world as it is." 24

Such concerns have, in fact, led a number of schools, including the M.B.A. programs at UCLA and the University of Virginia, to look into blocking Internet access during lectures. "I tell my students not to treat me like TV," says University of Wisconsin professor Aaron Brower, who has been teaching social work for 20 years. "They have to think of me like a real per- 25

Here Wallis focuses on the counterargument that a little stimulation can be good. How does she respond?

Why do you suppose Wallis uses headings throughout her essay?

Wallis shifts back to personal anecdotes to present her effects argument. Why does she use university professors to make her case?

son talking. I want to have them thinking about things we're talking about."

26   On the positive side, Gen M students tend to be extraordinarily good at finding and manipulating information. And presumably because modern childhood tilts toward visual rather than print media, they are especially skilled at analyzing visual data and images, observes Claudia Koonz, professor of history at Duke University. A growing number of college professors are using film, audio clips and PowerPoint presentations to play to their students' strengths and capture their evanescent attention. It's a powerful way to teach history, says Koonz. "I love bringing media into the classroom, to be able to go to the website for Edward R. Murrow and hear his voice as he walked with the liberators of Buchenwald." Another adjustment to teaching Generation M: professors are assigning fewer full-length books and more excerpts and articles. (Koonz, however, was stunned when a student matter-of-factly informed her, "We don't read whole books anymore," after Koonz had assigned a 350-page volume. "And this is Duke!" she says.)

27   Many students make brilliant use of media in their work, embedding audio files and video clips in their presentations, but the habit of grazing among many data streams leaves telltale signs in their writing, according to some educators. "The breadth of their knowledge and their ability to find answers has just burgeoned," says Roberts of his students at Stanford, "but my impression is that their ability to write clear, focused and extended narratives has eroded somewhat." Says Koonz: "What I find is paragraphs that make sense internally, but don't necessarily follow a line of argument."

28   Koonz and Turkle believe that today's students are less tolerant of ambiguity than the students they taught in the past. "They demand clarity," says Koonz. They want identifiable good guys and bad guys, which she finds problematic in teaching complex topics like Hutu-Tutsi history in Rwanda. She also thinks there are political implications: "Their belief in the simple answer, put together in a visual way, is, I think, dangerous." Koonz thinks this aversion to

What do these two paragraphs on the "positive side" (26 and 27) add to Wallis's argument?

Wallis returns to the dangers of multitasking, keeping her argument consistent. Upon what assumptions do you think this paragraph rests?

complexity is directly related to multitasking: "It's as if they have too many windows open on their hard drive. In order to have a taste for sifting through different layers of truth, you have to stay with a topic and pursue it deeply, rather than go across the surface with your toolbar." She tries to encourage her students to find a quiet spot on campus to just think, cell phone off, laptop packed away.

GOT 2 GO. TXT ME L8ER

Paragraphs 29–33 set out both benefits and dangers to adolescents from multitasking. How does Wallis enhance her credibility in these paragraphs?

But turning down the noise isn't easy. By the time 29 many kids get to college, their devices have become extensions of themselves, indispensable social accessories. "The minute the bell rings at most big public high schools, the first thing most kids do is reach into their bag and pick up their cell phone," observes Denise Clark Pope, lecturer at the Stanford School of Education, "never mind that the person [they're contacting] could be right down the hall."

Parents are mystified by this obsession with 30 e-communication—particularly among younger adolescents who often can't wait to share the most mundane details of life. Dominique Jones, 12, of Los Angeles, likes to IM her friends before school to find out what they plan to wear. "You'll get IMs back that say things like 'Oh, my God, I'm wearing the same shoes!' After school we talk about what happened that day, what outfits we want to wear the next day."

Turkle, author of the recently reissued *The Second* 31 *Self: Computers and the Human Spirit*, has an explanation for this breathless exchange of inanities. "There's an extraordinary fit between the medium and the moment, a heady, giddy fit in terms of social needs." The online environment, she points out, "is less risky if you are lonely and afraid of intimacy, which is almost a definition of adolescence. Things get too hot, you log off, while in real time and space, you have consequences." Teen venues like MySpace, Xanga and Facebook—and the ways kids can personalize their IM personas—meet another teen need: the desire to experiment with identity. By changing their picture, their "away" message, their icon or list of favorite bands, kids can cycle through different personalities. "Online life is like an identity workshop," says Turkle, "and that's the job of adolescents—to experiment with identity."

32   All that is probably healthy, provided that parents set limits on where their kids can venture online, teach them to exercise caution and regulate how much time they can spend with electronics in general. The problem is that most parents don't. According to the Kaiser survey, only 23% of seventh- to 12th-graders say their family has rules about computer activity; just 17% say they have restrictions on video-game time.

33   In the absence of rules, it's all too easy for kids to wander into unwholesome neighborhoods on the Net and get caught up in the compulsive behavior that psychiatrist Edward Hallowell dubs "screen-sucking" in his new book, *CrazyBusy*. Patricia Wallace, a techno-psychologist who directs the Johns Hopkins Center for Talented Youth program, believes part of the allure of e-mail—for adults as well as teens—is similar to that of a slot machine. "You have intermittent, variable reinforcement," she explains. "You are not sure you are going to get a reward every time or how often you will, so you keep pulling that handle. Why else do people get up in the middle of the night to check their e-mail?"

GETTING THEM TO LOG OFF

34 Many educators and psychologists say parents need to actively ensure that their teenagers break free of compulsive engagement with screens and spend time in the physical company of human beings—a growing challenge not just because technology offers such a handy alternative but because so many kids lead highly scheduled lives that leave little time for old-fashioned socializing and family meals. Indeed, many teenagers and college students say overcommitted schedules drive much of their multitasking.

35   Just as important is for parents and educators to teach kids, preferably by example, that it's valuable, even essential, to occasionally slow down, unplug

and take time to think about something for a while. David Levy, a professor at the University of Washington Information School, has found, to his surprise, that his most technophilic undergraduates—those majoring in "informatics"—are genuinely concerned about getting lost in the multitasking blur. In an informal poll of 60 students last semester, he says, the majority expressed concerns about how plugged-in they were and "the way it takes them away from other activities, including exercise, meals and sleep." Levy's students talked about difficulties concentrating and their efforts to break away, get into the outdoors and inside their head. "Although it wasn't a scientific survey," he says, "it was the first evidence I had that people in this age group are reflecting on these questions."

Why do you think Wallis chooses to conclude her essay with a passage from Hallowell about what you are *not* doing when you are multitasking?

For all the handwringing about Generation M, 36 technology is not really the problem. "The problem," says Hallowell, "is what you are not doing if the electronic moment grows too large"—too large for the teenager and too large for those parents who are equally tethered to their gadgets. In that case, says Hallowell, "you are not having family dinner, you are not having conversations, you are not debating whether to go out with a boy who wants to have sex on the first date, you are not going on a family ski trip or taking time just to veg. It's not so much that the video game is going to rot your brain, it's what you are not doing that's going to rot your life."

Generation M has a lot to teach parents and teach- 37 ers about what new technology can do. But it's up to grownups to show them what it can't do, and that there's life beyond the screen.

READING FOR MEANING

This section presents three activities that will help you think about the meanings in Wallis's speculation about the effects of multitasking. Your instructor may ask you to do one or more of these activities in class or online.

For more help with summarizing, see Chapter 10, pp. 518–19.

1. **Read to Summarize.** Write a sentence or two explaining what you learned about the effects of multitasking on Generation M.

Take a quiz to check your reading and vocabulary comprehension:
bedfordstmartins.com/readingcritically

2. **Read to Respond.** Write a paragraph analyzing your initial reactions to Wallis's effects essay. For example, consider anything that resonates with your experience or that seems contradictory, surprising, or fascinating, such as:

- Researchers' findings that "students are less tolerant of ambiguity" today than in the past and have an "aversion to complexity" (par. 28);

- Researchers' findings that people in Gen M tend to feel "almost a discomfort with not being stimulated" (par. 17) and that they can "get mental antsyness" (par. 23);

You may also try looking for patterns of opposition; see Chapter 10, pp. 525–26.

- The effect on you of Wallis's use of many different kinds of authorities, including the recipient of a MacArthur grant as well as several professors, authors of books, heads of foundations, and members of families.

3. **Read to Analyze Assumptions.** Write a paragraph or two analyzing an assumption you find intriguing in Wallis's essay. For example:

Assumptions about the value of thinking deeply. Wallis asserts that "the quality of one's output and depth of thought deteriorate as one attends to ever more tasks" (par. 17) and quotes Claudia Koonz, a professor of history, who says, "In order to have a taste for sifting through different layers of truth, you have to stay with a topic and pursue it deeply, rather than go across the surface with your toolbar" (par. 28). Wallis urges parents and educators to teach kids to "slow down, unplug and take time to think about something for a while" (par. 35). To think critically about the assumptions in this essay related to the value of thinking deeply, ask yourself questions like these:

- What evidence does Wallis provide that thinking deeply is a value her audience shares with her?

- What are the effects on society of its members' thinking deeply?

- How would you define "deep thinking" in your own words?

- What happens if you don't think deeply? Does it matter?

Assumptions about the value of face-to-face socializing. Wallis quotes Stephen Cox's complaint that his family members "'rarely have dinner together anymore.'... 'Everyone is in their own little world, and we don't get out together to have a social life'" (par. 15). Wallis also reports that researcher Elinor Ochs is concerned about "[w]hat happens ... as we replace side-by-side and eye-to-eye human connections with quick, disembodied e-exchanges ..." (par. 18). In addition, Wallis notes that "[m]any educators and psychologists" believe that parents "need to" help teens "spend time in the physical company of human beings" (par. 34), and she concludes her essay after a quotation from psychiatrist Edward Hallowell about social occasions teens are *not* engaging in when they are multitasking — family dinners, conversations, family ski trips — "'it's what you are not doing that's going to rot your life'" (par. 36). To think critically about the assumptions in this essay related to the value of face-to-face socializing, ask yourself questions like these:

- How is socializing via e-mail or Facebook or other online platforms different from socializing face-to-face?

You may also try evaluating the logic of an argument; see Chapter 10, pp. 530–31.

- What advantages does face-to-face socializing have over technological socializing? What are its disadvantages?

- Do you share Wallis's view that socializing face-to-face is superior to the alternative? Why or why not?

READING LIKE A WRITER

PRESENTING THE SUBJECT FAIRLY

When writers speculate about the effects of a trend, they must define or describe the trend so readers know that the trend actually exists. Readers are engaged by speculations if the trend is important to them personally or has a larger significance. Wallis knows that her readers are aware of the prevalence of technological devices, but they may not know just how much young people are using them, what is being sacrificed in favor of them, or what the consequences of using many of them at once — multitasking — might be. She therefore presents her subject through anecdotes, gives many examples, cites statistics, and quotes authorities, all to help the reader to see the negative effects of multitasking. Below you will explore just one of her approaches.

Analyze & Write ──────────────────────────────

Write a paragraph or two analyzing and evaluating how effectively Wallis presents her subject in the first several paragraphs:

1. Reread paragraphs 1–9. Make a list of all the tasks she attributes to the Cox twins, such as Piers being logged in to a MySpace chat room and AOL Instant Messenger (IM) (the equivalent of texting) (par. 1). How effectively do these paragraphs introduce Wallis's subject?

2. Now reread paragraph 11 and paragraphs 17–18. What effects does Wallis outline here? How do these effects relate to the causes she explored in paragraphs 1–9? How do they prepare the reader for the causes and effects she discusses in the rest of her essay? Think about the consequences that multitasking has had on the family as a whole and on the children in particular.

A Special Reading Strategy

Comparing and Contrasting Related Readings: Wallis's "The Multitasking Generation" and Turkle's "The Flight from Conversation"

Comparing and contrasting related readings is a critical reading strategy useful both in reading for meaning and in reading like a writer. This strategy is particularly applicable when writers present similar subjects, as is the case in the essays by Claudia Wallis (pp. 385–96) and Sherry Turkle (pp. 334–37). Both authors write about the impact of technology on social interactions. In fact, Wallis uses Turkle as a source (pars. 24, 28, and 31). To compare and contrast these two essays, think about issues such as these:

- Compare how the two writers handle what they perceive as threats from technology to social interaction. Think especially about how they approach the effects on people of relatively unrestrained use of technology. Do they have the same sense of alarm about it, or are their attitudes different? Do they provide a similar history of it? How similar are their examples?

- Read your responses to the "assumptions" sections in the material following both essays: In Turkle, you examined the role of conversation and of having control of oneself (and one's interactions); in Wallis, you examined the value of thinking deeply and of face-to-face socializing (pp. 397–98). What common ground do these two authors share?

See Chapter 10, pp. 527–30, for detailed guidelines on comparing and contrasting related readings.

Shankar Vedantam

The Telescope Effect

Shankar Vedantam (b. 1969) graduated from Stanford University with a master's degree in journalism. He is a science correspondent for National Public Radio and has worked for a number of major newspapers, including the Philadelphia Inquirer, Washington Post, *and* Newsday. *He has been honored with fellowships and awards by Harvard University, the World Health Organization, the Society of Professional Journalists, and the American Public Health Association. In addition to many articles, Vedantam has written plays and fiction, including his short-story collection* The Ghosts of Kashmir *(2005). "The Telescope Effect" is excerpted from his book* The Hidden Brain: How Our Unconscious Minds Elect Presidents, Control Markets, Wage Wars, and Save Our Lives *(2010).*

- • **Before you read,** *think about your own degree of empathy. When you feel empathy, you are able to feel the emotions and think the thoughts of beings other than yourself. You "get inside their skin." Is this quality something that comes naturally to you?*

- • **As you read,** *pay attention to how Vedantam supports his hypothesis about the "telescope effect."*

1   The *Insiko 1907* was a tramp tanker that roamed the Pacific Ocean. Its twelve-man Taiwanese crew hunted the seas for fishing fleets in need of fuel; the *Insiko* had a cargo of tens of thousands of gallons of diesel. It was supposed to be an Indonesian ship, except that it was not registered in Indonesia because its owner, who lived in China, did not bother with taxes. In terms of international law, the *Insiko 1907* was stateless, a two-hundred-sixty-foot microscopic speck on the largest ocean on earth. On March 13, 2002, a fire broke out in the *Insiko's* engine room. . . . The ship was about eight hundred miles south of Hawaii's Big Island, and adrift. Its crew could not call on anyone for help, and no one who could help knew of the *Insiko's* existence, let alone its problems.[1]

2   Drawn by wind and currents, the *Insiko* eventually got within two hundred twenty miles of Hawaii, where it was spotted by a cruise ship called the *Norwegian Star* on April 2. The cruise ship diverted course, rescued the Taiwanese crew, and radioed the United States Coast Guard. But as the *Norwegian Star* pulled away from the *Insiko* and steamed toward Hawaii, a few passengers on the cruise ship heard the sound of barking. The captain's puppy had been left behind on the tanker.

3   It is not entirely clear why the cruise ship did not rescue the Jack Russell mixed terrier, or why the Taiwanese crew did not insist on it. . . . Whatever the reason, the burned-out tanker and its lonely inhabitant were aban-

doned on the terrible immensity of the Pacific. The *Norwegian Star* made a stop at Maui. A passenger who heard the barking dog called the Hawaiian Humane Society in Honolulu. . . . The Humane Society alerted fishing boats about the lost tanker. Media reports began appearing about the terrier, whose name was Hokget.

Something about a lost puppy on an abandoned ship on the Pacific 4 gripped people's imaginations. Money poured into the Humane Society to fund a rescue. One check was for five thousand dollars. . . . "It was just about a dog," [Hawaiian Humane Society president Pamela] Burns told me. . . . "This was an opportunity for people to feel good about rescuing a dog. People poured out their support. A handful of people were incensed. These people said, 'You should be giving money to the homeless.'" But Burns felt the great thing about America was that people were free to give money to whatever cause they cared about, and people cared about Hokget. . . .

On April 26, nearly one and a half months after the puppy's ordeal began, 5 the *American Quest* found the *Insiko* and boarded the tanker. The forty-pound female pup was still alive, and hiding in a pile of tires. It was a hot day, so Brian Murray, the *American Quest*'s salvage supervisor, went in and simply grabbed the terrier by the scruff of her neck. The puppy was terrified and shook for two hours. Her rescuers fed her, bathed her, and applied lotion to her nose, which was sunburned.

Hokget, the rescued dog, with Dr. Becky Rhoades, the veterinarian with the Kauai (Hawaii) Humane Society who examined her

The story of Hokget's rescue is comical, but it is also touching. Human beings 6 from around the world came together to save a dog. The vast majority of people who sent money to the Humane Society knew they would never personally see Hokget, never have their hands licked in gratitude. Saving the dog, as Pamela Burns suggested to me, was an act of pure altruism, and a marker of the remarkable capacity human beings have to empathize with the plight of others.

There are a series of disturbing questions, however. Eight years before Hokget 7 was rescued, the same world that showed extraordinary compassion in the rescue of a dog sat on its hands as a million human beings were killed in Rwanda. . . . The twentieth century reveals a shockingly long list of similar horrors that have been ignored by the world as they unfolded. . . . Why have successive generations of Americans—a people with extraordinary powers of compassion—done so little to halt suffering on such a large scale? . . .

8   There are many explanations for the discrepancy between our response to Hokget and our response to genocide. Some argue that Americans care little about foreign lives—but then what should we make about their willingness to spend thousands of dollars to rescue a dog, a foreign dog on a stateless ship in international waters? Well, perhaps Americans care more about pets than people? But that does not stand up to scrutiny, either. Hokget's rescue was remarkable, but there are countless stories about similar acts of compassion and generosity that people show toward their fellow human beings every day. No, there is something about genocide, about mass death in particular, that seems to trigger inaction.

9   I believe our inability to wrap our minds around large numbers is responsible for our apathy toward mass suffering. We are unconsciously biased in our moral judgment, in much the same way we are biased when we think about risk. Just as we are blasé about heart disease and lackadaisical about suicide, but terrified about psychopaths and terrorists, so also we make systematic errors in thinking about moral questions—especially those involving large numbers of people.

10   The philosopher Peter Singer once devised a dilemma that highlights a central contradiction in our moral reasoning. If you see a child drowning in a pond, and you know you can save the child without any risk to your own life—but you would ruin a fine pair of shoes worth two hundred dollars if you jumped into the water—would you save the child or save your shoes?[2] Most people react incredulously to the question; obviously, a child's life is worth more than a pair of shoes. If this is the case, Singer asked, why do large numbers of people hesitate to write a check for two hundred dollars to a reputable charity that could save the life of a child halfway around the world—when there are millions of such children who need our help? Even when people are absolutely certain their money will not be wasted and will be used to save a child's life, fewer people are willing to write the check than to leap into the pond.

11   Our moral responsibilities feel different in these situations even though Singer is absolutely right in arguing they are equivalent challenges; one feels immediate and visceral, the other distant and abstract. We feel personally responsible for one child, whereas the other is one of millions who need help. Our responsibility feels diffused when it comes to children in distant places—there are many people who could write that check. But distance and diffusion of responsibility do not explain why we step forward in some cases—why did so many people come forward to save Hokget? Why did they write checks for a dog they would never meet? Why did they feel a single abandoned dog on a stateless ship was *their* problem?

I want to offer a disturbing idea. The reason human beings seem to care   12
so little about mass suffering and death is precisely *because* the suffering is
happening on a mass scale. The brain is simply not very good at grasping
the implications of mass suffering. Americans would be far more likely to
step forward if only a few people were suffering, or a single person were in
pain. Hokget did not draw our sympathies because we care more about
dogs than people; she drew our sympathies because she was a *single* dog
lost on the biggest ocean in the world. If the hidden brain biases our perceptions about risk toward exotic threats, it shapes our compassion into a
telescope. We are best able to respond when we are focused on a single
victim. We don't feel twenty times sadder when we hear that twenty
people have died in a disaster than when we hear that one person has
died, even though the magnitude of the tragedy *is* twenty times larger. . . .
We can certainly reach such a conclusion abstractly, in our conscious
minds, but we cannot *feel it viscerally*, because that is the domain of the
hidden brain, and the hidden brain is simply not calibrated to deal with
the difference between a single death and a million deaths.

But the paradox does not end there. Even if ten deaths do not make us   13
feel ten times as sad as a single death, shouldn't we feel five times as sad,
or even at least twice as sad? There is disturbing evidence that shows that
in many situations, not only do we not care twice as much about ten
deaths as we do about one, but we may actually care *less*. I strongly suspect that if the *Insiko* had been carrying a hundred dogs, many people
would have cared less about their fate than they did about Hokget. A hundred dogs do not have a single face, a single name, a single life story
around which we can wrap our imaginations—and our compassion. . . .

The evidence for what I am going to call the telescope effect comes from   14
a series of fascinating experiments.[3] At the University of Oregon, the psychologist Paul Slovic asked . . . groups of volunteers to imagine they were
running a philanthropic foundation. Would they rather spend ten million
dollars to save 10,000 lives from a disease that caused 15,000 deaths a
year, or save 20,000 lives from a disease that killed 290,000 people a year?
Overwhelmingly, volunteers preferred to spend money saving the ten thousand lives rather than the twenty thousand lives. Rather than tailor their
investments to saving the largest number of lives, people sought to save the
largest *proportion* of lives among the different groups of victims. An investment directed toward disease A could save two-thirds of the victims,
whereas an investment directed at disease B could save "only" seven percent of the victims.

We respond to mass suffering in much the same way we respond to   15
most things in our lives. We fall back on rules of thumb, on feelings, on
intuitions. People who choose to spend money saving ten thousand lives
rather than twenty thousand lives are not bad people. Rather, like those
who spend thousands of dollars rescuing a single dog rather than directing

the same amount of money to save a dozen dogs, they are merely allowing their hidden brain to guide them.

16   I have often wondered why the hidden brain displays a telescope effect when it comes to compassion. Evolutionary psychology tends to be an armchair sport, so please take my explanation for the paradox as one of several possible answers. The telescope effect may have arisen because evolution has built a powerful bias into us to preferentially love our kith and kin. It is absurd that we spend two hundred dollars on a birthday party for our son or our daughter when we could send the same money to a charity and save the life of a child halfway around the world. How can one child's birthday party mean more to us than another child's life? When we put it in those terms, we sound like terrible human beings. The paradox, as with the rescue of Hokget, is that our impulse springs from love, not callousness. Evolution has built a fierce loyalty toward our children into the deepest strands of our psyche. Without the unthinking telescope effect in the unconscious mind, parents would not devote the immense time and effort it takes to raise children; generations of our ancestors would not have braved danger and cold, predators and hunger, to protect their young. The fact that you and I exist testifies to the utility of having a telescope in the brain that caused our ancestors to care intensely about the good of the few rather than the good of the many.

17   This telescope is activated when we hear a single cry for help—the child drowning in the pond, the puppy abandoned on an ocean. When we think of human suffering on a mass scale, our telescope does not work, because it has not been designed to work in such situations.

18   What makes evolutionary sense rarely makes moral sense. (One paradox of evolution is that ruthless natural selection has produced a species that recoils at the ruthlessness of natural selection.) Humans are the first and only species that is even aware of large-scale suffering taking place in distant lands; the moral telescope in our brain has not had a chance to evolve and catch up with our technological advances. When we are told about a faraway genocide, we can apply only our conscious mind to the challenge. We can reason, but we cannot feel the visceral compassion that is automatically triggered by the child who is drowning right before us. Our conscious minds can tell us that it is absurd to spend a boatload of money to save one life when the same money could be used to save ten—just as it can tell us it is absurd to be more worried about homicide than suicide. But in moral decision-making, as in many other domains of life where we are unaware of how unconscious biases influence us, it is the hidden brain that usually carries the day.

Editor's Notes

1. Chris Lee and George Butler, "Complex Response to Tankship *Insiko 1907,*" *Proceedings of the Marine Safety Council,* Vol. 60, No. 1 (January–March 2003), pp. 49–51.

2. Peter Singer has mentioned the story about the drowning child in a number of publications, including his 2009 book, *The Life You Can Save*, Random House, Inc.

3. Paul Slovic, "'If I Look at the Mass I Will Never Act': Psychic Numbing and Genocide," *Judgment and Decision Making*, Vol. 2, No. 2 (April 2007), pp. 79–95.

READING FOR MEANING

This section presents three activities that will help you think about the meanings in Vedantam's causal argument. Your instructor may ask you to do one or more of these online.

1. **Read to Summarize.** Write a sentence or two explaining what you think is the main idea Vedantam wants his readers to understand about the *telescope effect*.

   For more help with summarizing, see Chapter 10, pp. 518–19.

2. **Read to Respond.** Write a paragraph analyzing your initial reactions to Vedantam's essay. For example, consider anything that resonates with your experience or that seems contradictory, surprising, or fascinating, such as:

   - The rescue of Hokget. Pamela Burns is quoted as saying, "This was an opportunity for people to feel good about rescuing a dog. People poured out their support." But she also notes, "A handful of people were incensed. These people said, 'You should be giving money to the homeless'" (par. 4). Which side do you come down on? Why?

   - Vedantam writes, ". . . there is something about genocide, about mass death in particular, that seems to trigger inaction. . . . Just as we are blasé about heart disease and lackadaisical about suicide, but terrified about psychopaths and terrorists, so also we make systematic errors in thinking about moral questions — especially those involving large numbers of people" (pars. 8–9). Are you persuaded by Vedantam's reasoning? Why or why not?

   You may also try reflecting on challenges to your beliefs and values; see Chapter 10, pp. 526–27.

3. **Read to Analyze Assumptions.** Write a paragraph or two analyzing an assumption you find intriguing in Vedantam's essay. For example:

   Assumptions about the effects of the "hidden brain" on our moral choices. Vedantam speculates that our "hidden brain" — his term for a host of unconscious mental processes that subtly bias our judgment — "shapes our compassion into a telescope. We are best able to respond when we are focused on a single victim" (par. 12). To think critically

Take a quiz to check your reading and vocabulary comprehension:
bedfordstmartins.com/readingcritically

about assumptions regarding the effects of the "hidden brain," ask yourself questions like these:

- Why does such brain behavior lead to more empathy for a few than the many? Do you agree with Vedantam that this is the result of our evolutionary past, or is it possible that we feel more empathy for the few because we believe we can more realistically help a single individual?
- Why does Vedantam call the telescope effect a form of "bias" (par. 12)?

Assumptions about money as a measure of compassion. Vedantam provides several examples to illustrate that donating money is evidence of human compassion: money for the dog, Hokget (par. 6); money (or the lack of money) for Rwanda genocide (par. 7); and money (or the lack of it) for children around the world (par. 10). He speculates that "many people could write that check" for faraway children, and that "distance and diffusion of responsibility do not explain why we step forward in some cases — why did so many people come forward to save Hokget? Why did they write checks for a dog they would never meet?" (par. 11). To think critically about assumptions regarding the expenditure of money as a measure of human compassion, ask yourself questions like these:

- If compassion correlates with generosity, then are people who make large donations more compassionate than those who make small donations or none at all? What else might affect how we choose to donate money? What other kinds of donations (of time, for example) might indicate generosity?
- Pamela Burns suggests that "the great thing about America was that people were free to give money to whatever cause they cared about . . ." (par. 4). Does this suggest that the Americans who donated to rescue Hogket are generally more compassionate than others?

READING LIKE A WRITER

MAKING A LOGICAL, WELL-SUPPORTED CAUSE OR EFFECT ARGUMENT

Although Vedantam is writing for a general audience, he does acknowledge his sources. In fact, Vedantam states at the beginning of paragraph 14 that psychologist Paul Slovic's research provides the main "evidence" supporting his favored cause and cites Slovic's research in the Editor's Notes.

Analyze & Write

Write a paragraph or two analyzing how Vedantam uses Slovic's research:

1. Reread paragraph 14. How does Vedantam use Slovic's research to support his causal analysis?

2. Reread paragraph 12 and paragraphs 15–18. What could Vedantam have added, if anything, to clarify the connection between Slovic's research and Vedantam's ideas about "the telescope effect" and "the hidden brain"?

Nicholas Carr

Is Google Making Us Stupid?

Nicholas Carr (b. 1959) attended Dartmouth College and received his MA in English and American literature and language from Harvard. He writes on the social, economic, and business implications of technology. Early in his career, he was executive editor of the Harvard Business Review *and a principal at Mercer Management Consulting. He is the author of* Does IT Matter? *(2004), on the economics of information technology;* The Big Switch: Rewiring the World, from Edison to Google *(2008), on cloud computing; and* The Shallows: What the Internet Is Doing to Our Brains *(2010). Carr has also written for many periodicals, including the* Atlantic Monthly, *the* New York Times Magazine, Wired, *the* Financial Times, *the* Futurist, *and* Advertising Age, *and has been a columnist for the* Guardian *and the* Industry Standard. *In addition, Carr has been a speaker at many academic, corporate, governmental, and professional events throughout the world. He is a member of the Encyclopaedia Britannica's editorial board of advisers and is on the steering board of the World Economic Forum's cloud computing project. You can learn more about Carr at his Web site, www.nicholasgcarr.com, and you can visit his blog,* Rough Type, *at www .roughtype.com.*

The essay below was the cover story of the Atlantic Monthly's Ideas *issue in 2008. In it, Carr argues that the Internet is having a disturbing effect on our cognitive activities — the work of our brains.*

- *Before you read, think about your own habits of concentration, considering whether you are able to focus deeply for long periods of time or whether you move from one idea to another fairly swiftly. Also think about whether concentration has to be sacrificed for the sake of acquiring more information.*

- *As you read, note how Carr mentions and responds to alternative ideas about the effect of the Internet on our thinking.*

1   "Dave, stop. Stop, will you? Stop, Dave. Will you stop, Dave?" So the supercomputer HAL pleads with the implacable astronaut Dave Bowman in a famous and weirdly poignant scene toward the end of Stanley Kubrick's *2001: A Space Odyssey.* Bowman, having nearly been sent to a deep-space death by the malfunctioning machine, is calmly, coldly disconnecting the memory circuits that control its artificial "brain." "Dave, my mind is going," HAL says, forlornly. "I can feel it. I can feel it."

2   I can feel it, too. Over the past few years I've had an uncomfortable sense that someone, or something, has been tinkering with my brain, remapping the neural circuitry, reprogramming the memory. My mind isn't going—so far as I can tell—but it's changing. I'm not thinking the way I used to think. I can feel it most strongly when I'm reading. Immersing

myself in a book or a lengthy article used to be easy. My mind would get caught up in the narrative or the turns of the argument, and I'd spend hours strolling through long stretches of prose. That's rarely the case anymore. Now my concentration often starts to drift after two or three pages. I get fidgety, lose the thread, begin looking for something else to do. I feel as if I'm always dragging my wayward brain back to the text. The deep reading that used to come naturally has become a struggle.

I think I know what's going on. For more than a decade now, I've been   3
spending a lot of time online, searching and surfing and sometimes adding to the great databases of the Internet. The Web has been a godsend to me as a writer. Research that once required days in the stacks or periodical rooms of libraries can now be done in minutes. A few Google searches, some quick clicks on hyperlinks, and I've got the telltale fact or pithy quote I was after. Even when I'm not working, I'm as likely as not to be foraging in the Web's info-thickets, reading and writing e-mails, scanning headlines and blog posts, watching videos and listening to podcasts, or just tripping from link to link to link. (Unlike footnotes, to which they're sometimes likened, hyperlinks don't merely point to related works; they propel you toward them.)

For me, as for others, the Net is becoming a universal medium, the con-   4
duit for most of the information that flows through my eyes and ears and into my mind. The advantages of having immediate access to such an incredibly rich store of information are many, and they've been widely

$$Ax^2 + Bx + C = 0$$
$$A^2 + B^2 = C^2$$

"The Cloud ate my homework."

described and duly applauded. "The perfect recall of silicon memory," *Wired*'s Clive Thompson has written, "can be an enormous boon to thinking." But that boon comes at a price. As the media theorist Marshall McLuhan pointed out in the 1960s, media are not just passive channels of information. They supply the stuff of thought, but they also shape the process of thought. And what the Net seems to be doing is chipping away my capacity for concentration and contemplation. My mind now expects to take in information the way the Net distributes it: in a swiftly moving stream of particles. Once I was a scuba diver in the sea of words. Now I zip along the surface like a guy on a Jet Ski.

5   I'm not the only one. When I mention my troubles with reading to friends and acquaintances — literary types, most of them — many say they're having similar experiences. The more they use the Web, the more they have to fight to stay focused on long pieces of writing. Some of the bloggers I follow have also begun mentioning the phenomenon. Scott Karp, who writes a blog about online media, recently confessed that he has stopped reading books altogether. "I was a lit major in college, and used to be [a] voracious book reader," he wrote. "What happened?" He speculates on the answer: "What if I do all my reading on the web not so much because the way I read has changed, i.e., I'm just seeking convenience, but because the way I THINK has changed?"

6   Bruce Friedman, who blogs regularly about the use of computers in medicine, also has described how the Internet has altered his mental habits. "I now have almost totally lost the ability to read and absorb a longish article on the web or in print," he wrote earlier this year. A pathologist who has long been on the faculty of the University of Michigan Medical School, Friedman elaborated on his comment in a telephone conversation with me. His thinking, he said, has taken on a "staccato" quality, reflecting the way he quickly scans short passages of text from many sources online. "I can't read *War and Peace* anymore," he admitted. "I've lost the ability to do that. Even a blog post of more than three or four paragraphs is too much to absorb. I skim it."

7   Anecdotes alone don't prove much. And we still await the long-term neurological and psychological experiments that will provide a definitive picture of how Internet use affects cognition. But a recently published study of online research habits, conducted by scholars from University College London, suggests that we may well be in the midst of a sea change in the way we read and think. As part of the five-year research program, the scholars examined computer logs documenting the behavior of visitors to two popular research sites, one operated by the British Library and one by a U.K. educational consortium, that provide access to journal articles, e-books, and other sources of written information. They found that people using the sites exhibited "a form of skimming activity," hopping from one source to another and rarely returning to any source they'd already visited.

They typically read no more than one or two pages of an article or book before they would "bounce" out to another site. Sometimes they'd save a long article, but there's no evidence that they ever went back and actually read it. The authors of the study report:

> It is clear that users are not reading online in the traditional sense; indeed there are signs that new forms of "reading" are emerging as users "power browse" horizontally through titles, contents pages and abstracts going for quick wins. It almost seems that they go online to avoid reading in the traditional sense.

Thanks to the ubiquity of text on the Internet, not to mention the popularity of text-messaging on cell phones, we may well be reading more today than we did in the 1970s or 1980s, when television was our medium of choice. But it's a different kind of reading, and behind it lies a different kind of thinking—perhaps even a new sense of the self. "We are not only *what* we read," says Maryanne Wolf, a developmental psychologist at Tufts University and the author of *Proust and the Squid: The Story and Science of the Reading Brain.* "We are *how* we read." Wolf worries that the style of reading promoted by the Net, a style that puts "efficiency" and "immediacy" above all else, may be weakening our capacity for the kind of deep reading that emerged when an earlier technology, the printing press, made long and complex works of prose commonplace. When we read online, she says, we tend to become "mere decoders of information." Our ability to interpret text, to make the rich mental connections that form when we read deeply and without distraction, remains largely disengaged. 8

Reading, explains Wolf, is not an instinctive skill for human beings. It's not etched into our genes the way speech is. We have to teach our minds how to translate the symbolic characters we see into the language we understand. And the media or other technologies we use in learning and practicing the craft of reading play an important part in shaping the neural circuits inside our brains. Experiments demonstrate that readers of ideograms, such as the Chinese, develop a mental circuitry for reading that is very different from the circuitry found in those of us whose written language employs an alphabet. The variations extend across many regions of the brain, including those that govern such essential cognitive functions as memory and the interpretation of visual and auditory stimuli. We can expect as well that the circuits woven by our use of the Net will be different from those woven by our reading of books and other printed works. . . . 9

The human brain is almost infinitely malleable. People used to think that our mental meshwork, the dense connections formed among the 100 billion or so neurons inside our skulls, was largely fixed by the time we reached adulthood. But brain researchers have discovered that that's not the case. James Olds, a professor of neuroscience who directs the Krasnow Institute for Advanced Study at George Mason University, says 10 that even the adult mind "is very plastic." Nerve cells routinely break old connections and form new ones. "The brain," according to Olds, "has the ability to reprogram itself on the fly, altering the way it functions." . . .

11   The process of adapting to new intellectual technologies is reflected in the changing metaphors we use to explain ourselves to ourselves. When the mechanical clock arrived, people began thinking of their brains as operating "like clockwork." Today, in the age of software, we have come to think of them as operating "like computers." But the changes, neuroscience tells us, go much deeper than metaphor. Thanks to our brain's plasticity, the adaptation occurs also at a biological level.

12   The Internet promises to have particularly far-reaching effects on cognition. In a paper published in 1936, the British mathematician Alan Turing proved that a digital computer, which at the time existed only as a theoretical machine, could be programmed to perform the function of any other information-processing device. And that's what we're seeing today. The Internet, an immeasurably powerful computing system, is subsuming most of our other intellectual technologies. It's becoming our map and our clock, our printing press and our typewriter, our calculator and our telephone, and our radio and TV.

13   When the Net absorbs a medium, that medium is re-created in the Net's image. It injects the medium's content with hyperlinks, blinking ads, and other digital gewgaws, and it surrounds the content with the content of all the other media it has absorbed. A new e-mail message, for instance, may announce its arrival as we're glancing over the latest headlines at a newspaper's site. The result is to scatter our attention and diffuse our concentration.

14   The Net's influence doesn't end at the edges of a computer screen, either. As people's minds become attuned to the crazy quilt of Internet media, traditional media have to adapt to the audience's new expectations. Television programs add text crawls and pop-up ads, and magazines and newspapers shorten their articles, introduce capsule summaries, and crowd their pages with easy-to-browse info-snippets. When, in March of this year, the *New York Times* decided to devote the second and third pages of every edition to article abstracts, its design director, Tom Bodkin, explained that the "shortcuts" would give harried readers a quick "taste" of the day's news, sparing them the "less efficient" method of actually turning the pages and reading the articles. Old media have little choice but to play by the new-media rules.

15   Never has a communications system played so many roles in our lives—or exerted such broad influence over our thoughts—as the Internet does today. Yet, for all that's been written about the Net, there's been little consideration of how, exactly, it's reprogramming us. The Net's intellectual ethic remains obscure. . . .

Google's headquarters, in Mountain View, California—the Googleplex— 16
is the Internet's high church. . . . Google, says its chief executive, Eric
Schmidt, is "a company that's founded around the science of measurement,"
and it is striving to "systematize everything" it does. Drawing on the tera-
bytes of behavioral data it collects through its search engine and other sites,
it carries out thousands of experiments a day, according to the *Harvard Business Review*, and it uses the results to refine the algorithms that increasingly
control how people find information and extract meaning from it. . . .

The company has declared that its mission is "to organize the world's 17
information and make it universally accessible and useful." It seeks to
develop "the perfect search engine," which it defines as something that
"understands exactly what you mean and gives you back exactly what you
want." In Google's view, information is a kind of commodity, a utilitarian
resource that can be mined and processed with industrial efficiency. The
more pieces of information we can "access" and the faster we can extract
their gist, the more productive we become as thinkers.

Where does it end? Sergey Brin and Larry Page, the gifted young men 18
who founded Google while pursuing doctoral degrees in computer science at Stanford, speak frequently of their desire to turn their search engine
into an artificial intelligence, a HAL-like machine that might be connected
directly to our brains. "The ultimate search engine is something as smart as
people—or smarter," Page said in a speech a few years back. "For us,
working on search is a way to work on artificial intelligence." In a 2004
interview with *Newsweek*, Brin said, "Certainly if you had all the world's
information directly attached to your brain, or an artificial brain that was
smarter than your brain, you'd be better off." Last year, Page told a convention of scientists that Google is "really trying to build artificial intelligence
and to do it on a large scale."

Such an ambition is a natural one, even an admirable one, for a pair of 19
math whizzes with vast quantities of cash at their disposal and a small
army of computer scientists in their employ. A fundamentally scientific
enterprise, Google is motivated by a desire to use technology, in Eric
Schmidt's words, "to solve problems that have never been solved before,"
and artificial intelligence is the hardest problem out there. Why wouldn't
Brin and Page want to be the ones to crack it?

Still, their easy assumption that we'd all "be better off" if our brains 20
were supplemented, or even replaced, by an artificial intelligence is unset-
tling. It suggests a belief that intelligence is the output of a mechanical
process, a series of discrete steps that can be isolated, measured, and opti-
mized. In Google's world, the world we enter when we go online, there's
little place for the fuzziness of contemplation. Ambiguity is not an opening
for insight but a bug to be fixed. The human brain is just an outdated computer that needs a faster processor and a bigger hard drive.

21   The idea that our minds should operate as high-speed data-processing machines is not only built into the workings of the Internet, it is the network's reigning business model as well. The faster we surf across the Web—the more links we click and pages we view—the more opportunities Google and other companies gain to collect information about us and to feed us advertisements. Most of the proprietors of the commercial Internet have a financial stake in collecting the crumbs of data we leave behind as we flit from link to link—the more crumbs, the better. The last thing these companies want is to encourage leisurely reading or slow, concentrated thought. It's in their economic interest to drive us to distraction.

22   Maybe I'm just a worrywart. Just as there's a tendency to glorify technological progress, there's a countertendency to expect the worst of every new tool or machine. . . . Perhaps those who dismiss critics of the Internet as Luddites or nostalgists will be proved correct, and from our hyperactive, data-stoked minds will spring a golden age of intellectual discovery and universal wisdom. Then again, the Net isn't the alphabet, and although it may replace the printing press, it produces something altogether different. The kind of deep reading that a sequence of printed pages promotes is valuable not just for the knowledge we acquire from the author's words but for the intellectual vibrations those words set off within our own minds. In the quiet spaces opened up by the sustained, undistracted reading of a book, or by any other act of contemplation, for that matter, we make our own associations, draw our own inferences and analogies, foster our own ideas. Deep reading, as Maryanne Wolf argues, is indistinguishable from deep thinking. If we lose those quiet spaces, or fill them up with "content," we will sacrifice something important not only in our selves but in our culture. In a recent essay, the playwright Richard Foreman eloquently described what's at stake:

> I come from a tradition of Western culture, in which the ideal (my ideal) was the complex, dense and "cathedral-like" structure of the highly educated and articulate personality—a man or woman who carried inside themselves a personally constructed and unique version of the entire heritage of the West. [But now] I see within us all (myself included) the replacement of complex inner density with a new kind of self—evolving under the pressure of information overload and the technology of the "instantly available."

23   As we are drained of our "inner repertory of dense cultural inheritance," Foreman concluded, we risk turning into "'pancake people'—spread wide and thin as we connect with that vast network of information accessed by the mere touch of a button."

24   I'm haunted by that scene in *2001*. What makes it so poignant, and so weird, is the computer's emotional response to the disassembly of its mind: its despair as one circuit after another goes dark, its childlike pleading with

the astronaut—"I can feel it. I can feel it. I'm afraid"—and its final reversion to what can only be called a state of innocence. HAL's outpouring of feeling contrasts with the emotionlessness that characterizes the human figures in the film, who go about their business with an almost robotic efficiency. Their thoughts and actions feel scripted, as if they're following the steps of an algorithm. In the world of *2001*, people have become so machinelike that the most human character turns out to be a machine. That's the essence of Kubrick's dark prophecy: as we come to rely on computers to mediate our understanding of the world, it is our own intelligence that flattens into artificial intelligence.

READING FOR MEANING

This section presents three activities that will help you think about the meanings in Carr's effects argument, "Is Google Making Us Stupid?"

1. **Read to Summarize.** Write a sentence or two explaining Carr's concern regarding the Internet's effect on our ability to concentrate and think deeply.

   For more help with summarizing, see Chapter 10, pp. 518–19.

2. **Read to Respond.** Write a paragraph analyzing your reaction to Carr's essay. For example, consider anything that resonates with your experience or that seems contradictory, surprising, or fascinating, such as:

   - The role of Carr's anecdotes in the first six paragraphs. Do they draw the reader into the essay? Present the subject? Help readers identify with Carr? Provide hard evidence? What role(s) do they play?

     You may also try reflecting on challenges to your beliefs and values; see Chapter 10, pp. 526–27.

   - Your own experience with reading on the Internet, and whether you share Carr's concern that the kind of reading fostered there is undermining "deep reading" (par. 2).

3. **Read to Analyze Assumptions.** Write a paragraph or two analyzing an assumption you find intriguing in Carr's essay. For example:

   Assumptions about the value of sustained concentration. Carr returns again and again to ways the Internet is reducing our ability to sustain concentration and focus for an extended period of time. He reports that he and his friends "have to fight to stay focused on long pieces of writing" (par. 5), cites a study that finds "there are signs that new forms of 'reading' are emerging as users [of research sites] 'power browse' . . . going for quick wins" (par. 7), and states that "[t]he last thing these companies [Google and others] want is to encourage leisurely reading or slow,

Take a quiz to check your reading and vocabulary comprehension:
bedfordstmartins.com/readingcritically

concentrated thought" (par. 21). Finally, he summarizes the ideas of developmental psychologist Maryanne Wolf: "Deep reading . . . is indistinguishable from deep thinking. If we lose those quiet spaces, or fill them up with 'content,' we will sacrifice something important not only in our selves but in our culture" (par. 22). To think critically about the assumptions in this essay related to the value of sustained concentration, ask yourself questions like these:

- Cognitively, what are the differences between engaging in the intellectual activity of sustained concentration and the activity of acquiring many bits of information?

- How does Carr support his contention that we lose something valuable if we lose sustained concentration?

- Is there a compromise — a way to have both sustained concentration and all the knowledge we need?

Assumptions about the value of the human over the machine. Carr seems concerned that machines will replace human thought, and that we will lose something important to our humanity as a result. He says that in "Google's world," the human brain is "just an outdated computer that needs a faster processor and a bigger hard drive" (par. 20). In Carr's view, expanded knowledge from online "content" is not enough; we also need the "intellectual vibrations . . . words set off within our own minds" (par. 22). In his conclusion, Carr laments that in the movie *2001*, "people have become so machinelike that the most human character turns out to be a machine" (par. 24). To think critically about the assumptions in this essay related to the value of the human over the machine, ask yourself questions like these:

- How would you define "human" in the context of Carr's essay? What kind of threat is the "machine" to the "humans"?

You may also want to try recognizing emotional manipulation; see Chapter 10, pp. 536–37.

- What do you think of Carr's concerns about the danger that machines pose to humans, especially machines that mimic the human mind?

- What could be the long-lasting consequences of *not* prizing human qualities, like the ability to contemplate?

READING LIKE A WRITER

RESPONDING TO OBJECTIONS OR ALTERNATIVE SPECULATIONS

Writers speculating about effects must support their proposed effects, using all the relevant resources available to them — quoting authorities, citing statistics and research findings, comparing and contrasting, posing rhetorical questions, offering literary allusions, and crafting metaphors, among other strategies. (Carr uses all of these resources in his essay.) Writers know that at every point in the argument their readers will have objections, questions, and alternative effects in mind, and that they must anticipate and respond to them. Just as imaginatively as they argue for their proposed effects, writers in this genre attempt to answer readers' questions, react to their objections, and evaluate their preferred effects.

Analyze & Write

Write a paragraph or two analyzing how Carr anticipates his readers' objections and supports his response:

1. Reread paragraphs 4, 7, 8, 10, 17, 18, 19, and 22, in which Carr responds to alternative arguments, underlining the main objections that he anticipates his readers will have to his argument. For example, in paragraph 4, he anticipates readers' likely objection that having access to so much information is a terrific advantage.

2. Now examine how Carr manages readers' possible objections and questions. For at least three of the objections or questions you identified in the paragraphs you reread, notice the kinds of support he relies on to argue against each objection. How appropriate and believable do you find his support?

ANALYZING VISUALS

Write a paragraph analyzing the cartoon included in Carr's essay and explaining what it contributes to the essay. To do the analysis, you can use the Criteria for Analyzing Visuals chart in Chapter 12, on pp. 611–12. Don't feel you have to answer all of the questions in the chart; instead, focus on those that seem most productive in helping you write a paragraph-length analysis. To help you get started, consider adding these questions that specifically refer to the cartoon:

- Recall the old excuse, "The dog ate my homework." How does the cartoon play on that parody of an excuse for turning work in late?

- Consider the traditional appearance of the teacher, student, and classroom. How does the contrast between that traditional look and the caption help generate the cartoon's humor?

- The cartoon originally appeared in the *New Yorker* magazine, a periodical that appeals to a middle-aged, fairly well-to-do, and sophisticated readership. How does the cartoon appeal to this audience?

Sheila McClain

Fitness Culture: A Growing Trend in America

Sheila McClain wrote this essay speculating about the causes of the fitness culture for her first-year college composition course. Since then it has been updated to reflect more current statistics.

- ***Before you read,*** *consider what you know about this topic: Do you see fitness as a trend in America? Do you engage in exercise yourself? If so, where — at a health club, on your own, or as part of a group (such as a team)? If not, what keeps you from exercising?*

- ***As you read,*** *consider how McClain establishes her credibility as a writer about fitness culture. On what causes do you feel she can most be trusted?*

1   The exercise and fitness industry used to cater to a small, select group of hard-core athletes and bodybuilders. Now, physical fitness has an increasingly broad appeal to people of all ages, and the evidence can be seen everywhere. You cannot turn on the television without seeing an infomercial featuring the latest exercise machine. Sales of fitness equipment for home use—from home gyms to DVDs and fitness games like the Wii Fit—have been booming since the early 1990s. Fitness club membership, according to the International Health, Racquet and Sportsclub Association (IHRSA), jumped from 20 million in 1991 to over 40 million in 2006 ("U.S. Health Club Membership"; see fig. 1). Although club membership did not change significantly between 2006 and 2009, it leapt another 10 percent to 50.2 million in 2010 ("U.S. Health Club Membership"). As of September 30, 2011, as many as 16 percent of Americans were members of a health club ("IHRSA").

2   Research linking fitness to health and longevity has led to the growth of the "fitness culture" in America. Numerous clinical studies and scientific reports have been publicized confirming that exercise, together with a proper diet, helps prevent heart disease as well as many other serious health problems, and may even reverse the effects of certain ailments. According to Marc Leepson, historian and former staff writer for the *Congressional Quarterly*, "clinical studies in 1989 done by the United States Preventive Services Task Force, a government appointed panel of experts, found 'a strong association between physical activity and decreased risk of

For an additional student reading, go to **bedfordstmartins.com/readingcritically**.

FIG. 1. Number of Health Club Members in the United States by Year (in Millions)
(Source: The Active Network 2007, p. 4)

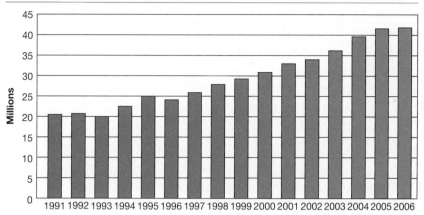

several medical conditions, as well as overall mortality'" (Leepson). Subsequent research has just heightened the association between fitness and longevity. A recent study reported in *Circulation: Journal of the American Heart Association* found that keeping fit or becoming more fit, regardless of your weight, can reduce your risk of dying. On the other hand, reducing your fitness correlated with increased risk ("Physical"). The federal government has tried to increase awareness about the benefits of fitness, including by promoting workplace wellness programs. "Hundreds of firms established in-house fitness centers or contracted with local gyms," because, as historian Marc Stern points out, exercise was assumed "to increase productivity, reduce absenteeism, enable recruitment and retention, and improve morale" (3–4).

3   As a nation, we have become much more aware of the ways that physical fitness contributes to health and longevity. In 2006, the Pew Research Center found that 86 percent of adults surveyed thought that "exercising for fitness improves a person's odds of a long and healthy life by 'a lot.' And, about six in ten believe that exercising has 'a lot' of impact on a person's attractiveness" (see Table 1, p. 420). Fifty-seven percent claim to do "some kind of exercise program to keep fit." Even so, "among these regular exercisers, about two-thirds (65%) admit that they aren't getting as much exercise as they should."

4   We all know why we should exercise, but why join a fitness club? Some of the answers may surprise you—such as to be part of a community, to reduce stress, to improve your body image, and simply to have fun. One reason people join fitness clubs is to fulfill the basic human desire for a sense of community and belonging. People today are more likely than in the past to stay at home, as Harvard professor Robert D. Putnam argued in

TABLE 1   The Benefits of Exercise

How much do you think exercising can impact . . .	a long and healthy life	attractiveness
A lot	86%	59%
A little	11	31
Not at all	1	6
It depends	1	2
Don't know	1	2
	100	100

Source: Pew Research Center

his best-selling book *Bowling Alone: The Collapse and Revival of American Community*. As a result, Americans have become more solitary. At the same time, they are growing more aware that they must stay fit to be healthy and realize that health clubs can have the added advantage of bringing them into contact with other people. Psychology professors Jasper A. J. Smits and Michael W. Otto, in their new book, *Exercise for Mood and Anxiety*, cite research showing that "one of the benefits of regular physical activity is feeling more connected to others" (7). Glenn Colarossi—a widely quoted authority on fitness, who has a master's degree in exercise physiology and is co-owner of the Stamford (Connecticut) Athletic Club—adds his own anecdotal evidence about why people join clubs: "People like to belong to something. They like the support and added incentive of working out with others" (qtd. in Glenn). Furthermore, Catherine Larner, a writer on health and lifestyle issues, considers "increasing one's circle of friends" among the benefits of going to the gym (1). Group exercise also fosters positive peer pressure that keeps people going when they might give up were they exercising alone at home.

5   Another even more surprising cause of the popularity of fitness clubs may be the anxiety about terrorism following 9/11. As Mary Sisson notes in an article in *Crain's New York Business*, health club chains saw an increase in revenues immediately after 9/11 and even expanded, one of them opening four new clubs, despite an economic downturn for most other industries. Sisson offers several plausible reasons why fear from the threat of terrorism on top of the normal stresses of modern life causes people to exercise more and to do so together: (1) under stressful conditions, people want the sense of community provided by gyms and classes; (2) working out gives people a sense of empowerment that counteracts feelings of helplessness; (3) traveling less provided many people with more leisure time to fill after 9/11; and (4) people make personal reassessments after a major catastrophe—such as the woman who realized how out-of-shape she was and joined a gym after descending forty flights of stairs to evacuate the World Trade Center.

Body image is a more predictable cause but may not actually play as central a role as most people think it does. A cynical friend of mine thinks that the fitness culture is fueled by women who are less interested in reducing their stress, improving their health, or joining a community than they are in wanting to look like the idealized images of celebrities and models they see in the media. I tried out this idea on my exercise physiology professor, and she agreed that some people—men as well as women—are motivated to begin exercise programs by the desire to reshape their bodies. The Pew Research Center poll showing people's opinions about the impact of exercising on attractiveness also seems to support this cause (see Table 1). However, my professor doubted that it could explain the huge increase in attendance at health clubs, because research in her field has shown that people with unrealistic goals are more likely to become discouraged easily and drop out of fitness classes (Harton). Skepticism about this cause is also evident in research by Laura Brudzynski and William P. Ebben, published in the *International Journal of Exercise Science*, showing that "body image may act as a motivator to exercise" but can also be "a barrier to exercise," particularly for those with a negative body image (15). So perhaps body image is not as significant a cause as many people assume.

A final cause worth noting is that fitness is becoming a lifestyle choice. As attitudes toward exercise are changing, health clubs may be becoming associated with fun instead of hard work. "No pain, no gain" used to be synonymous with exercise. But today exercise comes in many different forms, many of which are more engaging and gentler than in the past. The variety may also appeal to a wider range of people. Consider classes in belly dancing (you know what that is), strip tease aerobics (look it up!), and spinning (indoor group stationary cycling, led by an instructor)—these are just a few examples. David J. Glenn, writing in a business journal, points to the impact of these changing attitudes: "People look to personal fitness as a lifestyle and a way to enjoy life, not as a way to look like Arnold Schwarzenegger." Gabriela Lukas, a New Yorker who has been exercising regularly since 2001, finds it emotionally satisfying and says it makes her "feel alive" (qtd. in Sisson). When people are having fun, they are more likely to stick with exercise long enough to experience the body's release of endorphins commonly known as a "runner's high." More and more people are changing their attitudes about physical fitness as they recognize that they feel better, have more energy, and are actually improving the quality of their lives by exercising regularly.

The "fitness culture" in America continues to grow and shows no signs of slowing down anytime soon. As we become increasingly aware of the health benefits of fitness and as we continue to experience stress in our busy lives, we are bound to have even more need of the community support and the good fun of exercising with others at the local gym.

Works Cited

Active Marketing Group. "2007 Health Club Industry Review." *The Active Network.* The Active Network, 2007. Web. 4 Apr. 2012.

Brudzynski, Laura, and William P. Ebben. "Body Image as a Motivator and Barrier to Exercise Participation." *International Journal of Exercise Science* 3(1): 14–24, 2010. *WKU Top Scholar.* Web. 6 Apr. 2012.

Glenn, David J. "Exercise Activities Mellowing Out." *Fairfield County Business Journal* 2 June 2003: 22. *Regional Business News.* Web. 6 Apr. 2012.

Harton, Dorothy. Personal interview. 3 Apr. 2012.

International Health, Racquet & Sportsclub Association. "IHRSA Quarterly Consumer Study Available Free to IHRSA Members." *IHRSA,* 29 Nov. 2011. Web. 8 Apr. 2012.

---. "U.S. Health Club Membership Exceeds 50 Million, Up 10.8%; Industry Revenue Up 4% as New Members Fuel Growth." *IHRSA,* 5 Apr. 2011. Web. 5 Apr. 2012.

Larner, Catherine. "Will Gym Fix It for You?" *Challenge Newsline* 31.1 (2003): 1–2. *Academic Search Premier.* Web. 6 Apr. 2012.

Leepson, Marc. "Physical Fitness." *CQ Researcher* 2.41 (1992): 953–76. *CQ Researcher.* Web. 9 Apr. 2012.

Pew Research Center. "In the Battle of the Bulge, More Soldiers Than Successes." *Pew Research Center Publications.* Pew Research Center, 26 Apr. 2006. Web. 4 Apr. 2012.

"Physical Fitness Trumps Body Weight in Reducing Death Risks, Study Finds." *Science Daily.* Science Daily, 5 Dec. 2011. Web. 4 Apr. 2012.

Putnam, Robert D. *Bowling Alone: The Collapse and Revival of American Community.* New York: Touchstone-Simon and Schuster, 2001. Print.

Sisson, Mary. "Gyms Dandy." *Crain's New York Business* 26 Aug. 2002: 1–2. *Regional Business News.* Web. 3 Apr. 2012.

Smits, Jasper A. J., and Michael W. Otto. *Exercise for Mood and Anxiety.* New York: Oxford UP, 2011. Print.

Stern, Marc. "The Fitness Movement and the Fitness Center Industry, 1960–2000." *Business and Economic History On-Line* 6 (2008): 1–26. Business History Conference. Web. 5 Apr. 2012.

READING FOR MEANING

This section presents three activities that will help you think about the meanings in McClain's causal argument. Your instructor may ask you to do one or more of these activities in class or online.

For more help with summarizing, see Chapter 10, pp. 518–19.

1. **Read to Summarize.** Write a sentence or two explaining why McClain believes that the "fitness culture" has been growing.

Take a quiz to check your reading and vocabulary comprehension:
bedfordstmartins.com/readingcritically

2. **Read to Respond.** Write a paragraph analyzing your reactions to McClain's essay. For example, consider anything that resonates with your experience or that seems contradictory, surprising, or fascinating, such as:

   - McClain's argument that 9/11 could be one of the causes of this trend;
   - Your own experience — if you have any — with fitness clubs. Does it square with McClain's argument?

3. **Read to Analyze Assumptions.** Write a paragraph or two analyzing an assumption you find intriguing in McClain's essay. For example:

   Assumptions about the attractiveness of fitness clubs. Throughout her essay, McClain presents causes for increasing membership at U.S. fitness clubs. She argues that they may "fulfill the basic human desire for a sense of community and belonging" (par. 4), and they provide friends and "positive peer pressure" (par. 4). To think critically about the assumptions in this essay regarding the appeal of fitness clubs, ask yourself questions like these:

   - Whether or not you are a member of a fitness club, how convincing are the reasons McClain offers for increasing membership? What other reasons might explain this trend?
   - Do fitness clubs mirror the neighborhoods in which they are located? If they do, how might the causes for their appeal differ?

   Assumptions about people's motivations to exercise. McClain claims that people who are motivated to exercise to improve their body image are unlikely to sustain an exercise regimen (par. 6). She also states that "'No pain, no gain' used to be synonymous with exercise" (par. 7) and that such conditions kept people away from exercising, but that "today exercise [at fitness clubs] comes in many different forms, many of which are more engaging and gentler than in the past. The variety may also appeal to a wider range of people" (par. 7). To think critically about the assumptions in this essay regarding motivations to exercise, ask yourself questions like these:

   - Why might having fun while exercising be a better motivator than vanity?
   - Do you agree with Harton (McClain's exercise physiology professor) that people who exercise only to achieve a more attractive body are less likely to sustain exercise? Why or why not?

A Special Reading Strategy

Evaluating the Logic of an Argument

To **evaluate the logic of an argument** speculating about causes or effects, ask yourself three basic questions:

- How appropriate is the support for each cause or effect being speculated about?
- How believable is the support?
- How consistent and complete is the overall argument?

Such an evaluation requires a comprehensive and thoughtful critical reading, but your efforts will help you understand more fully what makes a causal argument successful. To evaluate the logic of McClain's argument, follow the guidelines in Chapter 10 (pp. 530–32). There you will find definitions and explanations as well as an illustration based on an excerpt from a famous essay by Martin Luther King Jr. (The excerpt appears on pp. 509–14).

READING LIKE A WRITER

ESTABLISHING CREDIBILITY TO PRESENT THE WRITER AS THOUGHTFUL AND FAIR

On a topic of national interest like the causes of the fitness culture, writers either have to be expert in the subject or have to do research to become expert enough to convince their readers that they should be taken seriously. To seem credible

- they must not oversimplify, trivialize, or stereotype their subject;
- they must not overlook possible objections or alternative causes or effects that will occur to readers;
- they must show that they have thought about their subject deeply and seriously.

Analyze & Write

Write a paragraph or two analyzing McClain's strategies to establish her credibility:

1. Reread "Fitness Culture: A Growing Trend in America," and annotate it for evidence of credibility or lack of it. How knowledgeable does McClain seem about the subject? Which paragraph most impresses you with her authority?

Where does her argument seem thin? Consider especially how she presents the subject and trend in paragraph 1 with its accompanying chart (fig. 1). Assess the sources she relies on and how effectively she uses them.

2. Consider how McClain's response to an alternative argument (par. 6) influences your judgment of her credibility.

3. Examine McClain's approach to readers. What assumptions does she make about their knowledge and beliefs? What attitude does she have toward her readers?

Reviewing What Makes Speculative Arguments Effective

Writers of essays speculating about causes or effects

- present the subject fairly;

- make a logical, well-supported cause or effect argument;

- respond to readers' likely objections or alternative speculations;

- establish their credibility.

Analyze & Write

Write a brief evaluation—positive, negative, or mixed—of one of the readings in this chapter, explaining why you think it succeeds or fails as an argument speculating about causes or effects. Be sure to consider the characteristics that distinguish cause or effect writing, as well as how successful the writer has been in communicating his or her purpose to the intended audience. You may also want to consider the effect the medium of presentation had on decisions the writer made.

A GUIDE TO WRITING ESSAYS SPECULATING ABOUT CAUSES OR EFFECTS

As you've read and discussed the reading selections in this chapter, you have probably done a good deal of analytical writing. Your instructor may assign a capstone project of your own to write a brief speculative essay arguing for your preferred causes or effects of an event, a phenomenon, or a trend. Having learned how writers present the subject, support and defend their preferred causes or effects, and persuade their readers that they are credible, you can now approach arguments speculating about causes or effects confidently as a writer. This Guide to Writing offers detailed suggestions for writing such arguments and resources to help you meet the special challenges this kind of writing presents.

THE WRITING ASSIGNMENT

Write an essay arguing for your preferred causes or effects for an event, a phenomenon, or a trend.

- Choose a subject that invites you to speculate about its causes or effects: why it may have happened or what its effects may be.

- Research the subject, gathering detailed information from appropriate sources, and present that information in a clear, logical way.

- Establish the existence and significance of the subject.

- Convince readers that the causes or effects you propose are more plausible than the alternatives.

WRITING A DRAFT

INVENTION, PLANNING, AND COMPOSING

The following activities will help you find a subject, consider what you and your readers need to know, determine your approach — cause or effect — and gather and sort through the information you need to present your speculation clearly, logically, and convincingly. To achieve these goals, you might analyze opposing arguments to identify potential areas of agreement based on shared concerns and values and overlapping interests and priorities. Writers strive not only to understand why people disagree, but also to find points on which they may agree — **common ground**.

Choosing a Subject

Rather than limiting yourself to the first subject that comes to mind, take a few minutes to consider your options. When choosing a subject, keep in mind that it must be

- one that you can show exists (such as with examples or statistics);
- one that has no definitive, proven cause or effect;
- one that you can research, as necessary, in the time you have;
- one that will puzzle — or at least interest — you and your readers.

Here are some ideas that may help you find a subject.

Trends

- changing patterns in leisure, entertainment, lifestyle, religious life, health, or technology
- completed artistic or historical trends (art movements or historical changes)
- long-term changes in economic conditions or political behavior or attitudes

Events

- a recent national or international event that is surrounded by confusion or controversy
- a recent surprising or controversial event at your college or in your community, such as the closing of a tutorial or health service, the loss of a game by a favored team, a change in traffic or zoning rules, or the banning of a book from school libraries
- a historical event about which there is still some dispute as to its causes or effects

Phenomena

- a social problem, such as discrimination, homelessness, high-school or college dropout rates, youth suicides, or teenage pregnancy
- one or more aspects of college life, such as libraries too noisy to study in, large classes, lack of financial aid, difficulties in scheduling classes, or insufficient availability of housing
- a human trait, such as anxiety, selfishness, fear of success or failure, leadership, jealousy, insecurity, envy, opportunism, curiosity, or restlessness

Because an authoritative essay arguing for preferred causes or effects requires sustained thinking, drafting, revising, and possibly research, you will want to choose a subject for which you have enough time and interest.

Consider carefully whether you are more interested in the causes or the effects of the event, trend, or phenomenon. Some subjects may invite speculation about either their causes or their effects, while others may preclude speculation about one or the other. For example, you could speculate about the causes of increasing membership in your church, whereas the effects of the increase might for now be so uncertain as to discourage plausible speculation. Some subjects invite speculation about both their causes and their effects. For this assignment, however, you need not do both.

You may find it useful to frame your topic in question form:

▶ Cause: Why is .... the most popular major at College X?

▶ Effect: How will the cancellation of the .... at X University affect students' employment prospects after graduation?

Making a chart listing subjects that interest you and their possible causes or effects can help you decide which subject is most promising.

Subject	*Possible Causes or Effects*
Example: Why do students often procrastinate in writing papers or studying for exams?	They have better things to do.
	The project seems overwhelming.
	They have many responsibilities and the one with the latest deadline suffers / the most difficult task gets done last.
	They are lazy.
Example: What would be the effect of making all science classes in middle school gender-specific?	Children might perform better.
	Courses for boys (or girls) might receive better funding.
	Children may not get used to studying side by side with children of the other sex and face more difficulties in high school or college.
	The types of instruction boys and girls receive may differ.

Analyzing Your Readers

Now that you have a potential subject, write for a few minutes, analyzing your potential readers.

● What might my potential readers already know about the event, phenomenon, or trend? (Even if you are writing only for your instructor, you should consider what he or she knows about your subject.)

- What kinds of examples or information could I provide that readers will find new, useful, interesting, or amusing? How might I clarify misconceptions or faulty assumptions?

- Will a more or less formal writing style be appropriate for my readers?

- What kinds of sources will my readers find credible?

- What questions might they ask? What might they be interested in learning more about?

Exploring Your Subject

You may discover that you know more about your subject than you suspect if you write about it for a few minutes without stopping. This brief sustained writing will stimulate your memory, help you probe your interest in the subject, and enable you to test your choice. As you write, consider the following questions:

- What about this subject interests me? What about it will interest my readers?

  ▶ I think the [subject] is important because ....

  ▶ My readers are likely to be curious about the subject because .... [Examples: it affects them personally/it raises important moral, psychological, or other questions they will find intriguing].

- What do I already know about the subject? What do my readers already know?

  ▶ I know what the obvious causes of [the subject] are, but I'm curious about the underlying [cultural/psychological/ideological] causes because ....

  ▶ The subject [has been in the news or is so well-known] that I expect my readers will know .... but not ....

Considering Causes or Effects

Discovering and analyzing the causes or effects you can already imagine can give your research (should you need to conduct research) direction and can also help you develop a list of the most (and least) plausible ones.

Discovering Causes or Effects. Brainstorm a list of possible causes or effects. For causes, consider underlying or background causes as well as immediate or instigating causes. For example, say you have noticed that the number of students in your classes has increased sharply in the past year.

- An underlying cause could be that a few years ago the voters in your state passed a bill that sharply reduced income for public colleges, and now the effects are beginning to show;

- An immediate cause could be that the college has had to lay off one-third of its faculty.

For effects, consider both short-term and long-term consequences, as well as how one effect may lead to another in a kind of chain reaction. Try to think of obvious causes or effects and also of those that are likely to be overlooked in a superficial analysis of your subject.

Considering how your subject is similar to or different from related subjects may also help you come up with causes or effects to add to your list:

▶ .... [name subject] is like .... [name other subject] in that they are both caused by ....

▶ Whereas .... [the other subject] is .... , ... [my subject] is ....

Conducting Research. Research can give you a greater understanding of an event, trend, or phenomenon and may suggest to you plausible causes or effects you have overlooked. (In addition, you may find support for your responses to readers' objections or to others' proposed causes or effects.) Enter keywords or phrases related to your cause or effect subject into the search box of

- an all-purpose database such as *Academic OneFile* (InfoTrac) or *Academic Search Complete* (EBSCOHost) to find relevant articles in magazines and journals

- a database like *LexisNexis* to find articles in newspapers

- a search engine like *Google* or *Yahoo!* to find relevant Web sites, blogs, podcasts, and discussion lists

To learn more about finding sources, consult Chapter 11, pp. 548–54.

- your library's catalog or WorldCat (www.worldcat.org) to find books and other resources on your topic

To locate numerical or statistical evidence that you could use as evidence or to draw graphs or tables, try the following sites:

- U.S. government official Web portal (www.usa.gov); for information about the federal government

- Library of Congress page on state government information (www.loc.gov/rr /news/stategov/stategov.html); follow the links for information on state and local government

- U.S. Census Bureau (www.census.gov), especially the Quick Facts and Fact Finder pages and the Statistical Abstracts for various years (to compare years); for demographic information

- Centers for Disease Control and Prevention (www.cdc.gov), especially the FastStats pages; for statistics about diseases and illnesses

- National Center for Education Statistics (nces.ed.gov); for reports such as "America's Youth: Transitions to Adulthood"

- Pew Research Center (www.pewresearch.org); for research data or public opinion polling data
- Rasmussen Reports (www.rasmussenreports.com), or Gallup (www .gallup.com); for public opinion polling data

Bookmark or keep a record of the URLs of promising sites. If you find useful information, you may want to download or copy information to use in your essay. When available, download PDF files rather than HTML files, because PDFs are likely to include visuals such as graphs and charts. If you copy and paste relevant information from sources into your notes, be careful to distinguish carefully between all material from sources and your own ideas. Remember to record source information with care and to cite and document any sources you use, including visuals and interviews.

For more on field research, turn to Chapter 11, pp. 555–67.

Another option is to conduct field research and use personal experience.

Analyzing Causes or Effects. Once you have come up with a number of causes or effects, identify the most convincing (and surprising) ones. Remember that cause or effect essays often speculate about several possible causes or effects but usually also argue for one that is especially interesting or plausible. You may want to try several of the sentence strategies below to help you determine which of your causes or effects will be most convincing:

- ▶ Why do I/my readers think .... [cause] could have resulted in .... [name subject]?
- ▶ Why do I/my readers think .... [effect] could have caused .... [name subject]?
- ▶ Is .... [cause] necessary to bring about .... [effect]; that is, could .... [effect] not happen without it? Is .... [cause] sufficient—enough in itself—to cause .... [effect]?
- ▶ Is .... [effect] inevitable for .... [cause]; are other effects more plausible?
- ▶ If .... [cause] is one of several contributing factors, what role does it play? For example, is it a minor or major cause, an obvious or hidden cause, a triggering cause (the one that got the cause-effect process started) or a continuing cause (the one that keeps it going)?
- ▶ If .... [effect] is one of several, what role does it play? Is it a minor effect, not very important, or is it a major effect not given proper attention?
- ▶ What kinds of evidence could I use to argue in favor of or to argue against .... [cause/effect]?

Now classify the causes or effects you plan to discuss in your essay into three categories: plausible cause(s) or effect(s) you want to argue for, causes or effects your readers may favor that you can concede but put aside as obvious or minor, and causes or effects you should refute because your readers are likely to think they are important.

Plausible Causes to Argue For	Readers' Causes to Concede/Put Aside	Readers' Causes to Refute

Remember that the only category you *must* include in your essay is the first: one or more causes or effects you will argue played a major, and perhaps, surprising role.

Considering Your Purpose

Write for several minutes about your purpose for writing this essay. The following questions will help you think about your purpose:

- What do I hope to accomplish with my readers? What one big idea do I want them to grasp and remember?

- How can I interest readers in my subject? How can I help them see its importance or significance? How can I convince them to take my speculations seriously?

- How much resistance should I expect from readers to each of the causes or effects I propose? Will my readers be largely receptive? Skeptical but convincible? Resistant and perhaps even antagonistic?

Formulating a Working Thesis Statement

Once you have identified one or more interesting and plausible causes or effects that could be the focus of your analysis, try drafting a working thesis. To get an idea about how you might formulate your thesis, take a look at the thesis statements from the reading selections you've studied in this chapter. Here are two:

> The mythic horror movie, like the sick joke, has a dirty job to do. It deliberately appeals to all that is worst in us. It is morbidity unchained, our most base instincts let free, our nastiest fantasies realized . . . and it all happens, fittingly enough, in the dark. (King, par. 12)

> We all know why we should exercise, but why join a fitness club? Some of the answers may surprise you — such as to be part of a community, to reduce stress, to improve your body image, and simply to have fun. (McClain, par. 4)

Now draft your own thesis statement, either using the sentence strategies below as a jumping-off point (you can put them into your own words when you revise) or using your own words and sentence patterns:

- ▶ The cause(s)/effect(s) of .... may be [surprising/alarming/disturbing/amazing], but they are clear: .... [state cause(s) or effect(s)].

- ▶ .... [state cause or effect] plays a [surprising/alarming/disturbing/amazing] role in [our lives/our families/our communities/our workplaces]: It [does/is/provides] .... [describe role].

- ▶ For many years, [name group] has believed that .... Now there is research supporting this claim, but not for the reasons you may think. It's not .... that has been causing this phenomenon but .... / It's not .... that has resulted from .... , it's ....

Working with Sources
Citing a Variety of Sources

Writers of essays speculating about causes or effects often rely on evidence from experts to support some causes or effects and refute others. For college assignments, your instructor may require that certain kinds of sources be used and may even specify that you should not consult sources. But for most writing situations, you will have to decide whether sources will make your speculations more convincing, what types of sources might be appropriate, and how many would be sufficient. Using too few sources or sources that are too narrow in scope can undercut the persuasiveness or credibility of your analysis. Consequently, it can be important to offer information from a number of sources and from sources that reflect a variety of areas of expertise.

Look, for example, at Sheila McClain's essay, "Fitness Culture: A Growing Trend in America" (pp. 418–22). McClain uses a number of different sources to support her causal analysis. Because she is writing for a class, McClain includes both in-text citations and a list of works cited. She uses signal phrases to provide the credentials of her sources. McClain uses health club statistics from industry Web sites, but she does not rely solely — or even primarily — on industry or business sources. She also cites independent sources her readers are likely to find credible, such as the Pew Research Center, a university press book, and several newspaper and academic articles. McClain also refers to an

(continued)

interview she did with her exercise physiology professor. The number of sources, their authority, and their variety lend credibility to McClain's own speculations.

As you determine how many and what kinds of sources to cite in your essay, keep in mind that readers of essays speculating about causes or effects are more likely to be persuaded if the sources you rely on are neither too few nor too narrowly focused. If, when you begin to draft, you find that your research seems skimpy, you may need to do further research.

Responding to Readers' Likely Objections or Preferred Causes

When drafting a response to objections that readers are likely to raise, or causes your readers are likely to prefer, start by analyzing your readers' likely reasons, and then consider ways you might respond:

Analyzing and Responding to Your Readers' Likely Objections. For each of your preferred causes or effects, consider the questions your readers might raise. Some possibilities include the following:

▸ Even if you can prove that .... and .... increased/decreased at the same time, how do you know .... actually caused/resulted from .... ?

▸ Even if you can prove that .... occurred after ...., how do you know that .... actually caused/resulted from ....? Could .... have been caused by/have resulted from something else altogether?

▸ .... seems to have been a cause/effect of ...., but was it really a major cause/effect or just one of many contributing factors?

Now consider how you might respond to the strongest of your readers' likely objections:

▸ The objection that .... can be caused by/can result from things other than .... may be true. But there is strong evidence showing that .... played a central role by ....

▸ Researchers studying .... have shown a causal connection between .... and .... They claim .... [quote/paraphrase/summarize information from source] (cite source).

▸ A large number of people have been polled on this question, and it appears that .... was an important factor in their decision to ....

Refuting or Conceding Readers' Preferred Causes or Effects

In the preceding section, you analyzed and drafted a response to the objections your readers are likely to raise. Now determine how you might respond to, concede, or refute your readers' preferred causes or effects.

First, choose an alternative cause or effect, and summarize it. Be sure to summarize it accurately and fairly. Do not commit the **"straw man" fallacy** of knocking down something that no one really takes seriously.

To learn more about fallacies, see Chapter 10, pp. 532–36.

Next, decide whether you can refute the alternative cause or effect or you need to concede it. Refute it if you can show that the alternative cause or effect lacks credible support or if the reasoning underlying the cause or effect is flawed.

▶ The .... [scenario or anecdote] others sometimes give to support this cause/effect certainly helps dramatize the subject, but it doesn't really explain ....

▶ If .... caused/resulted from ...., then one would expect .... to happen, but [it hasn't/the opposite has happened].

▶ The research showing .... is questionable because it is based on [a small or unrepresentative sample/anecdotal evidence].

Concede it by pointing out that the cause or effect is obvious and setting it aside, or by showing that it plays a less important role than the cause or effect you are championing.

▶ An obvious explanation is .... But if we dig deeper, we find that ....

▶ .... is one of the answers, but may actually not play as central a role as most people think it does.

▶ .... may have kept the process going, but .... was the trigger: Without it, ... [subject] would never have gotten started.

Including Visuals or Other Media

If appropriate to your rhetorical situation, consider whether visuals — especially tables and static or animated graphics — would strengthen your argument. You could construct your own visuals, scan materials from books and magazines, or download them from the Internet.

Note: Be sure to cite the source of visual or audio elements you did not create, and get permission from the source if your essay is going to be published on a Web site that is not password-protected.

Organizing Your Speculative Argument Effectively for Your Readers

Whether you have rough notes or a complete draft, making an outline of what you have written can help you organize your essay effectively for your audience. You may want to draft a sentence that forecasts the elements of your argument to alert your readers to your main points (and give yourself a tentative outline). Putting your points in a logical order (from least to most effective, for example) will make it easier for you to guide your readers from point to point. A cause or effect analysis may contain as many as four basic parts:

1. a presentation of the subject

2. plausible causes or effects, logically sequenced

3. convincing support for each cause or effect

4. a consideration of readers' questions, objections, and alternative causes or effects

These parts can be organized in various ways: If your readers are not likely to agree with your speculations about causes or effects, you may want to anticipate and respond to their possible objections just before you present the evidence in favor of your argument. If you expect readers *are* likely to favor your speculations, you may want to concede or refute alternatives after offering your own reasons. Either way, you may want to emphasize the common ground you share and conclude by emphasizing that your argument takes into account your shared values. You might want to make two or three different outlines before choosing the organization that looks most promising.

For more on outlining, see Chapter 10, pp. 515–17. Never be a slave to an outline: As you draft, you may see ways to improve your original plan, and you should be ready to revise your outline, shift parts around, or drop or add parts as needed. If you use the outlining function of your word processing program, changing your outline will be easy, and you may be able to write the essay simply by expanding that outline.

Drafting Your Cause or Effect Argument

By this point, you have done a lot of writing

- to present the subject fairly;

- to make a logical argument and support your preferred causes or effects with evidence your readers will find persuasive;

- to respond to objections and alternative speculations;

- to establish your credibility by presenting yourself as thoughtful and fair.

Now stitch that material together to create a draft. The next two parts of this Guide to Writing will help you evaluate and improve it.

Considering a Useful Sentence Strategy

As you draft your essay, you will want to help your readers recognize the stages of your argument and the support you offer for each proposed cause or effect. One effective way to do so is to use clear topic sentences, especially ones that are grammatically parallel.

Topic sentences usually open the paragraph or are placed early in the paragraph. They can announce a new cause or effect, introduce responses to readers' likely objections or alternative causes or effects, or identify different parts of the support for a cause, an effect, or a response. Topic sentences may also include key terms that you introduced in a thesis statement at the beginning of the essay, and they may take identical or similar sentence forms so that readers can recognize them more easily.

The following topic sentences from Stephen King's essay identify what King believes to be the three main causes for many moviegoers' attraction to horror movies:

> To show that we can, that we are not afraid, that we can ride this roller coaster. (par. 3)
>
> We also go to re-establish our feelings of essential normality . . . (par. 4)
>
> And we go to have fun. (par. 5)

King assists readers in identifying each new stage of his argument by introducing the grammatical subject *we* in the first topic sentence and then repeating it to signal the next two stages: "we can," "We also go," "And we go." He also uses verbs in the infinitive form: *To show, to re-establish, to have fun.*

While King relies on topic sentences within paragraphs to signal the stages in his argument (as do all the writers in this chapter), Carr uses them also to signal a change from citing his own personal experience as evidence to citing the experience of others. After his initial paragraph about HAL, the computer that is being dismantled in *2001*, Carr introduces each of the next four paragraphs with a reference to himself:

> I can feel it, too. (par. 2)
>
> I think I know what's going on. (par. 3)
>
> For me, as for others, the Net is becoming a universal medium, the conduit for most of the information that flows through my eyes and ears and into my mind. (par. 4)
>
> I'm not the only one. (par. 5)

Like King's, these topic sentences are not strictly parallel grammatically, but three of them create a parallel effect because they are all very short

(continued)

and begin with *I*. In the last two, Carr begins to refer to the experiences of others as well as himself. After that, his essay proceeds with little reference to himself and a great deal of support—as well as responses to alternative arguments—from third parties.

EVALUATING THE DRAFT

GETTING A CONSTRUCTIVE CRITICAL READING

Getting a critical reading of your draft will help you see how to improve it. Your instructor may schedule class time for reading drafts, or you may want to ask a classmate or a tutor in the writing center to read your draft. Ask your reader to use the following guidelines and to write out a response for you to consult during your revision.

READING A DRAFT CRITICALLY

Read for a First Impression

1. **Read the draft without stopping, and then write a few sentences giving your general impression.**

2. **Identify one aspect of the draft that seems particularly effective.**

Read Again to Suggest Improvements

1. **Recommend ways to make the presentation of the subject more effective.**

   - Read the opening paragraphs that present the subject to be speculated about, and then tell the writer what you find most interesting and useful there.

   - Point out one or two places where a reader unfamiliar with the subject might need more information.

   - Suggest ways the writer could make the subject seem more interesting or significant.

   - If the subject is a trend, explain what you understand to be the increase or decrease and let the writer know whether you think further evidence is required to demonstrate conclusively that the subject is indeed a trend.

   - If the beginning seems unlikely to engage readers, suggest at least one other way of beginning.

2. **Suggest ways to strengthen the cause or effect argument.**

   - List the causes or effects. Are there too many, too few, or just about the right number? Identify any cause or effect that seems especially imaginative or surprising and any that seems too obvious. Make suggestions for dropping or adding causes or effects.

   - Evaluate the support for each cause or effect separately. To help the writer make every cause or effect plausible to his or her intended readers, point out where the support seems thin or inadequate, irrelevant, hard to believe, or inconsistent with other support. Consider whether the writer has overlooked important sources of support: anecdotes, examples, statistics, analogies, or quotations from publications or interviews.

3. **Suggest ways to strengthen the responses to alternative arguments.**

   - Locate every instance of response to readers' objections or their preferred alternative causes or effects. Mark these in the margin of the draft. Review these as a set, and then suggest objections and alternative causes or effects the writer seems to have overlooked.

   - Identify responses that seem weakly supported, and suggest ways to strengthen the support.

   - If any of the refutations attack or ridicule readers, suggest ways the writer could refute without insulting or unduly irritating readers.

4. **Suggest how credibility can be enhanced.**

   - Tell the writer where the intended readers are likely to find the essay most or least knowledgeable and authoritative.

   - Identify places where the writer seeks common ground — shared values, beliefs, and attitudes — with readers. Try to identify other places where the writer might do so.

5. **Suggest how the organizational plan could be improved.**

   - Indicate whether a thesis is needed or whether it could be improved; consider whether a forecasting statement is needed.

   - Consider the overall plan, perhaps by making a scratch outline (see Chapter 10, pp. 515–17).

   - Analyze the progression of the proposed causes or effects, and decide whether they follow a logical sequence. If not, suggest ways they might be more logically sequenced, such as by putting them in chronological order or the order of their importance.

(continued)

- Review the places where responses to alternative arguments appear and consider whether they are smoothly woven into the writer's argument. If not, suggest places where he or she might move them.

- Indicate where new or better transitions might clearly cue the steps in the argument and keep readers on track.

6. **Evaluate the effectiveness of visuals.**

- Look at any visuals in the essay, and tell the writer what they contribute to your understanding of the writer's speculations.

- If any visuals do not seem relevant, explain your thinking.

IMPROVING THE DRAFT

REVISING, EDITING, AND PROOFREADING

Start improving your draft by reflecting on what you have written thus far:

- Review critical reading comments from your classmates, instructor, or writing center tutor. What are your readers getting at?

- Take another look at your notes and ideas. What else should you consider?

- Review your draft: What else can you do to make your essay clearer and more convincing to your readers?

Revising Your Draft

Revising means reenvisioning your draft, trying to see it in a new way, given your purpose and readers, in order to strengthen your cause or effect argument. Think imaginatively and boldly about cutting unconvincing material, adding new material, and moving material around. The suggestions in the chart that follows may help you solve problems and strengthen your essay.

TROUBLESHOOTING YOUR DRAFT

To Present the Subject More Effectively

Problem	Suggestions for Revising
Readers unfamiliar with the subject don't understand it readily.	• Provide more introductory information about the subject.
The significance of the subject is not clear.	• Dramatize its significance with an anecdote. • Highlight its social or cultural implications.
The subject is a trend, but its existence is not established.	• Show evidence of a significant increase or decrease over time. • Include a graphic to make the trend visible.

To Strengthen the Cause or Effect Argument

Problem	Suggestions for Revising
There are too many proposed causes or effects.	• Clarify the role of each one and the way it is related to others. • Drop one or more that seem too obvious, obscure, or minor.
A cause or effect lacks adequate support.	• Provide further examples, anecdotes, statistics, or quotations from authorities. • Drop it if you cannot find more support.

To Strengthen the Responses to Alternative Views

Problem	Suggestions for Revising
A likely question or objection readers will have is not addressed.	• Add information to answer the question. • Accommodate the objection by conceding the point and making it part of your own argument. • Refute the objection, arguing that it need not be taken seriously.
An alternative cause or effect readers would propose is not addressed.	• Concede or refute it.
Readers are attacked or ridiculed in a refutation.	• Refute ideas decisively while showing respect for your readers as people. • Use the sentence strategy of concession and refutation (pp. 367–68).

To Enhance Credibility

Problem	Suggestions for Revising
The essay does not establish common ground with readers.	• Figure out what you might have in common with your audience—some shared values, attitudes, or beliefs—and include them in your argument.
Readers question your credibility.	• Learn more about your subject, and use what you learn to support your argument more fully. • Address more of readers' likely questions, objections, and alternatives. • Talk with others who can help you think more imaginatively about your speculations. • Adjust your tone to make it civil and to clarify that you respect those who hold alternative views.

To Make the Organization More Effective

Problem	Suggestions for Revising
The causes or effects are not presented in a logical sequence.	• Change the sequence into some kind of logical order, such as chronological or least to most effective. You may find that you need to add or drop certain causes or effects.
Connections between ideas are not clear.	• Provide clearer transitions (*first, second, moreover, in addition*) to guide readers from one step in the argument to the next. • Use clear topic sentences to signal the stages of your argument and the support you provide for each cause or effect.
Your responses to alternative arguments are introduced awkwardly or unexpectedly.	• Move them around or add transitions to integrate them more smoothly.

Editing and Proofreading Your Draft

Check for errors in usage, punctuation, and mechanics, and consider matters of style. If you keep a list of errors you typically make, begin by checking your draft against this list. Ask someone else to proofread your essay before you submit it to your instructor.

From our research on student writing, we know that essays speculating about causes or effects have a high percentage of errors in the use of numbers and "reason is because" sentences. Because writers are usually drawn into "reason is because" sentences when making a causal argument, you will need to know options for revising such sentences. And, because you must usually rely on numbers to present statistics when you support your argument or demonstrate the existence of a trend, you will need to learn and follow the conventions for presenting different kinds of numbers. Check a writer's handbook for help with these potential problems.

Reflecting on What You Have Learned

Speculating about Causes or Effects

In this chapter, you have read critically several essays that speculate about causes or effects and have written one of your own. To better remember what you have learned, pause now to reflect on the reading and writing activities you completed in this chapter.

1. Write a page or so reflecting on what you have learned. Begin by describing what you are most pleased with in your essay. Then explain what you think contributed to your achievement. Be specific about this contribution.

   - If it was something you learned from the readings, indicate which readings and specifically what you learned from them.

   - If it came from your invention writing, point out the section or sections that helped you most.

   - If you got good advice from a critical reader, explain exactly how the person helped you — perhaps by helping you understand a problem in your draft or by helping you add a new dimension to your writing.

   - Try to write about your achievement in terms of what you have learned about the genre.

2. Reflect more generally on speculating about causes or effects, a genre of writing that plays an important role in social life and public policy in the United States. Consider some of the following questions:

   - Do you tend to adopt a tentative or an assertive stance when making such speculations about public issues? Why?

(*continued*)

- How might your personal preferences and values influence your speculations about, for example, the causes of health-care cost inflation or the effects of same-sex marriage? How about your gender, ethnicity, religious beliefs, age, or social class?

- What contribution might writing that speculates about causes or effects make to our society that other genres cannot make?

Proposal to Solve a Problem

A proposal can help us analyze a problem, evaluate the feasibility of alternative solutions, and ultimately move readers to take particular actions to solve the problem. Whether the proposal is written in college (for example, to research an indigenous language or to prohibit the sale of genetically manufactured foods on campus), in the broader community (for example, to install audible traffic signals for the visually impaired or to improve community policing), or in the workplace (for example, to bid for a service contract or to institute an employee wellness program), proposals enable us to take pragmatic action to address pressing problems.

This chapter offers several brief proposals for you to enjoy and analyze, with exploratory activities that will help you learn to read critically and write well. The Reading for Meaning and Reading Like a Writer activities following each selection invite you to analyze and write about the reading's ideas and writing strategies. You can also use the brief Guide to Writing toward the end of the chapter to help you identify a problem you care about and write a proposal to solve it.

RHETORICAL SITUATIONS FOR PROPOSALS

Proposals appear in a wide variety of contexts and media. Here are just a few examples:

- A blogger posts a proposal to solve the problem of the rising college loan default rate, which she illustrates with statistics and graphs from the U.S. Department of Education and a recent Senate report. She concedes one reason why the problem is worst at for-profit colleges: they enroll a larger proportion of working parents and first-generation college students — who have greater financial challenges compared to the majority of traditional public and private college students. Nevertheless, the blogger argues that many for-profit colleges make the problem worse by using advertising to lure potential students with the promise of a college program many students cannot complete and a well-paying job the colleges cannot guarantee. She proposes that truth-in-advertising laws be used to crack down on the aggressive recruiting tactics of for-profits that target low-income students.

• Frustrated by what they see as the failure of local high schools to prepare students for the workplace, several department managers of a pharmaceutical company, along with the firm's lead technical writer, develop a proposal to move vocational and technical training out of an ill-equipped high-school system and onto the plant's floor. They read about other on-the-job training programs, and interview selected high-school teachers and current employees who attended the high-school program they want to replace. After several weeks' research, they present to the company's chief executive officer and to the school board a proposal that includes their reasons, plus a timetable for implementing their solution and a detailed budget.

• For a political science class, a college student proposes that a direct popular vote replace the Electoral College system for electing the president because the Electoral College is undemocratic. He points out that several times in our history, for example in 2000, a candidate who lost the popular vote has become president. The fact that most states allocate electors on a winner-take-all basis, with all of the state's votes going to the winner even if the margin of victory is 50.1 percent to 49.9 percent, makes the system especially undemocratic. The student argues that using the direct popular vote instead would be the surest and simplest way to solve the problem, and voters would be likely to support this solution because it is based on the core American principle of "one person, one vote."

Thinking about the Genre

Proposals

Before studying a type of writing, it is useful to spend some time thinking about what you already know about it. You may have discussed with friends or seen online an idea you thought would help solve a problem. For class or at work, you may have written or read proposals.

Recall one occasion when you heard or read a proposal, or proposed a solution yourself orally or in writing. Use the following questions to develop your thoughts. Your instructor may ask you to write about your experience or discuss it with others in class or online.

• Who was the *audience*? How do you think communicating to this audience influenced what was told or how it was told? For example, if the audience was not personally affected by the problem, how were they inspired to care about solving the problem?

- What was the *purpose*? What did you — or the other writer or speaker — hope to achieve? For example, was the primary purpose to inspire the audience to vote a certain way or urge people in a position of power to take a particular action?

- How might a different audience or purpose have changed the proposal? For example, if the proposal were to be addressed to someone who could solve the problem, should it emphasize the proposed solution's feasibility or practicality? Also think about how changing the medium of presentation would affect the proposal. For example, if it were posted on a Web site, would it be desirable to link to a video showing how a similar solution works elsewhere?

A GUIDE TO READING PROPOSALS

This guide introduces you to proposal writing by inviting you to analyze a surprising proposal by David Bornstein, first by *reading for meaning* and then by *reading like a writer.*

- *Reading for meaning* will help you understand how Bornstein proposes to solve the problem of bullying.

- *Reading like a writer* will help you learn how Bornstein employs the strategies typical of proposal writing to makes his essay persuasive, such as

    1. demonstrating that the problem exists and is serious

    2. showing how his proposal would help solve the problem and is feasible

    3. responding to objections and alternative solutions

    4. organizing the proposal in a way that is clear, logical, and convincing

David Bornstein

Fighting Bullying with Babies

David Bornstein blogs regularly for the New York Times, *and his articles have appeared in other major venues as well. He has written several books about solving social problems, including* How to Change the World: Social Entrepreneurs and the Power of New Ideas *(2007) and* Social Entrepreneurship: What Everyone Needs to Know *(2010). The recipient of several awards (for example, from Duke University's Fuqua School of Business), Bornstein co-wrote the PBS documentary* To Our Credit *and founded Dowser.org to answer the question "Who's solving what and how?" Bornstein originally posted his proposal "Fighting Bullying with Babies" in 2010. We have converted Bornstein's links to in-text citations and have provided a list of the links at the end of the selection.*

- *Before you read, think about Bornstein's title and the tone created by his opening journalistic hook: "Imagine there was a cure for meanness. Well, maybe there is." Given his original* New York Times *blog audience, why do you think Bornstein begins his proposal this way?*

- *As you read, notice the two photographs we added from the Roots of Empathy site and consider what, if anything, they contribute to Bornstein's essay.*

1   Imagine there was a cure for meanness. Well, maybe there is. Lately, the issue of bullying has been in the news, sparked by the suicide of Tyler Clementi ("Tyler"), a gay college student who was a victim of cyber-bullying, and by a widely circulated *New York Times* article that focused on "mean girl" bullying in kindergarten (Paul). The federal government has identified bullying as a national problem. In August, it organized the first-ever "Bullying Prevention Summit," and it is now rolling out an anti-bullying campaign aimed at 5- to 8-year-old children (White House). This past month the Department of Education released a guidance letter ("Guidance") urging schools, colleges and universities to take bullying seriously, or face potential legal consequences.

2   The typical institutional response to bullying is to get tough. In the Tyler Clementi case, prosecutors are considering bringing hate-crime charges (Dolnick).[1] But programs like the one I want to discuss today show the potential of augmenting our innate impulses to care for one another instead of just falling back on punishment as a deterrent. And what's the secret formula? A baby.

3   We know that humans are hardwired to be aggressive and selfish. But a growing body of research is demonstrating that there is also a biological basis for human compassion (Angier). Brain scans reveal that when we contemplate violence done to others we activate the same regions in our brains that fire up when mothers gaze at their children, suggesting that caring for strangers may be instinctual. When we help others, areas of the brain associated with pleasure also light up. Research by Felix Warneken and Michael Tomasello indicates that toddlers as young as 18 months behave altruisti-

---

[1]Tyler Clementi's roommate, Dharun Ravi, was found guilty in March 2010 of fifteen counts, including invasion of privacy, tampering with evidence, and bias intimidation. [Editor's note]

cally. (If you want to feel good, watch one of their 15-second video clips [Warneken]. . . .)

More important, we are beginning to understand how to nurture this biological potential. It seems that it's not only possible to make people kinder, it's possible to do it systematically at scale—at least with school children. That's what one organization based in Toronto called Roots of Empathy has done. Roots of Empathy was founded in 1996 by Mary Gordon, an educator who had built Canada's largest network of school-based parenting and family-literacy centers after having worked with neglectful and abusive parents (Toronto District School Board). Gordon had found many of them to be lacking in empathy for their children. They hadn't developed the skill because they hadn't experienced or witnessed it sufficiently themselves. She envisioned Roots as a seriously proactive parent education program—one that would begin when the mothers- and fathers-to-be were in kindergarten. Since then, Roots has worked with more than 12,600 classes across Canada, and in recent years, the program has expanded to the Isle of Man, the United Kingdom, New Zealand, and the United States, where it currently operates in Seattle. Researchers have found that the program increases kindness and acceptance of others and decreases negative aggression.

Here's how it works: Roots arranges monthly class visits by a mother and her baby (who must be between two and four months old at the beginning of the school year). Each month, for nine months, a trained instructor guides a classroom using a standard curriculum that involves three 40-minute visits—a pre-visit, a baby visit, and a post-visit. The program runs from kindergarten to seventh grade. During the baby visits, the children sit around the baby and mother (sometimes it's a father) on a green blanket (which represents new life and nature) and they try to understand the baby's feelings. The instructor helps by labeling them. "It's a launch pad for them to understand their own feelings and the feelings of others," explains Gordon. "It carries over to the rest of class" (Gordon).

I have visited several public schools in low-income neighborhoods in Toronto to observe Roots of Empathy's work. What I find most fascinating is how the baby actually changes the children's behavior. Teachers have confirmed my impressions: tough kids smile, disruptive kids focus, shy kids open up. In a seventh grade class, I found 12-year-olds unabashedly singing nursery rhymes. The baby seems to act like a heart-softening magnet. No one fully understands why. Kimberly Schonert-Reichl, an applied developmental psychologist who is a professor at the University of British Columbia, has evaluated Roots of Empathy in four studies. "Do kids become more empathic and understanding? Do they become less aggressive and kinder to each other? The answer is yes and yes," she explained. "The question is why?" (Schonert-Reichl).

Photographs from the Roots of Empathy Web site showing the program in action

7   C. Sue Carter, a neurobiologist based at the University of Illinois at Chicago, who has conducted pioneering research into the effects of oxytocin, a hormone that has been linked with caring and trusting behavior, suspects that biology is playing a role in the program's impact (Angier). "This may be an oxytocin story," Carter told me. "I believe that being around the baby is somehow putting the children in a biologically different place. We don't know what that place is because we haven't measured it. However, if it works here as it does in other animals, we would guess that exposure to an infant would create a physiological state in which the children would be more social."

8   To parent well, you must try to imagine what your baby is experiencing. So the kids do a lot of "perspective taking." When the baby is too small to raise its own head, for example, the instructor asks the children to lay their heads on the blanket and look around from there. Perspective taking is the cognitive dimension of empathy—and like any skill it takes practice to master. Children learn strategies for comforting a crying baby. They learn that one must never shake a baby. They discover that everyone comes into the world with a different temperament, including themselves and their classmates. They see how hard it can be to be a parent, which helps them empathize with their own mothers and fathers. And they marvel at how capacity develops. Each month, the baby does something that it couldn't do during its last visit: roll over, crawl, sit up, maybe even begin walking. Witnessing the baby's triumphs—even something as small as picking up a rattle for the first time—the children will often cheer.

9   Ervin Staub, professor emeritus of psychology at the University of Massachusetts, has studied altruism in children and found that the best way to create a caring climate is to engage children collectively in an activity that benefits another human being ("Biographical Note"). In Roots, children are enlisted in each class to do something to care for the baby, whether it is

to sing a song, speak in a gentle voice, or make a "wishing tree." The results can be dramatic. In a study of first- to third-grade classrooms, Schonert-Reichl focused on the subset of kids who exhibited "proactive aggression"—the deliberate and cold-blooded aggression of bullies who prey on vulnerable kids (Schonert-Reichl et al.). Of those who participated in the Roots program, 88 percent decreased this form of behavior over the school year, while in the control group, only 9 percent did, and many actually increased it. Schonert-Reichl has reproduced these findings with fourth- to seventh-grade children in a randomized controlled trial. She also found that Roots produced significant drops in "relational aggression"—things like gossiping, excluding others, and backstabbing. Research also found a sharp increase in children's parenting knowledge. "Empathy can't be taught, but it can be caught," Gordon often says—and not just by children. "Programmatically my biggest surprise was that not only did empathy increase in children, but it increased in their teachers," she added. "And that, to me, was glorious, because teachers hold such sway over children."

When the program was implemented on a large scale across the province of Manitoba—it's now in 300 classrooms there—it achieved an   10
"effect size" that Rob Santos, the scientific director of Healthy Child Manitoba, said translates to reducing the proportion of students who get into fights from 15 percent to 8 percent, close to a 50 percent reduction (Healthy Child Manitoba). "For a program that costs only hundreds of dollars per child, the cost-benefit of preventing later problems that cost thousands of dollars per child, is obvious," said Santos. Follow-up studies have found that outcomes are maintained or enhanced three years after the program ends. "When you've got emotion and cognition happening at the same time, that's deep learning," explains Gordon. "That's learning that will last."

Links

Angier, Natalie. "The Biology behind the Milk of Human Kindness." *New York Times*. New York Times, 23 Nov. 2009. Web. 27 Mar. 2012.

Carter, Sue C. Personal interview. N.d.

Dolnick, Sam. "2 Linked to Suicide Case Withdraw from Rutgers." *New York Times*. New York Times, 29 Oct. 2010. Web. 27 Mar. 2012.

Gordon, Mary. Personal interview. N.d.

Healthy Child Manitoba. "Putting Children and Families First." Province of Manitoba, n.d. Web. 27 Mar. 2012.

Paul, Pamela. "The Playground Gets Even Tougher." *New York Times*. New York Times, 8 Oct. 2010. Web. 27 Mar. 2012.

"Roots of Empathy: From Research to Recognition." *Roots of Empathy*. Roots of Empathy, 2012. 27 Mar. 2012.

Schonert-Reichl, Kimberly. Personal interview. N.d.

Schonert-Reichl, Kimberly, et al. "Contextual Considerations in the Evaluation of a School-Based Social Emotional Competence Program." American Educational Research Association, Apr. 2009. Print.

Staub, Ervin. "Biographical Note." *Ervinstaub.com*. Ervinstaub.com, n.d. Web. 27 Mar. 2012.

Toronto District School Board. "Parenting and Family Literacy Centres." Toronto District School Board, n.d. Web. 27 Mar. 2012.

"Tyler Clementi." Times Topics. *New York Times*. New York Times, 16 Mar. 2012. Web. 27 Mar. 2012.

United States. Dept. of Education. "Guidance Targeting Harassment Outlines Local and Federal Responsibility." *Ed.gov*. Dept. of Education, 26 Oct. 2010. Web. 27 Mar. 2012.

———. Dept. of Health and Human Services. "Stop Bullying Now." *TFK Extra!* Health Resources and Services Administration, Dept. of Health and Human Services, n.d. Web. 27 Mar. 2012.

———. White House Conference on Bullying Prevention. *White House*. White House, 14 Oct. 2010. Web. 27 Mar. 2012.

Warneken, Felix. "Videoclips." Dept. of Developmental and Comparative Psychology, Max Planck Institute for Evolutionary Anthropology. Max Planck Institute, n.d. Web. 27 Mar. 2012.

Warneken, Felix, and Michael Tomasello. "Altruistic Helping in Human Infants and Young Chimpanzees." *Science* 311.5765 (2006): 1301–3. *Academic Search Complete*. Web. 27 Mar. 2012.

READING FOR MEANING

This section presents three activities that will help you think about the meanings in Bornstein's proposal. Your instructor may ask you to do one or more of these activities in class or online.

For more help with summarizing, see Chapter 10, pp. 518–19.

1. **Read to Summarize.** Reading to summarize involves asking yourself what the main point of the reading is. To explore Bornstein's proposal, write a sentence or two explaining how the proposed solution will help solve the bullying problem.

2. **Read to Respond.** Reading to respond asks you to explore your reactions to a text in light of your own knowledge or experience. To explore this proposal, write a paragraph analyzing your initial reactions to Bornstein's blog post. For example, consider anything that resonates with your experience or that seems contradictory, surprising, or fascinating, such as:

   - The fact that "a guidance letter" was sent to urge "schools, colleges and universities to take bullying seriously" (par. 1), perhaps in relation to how schools you're familiar with handle the problem of bullying;

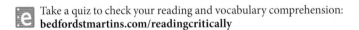 Take a quiz to check your reading and vocabulary comprehension:
bedfordstmartins.com/readingcritically

- The research Bornstein cites to show that the children taking part in the Roots program "become less aggressive and kinder to each other" (par. 6), focusing on one of the program's methods you find intriguing.

3. **Read to Analyze Assumptions. Assumptions** are ideas, beliefs, or values that are taken for granted as commonly accepted truths. The assumptions in a text usually reflect the writer's own attitudes or cultural traditions, but they may also represent other people's views. Reading to analyze assumptions asks you to uncover these perspectives as well as to probe your own. Sometimes the assumptions are stated explicitly, but often you will have to infer them (or figure them out) because they are only implied or hinted at through the writer's choice of words or examples. Write a paragraph or two analyzing an assumption you find intriguing in Bornstein's essay. For example:

Assumptions about bullying. When Bornstein asserts as common knowledge the idea that "humans are hardwired to be aggressive and selfish," he seems to assume that meanness or bullying has a "biological," even an evolutionary, basis in human development (par. 3). To think critically about the assumptions in this proposal related to bullying, ask yourself questions like these:

- How might traits like aggressiveness and selfishness have been beneficial to us in the past? In our society today, how are they advantageous or disadvantageous?

- If aggressiveness and selfishness are biological traits, why do you think Bornstein assumes bullying is a problem that can be solved?

- What does Bornstein assume about nature and nurture? Does he see them as opposite or complementary? What role does nurture play in causing bullying and what role could it play in preventing bullying?

Assumptions about empathy. The goal of Bornstein's model solution to the problem of bullying — Roots of Empathy — is to cultivate empathy, to plant a seed and help it grow. To think critically about the assumptions in this essay related to empathy, ask yourself questions like these:

You may also try contextualizing; see Chapter 10, pp. 522–23.

- Bornstein quotes Roots of Empathy founder Mary Gordon as frequently saying: "Empathy can't be taught, but it can be caught" (par. 9). What do you think she means?

- One of the tools the Roots of Empathy program uses to cultivate empathy is "perspective taking" (par. 8). Is it really possible to see things from another person's point of view and to understand their feelings? Why or why not?

READING LIKE A WRITER

DEMONSTRATING THE PROBLEM EXISTS AND IS SERIOUS

Every proposal begins with a problem. What writers say about the problem and how much space they devote to it depend on what they assume their readers know and think about the problem. Some problems require more explanation than others. Obviously, if readers are already immersed in discussing the problem and possible solutions, then the writer may not have to say much to introduce the problem. Nevertheless, savvy proposal writers try to present even familiar problems in a way that alerts readers to a problem's seriousness and prepares them for the writer's preferred solution.

| Analyze & Write |

Write a paragraph or two analyzing and evaluating how Bornstein presents the problem and establishes its seriousness:

1. Reread the title and first paragraph. How do the title and the opening sentences hook readers?

2. Why do you think Bornstein refers to a White House conference and the Department of Education's "guidance letter" (par. 1)? How do these references help him define the problem and excite readers' interest in his solution?

3. Note that Bornstein does not directly define *bullying*. Assuming that bullying is a rather wide and varied class of behaviors, how important is it that Bornstein clarify what he means by bullying? How does he give readers a sense of what bullying involves?

Showing How the Proposed Solution Would Help Solve the Problem and Is Feasible

The proposal writer's primary purposes are twofold:

1. To convince readers that the proposed solution would be **effective** — that it would help solve the problem, even if it would not eliminate it altogether

2. To convince readers that the proposed solution is **feasible** — that it can be implemented fairly easily and is cost-effective

For proposed solutions that already exist, the writer may need only to give the solution a name and give examples of where it is being applied successfully. For example, in "Fighting Bullying with Babies," Bornstein centers his argument on the example of the Roots of Empathy program in Toronto. Writers may also support their claims about the solution's effectiveness and feasibility with such evidence as statistics, research studies, and quotations from authorities.

| Analyze & Write |—————————————————————

Write a paragraph or two analyzing and evaluating Bornstein's use of evidence, particularly his use of the Roots of Empathy program, to support his proposal:

1. Reread paragraph 5, noting the details Bornstein shares with readers about how the Roots of Empathy program works.

2. Also skim paragraphs 6–10 to see what kinds of evidence Bornstein uses to support his argument that the Roots of Empathy model really can help to solve the problem of bullying and can be implemented on a wide scale fairly easily and inexpensively.

3. What do you think is most and least convincing about Bornstein's argument? Why?

Responding to Objections and Alternative Solutions

As they introduce the problem and then argue for the solution, proposal writers need to anticipate readers' possible objections to their argument as well as alternative solutions readers may prefer. Ignoring likely objections or alternative solutions is not a wise strategy because it gives the impression that the writer either does not fully understand the issue or cannot counter criticism. Writers have two options. They may:

1. *Concede* (or acknowledge) that an objection or alternative solution has some value and modify their proposed solution to accommodate it

2. *Refute* (or argue against) objections and alternative solutions by demonstrating that an objection is mistaken or that an alternative solution would not solve the problem or is inferior to the solution being proposed

---

| Analyze & Write |—————————————————————

Write a paragraph analyzing and evaluating how Bornstein responds to an alternative solution:

1. Reread paragraph 2, looking closely at the way Bornstein introduces and describes "the typical institutional response to bullying." Notice that he labels this alternative solution as "typical," but he doesn't specify what getting tough involves. What do you imagine Bornstein's original *New York Times* readers assumed were the ways a school usually gets tough with bullies? What would your school do? Note that Bornstein singles out only one extreme example of punishment. Why?

(*continued*)

2. Consider the words Bornstein uses to describe getting tough: "just falling back on punishment as a deterrent" (par. 2). *Deterrent* may remind older readers of the cold war strategy of mutual assured destruction (appropriately called MAD), the threat to use nuclear weapons in retaliation if the other side used them first. What effect would this connotation be likely to have on Bornstein's *New York Times* readers' ideas about the alternative solution Bornstein is refuting? What effect do they have on you?

3. Finally, reread paragraph 3. How does Bornstein use the fact that "humans are hardwired to be aggressive and selfish" to argue against getting tough? Why is this a strong or a weak argument?

Organizing the Proposal in a Way That Is Clear, Logical, and Convincing

To help readers identify the parts of the proposal, writers often use *cues* or signposts. For example, Bornstein introduces the problem and solution in his title — "Fighting Bullying with Babies." He uses a **rhetorical question** (a question he answers for readers) to reiterate this solution: "what's the secret formula? A baby" (par. 2). But Bornstein makes this assertion early in the essay as a teaser to keep people reading. His thesis statement requires a couple of paragraphs to explain because it not only asserts the solution but also the reasoning behind it:

Transitions   We know that humans are hardwired to be aggressive and selfish. But a growing body of research is demonstrating that there is also a biological basis for human compassion. . . .

More important, we are beginning to understand how to nurture this biological potential. (pars. 3–4)

Notice how the transitions help orient readers to the twists and turns of Bornstein's argument. "More important," for example, emphasizes the crucial part of the proposal: that something can be done to influence human behavior even if it is "hardwired."

Topic sentences, sentences that state the main idea of a paragraph or group of paragraphs, can be especially helpful to readers trying to follow the logic of a proposal. For example, notice how Bornstein uses topic sentences to indicate the alternative solution he is refuting (par. 2) and the explanation of how his proposed solution can be implemented (par. 5):

The typical institutional response to bullying is . . . (par. 2)

Here's how it works: (par. 5)

Analyze & Write ——————————————————————————

Write a couple of paragraphs analyzing and evaluating Bornstein's uses of cueing to help readers follow his argument:

1. Reread paragraphs 7–9 to see how Bornstein answers the rhetorical question "Why does the solution work?"

2. Look particularly at each of the topic sentences in these paragraphs to see how well he announces the answers.

3. Given Bornstein's purpose and audience, how clear and comprehensible is the logic of this proposal argument? If you were to give Bornstein advice on revising this proposal, what, if anything, would you recommend?

A Special Reading Strategy ————————————————

Comparing and Contrasting Related Readings: David Bornstein's "Fighting Bullying with Babies" and Excerpts on Bullying in Chapter 1

Comparing and contrasting related readings is a critical reading strategy useful both in reading for meaning and in reading like a writer. This strategy is particularly applicable when writers present similar subjects, as is the case in the essay by David Bornstein and the excerpts on bullying in Chapter 1 by Ron Banks (pp. 3–4), Tara L. Kuther (p. 6), Colleen Newquist (pp. 6–7), and Paul R. Smokowski and Kelly Holland Kopasz (p. 7). The genres differ — the excerpts are cause-effect analyses and Bornstein's is a proposal — but like many proposals, "Fighting Bullying with Babies" includes causal analysis. Choose one of the excerpts from Chapter 1 to compare and contrast to "Fighting Bullying with Babies," considering topics such as these:

- The way the authors define bullying and establish that it exists and is serious. For example, what do they assume readers already know about bullying? Do they cite examples of bullying, and if so, how much detail do they give? What kinds of evidence do they provide to persuade readers that the problem is serious?

- The causes and/or effects bullying has on the victims and/or the bullies themselves. What similarities and differences do you find in how the two readings analyze causes and effects? How do they support their cause-effect analysis?

For detailed guidelines on comparing and contrasting related readings, see Chapter 10, pp. 527–30.

ANALYZING VISUALS

Write a paragraph analyzing the visuals we added to Bornstein's proposal and explaining what, if anything, they contribute to the argument. To do the analysis, you can use the Criteria for Analyzing Visuals chart in Chapter 12 on pp. 611–12. Don't feel you have to answer all of the questions in the chart; focus on those that seem most productive in helping you write a paragraph-length analysis. To help you get started, consider adding these questions that specifically refer to the visuals included here:

- Compare the two photographs. What does each one show readers? How are they different? Similar?

For detailed guidelines on analyzing visuals, see Chapter 12, pp. 609–21.

- The photographs are not referred to in the proposal, but what in the text do you think they illustrate? What additional information, if any, do readers learn from the photos that is not in the text itself?

READINGS

William F. Shughart II

Why Not a Football Degree?

William F. Shughart II (b. 1947) has a PhD in economics from Texas A&M University. A distinguished professor at the University of Mississippi and a senior fellow at the Independent Institute, Shughart serves as the editor-in-chief of the scholarly journal Public Choice *and is also the associate editor of the* Southern Economic Journal. *His honors include the University of Mississippi Outstanding Researcher Award, the Sir Anthony Fisher International Memorial Award, and the* Business Week *Award. Shughart has written many books, including* Policy Challenges and Political Responses: Public Choice Perspectives on the Post–9/11 World *(2005) and* The Economics of Budget Deficits *(2002). He also publishes in popular newspapers such as the* Wall Street Journal, *in which this proposal appeared.*

- *Before you read,* note that the title asks the question "Why Not a Football Degree?" What problem do you imagine a college degree in football would solve?

- *As you read,* consider that this proposal was written originally for the Wall Street Journal, *a newspaper concerned primarily with business and financial matters. How do you think Shughart appeals to the interests and concerns of his original audience?*

1 The college football career of 2006's Heisman Trophy winner, Ohio State University quarterback Troy Smith, nearly was cut short at the end of his sophomore year following allegations that he had accepted $500 from a Buckeye booster. He was barred from playing in the 2005 Alamo Bowl and the next season's opener against Miami (Ohio). Quarterback Rhett Bomar was dismissed from the University of Oklahoma's football team after it was disclosed that he had earned substantially more than justified by the number of hours worked during the summer of 2006 at a job arranged for him by a patron of OU athletics. As a result of charges that, from 1993 to 1998, Coach Clem Haskins paid to have more than 400 term papers ghost-written for 18 of his players, the post-season tournament victories credited to the University of Minnesota's basketball team were erased from the NCAA's record books and the program was placed on

How does knowing that this is a proposal affect your understanding of the title and opening paragraph?

a four-year probation from which it has not yet recovered. In recent years, gambling and point-shaving scandals have rocked the basketball programs at Arizona State, Northwestern, and Florida; player suspensions and other penalties have been handed out for illegal betting on games by members of the Boston University, Florida State, and University of Maryland football teams.

Each of these events, which are only the latest revelations in a long series of NCAA rule violations, has generated the usual hand-wringing about the apparent loss of amateurism in college sports. Nostalgia for supposedly simpler times when love of the game and not money was the driving force in intercollegiate athletics has led to all sorts of reform proposals. The NCAA's decision in the late 1980s to require its member institutions to make public athletes' graduation rates is perhaps the least controversial example. Proposition 48's mandate that freshman athletes must meet more stringent test score and grade point requirements to participate in NCAA-sanctioned contests than is demanded of entering non-student-athletes has been criticized as a naked attempt to discriminate against disadvantaged (and mostly minority) high-school graduates who see college sports as a way out of poverty.

Why does Shughart mention these two earlier reforms before he explains his own proposed solution?

But whether or not one supports any particular reform proposal, there seems to be a general consensus that something must be done. If so, why stop at half-measures? I hereby offer three suggestions for solving the crisis in college athletics.

1. *Create four-year degree programs in football and basketball.* Many colleges and universities grant bachelor's degrees in vocational subjects. Art, drama, and music are a few examples, but there are others. Undergraduates who major in these areas typically are required to spend only about one of their four years in introductory English, math, history and science courses; the remainder of their time is spent in the studio, the theater or the practice hall honing the creative talents they will later sell as professionals.

Although a college education is no more necessary for success in the art world than it is in the world of sports, no similar option is available for students whose talents lie on the athletic field or in the gym.

Majoring in physical education is a possibility, of course, but while PE is hardly a rigorous, demanding discipline, undergraduates pursuing a degree in that major normally must spend many more hours in the classroom than their counterparts who are preparing for careers on the stage. While the music major is receiving academic credit for practice sessions and recitals, the PE major is studying and taking exams in kinesiology, exercise physiology and nutrition. Why should academic credit be given for practicing the violin, but not for practicing a three-point shot?

6   2. *Extend the time limit on athletic scholarships by two years.* In addition to practicing and playing during the regular football or basketball season, college athletes must continue to work to improve their skills and keep in shape during the off-season. For football players, these off-season activities include several weeks of organized spring practice as well as year-round exercise programs in the weight room and on the running track. Basketball players participate in summer leagues and practice with their teams during the fall. In effect, college athletes are required to work at their sports for as much as 10 months a year.

7   These time-consuming extracurricular activities make it extremely difficult for college athletes to devote more than minimal effort to the studies required for maintaining their academic eligibility. They miss lectures and exams when their teams travel, and the extra tutoring they receive at athletic department expense often fails to make up the difference.

8   If the NCAA and its member schools are truly concerned about the academic side of the college athletic experience, let them put their money where their collective mouth is. The period of an athlete's eligibility to participate in intercollegiate sports would remain at four years, but the two additional years of scholarship support could be exercised at any time during the athlete's lifetime. Athletes who use up their college eligibility and do not choose careers in professional sports would be guaranteed financial backing to remain in school and finish their undergraduate degrees. Athletes who have the talent to turn pro could complete their degrees when their playing days are over.

How convincing is this argument based on an analogy between the arts and sports?

This suggestion is likely to be controversial. How well do you think Shughart supports it?

3. *Allow a competitive marketplace to determine* 9
the compensation of college athletes. Football and
basketball players at the top NCAA institutions produce millions of dollars in benefits for their respective
schools. Successful college athletic programs draw
more fans to the football stadium and to the basketball arena. They generate revenues for the school
from regular season television appearances and from
invitations to participate in postseason play. There is
evidence that schools attract greater financial support
from public and private sources—both for their athletic and academic programs—if their teams achieve
national ranking. There even is evidence that the quality of students who apply for admission to institutions
of higher learning improves following a successful
football or basketball season.

Despite the considerable contributions made to the 10
wealth and welfare of his or her school, however, the
compensation payable to a college athlete is limited
by the NCAA to a scholarship that includes tuition,
books, room and board, and a nominal expense
allowance. Any payment above and beyond this
amount subjects the offending athletic program to
NCAA sanctions. In-kind payments to players and
recruits in the form of free tickets to athletic contests,
T-shirts, transportation and accommodations likewise
are limited. These restrictions apply to alumni and fans
as well as to the institutions themselves. The NCAA
also limits the amount of money athletes can earn outside of school by curtailing the use of summer jobs as
a means by which coaches and boosters can pay athletes more than authorized.

The illegal financial inducements reported to be 11
widespread in collegiate football and basketball supply conclusive evidence that many college athletes
are now underpaid. The relevant question is whether
the current system of compensation ought to remain
in place. Allowing it to do so will preserve the illusion
of amateurism in college sports and permit coaches,
athletic departments and college administrators to
continue to benefit financially at the expense of the
players. On the other hand, shifting to a market-based
system of compensation would transfer some of the

How convincing is
Shughart's strategy of
referring to "evidence"
here?

Why do you think Shughart
calls amateurism in college
sports an "illusion"?

wealth created by big-time athletic programs to the individuals whose talents are key ingredients in the success of those programs.

12   It would also cause a sea change in the distribution of power among the top NCAA institutions. Under the present NCAA rules, some of the major college athletic programs, such as Southern Cal, LSU and Florida in football, and Duke, North Carolina and Florida in basketball, have developed such strong winning traditions over the years that they can maintain their dominant positions without cheating.

13   These schools are able to attract superior high-school athletes season after season by offering packages of non-monetary benefits (well-equipped training facilities, quality coaching staffs, talented teammates, national exposure and so on) that increases the present value of an amateur athlete's future professional income relative to the value added by historically weaker athletic programs. Given this factor, along with NCAA rules that mandate uniform compensation across the board, the top institutions have a built-in competitive advantage in recruiting the best and brightest athletes.

14   It follows that under the current system, the weaker programs are virtually compelled to offer illegal financial inducements to players and recruits if they wish to compete successfully with the traditional powers. It also follows that shifting to a market-based system of compensation would remove some of the built-in advantages now enjoyed by the top college athletic programs. It is surely this effect, along with the reductions in the incomes of coaches and the "fat" in athletic department budgets to be expected once a competitive marketplace is permitted to work, that is the cause of the objection to paying student-athletes a market-determined wage, not the rhetoric about the repugnance of professionalism.

Shughart's phrase *It follows* suggests that his conclusion is logical, perhaps even inevitable. How convincing do you find it?

15   It is a fight over the distribution of the college sports revenue pie that lies at the bottom of the debate about reforming NCAA rules. And notwithstanding the high moral principles and concern for players usually expressed by debaters on all sides of the issue, the interests of the athlete are in fact often the last to be considered.

Why do you think Shughart ends his essay this way? How effective is this ending?

READING FOR MEANING

This section presents three activities that will help you think about the meanings in Shughart's proposal essay. Your instructor may ask you to do one or more of these activities in class or online.

1. **Read to Summarize.** Write a sentence or two summarizing Shughart's proposed solution.

2. **Read to Respond.** Write a paragraph analyzing your initial reactions to Shughart's essay. For example, consider anything that resonates with your experience or that seems contradictory, surprising, or fascinating, such as:

   - The rules violations that Shughart lists in the first paragraph, perhaps adding other, more recent violations with which you are familiar;

   - Shughart's idea that academic credit should be given to "practicing a three-point shot" (par. 5);

   - Shughart's observation that playing and practicing sports "make it extremely difficult for college athletes to devote more than minimal effort" to their studies (par. 7), perhaps in relation to your own experience as an athlete in college or high school.

3. **Read to Analyze Assumptions.** Write a paragraph or two analyzing an assumption you find intriguing in Shughart's essay. For example:

   Assumptions about the benefits of amateurism. NCAA rules require that to play college sports, athletes must retain amateur status, meaning that they cannot be paid by recruiters or sponsors and that their scholarships can cover only such things as tuition and housing. Shughart argues, however, that amateurism in college sports is an "illusion" (par. 11). To think critically about the assumptions in this essay related to amateurism, ask yourself questions like these:

   - Who, according to Shughart, benefits from keeping college athletes amateurs, and who would benefit if they were allowed to become professionals?

You may also try looking for patterns of opposition; see Chapter 10, pp. 525–26.

   - If the NCAA assumes that amateur status protects college athletes and perhaps also college sports, what is it supposed to protect them from, and how effective has this protection been?

   - What values are associated with the terms *amateur* and *professional*?

   Assumptions about the purpose of college. Although he concedes that the physical education major is "hardly a rigorous, demanding discipline" (par. 5), Shughart proposes that football be a major in its own right. His

Take a quiz to check your reading and vocabulary comprehension:
bedfordstmartins.com/readingcritically

argument hinges on the comparison of football to music and other performance arts in which students receive "academic credit for practice sessions and recitals" (par. 5). He calls them "vocational subjects" (par. 4) because their purpose is job training. To think critically about the assumptions in this proposal related to the purpose of college, ask yourself questions like these:

- In conceding that the physical education major is "hardly a rigorous, demanding discipline" (par. 5), Shughart appears to think his readers are likely to assume disciplines or subjects studied in college should be rigorous and demanding. Do you share this assumption? Why or why not?

- By calling football a "vocational subject" and proposing that there be a major in football, Shughart seems to assume the primary purpose of a college education should be job training. What other reasons, if any, might people choose to go to college?

You may also try reflecting on challenges to your beliefs and values; see Chapter 10, pp. 526–27.

READING LIKE A WRITER

SHOWING HOW THE PROPOSED SOLUTION WOULD HELP SOLVE THE PROBLEM AND IS FEASIBLE

"Why Not a Football Degree?" dismisses as "half-measures" previous efforts by the National Collegiate Athletic Association (NCAA) to solve what Shughart calls "the crisis in college athletics" (par. 3). He identifies an array of problems in college sports, including evidence that some athletes are being paid although they are supposed to be amateurs, not professionals; others are getting college credit they have not earned, for example for plagiarized papers; and still others are illegally betting on games. To address problems like these, Shughart makes a three-pronged proposal designed to help student athletes succeed in their academic studies as well as in their collegiate sports careers, and also eliminate "illegal financial inducements" (par. 11) while removing the "built-in advantages" (par. 14) of the most successful college sports programs.

| Analyze & Write |

Write a paragraph or two analyzing Shughart's argument in support of his proposed solution:

1. First, choose one of Shughart's "three suggestions" (par. 3) to analyze, and evaluate Shughart's argument. What kinds of support does the author provide? What are the strengths and weaknesses of this part of his argument?

2. Then consider how well the three parts of the proposal work together to offer a comprehensive solution to the problem as Shughart has defined it.

Kelly D. Brownell and Thomas R. Frieden

Ounces of Prevention— The Public Policy Case for Taxes on Sugared Beverages

Kelly D. Brownell (b. 1951) is a professor of psychology as well as a professor of epidemiology and public health at Yale, where he is also director of the Rudd Center for Food Policy and Obesity. An international expert who has published numerous books and articles, including Food Fight: The Inside Story of the Food Industry, America's Obesity Crisis, and What We Can Do About It *(2003), Brownell received the 2012 American Psychological Association Award for Outstanding Lifetime Contributions to Psychology. He was also featured in the Academy Award–nominated film* Super Size Me.

Thomas R. Frieden (b. 1960), a physician specializing in public health, is the director of the U.S. Centers for Disease Control and Prevention (CDC) and served for several years as the health commissioner for the City of New York.

Their proposal "Ounces of Prevention—The Public Policy Case for Taxes on Sugared Beverages" was originally published in 2009 in the highly respected New England Journal of Medicine, *which calls itself "the most widely read, cited, and influential general medical periodical in the world."*

- *Before you read, think about how the reputation of the publication in which this proposal first appeared, together with Brownell and Frieden's credentials, might have influenced the original audience as well as how it may affect college students reading the proposal today.*

- *As you read, notice that Brownell and Frieden include graphs and cite their sources. How do you think these features of their proposal might influence readers?*

Sugar, rum, and tobacco are commodities which are nowhere necessaries of life, which are become objects of almost universal consumption, and which are therefore extremely proper subjects of taxation.

—Adam Smith, *The Wealth of Nations*, 1776

1   The obesity epidemic has inspired calls for public health measures to prevent diet-related diseases. One controversial idea is now the subject of public debate: food taxes. Forty states already have small taxes on sugared beverages and snack foods, but in the past year, Maine and New York have proposed large taxes on sugared beverages, and similar discussions have begun in other states. The size of the taxes, their potential for generating revenue and reducing consumption, and vigorous opposition by the bev-

erage industry have resulted in substantial controversy. Because excess consumption of unhealthful foods underlies many leading causes of death, food taxes at local, state, and national levels are likely to remain part of political and public health discourse.

Sugar-sweetened beverages (soda sweetened with sugar, corn syrup, or other caloric sweeteners and other carbonated and uncarbonated drinks, such as sports and energy drinks) may be the single largest driver of the obesity epidemic. A recent meta-analysis found that the intake of sugared beverages is associated with increased body weight, poor nutrition, and displacement of more healthful beverages; increasing consumption increases risk for obesity and diabetes; the strongest effects are seen in studies with the best methods (e.g., longitudinal and interventional vs. correlational studies);* and interventional studies show that reduced intake of soft drinks improves health.[1] Studies that do not support a relationship between consumption of sugared beverages and health outcomes tend to be conducted by authors supported by the beverage industry.[2] Sugared beverages are marketed extensively to children and adolescents, and in the mid-1990s, children's intake of sugared beverages surpassed that of milk. In the past decade, per capita intake of calories from sugar-sweetened beverages has increased by nearly 30 percent (see bar graph Daily Caloric Intake from

2

Daily Caloric Intake from Sugar-Sweetened Drinks in the United States. Data are from Nielsen and Popkin.[3]

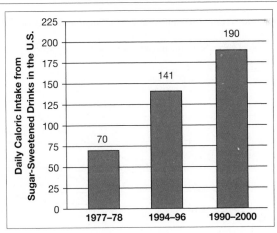

*In a *longitudinal* study, researchers observe changes taking place over a long period of time; in an *interventional* study, investigators give research subjects a measured amount of whatever is being studied and note its effects; and in a *correlational* study, researchers examine statistics to see if two or more variables have a mathematically significant similarity. [Editor's note]

Sugar-Sweetened Drinks in the United States);[3] beverages now account for 10 to 15 percent of the calories consumed by children and adolescents. For each extra can or glass of sugared beverage consumed per day, the likelihood of a child's becoming obese increases by 60 percent.[4]

3   Taxes on tobacco products have been highly effective in reducing consumption, and data indicate that higher prices also reduce soda consumption. A review conducted by Yale University's Rudd Center for Food Policy and Obesity suggested that for every 10 percent increase in price, consumption decreases by 7.8 percent. An industry trade publication reported even larger reductions: as prices of carbonated soft drinks increased by 6.8 percent, sales dropped by 7.8 percent, and as Coca-Cola prices increased by 12 percent, sales dropped by 14.6 percent.[5] Such studies—and the economic principles that support their findings—suggest that a tax on sugared beverages would encourage consumers to switch to more healthful beverages, which would lead to reduced caloric intake and less weight gain.

4   The increasing affordability of soda—and the decreasing affordability of fresh fruits and vegetables (see line graph)—probably contributes to the rise in obesity in the United States. In 2008, a group of child and health care advocates in New York proposed a one-penny-per-ounce excise tax on sugared beverages, which would be expected to reduce consumption by 13 percent—about two servings per week per person. Even if one quarter of the calories consumed from sugared beverages are replaced by other

Relative Price Changes for Fresh Fruits and Vegetables, Sugar and Sweets, and Carbonated Drinks, 1978–2009.
Data are from the Bureau of Labor Statistics and represent the U.S. city averages for all urban consumers in January of each year.

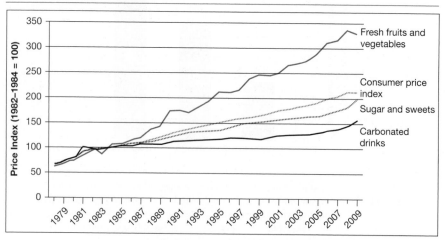

food, the decrease in consumption would lead to an estimated reduction of 8,000 calories per person per year—slightly more than 2 pounds each year for the average person. Such a reduction in calorie consumption would be expected to substantially reduce the risk of obesity and diabetes and may also reduce the risk of heart disease and other conditions.

Some argue that government should not interfere in the market and that 5 products and prices will change as consumers demand more healthful food, but several considerations support government action. The first is externality—costs to parties not directly involved in a transaction. The contribution of unhealthful diets to health care costs is already high and is increasing—an estimated $79 billion is spent annually for overweight and obesity alone—and approximately half of these costs are paid by Medicare and Medicaid, at taxpayers' expense. Diet-related diseases also cost society in terms of decreased work productivity, increased absenteeism, poorer school performance, and reduced fitness on the part of military recruits, among other negative effects. The second consideration is information asymmetry between the parties to a transaction. In the case of sugared beverages, marketers commonly make health claims (e.g., that such beverages provide energy or vitamins) and use techniques that exploit the cognitive vulnerabilities of young children, who often cannot distinguish a television program from an advertisement. A third consideration is revenue generation, which can further increase the societal benefits of a tax on soft drinks. A penny-per-ounce excise tax would raise an estimated $1.2 billion in New York State alone. In times of economic hardship, taxes that both generate this much revenue and promote health are better options than revenue initiatives that may have adverse effects.

Objections have certainly been raised: that such a tax would be regres- 6 sive, that food taxes are not comparable to tobacco or alcohol taxes because people must eat to survive, that it is unfair to single out one type of food for taxation, and that the tax will not solve the obesity problem. But the poor are disproportionately affected by diet-related diseases and would derive the greatest benefit from reduced consumption; sugared beverages are not necessary for survival; Americans consume about 250 to 300 more calories daily today than they did several decades ago, and nearly half this increase is accounted for by consumption of sugared beverages; and though no single intervention will solve the obesity problem, that is hardly a reason to take no action.

The full impact of public policies becomes apparent only after they take 7 effect. We can estimate changes in sugared-drink consumption that would be prompted by a tax, but accompanying changes in the consumption of other foods or beverages are more difficult to predict. One question is whether the proportions of calories consumed in liquid and solid foods would change. And shifts among beverages would have different effects depending on whether consumers substituted water, milk, diet drinks, or equivalent generic brands of sugared drinks.

8   Effects will also vary depending on whether the tax is designed to reduce consumption, generate revenue, or both; the size of the tax; whether the revenue is earmarked for programs related to nutrition and health; and where in the production and distribution chain the tax is applied. Given the heavy consumption of sugared beverages, even small taxes will generate substantial revenue, but only heftier taxes will significantly reduce consumption. Sales taxes are the most common form of food tax, but because they are levied as a percentage of the retail price, they encourage the purchase of less-expensive brands or larger containers. Excise taxes structured as a fixed cost per ounce provide an incentive to buy less and hence would be much more effective in reducing consumption and improving health. In addition, manufacturers generally pass the cost of an excise tax along to their customers, including it in the price consumers see when they are making their selection, whereas sales taxes are seen only at the cash register.

9   Although a tax on sugared beverages would have health benefits regardless of how the revenue was used, the popularity of such a proposal increases greatly if revenues are used for programs to prevent childhood obesity, such as media campaigns, facilities and programs for physical activity, and healthier food in schools. Poll results show that support of a tax on sugared beverages ranges from 37 to 72 percent; a poll of New York residents found that 52 percent supported a "soda tax," but the number rose to 72 percent when respondents were told that the revenue would be used for obesity prevention. Perhaps the most defensible approach is to use revenue to subsidize the purchase of healthful foods. The public would then see a relationship between tax and benefit, and any regressive effects would be counteracted by the reduced costs of healthful food.

10   A penny-per-ounce excise tax could reduce consumption of sugared beverages by more than 10 percent. It is difficult to imagine producing behavior change of this magnitude through education alone, even if government devoted massive resources to the task. In contrast, a sales tax on sugared drinks would generate considerable revenue, and as with the tax on tobacco, it could become a key tool in efforts to improve health.

References

1. Vartanian LR, Schwartz MB, Brownell KD. Effects of soft drink consumption on nutrition and health: a systematic review and meta-analysis. Am J Public Health 2007;97:667–675.

2. Forshee RA, Anderson PA, Storey ML. Sugar-sweetened beverages and body mass index in children and adolescents: a meta-analysis. Am J Clin Nutr 2008;87:1662–71.

3. Nielsen SJ, Popkin BM. Changes in beverage intake between 1977 and 2001. Am J Prev Med 2004;27:205–210.

4. Ludwig DS, Peterson KE, Gortmaker SL. Relation between consumption of sugar-sweetened drinks and childhood obesity: a prospective, observational analysis. Lancet 2001;357:505–508.
5. Elasticity: big price increases cause Coke volume to plummet. Beverage Digest. November 21, 2008:3–4.

READING FOR MEANING

This section presents three activities that will help you think about the meanings in Brownell and Frieden's proposal. Your instructor may ask you to do one or more of these activities in class or online.

1. **Read to Summarize.** Write a sentence or two briefly summarizing Brownell and Frieden's proposed solution.

For more help with summarizing, see Chapter 10, pp. 518–19.

2. **Read to Respond.** Write a paragraph analyzing your initial reactions to Brownell and Frieden's essay. For example, consider anything that resonates with your experiences or that seems contradictory, surprising, or fascinating, such as:

   - The idea that sports and energy beverages that are sugar-sweetened may not be good for you, perhaps in relation to your own consumption of such drinks;

You may also try reflecting on challenges to your beliefs and values; see Chapter 10, pp. 526–27.

   - The assertion that taxes on tobacco products "have been highly effective in reducing consumption" (par. 3), considering how many of your peers have chosen to be smokers or nonsmokers.

3. **Read to Analyze Assumptions.** Write a paragraph or two analyzing an assumption you find intriguing in Brownell and Frieden's proposal. For example:

   Assumptions about the government's role in solving health problems. Brownell and Frieden explicitly argue in favor of federal and/or state government actions to address public health problems such as those related to obesity and tobacco use. To think critically about assumptions in this essay related to the government's role in solving health problems, ask yourself questions like these:

   - Why do Brownell and Frieden assume that government should have a role in influencing people's decisions about their own health? In other words, why is the so-called "obesity epidemic" a public policy problem?

   - Imposing taxes is one thing government can do. What other actions could or should the government do to solve public health problems?

Take a quiz to check your reading and vocabulary comprehension:
bedfordstmartins.com/readingcritically

Assumptions about research studies. Brownell and Frieden cite a number of research studies, including a "meta-analysis," a study of studies. To think critically about assumptions in this essay related to research studies, ask yourself questions like these:

- Brownell and Frieden explain that the meta-analysis on which they are relying examined studies that took three different approaches — longitudinal, interventional, and correlational — to determine whether there is a cause-effect relationship between consuming sugar-sweetened beverages and obesity (par. 2). Why do Brownell and Frieden assume it is important to take a variety of approaches to a question like this? Do you agree or disagree?

- Brownell and Frieden also call into question studies that arrived at a different "outcome," arguing that these studies "tend to be conducted by authors supported by the beverage industry" (par. 2). Why do Brownell and Frieden assume it matters who funded the research? Should it matter?

READING LIKE A WRITER

RESPONDING TO OBJECTIONS AND ALTERNATIVE SOLUTIONS

Proposal writers usually try to respond to readers' likely objections and questions by conceding or refuting them. How writers handle objections and questions affects their credibility with readers, who usually expect writers to be respectful of other points of view and to take criticism seriously, while still arguing assertively for their solution. Brownell and Frieden respond to five possible objections. Notice that even though they devote more space to the first objection, they present all of the objections and their refutations using the same basic sentence pattern:

Transitions signaling an opposing point

Some argue that . . . , but . . . (par. 5)

Objections have certainly been raised: that . . . , that . . . , that . . . , and that. . . . But . . . , . . . , and . . . (par. 6)

┌─────────────────┐
│ **Analyze & Write** │
└─────────────────┘

Write a paragraph or two analyzing and evaluating how Brownell and Frieden respond to possible objections:

1. Reread paragraph 5. First, summarize the objection and Brownell and Frieden's reasons for refuting it. What cues do they provide to signal that an objection is coming and to highlight their reasons? Why do you think they call their reasons "considerations"? How convincing do you think these particular considerations were likely to be for their original *New England Journal of Medicine* audience?

2. Reread paragraph 6, in which the authors respond to four other objections. What cues do they provide to help you follow their argument? What reasons do Brownell and Frieden give to refute these objections? Which refutations, if any, do you think need further elaboration or support?

3. Given their purpose and audience, why do you think Brownell and Frieden focus so much attention on the first objection, but choose to group the other four objections together in a single paragraph?

Karen Kornbluh

Win-Win Flexibility

Karen Kornbluh (b. 1963) earned a Master of Public Policy degree from the John F. Kennedy School of Government at Harvard. After working for a number of years in the private sector as an economist and management consultant, Kornbluh has held a number of positions in the public sector, including deputy chief of staff at the Treasury Department and ambassador to the Organization for Economic Co-operation and Development.

As director of the Work and Family Program at the New America Foundation, a nonprofit, nonpartisan institute that sponsors research and conferences on public policy issues, Kornbluh led an effort to change the American workplace to accommodate what she calls the new "juggler family," in which parents have to juggle their time for parenting, caregiving, and work. Her book Running Harder to Stay in Place: The Growth of Family Work Hours and Incomes *was published in 2005 by the New America Foundation, and Kornbluh's articles have appeared in such venues as the* New York Times, Washington Post, *and* Atlantic Monthly. *The following proposal was published in 2005 by the Work and Family Program.*

- *Before you read,* think about your own experiences as a child or a parent and the ways that you or your parents have had to juggle time for parenting and work.

- *As you read,* consider who Kornbluh thinks her audience is likely to be. With this audience in mind, think about why she titles her proposal "Win-Win Flexibility."

INTRODUCTION

1   Today fully 70 percent of families with children are headed by two working parents or by an unmarried working parent. The "traditional family" of the breadwinner and homemaker has been replaced by the "juggler family," in which no one is home full-time. Two-parent families are working 10 more hours a week than in 1979 (Bernstein and Kornbluh).

2   To be decent parents, caregivers, and members of their communities, workers now need greater flexibility than they once did. Yet good part-time or flex-time jobs remain rare. Whereas companies have embraced flexibility in virtually every other aspect of their businesses (inventory control, production schedules, financing), full-time workers' schedules remain largely inflexible. Employers often demand workers be available around the clock. Moreover, many employees have no right to a minimum number of sick or vacation days; almost two-thirds of all workers—and an even larger percentage of low-income parents—lack the ability to take a day off to care for a family member (Lovell). The Family and Medical Leave Act (FMLA) of 1993 finally guaranteed that workers at large companies

could take a leave of absence for the birth or adoption of a baby, or for the illness of a family member. Yet that guaranteed leave is unpaid.

Many businesses are finding ways to give their most valued employees   3
flexibility but, all too often, workers who need flexibility find themselves shunted into part-time, temporary, on-call, or contract jobs with reduced wages and career opportunities—and, often, no benefits. A full quarter of American workers are in these jobs. Only 15 percent of women and 12 percent of men in such jobs receive health insurance from their employers (Wenger). A number of European countries provide workers the right to a part-time schedule and all have enacted legislation to implement a European Union directive to prohibit discrimination against part-time workers.

In America, employers are required to accommodate the needs of   4
employees with disabilities—even if that means providing a part-time or flexible schedule. Employers may also provide religious accommodations for employees by offering a part-time or flexible schedule. At the same time, employers have no obligation to allow parents or employees caring for sick relatives to work part-time or flexible schedules, even if the cost to the employer would be inconsequential.

In the twenty-first-century global economy, America needs a new approach that allows businesses to gain flexibility in staffing without sacrificing their competitiveness and enables workers to gain control over their work lives without sacrificing their economic security. This win-win flexibility arrangement will not be the same in every company, nor even for each employee working within the same organization. Each case will be different. But flexibility will not come for all employees without some education, prodding, and leadership. So employers and employees must be required to come to the table to work out a solution that benefits everyone. American businesses must be educated on strategies for giving employees flexibility without sacrificing productivity or morale. And businesses should be recognized and rewarded when they do so.

America is a nation that continually rises to the occasion. At the dawn   6
of a new century, we face many challenges. One of these is helping families to raise our next generation in an increasingly demanding global economy. This is a challenge America must meet with imagination and determination.

BACKGROUND: THE NEED FOR WORKPLACE FLEXIBILITY

Between 1970 and 2000, the percentage of mothers in the workforce   7
rose from 38 to 67 percent (Smolensky and Gootman). Moreover, the number of hours worked by dual-income families has increased dramatically. Couples with children worked a full 60 hours a week in 1979. By 2000 they were working 70 hours a week (Bernstein and Kornbluh). And more parents than ever are working long hours. In 2000, nearly 1 out of every

8 couples with children was putting in 100 hours a week or more on the job, compared to only 1 out of 12 families in 1970 (Jacobs and Gerson).

8   In addition to working parents, there are over 44.4 million Americans who provide care to another adult, often an older relative. Fifty-nine percent of these caregivers either work or have worked while providing care ("Caregiving").

9   In a 2002 report by the Families and Work Institute, 45 percent of employees reported that work and family responsibilities interfered with each other "a lot" or "some" and 67 percent of employed parents report that they do not have enough time with their children (Galinksy, Bond, and Hill).

10   Over half of workers today have no control over scheduling alternative start and end times at work (Galinksy, Bond, and Hill). According to a recent study by the Institute for Women's Policy Research, 49 percent of workers—over 59 million Americans—lack basic paid sick days for themselves. And almost two-thirds of all workers—and an even larger percentage of low-income parents—lack the ability to take a day off to care for a family member (Lovell). Thirteen percent of non-poor workers with caregiving responsibilities lack paid vacation leave, while 28 percent of poor caregivers lack any paid vacation time (Heymann). Research has shown that flexible arrangements and benefits tend to be more accessible in larger and more profitable firms, and then to the most valued professional and managerial workers in those firms (Golden). Parents with young children and working welfare recipients—the workers who need access to paid leave the most—are the least likely to have these benefits, according to research from the Urban Institute (Ross Phillips).

11   In the U.S., only 5 percent of workers have access to a job that provides paid parental leave. The Family and Medical Leave Act grants the right to 12 weeks of unpaid leave for the birth or adoption of a child or for the serious illness of the worker or a worker's family member. But the law does not apply to employees who work in companies with fewer than 50 people, employees who have worked for less than a year at their place of employment, or employees who work fewer than 1,250 hours a year. Consequently, only 45 percent of parents working in the private sector are eligible to take even this unpaid time off (Smolensky and Gootman).

12   Workers often buy flexibility by sacrificing job security, benefits, and pay. Part-time workers are less likely to have employer-provided health insurance or pensions and their hourly wages are lower. One study in 2002 found that 43 percent of employed parents said that using flexibility would jeopardize their advancement (Galinksy, Bond, and Hill).

13   Children, in particular, pay a heavy price for workplace inflexibility (Waters Boots 2004). Almost 60 percent of child care arrangements are of poor or mediocre quality (Smolensky and Gootman). Children in low-income families are even less likely to be in good or excellent care

settings. Full-day child care easily costs $4,000 to $10,000 per year—approaching the price of college tuition at a public university. As a result of the unaffordable and low-quality nature of child care in this country, a disturbing number of today's children are left home alone: Over 3.3 million children age 6–12 are home alone after school each day (Vandivere et al.).

Many enlightened businesses are showing the way forward to a twenty-first-century flexible workplace. Currently, however, businesses have little incentive to provide families with the flexibility they need. We need to level the playing field and remove the competitive disadvantages for all businesses that do provide workplace flexibility.   14

This should be a popular priority. A recent poll found that 77 percent of likely voters feel that it is difficult for families to earn enough and still have time to be with their families. Eighty-four percent of voters agree that children are being short-changed when their parents have to work long hours. . . .   15

PROPOSAL: WIN-WIN FLEXIBILITY

A win-win approach in the U.S. to flexibility . . . might function as follows. It would be "soft touch" at first—requiring a process and giving business an out if it would be costly to implement—with a high-profile public education campaign on the importance of workplace flexibility to American business, American families, and American society. A survey at the end of the second year would determine whether a stricter approach is needed.   16

Employees would have the right to make a formal request to their employers for flexibility in the number of hours worked, the times worked, and/or the ability to work from home. Examples of such flexibility would include part-time, annualized hours,[1] compressed hours,[2] flex-time,[3] job-sharing, shift working, staggered hours, and telecommuting.   17

The employee would be required to make a written application providing details on the change in work, the effect on the employer, and solutions to any problems caused to the employer. The employer would be required to meet with the employee and give the employee a decision on the request within two weeks, as well as provide an opportunity for an internal appeal within one month from the initial request.   18

The employee request would be granted unless the employer demonstrated it would require significant difficulty or expense entailing more than ordinary costs, decreased job efficiency, impairment of worker safety,   19

[1]*Annualized hours* means working different numbers of hours a week but a fixed annual total.

[2]*Compressed hours* means working more hours a day in exchange for working fewer days a week.

[3]*Flex-time* means working on an adjustable daily schedule.

infringement of other employees' rights, or conflict with another law or regulation.

20   The employer would be required to provide an employee working a flexible schedule with the same hourly pay and proportionate health, pension, vacation, holiday, and FMLA benefits that the employee received before working flexibly and would be required thereafter to advance the employee at the same rate as full-time employees.

21   *Who would be covered:* Parents (including parents, legal guardians, foster parents) and other caregivers at first. Eventually all workers should be eligible in our flexible, 24 × 7 economy. During the initial period, it will be necessary to define non-parental "caregivers." One proposal is to define them as immediate relatives or other caregivers of "certified care recipients" (defined as those whom a doctor certifies as having three or more limitations that impede daily functioning—using diagnostic criteria such as Activities of Daily Living (ADL)/Instrumental Activities of Daily Living (IADL)—for at least 180 consecutive days). . . .

22   *Public Education:* Critical to the success of the proposal will be public education along the lines of the education that the government and business schools conducted in the 1980s about the need for American business to adopt higher quality standards to compete against Japanese business. A Malcolm Baldrige–like award[4] should be created for companies that make flexibility win-win. A public education campaign conducted by the Department of Labor should encourage small businesses to adopt best practices of win-win flexibility. Tax credits could be used in the first year to reward early adopters.

Works Cited

Bernstein, Jared, and Karen Kornbluh. "Running Harder to Stay in Place: The Growth of Family Work Hours and Incomes." *New America Foundation*. New America Foundation, n.d. Web. 1 June 2005.

"Caregiving in the U.S." *The National Alliance for Caregiving* and *AARP*. Met Life Foundation, n.d. Web. 6 June 2005.

Galinksy, Ellen, James Bond, and Jeffrey E. Hill. "Workplace Flexibility: What Is It? Who Has It? Who Wants It? Does It Make a Difference?" *Families and Work Institute*. Families and Work Institute and IBM, n.d. Web. 1 June 2005.

Golden, Lonnie. "The Time Bandit: What U.S. Workers Surrender to Get Greater Flexibility in Work Schedules." *Economic Policy Institute*. Economic Policy Institute, n.d. Web. 1 June 2005.

Heymann, Jody. *The Widening Gap: Why America's Working Families Are in Jeopardy — and What Can Be Done about It*. New York: Basic, 2000. Print.

[4]The Malcolm Baldrige National Quality Award is given by the U.S. president to outstanding businesses.

Jacobs, Jerry, and Kathleen Gerson. *The Time Divide: Work, Family and Gender Inequality*. Cambridge: Harvard UP, 2004. Print.

Lovell, Vicky. "No Time to Be Sick: Why Everyone Suffers When Workers Don't Have Paid Sick Leave." *Institute for Women's Policy Research*. Institute for Women's Policy Research, n.d. Web. 3 June 2005.

Phillips, Katherin Ross. "Getting Time Off: Access to Leave among Working Parents." *Urban Institute*. Urban Institute, n.d. Web. 3 June 2005.

Smolensky, Eugene, and Jennifer A. Gootman, eds. *Working Families and Growing Kids: Caring for Children and Adolescents*. Washington, DC: National Academies P, 2003. Print.

Vandivere, Sharon, et al. "Unsupervised Time: Family and Child Factors Associated with Self-Care." *Urban Institute*. Urban Institute, n.d. Web. 1 June 2005.

Waters Boots, Shelley. "The Way We Work: How Children and Their Families Fare in a Twenty-first-Century Workplace." *New America Foundation*. New America Foundation, n.d. Web. 3 June 2005.

Wenger, Jeffrey. "Share of Workers in 'Nonstandard' Jobs Declines." *Economic Policy Institute*. Economic Policy Institute, n.d. Web. 1 June 2005.

READING FOR MEANING

This section presents three activities that will help you think about the meanings in Kornbluh's essay. Your instructor may ask you to do one or more of these activities in class or online.

1. **Read to Summarize.** Write a sentence or two summarizing Kornbluh's proposed solution.

   For more help with summarizing, see Chapter 10, pp. 518–19.

2. **Read to Respond.** Write a paragraph or two analyzing your initial reactions to Kornbluh's essay. For example, consider anything that resonates with your experience or that seems contradictory, surprising, or fascinating, such as:

   - Kornbluh's assertion that the "'traditional family' of the breadwinner and homemaker has been replaced by the 'juggler family,' in which no one is home full-time" (par. 1);

   - The fact that "[p]arents with young children and working welfare recipients — the workers who need access to paid leave the most — are the least likely to have" flexible arrangements at work (par. 10);

   - The idea that "[c]hildren, in particular, pay a heavy price for workplace inflexibility" (par. 13), perhaps in relation to your own experience as a child or a parent.

Take a quiz to check your reading and vocabulary comprehension:
bedfordstmartins.com/readingcritically

3. **Read to Analyze Assumptions.** Write a paragraph or two analyzing an assumption you find intriguing in Kornbluh's proposal. For example:

Assumptions about the poor quality of U.S. child-care arrangements. In paragraph 13, Kornbluh cites research that finds that "[a]lmost 60 percent of child care arrangements are of poor or mediocre quality." She concludes that "[a]s a result of the unaffordable and low-quality nature of child care in this country, a disturbing number of today's children are left home alone: Over 3.3 million children age 6–12 are home alone after school each day (Vandivere et al.)." Note that Kornbluh seems to assume that readers will accept the research she cites and yet gives no information about the standards used to evaluate different child-care arrangements. To think critically about assumptions in this essay related to child care, ask yourself questions like these:

- What criteria would you apply? What assumptions do you make about the quality of different child-care arrangements — such as a relative's or a teenager's babysitting or various kinds of private or public day-care facilities?
- Kornbluh also assumes that being "home alone after school" is bad for children age six to twelve (par. 13). At what age do you think it is advisable to leave children home alone? What age do other people you know (including, perhaps, your parents) consider appropriate?

Assumptions about motivating American business. Kornbluh asserts that companies have been "largely inflexible" regarding "full-time workers' schedules" (par. 2). But she seems to assume that if companies were educated and prodded as well as "rewarded," they would give "employees flexibility without sacrificing productivity or morale" (par. 5). To think critically about the assumptions in this essay related to American business, ask yourself questions like these:

- Why do you think Kornbluh assumes companies would respond to government leadership, including education and prodding?
- Why would businesses need to be recognized and rewarded for doing something that does not sacrifice, and actually might improve, worker productivity or morale?

READING LIKE A WRITER

DEMONSTRATING THAT THE PROBLEM EXISTS AND IS SERIOUS

For problems that are new to readers, writers not only need to explain the problem but to convince readers that it exists and is serious enough to justify the actions the writer thinks are necessary to solve it. Kornbluh assumes readers will not be familiar with the problem she is writing about or take it seriously. The success of Kornbluh's proposal depends on her ability to persuade readers that the problem not only exists, but is also serious and widespread enough to require a solution. As her very first paragraph illustrates, Kornbluh cites statistics to convince readers there is a significant problem that requires their attention:

Percentage shows problem is widespread

Number shows change over time

Today fully 70 percent of families with children are headed by two working parents or by an unmarried working parent. The "traditional family" of the breadwinner and homemaker has been replaced by the "juggler family," in which no one is home full-time. Two-parent families are working 10 more hours a week than in 1979 (Bernstein and Kornbluh).

Notice that Kornbluh cites the source for these statistics. The fact that the first source is her own book may help convince readers that Kornbluh is an expert. Kornbluh also provides a works-cited list, identifying her sources so that readers can check to determine whether they are reliable. Some of Kornbluh's sources are books published by major publishers (Harvard University Press and Basic Books, for example), which helps establish their credibility. Other sources she cites are research institutes (such as New America Foundation, Economic Policy Institute, and Families and Work Institute) that readers can easily check on the Internet. Another factor that adds at least to the appearance of reliability is that Kornbluh cites statistics from a range of sources instead of relying on only one or two sources.

Analyze & Write

Write a couple of paragraphs analyzing and evaluating Kornbluh's use of statistics to present the problem:

1. First, reread paragraph 7, in which Kornbluh cites statistics from two different time periods. What does this comparison contribute to her presentation of the problem?

2. Next examine paragraph 9, in which Kornbluh cites research results. What do you think is Kornbluh's purpose in citing this report?

3. Finally, skim Kornbluh's proposal to find places where she cites raw numbers together with percentages. Here's one example:

   According to a recent study by the Institute for Women's Policy Research, 49 percent of workers—over 59 million Americans—lack basic paid sick days for themselves. (par. 10)

   How, if at all, does giving statistics in both forms help readers?

For more on the use of statistics, see Working with Sources, pp. 498-99.

A Special Reading Strategy

Recognizing Emotional Manipulation

Proposals sometimes try to arouse emotion in readers to fuel their desire to solve the problem or to urge readers to take a particular action. Following the guidelines for recognizing emotional manipulation (Chapter 10, pp. 536–37), analyze Kornbluh's use of emotion in this proposal, and write a few sentences exploring what you have learned.

Instructor's Manual

TENTH EDITION

Reading Critically
Writing Well

A READER AND GUIDE

with INTEGRATED MEDIA

Rise B. Axelrod

Charles R. Cooper

Alison M. Warriner

Lawrence Barkley
Gray Scott
Leona Fisher

INSTRUCTOR'S MANUAL for

READING CRITICALLY
WRITING WELL

A Reader and Guide

TENTH EDITION

INSTRUCTOR'S MANUAL for

READING CRITICALLY
WRITING WELL

A Reader and Guide

TENTH EDITION

Rise B. Axelrod

*University of California,
Riverside*

Lawrence Barkley

Mt. San Jacinto College — Menifee

Charles R. Cooper

*University of California,
San Diego*

Gray Scott

*University of California,
Riverside*

Alison M. Warriner

*California State University,
East Bay*

Leona Fisher

Chaffey College

Bedford/St. Martin's   Boston ◆ New York

Manufactured in the United States of America.

8 7 6 5 4 3
f e d c b a

For information, write: Bedford/St. Martin's, 75 Arlington Street, Boston, MA 02116
(617-399-4000)

ISBN 978-1-4576-6229-4

CONTENTS

Part 1 PURPOSE AND OVERVIEW OF THIS MANUAL   1

Part 2 RATIONALE FOR THE BASIC FEATURES OF THE TEXT   1

Relating Reading and Writing by Genre   1
Critical Reading   2
Writing Instruction   3
Chapter Sequence   4
Emphasis on Library, Internet, and Field Research   5

Part 3 SUGGESTED COURSE PLANS   6

One-Semester Plan: Six Assignments   6
Two-Semester Plan: Ten Assignments   7
Semester Plan for an Argument Course   8
Quarter Plan: Four Assignments   8
Two-Quarter Plan: Eight Assignments   8
What about the Research Paper?   9

Part 4 TEACHING ACTIVITIES FOR A COURSE USING THIS TEXT   9

Presenting and Discussing Readings   10
Organizing Draft Workshops   16
Holding Conferences   19
Evaluating Student Writing and Keeping Records   21

Part 5 TEACHING CHAPTER 1   26

Part 6 TEACHING CHAPTERS 2–12   27

Overview of Chapter Structure   27
Teaching the Chapter Introductions   27
Teaching the Guides to Reading   29
Teaching the Other Readings   31
Special Reading Strategy Activities   31
Teaching the Reflective Activity
  "Reviewing What Makes an Essay Effective"   31
Teaching the Guides to Writing   32
Teaching the Reflective Activity
  "Reflecting on What You Have Learned"   34
Chapter 2 Autobiography   34
Chapter 3 Observation   46
Chapter 4 Reflection   58
Chapter 5 Explaining Concepts   68
Chapter 6 Evaluation   79
Chapter 7 Arguing for a Position   90
Chapter 8 Speculating about Causes or Effects   101
Chapter 9 Proposal to Solve a Problem   113
Chapter 10 A Catalog of Reading Strategies   124
Chapter 11 Strategies for Research and Documentation   125
Chapter 12 Strategies for Analyzing Visuals   126

INSTRUCTOR'S MANUAL for

READING CRITICALLY
WRITING WELL

A Reader and Guide

TENTH EDITION

Part 1 PURPOSE AND OVERVIEW OF THIS MANUAL

This *Instructor's Manual* supports teaching with *Reading Critically, Writing Well*, Tenth Edition. Beginning teachers will find comprehensive support for planning a course, presenting and discussing the readings, and giving and evaluating writing assignments. Experienced instructors will find resources to complement their teaching styles and to orient them quickly to the readings. Online teachers and teachers using course management systems such as Blackboard to enhance their on-campus classes will find examples of how to use the text in an online learning environment.

Part 2 of the manual offers a rationale for basic features of the text, and Part 3 outlines alternative course plans. Part 4 presents teaching activities to support your work with this text—activities like presenting and discussing readings, assigning journal work, organizing students to work collaboratively, organizing draft workshops, conferencing, evaluating students' work, and managing the workload. Instead of giving general advice, we share specific strategies and activities we have developed in our own programs. If you are a beginning instructor, you will find Part 4 particularly helpful. It will enable you to approach your course confidently and to get good work from your students right away. Part 5 discusses Chapter 1, which introduces students to the kinds of work they will be doing in each subsequent chapter.

Part 6, the longest part, discusses the genre chapters (Chapters 2–9) in general and then each chapter in turn, providing an orientation to the writing assignment, an overview of the readings, resources for teaching the Reading for Meaning and Reading like a Writer activities following the readings, and an outline of A Guide to Writing. A brief discussion of when best to teach Chapters 10-12 is also included.

Part 2 RATIONALE FOR THE BASIC FEATURES OF THE TEXT

This part explains briefly why we wrote *Reading Critically, Writing Well* the way we did. Our discussion of the ideas behind the text takes up the following topics:

- the relation between reading and writing in a writing course;
- the rationale for teaching critical reading strategies for both texts and visuals and the way that practicing critical reading strategies contributes to writing development;
- the reasons students need a comprehensive framework of support as they draft and revise, with a focus on systematic invention;
- the text's chapter sequence and relations among the chapters; and
- the possibilities for library, Internet, and field research in a course using this text.

RELATING READING AND WRITING BY GENRE

Schemas—memory for text—guide our reading and writing. Novice writers must develop schemas for the genres they will read and write in college and on the job. These schemas are learned through reading many essays in a genre, by analyzing selected essays rhetorically and stylistically, and by writing and revising essays with genre criteria in mind. Genre schemas permit more confident, efficient reading and foster productive invention, planning, critical reading of drafts, and revising.

We understand a genre to be a social construct that has evolved over time to meet writers' needs in recurring and now familiar rhetorical situations. Genres make communication possible within a particular culture or society. From a writer's point of view, genres are useful tools that enable and facilitate composing. While there can be a wide variety of form and strategy within a genre—as readings in this text illustrate—experienced readers and writers in a culture recognize paradigmatic instances. Though genres are stable over time—communication requires them to be—a particular genre may change or even disappear in response to a culture's changing rhetorical demands.

Current discourse theory and professional writers' experience confirm that each of the genres explored in Chapters 2 to 9—autobiography, observation, reflection, explaining concepts, evaluation, position paper, speculation about causes or effects, and proposal to solve a problem—requires of students a special way of thinking and composing. In each genre, students must solve unique rhetorical problems and use information, memories, or arguments in particular ways.

Unless they read widely and critically on their own or come from high schools with comprehensive writing programs where teachers understand the instructional implications of genre theory, students will need careful, focused instruction in the reading and writing of genres. This text provides the materials, activities, and assignments for such instruction.

Using this text, students write autobiography as they are reading it, or they write proposals to solve problems as they are reading problem-solution essays. The readings collected in each of the chapters (2–9) illustrate a wide range of strategies used by writers of that genre for different rhetorical purposes. Students observe many ways to begin, end, pattern, and develop a genre. They see writers solving predictable problems in different ways. This close matching of reading and writing by genre is the best way to realize fully the contribution reading can make to writing development in a composition course.

The text does more than simply match reading and writing by genre, however. An activity we call Reading like a Writer, which follows each reading, helps students understand the constraints and possibilities of a genre. They learn to read a genre—and they learn to read it the way a writer does.

CRITICAL READING

Reading critically, we believe, is a skill students can learn. We don't promise to make critical reading easy. In fact, we make reading harder and slower—but more productive. For every selection in the text, we invite students first to read for meaning and then to read like writers. And we ask them to read with pencil in hand, annotating the text from these two perspectives. Most important, we ask them to write about what they discover, using writing itself to explore ideas and to consolidate what they have learned. Writing becomes part of critical reading—an essential activity that provides a tentative record of meanings and insights students can then share with others and thereby further enlarge what they can learn from reading.

ADDITIONAL CRITICAL READING STRATEGIES In addition to these two critical reading strategies—Reading for Meaning and Reading like a Writer—we provide a Catalog of Reading strategies in Chapter 10 in the text:

- Annotating
- Taking inventory
- Outlining
- Summarizing
- Paraphrasing
- Synthesizing
- Contextualizing
- Exploring the significance of figurative language
- Looking for patterns of opposition

2

- Reflecting on challenges to your beliefs and values
- Comparing and contrasting related readings
- Evaluating the logic of an argument
- Recognizing logical fallacies
- Recognizing emotional manipulation
- Judging the writer's credibility

Each genre chapter includes reading activities that apply one or two of the listed methods to specific readings. You may assign those readings and reading activities in order to give students more exposure to the sorts of reading strategies just listed. Some of these strategies engage students in comparing and contrasting related readings as part of this edition's emphasis on linked readings. You may, of course, decide to have students use a strategy from this chapter with other readings.

The comprehensive, approachable, theory-based, and research-supported program of critical reading offered in the text provides no panacea, however. We know that what students get from a reading depends in part on what they bring to it. Consequently, when students read headnotes, we invite them to reflect on their knowledge of a reading's subject, and we offer them one purpose for reading. We also know that reading can be considerably enriched by discussion: textual meaning making at its best is in part a social activity. Consequently, we make it easy for you to help students share their writing in response to the Reading for Meaning and Reading like a Writer activities following every reading.

STRATEGIES FOR ANALYZING VISUALS Readers today must be skilled and savvy readers of visuals as well as of language, thanks to the Information Age's frequent marriage of text and visuals. For this reason, *Reading Critically, Writing Well* includes guidance for students on how to critically "read" images online, in film, or in other media. Instructors interested in having students practice or hone such skills may want to assign and discuss Chapter 12, Strategies for Analyzing Visuals, and follow up with any of the Analyzing Visuals activities in the genre chapters (2–9). The Analyzing Visuals activities for individual genre chapters are discussed in each of the associated sections of Part 6 in this manual.

WRITING INSTRUCTION

The pencil-in-hand critical reading strategies discussed above contribute directly to students' writing development. Though critical reading is necessary for developing writing skills in a genre, it is not sufficient. Students also need comprehensive support for invention, drafting, and revising an essay in a genre. This text provides such support through activities and guides.

READING LIKE A WRITER Students complete a full rhetorical analysis of each chapter's opening sample essay in A Guide to Reading. In addition, they analyze a key rhetorical strategy of each subsequent reading in a chapter. If they complete these activities for every reading, they learn about all the basic features and writing strategies of a genre. What they learn greatly improves the chances for successful peer critique. (Part 4 discusses ways to organize peer critiques, or *draft workshops*, as we call them.)

GUIDES TO WRITING Each genre chapter (2–9) concludes with A Guide to Writing, which is concise but comprehensive. This guide leads (and encourages) students through the writing process: writing a draft; evaluating the draft with feedback from others; improving the draft through revising, editing, and proofreading; and reflecting on what you have learned. There now is solid evidence that guided, systematic drafting enables students to write better. Therefore, each chapter provides genre-specific activities that are based on established heuristics like freewriting, answering questions, list making, outlining, and analyzing readers. Each activity requires only a few minutes (as few as one or two and rarely more than thirty). (See Part 4 of this manual for a discussion about assigning and encouraging drafting activities.)

The Writing a Draft activities enable students to find a subject, generate ideas about it, explore their rhetorical situation fully, and even carry out any necessary research. These writings may record several days of a potentially rich invention process. Students who use the full resources for invention compose first drafts that are longer, more thoughtful, more interesting, and closer to their best work on a subject.

The guides also help students give and get critical readings of their drafts, set goals before and during drafting, and organize their essays prior to drafting. Each guide concludes with advice about revising to strengthen the essay and improve its readability, suggestions for editing and proofreading the revised essay, and an invitation to reflect on what has been learned.

These Guides to Writing complement the critical reading strategies. Together, they provide a comprehensive program in reading and writing. They bring reading and writing together in a way that gives every student a chance to become more literate.

CHAPTER SEQUENCE

Although the genre chapters can be presented in different sequences (see the discussion of various course plans in Part 3), we offer here a brief rationale for the text sequence. These are the chapters:

Chapter 2: Autobiography
Chapter 3: Observation
Chapter 4: Reflection
Chapter 5: Explaining Concepts
Chapter 6: Evaluation
Chapter 7: Arguing for a Position
Chapter 8: Speculating about Causes or Effects
Chapter 9: Proposal to Solve a Problem

The sequence moves from experiential, observational, and explanatory writing (2–5) to persuasive or argumentative (6–9) writing. While an autobiographical essay is not necessarily easier to write than a position paper, there are certain advantages to our sequence. If students begin with autobiography, firsthand observation, and reflection, they need not struggle with library and Internet research. Instead, students work with familiar or immediately available material and learn to value their own memory and perception—developing a confident, assertive voice in their writing. Strategies of description and narration practiced in autobiography are central to observation and reflection. The anecdotes important to autobiography and reflection can emerge again very usefully in certain arguments.

Observation, reflection, and explanation offer opportunities for students to organize their material topically, use explicit topic sentences and cueing devices, and employ a variety of strategies (or modes) for developing their subjects and achieving their rhetorical purposes. Even autobiography that focuses on a remembered person typically is organized topically.

Chapter 6 begins an argument sequence that consists of half the genre chapters in the text. This sequence begins with evaluation and position papers to give students practice at expressing and defending judgments before they move on to more complicated genres of argument: speculating about causes and effects, and proposing solutions. The sequence closes with proposing solutions, because this genre incorporates those that have gone before it. For example, when students write a proposal to solve a problem in Chapter 9, they may argue the causes or effects of the problem and evaluate alternative solutions.

The argument chapters emphasize strategies for devising plausible arguments for particular readers. The students' rhetorical situation in each chapter can be viewed as follows:

- demonstrating the validity of a judgment (Chapter 6),
- defending a position on an issue (Chapter 7),
- conjecturing about possible causes or effects (Chapter 8),
- arguing the feasibility of a solution to a problem (Chapter 9).

This sequence provides a challenging introduction to the critical reading and writing of argumentation.

This edition of *Reading Critically, Writing Well* also includes three new chapters, included in previous editions as appendices:

Chapter 10: A Catalog of Reading Strategies
Chapter 11: Strategies for Research and Documentation
Chapter 12: Strategies for Analyzing Visuals

These chapters may be taught effectively on their own, but many instructors find it productive to pair them with the genres taught in Chapters 2–9. Chapter 10, for example, may be taught in conjunction with any of these chapters but can work well if taught early on. Students may find the material in Chapter 11 helpful as they are speculating about causes or effects (Chapter 8) or proposing solutions (Chapter 9). Chapter 12 can be taught well as a genre in its own right; however, many instructors and students have found it valuable to include visuals as part of any number of assignments, including the reflection essays (Chapter 4) or the essays explaining a concept (Chapter 5).

EMPHASIS ON LIBRARY, INTERNET, AND FIELD RESEARCH

Since research can strengthen student writing in Chapters 3 and 5 to 9, the text regularly invites library, Internet, or field research. In addition, Chapter 11 provides guidance with these three kinds of research. Although research can be emphasized toward the end of a course, students have so much to learn about finding and evaluating sources, integrating sources into their essays, and citing sources properly that we believe they should be doing some research early in the course. Hence, the text features field research in Chapter 3: Observation and library and Internet research in Chapter 5: Explaining Concepts. All subsequent chapters regularly invite students to do research. Such an emphasis on research provides a realistic introduction to writing in academic and professional situations. Many of the readings, including student readings, use and cite sources. Nevertheless, in a writing program that does not require students to use sources or does not take up sources until the second semester, students can easily skip the research steps in every chapter's Guide to Writing. They can instead support their arguments from personal experience and present knowledge.

5

Composition instructors typically organize their courses around writing assignments. Because *Reading Critically, Writing Well* covers eight genres and includes many ideas for writing in each genre chapter, it offers different possibilities for designing a course. This part describes a variety of course plans you can use as the basis of your own syllabus, beginning with a six-assignment plan. Then come plans for a two-semester program, a one-semester argument course, a quarter program, and a two-quarter program. Finally, we discuss the opportunities for research with the text, including an extended library and Internet research paper.

ONE-SEMESTER PLAN: SIX ASSIGNMENTS

This plan permits six essay assignments from Chapters 2 to 9. Though this plan does not include a formal, extended research paper, many assignments invite research. For example, beginning with Chapter 5, every chapter invites students to carry out library or Internet research.

From this plan, you could readily devise a syllabus for your course. All the suggested course plans in this section assume that you might be requiring frequent writing in a journal, making collaborative-learning assignments, arranging in-class workshops for peer critiques of drafts, or holding conferences over drafts. Part 4 offers advice on all these activities.

Here are the essay assignments, by chapter title, in this plan:

Autobiography (Chapter 2)
Observation (Chapter 3)
Reflection (Chapter 4)
Explaining Concepts (Chapter 5)
Evaluation (Chapter 6)
Proposal to Solve a Problem (Chapter 9)

This plan gives balanced attention to personal writing (Chapters 2, 4), explanatory writing (Chapters 3, 5), and argument (Chapters 6, 9). It uses all chapters except Chapter 7: Arguing for a Position and Chapter 8: Speculating about Causes or Effects. Chapters 7 and 8 could be substituted for Chapters 6 and 9.

Keeping in mind that each of our assignment chapters offers many critical reading and writing activities, you might want to allow as much as three weeks for each assignment, especially if you ask students to revise their essays. Here's how one assignment sequence might play out over a three-week period in a class meeting three times weekly:

Week 1
M: Discuss the chapter opening and rhetorical situations.
    Do in class the reflective activity, Thinking about the Genre.
    Assign the introductory reading and Reading for Meaning activity.
W: Discuss Reading for Meaning writing.
    Do in class one of the Reading like a Writer activities.
    Assign the remaining Reading like a Writer activities.
F: Discuss Reading like a Writer activities.
    Discuss possible essay subjects following each reading.
    Assign the first Invention and Research activities in A Guide to Writing.
    Assign the second and third readings and their Reading for Meaning and Reading like a Writer activities.

Week 2

M: Discuss the second and third readings and reading activities.
Evaluate subjects for essays.
Discuss Writing a Draft activities.
Assign the fourth and fifth readings and reading activities.

W: Discuss the fourth and fifth readings and reading activities.
Do in class a Writing a Draft activity from A Guide to Writing. Assign other Writing a Draft activities.
Do in class as a group activity Reviewing What Makes an Effective Essay.
Discuss possible organizational plans.

F: Assign the remainder of the Writing a Draft activities.
Assign the first draft.

Week 3

M: Hold a workshop on drafts.

W: Hold a further workshop on drafts or in-class work on revising drafts.

F: The revision is due.
Conduct in-class editing and proofreading exercises.
Do the Reflecting on What You Have Learned activity.

TWO-SEMESTER PLAN: TEN ASSIGNMENTS

Several colleges use *Reading Critically, Writing Well* as the basic text, usually along with a handbook or one or more trade books, for a two-semester writing program. A capacious two-semester plan like the following allows multiple resources in certain chapters to be used to the fullest. Here we list a possible essay sequence, assuming a pattern of course activities and assignments like that of the one-semester plan detailed above.

Assignment	*Chapter*
1	2, Autobiography: Narrating the Story
2	2, Autobiography: Describing Places
3	3, Observation
4	4, Reflection
5	5, Explaining Concepts
6	6, Evaluation
7	7, Arguing for a Position
8	8, Speculating about Causes or Effects (speculating about causes)
9	8, Speculating about Causes or Effects (speculating about effects)
10	9, Proposal to Solve a Problem

A variation on this plan is to do one autobiography assignment and then assign an observation, a reflection, or an evaluation essay centered on some part of the writing process. Students might reflect, in a formal graded essay, on their experiences writing a previous paper, or they might observe the writing process of a classmate or a team and write an observation paper about it, or they might write formal evaluations of essays written by classmates (as Christine Romano does in Chapter 6, where she evaluates Jessica Statsky's position paper from Chapter 7).

SEMESTER PLAN FOR AN ARGUMENT COURSE

The text includes enough material on argument to fill a one-semester course concerned solely with argument or persuasion:

Assignment	Chapter
1	6, Evaluation
2	7, Arguing for a Position (without research)
3	7, Arguing for a Position (with research)
4	8, Speculating about Causes or Effects (speculating about causes)
5	8, Speculating about Causes or Effects (speculating about effects)
6	9, Proposal to Solve a Problem

This plan could make good use of the critical reading strategies—such as Evaluating the Logic of an Argument; Testing Appropriateness, Believability, and Consistency and Completeness; Recognizing Emotional Manipulation; Testing for Knowledge, Common Ground, and Fairness; and Judging the Writer's Credibility—in Chapter 10. At the instructor's or student's discretion, some assignments might call for students to analyze visuals, using the strategies in Chapter 12. Assignments 1, 4, and 5 above are particularly well suited for visual analysis, as students could evaluate the effectiveness of a visual or craft arguments about the possible effects of the visual or the causes of particularly common visual elements.

QUARTER PLAN: FOUR ASSIGNMENTS

One-quarter courses can accommodate four of our assignments, though some courses that use our text give three or five assignments. Many programs at quarter-system campuses require students to complete two quarters of composition.

A one-quarter program faces hard choices. A sampling of personal, explanatory, and persuasive writing might look like this:

Assignment	Chapter
1	2, Autobiography
2	3, Observation
3	7, Arguing for a Position
4	9, Proposal to Solve a Problem

TWO-QUARTER PLAN: EIGHT ASSIGNMENTS

A two-quarter program, with four assignments each quarter, might be organized as follows:

Assignment	Chapter
1	2, Autobiography
2	3, Observation
3	4, Reflection
4	5, Explaining Concepts
5	6, Evaluation
6	7, Arguing for a Position
7	8, Speculating about Causes or Effects
8	9, Proposal to Solve a Problem

WHAT ABOUT THE RESEARCH PAPER?

Except for the Chapter 3 observational essay, which requires observing and interviewing, every essay arising from Chapters 2 to 9 can be completed without research. In fact, the choosing-a-subject section at the beginning of the Writing a Draft sequence of each Guide to Writing are designed to suggest many possibilities for writing that allow students to rely on their own present knowledge, experience, and resources. At the same time, every chapter except Autobiography can engage students in research, if the instructor wishes. We expect at least limited research with nearly all the assignments in our own programs. Here we briefly outline the possibilities:

Chapter 3, Observation: Visiting a place, observing, interviewing, taking notes

Chapter 5, Explaining Concepts: Library research on the concepts that students explain

Chapter 6, Evaluation: Reseeing, revisiting, or rereading the subject being evaluated and taking notes

Chapter 7, Arguing for a Position: Library research on an issue to define and describe it adequately and to assess others' positions

Chapter 8, Speculating about Causes or Effects: Library research on the event, trend, or phenomenon speculated about to describe it fully and to survey others' proposed causes or effects

Chapter 9, Proposal to Solve a Problem: Interviewing people to understand more fully a problem affecting them and to anticipate their preferred solutions; research on methods of implementing a proposed solution

Chapter 11, Strategies for Research and Documentation, provides comprehensive support for field (observing and interviewing), library, and Internet research.

If your program requires an extended library-research paper, the most likely candidates in the text are Chapters 5 and 9—the one explanatory, the other argumentative. These chapters, along with Chapter 11, provide full support for an extended research essay. Any of our proposed plans, above, could be adjusted to allow time during the final three or four weeks of a course for a library-research paper.

Part 4 TEACHING ACTIVITIES FOR A COURSE USING THIS TEXT

This part outlines basic teaching activities to support your work with this text. These activities, we believe, are important to the success of any composition course, whatever the textbook or other materials.

If you are a beginning instructor, you will find this section particularly helpful. Along with a syllabus based on one of our course plans in Part 3, the activities outlined in this part permit you to organize a complete course from start to finish: schedule, assignments, classroom and homework activities, evaluation of student writing, and record keeping. Instead of offering general advice in this part, we share activities, assignments, and materials we have used in our own programs along with at least a hundred instructors who have worked with us over the years.

Note: This part presents proven teaching activities; the final two parts of this manual (Parts 5 and 6) provide specific support for teaching the introductory chapter and each genre chapter.

PRESENTING AND DISCUSSING READINGS

If students are to succeed with an essay assignment in one of our genre chapters, they should read—and critically reread—the selections in that chapter. They should compare and contrast readings to see the full range of possibilities for their own essay in a genre. Class discussions of readings should be focused, productive, and encouraging to students as writers. How might you ensure such critical reading and discussions? This section offers suggestions.

GIVING CLEAR AND COMPLETE ASSIGNMENTS Even in a casual, slow-moving course using *Reading Critically, Writing Well*, assignments will be frequent: both the writing and the reading call for almost daily student work. If you find our other recommendations in this section persuasive, you can pursue several complementary strands of work, engaging students in a variety of out-of-class assignments each week.

Probably the most effective way to give assignments is to prepare a once-a-week handout, or online announcement if your campus uses Blackboard or some other Internet-based course management system. Even though we give students a detailed course syllabus, we further detail assignments for each week. We put assignments in writing because students do not all hear the same thing, it seems, when we give assignments orally and also because we want to save class time by not dictating assignments or writing them on the board. The weekly assignment handout precludes giving hasty last-minute assignments orally as students gather up books and head for the door. Most important, we think, preparing the weekly assignment handout gives us an opportunity to think through carefully what we want to accomplish in a given week.

Except for drafting and revising full essays, assignments in a course using this text are relatively brief. For example, a single selection and its reading activities might take an hour. After a reading, exploring in one's journal an idea for writing might take ten or fifteen minutes. Each chapter's introductory reading and related activities might require two hours, time best divided into two or more working periods during one or two days, and some of these activities might even be conducted in class.

In A Guide to Writing in any genre chapter, invention work entails brief writings spread over two or three days. Such frequent writing—our goal for students is *daily* writing—lets the mind work on the readings, consolidate new rhetorical learning, and produce ideas for writing. Consequently, *frequency* and *variety* of writing are essential. Pacing work during the week and from week to week is crucial. Your weekly assignment handout can pace, sequence, and clarify this work. As a result, students can efficiently use their limited time to prepare for class.

We give weekly assignments at the beginning of the first class meeting of each week and take a few minutes to go over the assignments and answer any questions. Because we provide the handout, students who come late rarely take our time after class to discuss assignments. A student who must be absent can later pick up the assignment handout or download it.

Some instructors add to the assignment handout comments reiterating course goals, previewing an especially challenging assignment, forecasting a change of pace, praising or exhorting the class, summarizing progress and anticipating next developments, relating concepts and assignments to give students a larger view of the course, and so on.

PREVIEWING READINGS Most of the readings are preceded by "before you read" and "as you read" suggestions and questions. These questions are designed to help students activate prior knowledge of the subject and read more purposefully. These questions enrich readings, and they may also entice or invite students to read a reading. As you assign a reading, however, you can do still more to entice students to read it:

- Tell them some things you may know about the historical or cultural context of the reading.

- Tell them something about the author, or read a brief excerpt from one of the author's books. (For example, when you assign "An American Childhood" by Annie Dillard in Chapter 2, read aloud a few of Dillard's arresting, memorable aphorisms and analogies about writing from her best-selling book *The Writing Life*.)
- Show them the book or an issue of the magazine from which the reading was selected, and talk about the impact of the book, what you learned from it, or the purpose and readership of the magazine.
- Preview what they will learn as writers from the reading.
- Relate the reading to other readings in the chapter.

These enticements take only a few minutes, but they can increase students' willingness to begin a reading in the odd moments and places where homework gets done.

SETTING UP A READING JOURNAL A reading journal and collaborative reading/learning assignments (described later in this section) are essential features of our courses.

A reading journal differs from a personal journal, a writer's journal, or an exploratory dialogic (or double-entry) journal. It is concerned mainly or exclusively with using writing to learn about reading, through goal-focused journal tasks assigned by the instructor. For students keeping reading journals in a course using this text, the frequent journal writings assist them in learning from their reading what a *writer* needs to know. This is a special kind of rhetorical learning. It is based on critical reading (and especially on critical rereading). Its mode is analytic, and its outcome is conceptual.

One of us has completed research (with Susan McDonald) suggesting that in an assigned-readings course in which a particular type of writing is to be the outcome, the reading journal we are proposing teaches students far more than an exploratory journal in which students initiate all the writing. (A dialogic or personal journal could be just the right choice for a different course.)

How do you set up a reading journal? After much trial and error over several years, we have discovered what works best for us and our instructors. Students buy a special loose-leaf three-ring binder and label it *Reading Journal*. (We recommend an inexpensive version with half-inch rings and a flexible cover; this size is more portable than heavy-duty binders.) Each journal entry begins on a separate piece of paper labeled with the student's name, the date, the source of the entry (e.g., Chapter 2, Dillard, Reading like a Writer), and any other information that will facilitate your record keeping.

Give reading journal assignments once a week as part of your weekly assignment handout. By going week by week, rather than planning journal assignments for a longer period, you have flexibility to speed or slow the pace, to insert assignments that arise from special problems or opportunities, and, most important, to match the assignments precisely to the week's sequence of reading and writing activities.

We collect loose-leaf journal entries every week or two and return them to students to reinsert in their binders at the next class meeting. The first time we collect journal entries, we spend more time reading and commenting than we do later: we want to be sure students know what we expect of their reading journals. If the entries are brief and thin, we insist on more writing in future journal entries. If the writing seems too serious, cautious, or planned, we encourage exploration, risk taking, digressions, even playfulness.

If you number your journal assignments sequentially from the beginning to the end of your course and ask students to do the same in their journals, then you always know where each student is in the sequence and whether at the midpoint or end of the course students have completed all assignments.

The reading journal also works well in a course management system (CMS) such as Blackboard. Students post their weekly journal entries in the discussion thread section of the CMS. One advantage to this system is transparency: you can assign students to read each other's work, so you can easily reference emerging themes or other characteristics within a specific journal assignment. You can even identify samples of exemplary work online and direct students to read them as examples of good reading-journal entries. If you are giving the plus, check, or minus response, you can enter your responses into the CMS's grading system, which remains available only to the student being graded, unlike the journal posts, which are available to the class.

Consider weighting the reading journal as 20 percent or 25 percent of the course grade. We tell students that they must complete all journal assignments in a timely fashion to receive a C in the course. We do not actually grade the journal. Instead, we skim it quickly at the end of the course and decide whether it is exemplary, very good, acceptable, or complete but thin and perfunctory; we inform students of our judgment in a brief final note.

The goal is to spend as little time as possible reading journals while still encouraging students to sustain their work in the journal.

How should students approach reading-journal assignments? We outline various types of journal assignments below, each requiring a different approach. We can say in general, however, that journal writing is relatively informal. It is first-draft writing, not painstakingly planned, tight, or cautious. It is exploratory, discursive, digressive, and associational. A student may begin a journal entry with one idea and end it with quite a different one. In the reading journal, a student *writes to learn*, not merely to report what has been learned.

Handwritten journal entries may (and probably *should*) exhibit crossed-out (less time-consuming than erasing) phrases or sentences, marginal or interlinear additions, one or more parts added later to the end. While journal entries generated electronically will not show the same traces of revision, they will demonstrate the same benefits of reworking and developing ideas as do handwritten entries. They should not strike the reader as perfunctory. Instead, they should show evidence of commitment to learning through writing—of insight, discovery, confusion, and questioning.

What kinds of reading-journal assignments might you give? We recommend three basic kinds:

1. *Critical reading activities from the genre chapters* Keep in mind that our critical reading activities—Reading for Meaning and Reading like a Writer—require writing. The reading journal collects and organizes *all* critical reading activities—no small convenience for you when, in a semester plan, students may complete thirty to forty critical reading activities. The loose-leaf format enables students to exchange single entries, and you can evaluate one or more activities at a time, much in the same way the online journal allows you to selectively evaluate specific activities.

2. *Copy and comment* (as in the Commonplace Book, a staple of liberal arts education since the Middle Ages) Students occasionally copy a particularly striking sentence or brief passage from one of the readings and then comment, react, or analyze for a page or so. You could make a copy-and-comment assignment once with each genre chapter. In this way, the reading journal poses an activity prized by advocates of the dialogic journal.

3. *Reflections on learning and on the course* Recent research demonstrates that when students step back and review what they are learning, they remember it longer and put it to better use. In a course using this text, students learn how to read and write certain genres. To put it another way, they acquire rhetorical or textual knowledge.

Each genre chapter offers students activities for reflecting, which you can assign as journal entries. The reflecting activities appear at the very end of the chapter, following A Guide to Writing [the Genre]. They give students an opportunity to look back on their experiences reading and writing essays in the genre and to reflect on what they have learned.

These metacognitive activities focus on the kind of writing students are learning about in a particular chapter, but you can add another reflecting activity that asks students to relate what they have learned from previous chapters to what they are learning in a current chapter. For example, students reflecting on what they have learned in Chapter 3: Observation can be asked which rhetorical concepts from Chapter 2: Autobiography informed their reading and writing of the observational essay, or students moving through the argument chapters (6–9) can be asked to compare and contrast the different types of argument.

Students might also be asked to comment on the course. With these tasks, you want to deflect personal evaluations of other students and of you and invite frank assessments of progress, problems with assignments or materials, misunderstandings, special insights, and frustrations. Questions like these, in various combinations, have worked very well for us:

- What has most surprised you so far about this course? Account for your surprise. (We ask this question and the next two early in a course.)
- What has most pleased you so far about this course? Most disappointed you? Account for your pleasure and disappointment.
- How is this course different from your high-school English courses, and how is it similar to them?
- How is this course influencing your reading and writing in your other courses? Give specific examples.
- How are your reading and writing changing as a result of this course? Give specific examples.
- We are now at the halfway point in the course. What are you most pleased with about your development as a reader and writer? What are your goals for the second half of the course?
- What one thing could I do to make the course more satisfying for you? What one thing could you do? Explain why these changes could be important for you.

We like to pose a journal task like this every two weeks or so. From students' writing, we learn a lot about the students and the course. You will readily think of other questions to ask as you get to know your students.

GIVING QUIZZES For many years, we resisted quizzing students to discover whether they had completed our reading assignments, assuming they had developed a mature understanding of the consequences of neglecting to do the reading. Now we collect or ask them to post in the class's course management system their Reading for Meaning activities—particularly, the Read to Summarize activity—or give a quiz at the beginning of most class meetings or at the start of online sections for which readings have been assigned.

The reasons we changed our position are that (1) we came to recognize the competing demands on students' time and (2) we understand how important thoughtful critical reading is to students' development as writers. Therefore, we now provide every possible encouragement for students to complete reading assignments.

Giving clear reading assignments, previewing readings enticingly, and giving reading-journal assignments on the readings provide much of the encouragement. Quizzes provide the rest. Students rarely come to our reading-day discussions unprepared. And as a consequence, their essays are informed by rhetorical strategies from the assigned readings—and, therefore, stronger.

We rely on three basic quiz questions, which we give orally (we give only *one* on a quiz):

1. Summarize selection X.
2. What can a writer learn from selection Y? (based on the Reading like a Writer activity)
3. How are selections X and Y alike and different? (based on the Special Reading Strategy: Comparing and Contrasting Related Readings)

Students write quickly for five or ten minutes. Students who are tardy or absent may not make up a missed quiz. We collect the quizzes and file them with other quizzes in a folder for each student. We do not grade or return them. Instead, we may periodically review these folders and write a note to (or chat with) a student whose quizzes are unsatisfactory. Most students write satisfactory quizzes. In one or two minutes, you can skim a quiz folder to tell any anxious student how well he or she is doing on the quizzes.

At the end of the course, you can just as quickly tell which students have consistently performed well on the quizzes. You can overlook one or two missing quizzes. To encourage students, you might weight quizzes 10 percent of the final grade.

Early in the course you can read aloud a few outstanding quizzes to give students an idea of what you expect. Be firm about the quizzes. Tell students why you give them: quizzes are only one small means toward a consequential end—better essays.

Available with this edition of *Reading Critically, Writing Well* is a series of quizzes for each professional selection (Chapters 2–9) in the print text and e-Pages: an auto-graded comprehension quiz and summary and vocabulary quizzes with automatic feedback. These quizzes may be accessed through the e-Pages, free with each new copy of the book: bedfordstmartins.com/readingcritically.

GIVING COLLABORATIVE-LEARNING ASSIGNMENTS We believe that collaborative-learning activities can contribute to students' understanding of what the readings offer them as critical readers and writers. We have students discuss readings in small groups to elaborate and consolidate their learning. Each student reads assigned selections and then meets with his or her collaborative-learning group to complete tasks we pose. These meetings are occasions primarily for rereading and talking, though some writing usually results as well. We sometimes talk about these groups as collaborative-reading groups.

Here are our two basic activities. We try to assign one or the other in each genre chapter, and both work well in online groups:

Group Report on a Reading

Carefully read the essay assigned to your group, and then meet with your group to work together on Read to Analyze Assumptions or the Reading like a Writer activity and to prepare a presentation for the rest of the class.

You will then share what you have learned. You should expect other members of the class to be familiar with the essay you will present. Needless to say, be sure that you are familiar with the essays assigned to the other groups. You must be prepared to participate in the discussion about the essays that the other groups present.

Group Evaluation of Two Readings

Your group has been assigned two readings. Carefully read the two assigned essays before you meet with your group. Decide on your own which reading you think is the better example of the genre.

Then meet with your group and discuss each person's choice of the better example. Prepare an oral report about your group's evaluation for the rest of the class.

In your report, you should explain your group's judgment and the reasons for making it. Be sure that you refer to the basic features of the genre. If one or two of your group cannot agree with the other members, give the class both minority and majority reports.

You should expect other members of the class to be familiar with these essays. Likewise, be sure that you are familiar with the essays assigned to the other groups. You must be able to participate in the other groups' presentations of their evaluations.

You will see many possible variations on these basic group activities. For example, you can use the Comparing and Contrasting Related Readings activity as a group activity to report on similarities and differences between the two readings rather than to argue that one is better. Or student teams might speculate about the possible causes or origins of genre features they identify in one or more readings.

Avoid assigning members to groups randomly or letting students assign themselves. Instead, as soon as possible, assign each student to a group of four. If students drop out during the term, you may need to combine reduced groups. In assigning members to groups, try to avoid homogeneous group-ings. We recommend a mix of genders, cultural backgrounds, ages, or other factors that will ensure a heterogeneous group. You may also want to ensure a range of writing abilities in each group, because research shows that diversity in ability increases explanation in a group and improves learning.

If groups meet during class time, try to encourage full participation by all group members, possibly by listening in for a minute and then asking one of the quieter members a question. Research strongly suggests that the students who benefit most from group activities are the ones who spend group time explaining things. If group work requires more time than you can afford in class, you can ask students to schedule a regular time to meet outside class, or you can create group meeting spaces in a course management system.

Explain to students that the collaborative discussion of readings will contribute to their success in your course, and offer them general guidelines for collaboration. Their goal—at least in these two basic activities—is to prepare a brief report (five to eight minutes or a three- to four-page post in a course management system, depending on how many groups you have and how long your class meets) on what they learned about the readings. Tell them they must report as a *panel*, with each person con-tributing. Since the reports tend to sprawl, you will have to enforce time limits for in-class reports so that all groups may report but you will still have time for other activities.

FACILITATING CLASSROOM DISCUSSION OF READINGS The day arrives when students come to class to discuss the readings—a crucial moment in a course that helps students read critically and write well. This is potentially the *worst* moment in a writing course. Students look at the floor, or there is little activity in the course management system. No one volunteers to take your first question or post a first response. The first person you call on was not able to do the reading. The second person you call on thought the readings were assigned for the next class meeting. The third person you call on seems to have misread or only partially read the reading. The mood changes. You feel grim. The students feel embarrassed. What to do? Probably the only thing to do is to allow time for everyone to read a reading before you attempt to discuss it. As a result, only one of the readings you assigned receives any attention.

This nightmare scenario will likely never materialize in your course if in your planning and assignments you take the advice we suggest in earlier sections:

- reading assignments that you give on a weekly handout,
- enticing previews to motivate students to read,
- reading-journal assignments to complete the critical reading activities following assigned readings,
- a collaborative-learning assignment on the readings, and
- a quiz on the readings.

Here's the plan we find most productive for a class meeting about assigned readings:

- quiz
- reading aloud of journal entries, or Read to Summarize and/or Read to Respond sections of the Reading for Meaning activity (two to four students)
- discussion of Read to Analyze Assumptions
- collaborative-learning reports on Read to Analyze Assumptions or the Reading like a Writer activity

- discussion
- your own close reading of a particular writing strategy exemplified in the reading or a brief explanation from you about the context of a reading, its author, its major ideas, and so on
- discussion of the rhetorical features in relation to the students' own writing

Notice that even though students have prepared carefully and must contribute to the presentation and discussion of readings, you still have a major role to play. Experienced teachers can arrange for students to say most of what needs to be said about readings, but they can rarely get them to say *all* that needs to be said. And so you say what they are not yet prepared to say. You make connections that will not be apparent to them as they are beginning to study a genre. They especially need your help in looking closely at features of a particular essay. As they observe you reading critically—reading rhetorically, reading like a writer—they learn to do it themselves.

It is important to begin each discussion by reminding students of the purpose for discussing the readings—to examine the basic features of and writers' strategies in a particular genre and to improve students' own writing as a result of this examination. As the discussion progresses, keep reminding students of the connections between the various readings and their own writing.

To complete the discussion of each reading, ask students to summarize the main things they have learned. You can then reiterate the main points of the discussion and help students to see the connections between the current reading and earlier ones. An in-class or online journal question can help students focus and reflect on what they have learned during the discussion.

Give up on discussions that do not seem to be going anywhere or that are not engaging most of the students. Do not stay on a single point (or a single essay) for too long.

Try to involve every student in every discussion so that a few students are not doing all the talking or posting. Many students are somewhat shy about speaking in class, so getting them to participate may take some special effort on your part. One way to elicit a spoken or posted response from even the shyest of students is to ask a simple, low-key question such as, What do you remember best about this selection? Most students should be able to answer this question on the spot, and they can then be encouraged to speculate about why a certain feature makes the selection memorable. If students have written responses to the Reading for Meaning and Reading like a Writer activities in class or as homework, you can ask them to read what they have written.

ORGANIZING DRAFT WORKSHOPS

The draft, or peer-critique workshop, brings class members together to read and respond to work in progress—usually, first or second drafts. In this section, we describe two workshop formats: (1) Two or three students bring copies of their drafts for the whole class and read their drafts aloud; then the whole class discusses the drafts. (2) Two students exchange drafts and write an analysis of each other's work; this format works well in a course management system. You could use one of these formats at one class meeting and the other at the next.

We recommend that you begin with whole-class discussion rather than with written analysis so that you can review the basic issues and requirements of the assignment. Even with the help of the chapter's Guide to Writing, there will still be students who have not quite brought the assignment into focus. By concentrating initially on one or two papers with the whole class, you can remind students of the basic issues of the kind of writing under discussion. At the end of the discussion, you can summarize these basic issues on the board and relate them to points in the chapter's Evaluating the Draft: Getting a Constructive Critical Reading. This flow should give students more confidence in helping each other and keep them focused on the central rhetorical issues of the assignment rather than the peripheral ones.

DISCUSSION FORMAT Arrange in advance for one or two students to post their essays in the course management system or to bring enough copies of their drafts for every two students to share. Alternatively, you can display the draft for the whole class to read, using a computer and projector or an overhead projector. The writer tells the class about any particular problems he or she has had in the draft and then reads it aloud while the rest of the class follows along on the copies, making marginal notes, or on the projected image. Class members will respond better if they hear and see the draft simultaneously. At the end of the oral reading, the instructor chairs a discussion of the draft, appointing a scribe to record specific suggestions for revisions on behalf of the writer. The activities in Evaluating the Draft can form the basis of this discussion. At the end of the discussion, the scribe gives the writer the discussion notes, and other students pass along their copies with marginal notes.

This whole-class discussion of one draft at a time simulates the traditional writers' workshop widely used in graduate programs. Many instructors using this workshop format ask that the writer not participate in the discussion. There are good reasons for this rule. At the draft stage, writers need to listen to the discussion and to reflect thoughtfully on what readers say, why they misunderstand, and what they have questions about. From listening to this sort of discussion of one's draft, a writer can know whether it struck readers as honest, engaging, authentic, informative, or convincing.

Working with the whole class on one draft allows you to guide the discussion and make observations that are relevant to the assignment and not just to the draft at hand. An alternative is to divide the class into small groups of four or five, with one member of each group bringing copies of his or her draft for the others in the group and reading it aloud to them. In a large class, this approach allows more students to receive group responses to their drafts and encourages the more reticent students to participate in the discussion. You can join one group or move among the groups. This format works best when students know what is expected and can work productively without your guidance.

WRITTEN-ANALYSIS FORMAT We typically begin by asking students to exchange drafts with another class member. Each student then spends the first twenty or twenty-five minutes reading the partner's draft silently and writing a critical response to it. Activities to guide this process can be found under Evaluating the Draft in the chapter's Guide to Writing. As students first exchange drafts, they brief their partners on particular points they would like the partners to critique. The respondents write their responses on separate sheets of paper, labeled at the top to look like this:

Autobiographical Essay Draft
Workshop Response for John Smith by Yolanda Jenkins

During the first part of the workshop, while pairs of students are working silently on each other's drafts, you may choose to move among them to offer advice. Alternatively, you can arrange in advance for students to bring additional copies of their drafts for you to review during this time. When students have finished their written responses, each partner returns the draft and response to the other, and then they can discuss their responses.

To facilitate this critical exchange, you may want to pair students according to their writing abilities, changing the pairs so that each student receives responses from several others during the course.

In the online environment, we pair students according to their writing abilities. Paired students post their drafts in the discussion thread section of the course management system; their posts include notes on particular aspects on which they would like feedback. We offer comments as students post their work at varying intervals prior to the assignment due date.

Student writers tend to write their first workshop responses with some anxiety. A few will launch into devastatingly honest evaluations of a partner's draft, but most err on the side of conciliation. Influenced perhaps by the knowledge that their own drafts are undergoing similar scrutiny, they are usually eager to praise and offer little substantial criticism. At the beginning of the course, they also lack the experience to make recommendations to the writer.

One way to address this problem in the first workshop is to take students through Evaluating the Draft, modeling for them the kind of critique that lets the writer know what works, what needs work, and what to do about weaknesses. A good response points to specific words in the draft, describes their effect on the reader tactfully but honestly, and suggests options the writer might consider. Questions to the writer beginning with "How about . . . ?" are often useful. To model such a critique, you can use copies of a class member's draft or copies of an anonymous draft written for a similar assignment in a previous course.

Student pairs could arrange to meet outside of class, exchange drafts, and complete a written analysis. Arriving in class with analyses in hand, they could review and discuss them and then move on to analyze still another student's draft in class or to discuss a draft with the whole class. As attractive as this alternative may seem—it can save class time for other matters—it has not worked well for us. Student pairs do not seem to finish their drafts very far in advance of the workshop class itself, or one student in a pair finishes in time for the scheduled exchange of drafts, and the other does not. All students seem to benefit from the same specific deadline: a draft must be completed by the time of the workshop class. (We accept partial drafts for workshops on the grounds that it is better for a student to get some advice on work in progress than no response at all, especially if he or she is struggling to understand the genre or to pull off a challenging rhetorical move, like integrating counterargument into an argument or interview notes into a profile.) In class, you can review with all students the criteria for an analysis and coach them in making a useful analysis.

PRACTICAL CONSIDERATIONS When a student comes to class late or without a draft, you have several options, depending on which workshop format the class is using:

- Have the student work on his or her own draft.
- Have the student join a pair and read a draft page by page as one partner finishes.
- Have the student wait for another late student to show up.
- Have the student respond to a copy of a draft that has been duplicated for the whole class.

In all these cases, the student must be reminded that he or she is responsible for obtaining another student's response to his or her own draft.

When the first and second drafts of the same assignment are read in subsequent workshops, some instructors ask students to choose a different partner to respond to the second draft. Other instructors allow students to use the same partners to read the second drafts so that the partners can comment on the progress made since the first drafts.

Some instructors find it useful to have students put their phone numbers or email addresses on their workshop responses so that writers can communicate with their workshop partners if they find they have questions as they revise their drafts. (If you are using Blackboard or another course management system, responding might be as simple as clicking "reply," but even if students are not engaging in online workshops, most CMS programs offer students the ability to email classmates. We find, however, that students are seldom aware of this feature, so it can be helpful to point it out or to have students write their email addresses on papers anyway.)

Some instructors ask all students to bring an extra copy of their drafts. During the pair workshop, while pairs are quietly writing their critiques of each other's drafts, the instructor quickly reviews all drafts, looking for the easy-to-spot problems.

HOLDING CONFERENCES

Conferences with students are time-consuming and difficult to schedule when classes are large, but we recommend them highly as a teaching practice, even if you can see students individually only once or twice during the course. Conferences allow you to develop a rapport with students, thus building the trust and self-confidence that many students need before they will take the risks in their writing that lead to real progress. For many students, these conferences are their only opportunities to work individually with a college instructor.

A conference may be scheduled at any time during the composing process. We find that the most useful time is after the first or second draft of an essay has been written, at a point when the student has spent some time thinking about the assignment, generating invention notes, and making at least one attempt to put the ideas into draft form but before the student has finished work on the essay. Ideally, the first draft is discussed in a conference and the second draft in a workshop with other students, or vice versa, before the student writes the final revision of the essay.

In the one-quarter courses we teach, we like to see each student in conference three times. The second of these, the midterm conference, allows us to review the student's progress and discuss the goals for the remainder of the course.

INDIVIDUAL DRAFT CONFERENCES We find individual conferences of fifteen minutes are useful if the time is spent carefully.

The student comes to the conference with a draft in hand and may at first expect you to play the role of mechanic, making the necessary repairs on it while he or she waits in anxious silence. It is often tempting to take the draft from the student and go to work on it, but this defeats the objective of conferencing, which is to help students learn to work on their own drafts. To this end, we leave the draft in the student's hands for most of the conference and usually begin by asking the student either to read it aloud or talk about it. In the most successful conferences, the students do at least half the talking; our comments merely draw them out and let them make discoveries for themselves.

Because our questions at the beginning of the conference, or after the student has read the draft aloud, tend to be the same, we give them to students in advance on a handout, leaving space between questions for their notes. This means that students come to the conference prepared with a list of things to say and questions to ask, and we can begin work immediately. This also saves precious time. Following are general questions we might ask students:

1. What pleases you most about this draft? Which part seems most successful?
2. Which areas of the draft do you feel need work, and why? What would your toughest reader be likely to say about the draft?
3. Which were the hardest and easiest parts to write?
4. What did you notice when you read this draft aloud to a friend?
5. What have you learned from this assignment so far?
6. What changes are you considering for the next draft?
7. What new writing strategy were you trying to use in this draft?
8. What question would you like to ask me about this draft?

Here are questions we ask students about a draft of an essay analyzing the causes of a trend in response to the assignment in Chapter 8. You could readily write such questions for any genre assignment.

1. What trend are you analyzing?
2. Why is it a trend, as opposed to a fad or a phenomenon?
3. What causes are you presenting to explain this trend? Which causes seem to you to be the strongest? Weakest?

19

4. Do you have a strongest or most convincing cause? Why have you selected this one particular cause as likely to be most convincing for your readers?

5. What have you done thus far in this assignment that you feel confident about? It can be anything from your research to the ideas you've developed to explain the trend you're writing about.

6. What problems are you having with this essay? Do they have to do with library research, listing possible causes, or evaluating causes? Are you unsure as to whether you are talking about a trend or a fad? In what specific ways can I help you?

Questions like these provide a good starting point for discussion, and they encourage students to take responsibility for their writing and assume an active role in improving it.

SMALL-GROUP DRAFT CONFERENCES An alternative to the individual conference is the small-group conference. Instead of meeting with each student for fifteen minutes the instructor meets with three students for half an hour or so, spending ten to fifteen minutes on each student's draft. In a typical group conference, each student brings copies of the draft for the other two students and the instructor. They each in turn read their drafts aloud while listeners make notes on their copies. At the end of each reading, the instructor and the writer talk about the draft. The other two students may quietly audit the discussion or contribute their views and suggestions. After ten or fifteen minutes, the writer collects the annotated copies, and attention turns to the next student's draft.

The group conference lacks the privacy of an individual conference, an important consideration for shy students. On the other hand, the group may generate ideas that would not emerge in a one-on-one conference. Some of the comments we make about the first student's draft usually apply to the other two as well, and students often decide to revise their own drafts in ways inspired by the discussion of another student's draft. Neither conference format is inherently better than the other; we recommend that you try both to decide which you prefer.

SCHEDULING CONFERENCES One way of scheduling conferences is to have students sign up for time slots in the class meeting before conference week, writing down their names and phone numbers on a sheet that you can then post on the door of your office or on an online course management system like Blackboard. If students find that they cannot keep the conference appointment, they locate a classmate who might change appointments with them. In this way, students are able to take care of rescheduling largely on their own, without having to call you.

One instructor finds it helpful to have students sign up for conference times *two* class meetings in advance—in pencil. She brings the list to the last meeting before the conference and circulates it once more so that students can double-check times and location and reschedule if necessary. Another keeps a running schedule on a course management system, using the discussion board format for students to request particular times, announce rescheduling needs, and check the schedule for their appointment times if they forget when to show up.

Students should be reminded to be on time for conference meetings, as even a few minutes can throw off your carefully planned schedule. If your office is difficult to locate, consider handing out a map or posting one online.

Of course, one could also simply hold conferences online, and skip the map altogether. Individual conferences on discussion boards do not require such detailed scheduling. We provide due dates and times for initial conference posts and subsequent responses so that students have enough time to consider offered feedback as they work on later drafts. The questions used in individual on-campus conferences also work well online, as do small-group conferences held in discussion threads. Finally, some course management systems have virtual-classroom or chat-room functions that enable instructors to meet with students online in real time, and some instructors teaching hybrid classes find these virtual meeting spaces effective.

EVALUATING STUDENT WRITING AND KEEPING RECORDS

Students completing an essay assignment will have generated a good deal of writing. We find it important to have a system of accounting for all the writing turned in and a method of reading and responding to it that allows us to give students helpful feedback while processing student work in a reasonable amount of time. Many instructors have students submit all their writing online, and they respond online as well. The suggestions in this section call for submission of writing the old-fashioned way, with hard copies.

At the beginning of the course, we give students a handout that specifies what they are to turn in for each writing assignment. Here is an example:

When you finish each assignment, you will turn in not only the final revision but *all* the writing you did for the assignment. Put this work in a flexible file folder with your name, your section, and the assignment written clearly on the outside. Each folder you turn in should contain the following five parts:

1. *Drafting* Numerous pages of rough, unpolished invention based on the activities in the chapter's A Guide to Writing [the Genre] for the assignment in *Reading Critically, Writing Well*, as well as one or two rough exploratory drafts, depending on the length of the assignment. The drafts should be legible and labeled with your name, the assignment title, the draft number, and page numbers.

2. *Workshop response* The response written on one of your drafts by a classmate during the workshop. The classmate's name should be on the response.

3. *Revising* The final, revised version of the essay. This should be printed and proofread with any errors neatly corrected. Double-space, print on one side of the page only, and number each page. The title page should be labeled in the top right-hand corner like this:

   [Your name]
   [Chapter title for the assignment]
   Revision
   [Date]

4. *Reflecting on What You Have Learned* Follow the guidelines in the activity of this name at the end of each genre chapter.

This handout gives students a checklist of all the work they are to turn in. We find it reduces confusion, eases our management of the large amounts of writing, and speeds the reading and response process.

When we pull the handful of work from each student's folder, we skim to check that all the assigned writing is there and to see what the student has accomplished in the invention and drafts. The invention tends to be a good indicator of the depth and thoroughness of the revised essay, and problems in the revision can often be traced to deficiencies in the invention. We try to make this connection clear to students early in the course.

To keep track of the student's performance in the various stages of the composing process for each assignment, we use a record sheet. This sheet is for our own records, and the student does not see it.

The self-evaluation (Reflecting on What You Have Learned) asks the student to reflect critically on the composing process and to think about and take responsibility for the decisions he or she has made. At its worst, a self-evaluation will say no more than "Here it is. I like it. I hope you do too," as the student declines the invitation to take responsibility. At its best, however, it provides the student with an account of his or her composing process, and it provides you with a critical introduction to the essay. It can also clearly indicate the student's level of involvement with the assignment. We usually first skim the whole package and then read the self-evaluation carefully.

We then focus on the final revision. We make a few comments in the margins, noting both strong and weak points in the writing, and add a few sentences or a paragraph of comments at the end or on a separate piece of paper. You may want to keep a copy of these comments for your own records. We often use the computer to compose comments and save a file for each assignment. We try to find something in the essay to praise, and we find that critical comments work best when phrased in terms of what the student might have done in the essay or should try to do in the next one. Questions are useful, too, when they lead students to think about ways they might have addressed the problems in the paper. This approach casts the instructor in the role of expert adviser rather than hanging judge.

Our response to a student's essay is influenced by its location in the sequence of assignments. Our comments will be different in each of the following situations:

1. The student is to revise the essay one more time.
2. We plan to repeat the assignment.
3. The assignment will not be made again in the course, and we want to summarize the student's achievement.
4. The assignment is the first or last in a series of related writing assignments (for example, the assignments in Chapters 6 to 9 on argument).

When time is limited, we respond to features in the essay in order of priority. In an autobiographical essay, we begin by considering the larger rhetorical issues—the writer's goals in telling the story, its structure, the beginning and ending, and the pacing of the narrative. Next, we look at some particular feature of the genre—the quantity and vividness of descriptive details, the writer's recollection of feelings at the time of the event or toward the person, the use of dialogue, and the proportion of narration, description, and commentary in the story. Finally, we comment on the writer's style, diction, and sentence structure.

We do not comment on everything that could be improved in a paper. An inexperienced writer can be easily overwhelmed by too much criticism and become too discouraged to work on any of the problems. Rather, we try to focus on a few of the most important things that need attention, thereby giving the student achievable goals. We follow the same policy with mechanical errors and stylistic infelicities, assuming that if we mark every transgression in a weak writer's paper, the student will most likely attend to none of the problems. Instead, we mark every error in a particular section—a whole page or one or two paragraphs on a page—by placing a check mark in the margin next to the line where the error occurs. We put parentheses around long phrases or whole sentences that need to be revised. This conveys the message that the mechanics and style need serious attention, draws the student's attention to some particular examples, and saves us the bother of marking every mistake in the entire essay.

Then, most important, we ask students to identify and correct their mistakes. If you include the appropriate correction symbol from your handbook with each marginal check mark or set of parentheses, then students can go to the handbook for assistance in identifying the mistake and correcting it. We ask them to rewrite on the revision any sentence containing an error. If the error rate is high, a whole section may need to be rewritten. We check these rewrites as soon as possible, asking students to rewrite still again any errors that remain uncorrected. After two or three revisions have been marked and corrected in this way, we ask students to identify and analyze their own error patterns. They list and classify their errors, again using the handbook for assistance, and then write up briefly what they have learned. The result is that students begin to take responsibility for reducing the number of errors, syntactic garbles and awkwardness, and stylistic infelicities in their own writing—and they learn to use a handbook.

Finally, we do not hesitate to ask a student to revise still again an essay that fails to meet minimal requirements established by the chapter's readings and A Guide to Writing. This request sets standards more effectively than a low grade.

We usually do not grade individual essays but use a portfolio method of grading. We recognize, however, that students need some indication of their progress before the obligatory grades at the end of the course, so we fill out for all students midterm progress reports with grades that indicate what they can expect at the end of the course if they continue at their present levels of performance. This form shows students where they need to focus their attention in the remainder of the course. (An example appears on page 24.)

At the end of the course, we use a final course report to write a response to the final essay submitted and an evaluative summary of the student's performance in the whole course. (An example of this form appears on page 25.) This summary and the course grade are based on a quick review of a student's portfolio of revised essays. We ask that the portfolio be turned in along with the revision of the final essay.

We also review our records of a student's attendance, reading-journal entries, quizzes, workshop responses, and any other work we might have assigned. Then we give a final grade based on three criteria:

1. whether all the assigned work has been completed in a timely fashion;
2. whether the work has improved during the course; and
3. whether revised essays are fully realized rhetorically—that is, whether the student's revisions reveal substantial learning about the rhetorical and composing possibilities of the various genres assigned in the course.

Keep in mind that standards of success on the assignments in *Reading Critically, Writing Well* are comprehensively established by the readings in each chapter, the activities at the beginning of each chapter and following each reading, A Guide to Writing at the end of each chapter, and the peer-critique guide Evaluating the Draft.

Here is an alternative:

1. Students put together a portfolio of their work to give you at the end of the course. The form of portfolio grading you might consider could include
   - all revisions,
   - all revisions, with one of them revised still further, and
   - a small selection of the best work that includes at least one revision, one workshop response, one complete writing process (invention, drafts, revision), and some small number of reading-journal entries. (You will no doubt think of other variations.)
2. Students write a reflective essay analyzing and evaluating their portfolio work. You will need to provide careful guidelines to engage students in thoughtful reflection on their learning in the whole course. The three reflective activities in each genre chapter can be helpful.
3. You review the portfolio and respond in writing.

The portfolio, especially if it includes further revised work, might be the culminating assignment in your course. Students could confer with each other and with you about portfolio selections and about further revision of one essay.

MIDTERM PROGRESS REPORT

Student _____   Instructor _____

Course _____   Date _____

Term _____   Section _____

QUANTITY OF WORK: Has the student completed all the assignments?

Invention _____

Drafts and revisions _____

Quizzes _____

Workshop responses _____

Critical reading activities _____

Self-evaluations _____

Attendance _____

QUALITY OF WORK: Has the student

used the guides to writing creatively? _____

revised drafts substantially? _____

given helpful workshop responses? _____

written perceptive self-evaluations? _____

edited and proofread carefully? _____

completed thoughtfully the critical reading activities? _____

participated in class discussions? _____

These areas need special attention in the remainder of the course:

_____

_____

_____

Midterm grade _____

FINAL COURSE REPORT

Student _____   Instructor _____

Course _____   Date _____

Term _____   Section _____

REMARKS ON FINAL ESSAY

_____

_____

_____

_____

_____

_____

_____

_____

_____

REMARKS ON THE PORTFOLIO

_____

_____

_____

_____

_____

_____

_____

_____

_____

_____

Final grade _____

Chapter 1 is designed to catapult students quickly into the course. Through six short, easy, inter-connected activities, it introduces students to a variety of "academic habits of mind" expected of them in college settings—habits that can help them to achieve the two goals indicated in the book's title, reading critically and writing well. In the process, while the text walks the students along a single thread of inquiry on the subject of bullying, they briefly encounter such crucial concepts as the mean-ing of critical thinking, genre, rhetorical sensitivity, styles of discourse, and writing as a generative activity, and to such essential moves as reading for meaning, reading like a writer, appreciating other viewpoints, forming hypotheses, reporting facts, synthesizing sources, and editing.

The chapter has five sections. The first three—a series of Thinking and Reading Critically activities—acquaint students with college instructors' expectations for student thinking. The sec-tions quickly introduce academic habits of mind, all connected to the common and approachable theme of *curiosity*. These sections also introduce students to two reading strategies they will be asked to use after each selection in the text: Reading for Meaning and Reading like a Writer. The last two sec-tions of the chapter—From Reading Critically to Writing Well and The Writing Process—help stu-dents begin to understand more specific ways in which they need to learn and apply academic habits of mind: in gaining an understanding of the distinctive discourse of the academy, using critical-thinking skills in their reading, and applying the knowledge and skills they have mastered in all these areas to the task of writing effectively.

INTRODUCTION Activity 1, which can be an effective in-class assignment for the first day of class, asks students to think about the habits of mind they may already possess by considering the ways they have previously familiarized themselves with a subject they were curious about. (They may revisit what they write for this exercise in Activity 6 at the end of the chapter, if you choose to use both activities.)

THINKING AND READING CRITICALLY In the Thinking and Reading Critically sections, a series of short passages about the possible causes of bullying, by four authors, provides the class with a quick introduction to the idea of *genres*, along with a series of examples of one genre: speculating about causes and effects.

As they read, students are encouraged to imagine the curiosity-driven questions that the authors must have had when they were researching and writing. Activity 2 asks students to select excerpts from the readings with different audiences in mind. You might consider conducting Activity 2 in class, with students writing individually at first, then teaming up to create group lists of excerpts that can be presented to the class.

ANALYZING IDEAS CRITICALLY AND WITH CIVILITY Activity 3 gives students the opportunity to discuss the issue of bullying with their classmates or families in the context of the reading they've been doing. In their discussions as part of this activity, students are encouraged to practice some of the genres they may encounter later on in the book, including explaining a concept, speculating about causes, and proposing a solution.

FROM READING CRITICALLY TO WRITING WELL This section can help to allay students' fears or apprehensions by reminding them of the experience they already have as both readers and writers. Stu-dents are asked to see reading and writing as interrelated activities that mutually reinforce and strengthen each other. This section also emphasizes the importance of intellectual curiosity, critical analysis, civility, and rhetorical sensitivity as integral to both the reading and writing process. You may want to discuss with your students why each of these traits is important to both readers and writers.

THE WRITING PROCESS This section emphasizes the oft-noted link between reading much and writing effectively, the recursive nature of writing, and the generative nature of writing. Activity 6, which is best conducted as an in-class writing exercise, gives students a chance to experience the generative nature of writing firsthand through *freewriting*. Again, students are asked to focus on the subject of bullying, and the activity provides a list of questions about experiences they may have had with bullies or bullying. The last step of the activity is critical: students are asked whether they surprised themselves with any of the material they created. You might consider having students share their answers to this final question with the class and listing some of the generated ideas, if students are willing to share them.

To get the best results with this initial freewrite, it is sometimes a good idea to let students know at the outset what the purpose of the activity is, perhaps by asking them how often they have found themselves coming up with new ideas while in the middle of writing a paper—ideas that maybe they wish they'd had before they started. (Many students have had this experience, often at about 4 a.m.) Mention that the goal of the exercise is to write until they come up with something promising that they hadn't originally thought of. Not all of them will reach that point, but some students should.

The rest of this section gives students an overview of other parts of the writing process: drafting, getting feedback from others, revising, editing, and proofreading. Activity 5 can help students generate the kinds of questions that can lead to good writing.

Activity 6 asks students to revisit what they wrote in Activity 1 and what they have learned since. Students should write to a younger student, identifying habits of mind he or she ought to be practicing to prepare for college. This metacognitive activity, which could be written as a journal entry or discussion-board posting, prompts students to crystallize what they have learned so far and increases the likelihood they will make connections between this chapter and the rest of the book.

Part 6 TEACHING CHAPTERS 2–12

In Part 6, we begin with general suggestions for teaching the elements in Chapters 2 to 12. Then we discuss each of the chapters, providing specific suggestions for using the reading and writing activities following each essay as well as the chapter's Guide to Writing.

OVERVIEW OF CHAPTER STRUCTURE

Each chapter in the student book other than Chapter 1 follows the same pattern:

- brief introduction to the genre and rhetorical situation
- A Guide to Reading [the Genre]
- readings
- Reviewing What Makes [Genre] Effective
- A Guide to Writing [the Genre]
- Reflecting on What You Have Learned

In the following paragraphs, we introduce these sections and discuss how you might teach them.

TEACHING THE CHAPTER INTRODUCTIONS

Each chapter introduction includes the following four features: a brief discussion of the genre's importance, the writing assignment, examples of rhetorical situations in which the genre is used, and a reflective activity inviting students to think about their prior experience with the genre.

27

DISCUSSION OF THE GENRE'S IMPORTANCE The opening paragraphs usually describe the genre and discuss its importance for writers and readers. You will notice that the description previews the chapter's key terms and concepts. For example, in Chapter 2: Autobiography, the first paragraph focuses on telling stories and describing people, creating a vivid impression through sensory detail, and understanding the important concept of autobiographical significance.

The introduction also both contextualizes the genre and raises issues. For example, in Chapter 2: Autobiography, the issues of diversity and privacy are introduced. These are issues you may want to explore with your students as they read the autobiographical essays in the chapter and write their own. Similarly, the opening paragraphs of Chapter 7: Arguing for a Position make a distinction between rhetorical situations in which people argue primarily to vent strong feelings and those in which people argue to reason and deliberate, examining their own as well as others' arguments with a critical eye.

You can have students read these introductory paragraphs on their own or you can go over them in class, where you can emphasize key terms and concepts and facilitate a discussion about the issues.

RHETORICAL SITUATIONS FOR [THE GENRE] Each chapter opens with typical writing assignments from college courses across the disciplines and from professional life. These examples show diverse contexts in which students are likely to encounter the chapter's genre. We made up very few of the academic assignments: nearly all came from current academic texts or instructor's manuals. We did revise several of them to foreground aspects of the rhetorical situation or to make explicit what the student is expected to know and do. Unfortunately, not all academics consistently make clear to students what is required in answering essay-exam questions or in selecting subjects for papers. You might wish to discuss these issues with your students as they prepare for midterms or final exams in their other courses.

There is much you can do to involve students in analyzing the different contexts in which the genre may appear. Here are a few possibilities:

- You can analyze one situation as a demonstration, emphasizing its thinking and writing demands, and then have students analyze another (either in small groups or as a class).
- You can ask each student to find an assignment in another course that calls for the genre under study.
- You can ask students to bring in examples from other contexts in which the genre may work (such as family, social, or religious contexts).
- You can have students research the profession or graduate study they are interested in to discover which genres are commonly used. (You also might consider making this research part of their Observation essay for Chapter 3.)

THINKING ABOUT THE GENRE This is the first of three reflective, or metacognitive, activities in the chapter. This activity invites students to think about their prior experience with the genre. The second reflective activity, Reviewing What Makes [Genre] Effective, follows the readings and precedes A Guide to Writing; the activity helps students make the transition from reading to writing. The third activity, Reflecting on What You Have Learned, comes at the end of A Guide to Writing and is designed to help students consolidate what they have learned—not only about the genre but also about reading critically and writing well. Taken as a set, these three activities empower students by making them aware that they have been learning from the reading selections, the reading apparatus, and their own writing.

You can use this first activity, Thinking about the Genre, to spur class discussion when you are introducing the genre. This activity allows students to realize they have some familiarity, possibly more than they expected, with the genre, thereby reducing the anxiety that typically accompanies any new writing assignment.

Consider having students write for a few minutes and then, to launch the discussion, having a few read aloud what they have written. Notice that the questions prompt students to think about their oral *and* written experiences with the genre. Students are asked to think about the rhetorical situation in which they or someone else used the genre, considering the audience's expectations as well as the writer's purpose.

TEACHING THE GUIDES TO READING

A Guide to Reading [the Genre] in each chapter focuses on one selection. It introduces students to the two types of critical reading activities presented throughout the book: Reading for Meaning and Reading like a Writer. These critical reading activities provide students with a full introduction to the genre they will be reading and writing. The reading selection together with critical reading activities illustrates for students the work they will do with each reading selection in the chapter. In A Guide to Reading, we survey all the major features of the genre in four or five Reading like a Writer activities. In the readings that follow, each reading has just one Reading like a Writer activity, which singles out an important rhetorical feature of that reading. If you cannot use all the readings in a chapter, you may want to choose readings based on the rhetorical features you want to emphasize. The discussion of each chapter, which follows, identifies the Reading like a Writer topics in that chapter.

THE FIRST READING SELECTION The selection we have chosen to serve as the sample is fairly brief, and we find it interesting. But more important, the sample reading illustrates all the rhetorical features typical of the genre. Because it introduces students to the full array of Reading like a Writer activities they will study in the other chapter readings, instructors seldom skip this first exemplary reading.

READING FOR MEANING In A Guide to Reading, Reading for Meaning consists of three parts: Read to Summarize, Read to Respond, and Read to Analyze Assumptions. These parts call for students to read and reread the selection for different purposes. Although the goal is for students eventually to read for all these purposes at the same time, we find that it helps students to practice reading for one purpose at a time. Of course, you may choose which parts your students do and the order in which they do them. Some instructors prefer to begin by having students respond to the reading, but instructors whose students have difficulty with basic comprehension may choose to focus on the first activity, even using it as the basis for a reading test. Read to Analyze Assumptions may be used as a reflective exercise after the reading has been discussed in class.

In our classes, we encourage students to annotate as they read. If you think annotating is as useful as we think it is, you may want to demonstrate—perhaps by means of an overhead projector—how students can layer their annotations as they reread for comprehension, response, and analysis. The section on annotating in Chapter 10, A Catalog of Reading Strategies, illustrates a number of ways to annotate. After demonstrating annotation techniques at the class level, we find it useful to have students practice annotating in small groups.

Following are general ideas for teaching Reading for Meaning. Again, the chapter-specific pages in this manual provide suggestions for teaching each reading.

Read to Summarize

This activity asks students to write a few sentences summarizing the reading or an important element of it. If you want to emphasize summarizing, you can extend this activity by using the section on summarizing in Chapter 10, A Catalog of Reading Strategies, which provides suggestions on summarizing long passages or whole essays. Summarizing can be an in-class writing activity, whether students are writing just a few sentences or longer, more expanded summaries. Ask a few students to read their summaries aloud and to explain what they have chosen to emphasize and why. Sharing students' summaries on a regular basis will reinforce the importance of summarizing, give students a variety of strategies for summarizing, and ultimately make students more adept at summarizing. Summarizing, of course, is not simply a useful critical reading strategy but also a valuable writing strategy that can be used in all the kinds of writing covered in *Reading Critically, Writing Well*.

Read to Respond

This activity acknowledges that reading for meaning involves, at least in part, actively responding to the text. A reader's mind is not a tabula rasa. Rather, the reader brings to the text a range of potential meanings based on his or her personal, cultural, and linguistic experiences. Consequently, readers need to analyze their own thoughts and feelings as they read, first by identifying what in the text seems salient or significant and then by trying to understand why they respond as they do.

This activity invites students to begin by focusing on anything in the text that stands out, resonates with their own experiences, or puzzles them. We offer several bulleted suggestions, but it is best if students relate to the text on their own terms. Students may feel self-conscious at first, but you can put them at ease by demonstrating that there really is no right or wrong answer. What counts is that students find a way to connect to something in the text and use that connection to explore the meanings created through their interaction with the text.

If you have students share their responses, they may discover that others in the class react in similar ways. They may also learn that still other students have very different responses based on the personal, cultural, and linguistic experiences that they bring to their reading. Seeing that readers find or make meaning in different ways will help students develop sensitivity as readers and will also make them more rhetorically aware writers.

You could discuss one or more of the bulleted items as a class. Most were chosen because they focus students' attention on significant or problematic aspects of the reading. The chapter-specific pages in this manual sometimes offer suggestions to supplement those in the text.

Read to Analyze Assumptions

This activity is the most challenging part of the Reading for Meaning sequence. It asks students to examine with a critical eye one or more of the assumptions, values, or beliefs underlying the reading. It also invites readers to think critically about their own assumptions. We open the activity with a paragraph or two modeling an analysis of one of the reading's assumptions. We also urge students to pay close attention to the writer's word choice and selection of examples, suggesting that these often signal underlying beliefs or values. The suggestions offered in the bulleted items focus on particular passages in the reading. In the chapter suggestions in this manual, we usually point to additional language in the reading you can use to stimulate further discussion in class.

We find that some students start out having difficulty with the concept of assumptions. They may skim the surface and even actively resist "reading too much into the text," as they sometimes say. Yet students usually catch on when you and other students in the class model reading for assumptions during class discussions and activities. Therefore, you might want to put off assigning this activity to students individually until you have spent considerable class time discussing some of the bulleted items and your students have worked in pairs or small groups on a passage they find interesting, exploring the possible underlying meanings together and then reporting to the rest of the class.

The critical reading strategies that we list in Chapter 10 may prove especially helpful for those students who initially struggle to analyze assumptions. You might want to have students practice one or more of these activities in small groups as well.

READING LIKE A WRITER A Guide to Reading in each chapter presents an array of Reading like a Writer activities. Taking the time to work through the entire set of activities as a class gives students an in-depth introduction to the rhetorical features and strategies typical of the genre. Each activity begins with a brief introduction, guides students through an analysis of a small part of the text, and concludes by asking students to write briefly about what they have learned, using specific examples from their textual analysis to support their conclusions. These analyses are designed to be easy for students to do. What is special about them is that they focus students' attention on the text. Perhaps for the first time, students look closely at the craft of writing. Seeing how a writer did what he or she did is one of the first steps students take as they expand their own repertoire of writing skills. You can help students make the connection between their reading and their writing by asking them to try out what they have learned as they plan and draft their essays.

As we recommend in Part 3 of this manual, you can easily devote two one-hour class meetings to these activities. We urge you not to rush through them. First-year students have very little experience with close textual analysis, and the skills they will learn from the close reading required by these activities will help them in many contexts, both within and beyond the academic world. You might do one or two activities as a class when you assign A Guide to Reading, just to get everyone started. Or you could give students time, in groups of two or three, to make notes toward an analysis they later write individually.

Students will need encouragement. At first, they may not go deep enough in their rhetorical analysis, but if you select and read aloud two or three strong examples, they will get the idea.

TEACHING THE OTHER READINGS

Each chapter usually has three additional professional publications and one student essay, with one essay often accompanied by an image and an Analyzing Visuals activity. If you cannot teach all the readings, you may want to choose readings either for their potential interest to your students or for the rhetorical features covered in the Reading like a Writer activities following the readings. This manual provides a brief description of each reading and a list of rhetorical features matched to each to help you decide. Notice also that the readings vary in length and difficulty.

Every reading is introduced by a headnote that tells about the writer and contextualizes the reading. The headnote concludes with prereading advice suggesting what students might look for as they read the selection for the first time.

All the readings are followed by the same three-part apparatus: a complete Reading for Meaning activity and a Reading like a Writer activity, which focuses on a feature of the reading that is especially illustrative. The Analyze & Write apparatus stimulates students' thinking and drives them to analyze writing strategies that they can later use in their own writing.

SPECIAL READING STRATEGY ACTIVITIES

Each chapter includes one or more Special Reading Strategy boxes. (A list of each of these Special Reading Strategy boxes appears following the table of contents in the text.) Each activity asks students to use one of the special reading strategies in Chapter 10 to analyze a reading in the chapter. These activities work in concert with the Reading for Meaning activities following the readings and may also be applied to the selections available through the e-Pages. You might encourage students to draw from the catalog of strategies in Chapter 10 on a regular basis, so that they learn to apply these strategies to any reading they encounter.

TEACHING THE REFLECTIVE ACTIVITY:
REVIEWING WHAT MAKES AN ESSAY EFFECTIVE

This is the second reflective activity (see Thinking about the Genre on p. 28 of this manual). It helps students consolidate what they have learned from the readings about the genre and helps them transition from reading to writing. As we suggest in the text, this activity can be done individually or in small groups. You could even make it a kind of debate, with one group arguing the benefits of their favorite reading and another pointing out its shortcomings. If you are going to have students write evaluation essays, such a debate will help them rehearse. Finally, you might consider having students do oral presentations in which they discuss their findings for this activity and, if they have already picked their own essay topics or written drafts, how their understanding of one of the readings influenced their own work. You could spread out these oral presentations over an entire term so that several students present on each genre, rather than having everyone present on the same genre.

THE WRITING ASSIGNMENT We place the Writing Assignment right at the beginning of the Guide to Writing so that students will have the assignment in front of them as they begin drafting. These writing assignments are presented in general terms, identifying the basic features and strategies of the genre and suggesting the purpose for writing in that genre for one's particular readers. In the chapter's Guide to Writing, we offer specific subject suggestions. In addition, the chapter-specific pages in this manual discuss some of the problems students may have with each assignment, including problems with choosing a subject.

TEACHING THE GUIDES TO WRITING

Every assignment chapter concludes with A Guide to Writing, which leads students through a systematic composing process. A Guide to Writing is just that—a guide, not a set of inflexible orders. It is designed to help students ask themselves an array of questions and respond to those questions in writing, thereby generating drafts that are increasingly more complete and more coherent. Each guide is divided into five parts: Writing a Draft, Evaluating the Draft, Reading a Draft Critically, Improving the Draft, and Reflecting on What You Have Learned.

ENCOURAGING INVENTION AND RESEARCH The Writing a Draft: Invention, Planning, and Composing section in each Guide to Writing includes a sequence of invention and research activities designed to help students generate ideas and writing useful for their essays. In the previous edition, we labeled some of these activities "Invention and Research," but we found that many students were resistant to spending time in this stage of the writing process. We have also found that writing with a word processor makes students much more likely to practice invention while they are actively engaged in drafting. Thus, we combined Invention and Research with the Drafting section, so students will come to see invention and research as part of the writing process, rather than as a stage that could be dispensed with.

As teachers, we are especially careful to introduce our students to the activities in this part of the Guide to Writing because so few of them have ever participated in systematic invention. We ask our students to open their books to the Writing a Draft: Invention, Planning, and Composing section, and then we briefly explain the purpose of each activity. By having students turn the pages and skim the activities while you discuss them, you will be able to reduce students' apprehension about these unfamiliar activities and greatly increase the probability that they will successfully complete them.

We either have students do the activities in class or have them write out of class and then discuss their writing in class. You could do the Choosing a Subject activity as a class or as a brainstorming activity in small groups. Students can also do invention in small groups or share their work with their peers. For example, even though students are working on different subjects, we might first have them write individually and then talk with other students about their purpose or about the visuals they are thinking of using. We find that making invention and research activities a regular part of class, rather than simply out-of-class requirements, ensures that students do the work and also makes the activities more productive. Spreading the invention phase over several class sessions also tends to give ideas time to percolate. Once students become immersed in invention through regular class activities, student writers often find themselves thinking of details to add to their drafts or solutions to problems in their writing when they are otherwise engaged.

Research is comfortably included in our broad definition of invention—everything writers do before and during writing to produce ideas and evaluate them. You can decide how much library or Internet research your students should do or leave it to them to decide. We provide detailed guidance to help students find and cite sources in Chapter 11, Strategies for Research and Documentation.

MAKING DRAFTING PRODUCTIVE Invention may produce a number of complete paragraphs, several lists, a page of freewriting, an interview, or notes on library or Internet research—a plethora of material that must be organized before the student can write a draft. This much material poses a new problem for many students: What should they do with all of it?

A Guide to Writing in each chapter urges students to consider several alternative plans before settling on one. Often students are unaware of alternatives; we find it helpful to illustrate several, sometimes from the reading selections and sometimes from subjects suggested by students.

Each planning section reminds students, as they go on to draft, that what they have developed during the invention process is only a plan. In other words, it is expendable. The final test for the draft is not whether it follows the outline developed during invention but whether it works. The planning section, like many other parts of A Guide to Writing, requires that inexperienced writers sometimes try a new approach.

The box titled Working with Sources in each chapter offers students strategies for finding, evaluating, and integrating genre-specific sources into their writing. Students are often unfamiliar with the differences between genre-specific sources. At the start of the term, you might go over the Working with Sources boxes in class so that students learn to take genre-specific approaches to working with sources.

The drafting section called Considering a Useful Sentence Strategy (for example, p. 61) illustrates a sentence pattern that is commonly used in each genre. Here is a list of the strategies:

Chapter 2: Autobiography. Using participial phrases to show simultaneous action, to make an action or image more specific and vivid, or to relate what the writer or someone else was thinking or feeling at the time of an action.

Chapter 3: Observation. Using absolute phrases to show simultaneous parts of a complex action or to detail observations of a person or an object.

Chapter 4: Reflection. Using parallel grammatical structures to connect related ideas or examples.

Chapter 5: Explaining Concepts. Using appositives to identify people, introduce terms, and present details.

Chapter 6: Evaluation. Using sentences that express comparisons and contrasts, specifically ones that contrast criticism with praise and vice versa.

Chapter 7: Arguing for a Position. Conceding the value of a likely criticism and then refuting it immediately, either in the same sentence or the next one.

Chapter 8: Speculating about Causes or Effects. Using clear topic sentences, especially ones that are grammatically parallel, to signal the stages of an argument.

Chapter 9: Proposal to Solve a Problem. Using rhetorical questions to engage and orient readers, to introduce and emphasize parts of an argument, to appeal to readers' emotions, and to provide transitions from problem to solution or among aspects of the proposal.

GIVING AND GETTING CRITICAL COMMENTS The box titled Reading a Draft Critically (for example, p. 62) poses a truly valuable critical reading task for students, especially for those who have experience only with simplified all-purpose peer-critique guidelines, which often appear in checklist form.

In *Reading Critically, Writing Well*, the peer reviewer's analysis is based on identifying and evaluating features of the genre that have been introduced and illustrated throughout the chapter. The goal is to have students read a draft closely in light of what they have learned about the genre and then write a response that describes the draft, evaluates it using criteria appropriate to the genre, and recommends possible revisions.

It is important to coach students to read a draft critically. Use modeling and explanation.

We recommend that you talk students through at least one step of the analysis the first time you assign them to do a critical reading of one another's drafts. When they complete their first critical reading, you can then select some expansive, helpful sections of analysis to share with them as examples of what you expect from all of them.

See Organizing Draft Workshops in Part 4 of this manual for more ways to use Reading a Draft Critically.

REVISING DEEPLY Research has shown that the more examples writers have seen of a genre, the larger the repertoire of strategies they can draw on to achieve their particular purpose. To help students make connections among their readings and the papers they are revising, the Troubleshooting Your Draft table included in each chapter (for example, p. 64) identifies common problems and strategies for dealing with them. If you go over the table with the class and highlight the ways these strategies connect back to the readings they have studied, they will be more likely to see the table as helpful and to focus on the sorts of global issues that are most critical at this stage, instead of only on sentence-level errors and infelicities.

Peer-critique draft workshops and student-teacher conferences are also invaluable in teaching students to revise. For information on class activities to support students' revising, see Organizing Draft Workshops and Holding Conferences in Part 4 of this manual.

TEACHING THE REFLECTIVE ACTIVITY: REFLECTING ON WHAT YOU HAVE LEARNED

A Guide to Writing in each chapter concludes with Reflecting on What You Have Learned. This activity has two parts. The first asks students to think about their composing process, including what they learned from reading examples of the genre and how their revision was influenced by readers of their drafts. The second part invites students to reflect on the role that the genre they just wrote plays in society, to consider its contributions, and to articulate the feelings, anxieties, or preferences they have when writing in the genre.

If students reflect in thoughtful detail on their own reading and writing processes, they can learn much about how they read and write. Students' responses to this activity can also help guide your comments on their papers. The student who has written a miserable paper and is miserable about it might get very different treatment from one who has done poorly but is uncritical. We believe that there is pedagogical value in responding directly to the student's reflections so that the teacher's comments are not self-contained but are part of a dialogue about the paper.

Chapter 2 AUTOBIOGRAPHY

Students usually find the readings in this chapter accessible and engaging, and they typically find it easy to recall significant events and people to write about. You will want to emphasize, as we do in the introduction and throughout the chapter, that good autobiographical writing should be both vivid and meaningful. It should enable readers to imagine what happened and what the people were like, but it also should convey to readers the significance of these subjects. The strategies of narrating a story and describing a person must serve the larger purpose of conveying to readers the event's or person's autobiographical significance. That is, the autobiographer's purpose is not just to present the event or person but also to help readers understand its importance in the writer's life.

This chapter can teach students to

- select personal experiences that represent themselves to others;
- practice strategies for narrating and describing;
- probe the significance of particular experiences and relationships;
- show significance through word choice, dramatic action, and vivid detail; and
- organize an essay narratively or topically.

You may want to emphasize the first item in the list above because the assignment to write something autobiographical can be misperceived by students as a requirement to make public something private. Students must be reminded that they are the ones who decide how they will represent themselves in their essays. They choose the person or event that lets them make this self-presentation. Students should not feel compelled to write about something they do not feel comfortable sharing. You could read aloud and discuss this passage from the first paragraph of the chapter introduction:

Writing and reading about the memorable events and people in our lives can be exhilarating, leading us to think deeply about why certain experiences have meaning for us. It can also help us understand the cultural influences that helped shape who we are and what we value. Whether you are reading or writing, however, it is important to remember that, as a genre, autobiography is public, not private like a diary. Although it involves self-presentation and contributes to self-knowledge, autobiography does not require unwanted self-disclosure. Readers expect autobiographers to portray themselves purposely for their readers, in other words, to write with an awareness of the rhetorical situation. For example, writing about yourself for a college admissions essay, you undoubtedly want to impress readers with such qualities as your thoughtfulness, diligence, social responsibility, and ambition. Writing for friends and family about a dodgy experience, you may want to share your anxieties but also show how you handled the situation.

WRITING ASSIGNMENT: AUTOBIOGRAPHY (p. 55)

Here is the writing assignment for Chapter 2 as it appears in the book:

Write an autobiographical essay about a significant event or person in your life.

- Choose an event or person that you feel comfortable writing about for this audience (your instructor and classmates), given your purpose (to present something meaningful).
- Consider how you can tell the story dramatically or describe a person vividly.
- Try to convey the meaning and importance in your life—what we call the **autobiographical significance**—of the event or person you've chosen to write about. Think about how you can lead readers to understand you better, to reflect on their own lives, to become aware of social and cultural influences, or to gain some other insights.

Problems Students May Have with This Assignment

We have noticed that students who try to write an autobiographical essay for the first time tend to have some predictable problems, especially with (1) developing a well-paced, dramatic narrative that also conveys the significance of the event or (2) putting together revealing anecdotes with interesting dialogue and vivid descriptions that show the relationship between the autobiographer and the remembered person. Students usually err by either telling without showing or showing without telling. Drawing on what they know of essayist conventions, students may frame the subject by opening with an introductory statement that announces the subject's general significance and ending with a pat and reductive moral. Students may also be so intent on making their story dramatic or description vivid that they forget to invest their narration and description with significance or to let readers know how the event or person affected them. If your students have either of these problems, direct them to the Writing a Draft activities (pp. 55–61), which will help them rethink their approach.

A third common problem, more related to surface features than to substance, is the formatting conventions of dialogue; students may present entire conversations as single paragraphs, or turn speaker tags into separate sentences. Tom Ruprecht's "In Too Deep" provides an effective introduction to conventions of dialogue, and the Using Dialogue section in A Guide to Writing Autobiography (p. 58) provides another example. You might have students practice reconstructing dialogue in class. Ask for some volunteers to share their material, and slowly work through it with the class, showing how the dialogue might be structured and formatted.

RESOURCES IN CHAPTER 2 FOR TEACHING AUTOBIOGRAPHY

Quizzes for each of the readings in the text and e-Pages are included in the e-Pages. The auto-graded multiple-choice comprehension quiz or the summary quiz with a sample summary as feedback may be used to provide an additional incentive to students to complete the reading. The vocabulary quiz (with feedback) may be used with students to help students build a college-level vocabulary.

FINDING SUBJECTS

Rhetorical Situations for Autobiography (p. 20)

These three examples show both academic and nonacademic occasions for autobiographical writing. You might want to use these examples to point out the writers' different purposes and audiences and the different ways they achieve the self-disclosure and depth of insight appropriate to the particular rhetorical situation in which they are writing.

You may also emphasize the way the author might create vivid impressions and highlight autobiographical significance by asking questions like, What sorts of details would be most important to the admissions essay about breakfast cereals? and What is the autobiographical significance of that event? The third example provides students with another illustration of the generative power of writing, an aspect you might draw attention to by asking whether the executive would have changed his management style if he had not written about his role model.

Choosing a Subject (p. 55)

Choosing a Subject is the first activity under Writing a Draft, the opening section of A Guide to Writing Autobiography. Students are offered bulleted lists of suggested subjects and are asked to make their own list of possible subjects. You might urge students from day one to begin compiling a list of possibilities.

Problems Students May Have Choosing a Subject

The writing assignment in this chapter gives students a wide choice of subjects. This choice, as students soon discover, presents problems as well as opportunities. When asked to choose a significant event or person, students frequently want to write about the first subject that comes to mind, often a recent experience or a traumatic one. An event that happened recently may appear to be important only because it is on the writer's mind. While writing about such an event will help the writer understand it, the event may turn out not to have much meaning after all. Traumatic events may also be problematic, not because they lack significance but because they are too significant. Writing about a traumatic event may involve more self-disclosure than seems appropriate given the rhetorical situation. On the other hand, the student may decide that writing about a traumatic event such as the death of a loved one can be therapeutic.

Some students will also, understandably, want to write about major emotional landmarks such as high-school graduation, being selected for a team, surviving an accident, or failing a big test. Some of these peak experiences represent initiations or rites of passage. They are prominent in the minds of many students and, properly handled, can make excellent subjects. Many such events, however, lack conflict—an essential ingredient in effective narrative. Another problem is that they are common experiences, familiar to almost everyone. The challenge in writing about such events is to find a conflict to focus on and to avoid clichés by finding something unusual in the experience or by giving readers a new perspective on it. For these reasons, we encourage students to think twice before writing about their first thrilling experience on the ski slopes, the prom that was all it promised to be, or an event that would have embarrassed anyone. Experiences that exactly match expectations contain nothing surprising and no new insights about the writer or about human nature.

When students write about people, rather than events, they are sometimes most tempted to write about people for whom their feelings are clear and unalloyed, people for whom they feel nothing but adoration or nothing but contempt. The resulting essays can sound more like political ads than rich autobiography, however, and offer writers few opportunities to explore or express complicated ideas.

Students do best when they look beyond the obvious and consider the subtler experiences or relationships they have had—events that led to a discovery or realization, important changes within themselves or within people close to them, people with whom they had complicated relationships or about whom they had ambivalent feelings, or relationships that caused them to learn something new about themselves.

THINKING ABOUT THE GENRE: AUTOBIOGRAPHY (p. 21)

This activity allows students to realize they have a familiarity, possibly greater than they expected, with the genre, reducing the anxiety that typically accompanies composing an essay and making the remaining activities in this chapter easier.

CHOOSING READINGS

The reading selections in this chapter represent two major types of autobiographical subjects—remembered events and remembered people. Annie Dillard, Saira Shah, Jenée Desmond-Harris, and Kate Beaton and Shannon Lewis (e-Pages) focus on events in their childhoods. Tom Ruprecht takes a seemingly trivial event and uses it to explore a side of himself to which readers may relate, and Brad Benioff presents a person who played an important role in his life.

If you cannot teach all of the readings in this chapter, you will have to make some choices. There are at least two principles that may guide your selection—(1) the interest level of the reading and its usefulness in suggesting subjects for your students' essays and (2) the basic features covered in each of the Reading like a Writer activities.

INTEREST LEVELS OF THE READINGS

Here are brief descriptions from the table of contents to help you choose readings that might be of interest to your students:

Annie Dillard, **An American Childhood.** A celebrated essayist remembers, with strange affection, a childhood prank and its scary consequences. (p. 22)

Tom Ruprecht, **In Too Deep.** A writer nominated for an Emmy for his work on *The Late Show with David Letterman*, Ruprecht uses humor to explore an ill-advised attempt to look good in the eyes of others. (p. 32)

Saira Shah, **Longing to Belong.** An award-winning journalist and documentary filmmaker recounts how events forced her to recognize the naïveté of her fairy-tale vision of her homeland. (p. 37)

Jenée Desmond-Harris, **Tupac and My Non-Thug Life.** A prominent writer and Harvard Law graduate, Desmond-Harris reflects about the effect of the death of the rapper Tupac Shakur on her and the formation of her identity. (p. 42)

Brad Benioff, **Rick.** A freshman composition student looks back at his complex relationship with a demanding, sometimes abusive, high-school coach. (p. 49)

Shannon Lewis, **We Were There.** Lewis, a student writer, recalls taking her children on a trip through historic Philadelphia that retraced a trip she took with her father as a teenager. (**e**)

Kate Beaton, **Treasure.** In this graphic memoir, a woman remembers and reflects on a time that she, as a child, buried a jar in the backyard. At first she regards her younger self with skepticism, but later she digs up the jar, implying some value or understanding that her younger self possessed and with which she is trying to reconnect. (**e**)

READING LIKE A WRITER ACTIVITIES

The first reading, Dillard's "An American Childhood," introduces the major features of autobiography through its Reading like a Writer activities. The student essay by Shannon Lewis in the e-Pages ("We Were There") does not specify Reading like a Writer Activities but invites analysis for all the basic features in the chapter. Each of the other readings has one Reading like a Writer activity. Here is a list of these activities.

Narrating the Story: Tom Ruprecht, "In Too Deep" (p. 35)

Presenting People: Saira Shah, "Longing to Belong" (p. 40)

A Special Reading Strategy: Comparing and Contrasting Related Readings: Shah's "Longing to Belong" and Desmond-Harris's "Tupac and My Non-Thug Life" (p. 41)

Conveying the Autobiographical Significance: Jenée Desmond-Harris, "Tupac and My Non-Thug Life" (p. 47)

Presenting People: Brad Benioff, "Rick" (p. 53)

Conveying the Autobiographical Significance: Kate Beaton, "Treasure" (**e**)

A GUIDE TO READING AUTOBIOGRAPHY (p. 22)

The essay that is the focus of A Guide to Reading Autobiography is Dillard's "An American Childhood."

e bedfordstmartins.com/readingcritically

Here are suggestions for teaching the Reading for Meaning activities following Dillard's reading.

Read to Summarize (p. 26)

For this activity, you will want to keep your students from writing mere plot summaries. Direct your students to identify the meaning—for Dillard—of the experience she describes. You can then use their observations as a springboard to a discussion on the autobiographical significance of Dillard's essay. This discussion, in turn, will help prepare students to discover and convey the autobiographical significance of their own upcoming essays. (A sample summary, which may be used as feedback, is available by assigning students to take the summary quiz for the Dillard reading that appears in the e-Pages: bedfordstmartins.com/readingcritically.)

Words that some students may find challenging (*translucent* [par. 6], *immense* [par. 13], and *piecemeal* [par. 20]) are included in a vocabulary quiz in the e-Pages. Other words students may need to define include *mazy* (par. 12), *impelled* (par. 14), *labyrinths* (par. 15), *cherishing* (par. 16), and *prow* (par. 16). Defining these words can lead naturally into a discussion of Dillard's use of metaphor.

Once the students have used one or more of the critical reading strategies to respond to "An American Childhood," you may wish to ask them to use the same strategy or strategies to explore the autobiographical event they plan to write about or in response to drafts by classmates during peer reviews. They could outline their own event's plot, summarize the autobiographical significance of a classmate's essay, paraphrase one of its scenes or some of its dialogue, or compose questions that will help them understand and remember it.

Read to Respond (p. 26)

Another passage you might ask students to respond to is Dillard's opening description of what she learned from the neighborhood boys about playing football:

> Best, you got to throw yourself mightily at someone's running legs. Either you brought him down or you hit the ground flat out on your chin, with your arms empty before you. It was all or nothing. If you hesitated in fear, you would miss and get hurt: you would take a hard fall while the kid got away, or you would get kicked in the face while the kid got away. But if you flung yourself wholeheartedly at the back of his knees—if you gathered and joined body and soul and pointed them diving fearlessly—then you likely wouldn't get hurt, and you'd stop the ball. Your fate, and your team's score, depended on your concentration and courage. Nothing girls did could compare with it. (par. 1)

You might ask your students about their own experiences—with sports or any other interest that they have pursued "body and soul." Try to get them to talk or write about what is involved in the total absorption and commitment that allow us to ignore what we might lose and think only about what we are trying to do. Many of us enjoy this focus in creative or intellectual activities such as writing, programming, or sewing.

Of course, students are likely to want to respond to Dillard's final comment, "Nothing girls did could compare with it." (Pointing out that the event she describes took place in 1952 might help students put the comment in context.) Discussing this comment provides a natural transition to the section Read to Analyze Assumptions, since the text of that section prompts students to think about the assumptions behind Dillard's remark.

Read to Analyze Assumptions (p. 26)

Before students engage with the assumptions categories, such as "assumptions about the value of rules and fair play," you might have a class discussion or a threaded discussion in a course management system (CMS) on how Dillard uses the ideas of *courage* and *heroism*. The discussion will prepare students for further identification and analysis of other assumptions in Dillard's essay, after which you might ask students to generate their own lists of assumptions they identify in Dillard's essay. As students work with the assumption categories, you might ask them to evaluate which assumptions on their lists fit into our three assumptions categories: "assumptions about the value of rules and fair play," "assumptions about the superiority of boys' play," and "assumptions about the desirability of committing yourself 'wholeheartedly.'"

The final activity in this section asks students to try out a critical reading strategy from Chapter 10—reflecting on challenges to your beliefs and values, exploring the significance of figurative language, or looking for patterns of opposition. Each of these strategies helps readers identify the assumptions and values of an author, and see how those sometimes hidden perspectives influenced the text, providing students with a natural transition to Reading like a Writer.

READING LIKE A WRITER (p. 27)

The four Reading like a Writer activities following Dillard's essay give students a thorough introduction to the craft of writing autobiography. You can have students do some or all of the activities here before going on to do selected Reading like a Writer activities for the subsequent readings. With the Dillard essay, students are introduced to major features of autobiographical writing—narrating the story, presenting people, describing places, and conveying the autobiographical significance. Each feature carries a reading and a writing activity that help students focus on Dillard's writing strategies.

Narrating the Story (p. 27)

After introducing students to such narrative concepts as *identification* and *surprise*, this section discusses the roles of verbs and verbals in describing the action. Many students naturally want to focus on adjectives and adverbs when they first attempt to write narratively, but ultimately stories are about actions, so the verbs they choose are crucial.

To illuminate this characteristic, the activity that follows this discussion asks students to consider how Dillard uses verbs and verbals to make her story dramatic. Before students begin analyzing the text on their own, you might quickly review these terms and help students locate the verbs and verbals in a brief passage (par. 16, perhaps). This review will give them confidence when they begin to analyze verb use in paragraphs 11 to 15 and in the essay as a whole for verbals. You might consider having them make their lists of verbs and verbals in class, and then go around the room, asking students to pick examples from their lists to put on the board for discussion.

Students will probably note that a high percentage of Dillard's verbs and verbals show action. They might also note that many of these words are simple ("ran," "chased") and that she repeats some of them. You might want to discuss why Dillard has not chosen more elaborate verbs and how the repetition speeds up the drama.

Have your students look at the last clauses of paragraph 13: "you have to fling yourself at what you're doing, you have to point yourself, forget yourself, aim, dive." Ask students if the verbs and verbals here are propelling the action or serving another function. They should see that these words are an important way that Dillard conveys her "immense discovery," the significance of this event for her at the time.

Describing Places (p. 29)

Students may be familiar with the general concept of using details, but they might not understand the difference between *naming* and *detailing*. If they are struggling, you may want to offer examples: "tire chains" (naming) and "clanking from afar" (detailing) from paragraph 7, "door" (naming) and "wide black" (detailing) from paragraph 9, and "trees" (naming) and "messy winter" (detailing) from paragraph 16. After seeing more examples, they may more easily see that describing requires both naming objects and including details that allow a reader to experience that object the way the writer has intended.

Likewise, some students may not be trained to notice figurative language. You might have them report to the class whether the single comparison they chose to analyze is a simile or a metaphor so that they can be aware of that kind of comparison throughout Dillard's essay. Discuss which comparisons are particularly effective in helping them imagine the place. This discussion might lead into a more general discussion about the value of metaphor and simile and what description by comparison offers that literal description does not. You might follow up on the activity by having students brainstorm new comparisons as possible replacements for the ones used by Dillard and then evaluate them so that they develop some experience formulating and appraising new expressions.

Presenting People (p. 30)

After completing this activity, students should see that experienced writers often use only a few well-chosen physical details rather than exhaustive lists to describe their characters. They should also note that presenting a character will involve a combination of strategies—physical description, characterization or evaluation, and dialogue.

Students should have marked only a few words and phrases in each paragraph they analyzed. You might ask them to speculate about how the essay would change if Dillard devoted an entire paragraph of description to the man who chased the kids. What would happen to the pace of her tale? You could also ask students to record in their own words their impressions of this man, then to go back to the essay to analyze what words and strategies gave them their impressions. Discuss the words Dillard uses to characterize the man: a "thin" man "in city clothes" (par. 10), with an "ordinary Pittsburgh accent" (par. 20), but also "our hero" (par. 16) and "sainted" (par. 21). Ask students to consider how Dillard wants us to view this man and how her depiction of him allows us to begin to see the significance of the entire event.

Conveying the Autobiographical Significance (p. 31)

This activity helps students understand how a writer communicates autobiographical significance by describing remembered feelings and implying present perspectives. By analyzing specific words the author has chosen, students will discover how to infer the feelings of the writer at both the time of the event and the time of the writing. You might have students meet in small groups to list words and phrases in paragraphs 19 to 21 that reveal Dillard's childhood perception of the event as well as her changed perception of it as an adult. Then have the groups report while you make a master list on the board or with a projector. As a whole class, discuss how Dillard's word choice and view of the event change from childhood to adulthood.

To prepare students for their own autobiographical writing, you might ask them to start thinking about childhood experiences that impressed them in one way when they were children but that appear different now. Discuss some of their examples, and advise them to look for this dual perspective in other essays from this chapter.

READINGS

Tom Ruprecht, "In Too Deep" (p. 32)

Reading for Meaning (p. 34)

Read to Summarize (p. 34)

In addition to briefly summarizing the story, students might also pay attention to the way that Ruprecht uses transitions. Many students will choose to narrate their own essays chronologically, as Ruprecht does, and so Ruprecht's use of transitions can be instructive. (A sample summary, which may be used as feedback, is available by assigning students to take the e-Pages summary quiz for the Ruprecht reading: bedfordstmartins.com/readingcritically.)

Words that some students may find challenging (*rugged* [par. 1], *spelunker* [par. 4], *pre-emptively* [par. 6]) are included in a vocabulary quiz in the e-Pages.

Read to Respond (p. 34)
Students may also respond to

- Ruprecht's last line comparing himself to "the proudest little kindergartner you've ever seen"
- a time when they did something because of the way they thought they'd be perceived by others

Read to Analyze Assumptions (p. 34)
The assumptions the students are asked to explore here surround the idea of *carpe diem* (seize the day) and wanting to impress others. Both are themes to which students will relate and probably have experience. Another assumption that students may have about the Remembered Event genre is that the experience written about must be traumatic or life-altering. You might ask students what this essay does (or doesn't do) to dispel that assumption.

READING LIKE A WRITER: NARRATING THE STORY (p. 35)

These activities help students to see what strategies and tools Ruprecht uses to construct his narrative including prepositional phrases to orient the reader, and repetition of key words and phrases.

ANALYZE AND WRITE (p. 36)

Students are encouraged to explore Ruprecht's use of the dramatic arc. If students are beginning drafting work on their own essays, this activity could make a good transition into plotting the dramatic arc of their own narratives.

Saira Shah, "Longing to Belong" (p. 37)

READING FOR MEANING (p. 39)

Read to Summarize (p. 39)
To be sure your students go beyond surface observation, you could ask the following questions: Why did Shah at first embrace the romantic, fairy-tale vision of becoming an Afghan bride? How was that vision (and her attitude) changed by her experience? (A sample summary, which may be used as feedback, is available by assigning students to take the e-Pages summary quiz for the Shah reading: bedfordstmartins.com/readingcritically.)

Words that some students may find challenging (*luxuriant* [par. 4], *tableau vivant* [par. 5], and *putative* [par. 15]) are included in a vocabulary quiz in the e-Pages.

Other words that students may need to define are *visceral* (par. 2), *sanctum* (par. 3), *demurely* (par. 4), *piety* (par. 5), *chaff* (par. 7), and *salvo* (par. 7). The last two terms, once defined, might make students more aware of the ongoing warfare metaphor in that paragraph, as seen in the later "heaviest guns."

Read to Respond (p. 39)
Another dimension of the story to which you may wish to direct your students is Shah's portrayal of her female relatives' behavior. Shah writes that when her fiancé would walk into a room, a child would be

placed in his arms and he would "pose with it, whiskers twitching, while the women cooed their admiration" (par. 3). What does Shah's choice of words reveal about her opinion of these staged moments?

Read to Analyze Assumptions (p. 39)

As a follow-up to the assumptions about the values underlying cultural differences, you might ask the class what assumptions Shah has made about the cultural backgrounds of her readers and their likely reactions to the details of her story, originally published in the *New York Times Magazine*. For the discussion of assumptions about the influence of fairy tales, you might expose students to some actual fairy tales from the Brothers Grimm tradition, which are considerably darker and less inviting than the "fairy tales" to which Shah obviously intends to allude. Finally, you might also direct students to her sudden recognition of her own assumptions, as she realizes that the teller of the stories she had in mind "was a man" (par. 5).

READING LIKE A WRITER: PRESENTING PEOPLE (p. 40)

This Reading like a Writer activity helps students understand how authors combine narration and description to describe a person and reinforce the dominant impression. To help students understand how the author uses these techniques to reinforce the dominant impression, call attention to words in the passage that help create the tone, such as *luxuriant*, *lack of height*, *twitching*, *would fling*, and *cooed*, and ask them to explain the dominant impression these details conjure up.

Jenée Desmond-Harris, "Tupac and My Non-Thug Life" (p. 42)

READING FOR MEANING (p. 45)

Read to Summarize (p. 45)

In addition to summarizing what the story is about, students may want to outline the story or comment on its organization. You might ask your students to consider, for example, Desmond-Harris's use of headings as a means of organizing her essay. (A sample summary, which may be used as feedback, is available by assigning students to take the e-Pages summary quiz for the Desmond-Harris reading: bedfordstmartins.com/readingcritically.)

Words that some students may find challenging (*taboo* [par. 1], *libation* [par. 4], and *premonitions* [par. 5]) are included in a vocabulary quiz in the e-Pages.

Read to Respond (p. 46)

Students may also respond to

- a moment in history, or perhaps even a celebrity death, that had a profound impact on their lives
- the feelings they have about their behavior or responses to certain events when they were younger and why

Read to Analyze Assumptions (p. 46)

This activity asks students to consider assumptions about celebrity and assumptions about identity. If students have not yet reflected on their personal experience, these activities may allow them to do so and could lead students to possible events for their own essays.

READING LIKE A WRITER: CONVEYING THE AUTOBIOGRAPHICAL SIGNIFICANCE (p. 47)

The instructions here point out that events that have lasting significance are almost always charged with ambivalent or conflicting emotions. This is something that students may struggle to depict in their own writing. The activities included here ask students to look at the way that Desmond-Harris conveys multiple layers of meaning to readers.

ANALYZING VISUALS (p. 48)

Students have a great deal of exposure to visuals but not a lot of practice in analyzing them for a class, so they may approach this task with anxiety or uncertainty, even though they may prove to have a lot to say on visuals once they get started. It might be a good idea, for this reason, to start small, with simple observations: Do the subjects in the photos look happy? What are they doing? Are the shots candid or posed? Who do they think took the photographs? Who seems to be the focus of the two photographs, taken together? Build from there to the questions posed in the text, and break for a moment to let students work on their answers to them. Remind the students that there are no official, right answers to these questions and that they should feel free to speculate.

Brad Benioff, "Rick" (p. 49)

READING FOR MEANING (p. 52)

Read to Summarize (p. 52)
Because readers' personal experiences will largely shape what they believe, encourage students to provide textual evidence to support their explanations so that they do not merely exchange their experiences with Benioff's.
Words students may need to define include *maces* (par. 6) and *jovial* (par. 6).

Read to Respond (p. 52)
Students may also respond to Benioff's mounting feelings of inadequacy as Rick silently evaluates him or to Benioff's epiphany in paragraph 25.

Read to Analyze Assumptions (p. 52)
Another assumption about masculinity your students may consider is the notion that anger, revenge, and hatred can drive a person to achieve greatness.

READING LIKE A WRITER: PRESENTING PEOPLE (p. 53)

This Reading like a Writer activity asks students to focus specifically on the describing strategies Benioff uses in paragraph 6—detailing and comparing. Students should realize that Benioff's description is purposeful—to give readers an impression of Rick and an understanding of his significance.

Shannon Lewis, "We Were Here" (student essay, 🄴)

The "As you read" activity included in the e-Pages invites students to focus on the various perspectives that Lewis writes from: as a child with her father, and later as a parent herself, reflecting on what the trip must have been like for her father. In focusing on these perspectives, students will have the opportunity to explore the main features of this assignment, particularly the autobiographical significance feature. You may also want to call students' attention to Lewis's vivid descriptions throughout the essay.

🄴 bedfordstmartins.com/readingcritically

Kate Beaton, "Treasure" (interactive graphic memoir, e)

The graphic novel and graphic memoir have become increasingly popular mediums, and ones with which our students may have some experience. By exploring how the main features of the Remembered Event genre are evident in Kate Beaton's "Treasure," students may get new perspective into writing essays. For example, many students will choose to write their remembered event essays about events that occurred in their younger years. The Beaton reading can help students to think about the kinds of details to include in such an essay and can help them begin to reflect on the significance of such events. The e-Page for this reading features an enhanced version of Kate Beaton's cartoon that allows students to zoom in and explore individual graphics in terms of the genre's major features.

Reading to Summarize (e)
A sample summary, which may be used as feedback, is available by assigning students to take the e-Pages summary quiz for the Beaton reading: bedfordstmartins.com/readingcritically.

READING LIKE A WRITER: CONVEYING THE AUTOBIOGRAPHICAL SIGNIFICANCE (e)

This activity asks students to analyze how the cartoonist uses words and images to convey the autobiographical significance. It may be useful to point out that writing can also subtly convey significance through the way in which people and events are described. The main point may be implied rather than stated outright.

REVIEWING WHAT MAKES AUTOBIOGRAPHY EFFECTIVE (p. 54)

This reflective activity makes a great transition from reading to writing. As the text suggests, this activity can be done individually or in small groups. As the introduction to Part 6 of this manual notes, you can also assign it as an oral presentation for a few students, with other students doing similar presentations on later genres at other points during the term.

A GUIDE TO WRITING AUTOBIOGRAPHY (p. 55)

To represent an event or person vividly, students will need to generate many concrete details. You may need to encourage students to complete the invention activities fully and thoughtfully, pointing out that although they are unlikely to use all the details they generate during invention it will be to their benefit to have a wealth of details from which to choose as they draft their essays. Additionally, you may want to take a few minutes of class time to allow your students to list the different resources they have available to them when writing autobiographical essays — such as memory, others' statements, and memorabilia.

Whether they are writing about an event or a person, many students tend to opt for the simplest structure — a chronological organization — without stopping to consider alternatives. A chronological organization is acceptable, and many of the readings follow a chronological order. Essays about remembered persons may be more effective if they follow topical organizations, however, and even students writing about events should realize that they need not begin their stories at the beginning and follow them all the way through to the end. A simple variation, for instance, is to begin the essay by engaging readers with some dialogue, action, or vivid description before filling in the context. And

e bedfordstmartins.com/readingcritically

45

even if they do choose to follow a strict chronological sequence, students should remember that they can control the pace of the narrative, slowing down to present details about important parts and picking up the pace by summarizing less important parts. Students often spend too much time on less significant, preliminary incidents and not enough time on the most important moments.

Here is an outline of A Guide to Writing Autobiography:

Writing a Draft: Invention, Planning, and Composing
    Choosing a Subject
    Shaping Your story
        Sketching Out the Exposition, or Backstory
        Drafting the "Inciting Incident"
        Dramatizing the Rising Action or Climax
        Experimenting with Endings
    Presenting Important People and Places
        Using Naming, Detailing, and Comparing
        Using Dialogue
        Detailing Important Places
        Including Visuals
    Reflecting on Your Subject
        Reviewing the Dominant Impression Your Description and Narration Create
        Exploring How You Felt at the Time
        Exploring Your Present Perspective
        Considering Your Purpose and Audience
        Formulating a Working Thesis
    Drafting Your Story
    Considering a Useful Sentence Strategy

Evaluating the Draft: Getting a Constructive Critical Reading
    Reading a Draft Critically (box)

Improving the Draft: Revising, Editing, and Proofreading
    Revising Your Draft
    Troubleshooting Your Draft (table)
        To Make the Narrative More Dramatic
        To Present People Vividly
        To Describe Places Vividly
        To Convey the Autobiographical Significance
        To Make the Organization More Effective
    Editing and Proofreading Your Draft

Reflecting on What You Have Learned: Autobiography (box)

Chapter 3 OBSERVATION

Observation, the genre featured in this chapter, is closely related to the genres in the preceding chapter and in the two subsequent ones. The discussion of Chapter 5 in this manual covers some differences between observational, reflective, and explanatory writing. Here we point out the key difference between observational and autobiographical writing: Whereas autobiographical writing attempts to find personal meaning in experience and to transmit that meaning to readers through vivid storytelling, observational writing aims to present what writers have discovered about a subject foreign to them by observing it firsthand. Informing readers about the subject in a vivid, engaging way is the main purpose of observational writing.

This chapter can teach students to

- identify a place that may interest readers;
- interview people and integrate what they say into an essay;
- observe people closely and present them and their activities at a particular location vividly;
- practice strategies for describing, narrating, controlling the point of view, and creating a dominant impression; and
- organize an essay narratively or topically.

You may want to emphasize the firsthand research strategies of observing and interviewing. Chapter 11, Strategies for Research and Documentation, devotes several pages to these field-research methods. Because research—particularly, field research like interviewing—can be time-consuming, students will have to plan and manage their time carefully. You might want to reassure them that if they choose a subject that truly interests them, the time they spend on research will be fascinating.

WRITING ASSIGNMENT: OBSERVATION (p. 112)

Here is the writing assignment as it appears in the Guide to Writing in Chapter 3:

Write an observational essay about an intriguing or unusual place, person, or activity.

- Choose a subject that is relatively unfamiliar to your audience or a familiar subject that you can present in a fresh and surprising way, perhaps focusing on a little noticed or poorly understood aspect of the subject.
- Research the subject, gathering detailed information primarily from close observations and interviews, and present that information in a clear, logical way that is entertaining as well as informative.
- Analyze and interpret the subject so that you can take readers behind the scenes, giving them insight into the subject's cultural significance.

Problems Students May Have with This Assignment

There are typically two problems students have with this assignment. The first has to do with focus of the essay and the other with scheduling.

The focusing problem comes from the overwhelming quantity of information that students usually gather. One of the best ways to focus an observational essay is to organize it around a dominant impression of the subject. By this we mean a unique or fresh perspective that reveals a new or unexpected insight into a given subject.

Writing up their notes from observations and exchanging these write-ups with others in the class can also help students focus their observations. The more they work with their material—analyzing it, writing about it, finding connections and patterns within it—the more cohesive their essays will be. As their drafts become more organized and cohesive, students will also be able to discover and develop the impressions they wish to convey.

The scheduling problem arises from the difficulty many students have in sustaining a long research project. In A Guide to Writing Observational Essays (p. 112), we recommend that students establish their own research schedules. But we also suggest that you set up deadlines for various stages of the project—writing notes on observational visits and interviews, preparing an outline, and writing the first draft—to help students keep on schedule. You could easily have students write their observations and interviews outside of class and then use class time for peer workshops on these write-ups.

RESOURCES IN CHAPTER 3 FOR TEACHING OBSERVATION

Quizzes for each of the readings in the text and e-Pages are included in the e-Pages. The auto-graded multiple-choice comprehension quiz or the summary quiz with a sample summary as feedback may be used to provide an additional incentive to students to complete the reading. The vocabulary quiz (with feedback) may be used with students to help students build a college-level vocabulary.

Finding Subjects

Rhetorical Situations for Observations (p. 68)

The situations that open this chapter suggest some of the possibilities for this kind of writing. Students can see right away that a profile may focus on an activity (mural painting), a person (CEO), or a place (urban renewal project). But they should also see that these categories overlap. Writing about a place involves presenting people and their activities; writing about a person involves describing the person's activities and the places in which they occur; writing about an activity involves the people who are doing the activity and the places where it occurs. In addition, the third example, in which the student reads newspaper accounts of the urban renewal project, illustrates the ways that observational reporting can build on research. Finally, these situations show that observational writing may contrast the writer's expectations with the actual situation (visit with the CEO), uncover a controversy (the urban renewal project), or simply present something fascinating (mural painting).

Choosing a Subject

Choosing a Subject is the first activity under Writing a Draft, the opening section of A Guide to Writing Observations (p. 112). Students are offered bulleted lists of suggested topics and are asked to make their own list of possible subjects. You might urge students from day one to begin compiling a list of possibilities. Ideas inspired by the suggestions in Considering Ideas for Your Own Writing could be part of this list.

Problems Students May Have Choosing a Subject

Choosing a suitable subject is particularly important for this assignment because students will invest a good deal of their time visiting the place or person, conducting interviews, and doing library or Internet research. Point out the suggestions under Choosing a Subject in A Guide to Writing Observational Essays.

For students who have just arrived at a university (or a new city), the observational essay offers an ideal chance for exploration. Students should be encouraged to seek out unusual activities, people, or places. Most campus Web pages have lists and directories of facilities, institutes, specialized libraries, exhibits, and activities located on campus, and students have written very good essays in the past about map libraries, other special collections, exhibits of old printing presses, and even the morning cleaning staff of their dormitories. The Yellow Pages provide a ready-made list of potential topics ranging from jewelry designers to printing companies. A map of the area or a local newspaper can also reveal interesting places to investigate.

When you give the assignment, urge students to avoid subjects with which they are overly familiar (for example, the summer job they have had for the last four years or their college dorm). If your students are writing a longer profile, they will need to pick a subject with plenty of activity, enough people for several interviews, and a circumscribed place that can be described specifically (profiles about "the beach" or "downtown" generally don't work, for instance).

Two other problems with selecting a subject are those of accessibility and security. Subjects that may sound exciting in theory may not be possible or appropriate in practice. A doctor or scientist may not be available for interviews; most elementary and high-school campuses have highly restricted access; legal considerations might prevent a student from profiling an emergency room; a military installation or a nuclear power plant may be inaccessible to the general public. Similarly, you may want to discourage students from exploring potentially dangerous subjects. It is natural, even commendable, for some people to want to do something a little daring, but it is not always a good idea. Students should think twice about profiling something like the county jail (which may be unavailable, anyway), a place in a neighborhood with a high incidence of crime, or an activity that presents a health or safety hazard. On the one hand, you do not want your students to select mundane or drab subjects; on the other hand, you should urge them to use discretion when picking a subject. All you really need to do is to encourage them to explore unfamiliar places or activities: the experience of discovery should be enough to yield a fresh and insightful angle. Part of the task, of course, is for students to get beneath the surface of whatever they are observing. You might suggest they think about people or places that once aroused curiosity in them but that they never had a chance to investigate. Students in our classes, for instance, have gone back to tiny desert towns where their cars have broken down to learn who lives there, or ventured off the freeway to investigate strange sights they had often wondered about during their regular commute.

One way to help students gather rich feedback on their prospective subjects is to circulate subject sheets and have the students evaluate one another's ideas. You can easily do this in one of two ways. At the top of a sheet of paper, students write a tentative title for their essay. Then they describe in two or three sentences the person, place, or activity that will be the subject of their essay. In one sentence, they identify possible readers (class members, readers of a particular newspaper or magazine, or perhaps a special group of readers with a need to know what the writer will discover). These sheets then circulate around the class, with students writing questions or comments (and even commenting on other students' comments). Then you can invite each student to identify the subject he or she is eager to read about. Alternatively, you can accomplish the same objectives by having students post the same information in a course management system discussion board. Classmates can post questions and comments about students' initial posts and suggest relevant resource links that relate to students' subjects for the essay.

We encourage you to work closely with your students on this project, especially during this first stage of invention. Because students are unlikely to have previously undertaken a writing project like this, they need extra encouragement and scaffolding throughout the process.

THINKING ABOUT THE GENRE: OBSERVATION (p. 69)

This activity will allow students to realize they have a familiarity, possibly greater than they expected, with the genre, reducing the anxiety that typically accompanies composing an essay and making the remaining activities in this chapter easier. In particular, students often have great familiarity with observational reporting because they have watched such reporting on television or online. Television shows like *Dirty Jobs*, for which clips are available on YouTube, are particularly popular among teachers of observational reporting because they show students they have been watching observational reports of various sorts for most of their lives.

CHOOSING READINGS

If you cannot teach all the readings in this chapter, you will have to make some choices. There are at least three principles that may guide your selection: the type of observation, the interest level of the reading and its usefulness in suggesting subjects for your students' essays, and the basic features focused on in the Reading like a Writer activities.

Type of Observation

The reading selections in this chapter, beginning with the sample *New Yorker* essay, "Soup," focus on one of three common observational subjects—people (or animals), places, and activities. "Soup" focuses on a person, the restaurant owner and chef Mr. Yeganeh. The essays by John T. Edge and Gabriel Thompson present activities. Peggy Orenstein's essay observes many people in an eighth-grade math classroom. The student-authored selections by Brian Cable and Brianne O'Leary (e-Pages) profile a place.

Interest Levels of the Readings

Here are brief descriptions from the table of contents to help you choose readings that might be of interest to your students:

The New Yorker, **Soup.** A magazine writer profiles a restaurateur—a temperamental master of the art of soup making—along with his tiny storefront establishment. (p. 71)

John T. Edge, **I'm Not Leaving Until I Eat This Thing.** Daring himself to eat a food product that makes him queasy, an expert on Southern food observes a factory that processes and bottles pig lips. (p. 80)

Gabriel Thompson, **A Gringo in the Lettuce Fields.** A prolific writer and community organizer, Thompson writes about the hard life of a fieldworker while doing the work himself. (p. 89)

Peggy Orenstein, **The Daily Grind: Lessons in the Hidden Curriculum.** An investigative reporter profiles an eighth-grade math class, revealing how gender affects students' interactions with one another and with their teacher. (p. 96)

Brian Cable, **The Last Stop.** A first-year composition student observes the unfamiliar world of a mortuary, ending up in the embalming room, which he leaves only after placing his finger on the firm, cold skin of a dead body. (p. 104)

Brianne O'Leary, **Fatty's Custom Tattooz and Body Piercing.** A first-year composition student observes a tattoo parlor, along with its customers and idiosyncratic owner and tattoo artist. (**e**)

Sarah Kate Kramer, **Niche Market: Fountain Pen Hospital.** For a local public radio station, Kramer profiles a store in New York City that exists by repairing and selling fountain pens. (**e**)

Reading like a Writer Activities

The first reading, "Soup," introduces the major features of observation through its Reading like a Writer activities. The student essay in the e-Pages (by Brianne O'Leary) does not specify Reading like a Writer activities but invites students to choose a feature of the reading they think is worth analyzing. Each of the other readings has one Reading like a Writer activity. Below is a list of these activities.

Presenting Information about the Subject: John T. Edge, "I'm Not Leaving Until I Eat This Thing" (p. 86) and Sarah Kate Kramer, "Niche Market: Fountain Pen Hospital" (**e**)

Adopting an Authorial Role: Gabriel Thompson, "A Gringo in the Lettuce Fields" (p. 95)

Conveying a Perspective on the Subject: Peggy Orenstein, "The Daily Grind: Lessons in the Hidden Curriculum" (p. 101)

Organizing the Information: Brian Cable, "The Last Stop" (p. 110)

e bedfordstmartins.com/readingcritically

A GUIDE TO READING OBSERVATIONS (p. 70)

The essay that is the focus of A Guide to Reading Observations is "Soup."

READING FOR MEANING (p. 74)

Here are suggestions for teaching the Reading for Meaning activities following "Soup."

Read to Summarize (p. 74)

To help guide students, you may suggest they describe Yeganeh's attitude toward his customers as well as toward other restaurants. (A sample summary, which may be used as feedback, is available by assigning students to take the e-Pages summary quiz for "Soup": bedfordstmartins.com/readingcritically.)

Words that some students may find challenging (*alchemist* [par. 1], *concoctions* [par. 1], and *staccato* [par. 2]) are included in a vocabulary quiz in the e-Pages.

Read to Respond (p. 74)

How do the students respond to Yeganeh's manner? Is his soup kitchen a place they would like to buy food? Some instructors bring in the DVD of the *Seinfeld* episode inspired by Yeganeh and his Soup Kitchen International and show it to students (who, in most classes, are likely to have been born after the episode aired). If you use the DVD, you may follow up by asking students to compare and contrast the characterization of Yeganeh and his storefront kitchen in the article with that in the episode.

Read to Analyze Assumptions (p. 74)

Students are familiar with bosses, coaches, teachers, and parents exercising power, and they also have a lot of experience with the restaurant industry, as customers if not as employees, so they should have a lot to say in response to the assumptions about power and the assumptions about customer service. Another assumption about customer service appears in the following sentence:

The order of any well-behaved customer is accompanied by little waxpaper packets of bread, fresh vegetables (such as scallions and radishes), fresh fruit (such as cherries or an orange), a chocolate mint, and a plastic spoon. (par. 5)

The accompaniment seems to say something about Yeganeh's beliefs about human nature, reward, and punishment. You might ask students: How may these additional vegetables and fruit help condition Yeganeh's patrons to abide by the "strict rules for conduct in line" (par. 1)? Is there a sense that Yeganeh treats and responds to his patrons as if they were children?

READING LIKE A WRITER (p. 75)

The four Reading like a Writer activities following "Soup" introduce students to the basic features and strategies of observational essays—presenting information about the subject, organizing the information, adopting an authorial role, and conveying a perspective on the subject. Each feature carries a reading and a writing activity that help students focus on the writing of the sample essay, "Soup."

Presenting Information about the Subject (p. 75)

This activity focuses on ways in which writers of observation vividly present their subjects. The introductory remarks connect what students learned in Chapter 2: Autobiography to what they learn in this chapter as they analyze observational essays like "Soup." In fact, like the activity in Chapter 2 following Brad Benioff's essay, "Rick," this activity asks students to survey the ways an author describes his or her subject. Unlike the Chapter 2 activity, however, this one encourages students initially to look at the way the author portrays Yeganeh mostly through his behavior, gestures, and speech rather than through visual description. As they write briefly about their analyses, students should be able to report that the behavioral details contribute to the readers' sense of who Yeganeh is. In the second task, students focus on the different senses that the article invokes in order to give readers a sense of the storefront as a location.

Organizing the Information (p. 76)

This activity draws students' attention to the different ways in which observational writers gather and present information from field and background research. As students plan their observational essays, they will have to decide on the types of information to seek and how to organize their material. Students are introduced here to two of the basic methods of organizing observational essays—narrative and topical. As they plan and write their own observational essays, students will probably need to choose between these two methods or some combination of the two. The anonymous *New Yorker* author of "Soup" organizes observations topically, whereas Gabriel Thompson, the author of a later essay in this chapter, organizes his essay narratively, while John Edge, the author of another essay in this chapter, uses a hybrid approach.

To analyze the organization of "Soup," students are asked to make a scratch outline identifying the topics in the first six paragraphs. Students tend to identify the same main topics, although they may use different words to name them and may identify different subtopics.

You might follow up by asking students to identify what the sources appear to be for each piece of information or quote in the section they studied. Identifying sources of information in the essay helps students see that to make their presentation coherent and interesting writers of observational essays must select details from the hodgepodge of information they initially collect.

Adopting an Authorial Role (p. 77)

This passage helps students think about how observational writers choose roles as spectator observers or participant observers. (Later in the chapter, John T. Edge in his essay "I'm Not Leaving Until I Eat This Thing," combines roles.) Students are asked to explore the benefits and challenges of the two roles in preparation for the activity. We have found that most students are familiar with the spectator role, in which the writer reports about but is not a part of the activity. You may need to remind students who want to write as participant observers to include sufficient detail for readers unfamiliar with the subject. In this case, the author of "Soup" has adopted a spectator observer role, but you might find it worthwhile to have the class search the text for evidence to support this classification—doing so can help students cement what otherwise is a fairly abstract concept.

After reading this passage, consider having students share their responses to the analytical activity (or generate those responses): What would a participant-observer essay have looked like, and what might readers have learned from that perspective? Why do they think the author chose a spectator role?

Conveying a Perspective on the Subject (p. 78)

This activity helps students think about how observational writers use details to convey what they find interesting about the subject. As we indicate in the text, the writer's angle on the subject may be stated directly or implied. Although students choose what they include in their observational essays, the main focus of the essay should, nevertheless, be descriptions of the subject and not students' evaluations or interpretations of the subject.

In analyzing "Soup," students are asked to mark places where the writer's attitudes and ideas come across. An additional activity for conveying a dominant impression of the subject follows Cable's essay later in the chapter.

Note that these activities build on what students who studied autobiography in Chapter 2 learned about conveying significance by showing and telling. You could take this opportunity to preview assignments in later chapters that require students to make explicit their point of view and argue for it.

READINGS

John T. Edge, "I'm Not Leaving Until I Eat This Thing" (p. 80)

READING FOR MEANING (p. 84)

Read to Summarize (p. 84)

In addition to having students explain how Farm Fresh Food Supplier obtains and packs pig lips, you may also have them briefly describe the essay's organization (the spectator segment of the essay is bracketed by segments involving the author's participation). (A sample summary, which may be used as feedback, is available by assigning students to take the e-Pages summary quiz for the Edge reading: bedfordstmartins.com/readingcritically.)

Words that some students may find challenging (*globular* [par. 5], *viscera* [par. 6], and *flaccid* [par. 18]) are included in a vocabulary quiz in the e-Pages. Additional words that some students may struggle with include *slurry* (par. 4), *carrion* (par. 5), *cordovan* (par. 8), *tinged* (par. 11), and *reverie* (par. 14).

Read to Respond (p. 85)

Students also may respond to

- the mass slaughter of animals for consumption (factory farming);
- the fact that the selling of down-home merchandise ("Jason's Pickled Pig Lips") is still a rather competitive business ("We do our best to corner the market on lips" [par. 11]).

Read to Analyze Assumptions (p. 85)

In addition to the assumptions called out by the text, students might discuss Edge's assumption that he *ought* to try the pickled pig lip. Technically, nothing is forcing him to do so, but he seems to assume the obligation. Why? A further assumption you may wish to have your students explore is the perceived role of women and work. Point out to students that men now manage and will continue to manage Farm Fresh Food Supplier ("after he graduates from business school, Lionel's younger son, Matt, will take over operations at the plant" [par. 10]). Ask students to identify, in contrast, the roles of women in the essay, including Lionel Dufour's own daughter, Dana, "a button-cute college student who has won numerous beauty titles" (par. 10).

ANALYZING VISUALS (p. 86)

Students pursuing the questions listed under this activity might jump to the easy conclusion that Edge is reminding us that the pig was once an animal rather than food, and there is certainly nothing wrong with that interpretation. However, other valid answers are possible and might emerge if students are asked additional questions, like "Would many readers recognize pickled pig lips as pig lips if they were in a jar or on a plate?" As an additional exercise, you might ask students to search online for images they think could have been used with this article (or with another essay) and post them in a course-management system such as Blackboard. Then, in class, you and the students could look them over on an overhead projector, discussing the ways the different images might modify the message or impact of Edge's article.

This Reading like a Writer activity focuses on Edge as a participant in the subject he is observing. Students are asked to review the introduction, paragraphs 1 and 2, to analyze how Edge sets up time and place in the essay. Students are also asked to evaluate how the sections in paragraphs 3 to 12 inform paragraphs 13 to 19, where Edge resumes his story about eating a pig lip. They should recognize that his discussion of the production of carrion products tells readers little about their appeal or taste, and that this discussion puts his attempt to eat a pig lip in context so that when he comes back to the bar in paragraph 13, we know what it is that he is trying to learn. You may also want to discuss how the essay would be different if the author were not a participant and what kinds of subjects benefit from author participation.

This activity introduces students to the ways Edge uses his interview in his observation. The activity covers the techniques of quoting, paraphrasing, and summarizing, and can help students to make strategic choices about which parts of interviews they conduct to excerpt and how. You may want to discuss in class the reasons why a writer like Edge might choose one technique over the other. In the activity, students are asked to analyze, in writing, Edge's choices to quote, paraphrase, and summarize those whom he observed. You might invite students to share their responses and discuss how they might apply what they've discovered to their own writing.

A SPECIAL READING STRATEGY—COMPARING AND CONTRASTING RELATED READINGS: "SOUP" AND EDGE'S "I'M NOT LEAVING UNTIL I EAT THIS THING" (p. 87)

In this chapter, a special reading strategy follows Edge's observational essay, comparing it with the earlier observational essay, "Soup." If your students have not read and discussed the section on comparing and contrasting related readings in Chapter 10, A Catalog of Reading Strategies, you might want to take the time now to do so.

To get students to think about the similarities and differences between "Soup" and Edge's essay, we invite students to compare the two essays in terms of their cultural contexts, organization, and the roles taken by the writers. This is a lot of territory for students to cover. You might want to divide the class into groups, asking each group to address one of these topics and report their findings to the class as a whole.

Gabriel Thompson, "A Gringo in the Lettuce Fields" (p. 89)

READING FOR MEANING (p. 93)

Read to Summarize (p. 93)
In addition to having students briefly explain the work migrant lettuce pickers do, you might also have students look back through the previous readings, exploring how the writers' organizational choices highlight certain elements of each profile. (A sample summary, which may be used as feedback, is available by assigning students to take the e-Pages summary quiz for the Thompson reading: bedfordstmartins.com/readingcritically.)

Words that some students may find challenging (*gingerly* [par. 2], *jeers* [par. 5], and *tentative* [par. 8]) are included in a vocabulary quiz in the e-Pages.

Read to Respond (p. 94)
Students may also respond

- by discussing unfamiliar experiences they may have had, such as exposures to other cultures or unfamiliar activities
- by exploring the differences between information that comes from an interview and information that comes from observation

Read to Analyze Assumptions (p. 94)

This section invites students to explore the ethical implications of pieces like Thompson's that use an immersion approach. Students are also invited to consider the status of immigrant workers. Given the sensitivity of these issues and of Thompson's outsider status, the conversation that may come of these questions is probably an important one to have.

READING LIKE A WRITER: ADOPTING AN AUTHORIAL ROLE (p. 95)

This section can direct students' attention to the ways that Thompson reminds readers of his outsider status and can serve as a reminder to students that even if they choose to adopt a participant role, they will always be, like Thompson, outsiders looking in on the activities they profile and should think of themselves as participant-observers.

This activity could lead you and your students to discuss which strategies they might use in their own essays to convey effectively their roles as observers. For example, would highlighting their own difficulties with an activity, as Thompson did, be effective? Or would some students be better served by focusing on exotic descriptions of the subject, like Edge?

Peggy Orenstein, "The Daily Grind: Lessons in the Hidden Curriculum" (p. 96)

READING FOR MEANING (p. 100)

Read to Summarize (p. 100)

You may wish to indicate to students that while Orenstein's essay focuses primarily on a specific class, she uses detailed descriptions of the students' appearances and mannerisms to help differentiate the students from one another. (A sample summary, which may be used as feedback, is available by assigning students to take the e-Pages summary quiz for the Orenstein reading: **bedfordstmartins .com/readingcritically**.)

Words that some students may find challenging (*brassy* [par. 5], *sanguine* [par. 10], and *largesse* [par. 20]) are included in a vocabulary quiz in the e-Pages. Additional words that some students may need to look up include *reigning* (par. 1), *gawky* (par. 10), and *rebuke* (par. 18).

Read to Respond (p. 100)
Students may also respond to

- how a teacher's attention shapes a student's learning;
- the idea of choosing to remain quiet in class;
- Orenstein's choosing to narrate Amy's answer as a mistake (par. 19).

Read to Analyze Assumptions (p. 100)
Students might also discuss whether Orenstein's description of Amy is based on an assumption that people tend to be consistent, or ought to be consistent, and whether they agree with such an assumption. Orenstein also appears to assume that Mrs. Richter's class is behaving the way it usually does — that it is not behaving differently because a strange observer (Orenstein) is there. What evidence can students find to defend or challenge such an assumption? If students conclude that Orenstein's presence is affecting behavior, what assumptions might they make (or retract) about Mrs. Richter's teaching performance?

READING LIKE A WRITER: CONVEYING A PERSPECTIVE ON THE SUBJECT (p. 101)

The Reading like a Writer activity asks students to analyze the words and phrases that Orenstein uses to suggest what she thinks or feels about her subject. We highlight how Orenstein's use of contrast and juxtaposition may give readers an indication of the author's perspective on her subject.

This activity invites students to look at the ways that Orenstein draws contrasts as she portrays her subject and asks students to think about what those contrasts might help readers to understand. After the students analyze Orenstein's essay, you might invite them to think of ways that drawing contrasts in their own writing can help them to emphasize important ideas or themes.

Brian Cable, "The Last Stop" (p. 104)

Reading for Meaning (p. 109)

Read to Summarize (p. 109)

Cable's essay is organized spatially. In his exploration of Goodbody Mortuaries, Cable moves from room to room. You may wish to have students use this organization to structure their summary of this selection. Students can describe the route Cable takes in his exploration, noting especially where he begins once inside and where he ends up before leaving. You may also wish to ask students how Cable's organizational strategy allows them, as readers, to better understand Cable's observations.

Read to Respond (p. 109)

Students may also respond to

- the epigraph (the Mark Twain quotation) at the top of the essay;
- the cost of burying someone;
- the idea that one may study to become a mortician, "with courses in anatomy and embalming as well as in restorative art" (par. 25).

Read to Analyze Assumptions (p. 109)

You might start off a discussion of the assumptions (or a discussion of what students have written about assumptions) by asking students what assumptions of theirs were challenged by Cable's essay. Students might also explore the underlying cultural acceptance of humor in association with death and dying. One example appears in paragraph 25, in which Tim tells the author that becoming a mortician was "a profession I could live with." Twain's aforementioned quotation, in the epigraph at the top of the essay, provides another such instance.

Reading like a Writer: Organizing the Information (p. 110)

This section introduces students to the ways that observations may be organized: topically, narratively, and spatially. You might discuss why each of the authors in this chapter chose to organize their essays as they did. Now may also be a good time to allow students to reflect on which method of organization might serve their own essays well and why. It also asks students to explore the ways that Cable uses transitions to move students both through the space he is describing and through his essay, and to evaluate the effectiveness of these transitions.

Brianne O'Leary, "Fatty's Custom Tattooz and Body Piercing" (student essay, e)

The "As you read" activity asks students to consider the effect of O'Leary's question to herself at the beginning of her profile and how this question shapes the rest of the essay. The question and the

e bedfordstmartins.com/readingcritically

56

answers to this question help to solidify the profile's perspective and establish a clear dominant impression. You could encourage students to use this technique to help them focus their own essays.

Sarah Kate Kramer, "Niche Market: Fountain Pen Hospital" (Web page with photo slideshow, ⊖)

Kramer's profile is supplemented with photographs she took during her observation of the Fountain Pen Hospital. The Analyze and Write activities ask students to consider how textual and visual details combine to convey a dominant impression and fulfill the author's purpose in writing the text.

Students may want to consider bringing cameras or taking pictures with their phones when they conduct observations. It is probably a good idea to remind students that they should ask for permission before taking photos. If you choose to allow students to use images as part of their profiles, analyzing Kramer's piece could prove especially valuable.

REVIEWING WHAT MAKES OBSERVATION EFFECTIVE (p. 111)

This reflective activity makes a great transition from reading to writing. As the text suggests, this activity can be done individually or in small groups.

A GUIDE TO WRITING OBSERVATION ESSAYS (p. 112)

As students begin to investigate their subjects, you will want to stress the importance of field research in observational writing. Field research is an essential part of the work students will do for this assignment. Depending on their subjects, students are likely to use both observation and interviews. Few students will have much experience with either. In Chapter 11, Strategies for Research and Documentation, we give students a detailed overview of these types of research. We lead students through the observation and interview processes, and while some of this advice may seem like common sense (take a writing implement, prepare some questions in advance), most students find it useful. You might emphasize the importance of reflecting on their observations and interviews immediately after completing them, reviewing and adding to their notes while the memory of the experience is still fresh rather than after their memory of the event has faded.

Students often have difficulty deciding what impression they want to convey in their observational essays. You may want to devote some class time to having students complete the activities in the section Developing Your Perspective on the Subject. At this stage in the composing process, the impressions students develop need only be provisional; reassure them that they can change impressions as they learn more about their subjects.

When planning their essays, students often organize information in the order in which they discovered it. Remind them that the writers they read organize their observational essays narratively, topically, spatially, or through a blend of these approaches. If students opt for a purely chronological organization, they should do so because that is the best way to present their information, not because it is the only option they have considered. Likewise, remind students of the variety of beginnings demonstrated by the selections in this chapter, and tell them that they need not wait for the ideal beginning before they start drafting.

We try to help our own students submit their revised and edited essays for publication and award extra credit to students whose work is published. You might suggest that students submit their

⊖ bedfordstmartins.com/readingcritically

finished pieces to a local newspaper or magazine that publishes observational articles, or you might let students identify the publication they would like to write for.

Here is an outline of A Guide to Writing Observation Essays:

Writing a Draft: Invention, Planning, and Composing
 Choosing a Subject
 Researching Your Subject
  Making a Schedule
  Setting Up, Preparing for, and Conducting Interviews and Observations
  Reflecting on What You Learned
 Working with Sources: Integrating Quotations from Interviews (box)
 Developing Your Perspective on the Subject
  Exploring Your Perspective
  Defining Your Purpose for Your Readers
  Considering Your Main Point
  Clarifying the Dominant Impression
 Adopting a Role
  Considering Your Role
  Using Your Role
 Formulating a Working Thesis
 Considering Adding Visuals or Other Media
 Organizing Your Draft
 Drafting Your Observational Essay
 Considering a Useful Sentence Strategy

Evaluating the Draft: Getting a Constructive Critical Reading
 Reading a Draft Critically (box)

Improving the Draft: Revising, Editing, and Proofreading
 Revising Your Draft
 Troubleshooting Your Draft (table)
  To Present the Information More Clearly and Vividly
  To Organize the Observation More Clearly and Effectively
  To Make the Essay More Engaging and Informative
  To Strengthen the Writer's Perspective on the Subject
 Editing and Proofreading Your Draft

Reflecting on What You Have Learned: Observation (box)

Chapter 4 REFLECTION

What distinguishes the reflective essay is, to borrow Virginia Woolf's words, its "fierce attachment to an idea." In introducing reflection, you might help students make connections between this assignment and those in the two previous chapters. While autobiographers tell about significant events and people in their lives and writers of observation present what they have discovered about a subject firsthand, writers of reflection spin webs of ideas.

Reflective writing is a natural outgrowth of both autobiographical and observational writing. All three have their roots in personal experience, and all are concerned with the meaning or significance of that experience. But whereas autobiographers and observational writers need only present their experience vividly to show its significance, reflective writers must explore and elaborate on the meanings they find.

Autobiographers bring out personal significance; reflective writers (like writers of observation) look for general implications. Reflection stems from an observation or experience that raises a question or leads to an insight about the human condition. Reflective essayists write about the ways in which we live and interact, the goals toward which we strive, and the shortcomings that hobble us. The reflective essay is typically a public meditation on what makes us human. The reading and writing activities in this chapter should help students begin to appreciate the value of this genre.

This chapter can teach students to

- select personal experiences or observations that may have implications for social life;
- connect personal experiences and observations to larger social realities;
- practice strategies for narrating and describing; and
- organize an essay through thematic coherence.

Drawing out the implications of what one has seen or heard tends to be the greatest challenge of reflective writing, especially for young writers who lack confidence in their ideas or feel that teachers (or adults generally) are not interested in what they have to say. Success not only in this kind of writing but also in their other classes requires students to have confidence in their abilities to develop interesting ideas and to express them in engaging ways. Although challenging, this assignment can help students build their confidence.

WRITING ASSIGNMENT: REFLECTION (p. 167)

Here is the writing assignment in the Guide to Writing in Chapter 4:

Write a reflective essay that grows out of a specific occasion or event.

- Choose an occasion or event that you feel comfortable writing about for this audience (your instructor and classmates). You may want to select the general subject that you want to reflect on first, and then choose an event or occasion that effectively particularizes this subject.
- Consider how you can depict the occasion or event vividly so that readers can imagine what you experienced. Try to create a voice or persona that will appeal to your audience.
- Develop your reflections, including insights that interest, surprise, or enlighten your readers.
- Organize your reflection so that readers will be able to follow your train of thought.

Problems Students May Have with This Assignment

In our experience, problems students have with this assignment fall into two fairly predictable categories—choosing workable subjects and developing reflections on them. In the latter area, students' difficulties have to do mainly with achieving some balance between particular material—in the form of occasions, examples, and illustrations—and general statements.

Exploratory drafts tend toward one extreme or the other. As our students begin writing, we often see first drafts that consist almost entirely of vague, abstract statements or that look very much like essays about events (especially if students have recently completed Chapter 2). A third type of problem draft comes from students who believe they need to reach a conclusion about their subject, perhaps anticipating upcoming argument assignments. All these problems can be minimized if you help students pay careful attention to both the general and the particular components of each reading selection as well as to both in their own developing essays.

Going over invention work early, in class, is particularly important with reflective writing. The discussion format of a draft workshop (see Part 4, Organizing Draft Workshops, p. 16) may also help students crystallize their understanding of the assignment's expectations and hone in on reflection in their invention materials.

RESOURCES IN CHAPTER 4 FOR TEACHING REFLECTION

Quizzes for each of the readings in the text and e-Pages are included in the e-Pages. The auto-graded multiple-choice comprehension quiz or the summary quiz with a sample summary as feedback may be used to provide an additional incentive to students to complete the reading. The vocabulary quiz (with feedback) may be used with students to help students build a college-level vocabulary.

FINDING SUBJECTS

Rhetorical Situations for Reflections (p. 130)

These three examples show both academic and nonacademic occasions for reflective writing. You might want to use these examples to point out the writers' different purposes and audiences, the different subjects they consider worth thinking and writing about, and the different ways they sustain their reflections. For instance, how might the first writer present himself differently for his alumni magazine than he might for, say, a guest column on the sports page of the local newspaper?

Choosing a Subject

Finding a Particular Occasion and a General Subject is the first activity under Writing a Draft, the opening section of A Guide to Writing Reflective Essays (p. 167). Here, students are shown how to make a chart that matches occasions and subjects they could consider writing about. As we suggested above, you could spend class time charting possible subjects on the board to help students see how general subjects for reflection can lead them to recall particular occasions they have observed and how particular occasions can lead to general reflections.

Because students often have difficulty choosing a suitable subject for reflection, it's advisable from day one to discuss possibilities with students. An easy way to do so is to ask students to keep a list of particular real-life occasions (such as overheard conversations or intriguing newspaper articles). Then you could lead the class in brainstorming general subjects suggested by these particular occasions. If you spend five to ten minutes of every class this way, your students will develop the habit of reflecting and begin to discover subjects they could develop into an essay. Similarly, during work in this chapter, you could have your students keep a daily journal in which they note things that happen to them or things they observe and the thoughts they have while dwelling on those experiences and observations. Sometimes the journal entries can become particular occasions or can remind students of occasions or subjects they might want to address.

Problems Students May Have Choosing a Subject

Although students will have discussed various subjects, you may be surprised at the difficulty some students have in settling on an appropriate subject.

Students encounter two problems. Some try to write about abstract concepts (*love, truth, justice,* etc.) that they can't ground in concrete occasions, examples, and illustrations. Other students want to reflect on controversial issues, such as abortion or capital punishment, that lead them instead to take a position. Abstract concepts and controversial issues can lead to interesting reflective essays, but students tend to go astray unless instructors keep them focused on the basic features of reflective essays.

THINKING ABOUT THE GENRE: REFLECTION (p. 130)

This activity will allow students to realize they have a familiarity, possibly greater than they expected, with the genre, reducing the anxiety that typically accompanies composing an essay and making the remaining activities in this chapter easier.

CHOOSING READINGS

If you cannot teach all the readings in this chapter, you will have to make some choices. There are at least two principles that may guide your selection—(1) the interest level of the reading and its usefulness in suggesting topics for your students' essays, and (2) the basic features focused on in the Reading like a Writer activities.

INTEREST LEVELS OF THE READINGS

Here are brief descriptions from the table of contents to help you choose readings that might interest your students:

Brent Staples, **Black Men and Public Space**. A member of the *New York Times* editorial board notes how his presence on a city street triggers defensive reactions in white passersby and addresses the "alienation that comes of being ever the suspect." (p. 132)

Dana Jennings, **Our Scars Tell the Stories of Our Lives**. A newspaper columnist ponders the significance of his scars and the stories they tell. (p. 143)

Dan Zevin, **Father Shops Best**. An essayist known for his humor reflects on a shopping trip with his father and what it showed him about their relationship. (p. 149)

Rob Walker, **Replacement Therapy: Why Our Gadgets Can't Wear Out Fast Enough**. A prolific journalist speculates that we are secretly glad to have excuses to replace our quickly outdated technology—and this might be one of the reasons why technology becomes outdated so quickly. (p. 156)

Katherine Haines, **Whose Body Is This?** A first-year composition student considers society's obsession with the perfect body—especially, the perfect female body—and the negative pressures this obsession creates. (p. 161)

Wendy Lee, **Peeling Bananas**. A Chinese-American high-school student contemplates the positive and negative aspects of growing up as "a hybrid of two cultures." (**e**)

Francine Wheeler, **Sandy Hook Victim's Mother Delivers President Obama's Weekly Address, April 13, 2013**. A bereaved mother uses her experience to make an impassioned plea for gun control. (**e**)

READING LIKE A WRITER ACTIVITIES

The first reading, Staples's "Black Men and Public Space" (p. 132), introduces all the basic features of reflection through its Reading like a Writer activities. The final reading, Haines's "Whose Body Is This?" does not specify a Reading like a Writer activity but invites students to choose a feature of the reading they think is worth analyzing. Each of the other readings has one Reading like a Writer activity. Below is a list of these activities.

e bedfordstmartins.com/readingcritically

61

A Special Reading Strategy: Exploring the Significance of Figurative Language: Dana Jennings, "Our Scars Tell the Stories of Our Lives" (p. 147)

Presenting the Occasion: Dana Jennings, "Our Scars Tell the Stories of Our Lives" (p. 147)

Engaging Readers: Dan Zevin, "Father Shops Best." (p. 154)

Maintaining Coherence: Rob Walker, "Replacement Therapy: Why Our Gadgets Can't Wear Out Fast Enough" (p. 159)

Developing the Reflections: Katherine Haines, "Whose Body Is This?" (p. 165)

Reading like a Writer: Presenting the Occasion: Francine Wheeler, "Sandy Hook Victim's Mother Delivers President Obama's Weekly Address, April 13, 2013" (**e**)

A GUIDE TO READING REFLECTIVE ESSAYS (p. 131)

The essay that is the focus of A Guide to Reading Reflective Essays is Staples's "Black Men and Public Space."

READING FOR MEANING (p. 135)

Here are suggestions for teaching the Reading for Meaning activities following Staples's "Black Men and Public Space."

Read to Summarize (p. 135)

After students have explained ways Staples tries to alleviate people's fear of him and commented on Staples's feelings about his encounters with fearful passersby, you may ask students to consider the following: The United States is a culture of violence, and many people consciously try to appear capable of violence to deter violence against themselves. (A sample summary, which may be used as feedback, is available by assigning students to take the e-Pages summary quiz for the Staples reading: bedfordstmartins.com/readingcritically.) If Staples appears aggressive and antagonistic, why, in our culture of violence, does he wish to destroy that image?

Words that some students may find challenging (*discreet* [par. 1], *perilous* [par. 8], and *congenial* [par. 11]) are included in a vocabulary quiz in the e-Pages. Other words students may need to define include *uninflammatory* (par. 1), *warrenlike* (par. 5), *solace* (par. 5), *proprietor* (par. 9), and *skittish* (par. 11).

Read to Respond (p. 135)

Students may also respond to

- how they have reacted in the past, in situations similar to those of Staples's "victims";
- the measures Staples takes to make individuals and groups less anxious when he is present;
- Staples's belief that when he whistles melodies from classical composers people are less afraid of him.

Read to Analyze Assumptions (p. 135)

Students might also consider the set of cultural assumptions underlying why and how we respond to appearance. Using Staples's appearance and the reactions of people toward him as a starting point, you may ask students to explore and share their own experiences in responding to someone's appearance or receiving unwanted or unexpected responses because of their attire.

e bedfordstmartins.com/readingcritically

In these four Reading like a Writer activities, the focus shifts from the content and purpose of the essay to the specific strategies Staples uses to achieve his purpose. You can have students do some or all of the activities before doing the selected Reading like a Writer activities for the subsequent readings. In working on these four activities, students are introduced to the basic features of the reflective essay—presenting the particular occasion, developing the reflections, maintaining topical coherence, and engaging readers. Each feature carries a reading and a writing activity that help students examine Staples's writing strategies.

Presenting the Occasion (p. 137)

This activity asks students to reread the opening paragraph of Staples's essay and to analyze the strategies he uses to present his occasion. By marking the names, details, and actions Staples uses to identify the participants in the scene, students should notice that Staples creates a contrast between "the victim" and himself, the "youngish black man." This contrast creates tension that engages readers, and it also sets up the reflection that will follow.

Developing the Reflections (p. 137)

This section requires students to look at the strategies Staples uses in general and the examples he uses in particular to develop his reflections. Students may differ on which instances of development are most effective; however, they should notice that Staples usually mentions an action or behavior in a general statement before making it vivid through an example.

Maintaining Coherence (p. 138)

This activity will make students aware of how frequently Staples refers to time and place and how these markers keep a reader oriented. Some students may be anxious about providing order and structure in their own reflective writing. For that reason, this activity is important in showing how Staples achieves coherence and how they can as well. As a follow-up activity, you might have students note the way repeated wording helps maintain topical coherence. In addition to looking back at the activity's discussion of the "language of fear" and its associated words, students might look at the way Staples repeats words and themes related to race, darkness, or night.

Engaging Readers (p. 139)

This activity focuses on the ways Staples presents himself—his persona—as a means of engaging readers. Students should get the sense that Staples is reaching out to his readers. He wants them to view him as sensitive—"a softy who is scarcely able to take a knife to a raw chicken" (par. 2)—and reasonable—"I understand, of course, that the danger they perceive is not a hallucination" (par. 5). This persona is attractive to readers, especially because it contrasts so starkly with the frightening persona that Staples unintentionally projects to some people by his physical appearance.

Inexperienced writers often assume their reflections will automatically be of interest to readers. This activity will help students realize that they should make a conscious effort to engage readers.

A SPECIAL READING STRATEGY—COMPARING AND CONTRASTING RELATED READINGS: BRENT STAPLES'S "BLACK MEN AND PUBLIC SPACE" AND AN EXCERPT FROM HIS AUTOBIOGRAPHY, *PARALLEL TIME* (p. 140)

In this chapter, an additional reading activity follows the reflective essay by Staples. However, before having students complete this activity, you may wish to have them read and discuss the section on comparing and contrasting in Chapter 10, A Catalog of Reading Strategies. There students will find an explanation of comparing and contrasting and an annotated model. For this special reading strategy, we ask students to compare Staples's two selections in terms of the way the particular occasion is described, the descriptions of "the language of fear," and the way in which Staples has remembered his thoughts and feelings.

READINGS

Dana Jennings, "Our Scars Tell the Stories of Our Lives" (p. 143)

READING FOR MEANING (p. 145)

Read to Summarize (p. 145)

The first step in this activity draws attention to the particular occasions that students will study later in the Reading like a Writer activity for this reading. Mapping out the occasions on the board may help students analyze the essay later. (A sample summary, which may be used as feedback, is available by assigning students to take the e-Pages summary quiz for the Jennings reading: **bedfordstmartins .com/readingcritically**.)

Words that some students may find challenging (*parse* [par. 1], *motley* [par. 1], and *talismanic* [par. 11]) are included in a vocabulary quiz in the e-Pages. Other words that students may need to look up include *reigning* (par. 1), *gawky* (par. 10), *rebuke* (par. 18), *lunar* (par. 4), *Superfund* (par. 6), and *burnish* (par. 11).

Read to Respond (p. 145)

Students may also respond to

- the mystery scars from Jennings's childhood;
- the incidents and events that Jennings describes;
- his question, "How do any of us get out of childhood alive?" (par. 3)

Read to Analyze Assumptions (p. 146)

Your class might also discuss these two apparently dueling, contradictory assumptions: (1) Jennings's scars are unusual enough to be interesting to others; (2) his degree of childhood damage is common enough that he wonders how "any of us" survive adolescence. Do students think these are irreconcilable notions, or can they see ways they possibly complement each other in this essay? Do they think either proposition is vulnerable to a challenge?

A SPECIAL READING STRATEGY: EXPLORING THE SIGNIFICANCE OF FIGURATIVE LANGUAGE (p. 147)

The special reading strategy for Jennings's essay invites students to look at the ways writers use metaphors, similes, and symbols in reflective writing. If your students have not read and discussed the section on exploring the significance of figurative language in Chapter 10, A Catalog of Reading Strategies, you might take the time to do so now. The text shows that Jennings uses metaphors related to travel, but students are asked to identify other families of metaphors they find in his essay. Some of those metaphor groupings include *scars as text* (*footnotes* and *runes*, par. 1; *brand*, par. 6; *signposts*, par. 9; *signatures*, par. 12), and *scars as astronomical objects* (*starbursts*, par. 2; *lunar*, par. 4; *cratered*, par. 5).

READING LIKE A WRITER: PRESENTING THE OCCASION (p. 147)

This Reading like a Writer activity asks students to consider how Jennings presents his occasion, which, in this essay, is not a specific event (as it was with Staples). Instead, it's a specific observation: He tells what he thinks as he looks over the scars on his body. The activity asks students to notice how Jennings structures his essay, starting with his overall point and the observations and memories that prompted it, and then moving onto a holistic reflection about the tour he has just conducted. Students continue to reflect on Jennings's essay by identifying and considering Jennings's use of vivid details. You may want to discuss as a class the ways that certain details can help readers draw conclusions as to the purpose and significance of writers' reflections. As a follow-up activity, you could have students imitate these moves in a brief journal entry, giving a tour of what they are wearing or scars on their own body or what they see as they look around their dorm rooms, telling the stories behind the items they notice, and drawing some reflective conclusions. Conducting this sort of activity can help them spot the occasion in Jennings's essay, help them see the structure to his presentation of the occasion, and think (perhaps) of some occasions of their own, for their own essays.

Dan Zevin, "Father Shops Best" (p. 149)

READING FOR MEANING (p. 149)

Read to Summarize (p. 149)

This activity asks students to focus not only through the movement of the plot and the character but also on what the author learns. You might want to explore with students how they arrive at their conclusions as to what Zevin has learned. This could occasion a good discussion about the difference between showing and telling readers. (A sample summary, which may be used as feedback, is available by assigning students to take the e-Pages summary quiz for the Zevin reading: bedfordstmartins.com /readingcritically.)

Words that some students may find challenging (*numismatics* [par. 6], *spoils* [par. 19], and *inhibited* [par. 20]) are included in a vocabulary quiz in the e-Pages.

Read to Respond (p. 153)

You may also have students respond to

- experiences they've had with their own parents or other adult role models or moments when they could sense their relationships with their parents or role models changing
- activities or behaviors they admire or want to emulate in their parents or other role models

Read to Analyze Assumptions (p. 153)

These activities ask students to reflect on assumptions about heritage and the things passed from one generation to the other. While the questions in the book focus on the Zevin essay, this is usually a subject about which most of our students have a lot of personal experience to share; however, it can be a sensitive issue for some, too. If you'd like to encourage your students to discuss these issues from their own experience, you may want to frame the activity in terms of what the students themselves may pass down to future generations. The next activity asks the students to consider the advantages and possible disadvantages of using humor in the reflection genre.

READING LIKE A WRITER: ENGAGING READERS (p. 154)

This Reading like a Writer activity helps students understand how reflective writers may establish a tone or project a voice that will engage the reader. It asks students to evaluate Zevin's ability to do so. You might wish to discuss with students how Zevin uses familiar sights and experiences to engage his readers.

As with other attempts to analyze visuals, the answers to these questions may vary, and students should be encouraged to debate the merits of their interpretations without fear of an official response that trumps theirs. It might be best, however, if they take the questions in the order presented, whether they're working in groups, as a class, or individually.

Rob Walker, "Replacement Therapy: Why Our Gadgets Can't Wear Out Fast Enough" (p. 156)

READING FOR MEANING (p. 158)

Read to Summarize (p. 158)

Students are asked to summarize what Walker's essay is about. This essay may also be a good one to have the students practice outlining as Walker tends to take a topical approach to reflection with which many students may be less familiar.

Read to Respond (p. 158)

Students may also respond to

- The gadgets they have with them in class and how indispensible (or otherwise) they find them.
- Other objects that must or could be replaced because they have become "obsolete" (clothes, bags, etc.). Students might compare and contrast these objects with the "gadgets" Walker describes.

Read to Analyze Assumptions (p. 158)

This series of activities asks students to explore two assumptions that are sometimes at odds: "New is better" and "we should not be wasteful." You could have a discussion with your students about why it is that people often hold contradictory ideas. You might suggest that exploring a contradiction in human behavior is fertile ground for a reflection essay.

READING LIKE A WRITER: MAINTAINING COHERENCE (p. 159)

This Reading like a Writer activity focuses on how writers create coherence while covering new ground by using transitional words and phrases. Walker maintains coherence through the way he often addresses his readers at the beginning or end of a paragraph. You might have your students look at how often Walker begins or ends a paragraph by addressing the reader directly by using "you," or "we," and ask your students why they feel Walker chose this approach. If students are working on their own drafts at this point, a good follow-up activity might be to have them look at transitions or repetition of key words and phrases in their own essays.

Katherine Haines, "Whose Body Is This?" (p. 161)

READING FOR MEANING (p. 164)

This Reading for Meaning activity invites students to apply to Haines's essay what they have learned from the other readings in this chapter about reading to summarize, respond, and analyze assumptions. You might want to have your class suggest words to define, as well as brainstorm possibilities for response and analysis.

Read to Summarize (p. 164)

This activity asks students to speculate about what Haines wants her readers to understand from the experiences she shares in her essay. You might asks students to focus in particular on the framing narrative Haines uses to introduce and conclude her essay.

Read to Respond (p. 164)

Students may also respond to

- the way and the extent to which society puts pressure on men to conform to certain physical ideals
- other factors that promote an ideal body type for women in our society

Read to Analyze Assumptions (p. 164)

Students often have a lot to say about the two assumptions raised in this section. The first assumption relates to the value placed on high self-esteem. The second relates to the way the media can shape our behavior. In addition to the ideas suggested in the book, you may want to ask about the ways that the media have empowered women and/or fostered self-esteem, or you may want your students to explore the line between self-esteem and over-confidence or arrogance.

READING LIKE A WRITER: DEVELOPING THE REFLECTION (p. 165)

This activity asks students to consider Haines's use of examples and the ways that her reflection is enhanced through the examples she gives. You might assign your students to work on specific examples in groups, or you might use this activity as a springboard into a drafting activity like the cubing activity in the Guide to Writing for this chapter.

Wendy Lee, "Peeling Bananas" (student essay, e)

Students are asked to consider the values associated with words like "assimilation" and "heritage." The text tell students that the values associated with these words can be conflicting, and you may want to spend some time in class discussing with students the connotations these words have for them. Like Lee herself, many of us, including our students, can relate to having a hybrid or plural ethnic or national identity. The "As you read" activity for this text invites students to consider how heritage and assimilation affect them individually.

Francine Wheeler, "Sandy Hook Victim's Mother Delivers President Obama's Weekly Address, April 13, 2013" (video, e)

READING FOR MEANING (e)

A sample summary, which may be used as feedback, is available by assigning the students to take the summary quiz for the Wheeler reading that appears in the e-Pages.

READING LIKE A WRITER: PRESENTING THE OCCASION (e)

This activity asks students to consider how this video grabs and keeps the viewer's attention, focusing on how the camera work enhances its appeal. You may want to introduce the appeals of logos, ethos, and pathos during this discussion.

REVIEWING WHAT MAKES REFLECTION EFFECTIVE (p. 166)

This reflective activity makes a great transition from reading to writing. As the text suggests, this activity can be done individually or in small groups.

e bedfordstmartins.com/readingcritically

A GUIDE TO WRITING REFLECTIVE ESSAYS (p. 167)

Because this assignment is extremely challenging for many students, you may want to use class time helping students with Writing a Draft: Invention, Planning, and Composing, especially with choosing an occasion and shaping and developing their reflections. You could have students work in small groups to read aloud to one another what they have written in their two-column charts and then discuss possibilities for expanding their ideas. Discussing their ideas with peers could encourage students who lack confidence in their ideas and spur thinking while helping confident students further refine their ideas.

Here is an outline of A Guide to Writing Reflective Essays:

Writing a Draft: Invention, Planning, and Composing
    Choosing an Occasion and General Subject
    Shaping Your Reflection
    Developing Your Reflection
        Narrating an Event
        Describing What You Observed
        Cubing
        Exploring How You Felt at the Time and What the Occasion Made You Realize Later
        Considering Your Purpose and Audience
        Formulating a Working Thesis
        Considering Visuals
    Drafting Your Reflective Essay
    Considering a Useful Sentence Strategy

Evaluating the Draft: Getting a Constructive Critical Reading
    Reading a Draft Critically (box)
    Revising Your Draft
    Troubleshooting Your Draft (table)
        To Present the Particular Occasion More Effectively
        To Develop the Reflection More Fully
        To Strengthen Coherence
        To Better Engage Readers
    Editing and Proofreading Your Draft

Reflecting on What You Have Learned: Reflection (box)

Chapter 5 EXPLAINING CONCEPTS

If your students are going from Chapter 4 to Chapter 5, you might take time to discuss the similarities and differences between reflective and explanatory writing. Whereas the purpose of reflective writing is to try out ideas and help the reader see even the familiar in a new light, the purpose of explanatory writing is simply to explain something that is already well established. While explanatory writing may be every bit as entertaining and thought provoking as a reflective essay, it never loses sight of its primary goal—to inform the reader.

If your students are going directly from Chapter 3 to Chapter 5, you might want to point out some of the similarities and differences between observational and explanatory writing. Both present information in a way that readers find intelligible and interesting. Observational writing derives mainly from the writer's firsthand experiences and often relies on narrative and vivid description to communicate what the writer has learned about the subject. Although concept explanation may include the writer's personal experiences, it usually depends heavily on what the writer has learned from others. Writers of explanation synthesize, review, or summarize the work of others. They present information, draw connections, and discuss implications. They may also translate technical or specialized information into the language and contexts of readers outside the discipline.

In this chapter, we focus on one particular type of explanatory writing—writing to explain concepts. This focus enables students to work on the kind of explanation they are reading and writing in most of their courses. Throughout the disciplines, particularly in introductory courses, students are learning basic concepts. They learn by reading and writing. Understanding the rhetoric of explanatory discourse can help them become better learners as well as more effective explainers.

This chapter can teach students to

- identify a concept that may interest particular readers;
- narrow and research a concept;
- practice strategies of defining, illustrating, comparing or contrasting, classifying, narrating a process, or reporting causes or effects;
- organize an essay by classifying and dividing; and
- signal explicitly the move from one topic to the next.

The assignment to write essays explaining concepts can also be a good way to introduce students to library or Internet research. The student who knows little but is curious about a concept can gather information from the library, find information on the Internet, or talk with experts. Strategies for both firsthand and secondary-source research are covered in detail in Chapter 11, Strategies for Research and Documentation. You might want to refer students to this section early in the assignment.

WRITING ASSIGNMENT: EXPLAINING CONCEPTS (p. 230)

Here is the writing assignment that appears in the Guide to Writing in Chapter 5:

Write an explanation of a concept that interests you enough to study further.

- Choose a concept that you know a good deal about or about which you'd like to learn.
- Consider what your readers already know about the concept and how your explanation can add to their knowledge.
- Research material that helps clarify or provides examples of your concept.
- Consider the most effective writing strategies to convey your concept.
- Think about how to engage your readers' interest in your concept and guide them through your explanation

Problems Students May Have with This Assignment

In our experience, the main problems students have with this assignment involve choice of subject and organization. Students may fail to do sufficient research, or instead they may allow their own writing to be eclipsed by their sources. Their essays then become dumping grounds for unprocessed (and sometimes plagiarized or patchwritten) information. The purpose of the assignment is twofold—to give students an opportunity to analyze and synthesize information and to have them organize the information and present it in a way that makes it understandable and interesting. The greatest challenge of this assignment may not be the gathering of information but the presentation of it. To succeed with this challenge, students will need to help readers understand unfamiliar terminology, build readers' knowledge incrementally, and provide cues to help readers to follow the organization.

You may need to help students focus on suitable concepts (some instructors even require subject proposals from students in order to identify students having difficulty understanding the task); to walk them through research options available at your library; and to give them in-class practice with summarizing, paraphrasing, and documenting sources. Following the tips below and in Part 4, above, can help you build on these approaches so that students can produce better written work.

RESOURCES IN CHAPTER 5 FOR TEACHING EXPLAINING CONCEPTS

Quizzes for each of the readings in the text and e-Pages are included in the e-Pages. The auto-graded multiple-choice comprehension quiz or the summary quiz with a sample summary as feedback may be used to provide an additional incentive to students to complete the reading. The vocabulary quiz (with feedback) may be used with students to help students build a college-level vocabulary.

FINDING SUBJECTS

Rhetorical Situations for Concept Explanations (p. 178)
These three examples illustrate both academic and business occasions for writing that explains concepts. You might want to use these examples to point out some of the strategies writers use to present unfamiliar ideas. Note especially how often the writers in these examples use comparison and contrast to relate a new concept to another concept likely to be familiar. You might have students list questions they would have about these concepts, and have them decide which of the questions ought to be answered in a good explanation.

Choosing a Concept (p. 231)
Choosing a Concept is the first activity under Writing a Draft: Invention, Planning, and Composing, the opening section of A Guide to Writing Essays Explaining Concepts. Students are shown concepts grouped by fields of study. They are then asked to make a list of concepts they would consider writing about. You might urge students from day one to begin compiling a list of possibilities.

Problems Students May Have Choosing a Subject
One solution to the problem of subject choice is to encourage students to write about subjects introduced in their other courses. In the Invention and Research section, many concepts from academic subjects are suggested. If students lack confidence in writing about a concept from one of their academic subjects, you might allow them to write about concepts drawn from their extracurricular interests.

Students will need your help in finding a focus for their essays. Because many concepts are too big—too much is known about them—for most rhetorical situations, students need to focus their essays and write about one aspect of the concept. Notice how the Invention and Research activities are set up to lead students first to a broad overview of the concept and then to focus on one aspect of it. When we teach this assignment, we require students to describe both the concept and the aspect of it they will focus on, either to us or to the whole class during a subject discussion session.

THINKING ABOUT THE GENRE: CONCEPT EXPLANATION (p. 179)

This activity will allow students to realize they have a familiarity, possibly greater than they expected, with the genre, reducing the anxiety that typically accompanies composing an essay and making the remaining activities in this chapter easier.

CHOOSING READINGS

If you cannot teach all the readings in this chapter, you will have to make some choices. There are two main principles that may guide your selection—(1) the interest level of the reading and its usefulness in suggesting subjects for your students' essays and (2) the major features covered in each of the Reading like a Writer activities.

The reading selections in this chapter, beginning with the sample essay by Susan Cain, represent a variety of concepts and ways of explaining them. Nevertheless, all the concepts presented here refer to cultural or social phenomena: Cain on shyness, Tannen on marked forms, Bailey on dating, Hurley on intelligence, Ngo on cannibalism, and, Stone on continuous partial attention and Ton on hip-hop (e-Pages). However, articles and books on astronomy, biology, chemistry, and physics also lend considerable time to explaining concepts of natural science, and might be used as supplemental examples.

INTEREST LEVELS OF THE READINGS

Here are brief descriptions from the table of contents to help you choose readings that might be of interest to your students:

Susan Cain, **Shyness: Evolutionary Tactic?** A prominent author and journalist explains that shyness, far from being a debilitating social disadvantage, actually confers certain benefits like introspection and attentiveness. (p. 181)

Deborah Tannen, **Marked Women.** A linguist explains the linguistic concept of marked forms: "Each of the women at the conference had to make decisions about hair, clothing, makeup and accessories, and each decision carried meaning. Every style available to us was marked." (p. 192)

Beth L. Bailey, **Dating.** A sociologist explains the concept of dating and shows how courtship rituals have changed over the years—to the disadvantage of poor men and strong-minded women. (p. 201)

Dan Hurley, **Can You Make Yourself Smarter?** A science writer explains that intelligence, which people tend to think of as fixed, is subject to change. Hurley explains that it is, in fact, possible to make yourself (and others) smarter. (p. 212)

Linh Kieu Ngo, **Cannibalism: It Still Exists.** A first-year composition student explains the anthropological concept of cannibalism, delineating the three functional categories of survival, dietary, and ritual cannibalism. (p. 223)

Justin Ton, **Hip-Hop You Don't Stop.** A college student explains the origins and "four pillars" of hip-hop music, detailing its evolution and arguing that it turns young people away from violence and toward positive expression. (**e**)

Linda Stone, **Continuous Partial Attention.** A high-tech visionary, Linda Stone describes the phenomenon of continuous partial attention, the phenomenon created by the multitasking demanded by our fast-paced, digital culture. (**e**)

e bedfordstmartins.com/readingcritically

The first reading, Cain's "Shyness: Evolutionary Tactic?" introduces all the major features of the essay explaining a concept through its Reading like a Writer activities. Each of the other readings has one Reading like a Writer activity. Below is a list of these activities.

Engaging Readers' Interest: Deborah Tannen, "Marked Women" (p. 199)

Using Comparison and Contrast: Beth L. Bailey, "Dating" (p. 211)

Integrating Sources Smoothly: Dan Hurley, "Can You Make Yourself Smarter?" (p. 221)

Organizing the Information Clearly and Logically: Linh Kieu Ngo, "Cannibalism: It Still Exists" (p. 228)

A GUIDE TO READING CONCEPT EXPLANATIONS (p. 180)

Here are suggestions for teaching the Reading for Meaning activities following Cain's "Shyness: Evolutionary Tactic?"

READING FOR MEANING (p. 186)

Read to Summarize (p. 186)
This section asks students to explore the meaning of the essay by reflecting on the word "introversion" as Cain defines it. (A sample summary, which may be used as feedback, is available by assigning students to take the e-Pages summary quiz for the Cain reading: **bedfordstmartins.com/readingcritically**.)

Words that some students may find challenging (*insinuation* [par. 4], *meek* [par. 11], and *buoyant* [par. 23]) are included in a vocabulary quiz in the e-Pages.

Read to Respond (p. 186)
Students may also respond to

- shyness or introversion as they have experienced it or observed it in others
- being outgoing or extroverted and the possible benefits to these traits

Read to Analyze Assumptions (p. 186)
The assumptions in these activities ask the students to consider assumptions about medical conditions and the assumption that what is true for animals will also be true for humans. A belief at the root of the latter assumption is often, of course, the assumption that humans are animals. You may want to have students discuss this idea, or you could also suggest students list the kinds of assumptions people often make about shy people or extroverted people and discuss the extent to which these assumptions are true.

READING LIKE A WRITER (p. 187)

The four Reading like a Writer activities following Cain's essay give students a comprehensive introduction to the rhetorical features and writing strategies of essays explaining concepts. You can have students do some or all of the activities here before going on to do selected Reading like a Writer activities for the subsequent readings. With the Cain essay, students are introduced to major features of concept explanation—explaining using appropriate strategies, organizing the information clearly and logically, integrating sources smoothly, and engaging readers' interest. Each feature carries a reading and a writing activity that help students focus on Cain's writing strategies.

Using Appropriate Writing Strategies (p. 188)

This section lists some of the explaining strategies that writers use to define their concepts to readers: defining, illustrating, comparing and contrasting, and showing causes of effects. The strategies discussed here not only are central to essays explaining concepts but also figure prominently in position papers, which students are exposed to in Chapter 7. This section and the Analyze and Write activity focus specifically on comparing and contrasting.

This activity asks students to consider Cain's use of comparison and contrast as an explanatory strategy. It provides an example of Cain's use of comparison and asks students to identify an example of Cain's use of contrast, emphasizing the sentence strategies writers use in contrast. Finally, it asks students to consider why Cain finds contrast such a useful strategy. If students have begun writing their own concept explanation, you might ask them to write a paragraph comparing or contrasting their concept with another similar concept.

Organizing the Information Clearly and Logically (p. 188)

Here students are introduced to strategies and tools that can help them both to read and write well-organized explanations: forecasting statements, topic sentences, transitions, pronouns that refer back to nouns that appear earlier in the sentence, and summaries. Your students may be reluctant to use these sorts of road signs in their own writing for fear of being too blunt. The failure to be explicit plagues the explanatory essays of many inexperienced writers. You could discuss the issue and try to discover why some students shy away from stating their points directly. This section and the Analyze and Write activity that accompanies it provide students with some examples of these tools and a chance to see them at work in Cain's essay.

The example passage includes transitions, pronoun referents, key terms or their synonyms, summary, and forecasting. You might expand this activity by asking students to identify the organizational strategies they used in an earlier paper or by looking at the organizational strategies used in one or more successful student papers.

Integrating Sources Smoothly (p. 189)

This section refers students to Chapter 11: Strategies for Research and Documentation, and if you have not yet assigned students material to read from Chapter 11, now may be a good time to do so. Many students struggle to integrate source material into their writing smoothly and seamlessly. This section and the Analyze and Write activity that accompanies it introduces students to integrating sources through exploring how Cain includes sources in her essay.

This activity is designed to help students learn from professional writers some strategies for integrating from sources successfully into their own essays. The goal is to get them to see the importance of stating their own idea first and then using information from sources to support that idea, rather than having them use information from sources in place of their own ideas. As an extension of this activity, ask students to look at a passage in a paper of their own (or in a successful student essay from earlier in the semester or from another course) to analyze how well they have used information from sources to support their own ideas and how they might revise to emphasize their own idea as opposed to the ideas included in the source.

Engaging Readers' Interest (p. 190)

This section and the accompanying Analyze and Write activity introduce students to a variety of strategies for getting and keeping readers engaged. Many of the strategies listed in this section can work well in introductions to essays that explain concepts, and this activity could be used as a segue into an introduction drafting activity for the students' own papers where they might try out a few of the strategies listed here.

This activity could be extended by asking students to do the same kind of analysis on the strategies their fellow students use to engage the reader.

READINGS

Deborah Tannen, "Marked Women" (p. 192)

READING FOR MEANING (p. 198)

Read to Summarize (p. 198)
You might also ask students to describe Tannen's emotional response to the concept of "marking." Other words that students may need to define include *frivolousness* (par. 11), *parthenogenesis* (par. 26), and *apologist* (par. 33).

Read to Respond (p. 198)
Students may also respond to

- the fact that Tannen's conclusions are based primarily on her observations of three women and eight men at a conference;
- Tannen's assertion that when a woman takes her husband's surname, she announces that she has traditional values;
- an unaddressed question — if women are marked, who did the marking?

Read to Analyze Assumptions (p. 199)
You might also ask students to write about the cultural assumptions, values, and beliefs underlying Tannen's statement that women do not have the freedom to be unmarked, or her assumption that the men at her conference — despite their beards, differences in clothing, and other traits — were unmarked because she didn't recognize what they wore as symbolizing anything.

READING LIKE A WRITER: ENGAGING READERS' INTEREST (p. 199)

This Reading like a Writer activity focuses on Tannen's efforts to engage her readers. Students should recognize that Tannen's use of an informal, conversational tone and of the first-person pronoun *I* allows them greater accessibility than if she had used a formal, scholarly tone and more objective third-person pronouns. This exercise may be especially useful for students who have difficulty imagining an audience and who consequently assume that their subjects are engaging simply because they are writing about them.

Many students will shy away from using the first person in their own writing (and some instructors, especially in the sciences and social sciences, may discourage students from using the first person), so this activity could prompt a discussion of when use of the first person is appropriate and even helpful.

Beth L. Bailey, "Dating" (p. 201)

A Special Reading Strategy: Synthesizing Information from Sources (p. 209)

The information in this boxed text provides students with some information about synthesizing sources, and points out specific instances where Bailey synthesizes information in her essay. Chapter 10, A Catalog of Reading Strategies, includes a section on synthesizing (p. 520) which students may also find helpful, and the section in Chapter 11, Strategies for Research and Documentation, titled "Using Information from Sources to Support Your Claims" (p. 571) might also be of use.

Reading for Meaning (p. 210)

Read to Summarize (p. 210)
In addition to having students list the differences between calling and dating, you may wish to have students restate Bailey's thesis to help them better understand why Bailey is providing readers a brief history of dating. (A sample summary, which may be used as feedback, is available by assigning students to take the e-Pages summary quiz for the Bailey reading: bedfordstmartins.com/readingcritically.)

Words that some students may find challenging (*supplant* [par. 2], *fortnight* [par. 5], and *exotica* [par. 7]) are included in a vocabulary quiz in the e-Pages. Other words that students may need to look up include *waxed* (par. 3), *tantamount* (par. 3), *myriad* (par. 5), and *apocryphal* (par. 20).

Read to Respond (p. 210)
Students may also respond to

- the link between dating and prostitution;
- the idea that the advent of dating eventually further marginalized women, forcing "women to act as men's dependents" (par. 28);
- the fact that, as women have started to take more initiative in dating, they have not returned to the "calling" model of courtship.

Read to Analyze Assumptions (p. 210)
Another possibility includes considering the assumptions and values that at the turn of the twentieth century dictated the need for chaperones—or at least some type of supervision—for respectable middle- and upper-class young women on dates. Students might also analyze the assumptions of the historical men and women described by Bailey, such as the men who assumed they were not getting a fair deal out of the dating regime, or even the young man in the opening anecdote who assumed he could ask to call on the woman, and assumed he understood what her answer meant. What might his assumptions imply about the 1920s, when the joke was told, and what do those assumptions seem to imply to Bailey?

Reading like a Writer: Using Comparison and Contrast (p. 211)

This Reading like a Writer activity calls attention to the strategy of explaining something new by comparing or contrasting it with something known. We point out that Bailey reverses the typical strategy by explaining something known, dating, by relating it to something unknown, calling. You might ask students to find more typical examples of comparing or contrasting in the other essays that explain concepts. Anderson, for instance, compares the economics of online retailers with those of conventional brick-and-mortar stores, while Tannen explains the marked nature of women by drawing parallels with marked language, which may be more obvious to readers. Ngo compares and contrasts several categories of cannibalism.

This activity encourages students to analyze the way that Bailey uses comparison and contrast to deepen readers' understanding of her concept. If students have not yet practiced this technique in their own drafting, now might be a good time to refer them to an activity like "Using Appropriate Explanatory Strategies" (p. 234) in the Guide to Writing, especially the sentence strategies for comparing and contrasting.

Dan Hurley, "Can You Make Yourself Smarter?" (p. 212)

READING FOR MEANING (p. 219)

Read to Summarize (p. 219)
Here students are asked to explain "fluid intelligence" as Hurley describes this. Because this may be a new way to understand intelligence for some of our students, you may want to have them begin by discussing their own understanding of what intelligence is (or isn't). (A sample summary, which may be used as feedback, is available by assigning students to take the e-Pages summary quiz for the Hurley reading: bedfordstmartins.com/readingcritically.)

Words that some students may find challenging (*hunkered* [par. 1], *diligence* [par. 5], and *immune* [par. 11]) are included in a vocabulary quiz in the e-Pages.

Read to Respond (p. 219)
Students might also respond to

- other traits that people perceive as fixed rather than fluid (examples could include athletic ability, or talent for music) and whether or not those perceptions are accurate
- the ways traits like intelligence are measured and whether or not such measurements are accurate and why

Read to Analyze Assumptions (p. 220)
Here students are asked to consider our assumptions about the social-science based evidence. The value of such evidence is an assumption that many of our students are likely to take for granted so you may want to take some time in class to go through and discuss the material presented in this section in particular. The other assumption that students are asked to explore are assumptions about the validity of analogies. Now may be a good time to introduce students to evaluating logic, discussed in Chapter 10, A Catalog of Reading Strategies (p. 530), as students are sometimes prone to make such false analogies in their writing.

READING LIKE A WRITER: INTEGRATING SOURCES SMOOTHLY (p. 221)

Students are introduced to summarizing, paraphrasing, and quoting in this section, which refers to several of the chapter's previous readings. This section could also make an excellent segue to the relevant material on synthesizing sources in Chapter 11, Strategies for Research and Documentation (p. 569). Through this activity, students take a closer look at the way Hurley summarizes, paraphrases, and quotes his sources. If you want to give the students more practice looking at and analyzing these techniques, you could have students conduct the first activity in this section on one of the other readings in this chapter.

ANALYZING VISUALS (p. 221)

Students are asked to analyze the chart included with the Hurley reading. Many students could find such an exercise somewhat intimidating, so be sure to remind them that Chapter 12, Analyzing Visuals, includes information on reading and incorporating charts.

Linh Kieu Ngo, "Cannibalism: It Still Exists" (p. 223)

READING FOR MEANING (p. 227)

Read to Summarize (p. 227)
After asking students to explain the differences between the several types of cannibalism, you may also wish to ask them to clarify the cultural significance of each type.
Words that students may need to look up include *marsupials* (par. 9) and *avenged* (par. 12).

Read to Respond (p. 227)
Students may also respond to

- the theory Ngo suggests to explain why the Miyanmin society practices cannibalism (par. 9);
- the Bimin-Kuskusmin accounts involving the eating of parts of raw genitals to ensure fertility (13);
- the arrangement of Ngo's essay, especially the introductory anecdote meant to engage the reader and the closing proposition.

Read to Analyze Assumptions (p. 227)
You might also ask students to consider (1) the underlying values that explain why Vietnamese refugees "did not kill people to get human flesh for nourishment, but instead waited until the people had died" (par. 7) or (par. 2) the assumptions that Ngo makes about the reliability of his sources' descriptions of tribal practices in distant parts of the world—descriptions that might not have been fact-checked.

READING LIKE A WRITER: ORGANIZING THE INFORMATION CLEARLY AND LOGICALLY (p. 228)

Students often struggle with organizing their concept essays effectively. As we indicated earlier in the chapter, many of them shy away from the kinds of explicit organizational tools and strategies we advocate as instructors. To that end, we've reminded students of these strategies here and pointed out instances of them in Ngo's essay. It might help to remind students that Ngo himself was a student when he wrote this paper and to emphasize how effective Ngo's use of forecasting statements, topic sentences, brief summaries, and transitions is. If students have begun work on their own essays, this activity can transition nicely into a peer-review activity in which the students examine each other's essays for similar devices.

Justin Ton, "Hip-Hop You Don't Stop" (student essay, e)

The "Before you read" and "As you read" activities for this reading ask students to think about genres prominent in popular culture and the things that differentiate specific genres from each other. Because Ton writes about hip-hop, a genre with which most students have some familiarity, the "As you read" activity asks students to be aware of how what they already know about the hip-

e bedfordstmartins.com/readingcritically

hop genre informs their reading and expands their understanding. The "As you read" activity suggests annotating the text, which can be a helpful exercise and one that you could model with the students in class.

Linda Stone, "Continuous Partial Attention" (video, e)

READING FOR MEANING (e)

A sample summary, which may be used as feedback, is available by assigning the students to take the e-Pages summary quiz for the Stone reading that appears in the e-Pages.

READING LIKE A WRITER: EXPLAINING USING APPROPRIATE STRATEGIES (e)

This activity asks students to analyze separately how both the text and the visuals in the video work to explain the concept. You might also ask students to consider how they could use static visuals, such as photographs or flow charts, to help explain their concept.

REVIEWING WHAT MAKES CONCEPT EXPLANATIONS EFFECTIVE (p. 229)

This reflective activity makes a great transition from reading to writing. As the text suggests, this activity can be done individually or in small groups.

A GUIDE TO WRITING ESSAYS EXPLAINING CONCEPTS (p. 230)

The biggest challenge for writers of explanatory essays is selecting and arranging the material in a way that will be clear and interesting to readers. Three steps in the composing process address this problem — analyzing your readers (p. 232), formulating a working thesis (p. 234), and organizing your draft concept explanation effectively (p. 237) — and students should give them special attention. Thinking carefully about these three steps — and then following through with rich, exploratory invention writing — can help prevent students from submitting undigested reports of information.

Here is an outline of A Guide to Writing Essays Explaining Concepts:

Writing a Draft: Invention, Planning, and Composing
    Choosing a Concept
    Analyzing Your Readers
    Researching the Concept
        Determining What You Know (and What You Don't Know)
        Conducting Background Research
        Choosing an Aspect of Your Concept to Focus On
        Conducting Additional Research on Your Focused Concept
    Formulating a Working Thesis Statement
    Using Appropriate Explanatory Strategies
    Including Visuals
    Integrating Information from Sources
    Organizing Your Concept Explanation Effectively for Your Readers
    Drafting Your Concept Explanation
    Considering a Useful Sentence Strategy (box)

e bedfordstmartins.com/readingcritically

Evaluating the Draft: Getting a Constructive Critical Reading
     Reading a Draft Critically (box)

Improving the Draft: Revising, Editing, and Proofreading
     Revising Your Draft
     Troubleshooting Your Draft (table)
     Editing and Proofreading Your Draft

Reflecting on What You Have Learned: Explaining Concepts (box)

Chapter 6 EVALUATION

This is a pivotal chapter in the book because it is the first that deals with argument. The preceding chapters introduce types of personal and explanatory essays. In this chapter, students encounter essays that make and defend value judgments. Evaluation is one of the basic elements of argumentative writing, and students need to recognize the role that evaluation plays in the other types of argument that are treated in the remaining chapters of *Reading Critically, Writing Well*—Arguing for a Position (Chapter 7), Speculating about Causes or Effects (Chapter 8), and Proposal to Solve a Problem (Chapter 9). Essays speculating about causes or effects, for example, judge the relative value of alternative explanations or predictions. Similarly, proposals assess alternative solutions, and position papers gauge opposing positions.

This chapter begins with a discussion of the evaluations that students make every day and suggests academic and other occasions for evaluative writing. The purpose here is to remind students that they already know something about evaluative discourse—that is, they know when, why, by whom, and for whom evaluations are written. This chapter builds on and refines what most students already know.

The introduction also draws a distinction between evaluations and expressions of taste. Students could explore this distinction by defining terms such as *taste*, *preference*, and *judgment* and by conjecturing about the different purposes of expressing, explaining, justifying, and convincing. The main point is to help students classify the evaluative essay they will write as an argument because it requires that the writer's judgment—the thesis—be backed with reasons and support.

Students can learn a great deal from this challenging assignment, including how to

- choose an appropriate subject to evaluate;
- present a subject to readers;
- assert a clear, authoritative judgment, qualifying it as necessary;
- give reasons for a judgment, based on recognized standards;
- support reasons by providing evidence and by comparing or contrasting a subject to similar subjects;
- organize an essay through logically related reasons; and
- signal explicitly the stages of an evaluative argument.

WRITING ASSIGNMENT: EVALUATION (p. 295)

Here is the writing assignment that appears in the Guide to Writing in Chapter 6:

Write an evaluation supporting your judgment.

- Choose a subject that you can analyze in detail.
- Base your judgment on widely recognized criteria for evaluating a subject like yours.
- Marshall evidence to support your judgment.

- Consider possible objections your readers might raise as well as alternative judgments they might prefer.
- Organize your evaluation clearly and logically.

Problems Students May Have with This Assignment

This seems like a straightforward assignment—say whether you like or dislike something, and then say why—but it can go wrong in many ways the first time students try it. Students may not be willing to assert firm judgments, or they may not understand—even after the readings and Reading like a Writer activities in the text—that they are to make and defend their own judgments with reasons and support. In addition, because they are unaccustomed to being held to the rhetorical requirements of a specific rhetorical situation, student writers may overlook the requirement to describe the subject for readers unfamiliar with it. They may also unwittingly merge or blur their reasons because they lack confidence in them. Students also may not fully understand which standards for evaluating apply to their subjects, or they may assume mistakenly that their readers share the same standards. You might ask your class to brainstorm standards for several similar but different subjects (horror films and dramas, perhaps, or roadside cafes and five-star restaurants) to help students see that readers will expect them to use standards appropriate for their specialized subjects.

These problems suggest that before you ask students to analyze each other's drafts, you may want to model a critical reading of several students' drafts. This way you can emphasize the rhetorical requirements of the assignment. Furthermore, the challenging nature of evaluation makes it a good choice for assigning twice. You could first have everyone in the class evaluate the same subject— perhaps a short story or a movie you show in class. Many short films are now available online. Then students could do a second essay evaluating a subject of their own choice. (You need not *grade* both papers. The first attempt could be a practice run; you might even have students do the practice run in groups, and then use a projector to evaluate each group's evaluation.)

Another way to deal with the common instinct to simply express a verdict without supporting it is to encourage or require students to evaluate by comparing their subject with another appropriate subject in the same category: they might compare two Vietnamese restaurants near campus to determine which is the better deal for students, or compare two summer movies to determine which offers the better thrills. (See the third scenario in Rhetorical Situations for Evaluations, p. 246, for another example.) Students are used to breaking subjects down into points or subtopics for comparisons, and, for this reason, often find it easier to think of ways to back up their opinions in this format.

Perhaps the biggest problem that you need to anticipate arises when students risk doing this assignment from memory. A subject to be evaluated needs to be analyzed closely during invention and possibly reexamined during drafting and revising. Students should not evaluate a movie, for example, unless they can see it two or three times; nor should they evaluate a novel unless they have time to review it very carefully. Similarly, they should not evaluate a consumer product unless they are currently using it and are knowledgeable—or can quickly become knowledgeable—about the general type of product.

RESOURCES IN CHAPTER 6 FOR TEACHING EVALUATION

Quizzes for each of the readings in the text and e-Pages are included in the e-Pages. The auto-graded multiple-choice comprehension quiz or the summary quiz with a sample summary as feedback may be used to provide an additional incentive to students to complete the reading. The vocabulary quiz (with feedback) may be used with students to help students build a college-level vocabulary.

Rhetorical Situations for Evaluations (p. 246)

These three rhetorical situations illustrate a wide range of evaluations, academic and otherwise. Each product demonstrates the characteristics mentioned in the writing assignment by presenting a definitive judgment and backing it up with sound reasons and support. The third situation, in which a college student evaluates colleges for his younger brother, does not highlight judgment quite as prominently as the first two rhetorical situations do. In this situation, the writer offers his brother criteria by which he can make his own judgment. This example might be useful in introducing the central role that the strategy of comparison and contrast often plays in evaluative writing.

Choosing a Subject

Choosing a Subject is the first activity under Writing a Draft: Invention, Planning, and Composing, the opening section in A Guide to Writing Evaluations (p. 295). Students are shown a bulleted list of suggested subjects and are asked to make their own list of possible subjects. You might want to brainstorm with your students additional categories with which they are familiar.

Problems Students May Have Choosing a Subject

Our experience has shown that the most successful essays are those that draw heavily on an individual student's interest or expertise. Students who express an avid interest in skateboarding often write fine essays on skateboard magazines, skateboard parks, or skateboarding equipment. Not only are they familiar with the standards that are usually applied to that field of interest, but also they are able to make pertinent comparisons and contrasts. Even if they do not seem academic, subjects like these can be quite ambitious and demanding when students are enthusiastic and take them seriously. Students may even be able to publish authoritative evaluations of such topics in magazines or on the Web.

By and large, students have the least difficulty evaluating consumer products. Standards are fairly easy to establish, the essays themselves are not difficult to organize, and comparisons can be found easily. Still, there are some dangers in permitting students to write such essays. All too often, students slip into a kind of Madison Avenue prose, uncritically touting the virtues of their chosen product and making claims of comfort or style unsupported by any kind of evidence. Often, they frame details the same ways they have seen them framed in ads, press releases, and company Web sites, or even borrow language from these sources, without recognizing the impact such moves have on their credibility. Trivial criteria or judgments based on personal taste instead of on generally established standards are often applied to consumer-product evaluations, and students should be warned in advance about such potential problems.

Evaluations of people are likely to be successful only when students are careful to establish clear and reasonable standards that others share. Teachers are a popular choice but lend themselves to simplistic judgments ("He was a friend to his students as well as a teacher") that are supported only by personal experience.

We are also wary of attempts to evaluate abstract concepts such as friendship or greed. Though it is theoretically possible to write such evaluations, it is difficult to decide on appropriate standards. Even more difficult is determining the kind of support that might be brought to bear on such a topic. Our students have occasionally written credible essays evaluating capitalism or democracy, but the key to their success seems to lie in the fact that these concepts can be illustrated with specific examples. Evaluations of philosophical abstractions almost always lead to more problems than rewards.

Easily the most promising subjects are discrete, tangible objects or events that can be closely and repeatedly analyzed—a story or novel, movie, musical recording, concert, play performance, essay (perhaps in this book), magazine article, restaurant, computer program, or Web site. Before drafting, students can examine the subject, taking careful notes. They can revisit it once again before revising, keeping the subject present throughout the writing process. Such an immediate presence of subjects makes it easier for students to amass the supporting examples required in a strong evaluation essay.

THINKING ABOUT THE GENRE: EVALUATION (p. 247)

This activity will allow students to realize they have a familiarity, possibly greater than they expected, with the genre, reducing the anxiety that typically accompanies composing an essay and making the remaining activities in this chapter easier.

CHOOSING READINGS

The reading selections in this chapter, beginning with the sample essay by Amitai Etzioni, represent an array of subjects for evaluation. If you cannot assign all the readings in this chapter, you will have to make some choices. There are two main principles that may guide your selection—(1) the interest level of the reading and its usefulness in suggesting subjects for your students' essays and (2) the basic features covered in each of the Reading like a Writer activities.

INTEREST LEVELS OF THE READINGS

Here are brief descriptions from the table of contents to help you choose readings that would be of interest to your students:

Amitai Etzioni, **Working at McDonald's.** A respected sociologist argues that after-school jobs at fast-food restaurants are bad for teenagers. (p. 249)

Malcolm Gladwell, **What College Rankings Really Tell Us.** An award-winning author explains why consumers aren't getting the full picture when they look to rankings for an assessment of a complicated institution like a college or a university. (p. 260)

Christine Rosen, **The Myth of Multitasking.** A prominent writer and commentator on such subjects as bioethics, fundamentalism, feminism, and technology warns that "when people do their work . . . with crumbs of attention rationed out among many competing tasks, their culture may gain in information, but it will surely weaken in wisdom." (p. 270)

William Akana, *Scott Pilgrim vs. the World*: **A Hell of a Ride.** A student in a composition course concludes that *Scott Pilgrim vs. the World* succeeds on the strength of its innovative approach and its humor. Akana praises what he calls the film's great dialogue, inventive special effects, and artistic cinematography and direction. (p. 279)

Christine Romano, **Jessica Statsky's "Children Need to Play, Not Compete": An Evaluation.** A first-year college student applies critical reading skills to another student's essay and comes up with an assertive but carefully balanced evaluation. (p. 287)

Brittany Lemus, Requiem for a Dream: **Fantasy versus Reality.** A student in a composition class argues that the film *Requiem for a Dream* may have been initially off-putting but its memorable characters and central message have proved powerful over time. (**e**)

Marlon Bishop, **Gig Alert: Bright Eyes.** A brief, online review allows readers to decide for themselves whether seeing the band Bright Eyes is appealing by providing a sound file of one of the band's songs. (**e**)

e bedfordstmartins.com/readingcritically

82

The first reading, Etzioni's "Working at McDonald's," introduces all the major features of evaluation through its Reading like a Writer activities. Each of the other readings has one Reading like a Writer activity. Here is a list showing the activities following these readings.

Responding to Objections and Alternative Judgments: "What College Rankings Really Tell Us" (p. 267)

Supporting the Judgment: Christine Rosen, "The Myth of Multitasking" (p. 276)

Presenting the Subject: William Akana, *Scott Pilgrim vs. the World*: A Hell of a Ride" (p. 285)

Organizing the Evaluation: Christine Romano, "Jessica Statsky's 'Children Need to Play, Not Compete': An Evaluation" (p. 292)

Presenting the Subject: Marlon Bishop, "Gig Alert: Bright Eyes" (🄴)

A GUIDE TO READING EVALUATIONS (p. 248)

The essay that is the focus of A Guide to Reading Evaluations is Etzioni's "Working at McDonald's."

Reading for Meaning (p. 252)

Here are suggestions for teaching the Reading for Meaning activities following Etzioni's "Working at McDonald's."

Read to Summarize (p. 252)

You may ask students to reread the several places in the essay (pars. 8–9, 10, and 14) where Etzioni refers to studies, and then have students briefly summarize each study's argument and Etzioni's rebuttal to it.

You might also point out to students that the essay's opening sentence includes the use of the second-person possessive, *your*, and in this context suggests that Etzioni's audience is parents. However, the audience shifts in the concluding sentence to the teens about whom Etzioni has been writing. Point out that this sentence uses the second person: "Go back to school" (par. 22), with *you* being the understood subject. You might ask students why Etzioni would make a direct address to teens at the end of an essay primarily directed at parents. Note that the essay was originally published as an opinion piece in a newspaper. You might suggest that Etzioni includes teens as part of his audience from the beginning.

(A sample summary, which may be used as feedback, is available by assigning students to take the e-Pages summary quiz for the Etzioni reading: bedfordstmartins.com/readingcritically.)

Words that some students may find challenging (*folklore* [par. 4], *undermine* [par. 11], and *compliance* [par. 14]) are included in a vocabulary quiz in the e-Pages. Other words that students may need to look up include *gumption* (par. 7), *don* (par. 7), *affluent* (par. 13), and *intrinsic* (par. 19).

Read to Respond (p. 252)

Students may also respond to

- Etzioni's brusque and at times harsh tone (for example, the essay's opening sentence, "McDonald's is bad for your kids");

🄴 bedfordstmartins.com/readingcritically

- Etzioni's observations on the use and what he considers the general abuse (pars. 18-20) of the money the teens earn.

Read to Analyze Assumptions (p. 253)

You might also ask students to consider teens' underlying values and assumptions that would allow them to feel "they were entitled to $50 severance 'pay' on their last day on the job" (par. 16), or the assumption that Etzioni himself is challenging—the assumption that part-time jobs might be a good experience for a teenager.

READING LIKE A WRITER ACTIVITIES (p. 254)

This section helps students shift their focus from the content to how the writer presents his evaluation. Students are introduced here to four major elements of evaluative writing—presenting the subject, asserting an overall judgment, giving reasons and support, and anticipating objections and alternative judgments. Each feature carries a reading and a writing activity that help students focus on Etzioni's strategies.

Presenting the Subject (p. 254)

This activity asks students to reread and analyze specific paragraphs that present factual details describing the employees at fast-food restaurants and their work. In addition to locating the information in the essay, students are urged to speculate on how Etzioni gathered this information. They are also asked to evaluate the information and to imagine what he may have left out. Imagining what the writer omitted is a valuable critical reading activity, and it underscores a writer's need to make choices about what to include and what to leave out.

Supporting the Judgment (p. 255)

This task addresses the way that writers of evaluation assert their judgments. Students should note that Etzioni states his judgment emphatically at the beginning of the essay and in slightly different forms throughout the selection. For instance, in paragraph 11, he aims his thesis specifically toward minority youngsters. Students are asked to consider whether Etzioni modifies his judgment at any point. You might discuss with students the strategy of acknowledging both a subject's good and bad qualities instead of treating only one or the other.

Responding to Objections or Alternative Judgments (p. 256)

This activity leads students to notice how Etzioni deals with readers' likely objections or alternative judgments. You could divide the class into groups to focus on different counterarguments and then report their findings to the rest of the class. In small groups, students may feel more comfortable arguing with one another about a counterargument's strengths and weaknesses.

Organizing the Evaluation (p. 258)

This section invites students to analyze and evaluate one of Etzioni's reasons, along with the support he offers. Students are asked to consider the reason's appropriateness to Etzioni's overall argument and then to judge the reliability of the support. Some students may find that the three reasons—that fast-food jobs are too routinized, that these jobs interfere with education, and that on-the-job supervision is inadequate or inappropriate—seem calculated to appeal not to student workers but to parents. Students may also be critical of Etzioni's evidence to support these reasons. While the evidence of long hours and late closing times seems plausible in support of the second reason, the evidence in support of Etzioni's claims about routinization and supervision may strike some students as exaggerated, condescending, or both.

READINGS

Malcolm Gladwell, "What College Rankings Really Tell Us" (p. 260)

Reading for Meaning (p. 266)

Read to Summarize (p. 266)

This section asks students to summarize Gladwell's overall judgment (his thesis) and his main supporting reasons. In other words, students are asked to compose a very basic outline of the evaluation. You may want to suggest to students that this kind of a rough outline can be a very helpful reading strategy for other genres as well. (A sample summary, which may be used as feedback, is available by assigning students to take the e-Pages summary quiz for the Gladwell reading: bedfordstmartins .com/readingcritically.)

Words that some students may find challenging (*heterogeneous* [par. 2], *methodology* [par. 9], and *efficacy* [par. 11]) are included in a vocabulary quiz in the e-Pages.

Read to Respond (p. 266)

Students might also respond to

- the ways that they and their friends or classmates chose to attend their college or university
- other alternative criteria that could be used to rank colleges or universities
- the reasons why people value rankings, even those they recognize as arbitrary

Read to Analyze Assumptions (p. 266)

This section asks students to explore assumptions about ideology. Students may have some difficulty understanding what ideology is. Although the textbook does provide a definition (the ideas, beliefs, values, and concerns of an individual or a group), you may want to spend some time as a class talking about what ideology is before proceeding to the bulleted questions in this section of the text. The other set of assumptions that students are asked to explore in this Read to Analyze Assumptions section are assumptions related to the ideas of selectivity and efficacy.

Reading like a Writer: Responding to Objections and Alternative Judgments (p. 267)

Here students are introduced to the idea that their word choice and tone can cue readers as to a writer's views of alternative judgments or objections. The text cautions students that tone can put readers off, especially those who may not agree with the writer's refutation. Students are asked to look at the exchange between Gladwell and Morse in paragraphs 9–12, to analyze the tone, and to imagine how different groups of readers might respond. If students have begun work on their own essays, this activity could segue into an evaluation of tone in their own or in each other's essays.

Christine Rosen, "The Myth of Multitasking" (p. 270)

Reading for Meaning (p. 275)

Read to Summarize (p. 275)

In addition to asking students to explain why Rosen criticizes multitasking, you might also ask students to list reasons other people think of multitasking as good. (A sample summary, which may be used as feedback, is available by assigning students to take the e-Pages summary quiz for the Rosen reading: bedfordstmartins.com/readingcritically.)

Words that some students may find challenging (*undissipated* [par. 1], *agitation* [par. 1], and *ethos* [par. 4]) are included in a vocabulary quiz in the e-Pages.

Other words students may need to look up include *parallel processing* (par. 2), *perennial* (par. 4), and *extols* (par. 5).

Read to Respond (p. 275)

Students may also respond to

- the assertion in the title and in the Hallowell quote that multitasking is "mythical" (par. 5);
- the study that concluded workers lost twenty-five minutes after each interruption of concentration (par. 6).

Read to Analyze Assumptions (p. 276)

If students do not tackle the text's questions about the causes of unfocused attention, you might want to dedicate some time in class to them — not only will doing so give students good practice at identifying a shift in assumptions, it will also give them practice at speculating about causes, another genre of argument supported in Chapter 8. Another assumption that students might want to explore is the implied assumption by Rosen that because the term *multitasking* is a relatively recent invention, the phenomenon must also be new, or dramatically on the rise, rather than an old habit now backed by technology. Does Lord Chesterfield's quotation undermine such an assumption at all? In reading his advice to his son, should we assume the behavior he praises is common, or rare?

READING LIKE A WRITER: SUPPORTING THE JUDGMENT (p. 276)

This Reading like a Writer activity asks students to analyze Rosen's use of authorities — often university research studies — as support for her points. Students might discuss whether they find such studies persuasive. Would their opinions change if she had, instead, claimed support from articles in the *Los Angeles Times*, from *ABC News* polls, or from About.com? As a research exercise, you might also have students try to find one of the studies mentioned by Rosen and analyze it to see what information she left out. Do they think she represented the source material accurately and fairly? Did she leave out any information that they think might have made her argument stronger?

A SPECIAL READING STRATEGY: LOOKING FOR PATTERNS OF OPPOSITION (p. 278)

This special reading strategy invites students to look into the ways that Rosen frames (or reframes) *multitasking* and *focused attention* through word choices. Many students will find this task difficult and mystifying unless they use the two-column chart recommended in the instructions or have done this sort of thing before. You might find it helpful to have the students complete the first step on their own, then set up a chart on the board or project one and fill in the first couple of binary patterns from Chesterfield to get them started:

Focused Attention	Multitasking
"Steady and undissipated attention" *	"Hurry, bustle, and agitation"
"mark of a superior genius" *	"symptoms of a weak and frivolous mind"

After students have the idea, you might set them loose to work individually or in teams on the rest of the activity.

William Akana, "*Scott Pilgrim vs. the World*: A Hell of a Ride" (p. 279)

READING FOR MEANING (p. 283)

Read to Summarize (p. 283)

Like other Read to Summarize activities in this chapter, students are asked to make a rough outline of the evaluation, identifying Akana's overall evaluation and his main reasons. You could point out to students that Akana himself provides readers with just such an overview in the last sentence of paragraph 2 (Akana's thesis). Students could be encouraged at this point to draft or revise their own thesis statements.

Read to Respond (p. 284)

Students might also respond to

- the images included with Akana's essay (The Analyzing Visuals activity later on will ask students more specific questions about the screenshots included with Akana's essay, but some initial discussion of the visuals at this point may be helpful.)
- the aspects or elements of filmmaking that they appreciate or look for in films

Read to Analyze Assumptions (p. 284)

Here the students are asked to explore two sets of assumptions. The first activity asks the students to consider the value of special effects. Some instructors find that showing clips from dated films or television shows (*Star Trek*, the original series, or the first *Planet of the Apes* film, for example) helpful for this activity. Students can discuss what these effects add (or do not add) to the experience. You could then contrast one of the dated clips with a scene from a more recent film or television series. You could ask the students whether or not the impact of the special effects is the same. If it is not, why not? What about for the intended audiences of the clips?

The second set of assumptions that students are asked to consider is the idea of self-respect, which serves as a motivation for Scott Pilgrim, the main character in the film. Students are asked to consider whether or not the idea that "the only person you are fighting for is yourself" is as cliché as the idea that "love conquers all." Opinions here, of course, may vary. This conversation could even lead you and your students into a discussion about our assumptions about clichés. For example you could ask students if clichés appear over and over again because they are true. Or are they merely evidence our society is intellectually or ideologically lazy?

READING LIKE A WRITER: PRESENTING THE SUBJECT (p. 285)

Students are asked to explore how Akana provides the information readers will need about the subject. You may want to point out to students how even as Akana shares information about the film, he avoids too much summary. Many students struggle to understand the difference between summary and analysis, particularly with evaluations of films. Akana's presentation of the subject is relatively brief; he provides readers only the background they will need to understand his analysis. You may want to have students go through Akana's entire essay, looking for instances where Akana summarizes and where he analyzes. In order to help students understand the difference between summary and analysis, you may want to refer them to the relevant sections in Chapter 10: A Catalog of Reading Strategies.

ANALYZING VISUALS (p. 286)

The bulleted questions in the boxed text can produce some great conversations. You may want to divide students into groups and assign different questions to each group; afterward, you could discuss all of the questions as a class.

Christine Romano, "Jessica Statsky's 'Children Need to Play, Not Compete': An Evaluation" (p. 287)

READING FOR MEANING (p. 291)

Read to Summarize (p. 291)

Before having students explain the strengths and weaknesses of Statsky's arguments according to Romano, you may wish to have your students review scratch outlines, discussed in Outlining in Chapter 10, A Catalog of Reading Strategies. After students have reviewed Chapter 10, they can create scratch outlines of Romano's essay. Here's one possibility:

¶ 1 Overview of Statsky's essay
¶ 2 Thesis paragraph
¶ 3–6 Strengths in Statsky's essay according to Romano
¶ 7–9 Weaknesses in Statsky's essay according to Romano
¶ 10 Conclusion

You may wish to have students further detail paragraphs 3–6 and 7–9, but even a scratch outline will clarify for students the structure of Romano's essay.

Read to Respond (p. 291)

Students may also respond to

- the fact that Romano does not explain the logical fallacy "of failing to accept the burden of proof" (par. 7), which she accuses Statsky of committing;
- Romano's gross generalization that "most parents know that big cities receive special federal funding for evening, weekend, and summer recreation" (par. 7).

Read to Analyze Assumptions (p. 291)

Students may further consider the assumptions underlying Romano's criticism of Statsky for not addressing an audience who believes that competitive sports "create a sense of community with a shared purpose," "build character through self-sacrifice and commitment to the group," and "teach children to face their fears early" (par. 8).

READING LIKE A WRITER: ORGANIZING THE EVALUATION (p. 292)

In this Reading like a Writer section, students are asked to look carefully at the transitions that Romano uses in her essay. The activity covers logical transitions and explains to students the role that logical transitions can serve in helping readers understand the argument. This activity covers several different ways logical transitions may be used:

- To list items consecutively
- To call attention to additional points
- To introduce a contrast or an opposing point
- To signal a cause or effect
- To introduce an example

You may want to suggest to students that they could look for similar transitions in one of the chapter's previous readings. Students are also asked to analyze Romano's use of cueing strategies by looking carefully at her thesis statement and her subsequent references to her thesis throughout the essay. Performing similar analysis during a peer-review activity could be valuable for students.

Brittany Lemus, *"Requiem for a Dream*: Fantasy versus Reality" (student essay, e)

The "As you read" activities for this text asks the students to explore the ways that Lemus uses variations of the word "dream" throughout her essay. The students are also asked whether or not Lemus's essay makes them want to see the film. You may want to discuss this question as a class and have students point out specific passages that motivate them (or do not motivate them) to see the film. You could discuss together why such passages are effective (or ineffective). Since many students choose to write film reviews, exploring the effective strategies Lemus uses throughout her essay can be very beneficial to students.

Marlon Bishop, "Gig Alert: Bright Eyes" (Web page with sound file, e)

READING FOR MEANING (e)

A sample summary, which may be used as feedback, is available by assigning students to take the e-Pages summary quiz for the Bishop reading that appears in the e-Pages.

READING LIKE A WRITER: PRESENTING THE SUBJECT (e)

This activity asks students to evaluate the criteria used to evaluate the band Bright Eyes and also to consider how providing an MP3, so the audience can hear the band for themselves, affects the need for the writer to assert her or his opinion.

REVIEWING WHAT MAKES EVALUATIONS EFFECTIVE (p. 294)

This reflective activity makes a great transition from reading to writing. As the text suggests, this activity can be done individually or in small groups.

A GUIDE TO WRITING EVALUATIONS (p. 295)

Probably the most challenging Invention and Research activity is Developing the Reasons and Evidence Supporting Your Judgment (p. 299). Students tend to have two kinds of difficulty—identifying standards they and their readers are likely to share and marshaling specific support for their judgments.

You can address the first problem by having students in small groups discuss why they think readers will or will not find the writer's reasons appropriate. The second problem—finding support—requires students to have ready access to the subject that is being evaluated and take careful notes so that they can, for example, quote or paraphrase bits of dialogue from a movie.

Here is an outline of A Guide to Writing Evaluations:

> *Writing a Draft: Invention, Planning, and Composing*
> Choosing a Subject to Evaluate
> Assessing Your Subject and Considering How to Present It to Your Readers
> Considering Your Purpose for Your Audience

Formulating a Working Thesis Statement
Developing the Reasons and Evidence Supporting Your Judgment
Researching Your Evaluation
Responding to a Likely Objection or Alternative Judgment
Including Visuals or Other Media
Organizing Your Evaluation Effectively for Your Readers
Working with Sources: Using Summary to Support Your Evaluative Argument (box)
Drafting Your Evaluation
Considering a Useful Sentence Strategy

Evaluating the Draft: Getting a Constructive Critical Reading
Reading a Draft Critically (box)

Improving the Draft: Revising, Editing, and Proofreading
Revising Your Draft
Troubleshooting Your Draft (table)
Editing and Proofreading Your Draft

Reflecting on What You Have Learned: Evaluation (box)

Chapter 7 ARGUING FOR A POSITION

This is the second of four chapters that deal with important types of argument: Evaluation (Chapter 6), Arguing for a Position (Chapter 7), Speculating about Causes or Effects (Chapter 8), and Proposal to Solve a Problem (Chapter 9). At the heart of a position paper, there are nearly always ethical questions— questions of right and wrong —that can seldom be resolved by facts alone.

When students take a position on a controversial issue, they discover not only that people differ but also that they may have good reasons for their different views. Students learn to respect the complexity of the issues they read and write about as well as the subtlety of others' reasoning. This chapter's emphasis on the rhetorical aspects of argumentation helps students avoid polemics. Students learn to develop an argument that is responsive to their readers' concerns and that builds a bridge of shared values.

The writing assignment requires that students examine the issue critically as they write instead of framing an argument to support an already formed opinion. We encourage students to use the entire composing process to help them analyze and evaluate the issue and the different points of view on it. We urge them to examine their own underlying assumptions as critically as they would those of others. We want them to recognize the value of thinking through the issue and of basing their positions on solid reasoning and sound supporting evidence.

Students writing position papers can learn to

- choose an arguable issue and define it carefully;
- assert a position on an issue;
- give reasons that readers should take a position seriously;
- support each reason with examples, facts, analogies, statistics, anecdotes, or quotes from authorities;
- anticipate readers' questions and positions on an issue, counterarguing as needed;
- organize an essay through logically ordered reasons; and
- explicitly signal the stages in an argument taking a position.

WRITING ASSIGNMENT: POSITION ARGUMENT (p. 358)

Here is the writing assignment that appears in the Guide to Writing in Chapter 7:

Write an essay arguing a position on a controversial issue:

- Choose an issue either on which you have a position or that you'd like to investigate further.
- Consider what your readers might know about the issue, and what stance they might take towards it.
- Conduct research on the issue so you can support and clarify your own argument and also so that you can address the objections your readers might raise as well as the alternative positions they might prefer.
- Adopt a reasonable tone, one that will lend credibility to your position.

Problems Students May Have with This Assignment

Probably the greatest problem students encounter when they begin writing position papers is mistaking assertion for argumentation. This problem manifests itself in sweeping generalizations unsupported by reasons and evidence. Students with little experience developing an argument usually assume that all they need do is state what they think. They do not realize that they have to give reasons for their position and evidence to support it. Nor do they recognize how important it is to anticipate readers' objections and questions and then either to modify their own positions by acknowledging reasonable objections or to defend them by refuting unreasonable ones.

For some students, the essential problem is lack of experience in reasoning. Some students simply may be unused to setting out their reasons in a way that others can follow. For them, reading a diversity of arguments will provide instructive models. If, however, the problem stems from a lack of thoughtfulness—from the habit of relying on unexamined assumptions and biases—then the solution is more difficult. These students need first to accept the value of introspection and logical reasoning. They must recognize that the aim of argumentation is not merely to voice their own opinion but to examine it critically. The root of the problem for some students might be cognitive as well as emotional. Some students have little experience in self-analysis, let alone audience analysis. They may be able to assert their own opinions forcefully but tend to have difficulty looking critically at their own assumptions or describing carefully their own train of thought. In our experience, students with this kind of problem respond well when argumentative writing is presented as an act of communication rather than one of aggression. When the emphasis is on creating common ground instead of squashing opponents, students feel less defensive and more open to alternative ways of seeing.

RESOURCES IN CHAPTER 7 FOR TEACHING POSITION PAPERS

Quizzes for each of the readings in the text and e-Pages are included in the e-Pages. The auto-graded multiple-choice comprehension quiz or the summary quiz with a sample summary as feedback may be used to provide an additional incentive to students to complete the reading. The vocabulary quiz (with feedback) may be used with students to help students build a college-level vocabulary.

FINDING SUBJECTS

Rhetorical Situations for Position Papers (p. 312)

The three brief rhetorical situations presented early in the chapter demonstrate that writers argue for positions on controversial issues in both academic and nonacademic settings. The situations also suggest some of the many issues debated in position papers—the regulation of urban development, the cost of public education, and the right of public employees to strike. You might ask your students to brainstorm a list of other issues even before reading further in the chapter, or you might refer to these rhetorical situations just before asking students to list subjects on which they might consider writing. During discussion of these scenarios, you might draw attention to the research described in the second and third examples. The example of the economics student describes a range of sources, but you might ask students to think of others she might have tried. The example of the political science student describes interviews of family members, both of them public employees. You might ask students to debate the advantages and disadvantages of the student's choice of sources.

Choosing a Controversial Issue (p. 359)

Choosing an Issue is the first activity under Writing a Draft: Invention, Planning, and Composing, the opening section of A Guide to Writing Position Papers. Students are urged to list possible issues in the form of *should* questions and are shown a few examples. Then they are asked to choose an arguable issue—that is, an issue "that people disagree about but that cannot be resolved simply with facts or by authorities."

Problems Students May Have Choosing an Issue

We have found no simple rule for prejudging the promise of issues for position papers. The key is for students to do the work necessary to become informed about the different points of view that people take on the issue. If they are interested only in supporting their own positions and not in learning about other points of view, then their arguments are likely to be taken seriously only by those who already agree with them.

Without making the assignment a full-blown research project, you might encourage students to discuss the issue with others and to do some reading about it. Exploring opposing views should be a required part of the invention process. Sometimes, however, students make their research one sided. It is good to seek reasons and evidence to support a position, but writers also need to be able to anticipate objections and to appeal to values and concerns they might share with others. If you choose to make this assignment a substantial research project, you might require that your students explore a minimum of two sources presenting positions that oppose their initial positions.

In A Guide to Writing Position Papers, we offer a list of possibilities to get students thinking about issues they could write about. Many of the issues we suggest are ones we think students will know and care about. Caring about the issue is essential for good writing, particularly for argumentative writing. This requirement comes as a surprise to some students—and may even be threatening to them. We have been amazed at the number of students reluctant to express an opinion. Many have been taught that it is inappropriate for them to do so. Some have been made to feel that they know too little to have an opinion worth sharing. Others believe that they are in school to consume ideas and opinions, not to produce them. For these students, we emphasize the process over the product. We explain that taking a position teaches them to analyze issues critically and to evaluate arguments. With experience, students gain confidence in their reasoning abilities and come to enjoy developing a thoughtful, well-supported argument.

THINKING ABOUT THE GENRE: POSITION ARGUMENTS (p. 313)

This activity will allow students to realize they have a familiarity, possibly more than they expected, with the genre, reducing the anxiety that typically accompanies the composing of any essay and making easier the remaining activities in this chapter.

CHOOSING READINGS

If you cannot teach all of the readings in this chapter, you will have to make some choices. There are at least two principles that may guide your selection: first, the interest level of the reading and its usefulness in suggesting topics for your students' essays; second, the basic features focused on in the Reading like a Writer activities.

INTEREST LEVELS OF THE READINGS

The reading selections in this chapter, beginning with the sample essay by Brian Greene, present a variety of different issues and ways of arguing. Here are brief descriptions from the table of contents to help you choose readings that might be of interest to your students:

Brian Greene, **Put a Little Science in Your Life.** A scientist argues that science is "a way of life" and that to practice and understand it is to undergo a "transformation . . . that is empowering and emotional . . . and one of the most precious of human experiences." (p. 315)

Karen Stabiner, **Boys Here, Girls There: Sure, If Equality's the Goal.** A journalist defends the position that single-sex schools benefit girls, especially those in low-income families. (p. 325)

Sherry Turkle, **The Flight from Conversation.** An author and professor at MIT argues that our electronic tools from communication are diminishing our opportunities for in-person interactions and their richness and depth. (p. 334)

Daniel J. Solove, **Why Privacy Matters Even If You Have "Nothing to Hide."** A scholar and legal expert argues that even those who claim they have "nothing to hide" are hurt by invasions of privacy in the name of security. (p. 341)

Jessica Statsky, **Children Need to Play, Not Compete.** Documenting the excesses and dangers of competitive sports for children under the age of thirteen, a first-year college student argues for eliminating such programs in favor of programs "emphasizing fitness, cooperation, sportsmanship, and individual performance." (p. 349)

Tan-Li Hsu, **High on Caffeine: Regulating Energy Drinks.** Alarmed at the level of caffeine in popular energy drinks, a college student argues that the drinks put young people at risk and urges marketers to label cans and issue warnings accordingly. (**e**)

U. S. Department of Transportation/Ad Council, **The "It's Only Another Beer" Black and Tan.** This public service announcement uses the recipe genre to discourage drinking and driving. (**e**)

READING LIKE A WRITER ACTIVITIES

The first reading, Greene's "Put a Little Science in Your Life," introduces all the basic features of position papers through its Reading like a Writer activities. The final reading, Statsky's "Children Need to Play, Not Compete," does not specify a Reading like a Writer activity but invites students to choose a feature of the reading they think is worth analyzing. Each of the other readings has one Reading like a Writer activity. Here is a list of these activities.

Responding to Objections and Alternative Positions Fairly: Karen Stabiner, "Boys Here, Girls There: Sure, If Equality's the Goal" (p. 331)

Arguing Directly for the Position, and Supporting the Position with Reasonable Evidence: Sherry Turkle, "The Flight from Conversation" (p. 334)

e bedfordstmartins.com/readingcritically

Presenting the Controversial Issue Fairly and Credibly: Daniel J. Solove, "Why Privacy Matters Even if You Have 'Nothing to Hide'" (p. 348)

Asserting a Clear Position: Jessica Statsky, "Children Need to Play, Not Compete" (p. 355)

A GUIDE TO READING ESSAYS ARGUING FOR A POSITION (p. 314)

The essay that is the focus of A Guide to Reading Essays Arguing for a Position is Greene's "Put a Little Science in Your Life."

READING FOR MEANING (p. 318)

Here are suggestions for teaching the Reading for Meaning activities following the Greene essay.

Read to Summarize (p. 318)
To help students better understand Greene's purpose, have the class discuss the differences between the easy argument that Greene summarizes in paragraphs 4 and 5, and the more significant one he starts to make in paragraph 7. (A sample summary, which may be used as feedback, is available by assigning students to take the e-Pages summary quiz for the Greene reading: bedfordstmartins .com/readingcritically.)

Words that some students may find challenging (*debilitating* [par. 1], *dogma* [par. 7], and *esoteric* [par. 9]) are included in a vocabulary quiz in the e-Pages. Other words that students may need to look up include *ubiquity* (par. 4), *predictive* (par. 7), *relativity* (par. 8), and *paradigm* (par. 19).

Read to Respond (p. 318)
Students may also respond to

- Greene's occasional assertion that we enjoy the technological fruits of science even if we think science is "cold, distant and intimidating" (par. 10);
- the "big questions" he lists (par. 17).

Read to Analyze Assumptions (p. 319)
Students might also debate Greene's assumptions that, in today's educational environment, science needs better public relations, and that comparing science to the humanities is to science's advantage. A related assumption that might be discussed is Greene's clear implication that art, music, and literature hold value as practices that give life meaning—an assumption not always shared by those who shape the curriculum.

READING LIKE A WRITER (p. 320)

This section helps students move from examining the content and purpose of essays to analyzing the strategies used by writers to accomplish their purposes. The five Reading like a Writer activities following Greene's essay give students a comprehensive introduction to the basic features of essays arguing a position—presenting the issue; asserting a clear, unequivocal position; arguing directly for the position; counterarguing objections and opposing positions; and establishing credibility. Each feature carries a critical reading and a writing activity that help students focus on Greene's writing strategies.

Presenting the Controversial Issue Fairly and Credibly (p. 320)

This activity highlights the need for writers of position papers to inform their readers about the issue and to convince them that the issue is worth taking a position on. The activity focuses on the way Greene sets up the issue in his opening paragraphs, particularly in paragraphs 4 and 5. Students may be surprised that, in an argument about why science is important, he shows why people already believe it to be important. His position is that most people cite the wrong reasons, not that their conclusions are wrong. Students may find it productive to discuss the value of such arguments. Is it worthwhile to try to improve on an existing argument, as Greene is attempting?

Asserting a Clear Position (p. 321)

This section reminds students that although informing readers about the issue is certainly part of a writer's task in taking a position, a writer must also assert a definitive position on the issue. The idea that position papers need to be assertive may lead some students to think that complicated or nuanced theses are unacceptable, so you might want to take time to discuss with students the way this section of the text qualifies its death-penalty example, emphasizing that a clear position need not be simple or monolithic. Before having students move on to the tasks in this activity, you should make sure most of them are able to reconcile qualifying with assertively stating the thesis.

The activity asks students to notice where Greene states and restates his position and to examine the context of each restatement. Some students, especially those uncomfortable with the explicitness of most position papers, may think he is being unnecessarily repetitive. The challenge is getting them to consider why he chooses to repeat his thesis —what his rhetorical purpose might be for this particular move.

Arguing Directly for the Position, and Supporting the Position with Reasonable Evidence (p. 322)

This section lists various kinds of support that writers of position papers typically use. Students are then asked to analyze one of Greene's claims—that big questions are an important aspect of science—and the examples in paragraphs 17 and 18 that he uses to support the claim. Paragraph 17 presents examples of big questions that science poses. Paragraph 18 gives examples of theories that have recently emerged as possible answers in the field of physics. Finally, students are asked to assess the likely persuasiveness of this kind of support. As the text notes, examples are not proof (nor are they claimed by Greene to be), but they can persuade through emotions. The questions in paragraph 17, then, might be deemed effective if they awaken in readers a primal sense of awe or wonder. The list of theories in paragraph 18, however, includes no explanations or descriptions of those theories and thus might be persuasive only to readers already familiar with them. Then again, if Greene succeeds in generating a sense of mystery in paragraph 17, and readers are then surprised to hear there are possible answers to such questions in the theories he later names, they might look up those theories.

Responding to Objections and Alternative Positions Fairly and Credibly (p. 323)

Effective arguments also address alternative and opposing viewpoints, sometimes acknowledging them, sometimes accommodating, sometimes refuting. Arguments in this chapter as well as essays in the other argumentative chapters indeed address other viewpoints. In the paragraphs students are asked to analyze for this activity, Greene both accommodates and refutes opposing viewpoints. There are, essentially, two viewpoints that he addresses: first, that science is cold and impersonal; second, that science instruction should emphasize mastery of the technicalities. He sees the first as a "shame" (par. 10), but understandable in light of the second viewpoint, which he believes makes science seem so cold. In dealing with each argument, he concedes some ground—science is often presented as dull, technical facts, and these facts are indeed important to a scientific education—but he also counters that science education would engage students more if teachers addressed the big questions at the heart of scientific inquiry. By taking this approach, Greene shows himself to be understanding and sympathetic to those who might oppose him rather than deliberately confrontational, and as a result, his counterargument may seem to readers to be more an extension of some shared common ground than an attack. Students may be unfamiliar and uncomfortable with this kind of "yes, but" approach; they should be encouraged to try it and practice it. One way to do so might be to have students turn, at this point, to Considering a Useful Sentence Strategy (p. 367), to study and practice sentences that concede in part but follow up with immediate refutations.

READINGS

Karen Stabiner, "Boys Here, Girls There: Sure, If Equality's the Goal" (p. 325)

READING FOR MEANING (p. 330)

Read to Summarize (p. 330)

In addition to asking your students to explain why Stabiner favors single-sex schools for girls, you might also ask them to list the opposing arguments Stabiner identifies and responds to. (A sample summary, which may be used as feedback, is available by assigning students to take the e-Pages summary quiz for the Stabiner reading: bedfordstmartins.com/readingcritically.)

Words that some students may find challenging (*proselytize* [par. 4], *siphoning* [par. 9], and *wariness* [par. 10]) are included in a vocabulary quiz in the e-Pages. Other words that students may need to look up include *parochial* (par. 5), *stark* (par. 7), *bipartisan* (par. 9), *grudgingly* (par. 15), and *handmaidens* (par. 17).

Read to Respond (p. 330)

Students might also respond to

- any of Stabiner's points in light of experiences they have had with coeducation;
- Stabiner's suggestion that "the political debate about vouchers and school choice" (par. 19) may be shaping the discussion about single-sex schools;
- Stabiner's argument that "single-sex public schools and classes, as odd as it may sound, are about inclusion; any school district that wants one can have one and everyone can learn from the experience" (par. 20).

Read to Analyze Assumptions (p. 330)

You might also ask students to explore

- the assumptions behind Stabiner's use of the word *handmaiden* in her sentence "Will there be a group of educational handmaidens, girls who are consigned to coed schools to keep the boys from acting out?" (par. 17);
- the assumptions suggested by the comment after the dash in the following sentence: "The new educational reform law is called the No Child Left Behind Act, an irresistible sentiment with a chilling edge to it — did we ever actually intend to leave certain children behind?" (par. 21).

READING LIKE A WRITER: RESPONDING TO OBJECTIONS AND ALTERNATIVE POSITIONS FAIRLY (p. 331)

This Reading like a Writer activity focuses on Stabiner's strategy for responding to alternative positions and how she structures her argument in relation to likely objections from her readers. Students are asked to identify where Stabiner acknowledges, refutes, and concedes the objections. You might have a class discussion or use a course management system to have a discussion about how convincingly she frames the issue of same-sex schools when she addresses her opposition.

A SPECIAL READING STRATEGY — COMPARING AND CONTRASTING RELATED READINGS: ORENSTEIN'S "THE DAILY GRIND: LESSONS IN THE HIDDEN CURRICULUM" AND STABINER'S "BOYS HERE, GIRLS THERE: SURE, IF EQUALITY'S THE GOAL" (p. 332)

Orenstein's observational essay in Chapter 3 and Stabiner's position paper in Chapter 7 harmonize well, since both concern the ways that a mix of boys and girls in a classroom can complicate education. It may be tempting for students who read both essays to answer the first part of the activity with a simple, "Yes, Stabiner's single-sex classes would make Orenstein and her subject Amy Wilkinson happier," but the question also asks what girls like Wilkinson might lose in the switch to all-girl classrooms. There is no right or wrong answer to this question, but students should consider or even debate this part of the question before moving onto the second part of the activity. The second part gives students another opportunity to think about differences between the two essays, by considering their differing purposes and genres. Another way to express this question, if students seem stumped, is to ask, "What strategic advantages might Orenstein's observational essay have that Stabiner's does not? What advantages might an overt position paper like Stabiner's have over an observational essay?"

Sherry Turkle, "The Flight from Conversation" (p. 334)

READING FOR MEANING (p. 338)

Read to Summarize (p. 338)
Students are encouraged to explore Turkle's position through comparing and contrasting the ways she depicts digital interactions versus face-to-face conversations. (A sample summary, which may be used as feedback, is available by assigning students to take the e-Pages summary quiz for the Turkle reading: bedfordstmartins.com/readingcritically.)

A vocabulary quiz on words that some students may find challenging (*kinetic* [par. 13], *nuance* [par. 13], and *partisan* [par. 25]) are included in a vocabulary quiz in the e-Pages.

Read to Respond (p. 338)
Students may also respond to

- their own experiences with digital interactions
- what they may believe is gained through digital interactions (and here you could refer students to paragraphs like 10 or 20 where Turkle acknowledges some of the reasons why people are drawn to digital interaction)

Read to Analyze Assumptions (p. 338)
This set of exercises asks students to question the assumptions that good conversation contributes to well-being as well as a set of assumptions around the idea of the value of controlling ourselves. You could arrange students in groups and have them debate these ideas. For example, one group could generate ideas about the value of conversation, while another group could argue for the value of solitude. Another group might discuss the virtues of self-control while still another could discuss the potential value in letting go and acting on impulse.

Here students are reminded of the various types of evidence writers may provide: facts, statistics, examples, anecdotes, expert opinion, or analogies. The activity asks students to take a careful look at the kinds of evidence Turkle uses to make her argument and to evaluate the effectiveness of her evidence.

A SPECIAL READING STRATEGY: REFLECTING ON CHALLENGES TO YOUR BELIEFS AND VALUES (p. 340)

This section points out that sometimes reading arguments can be challenging, especially when arguments challenge our values or our beliefs. Students (most of us, in fact) are sometimes tempted to respond to arguments emotionally without analyzing the source of the emotional response let alone the merits of the argument. Here students are given a series of strategies for reflecting on the emotional responses arguments sometimes trigger and analyzing the source of such responses. You may want to give students some time in class to do the writing activity suggested at the end of this activity.

Daniel J. Solove, "Why Privacy Matters Even If You Have 'Nothing to Hide'" (p. 341)

READING FOR MEANING (p. 346)

Read to Summarize (p. 346)
In this activity students are asked to summarize Solove's position. You might also have them do a brief outline of Solove's reasons and evidence. (A sample summary, which may be used as feedback, is available by assigning students to take the e-Pages summary quiz for the Solove reading: **bedfordstmartins .com/readingcritically**.)

Words that some students may find challenging (*formidable* [par. 4], *dossier* [par. 7], and *incremental* [par. 15]) are included in a vocabulary quiz in the e-Pages.

Read to Respond (p. 346)
Students might also respond to:

- the concerns of balancing the value of security with the value of privacy
- the things they choose to share with the public (in conversation, in online profiles, etc.) and why

Read to Analyze Assumptions (p. 347)
The first assumption students are asked to interrogate is the assumption that "privacy is about hiding bad things." In addition to the discussion prompts in the text, you could ask students what elements of our culture reinforce this notion.

The second assumption is that people would try to curb violations of privacy more if they knew how the information gathered was used. Recent news stories in the past several years have underscored just how much information is collected by government agencies acting in the interest of "security." You might ask students to speculate about other applications to which information like phone records could be used besides security and whether or not they feel threatened by the possibilities of such applications of their information and why.

READING LIKE A WRITER: PRESENTING THE CONTROVERSIAL ISSUE FAIRLY AND CREDIBLY (p. 348)

Here students are given some sentence-level strategies for presenting their issues fairly and credibly. You may want to remind students that such strategies are merely suggestions to get them started and not rote formulas that must be followed. Students are also asked to further analyze how Solove presents his issue. This activity could transition nicely into a drafting activity that allowed students to practice presenting their own issues.

Jessica Statsky, "Children Need to Play, Not Compete" (p. 349)

READING FOR MEANING (p. 354)

This Reading for Meaning activity invites students to apply to Statsky's essay what they have learned from the other readings in this chapter about reading to summarize, reading to respond, and reading to analyze assumptions. You might want to have your class suggest words to define as well as brainstorm possibilities for response and analysis.

Read to Summarize (p. 354)
Students are asked to share what they've learned from Statsky's essay about children and sports. This may be a good time to point out to students that position papers often, in addition to making an argument, must educate readers on points that are obscure or not well understood.

Read to Respond (p. 354)
Students might also respond to

- their own experience with playing competitive sports as children
- the idea that sports is good preparation for life

Read to Analyze Assumptions (p. 354)
These activities ask students to explore the assumptions surrounding two values that are crucial to Statsky's argument: cooperation and inclusion. You may want to encourage students to respond to these assumptions with their own experience. You could ask them whether or not they have they found cooperation and inclusion to be valuable, and to explain their answers.

READING LIKE A WRITER: ASSERTING A CLEAR POSITION (p. 355)

Here students are asked to explore the ways that Statsky makes her position clear to readers. One of the ways she does this is by qualifying her position—a technique that students may want to use in their essays as well, and one you may want to go over in class. The activity asks students to take a closer look at Statsky's thesis and supporting reasons. If students have not yet drafted their own thesis statements, this could make a good segue into such an activity. If students are a bit farther along in the drafting process, you may want them to analyze their own or each other's thesis statements.

Tan-Li Hsu, "High on Caffeine: Regulating High Energy Drinks" (student essay, 🄔)

The "As you read" activity for this selection in the e-Pages encourages students to look for strategies in Hsu's essay that they have been learning about in class. The activity also encourages students to annotate the text as they spot these strategies. You could assign students to do this on their own, but you might also find that this is an activity that could work well performed in small groups or even as a whole class. Hsu's essay provides many excellent examples of strategies we encourage our students to use: he frames the issue well, he cites credible sources, he raises and responds to objections effectively (see par. 8). Reminding students that Hsu was a student when he wrote the essay can help students feel motivated and encouraged as they write their own position arguments.

🄔 bedfordstmartins.com/readingcritically

U.S. Department of Transportation/Ad Council, The "It's Only Another Beer" Black and Tan (interactive public service announcement, <img>)

READING FOR MEANING (<img>)

A sample summary, which may be used as feedback, is available by assigning students to take the summary quiz for U.S. Department of Transportation/Ad Council public service announcement. This interactive PSA provides pop-ups to help students analyze the PSA in terms of the major features of the genre.

READING LIKE A WRITER: RESPONDING TO OBJECTIONS AND ALTERNATIVE POSITIONS (<img>)

This activity asks students to analyze how effectively the PSA presents its message and to evaluate how effectively the visual and layout contribute to the ad's power. This activity could provide a good jumping-off point for a discussion of genre, especially of the flexibility of genre in the service of reaching one's audience. (You might want to point out that academic genres are not particularly flexible generally, so they should discuss any variations in form or content with their instructor in advance.)

The activity offers students an opportunity to focus on one of the strategies for writing position papers covered in this chapter—presenting the issue, asserting a clear and unequivocal position, arguing directly for a position, counterarguing objections and opposing positions, or establishing credibility.

ANALYZING VISUALS (p. 356)

Students may be inspired by Statsky's inclusion of a relevant cartoon to include cartoons or other art with their work as well. For this reason, discussing its connections to the text and what it adds to the argument may be worthwhile even if you are not regularly using the Analyzing Visuals features. The questions listed in the activity prompt are particularly well suited for exploring the connections between argument and cartoon, ending with an invitation to imagine another illustration, a move that can give students some practice in thinking about ways to illustrate an argument. (Some may decide that selecting an illustration is harder than it looks.)

The cartoon itself might also be analyzed more closely. For instance, you might ask students how they interpret these details:

- Mrs. Enright is already at the plate and ready to swing the bat;
- the coach is taking no actions, other than to speak to her politely;
- Tommy appears to be looking up (toward whom? with what sort of expression?);
- the catcher is ready to play, even with Mrs. Enright at bat, and most of the other characters in the background seem to be carrying on with business as usual.

REVIEWING WHAT MAKES POSITION ARGUMENTS EFFECTIVE (p. 357)

This reflective activity makes a great transition from reading to writing. As the text suggests, this activity can be done individually or in small groups.

A GUIDE TO WRITING POSITION ARGUMENTS (p. 358)

Throughout the guide, we encourage students to consider their purpose and audience, and we also emphasize the deliberative aspects of argumentation, asking students to explore their own perspectives as well as other points of view. When advising students on how to address readers, you might

<img> bedfordstmartins.com/readingcritically

want to discuss with them how likely it is that they will change their readers' minds. This is an important point because students often believe that the objective of a position paper is to prove the opposition wrong. In fact, many position papers have much more modest goals, such as merely to convince an entrenched opposition that the writer's position is reasonable and deserves serious consideration and respect. Readers may disagree with the writer, but a position paper serves a valuable purpose if readers gain a better understanding of the writer's view and a more tolerant attitude toward it.

Here is an outline of A Guide to Writing Position Papers:

Writing a Draft: Invention, Planning, and Composing
  Choosing a Controversial Issue
  Developing Your Argument
   Presenting the Issue
   Drafting a Working Thesis
   Developing the Reasons Supporting Your Position
   Researching the Issue
   Including Visuals
   Responding Fairly to Objections Your Readers Are Likely to Raise
   Considering Your Purpose
  Organizing Your Position Argument Effectively for Your Readers
  Drafting Your Position Argument
  Working with Sources: Using Sources to Reinforce Your Credibility (box)
  Considering a Useful Sentence Strategy

Evaluating the Draft: Getting a Constructive Critical Reading
  Reading a Draft Critically (box)

Improving the Draft: Revising, Editing, and Proofreading
  Revising Your Draft
  Troubleshooting Your Draft (table)
  Editing and Proofreading Your Draft

Reflecting on What You Have Learned: Arguing for a Position (box)

Chapter 8 SPECULATING ABOUT CAUSES OR EFFECTS

This is the third in a series of four chapters dealing with important types of argument: Evaluation (Chapter 6), Arguing for a Position (Chapter 7), Speculating about Causes or Effects (Chapter 8), and Proposal to Solve a Problem (Chapter 9). In this chapter, students learn about causal argument—argument about the influence of one thing on another, when the nature of this influence cannot be proved. Since this kind of argumentation concerns explanation and prediction, it is a crucial mode of inquiry and writing in the sciences and social sciences. Arguments about causes or effects, in turn, become important elements in proposals as writers use these arguments to explain what has caused a problem, what its effects will be if no solution is found, and what effects each possible solution is likely to have.

In discussing the introduction to this chapter, you should help students see that the focus is on analysis and argument about possible causes or effects of events, trends, or phenomena. The selections do not simply summarize others' proposed causes or effects but argue inventively for the writers' own beliefs about causes or effects for a subject that cannot presently (or perhaps ever) be explained definitively. Students' essays should also present speculative arguments. Students may very well research proposed causes or effects that they do not report in their essay. During research, they will weigh and evaluate each cause or effect in light of their understanding of the subject and their chosen argument. They should then argue for their preferred causes or effects, whether they discovered them on their own or turned them up in their research.

In the process of reading and writing essays that speculate on causes or effects, students learn a great deal. This chapter can teach students to

- choose an event, trend, or phenomenon that remains open to speculation about its possible causes or effects;
- present a subject to be speculated about;
- propose likely causes or effects;
- support proposed causes or effects with facts, examples, statistics, cases, quotes from authorities, or anecdotes;
- anticipate readers' questions and preferred causes or effects, counterarguing as needed;
- organize an essay through a logical sequence of causes or effects; and
- signal explicitly the stages of cause or effect reasoning.

You could emphasize that this assignment builds on what students have learned writing other genres in *Reading Critically, Writing Well*. Students may recall thinking and writing about causes or effects when writing autobiography (Chapter 2), observation (Chapter 3), reflection (Chapter 4), or explaining concepts (Chapter 5). When evaluating causes and effects proposed by others, students may need to remember what they learned when writing evaluations (Chapter 6). In previous chapters, students also gain considerable experience supporting assertions with facts, examples, anecdotes, and quotes from authorities. In addition, they have read and written essays that are organized logically by topic and cued explicitly. All this experience should increase students' confidence as they approach this challenging new assignment.

WRITING ASSIGNMENT: SPECULATING ABOUT CAUSES OR EFFECTS (p. 426)

Here is the writing assignment that appears in the Guide to Writing in Chapter 8:

Write an essay arguing for your preferred causes or effects for an event, a phenomenon, or a trend.

- Choose a subject that invites you to speculate about its causes or effects; why it may have happened or what its effects may be.
- Research the subject, gathering detailed information from appropriate sources, and present that information in a clear, logical way.
- Establish the existence and significance of the subject.
- Convince readers that the causes or effects you propose are more plausible than the alternatives.

Problems Students May Have with This Assignment

Speculating about causes or effects really requires making a double argument. The writer must first establish the existence of the event, phenomenon, or trend and then argue for possible causes or effects of it. Both parts are important, but students sometimes neglect one or the other. Students who choose a trend have the added burden of demonstrating that the rate of something actually is increasing over a specified time period. Students may need special encouragement and help to make sure that they do justice to both parts of the assignment.

Another common problem students may encounter involves presenting only predictable or obvious causes or effects, leading the reader to ask, So what? This particular problem is most likely to occur when students choose a widely recognized trend, event, or phenomenon. They rely on the obvious instead of coming up with more inventive or probing explanations. Students also go amiss when they mention alternative causes or effects but do not refute or give reasons for accepting them. An even more fundamental problem occurs when students fail to consider alternative causes or effects, merely presenting those they think are likely and ignoring other possibilities.

A Guide to Writing Essays Speculating about Causes or Effects (p. 426) has been devised to forestall problems like these, but your students may need extra coaching—especially, if you want them to write about causes, which tend to be more challenging than effects. Consider spending some class time on one or two students' subjects. List obvious causes or effects and then develop them with background causes or long-term effects. You might also consider having students do this assignment twice: in small groups with your active support and then by themselves. The first time around you could supply a rather circumscribed subject, possibly one that does not require research or for which you might provide research material.

RESOURCES IN CHAPTER 8 FOR TEACHING ESSAYS SPECULATING ABOUT CAUSES OR EFFECTS

Quizzes for each of the readings in the text and e-Pages are included in the e-Pages. The auto-graded multiple-choice comprehension quiz or the summary quiz with a sample summary as feedback may be used to provide an additional incentive to students to complete the reading. The vocabulary quiz (with feedback) may be used with students to help students build a college-level vocabulary.

FINDING SUBJECTS

Rhetorical Situations for Speculating about Causes or Effects (p. 375)
These three brief rhetorical situations demonstrate that writers analyze and explain the causes or effects of events, phenomena, and trends in both academic and nonacademic settings. The three situations also illustrate two important decisions students will make as they begin to consider writing their own essays: whether to write about causes or effects and whether to write about events, phenomena, or trends. The first rhetorical situation examines the causes of a phenomenon (which students may note might also have been treated as a trend), the second speculates about causes of a phenomenon and the third analyzes the effects of a subject that could be treated as a trend. Discuss the situations with the class, emphasizing both the particular decisions the writers had to make and the unique features of this kind of writing. While discussing these scenarios, consider asking students to speculate about alternative causes or effects for each of the three situations, and ask which alternatives probably ought to be addressed by each of the three authors.

Choosing a Subject (p. 427)
Choosing a Subject is the first activity under Writing a Draft: Invention, Planning, and Composing, the opening section of A Guide to Writing Essays Speculating about Causes or Effects. Students are shown possible subjects, grouped under the categories *trends*, *events*, and *phenomena*. You might urge students from day one to begin compiling a list of possibilities. You might spend a few minutes at the beginning of each class discussing their ideas.

Problems Students May Have Choosing a Subject
We have found that most of our students need careful guidance in choosing subjects for this assignment. You may need to steer them away from events with a single obvious cause or effect. For students who want to write about a phenomenon, you will probably need to remind them that they must demonstrate that their subjects involve established patterns of behavior and are not merely one-time events or trends. For those writing about a trend, you will almost certainly need to help them

establish that the pattern really is a significant trend, involving long-term changes in behavior rather than short-term, faddish shifts.

The following types of topics pose particular challenges for students:

- Causes or effects of historical events, phenomena, or past trends (for instance, an explanation of the increase in brain size during early human evolution). These subjects involve students in a different kind of research than that required by more current topics. These essays tend to read like research reports of others' observations. One way to help students stay on task is to encourage them to look for areas of dispute in the literature so that, at the very least, they are taking sides in a debate about causes and effects.
- Causes or effects of phenomena observed in personal life (competitiveness, procrastination, popularity, laziness). Students writing about these subjects may tend to rely exclusively on anecdotal information from their own experience rather than generalize from their own experiences to larger conclusions about the phenomenon.
- Causes of trends relating to technology (increasing use of scanners and digital cameras, declining cost of televisions). Students sometimes choose to write about these subjects because it is easy to document the existence of the trend itself; however, students often have difficulty going beyond the obvious explanation of technological advances in analyzing the causes of such trends.
- Subjects that could be approached as either phenomena or trends (teenage suicide, popular activities like windsurfing or snowboarding). Students will need to decide whether to treat the topic as a trend or as a phenomenon.

Since subject choice is so important and problematic, you might try this in-class activity. After discussing the readings, list several possible events, phenomena, or trends on the board. Ask small groups of students to choose a subject and prepare a defense of it for the class. They must argue that the subject is actually an event, a phenomenon, or a trend; that it is a researchable subject; and that its causes or effects are not already settled—that is, that they still require speculation.

THINKING ABOUT THE GENRE: SPECULATIONS ABOUT CAUSES AND EFFECTS (p. 376)

This activity will allow students to realize they have a familiarity, possibly greater than they expected, with the genre, reducing the anxiety that typically accompanies composing any essay and making the remaining activities in this chapter easier.

CHOOSING READINGS

If you cannot teach all the readings in this chapter, you will have to make some choices. There are at least three principles that may guide your selection: (1) the type of speculative essay; (2) the interest level of the reading and its usefulness in suggesting subjects for your students' essays; (3) the basic features focused on in the Reading like a Writer activities.

TYPES OF SPECULATIVE ESSAYS

The reading selections in this chapter, beginning with the sample essay by Stephen King, represent different types of speculative essays. One essay (Vedantam) explains an effect and looks at its causes. Two explain causes (King, McClain), and two explain effects (Wallis and Carr). Two treat established phenomena (King and Vedantam), and three treat ongoing trends (Wallis, Carr, and McClain). There are no examples of essays speculating on the causes or effects of a one-time event, although Vedantam analyzes a one-time event to explore the causes and effects of a broader phenomenon.

Here are brief descriptions from the table of contents to help you choose readings that might be of interest to your students:

Stephen King, **Why We Crave Horror Movies.** America's best-known writer of horror novels and film scripts speculates about why we continue "daring the nightmare" in order to watch horror movies. (p. 378)

Claudia Wallis, **The Multitasking Generation.** Questioning the idea that multitasking saves time, a writer and editor at *Time* magazine presents evidence that, for Generation M at least, multitasking has surprising and possibly alarming consequences. (p. 385)

Shankar Vedantam, **The Telescope Effect.** An award-winning journalist speculates about the reasons why people are often very generous in the face of an individual stranger's tragedy but often ignore tragedy on a massive scale. (p. 400)

Nicholas Carr, **Is Google Making Us Stupid?** An author and professional speaker wonders whether technology is changing our physical brains and the way we think, impairing our ability to concentrate, focus, and do research. (p. 408)

Sheila McClain, **Fitness Culture: A Growing Trend in America.** Composition student Sheila McClain speculates about the reasons for the growing popularity of fitness culture. (p. 418)

Michele Cox, **The Truth about Lying.** A student investigates the motivations for lying, backing up her assertions with findings from psychologists and other observers. (**e**)

On the Media, **The Reel Sounds of Violence.** A podcast from this National Public Radio show explores the trend of "sound inflation" in violent movies. (**e**)

The first reading, King's "Why We Crave Horror Movies," introduces all of the basic features of speculating about causes or effects through the Reading like a Writer activities. The final reading, McClain's "Fitness Culture: A Growing Trend in America," does not specify a Reading like a Writer activity but invites students to choose a feature of the reading they think is worth analyzing. Each of the other readings has one Reading like a Writer activity. Here is a list of these activities.

Presenting the Subject Fairly: Claudia Wallis, "The Multitasking Generation" (p. 398)

Making a Logical, Well-Supported Cause or Effect Argument: Shankar Vedantam, "The Telescope Effect" (p. 406)

Responding to Objections or Alternative Speculations: Nicholas Carr, "Is Google Making Us Stupid?" (p. 416)

Establishing Credibility to Present the Writer as Thoughtful and Fair: Sheila McClain, "Fitness Culture: A Growing Trend in America" (p. 424)

A GUIDE TO READING ESSAYS SPECULATING ABOUT CAUSES OR EFFECTS (p. 377)

The essay that is the focus of A Guide to Reading Essays Speculating about Causes or Effects is King's "Why We Crave Horror Movies."

e bedfordstmartins.com/readingcritically

READING FOR MEANING (p. 380)

Read to Summarize (p. 380)

To better enable students to understand King's essay, you may wish to have them, individually or in groups, identify the movies (you may wish for them to check The Internet Movie Database, http://www.imdb.com) and the people King references: Freda Jackson (par. 4); *Die, Monster, Die!* (par. 4); Robert Redford (par. 4); Diana Ross (par. 4); Cleveland Torso Murderer (par. 8); Jack the Ripper (par. 8); Leonard Nimoy (par. 9); *Dawn of the Dead* (par. 12); and Lennon and McCartney (par. 13). (A sample summary, which may be used as feedback, is available by assigning students to take the e-Pages summary quiz for the King reading: **bedfordstmartins.com/readingcritically**.)

Words that some students may find challenging (*squinch* [par. 1], *remonstrance* [par. 10], and *anarchistic* [par. 11]) are included in a vocabulary quiz in the e-Pages. Other words that students may need to look up include *reactionary* (par. 4), *status quo* (par. 9), and *morbidity* (par. 12).

Read to Respond (p. 380)

Students may also respond to

- King's informal, conversational style, or the voice (a little insane at times) King uses in composing the essay;
- King's contention that horror films are "innately conservative, even reactionary" (par. 4);
- the simile (pars. 12 and 13) in which King compares the human subconscious to a subterranean river infested with alligators.

Read to Analyze Assumptions (p. 381)

Students may also consider the assumptions underlying King's claim that "the potential lyncher is in almost all of us" (par. 9) and his comparison of our emotions and fears to a body needing exercise (par. 9).

READING LIKE A WRITER ACTIVITIES

The four Reading like a Writer activities following King's essay give students a thorough introduction to writing essays speculating about causes. This section introduces students to the major elements of writing about causes or effects — presenting the subject; making a logical, step-by-step cause-and-effect argument; counterarguing; and establishing credibility. Each feature carries a reading and a writing activity that help students focus on King's writing strategies.

Presenting the Subject Fairly (p. 382)

This activity leads students to look at the way King uses examples to present the subject and establish its importance. Students will notice that King presents his subject as a phenomenon rather than as a one-time event or a trend. Students should also note that King seems to assume that he doesn't have to prove that some people crave horror movies because the phenomenon is common knowledge.

Making a Logical, Well-Supported Cause or Effect Argument (p. 382)

This activity focuses on King's use of analogy, a special kind of comparison he uses to support his argument. We urge students to identify and test King's analogies. Because he is such an engaging, persuasive writer, you might need to spend some time getting students to think critically about King's use of analogy. Students need to be alert to the potential pitfalls of supporting an argument with analogy as well as other possible fallacies common to cause-and-effect argument, such as confusing correlation with cause or assuming that simply because one thing precedes another, the first causes the second.

Responding to Objections and Alternative Speculations (p. 383)

This section highlights the importance of anticipating objections readers might have to the argument. Students are asked specifically to consider the effectiveness of King's ventriloquizing the objection "Why bother?" (par. 13). This activity could generate some lively argument, depending to a large extent on students' own attitudes toward horror movies.

Establishing Credibility to Present the Writer as Thoughtful and Fair (p. 384)

This activity asks students to think about the ways King gains readers' confidence. Since King is a well-known writer of horror novels, several of which have been made into movies, the reader is clearly expected to consider him an authoritative source.

Students may or may not find this authority convincing on its own (or may not even recognize it, if they are unfamiliar with his work, as many students today may be). Some students may ask why King's argument makes no reference to the large body of psychological and social science research on this subject, while others may defend King's strategy, arguing that such a reference is neither neces-sary nor appropriate, given his original audience of *Playboy* magazine readers.

You could also point out that King attempts to bond with readers by linking his observations about human behavior to actions most people have experienced or witnessed: "We've all known people who talk to themselves" (par. 2); we've all heard "sick" jokes (par. 11); most of us have experienced emotions that might be called "uncivilized." King's recognition that these experiences are shared, which is reflected in his use of the first-person plural pronouns *we* and *us*, helps readers accept his argument.

READINGS

Claudia Wallis, "The Multitasking Generation" (p. 385)

Reading for Meaning (p. 396)

Read to Summarize (p. 396)

After having students explain Wallis's argument about the effects of multitasking, you might have them also identify the trend she describes (increasing multitasking) and the causes she credits for it. (A sample summary, which may be used as feedback, is available by assigning students to take the e-Pages summary quiz for the Wallis reading: bedfordstmartins.com/readingcritically.)

Words that some students may find challenging (*simultaneously* [par. 14], *prowess* [par. 15], and *compulsive* [par. 15]) are included in a vocabulary quiz in the e-Pages. Other words that students may need to look up include *space-time* (par. 2), *MacArthur "genius" grant* (par. 10), *perfunctory* (par. 11), *quaint* (par. 13), and *toggling* (par. 19).

Read to Respond (p. 397)

Students may also respond to

- Wallis's evidence that humans can't really multitask as they think they do;
- the idea that young people try on identities;
- Wallis's argument that human minds need breaks, or downtime.

Read to Analyze Assumptions (p. 397)

Students may also explore

- Wallis's apparent assumption that some of the tasks multitasked by Generation M cannot become "highly practiced" like slicing an onion;
- the assumption that there's a significant difference between "multitasking" and "sequential processing";
- the assumption that perceived lower tolerance for ambiguity (par. 28) is connected to multitasking.

This section with its accompanying Analyze and Write activity gives students the chance to explore the various techniques that Wallis uses to present her subject: anecdotes, examples, statistics, and quotes from authorities. This activity draws students' attention to the examples, statistics, and authorities Wallis uses in paragraphs 1–9 and 11 to present her subject, multitasking, and to show some of its impacts on family life. The final question asks students to find evidence of these effects repeated throughout the essay (say, in par. 34), but some students might skip or overlook the question. For this reason, you might wish to have students list the effects they've found and then, as a class, look through the essay for repeated themes and effects.

A SPECIAL READING STRATEGY — COMPARING AND CONTRASTING RELATED READINGS: WALLIS'S "THE MULTITASKING GENERATION" AND TURKLE'S "THE FLIGHT FROM CONVERSATION" (p. 399)

This special reading strategy following Wallis's essay provides an opportunity for students to see how writers use different genres to discuss the same subject. If your students have not read and discussed the section on comparing and contrasting related readings in Chapter 10, A Catalog of Reading Strategies, you might have them take the time to do so now. We ask students to explore the authors' definitions of *multitasking* and their approaches to the subject. If you find such activities productive, you might have students compare these two essays with Nicholas Carr's "Is Google Making Us Stupid?" later in this chapter. Carr's essay, like Wallis's, expresses alarm at the declining ability of people to focus deeply and also seems to link that decline to use of the Internet.

Shankar Vedantam, "The Telescope Effect" (p. 400)

READING FOR MEANING (p. 405)

Read to Summarize (p. 405)

Students are asked to identify the main idea that Vedantam wants his readers to understand. You might discuss here how authors of speculative essays often have motives beyond simply explaining the causes or effects of a phenomenon or trend. Vendantam, for example, may also be trying to get his readers to question and change their behavior. (A sample summary, which may be used as feedback, is available by assigning students to take the e-Pages summary quiz for the Vendantam reading: bedfordstmartins.com/readingcritically.)

Words that some students may find challenging (*incensed* [par. 4], *discrepancy* [par. 8], and *blasé* [par. 9]) are included in a vocabulary quiz in the e-Pages.

Read to Respond (p. 405)

Students might also respond to

- a time they found an individual stranger's story or circumstances compelling
- a time when, perhaps, they found "mass" tragedy compelling and were moved to action

Read to Analyze Assumptions (p. 405)

These activities ask students to reflect on the assumptions surrounding a "hidden brain" and around money as a measure of compassion. Students usually find these topics quite engaging and often have a lot to say. You may want to consider dividing the class into groups and assigning each group a different bulleted question.

READING LIKE A WRITER: MAKING A LOGICAL, WELL-SUPPORTED CAUSE OR EFFECT ARGUMENT (p. 406)

This activity focuses on Vedantam's use of sources, particularly psychologist Paul Slovic's work, to make the argument. It asks students to take a closer look at paragraphs 14, 12, and 15–18 in Vedantam's essay to analyze the way that Vedantam incorporates his secondary source material.

Nicholas Carr, "Is Google Making Us Stupid?" (p. 408)

READING FOR MEANING (p. 415)

Read to Summarize (p. 415)
In addition to having students summarize Carr's concerns, you might have them discuss the point Carr is trying to make with his allusions to *2001: A Space Odyssey*. (It might be helpful to find the scene online or bring in a DVD to play the scene in question.) (A sample summary, which may be used as feedback, is available by assigning students to take the e-Pages summary quiz for the Carr reading: bedfordstmartins.com/readingcritically.)

Words that some students may find challenging (*implacable* [par. 1], *malleable* [par. 10], and *gewgaw* [par. 13]) are included in a vocabulary quiz in the e-Pages. Other words students may need to look up include *staccato* (par. 6), *cognition* (par. 7), *consortium* (par. 7), *sea change* (par. 7), *plastic* (par. 10)—note that here it is used in a way that might be unfamiliar to students—*clockwork* (par. 11), *ethic* (par. 15), *Luddites* (par. 22), and *stoked* (par. 22).

Read to Respond (p. 415)
Students may also respond to

- their previous experiences with deep reading—not only of novels but of substantive nonfiction;
- the ambitions of Google's founders to augment our minds with artificial intelligence;
- the idea that the mind, even in adulthood, remains "plastic" (par. 10).

Read to Analyze Assumptions (p. 415)
You might also ask students to consider

- the assumption by both Carr and Wallis that ambiguity is a good thing that's not fully appreciated anymore;
- Carr's assumption about who his readers are, given his references to *2001*, the length of his article, and his frequent quoting of fellow writers who have made similar observations;
- the assumptions by Google's founders that we would be better off with much of our thinking handled or augmented by artificial intelligence.

READING LIKE A WRITER: RESPONDING TO OBJECTIONS OR ALTERNATIVE SPECULATIONS (p. 416)

This Reading like a Writer activity asks students to evaluate Carr's response to objections and alternative speculations and their support, an exploration that is useful training not only for this genre of writing but for the other argumentative genres as well. You might divide students into teams and have each team analyze and evaluate a response to an objection or an alternative speculation from a different paragraph.

Paragraph 7 is particularly interesting because in it Carr anticipates an objection to his *evidence* rather than to a specific point he has made ("Anecdotes alone don't prove much. . . ."). Astute students may notice, however, that he's using the anecdotes more for clarity and for ethos than for proof: His anecdotes all center on professional writers who once could read deeply but now struggle to do so rather than on young people who supposedly no longer read books. His choice of examples clarifies his concern—he's not saying that Johnny can't read but that he himself no longer can. This move changes the character of his argument from one about a supposed fault of others to a concern about a personal loss, which makes it harder to question or criticize and has the potential to disarm knee-jerk dismissals that might arise if he were simply to talk about "today's students" while not one himself.

As a follow-up to this activity, the class might look at the original article online, where they can read Carr's historical anecdotes about Plato reacting to the written word and Squarciafico responding to the invention of the printing press—a section that does not appear in our version. (Note: Wallis also alludes to the Plato example.) In this section, Carr acknowledges that each major invention in information technology raises concerns that are valid—but that also bring unforeseen benefits. He grants that the Internet may be no different. Students might find it worthwhile to discuss the ways in which this argument is a concession, and the ways in which it acts as a refutation. A good discussion should pick up on the fact that although the section appears to be mostly a concession, it also slides in evidence that critics of such technologies have historically been right in their indictments, implying that perhaps Carr, like them, is being prescient.

The full, online article can be found at http://www.theatlantic.com/magazine/archive/2008/07/is-google-making-us-stupid/6868/.

ANALYZING VISUALS (p. 417)

The cartoon that accompanies Carr's essay depicts a child in the classroom, explaining to the teacher why he doesn't have his homework. You might ask students whether the teacher and classroom depicted reflects their own experience in elementary school and to contrast their own experience with their parents'. (Or you might explain what your own, say, second grade teacher and classroom looked like.)

Sheila McClain, "Fitness Culture: A Growing Trend in America" (p. 418)

READING FOR MEANING (p. 422)

Read to Summarize (p. 422)
The activity here, which asks students to list some of the reasons McClain gives in her essay for the growth of fitness culture could easily be turned into an activity in which the students compose a more detailed outline of the essay. Outlining McClain's essay could give the students some ideas for organizing their own essays.

Read to Respond (p. 423)
Students might also respond to

- other trends or evidence they've seen for the growth of fitness culture
- any alternative views or objections they might have to McClain's essay

Read to Analyze Assumptions (p. 423)
The assumptions about the attractiveness of a fitness club and people's motivations for exercise are treated in this section. Students could discuss their own experience here with fitness clubs as well as their own motivations (or lack thereof) for exercise.

This activity asks students to apply the Evaluating the Logic of an Argument tests from Chapter 10, A Catalog of Reading Strategies to McClain's text. If your class has not yet used this analytical tool, you may want to work through the Martin Luther King Jr. example in the chapter before assigning students this section on McClain. However, resist the temptation to have students work in teams for this activity. If you do, the instinctive approach for most students will be to divide up the duties among team members, with each student taking one question—and students who divide to conquer often miss out on logical connections among the points. (Another option to consider may be to have students read Christine Romano's essay in Chapter 6, since it uses this test as its primary analytical tool.)

Reading like a Writer: Establishing Credibility to Present the Writer as Thoughtful and Fair (p. 424)

This Reading like a Writer activity engages readers in an extensive analysis and evaluation of the credibility of McClain's essay. Students are asked to examine credibility by assessing the writer on four elements—knowledge of the subject, representation of its complexity, use of explicit counterarguments, and implied attitudes and assumptions about readers. Working in groups on this activity might help students read closely. You could have each group find one example of each element in the text. Or you could divide the class into four groups and have each group examine one of four elements more extensively, finding several examples to support its judgment.

Along the way, students considering the first question are asked to evaluate McClain's sources and how she uses them. Students pursuing this thread may remark on

- the large number and diversity of sources she draws on (books, corporate Web pages, scholarly articles, Web pages of people identified in the essay as nutrition professors);
- her inclusion of an additional "works consulted" (which will probably be novel to many students);
- the frequency with which she paraphrases her information instead of quoting it; what this pattern suggests to them about her understanding of the subject;
- her organization of source material, weaving sources together by topic instead of talking first about one source and then about another (see paragraph 3, about high-fructose corn syrup, which cites four sources).

You may find that discussing McClain's use of sources before students tackle the exercise opens the door to a better analysis of her overall approach to credibility in student responses to the other three questions. Addressing the topic may also let you deal with some common unvoiced concerns that students have about sourcing—such as the popular assumption among writers-in-training that a student who cites sources "too frequently" looks to professors and graders like he or she is lazy and has not written an original paper. (This assumption drives many students not to cite sources as frequently as they ought to.) Focusing on McClain's arrangement and analysis of source material, her paraphrasing of that material, and the places in the text in which her own ideas shape the argument may help alleviate some of these anxieties about sourced work.

In this Reading like a Writer activity, students are reminded that the writer of an essay that speculates about causes should present him- or herself as thoughtful and fair. Students are warned against oversimplifying, trivializing, stereotyping, or overlooking possible alternative causes or effects that will occur to readers. They are also encouraged to show readers they have thought deeply and seriously about their topics. The activity asks students to annotate McClain's support and evidence for credibility, look at her response to an alternative argument (in par. 5), and examine the assumptions she makes about her readers and her attitude toward them. This kind of analysis could be done on any or all of the readings included in this chapter.

Michele Cox, "The Truth about Lying" (student essay, **e**)

The "As you read" activity asks students to reflect on their own experience with the reasons why they lie and to see how well Cox's speculation tallies with their experiences. You might also ask students to consider the motivations that Cox lists in her essay and have the students come up with examples of the kinds of lies that might fit with the motivations that Cox names in her essay.

On the Media, "The Reel Sounds of Violence" (podcast, **e**)

READING FOR MEANING (**e**)

A sample summary, which may be used as feedback, is available by assigning students to take the e-Pages summary quiz for the *On the Media* reading that appears in the e-Pages.

READING LIKE A WRITER: PRESENTING THE SUBJECT (**e**)

This activity asks students to analyze how effectively *Slate* editor Daniel Engber (a guest on the show being interviewed by the host, Brooke Gladstone) presents his subject, asking students to attend especially to his use of contrast. You might also ask students to analyze how effectively Engber uses evidence (recorded sound effects from movies) to make his case.

REVIEWING WHAT MAKES SPECULATIVE ARGUMENTS EFFECTIVE (p. 425)

This reflective activity makes a great transition from reading to writing. As the text suggests, this activity can be done individually or in small groups.

A GUIDE TO WRITING ESSAYS SPECULATING ABOUT CAUSES OR EFFECTS (p. 426)

Some students have trouble understanding the terms *trend* and *phenomenon*. Perhaps the simplest way to define and distinguish these terms would be to say that a trend is a changing pattern of human behavior, while a phenomenon is a pattern that remains constant.

Perennial traditions and persistent problems are phenomena; shifts in the pattern of human behavior and problems that are improving or deteriorating are trends. If your students find this distinction too subtle, illustrate it by discussing the difference between the causes of a long-standing local problem and the causes of a sudden worsening of this problem. Different reasons are needed to explain the changing situation.

Some students also have difficulty distinguishing between a trend and a fad. A trend has some momentum and staying power and reflects significant changes in behavior or circumstances. Fads may be widespread, but they tend to be short-lived and whimsical: Changes in fashion, for instance, are often caused simply by the desire for novelty.

When students start considering causes or effects, they may need some guidance to distinguish causes from effects and to distinguish various kinds of causes and effects from one another. Background causes precede and prepare indirectly for an event or a trend, immediate causes trigger it, and perpetuating causes sustain a trend or phenomenon.

If students are writing an analysis of effects, they should consider immediate, long-term, and indirect effects of their event, trend, or phenomenon. If it has been around for some time, they may also be able to consider past effects.

e bedfordstmartins.com/readingcritically

Ask students to work out the relationships among their causes or effects. For instance, are any of the causes connected? Are there chains of causes to be traced? Which are the most influential causes? These sorts of questions are particularly useful for students—and there will be many of them—who find evidence of multiple causes and are tempted to conclude simply that the answer is a combination of all of them. Instead of identifying a single cause, such students might consider trying to rank the multiple causes in order of significance (giving reasons for the rankings) or show how they are related. These kinds of moves can help students steer away from easy answers toward more intellectually rewarding analytical work.

Here is an outline of A Guide to Writing Essays Speculating about Causes or Effects:

Writing a Draft: Invention, Planning, and Composing
 Choosing a Subject
 Analyzing Your Readers
 Exploring Your Subject
 Considering Causes or Effects
  Discovering Causes or Effects
  Conducting Research
  Analyzing Causes or Effects
 Considering Your Purpose
 Formulating a Working Thesis Statement
 Working with Sources: Citing a Variety of Sources (box)
 Responding to Readers' Likely Objections or Preferred Causes
  Analyzing and Responding to Your Readers' Likely Objections
  Refuting or Conceding Readers' Preferred Causes or Effects
 Including Visuals or Other Media
 Organizing Your Speculative Argument Effectively for Your Readers
 Drafting Your Cause or Effect Argument
 Considering a Useful Sentence Strategy (box)

Evaluating the Draft: Getting a Constructive Critical Reading
 Reading a Draft Critically (box)

Improving the Draft: Revising, Editing, and Proofreading
 Revising Your Draft
 Troubleshooting Your Draft (table)
 Editing and Proofreading Your Draft

Reflecting on What You Have Learned: Speculating about Causes or Effects (box)

Chapter 9 PROPOSAL TO SOLVE A PROBLEM

This is the last in a series of four chapters dealing with important types of argument: Evaluation (Chapter 6), Arguing for a Position (Chapter 7), Speculating about Causes or Effects (Chapter 8), and Proposal to Solve a Problem (Chapter 9). Proposals are one of the most complex kinds of argument because they can incorporate so many other kinds of writing—in fact, most of the genres presented in this book. Proposal writers often use their own experiences or observations of other people to present a problem and establish its seriousness. They explain concepts needed to understand the problem. They both evaluate the problem to demonstrate that it is serious enough to require a solution and evaluate alternative solutions to show that the proposed solution is the best one. Finally, writers analyze the problem's causes and effects to argue that the proposed solution will remove the causes and have positive, not negative, effects.

Proposals are an important and common type of writing, and many students can expect to write proposals during their postcollege careers. Jobs in government, business, science, and technology often depend on proposal writing. Although students do not ordinarily read or write many proposals in school, they may write proposals for term papers, research projects, or student-government activities. Studying proposal writing helps students learn to reconceive situations in terms of problems and solutions. The educational system teaches students to think in terms of good and bad (appropriate to writing evaluations), cause and effect (appropriate to speculation about causes or effects), and right and wrong (appropriate to position papers) but not as often in terms of problem and solution (appropriate to proposals). Nevertheless, problem solving is basic to creativity and an invaluable guide to acting in the world.

This is an especially promising assignment for a course with a service-learning component. You could first assign an observation essay (Chapter 3) in which students visit and interview people at a local site — such as a literacy program at a library, an AIDS prevention hotline, a voter-registration and information group such as the League of Women Voters — to identify problems people at the site are trying to solve. These problems would then become the subjects of students' proposals.

Students writing proposals can learn to

- choose a problem that needs solving and come up with a feasible solution;
- describe a problem and solution;
- give readers reasons that they should support a solution;
- support each reason with examples, facts, analogies, cases, scenarios, statistics, quotes from authorities, or anecdotes;
- anticipate readers' questions and preferred solutions, counterarguing as needed;
- organize an essay through logically ordered reasons; and
- signal explicitly the stages in an argument to support a solution.

You might want to reassure students that they have already practiced giving reasons and support, anticipating readers' objections and counterarguing, organizing essays logically, and giving explicit cues. The complexity of proposal writing makes it challenging, but students who have worked through the other chapters in *Reading Critically, Writing Well* should be well prepared.

WRITING ASSIGNMENT: PROPOSAL TO SOLVE A PROBLEM (p. 491)

Here is the writing assignment that appears in the Guide to Writing in Chapter 9:

Write an essay proposing a solution to a problem.

- Choose a problem affecting a community or group to which you belong.
- Research the problem and possible solutions.
- Decide how to present the problem so that readers see it exists and is serious.
- Find a solution that would help solve the problem and could be implemented without being too costly or time-consuming.
- Address likely objections to your proposed solution as well as any alternative solutions readers might prefer.

Organize the proposal in a way that is clear, logical, and convincing.

Problems Students May Have with This Assignment

Difficulties students sometimes encounter as they write proposals involve the choice of subject and the need to establish the problem's existence and seriousness. Even though students are asked to write about a problem faced by a group to which they belong, they sometimes take on problems too abstract or complicated for them to research fully and handle effectively in a short time. It is understandable that students should want to solve the major problems our society faces—such as violence in schools, the widening gulf between rich and poor, or the general lack of civility. As much as we want to encourage students to explore these problems and try to help solve them, we also want students to have every chance of succeeding in their first effort at writing an effective proposal. Therefore, we encourage our students to choose problems that they can address at a local level and can write about in specific, rather than general, terms.

A good proposal needs to both argue for a solution and define and establish the problem. We have found that even the student who argues effectively for a solution may sometimes fail to establish the problem's existence and seriousness. This student might assume that the reader agrees there is a problem or that all readers will understand the problem in the same way. Defining the problem requires careful assessment of the rhetorical situation. Writers must gauge their readers' current understanding of the problem and construct an argument to convince readers that the problem needs and deserves their attention.

RESOURCES IN CHAPTER 9 FOR TEACHING PROPOSALS

Quizzes for each of the readings in the text and e-Pages are included in the e-Pages. The auto-graded multiple-choice comprehension quiz or the summary quiz with a sample summary as feedback may be used to provide an additional incentive to students to complete the reading. The vocabulary quiz (with feedback) may be used with students to help students build a college-level vocabulary.

FINDING SUBJECTS

Rhetorical Situations for Proposals (p. 445)
The chapter opens with three brief rhetorical situations that suggest a range of occasions for writing proposals—writing for a community cause, a business situation (one of the most common domains for proposal writing), and for a college political science course. You might want to use these situations in a discussion of possible subjects by pointing out the different purposes and audiences, the different kinds of problems, and the different ways writers support their arguments. You may also wish to have students identify the two parts to a proposal—the establishment of the problem and the proposed course of action—in each example.

Finally, it might be worth stressing to students that two of the examples showcase situations in which the authors did not start out with fully crystallized ideas of how they would solve their problems. Many students are uncomfortable picking subjects or problems for which they cannot think of obvious solutions. As a result, they sometimes gravitate toward topics that have already been heavily addressed by national public-awareness campaigns designed to change the habits of readers or viewers. Students uncomfortable with problems lacking obvious solutions also tend to propose raising awareness as a first-draft solution, essentially turning their papers (or the reading of them) into their solutions. A good first step toward making students more comfortable with uncertainty in their quest for a solution is to show them that other people have made that same journey.

Choosing a Problem (p. 492)
Choosing a Problem is the first activity under Writing a Draft: Invention, Planning, and Composing, the opening section of A Guide to Writing Proposals. Students are urged to list groups or organizations to which they belong and then think of problems faced by these institutions. We encourage students to choose problems plaguing communities in which they are actively involved—such as

their neighborhood, dorm, or sports team—both to motivate them and to provide a real-world context for their writing.

Problems Students May Have Choosing a Subject

Choosing an appropriate subject is probably the hardest part of proposal writing. Some students know immediately what they want to write about, while others struggle to find something appropriate. Perhaps the greatest stumbling block is abstraction. The more distant the problem is from personal experience, the harder it is to write about. That is why we urge students to choose a problem affecting a group to which they belong. Even the most abstract problems can be treated in a local context. Those concerned with broad educational problems, for example, might find evidence of the problem in their own high school or college. Those concerned with social and economic problems like homelessness and unemployment might look in their communities.

Writing about a problem of a group to which they belong will also help students with the crucial task of analyzing their readers. They can more easily anticipate possible objections to their solutions and alternative solutions readers might prefer. They can also draw on common values and experience to establish the seriousness of the problem and argue for the feasibility of the proposed solution.

THINKING ABOUT THE GENRE: PROPOSALS (p. 446)

This activity will allow students to realize they have a familiarity, possibly greater than they expected, with the genre, reducing the anxiety that typically accompanies composing an essay and making the remaining activities in this chapter easier.

CHOOSING READINGS

The reading selections in this chapter, beginning with the sample essay by David Bornstein, present a variety of different issues and ways of arguing. If you cannot teach all the readings in this chapter, you will have to make some choices. There are at least two principles that may guide your selection: (1) the interest level of the readings and their usefulness in suggesting subjects for your students' essays; (2) the basic features focused on in the Reading like a Writer activities.

INTEREST LEVELS OF THE READINGS

Here are brief descriptions from the table of contents to help you choose readings that might be of interest to your students:

David Bornstein, **Fighting Bullying with Babies.** An award-winning author and blogger proposes that one effective way to get children to stop bullying each other is to allow them to spend time getting to know and appreciate a baby and what it takes to raise one. (p. 447)

William F. Shughart II, **Why Not a Football Degree?** Impatient with what he calls "half-measures" that have been adopted or proposed to try to reform college sports, an economics professor recommends a three-pronged solution that treats the issue as a business proposition. (p. 459)

Kelly D. Brownell and Thomas R. Frieden, **Ounces of Prevention—The Public Policy Case for Taxes on Sugared Beverages.** A professor of psychology and a physician argue that one effective way to combat obesity and improve the health of the nation would be to tax sugared beverages. (p. 466)

Karen Kornbluh, **Win-Win Flexibility.** An economist and political activist proposes a solution to a problem faced by the new "juggler family," in which parents have trouble balancing their time between working and caring for their children and elderly parents. (p. 474)

Patrick O'Malley, **More Testing, More Learning.** In a strongly reasoned message to professors on his campus, a first-year college student advocates an increase in testing throughout the academic term. (p. 483)

Molly Coleman, **Missing the Fun.** A freshman student proposes blacking out dates for sporting events that conflict with major social occasions at school, so student-athletes don't have to miss out. (**e**)

Phoebe Sweet and Zach Wise, **The Problems with Lawns: The Transforming Landscape of Las Vegas.** Sweet and Wise review some of the ways Las Vegas has encouraged water conservation to keep this city in the desert alive. (**e**)

READING LIKE A WRITER ACTIVITIES

The first reading, Bornstein's "Fighting Bullying with Babies," introduces all the basic features of proposals through its Reading like a Writer activities. Each of the other readings has one Reading like a Writer activity. Here is a list of these activities.

Showing How the Proposed Solution Would Help Solve the Problem and Is Feasible: William F. Shughart II, "Why Not a Football Degree?" (p. 465)

Responding to Objections and Alternative Solutions: Kelly D. Brownell and Thomas R. Frieden, "Ounces of Prevention: The Public Policy Case for Taxes on Sugared Beverages" (p. 472)

Demonstrating that the Problem Exists and Is Serious: Karen Kornbluh, "Win-Win Flexibility" (p. 480)

Organizing the Proposal in a Way That Is Clear, Logical, and Convincing: Patrick O'Malley, "More Testing, More Learning" (p. 489)

Showing How the Proposed Solution Would Help Solve the Problem and Is Feasible: Phoebe Sweet and Zach Wise, "The Problem with Lawns: The Transforming Landscape of Las Vegas" (**e**)

A GUIDE TO READING PROPOSALS (p. 447)

The essay that is the focus of A Guide to Reading Proposals is Bornstein's "Fighting Bullying with Babies."

READING FOR MEANING (p. 452)

Here are suggestions for teaching the Reading for Meaning activities following "Fighting Bullying with Babies."

Read to Summarize (p. 452)

Students are asked to write down what they believe the main point of the reading is along with an explanation of how the proposed solution might solve the problem. If you would like students to construct a more detailed outline of Bornstein's essay, this activity could easily be expanded. (A sample

e bedfordstmartins.com/readingcritically

117

summary, which may be used as feedback, is available by assigning students to take the e-Pages summary quiz for the Bornstein reading: bedfordstmartins.com/readingcritically.)

Words that some students may find challenging (*proactive* [par. 4], *cognitive* [par. 8], and *altrusim* [par. 9]) are included in a vocabulary quiz in the e-Pages.

Read to Respond (p. 452)
Students may also respond to

- their own experiences with babies, and the emotions or reactions being with a baby triggered
- any alternative solutions they may have for the problem of bullying and whether or not such alternatives were or should have been addressed by Bornstein

Read to Analyze Assumptions (p. 453)
Students are asked to examine assumptions about bullying and assumptions about empathy. Since students in your class will surely have experience with each of these concepts, you may want to allow extra time for this discussion, or you may want students to work in partnerships or in groups to respond to the bulleted questions.

Students might also be interested in discussing the following assumptions:

- Bornstein's assumption that meanness and bullying are the same thing.
- His assumption that the change in the children's behavior has a biological cause.

READING LIKE A WRITER ACTIVITIES (p. 454)

The four Reading like a Writer activities following Bornstein's proposal give students a comprehensive introduction to proposals to solve problems and help students move from examining the content and purpose of essays to analyzing the strategies used by writers to accomplish their purposes. You can have students do some or all of these activities before doing selected Reading like a Writer activities for subsequent readings. Students are introduced to the major features and strategies of proposal writing: demonstrating the problem exists and is serious, showing how the proposed solution would help solve the problem and is feasible, responding to objections and alternative solutions, and organizing the proposal in a way that is clear, logical, and convincing. The tasks in this section directly anticipate the thinking that students will do as they read the other chapter selections and begin their own essays.

Demonstrating the Problem Exists and Is Serious (p. 454)
This Reading like a Writer section with its accompanying Analyze and Write activity focuses students' attention on Bornstein's efforts to present the problem of bullying and its seriousness. In their own essays, students will have to demonstrate the seriousness of their problem and importance of taking some steps toward a solution. Question 3 in the Analyze and Write activity points out that Bornstein never defines "bullying," assuming that his readers understand what the problem is. You may want to highlight to students that while establishing the existence and seriousness of the problem is important, defining it may not always be necessary.

Showing How the Proposed Solution Would Help Solve the Problem and Is Feasible (p. 454)
This section and the Analyze and Write activity underscore how important it is for authors to explain their solutions clearly and show how they will solve (or help solve) the problem. Students are asked to analyze several of Bornstein's paragraphs in which he explains his solution and its merits.

Responding to Objections and Alternative Solutions (p. 455)

In this section and the Analyze and Write activity students are reminded of the two basic strategies for responding to an argument: concession and refutation. Students are then asked to analyze a series of Bornstein's responses to objections and alternatives. You might remind students that the strategies that Bornstein uses are strategies they too may employ in their essays.

Organizing the Proposal in a Way That Is Clear, Logical, and Convincing (p. 456)

Here students are asked once again to look carefully at the ways that writers provide cues for readers in the form of clear thesis statements, topic sentences, and logical transitions. In the Analyze and Write activity, students are asked to give special focus to paragraphs 7–9, looking for ways that Bornstein's transitions and topic sentences guide readers through his argument.

A Special Reading Strategy: Comparing and Contrasting Related Readings: David Bornstein's "Fighting Bullying with Babies" and Excerpts on Bullying in Chapter 1 (p. 457)

This activity invites students to compare the Bornstein essay with the readings in the very first chapter of the book on bullying. If you did not assign the first chapter, you may still want students to do this exercise. In comparing one genre with another (the readings in Chapter 1 are cause-effect analyses), students will learn a lot about the proposal genre. This in turn will help them to draft stronger proposal essays.

Analyzing Visuals (p. 458)

The photographs that accompany Bornstein's essay depict the process prescribed by the organization Roots of Empathy. The activity asks students to analyze these photos using the criteria for analyzing visuals in Chapter 12. These photos were actually provided by Roots of Empathy, which includes them on its Web site. You might ask students to consider why Roots of Empathy included these photographs on their site. What elements of the photographs would help Roots of Empathy "sell" their program?

READINGS

William F. Shughart II, "Why Not a Football Degree?" (p. 459)

Reading for Meaning (p. 464)

Read to Summarize (p. 464)

Since Shughart starts by pointing to the many rule violations of the NCAA, you may wish to have students research, before they come to class to discuss this essay, whether such violations have increased in the past ten years. (A sample summary, which may be used as feedback, is available by assigning students to take the e-Pages summary quiz for the Shughart reading: **bedfordstmartins .com/readingcritically**.)

Words that some students may find challenging (*consensus* [par. 3], *nominal* [par. 10], and *mandate* [par. 13]) are included in a vocabulary quiz in the e-Pages. Other words students may need to define include *revelations* (par. 2), *extracurricular* (par. 7), and *inducements* (par. 11).

Read to Respond (p. 464)
Students may also respond to

- Shughart's belief that "a college education is no more necessary for success in the art world than it is in the world of sports" (par. 5);
- Shughart's assertion that students pursuing a stage career spend less time in the classroom than do PE majors (par. 5).

Read to Analyze Assumptions (p. 464)

You may also wish to ask students to examine the beliefs underlying Shughart's observation that "and notwithstanding the high moral principles and concern for players usually expressed by debaters on all sides of the issue, the interests of the athlete are in fact often the last to be considered" (par. 15).

READING LIKE A WRITER: SHOWING HOW THE PROPOSED SOLUTION WOULD HELP SOLVE THE PROBLEM AND IS FEASIBLE (p. 465)

This section provides students with some introductory analysis of Shughart's approach to establishing the viability and feasibility of his solution. Students are asked to begin by analyzing just one of Shughart's "three suggestions." Only after they have analyzed one suggestion in detail are they asked to consider the ways that the three suggestions work together. This could be a good time to let students know how you feel about allowing them to propose multiple, related solutions in their papers. This approach can be challenging to students who sometimes treat each of the solutions they propose too superficially. On the other hand, many problems do require a multifaceted approach, and learning how to propose such an approach is an important and valuable skill.

Kelly D. Brownell and Thomas R. Frieden, "Ounces of Prevention:
The Public Policy Case for Taxes on Sugared Beverages" (p. 466)

READING FOR MEANING (p. 471)

Read to Summarize (p. 471)

Students are asked to summarize Brownell and Frieden's solution in this activity. You could have them work this summary into a more detailed outline. (A sample summary, which may be used as feedback, is available by assigning students to take the e-Pages summary quiz for the Brownell and Frieden reading: bedfordstmartins.com/readingcritically.)

Words that some students may find challenging (*absenteeism* [par. 5], *regressive* [par. 6], and *incentive* [par. 6]) are included in a vocabulary quiz in the e-Pages.

Read to Respond (p. 471)

Students may also respond to

- Brownell and Frieden's claim that beverage marketers "exploit the vulnerabilities of young children" (par. 5)
- any recent attempts they may be aware of to limit or restrict people's consumption of sugared beverages, such as the recent attempt in New York City to limit the size of soft drinks for sale

Read to Analyze Assumptions (p. 471)

The first set of assumptions students are asked to explore are assumptions surrounding the government's role in public health. If your students are like ours, there may be wide and contentious difference in your classroom regarding the role of government. The first bulleted question is designed to ensure that the conversation stays directed toward analyzing the authors' assumptions, but the second one allows students to express their own views.

Another set of assumptions that students are asked to examine are assumptions about research studies. Many students will not have thought critically before about the kinds of questions this activity raises. Discussing them together as a class could work well.

In paragraphs 5 and 6, Brownell and Frieden raise objections and respond to them. This activity invites students to take a closer look at the way the authors do this. Question 3 is particularly interesting. Students are asked to consider why Brownell and Frieden spend so much time addressing the first objection they raise in comparison with the other objections (which are grouped into a single paragraph). You could remind students that audiences will not see all objections to a solution as equal, and you could ask your students what assumptions Brownell and Frieden are making about the objections of their audience. Do the students think they were right to make such an assumption?

Karen Kornbluh, "Win-Win Flexibility" (p. 474)

Reading for Meaning (p. 479)

Read to Summarize (p. 479)

After having students explain the proposed solution, you may also have them identify why Kornbluh proposes beginning with a "'soft-touch' at first" (par. 16). (A sample summary, which may be used as feedback, is available by assigning students to take the e-Pages summary quiz for the Kornbluh reading: bedfordstmartins.com/readingcritically.)

Words that some students may find challenging (*obligation* [par. 4], *morale* [par. 5], and *staggered* [par. 17]) are included in a vocabulary quiz in the e-Pages. Other words students may need to define include *sector* (par. 1) and *mediocre* (par. 13).

Read to Respond (p. 479)

Students may also respond to

- Kornbluh's use of statistics to support her proposed solution;
- Kornbluh's representation of life for employees without flexible work schedules.

Read to Analyze Assumptions (p. 480)

You might also ask students to examine

- Kornbluh's assumption that all workers would have the knowledge to "make a written application providing details on the change in work, the effect on the employer, and solutions to any problems caused to the employer" (par. 18);
- Kornbluh's statement that "to be decent parents, caregivers, and members of their communities, workers now need greater flexibility than they once did" (par. 2).

Reading like a Writer: Demonstrating That the Problem Exists and Is Serious (p. 480)

One way to establish that a problem is serious is to cite hard data, which is exactly what Kornbluh does in her essay. Students are encouraged to employ this technique in their own writing. The activity asks students to examine the places where Kornbluh cites statistics and survey results, and asks students to consider why such evidence is effective. If you have students conduct this activity in class, you may want to use it to segue into a discussion of how to find such evidence in their own research through using your college library's resources.

A Special Reading Strategy — Recognizing Emotional Manipulation (p. 482)

This special reading strategy following Karen Kornbluh's proposal asks students to think about the role of emotion, or pathos, in argumentation. Before assigning this section, you might want to have your students read and discuss the section on recognizing emotional manipulation in Chapter 10, A Catalog of Reading Strategies. A key question for students to address is the fine line between appropriate use of emotional content and manipulation. As readers, do students find that they start to resist an argument if they recognize emotional manipulation? As writers, what principles can they think of for using pathos so that their arguments are more, rather than less, likely to persuade?

Patrick O'Malley, "More Testing, More Learning" (p. 483)

Reading for Meaning (p. 488)

Read to Summarize (p. 488)

After having students explain the problem O'Malley identifies, the solution he proposes, and the alternative solutions he recognizes, you may wish to have them summarize the counterarguments O'Malley provides to refute the alternative solutions.

A word that students may need to define is *panacea* (par. 12).

Read to Respond (p. 488)

Students may also respond to

- the alternative solutions O'Malley recognizes and his counterarguments to them;
- O'Malley's use of personal experience as evidence.

Read to Analyze Assumptions (p. 488)

You might also ask students to explore the underlying values and assumed student behaviors revealed by this statement: "If students had frequent exams in all their courses, they would have to schedule study time each week and gradually would develop a habit of frequent study" (par. 5).

Once again we ask our students to pay attention to the cues that help a reader to understand an argument: a clear thesis, key terms, forecasting statements, and effective transitions. In this series of activities students are asked to pay special attention to paragraphs 6, and 8–12, looking for cues that O'Malley provides his readers. Students are then asked to evaluate the effectiveness of those cues and the extent to which they as readers are helped by them.

REVIEWING WHAT MAKES PROPOSALS EFFECTIVE (p. 490)

This reflective activity makes a great transition from reading to writing. As the text suggests, this activity can be done individually or in small groups.

Molly Coleman, "Missing the Fun" (student essay, e)

The "As you read" activities for this text ask students to pay attention to the ways that Coleman encourages her audience to identify with students and how she anticipates and responds to possible objections to her proposal. You might use the Coleman essay to begin a discussion with students about why it can be helpful to get readers to identify with those who are facing the problem their solutions address (because not all readers will have experienced the problem directly, because an emotional connection to the problem may motivate readers to take action). Similarly, you could use this essay to begin a discussion on effective technique for anticipating and responding to possible objections to students' solutions.

e bedfordstmartins.com/readingcritically

Phoebe Sweet and Zach Wise, "The Problem with Lawns: The Transforming Landscape of Las Vegas" (video, e)

READING FOR MEANING (e)

A sample summary, which may be used as feedback, is available by assigning students to take the e-Pages summary quiz for the Sweet and Wise selection that appears in the e-Pages.

READING LIKE A WRITER: SHOWING HOW THE PROPOSED SOLUTION WOULD HELP SOLVE THE PROBLEM AND IS FEASIBLE (e)

This activity asks students to analyze and evaluate how effectively the video demonstrates the ways in which the Las Vegas Water Authority is encouraging the citizens of Las Vegas to conserve water. You might ask students to analyze the visuals the video uses to make its case, in addition to the information and examples provided through interviews. After watching the video, you might ask students if they're persuaded that living in Las Vegas is truly feasible for the long haul.

A GUIDE TO WRITING PROPOSALS (p. 491)

Since we argue that proposal writing requires a strong sense of audience, peer critique can be especially useful. We encourage students in a draft workshop—see Reading a Draft Critically (p. 502)—to pretend they are the readers addressed in the proposal. Role-playing like this can be informative and fun. Having two or three students listen as the writer reads the draft aloud parallels the way proposals are often presented. The discussion that follows the reading could help the writer see how readers are likely to respond.

Here is an outline of A Guide to Writing Proposals:

Writing a Draft: Invention, Planning, and Composing
    Choosing a Problem
    Developing Your Proposal
        Analyzing the Problem
        Considering Your Readers
        Finding a Tentative Solution
        Researching Your Proposal
        Supporting Your Solution
        Anticipating Readers' Objections
        Responding to Alternative Solutions
        Formulating a Working Thesis
    Working with Sources: Citing Statistics to Establish the Problem's Existence
    and Seriousness (box)
    Including Visuals and Other Media
    Organizing Your Proposal Effectively for Your Readers
    Drafting Your Proposal
    Considering a Useful Sentence Strategy (box)

Evaluating the Draft: Getting a Constructive Critical Reading
    Reading a Draft Critically (box)

e bedfordstmartins.com/readingcritically

Improving the Draft: Revising, Editing, and Proofreading
    Revising Your Draft
    Troubleshooting Your Draft (table)
        To Introduce the Problem More Effectively
        To Strengthen the Support for the Proposed Solution
        To Improve the Response to Objections and Alternative Solutions
        To Make the Organizational Plan More Effective
    Editing and Proofreading Your Draft

Reflecting on What You Have Learned: Proposal to Solve a Problem (box)

Chapter 10 A CATALOG OF READING STRATEGIES

Chapter 10, which in previous editions of *Reading Critically, Writing Well* had appeared as an appendix, familiarizes students with strategies that can help them to read for meaning and analyze assumption. This chapter also provides students with an introduction logic and tools and strategies for argumentation. As such, parts of this chapter could be taught in conjunction with any or all of Chapters 2–9. Or, you may choose to take the approach of assigning parts or all of this chapter separately. You could, for example, assign the section on Annotating and the "Letter from Birmingham Jail" early on in the course to introduce students to the idea of annotating readers. Then, you might come back to Chapter 10's information on logic and argumentation later on as you begin to discuss strategies for reading and writing position papers (Chapter 7). Included below is an outline of the chapter:

A Catalog of Reading Strategies
    Annotating
        Martin Luther King Jr., *An Annotated Sample from "Letter from Birmingham Jail"*
    Taking Inventory
    Outlining
    Summarizing
    Paraphrasing
    Synthesizing
    Contextualizing
    Exploring the Significance of Figurative Language
    Looking for Patterns of Opposition
    Reflecting on Challenges to Your Beliefs and Values
    Comparing and Contrasting Related Readings
        Lewis H. Van Dusen Jr., *Legitimate Pressures and Illegitimate Results*
    Evaluating the Logic of an Argument
        Testing for Appropriateness
        Testing for Believability
        Testing for Consistency and Completeness
    Recognizing Logical Fallacies
        Slippery Slope
        Post Hoc, Ergo Propter Hoc
        False Dilemma (Either/Or Reasoning)
        Mistaking the Part for the Whole (Nonrepresentative Sample)
        Hasty Generalization
        Bandwagon Appeal
        Ad Hominem (or *Ad Personam*) Attack
        Straw Man (or Straw Person)

Begging the Question (Circular Reasoning)
Red Herring
Recognizing Emotional Manipulation
Judging the Writer's Credibility
Testing for Knowledge
Testing for Common Ground
Testing for Fairness

Chapter 11 STRATEGIES FOR RESEARCH AND DOCUMENTATION

Chapter 11, which in previous editions of *Reading Critically, Writing Well* had appeared as an appendix, provides students with information about conducting research. The chapter also includes information for citing and documenting source material in MLA and APA style. This chapter can be effective taught on its own; however, since research could be incorporated into nearly any of the reading and writing genres covered in Chapters 2–9, but may be especially helpful for Chapters 3 and 5–9, you may want to assign Chapter 11 in conjunction with one of these chapters, or you may want to assign different parts of Chapter 11 at different stages of the course. For example, you might choose to have students read only the Conducting Fieldwork section of Chapter 11 as they work on the reading and writing assignment discussed in Chapter 3: Observation. Then, later on in the course, as students work on writing assignments like the ones contained in Chapters 5–9, you might have the students read the rest of Chapter 11. Included below is an outline of the chapter:

Strategies for Research and Documentation

Planning a Research Project
    Analyzing Your Rhetorical Situation and Setting a Schedule
    Choosing a Topic and Getting an Overview
        Using General Encyclopedias
        Using Specialized Encyclopedias and Other Overview Resources
    Narrowing Your Topic and Drafting Research Questions
    Establishing a Research Log
    Creating a Working Bibliography
    Annotating Your Working Bibliography
    Taking Notes on Your Sources

Finding Sources
    Searching Library Catalogs and Databases
        Using Appropriate Search Terms
        Narrowing (or Expanding) Your Results
        Finding Books (and Other Sources) through Your Library's Catalog
        Finding Articles in Periodicals Using Your Library's Databases
    Searching for Government Documents and Statistical Information Online
    Searching for Web Sites and Interactive Sources
        Using *Google Scholar* and *Google Book Search*
        Using Other Search Options
        Using Interactive Sources

Conducting Field Research
    Conducting Observational Studies
        Planning an Observational Study
        Making Observations
        Writing Your Observational Study

     Conducting Interviews
         Planning the Interview
         Preparing for the Interview
         During the Interview
         Following the Interview
     Conducting Surveys
         Designing Your Survey
         Administering the Survey
         Writing the Report

Evaluating Sources
     Choosing Relevant Sources
     Choosing Reliable Sources
         Who Wrote It?
         When Was It Published?
         Is the Source Scholarly, Popular, or for a Trade Group?
         Who Published It?
         How Is the Source Written?
         What Does the Source Say?

Using Sources to Support Your Ideas
     Synthesizing Sources
     Acknowledging Sources and Avoiding Plagiarism
         Determining What Does (and Does Not) Need to Be Acknowledged
         Avoiding Plagiarism
     Using Information from Sources to Support Your Claims
         Deciding Whether to Quote, Paraphrase, or Summarize
         Altering Quotations Using Italics, Ellipses, and Brackets
         Using In-text or Block Quotations
         Using Punctuation to Integrate Quotations
         Paraphrasing Sources Carefully
         Summarizing to Present the Source's Main Ideas in a Balanced and Readable Way

Citing and Documenting Sources in MLA Style
     Using In-Text Citations to Show Where You Have Used Source Material
         Directory to In-Text Citation Models (box)
     Creating a List of Works Cited
         Directory to Works-Cited-List Models (box)

Citing and Documenting Sources in APA Style
     Using In-Text Citations to Show Where You Have Used Source Material
         Directory to In-Text-Citation Models (box)
     Creating a List of References
         Directory to Reference-List Models (box)

Chapter 12 STRATEGIES FOR ANALYZING VISUALS

The final chapter of *Reading Critically Writing Well*, Chapter 12, covers strategies for analyzing visuals. Many students come to us unused to the idea of "reading" visuals as "texts." However, the majority of our students have grown up in a society saturated with visual cues and messages. The material in this chapter can help students to become more cognizant and aware of the power of visual texts to convey ideas, feelings, and information. Because each of Chapters 2–9 include an Analyzing Visuals activity in association with one of the readings for each particular chapter, you may want to assign Chapter 12 early on in the semester or term. Other instructors have found that Chapter 12 can be taught as a genre unto itself and have assigned an analyzing a visual essay, similar to the student essay included in this chapter. Another approach would be to refer students to this chapter as a resource for the Analyzing Visuals activities in Chapters 2–9 as you assign those particular readings. Included below is an outline of the chapter:

Strategies for Analyzing Visuals
    Criteria for Analyzing Visuals
        Criteria for Analyzing Visuals (table)
    A Sample Analysis
        Paul Taylor's Analysis of *Emerging Man* (table)
        Paul Taylor, *The Rising* (student essay)

Patrick O'Malley

More Testing, More Learning

Patrick O'Malley wrote the following proposal when he was a first-year college student. To research the problem, he interviewed two professors, talked with several students, and read published research on testing. He cited these sources using APA style, as his instructor had requested. Because of his unusual rhetorical situation — a student advising teachers on how to plan their courses — O'Malley decided to make his essay an open letter to professors on his campus, a letter that might appear in the campus newspaper.

- *Before you read, think about your own experience with what O'Malley calls "major, infrequent, high-stakes exams" (par. 2). Do you think this kind of testing is a problem, and if so, why?*

- *As you read, consider O'Malley's decision to try to publish his proposal as an open letter in the campus newspaper. How well do you think he addresses the concerns of his readers, students as well as professors?*

It's late at night. The final's tomorrow. You got a C on the midterm, so this one will make or break you. Will it be like the midterm? Did you study enough? Did you study the right things? It's too late to drop the course. So what happens if you fail? No time to worry about that now — you've got a ton of notes to go over. 1

Although this last-minute anxiety about midterm and final exams is only too familiar to most college students, many professors may not realize how such major, infrequent, high-stakes exams work against the best interests of students both psychologically and cognitively. They cause unnecessary amounts of stress, placing too much importance on one or two days in the students' entire term, judging ability on a single or dual performance. Reporting on recent research at Cornell University Medical School, Sian Beilock, a psychology professor at the University of Chicago, points out that "stressing about doing well on an important exam can backfire, leading students to 'choke under pressure' or to score less well than they might otherwise score if the stakes weren't so high." Moreover, Cornell's research using fMRI brain scans shows that "the pressures of a big test can reach beyond the exam itself — stunting the cognitive systems that support the attention and memory skills every day" (Beilock, 2010). So, not only do high-stakes exams discourage frequent study and undermine students' performance, they also do long-term damage to students' cognitive development. If professors gave brief exams at frequent intervals, students would 2

For an additional student reading, go to
bedfordstmartins.com/readingcritically.

be spurred to learn more and worry less. They would study more regularly, perform better on tests, and enhance their cognitive functioning.

3   Ideally, a professor would give an in-class test or quiz after each unit, chapter, or focus of study, depending on the type of class and course material. A physics class might require a test on concepts after every chapter covered, while a history class could necessitate quizzes covering certain time periods or major events. These exams should be given weekly or at least twice monthly. Whenever possible, they should consist of two or three essay questions rather than many multiple-choice or short-answer questions. To preserve class time for lecture and discussion, exams should take no more than 15 or 20 minutes.

4   The main reason professors should give frequent exams is that when they do and when they provide feedback to students on how well they are doing, students learn more in the course and perform better on major exams, projects, and papers. It makes sense that in a challenging course containing a great deal of material, students will learn more of it and put it to better use if they have to apply or "practice" it frequently on exams, which also helps them find out how much they are learning and what they need to go over again. A 2006 study reported in the journal *Psychological Science* concluded that "taking repeated tests on material leads to better long-term retention than repeated studying," according to the study's co-authors, Henry L. Roediger and Jeffrey Karpicke (ScienceWatch.com, 2008). When asked what the impact of this breakthrough research would be, they responded: "We hope that this research may be picked up in educational circles as a way to improve educational practices, both for students in the classroom and as a study strategy outside of class." The new field of mind, brain, and education research advocates the use of "retrieval testing." For example, research by Karpicke and Blunt (2011) published in *Science* found that testing was more effective than other, more traditional methods of studying both for comprehension and for analysis. Why retrieval testing works is not known. UCLA psychologist Robert Bjork speculates that it may be effective because "when we use our memories by retrieving things, we change our access" to that information. "What we recall," therefore, "becomes more recallable in the future" (qtd. in Belluck, 2011).

5   Many students already recognize the value of frequent testing, but their reason is that they need the professor's feedback. A Harvard study notes students' "strong preference for frequent evaluation in a course." Harvard students feel they learn least in courses that have "only a midterm and a final exam, with no other personal evaluation." Students believe they learn most in courses with "many opportunities to see how they are doing" (Light, 1990, p. 32). In a review of a number of studies of student learning, Frederiksen (1984) reports that students who take weekly quizzes achieve higher scores on final exams than students who take only a midterm exam and that testing increases retention of material tested.

Another, closely related argument in favor of multiple exams is that they 6 encourage students to improve their study habits. Greater frequency in test taking means greater frequency in studying for tests. Students prone to cramming will be required—or at least strongly motivated—to open their textbooks and notebooks more often, making them less likely to resort to long, kamikaze nights of studying for major exams. Since there is so much to be learned in the typical course, it makes sense that frequent, careful study and review are highly beneficial. But students need motivation to study regularly, and nothing works like an exam. If students had frequent exams in all their courses, they would have to schedule study time each week and would gradually develop a habit of frequent study. It might be argued that students are adults who have to learn how to manage their own lives, but learning history or physics is more complicated than learning to drive a car or balance a checkbook. Students need coaching and practice in learning. The right way to learn new material needs to become a habit, and I believe that frequent exams are key to developing good habits of study and learning. The Harvard study concludes that "tying regular evaluation to good course organization enables students to plan their work more than a few days in advance. If quizzes and homework are scheduled on specific days, students plan their work to capitalize on them" (Light, 1990, p. 33).

By encouraging regular study habits, frequent exams would also de- 7 crease anxiety by reducing the procrastination that produces anxiety. Students would benefit psychologically if they were not subjected to the emotional ups and downs caused by major exams, when after being virtually worry-free for weeks they are suddenly ready to check into the psychiatric ward. Researchers at the University of Vermont found a strong relationship among procrastination, anxiety, and achievement. Students who regularly put off studying for exams had continuing high anxiety and lower grades than students who procrastinated less. The researchers found that even "low" procrastinators did not study regularly and recommended that professors give frequent assignments and exams to reduce procrastination and increase achievement (Rothblum, Solomon, & Murakami, 1986, pp. 393–394).

Research supports my proposed solution to the problem I have 8 described. Common sense as well as my experience and that of many of my friends support it. Why, then, do so few professors give frequent brief exams?

Some believe that such exams take up too much of the limited class time 9 available to cover the material in the course. Most courses meet 150 minutes a week—three times a week for 50 minutes each time. A 20-minute weekly exam might take 30 minutes to administer, and that is one-fifth of each week's class time. From the student's perspective, however, this time is well spent. Better learning and greater confidence about the course seem a good trade-off for another 30 minutes of lecture. Moreover, time lost to lecturing or discussion could easily be made up in students' learning on their own through careful regular study for the weekly exams. If weekly exams still seem too time-consuming to some professors, their frequency could be reduced to every other week or their length to 5 or 10 minutes. In courses where multiple-choice exams are appropriate, several questions could be designed to take only a few minutes to answer.

10   Moreover, professors object to frequent exams because they take too much time to read and grade. In a 20-minute essay exam, a well-prepared student can easily write two pages. A relatively small class of 30 students might then produce 60 pages, no small amount of material to read each week. A large class of 100 or more students would produce an insurmountable pile of material. There are a number of responses to this objection. Again, professors could give exams every other week or make them very short. Instead of reading them closely, they could skim them quickly to see whether students understand an idea or can apply it to an unfamiliar problem; and instead of numerical or letter grades, they could give a plus, check, or minus. Exams could be collected and responded to only every third or fourth week. Professors who have readers or teaching assistants could rely on them to grade or check exams. And the Scantron machine is always available for instant grading of multiple-choice exams. Finally, frequent exams could be given *in place of* a midterm exam or out-of-class essay assignment.

11   Since frequent exams seem to some professors to create too many problems, however, it is reasonable to consider alternative ways to achieve the same goals. One alternative solution is to implement a program that would improve study skills. While such a program might teach students how to study for exams, it cannot prevent procrastination or reduce "large test anxiety" by a substantial amount. One research team studying anxiety and test performance found that study skills training was not effective in reducing anxiety or improving performance (Dendato & Diener, 1986, p. 134). This team, which also reviewed other research that reached the same conclusion, did find that a combination of "cognitive/relaxation therapy" and study skills training was effective. This possible solution seems complicated, however, not to mention time-consuming and expensive. It seems much easier and more effective to change the cause of the bad habit rather than treat the habit itself. That is, it would make more sense to solve the problem at its root: the method of learning and evaluation.

12   Still another solution might be to provide frequent study questions for students to answer. These would no doubt be helpful in focusing students' time studying, but students would probably not actually write out the answers unless they were required to. To get students to complete the questions in a timely way, professors would have to collect and check the answers. In that case, however, they might as well devote the time to

grading an exam. Even if it asks the same questions, a scheduled exam is preferable to a set of study questions because it takes far less time to write in class, compared to the time students would devote to responding to questions at home. In-class exams also ensure that each student produces his or her own work.

Furthermore, professors could help students prepare for midterm and 13 final exams by providing sets of questions from which the exam questions will be selected or announcing possible exam topics at the beginning of the course. This solution would have the advantage of reducing students' anxiety about learning every fact in the textbook, and it would clarify the course goals, but it would not motivate students to study carefully each new unit, concept, or text chapter in the course. I see this as a way of complementing frequent exams, not as substituting for them.

From the evidence and from my talks with professors and students, I see 14 frequent, brief in-class exams as the only way to improve students' study habits and learning, reduce their anxiety and procrastination, and increase their satisfaction with college. These exams are not a panacea, but only more parking spaces and a winning football team would do as much to improve college life. Professors can't do much about parking or football, but they can give more frequent exams. Campus administrators should get behind this effort, and professors should get together to consider giving exams more frequently. It would make a difference.

References

Beilock, S. (2010, September 3). Stressing about a high-stakes exam carries consequences beyond the test [Web log post]. Retrieved from http://www.psychologytoday.com/blog/choke/201009/stressing-about-high-stakes-exam-carries-consequences-beyond-the-test

Belluck, P. (2011, January 20). To really learn, quit studying and take a test. *The New York Times*. Retrieved from http://www.nytimes.com

Dendato, K. M., & Diener, D. (1986). Effectiveness of cognitive/relaxation therapy and study skills training in reducing self-reported anxiety and improving the academic performance of test-anxious students. *The Journal of Counseling Psychology, 33*, 131–135.

Frederiksen, N. (1984). The real test bias: Influences of testing on teaching and learning. *American Psychologist, 39*, 193–202.

Karpicke, J. D., & Blunt, J. R. (2011, January 30). Retrieval practice produces more learning than elaborative studying with concept mapping. *Science Online* doi:10.1126/science.1199327

Light, R. J. (1990). *Explorations with students and faculty about teaching, learning, and student life*. Cambridge, MA: Harvard University Graduate School of Education and Kennedy School of Government.

Rothblum, E. D., Solomon, L., & Murakami, J. (1986). Affective, cognitive, and behavioral differences between high and low procrastinators. *Journal of Counseling Psychology, 33*, 387–394.

ScienceWatch.com (2008, February). Henry L. Roediger and Jeff Karpicke talk with ScienceWatch.com and answer a few questions about this month's fast breaking paper in the field of psychiatry/psychology [Interview]. Retrieved from http://sciencewatch.com/dr/fbp/2008/08febfbp /08febfbpRoedigerETAL

READING FOR MEANING

This section presents three activities that will help you think about the meanings in O'Malley's proposal. Your instructor may ask you to do one or more of these activities in class or online.

For more help with summarizing, see Chapter 10, pp. 518–19.

1. **Read to Summarize.** Write a sentence or two summarizing O'Malley's proposed solution.

2. **Read to Respond.** Write a paragraph analyzing your initial reactions to O'Malley's proposal. For example, consider anything that resonates with your experience or that seems contradictory, surprising, or fascinating, such as:

   - Whether O'Malley's solution, if it were adopted by professors, would make a difference in your own study habits or address any problems that you have with studying;

You may also try judging the writer's credibility; see Chapter 10, pp. 537–38.

   - The relation O'Malley attempts to establish between high-pressure exams and poor performance (par. 2), viewing it against your own experience;

   - The kinds of classes, in your experience, that are and are not suited to frequent brief exams.

3. **Read to Analyze Assumptions.** Write a paragraph or two analyzing an assumption you find intriguing in O'Malley's essay. For example:

   Assumptions about the relationship between motivation and procrastination. In paragraph 6, O'Malley argues that college students would be "strongly motivated — to open their textbooks and notebooks more often" if they had to take exams frequently. He explains that the assumption underlying this argument is that "students need motivation to study regularly." In the next paragraph, however, he reviews research on procrastination that "found that even 'low' procrastinators did not study regularly" (par. 7).

   To think critically about the assumptions in this essay related to motivation and procrastination, ask yourself questions like these:

   - What seems to be the relationship, if any, between motivation and procrastination?

- If even students categorized as "low" procrastinators "did not study regularly," does it make sense to assume, as O'Malley does, that frequent tests would motivate most students to study?

- Given your own experiences and observations of other students, what would be likely to motivate most students and overcome their tendency to procrastinate?

Assumptions about the "right way to learn." O'Malley claims, "Students need coaching and practice in learning. The right way to learn new material needs to become a habit" (par. 6). He seems to assume that studying regularly is the "right way to learn" and that cramming the night before an exam is the wrong way. To think critically about the assumptions in this essay related to the "right way to learn," ask yourself questions like these:

- Why does O'Malley assume that cramming is inferior to studying regularly? In your experience and observations of other students, to what extent, if any, does cramming result in poorer performance on exams?

- If students studied regularly, wouldn't they need to cram the night before the exam anyway to remind themselves of what they had studied days and weeks earlier?

- Do you think there is a single "right way" — or at least, a best way — for students to study? If so, what is it?

You may also try reflecting on challenges to your beliefs and values; see Chapter 10, pp. 526–27.

READING LIKE A WRITER

ORGANIZING THE PROPOSAL IN A WAY THAT IS CLEAR, LOGICAL, AND CONVINCING

Topic sentences — particularly when they repeat key terms (or synonyms) from the thesis and forecasting statement — can be especially helpful cues for readers. Notice how O'Malley uses this strategy in two paragraphs from his essay:

Thesis/key terms *Forecasting statement*	If professors gave brief exams at frequent intervals, students would be spurred to learn more and worry less. *They would study more regularly, perform better on tests, and enhance their cognitive functioning.* (par. 2)
Cue	The main reason professors should give frequent exams is that when they do and when they provide feedback to students on how well they are doing, students learn more in the course and perform better on major exams, projects, and papers. (par. 4)

Repetition of key terms along with transitions that identify the topic (such as *main reasons*) and indicate the logical relationships among sentences and paragraphs (such as *however, for example,* and *since*) are both helpful. They tie together the parts of an argument and help to make a proposal well organized, readable, and logical.

Analyze & Write

Write a paragraph analyzing and evaluating O'Malley's use of cues to help readers follow the logic of his proposal:

1. First, reread paragraph 6 and paragraphs 8–12, and highlight the cues O'Malley provides.

2. Then identify two or three examples of cueing that help make this part of his argument logical.

3. Finally, evaluate how well O'Malley's use of cueing in this section and throughout the proposal helps you as a reader. Point out any places where cues are needed or could be improved.

Reviewing What Makes Proposals Effective

An effective proposal

- identifies an existing problem and demonstrates its seriousness;

- proposes a solution and shows that it would help solve the problem and is feasible — not too costly or time-consuming;

- anticipates and responds to likely objections to the proposed solution as well as any alternative solutions readers might prefer;

- is organized clearly and logically, making it easy for readers to follow the argument.

Analyze & Write

Write a brief evaluation — positive, negative, or mixed — of one of the readings in this chapter, explaining why you think it succeeds or fails as a proposal. Be sure to consider the characteristics that distinguish proposals, as well as how successful the writer has been in communicating his or her purpose to the intended audience. You may also want to consider the effect the medium of presentation had on decisions the writer made.

A GUIDE TO WRITING PROPOSALS

As you've read and discussed the reading selections in this chapter, you have probably done a good deal of analytical writing. Your instructor may assign a capstone project to write a brief proposal of your own. Having learned how writers define the problem, argue in support of their solution, respond to possible objections and alternative solutions, and organize the proposal in a way that makes it clear and easy to follow, you can now approach proposals confidently as a writer. This Guide to Writing offers detailed suggestions for writing a proposal and resources to help you meet the special challenges this kind of writing presents.

THE WRITING ASSIGNMENT

Write an essay proposing a solution to a problem.

- Choose a problem affecting a community or group to which you belong.

- Research the problem and possible solutions.

- Decide how to present the problem so that readers see it exists and is serious.

- Find a solution that would help solve the problem and could be implemented without being too costly or time-consuming.

- Address likely objections to your proposed solution as well as any alternative solutions readers might prefer.

- Organize the proposal in a way that is clear, logical, and convincing.

WRITING A DRAFT

INVENTION, PLANNING, AND COMPOSING

The following activities will help you choose a problem, find the information you need to devise and support a feasible solution, and develop an effective response to objections or alternative solutions readers are likely to raise.

Choosing a Problem

Rather than limiting yourself to the first subject that comes to mind, take a few minutes to consider your options and list as many problems as you can. When choosing a subject, keep in mind that the problem must be

- important to you and of concern to others;
- solvable, at least in part;
- one that you know a good deal about or can research in the time you have.

Choosing a problem affecting a group to which you belong (for example, as a classmate, teammate, participant in an online game site, or garage band member) or a place you have worked (a coffee shop, community pool, or radio station) gives you an advantage: You can write as an expert. You know the history of the problem, you know who to interview, and perhaps you have already thought about possible solutions. Moreover, you know who to address and how to persuade that audience to take action on your proposed solution.

If you already have a problem and possible solution(s) in mind, skip this activity. If you need to find a problem, making a chart like the one below can help you get started exploring creative solutions to real-life problems related to your school, community, or workplace.

	Problems	*Possible Solutions*
School	Can't get into required courses	Make them large lecture courses.
		Make them online or hybrid courses.
		Give priority to majors.
Community	No safe place for children to play	Use school yards for after-school sports.
		Get high-school students or senior citizens to tutor kids.
		Make pocket parks for neighborhood play.
		Offer programs for kids at branch libraries.
Work	Inadequate training for new staff	Make a training video or Web site.
		Assign experienced workers to mentor trainees (for bonus pay).

Developing Your Proposal

The writing and research activities that follow will enable you to test your problem and develop an argument supporting your proposed solution.

Analyzing the Problem

Spend a few minutes thinking about what you and your readers know about the problem and how you can convince your readers that the problem you have identified is real and needs to be solved:

Brainstorm a List. Spend ten minutes listing everything you know about the problem. Write quickly, leaving judgment aside for the moment. After the ten minutes are up, you can review your list and highlight or star the most promising information.

Use Cubing. Probe the problem from a variety of perspectives:

- Describe the problem.
- Compare the problem to other, similar problems, or contrast it with other, related problems.
- Identify causes of the problem. (Consider immediate and deeper causes.)
- Consider the consequences of the problem. (Think about both short-term and long-term consequences.)
- Connect the problem to other problems in your experience.
- Analyze the problem to identify those most affected by it or any who benefit from it.
- Apply the problem to a real-life situation.

Prove the Problem's Existence and Seriousness. Use the sentence strategies below as a jumping-off point for demonstrating the existence and seriousness of the problem.

Give an example to make the problem specific

- ▶ Recently, ... has been [in the news/in movies/a political issue] because of .... [name event].

Use a scenario or anecdote to dramatize the problem

- ▶ Example: It's late at night. The final's tomorrow. You got a C on the midterm, so this one will make or break you. (O'Malley, par. 1)

Cite statistics to show the severity of the problem

▸ It has recently been reported that .... percent of .... [name group] are .... [specify problem].

Describe the problem's negative consequences

▸ According to .... [name expert/study], ... [state problem] is affecting .... [name affected group]: .... [insert quote from expert].

Show why readers should care about solving the problem

▸ We're all in this together. .... is not a win-lose proposition. If .... [name group] loses, we all lose.

▸ If we don't try to solve ...., no one else will.

▸ Doing nothing will only make .... worse.

▸ We have a moral responsibility to do something about ....

Considering Your Readers

With your understanding of the problem in mind, write for a few minutes to bring your intended readers into focus. Will you be writing to all members of your group or to only some of them (a committee that might supervise or evaluate the group, an individual in a position of authority)? Briefly justify your choice of readers.

Now gauge the impact of the problem on your readers and the attitudes they hold. How might these attitudes inform the solutions they are likely to prefer?

Freewriting. Write without stopping for five or ten minutes about the problem's direct or indirect impact on your readers. Don't stop to reflect or consider; if you hit a roadblock, just keep coming back to the topic or raise questions you could research later. At the end of the specified time, review your writing and highlight or underline promising ideas.

Considering Values. Comment on the values and attitudes of your readers and how they have responded to similar problems in the past. Use these sentence strategies as a jumping-off point:

▸ Some of my readers think .... is .... [someone else's responsibility/ not that big a problem].

▸ Others see .... as a matter of .... [fairness/human decency].

▸ Many complain about .... but do nothing because solving it seems [too hard/too costly].

Finding a Tentative Solution

List at least three possible solutions to the problem. You may want to consider using the following approaches to start:

- **Adapt a solution that has been tried or proposed for a similar problem.**

  Example: Bornstein's solution to bullying is to teach children empathy, as the Roots of Empathy program does.

- **Focus on eliminating a cause or minimizing an effect of the problem.**

  Example: O'Malley's solution to stressful high-stakes exams is to eliminate the cause of the stress by inducing instructors to give more frequent low-stakes exams.

- **See the problem as part of a larger system, and explore solutions to the system.**

  Example: Kornbluh's solution is for employers to work with employees to enhance job flexibility.

- **Focus on solving a small part of the problem.**

  Example: Brownell and Frieden's solution to obesity is to reduce the consumption of sugared beverages through taxation.

- **Look at the problem from different points of view.**

  Example: Consider what students, teachers, parents, or administrators might think could be done to help solve the problem.

- **Think of a specific example of the problem, and consider how you could solve it.**

  Example: O'Malley could have focused on solving the problem of high-stakes exams in one particular course.

Researching Your Proposal

In exploring the problem and considering possible solutions, you may have identified questions you need to research. Doing research with your questions and notes in mind will help you work efficiently. But recognize that you might also find contradictory evidence that leads you to rethink your ideas.

If you are proposing a solution to a problem about which others have written, use the research strategies below to help you find out what solutions others have proposed or tried. You may also use these strategies to find out how others have defined the problem and demonstrated its seriousness.

- Enter keywords or phrases related to your solution (or problem) into the search box of an all-purpose database such as *Academic OneFile* (InfoTrac) or

Academic Search Complete (EBSCOHost) to find relevant articles in magazines and journals; a database like *LexisNexis* to find articles in newspapers; or library catalogs to find books and other resources. (Database names may change, and what is available will differ from school to school. Some libraries may even combine all three into one search link on the library's home page. Ask a librarian if you need help.) Patrick O'Malley could have tried a combination of keywords, such as *learning* and *test anxiety*, or variations on his terms (*frequent testing, improve retention*) to find relevant articles.

- *Bookmark* or keep a record of the URLs of promising sites, and download or copy information you could use in your essay. When available, download PDF files rather than HTML files, because PDFs are likely to include visuals such as graphs and charts. If you copy and paste relevant information from sources into your notes, be careful to distinguish carefully between all material from sources and your own ideas. Remember to record source information with care and to cite and document any sources you use, including visuals and interviews.

To learn more about finding information, avoiding plagiarism, or documenting sources, see Chapter 11, pp. 548–80.

Supporting Your Solution

Write down every plausible reason why your solution should be heard or tried. Then review your list and highlight the strongest reasons, the ones most likely to persuade your readers. Write for a few minutes about the single most convincing reason. The sentence strategies below can help you explain how your solution could help solve the problem:

It would eliminate a cause of the problem

▸ Research by .... shows it would reduce ....

It has worked elsewhere

▸ It works in ...., ..., and ...., as studies evaluating it by .... and .... show.

It would change people's behavior

▸ .... would [discourage/encourage] people to ....

Anticipating Readers' Objections

Write a few sentences defending your solution against each of the following predictable objections:

- It won't really solve the problem.
- I'm comfortable with things as they are.

- We can't afford it.
- It will take too long.
- People won't do it.
- Too few people will benefit.
- It's already been tried, with unsatisfactory results.
- You're making this proposal because it will benefit you personally.

For your proposal to succeed, readers must be convinced to take the solution seriously. Try to imagine how your prospective readers will respond.

Responding to Alternative Solutions

Identify two or three other solutions that your readers may prefer. Choose the one that poses the most serious challenge to your proposed solution. Then write a few sentences comparing your solution with the alternative one, weighing the strengths and weaknesses of each. Explain how you might demonstrate to readers that your solution has more advantages and fewer disadvantages than the alternative. (You may need to conduct additional research to respond to alternative solutions.)

Formulating a Working Thesis

A working thesis will keep you focused as you draft and revise your essay. The thesis statement in a proposal should offer the solution and may also identify the problem. Although they are not required to do so, thesis statements may also forecast the main reasons in favor of the solution. (Forecasts can help guide readers.)

Here are two examples of thesis statements from the readings:

Problem Imagine there was a cure for meanness. Well, maybe there is. . . . And what's
Solution the secret formula? A baby. (Bornstein, pars. 1–2)

Forecast If professors gave brief exams at frequent intervals, students would be spurred to *learn more and worry less. They would study more regularly, perform better on tests, and enhance their cognitive functioning.* (O'Malley, par. 2)

As you draft your own thesis statement, pay attention to the language you use. It should be clear and unambiguous, emphatic but appropriately qualified. Although you will probably refine your thesis statement as you draft and revise your essay, trying now to articulate it will help give your planning and drafting direction and impetus.

Working with Sources

Citing Statistics to Establish the Problem's Existence and Seriousness

Statistics can be helpful in establishing that a problem exists and is serious. Patrick O'Malley, Kelly Brownell and Thomas Frieden, and Karen Kornbluh use statistics for this purpose. Note that Brownell and Frieden present some of their statistics in the form of graphs (see Including Visuals and Other Media, below). To define her problem, Kornbluh uses statistics in three different forms: percentages, numbers, and proportions. (Percentages are underlined, numbers are bold, and proportions are set in italics.)

> Between 1970 and 2000, the percentage of mothers in the workforce rose from <u>38</u> to <u>67 percent</u> (Smolensky and Gootman). Moreover, the number of hours worked by dual-income families has increased dramatically. Couples with children worked a full **60** hours a week in 1979. By 2000 they were working **70** hours a week (Bernstein and Kornbluh). And more parents than ever are working long hours. In 2000, nearly *1 out of every 8* couples with children was putting in **100** hours a week or more on the job, compared to only *1 out of 12* families in 1970 (Jacobs and Gerson). (par. 7)

Percentages can seem quite impressive, but sometimes, without the raw numbers, readers may not appreciate just how remarkable the percentages really are. In the following example, readers can see at a glance that the percentage Kornbluh cites is truly significant:

> In addition to working parents, there are over **44.4 million** Americans who provide care to another adult, often an older relative. <u>Fifty-nine percent</u> of these caregivers either work or have worked while providing care ("Caregiving"). (par. 8)

To establish that there is a widespread perception among working parents that the problem is serious, Kornbluh cites survey results:

> In a 2002 report by the Families and Work Institute, <u>45 percent</u> of employees reported that work and family responsibilities interfered with each other "a lot" or "some" and <u>67 percent</u> of employed parents report that they do not have enough time with their children (Galinsky, Bond, and Hill). (par. 9)

This example shows that nearly half of all employees have had difficulty juggling work and family responsibilities. The readers Kornbluh is addressing — employers — are likely to find this statistic important because it suggests that their employees are spending time worrying about or attending to family responsibilities instead of focusing on work.

For statistics to be persuasive, they must be from sources that readers consider reliable. Researchers' trustworthiness, in turn, depends on their credentials as experts in the field they are investigating and also on the degree to which they are disinterested, or free from bias. Kornbluh provides a list of works cited that readers can follow up on to check whether the sources are indeed reliable, for example from publishers and research institutes. Another factor that adds to the appearance of reliability is that Kornbluh cites statistics from a range of sources instead of relying on only one or two. Moreover, the statistics are current and clearly relevant to her argument.

To find statistics relating to the problem (or possible solution) you are writing about, explore the state, local, or tribal sections of www.usa .gov, the U.S. government's official Web portal, or visit the Library of Congress page State Government Information, www.loc.gov/rr/news /stategov/stategov.html, and follow the links. In particular, visit the U.S. Census Bureau's Web site (www.census.gov), which offers reliable statistics on a wide variety of issues.

Including Visuals and Other Media

Think about whether visuals — drawings, photographs, tables, or graphs — would strengthen your proposal. Notice the photographs we added to Bornstein's proposal (pp. 447–52), which came originally from the Roots of Empathy Web site. Also notice the two graphs Brownell and Frieden included in their proposal (pp. 466–71). Each graph has a heading and a caption that indicates where the data comes from. Brownell and Frieden apparently created the graphs themselves.

Consider constructing your own visuals, scanning materials from books and magazines, or downloading them from the Internet. If you submit your essay electronically to other students and your instructor or if you post it on a Web site, you might consider including video and audio clips as well as still images. Be sure to obtain permission, as we did, if your proposal will be read outside of your classroom.

Organizing Your Proposal Effectively for Your Readers

The basic parts of a proposal argument are quite simple:

1. the problem

2. the solution

3. the reasons in support of the solution

4. a response to objections or alternative solutions readers might propose

This simple plan is nearly always complicated by other factors, however. In outlining your material, you must take into consideration many other details, such as whether readers already recognize the problem, how much agreement exists on the need to solve the problem, how much attention should be given to alternative solutions, and how many objections and questions by readers should be expected. If you are writing primarily for readers who acknowledge that the problem exists and are open to your solution, you might begin with a brief introduction that ends with your thesis statement and conclude by urging your readers to action. If you are writing primarily for readers who do not recognize the problem or are likely to prefer alternative solutions, however, you may need to begin by establishing common ground and acknowledging alternative ways readers may see the problem, and then concede the strengths of alternative solutions before launching fully into your own proposal; you may want to conclude by reiterating the values you share with your readers.

Drafting Your Proposal

By this point, you have done a lot of writing

- to focus and define a problem, and develop a solution to it;

- to support your solution with reasons and evidence your readers will find persuasive;

- to refute or concede objections and alternative solutions;

- to organize your ideas to make them clear, logical, and effective for readers.

Now stitch that material together to create a draft. The next two parts of this Guide to Writing will help you evaluate and improve it.

Considering a Useful Sentence Strategy

As you draft your proposal, you will want to connect with your readers. You will also want readers to become concerned with the seriousness of the problem and thoughtful about the challenge of solving it. Sentences that take the form of rhetorical questions can help you achieve these goals.

A **rhetorical question** is a sentence that poses a question that the writer does not expect the reader to answer. (In most cases, a reader could not possibly answer it.) In proposals, however, rhetorical questions can do important rhetorical work — that is, they can

- engage readers—for example, by dramatizing the problem

    Will it be like the midterm? Did you study enough? Did you study the right things? It's too late to drop the course. So what happens if you fail? (O'Malley, par. 1)

- orient readers by introducing or emphasizing parts of the argument, cueing solutions or responses

    And what's the secret formula? A baby. (Bornstein, par. 2)

    If so, why stop at half-measures? (Shughart, par. 3)

    Why, then, do so few professors give frequent brief exams? (O'Malley, par. 8)

    Why should academic credit be given for practicing the violin, but not for practicing a three-point shot? (Shughart, par. 5)

Even though they are useful, rhetorical questions are not a requirement for a successful proposal and should be used only when appropriate to the rhetorical situation. They tend to be used sparingly in academic writing, and they should not be overused because readers may find them annoying and unnecessary.

EVALUATING THE DRAFT

GETTING A CONSTRUCTIVE CRITICAL READING

Getting a critical reading of your draft will help you see how to improve it. Your instructor may schedule class time for reading drafts, or you may want to ask a classmate or a tutor in the writing center to read your draft. Ask your reader to use the following guidelines and to write out a response for you to consult during your revision.

READING A DRAFT CRITICALLY

Read for a First Impression

1. **Read the draft without stopping, and then write a few sentences giving your general impression.**

2. **Identify one aspect of the draft that seems particularly effective.**

Read Again to Suggest Improvements

1. **Recommend ways to present the problem more effectively.**

   - Locate places in the draft where the problem is defined and described. Point to any places where you believe the intended readers will need more explanation or where the presentation seems unclear or confusing.

   - Consider whether the writer does enough to establish the seriousness of the problem, creating a sense of urgency to gain readers' support and excite their curiosity about solutions. If not, suggest ways to do so.

2. **Suggest ways to present the solution more effectively.**

   - Locate the solution, and decide whether it is immediately clear. If not, point to places where it should be made clearer, and suggest how, if possible.

   - If the draft does not lay out steps for implementation, advise the writer whether doing so would help.

3. **Recommend ways to strengthen the argument for the solution.**

   - List the reasons the writer gives for adopting the solution or considering it seriously. Point out the reasons most and least likely to be convincing. Let the writer know if there are too many or too few reasons. If the reasons are not in a logical order, suggest a new order.

   - Evaluate the support for each reason. Point out any passages where the support seems insufficient, and recommend further kinds of support. If necessary, tell the writer how to make the solution seem more practical, workable, and cost-effective.

4. **Suggest ways to extend and improve the response to objections or alternative solutions.**

   - Locate places where the writer anticipates readers' likely objections to the proposal. Evaluate how successfully the writer concedes or refutes each objection, and, if necessary, recommend ways to make the response to particular objections more convincing.

- Suggest any likely objections and questions the writer has overlooked.

- Identify any alternative solutions the writer mentions. If necessary, give advice on how the writer could present them more clearly and responsibly and could concede or refute them more convincingly.

5. **Suggest how the organization might be improved.**

- Consider the overall plan, perhaps by making a scratch outline. Decide whether the reasons and responses follow a logical sequence. Suggest a more logical sequence, if necessary.

- Indicate where new or better transitions might help identify steps in the argument and keep readers on track.

6. **Evaluate the effectiveness of visuals.**

- Look at any visuals in the essay, and tell the writer what they contribute to your understanding of the argument.

- If any visual does not seem useful, or if adding a visual would strengthen the argument, explain your thinking.

IMPROVING THE DRAFT

REVISING, EDITING, AND PROOFREADING

Start improving your draft by reflecting on what you have written thus far:

- Review critical reading comments from your classmates, instructor, or writing center tutor. What are your readers getting at?

- Take another look at your notes and ideas: What else should you consider?

- Review your draft: What else can you do to make your proposal clearer or more interesting to your readers?

Revising Your Draft

Revising means reenvisioning your draft, trying to see it in a new way, given your purpose and audience, in order to develop a clearer, more compelling proposal. Think imaginatively and boldly about cutting unconvincing or tangential material, adding new material, and moving material around. The suggestions in the chart that follows may help you solve problems and strengthen your essay.

TROUBLESHOOTING YOUR DRAFT

To Introduce the Problem More Effectively

Problem	Suggestions for Revising
Readers doubt that the problem exists or that it is very serious.	• Discuss the problem's history or describe its effects on real people. • Add information—statistics, examples, studies, and so on—that your audience is likely to find persuasive or that they can relate to. • Consider adding visuals, such as graphs, tables, or charts, if these would help clarify the problem for your audience.

To Strengthen the Support for the Proposed Solution

Problem	Suggestions for Revising
The solution being proposed is not clear.	• Describe the solution in more detail. • Outline the steps of its implementation. • Add a visual illustrating the solution.
Readers are not convinced that the proposed solution would solve the problem.	• Explain how the solution addresses specific aspects of the problem. • Point out where else the solution has worked. • Cite experts or research studies.

To Improve the Response to Objections and Alternative Solutions

Problem	Suggestions for Revising
Likely objections to the solution have not been adequately addressed.	• Acknowledge valid objections and modify your solution to concede them. • Refute invalid objections by presenting reasons and supporting evidence.
Alternative solutions preferred by readers have not been adequately addressed.	• Address alternative solutions directly, acknowledging their strengths as well as their weaknesses. • Try to show why your solution is preferable—for example, it is easier to implement, costs less, takes less time, has fewer negative side effects, would garner more support.

To Make the Organizational Plan More Effective	
Problem	**Suggestions for Revising**
The essay is hard to follow.	• Mark each part of the proposal more clearly with explicit topic sentences and transitions or headings. • Add a forecasting statement.

Editing and Proofreading Your Draft

Check for errors in usage, punctuation, and mechanics, and consider matters of style. If you keep a list of errors you typically make, begin by checking your draft against this list. Ask someone else to proofread your essay before you submit it to your instructor.

From our research on student writing, we know that proposal writers tend to refer to the problem or solution by using the pronoun *this* or *that* ambiguously. Edit carefully any sentences with *this* or *that* to ensure that a noun immediately follows the pronoun to make the reference clear. Check a writer's handbook for help with this potential problem.

Reflecting on What You Have Learned

Proposal to Solve a Problem

In this chapter, you have read critically several proposals and have written one of your own. To better remember what you have learned, pause now to reflect on the reading and writing activities you completed in this chapter.

1. Write a page or so reflecting on what you have learned. Begin by describing what you are most pleased with in your essay. Then explain what you think contributed to your achievement. Be specific about this contribution.

   - If it was something you learned from the readings, indicate which readings and specifically what you learned from them.

   - If you got good advice from a critical reader, explain exactly how the person helped you — perhaps by helping you understand a problem in your draft or by helping you add a new dimension to your writing.

   - Try to write about your achievement in terms of what you have learned about the genre.

   (continued)

2. Reflect more generally on proposals, a genre of writing that plays an important role in our society. Consider some of the following questions:

- How confident do you feel about making a proposal that might lead to improvements in the functioning of an entire group or community? Does your proposal attempt to bring about fundamental or minor change in the group?

- Whose interest would be served by the solution you propose? Who else might be affected? In what ways does your proposal challenge the status quo in the group?

- What contribution might essays proposing solutions to problems make to our society that other genres of writing cannot make?

CHAPTER

10

A Catalog of
Reading Strategies

Here we present fifteen strategies for reading critically that you can apply to the selections in this book as well as to your other college reading. Mastering these strategies will make reading much more satisfying and productive for you and help you handle difficult material with confidence:

- *Annotating:* Recording your reactions to, interpretations of, and questions about a text as you read it

- *Taking inventory:* Listing and grouping your annotations and other notes to find meaningful patterns

- *Outlining:* Listing the text's main ideas to reveal how it is organized

- *Summarizing:* Distilling the main ideas or gist of a text

- *Paraphrasing:* Restating what you have read to clarify or refer to it

- *Synthesizing:* Integrating into your own writing ideas and information gleaned from different sources

- *Contextualizing:* Placing a text in its historical and cultural context

- *Exploring the significance of figurative language:* Examining how metaphors, similes, and symbols are used in a text to convey meaning and evoke feelings

- *Looking for patterns of opposition:* Inferring the values and assumptions embodied in the language of a text

- *Reflecting on challenges to your beliefs and values:* Examining the bases of your personal responses to a text

- *Comparing and contrasting related readings:* Exploring likenesses and differences between texts to understand them better

- *Evaluating the logic of an argument:* Determining whether an argument is well reasoned and adequately supported

- *Recognizing logical fallacies:* Looking for errors in reasoning

- *Recognizing emotional manipulation:* Identifying texts that unfairly and inappropriately use emotional appeals based on false or exaggerated claims

- *Judging the writer's credibility:* Considering whether writers represent different points of view fairly and know what they are writing about

ANNOTATING

Annotations are the marks — underlines, highlights, and comments — you make directly on the page as you read. Annotating can be used to record immediate reactions and questions, outline and summarize main points, and evaluate and relate the reading to other ideas and points of view. Although this discussion of annotating assumes you are reading printed pages, you can also annotate many kinds of text on-screen by using your software's highlighting and commenting functions or simply by typing annotations into the text using a different color or font. If electronic annotation is not possible, print out the text and annotate by hand.

Your annotations can take many forms, such as the following:

- Writing comments, questions, or definitions in the margins

- Underlining or circling words, phrases, or sentences

- Connecting ideas with lines or arrows

- Numbering related points

- Bracketing sections of the text

- Noting anything that strikes you as interesting, important, or questionable

Most readers annotate in layers, adding further annotations on second and third readings. Annotations can be light or heavy, depending on your purpose and the difficulty of the material. Your purpose for reading also determines how you use your annotations.

The following selection, excerpted from Martin Luther King Jr.'s "Letter from Birmingham Jail," illustrates some of the ways you can annotate as you read. Add your own annotations, if you like.

Martin Luther King Jr.

An Annotated Sample from "Letter from Birmingham Jail"

Martin Luther King Jr. (1929–1968) first came to national notice in 1955, when he led a successful boycott against the policy of restricting African American passengers to rear seats on city buses in Montgomery, Alabama, where he was minister of a Baptist church. He subsequently formed the Southern Christian Leadership Conference, which brought people of all races from all over the country to the South to fight nonviolently for racial integration. In 1963, King led demonstrations in Birmingham, Alabama, that were met with violence; a bomb was detonated in a black church, killing four young girls. King was arrested for his role in organizing the protests, and while in prison, he wrote his "Letter from Birmingham Jail" to justify his strategy of civil disobedience, which he called "nonviolent direct action."

King begins his letter by discussing his disappointment with the lack of support he has received from white moderates, such as the group of clergy who published criticism of his organization in the local newspaper.

Read the following excerpt, paying attention to the following:

- *Try to infer what the clergy's specific criticisms might have been.*

- *Notice the tone King uses. Would you characterize the writing as apologetic, conciliatory, accusatory, or something else?*

1 I must confess that over the past few years I have been gravely disappointed with the white moderate. I have almost reached the regrettable conclusion that the Negro's [great stumbling block in his stride toward freedom] is not the White Citizen's Counciler or the Ku Klux Klanner, but the white moderate, who is more devoted to "order" than to justice; who prefers a negative peace which is the absence of tension to a positive peace which is the presence of justice; who constantly says: "I agree with you in the goal you seek, but I cannot agree with your methods of direct action"; who paternalistically believes he can set the timetable for another man's freedom; who lives by a mythical concept of time and who constantly advises the Negro to wait for a "more convenient season." Shallow understanding from people of good will is more frustrating than absolute misunderstanding from people of ill will. Lukewarm acceptance is much more bewildering than outright rejection.

¶1. White moderates block progress.

Contrasts: order vs. justice, negative vs. positive peace, goals vs. methods

(treating others like children)

more contrasts

¶2. What the moderates
don't understand

metaphor: law and order =
dams (faulty?)

I had hoped that the white moderate would under- 2
stand that <u>law and order exist for the purpose of
establishing justice</u> and that when they fail in this purpose they become the [dangerously structured dams
that block the flow of social progress.] I had hoped
that the white moderate would understand that the
<u>present tension</u> in the South is a <u>necessary phase of
the transition</u> from an [obnoxious <u>negative peace,</u>] in

repeats contrast
(negative / positive)

which the Negro passively accepted his unjust plight,
to a [substantive and <u>positive peace,</u>] in which all
men will respect the dignity and worth of human

Tension already exists: We
help dispel it. (True?)

personality. Actually, we <u>who engage in nonviolent
direct action are not the creators of tension. We
merely bring to the surface the hidden tension</u> that is
already alive. We bring it out in the open, where it

simile: hidden tension is
"like a boil"

can be seen and dealt with. [<u>Like a boil</u> that can never
be cured so long as it is covered up but must be
opened with all its ugliness to the natural medicines
of air and light, injustice must be exposed, with all
the tension its exposure creates, to the <u>light of human
conscience and the air of national opinion before it
can be cured.</u>]

¶3. Questions clergymen's
logic: condemning his
actions = condemning
robbery victim, Socrates,
Jesus.

In your statement you assert that <u>our actions,</u> even 3
though peaceful, must be <u>condemned</u> because they
precipitate violence. But is this a logical assertion?
<u>Isn't this like condemning</u> (a robbed man) because his
possession of money precipitated the evil act of rob-

repetition ("Isn't this
like . . .")

bery? <u>Isn't this like condemning</u> (Socrates) because his
unswerving commitment to truth and his philosophical inquiries precipitated the act by the misguided
populace in which they made him drink hemlock?
<u>Isn't this like condemning</u> (Jesus) because his unique
God-consciousness and never-ceasing devotion to
God's will precipitated the evil act of crucifixion? We
must come to see that, as the federal courts have consistently affirmed, it is wrong to urge an individual to
cease his efforts to gain his <u>basic constitutional rights</u>

(Yes!)

because the question may precipitate violence. [<u>Soci-
ety must protect the robbed and punish the robber.</u>]

example of a white
moderate's view

I had also hoped that the white moderate would 4
reject the <u>myth concerning time</u> in relation to the
struggle for freedom. I have just received a letter from
a white brother in Texas. He writes: "All Christians
know that the colored people will receive equal rights

eventually, but it is possible that you are in <u>too great a religious hurry</u>. It has taken Christianity almost two thousand years to accomplish what it has. The teachings of Christ take time to come to earth." Such an attitude stems from a tragic misconception of time, from the strangely irrational notion that there is something in the very flow of time that will inevitably cure all ills. (Actually, time itself is neutral; it can be used either destructively or constructively.) More and more I feel that the people of ill will have used time much more effectively than have the people of good will. We will have to repent in this generation not merely for the [hateful <u>words and actions</u> of the bad people] but for the [<u>appalling silence</u> of the good people.] Human progress never rolls in on [wheels of inevitability;] it comes through the tireless efforts of men willing to be co-workers with God, and without this hard work, time itself becomes an ally of the forces of social (stagnation.) [We must use time <u>creatively</u>, in the knowledge that <u>the time is always ripe to do right</u>.] <u>Now is the time</u> to make real the promise of democracy and transform our pending [national elegy] into a creative [psalm of brotherhood.] <u>Now is the time</u> to lift our national policy from the [quicksand of racial injustice] to the [solid rock of human dignity.]

5   You speak of our activity in Birmingham as <u>extreme</u>. At first I was rather disappointed that fellow clergymen would see my nonviolent efforts as those of an extremist. I began thinking about the <u>fact</u> that <u>I stand in the middle of two opposing forces in the Negro community</u>. One is a [force of complacency,] made up in part of Negroes who, as a result of long years of oppression, are so drained of self-respect and a sense of "somebodiness" that they have adjusted to segregation; and in part of a few middle-class Negroes, who because of a degree of academic and economic security and because in some ways they profit by segregation, have become insensitive to the problems of the masses. The other [force is one of bitterness and hatred,] and it comes perilously close to advocating violence. It is expressed in the various <u>black nationalist</u> [groups that are springing up] across the nation, the largest and best-known being <u>Elijah Muhammad's Muslim movement</u>. Nourished by the Negro's frustration over

¶4. Time must be used to do right.

Silence / passivity is as bad as hateful words and actions.

metaphor (mechanical?)

(stop developing)

metaphors (song, natural world)

King accused of being an extremist.

¶5. Puts self in middle of two extremes: complacency and bitterness.

Malcolm X?

the continued existence of racial discrimination, this movement is made up of people who have lost faith in America, who have absolutely repudiated Christianity, and who have concluded that the white man is an incorrigible "devil."

¶6. Offers better choice: nonviolent protest.

(How did nonviolence become part of King's movement?)

I have tried to stand between these two forces, say- 6
ing that we need emulate neither the "do-nothingism" of the complacent nor the hatred and despair of the black nationalist. For there is the more excellent way of love and nonviolent protest. I am grateful to God that, through the influence of the Negro church, the way of nonviolence became an integral part of our struggle.

¶7. Says movement pre-vents racial violence. (Threat?)

If this philosophy had not emerged, by now many 7
streets of the South would, I am convinced, be flow-ing with blood. And I am further convinced that if our white brothers dismiss as "rabble-rousers" and "out-side agitators" those of us who employ nonviolent direct action, and if they refuse to support our non-violent efforts, millions of Negroes will, out of frustra-

(comfort)

tion and despair, seek (solace) and security in black-nationalist ideologies—a development that would inevitably lead to a frightening racial nightmare.

(Oppressed people cannot remain oppressed for- 8
ever.) The yearning for freedom eventually manifests itself, and that is what has happened to the American Negro. Something within has reminded him of his birthright of freedom, and something without has reminded him that it can be gained. Consciously or

(spirit of the times)

unconsciously, he has been caught up by the (Zeitgeist,) and with his black brothers of Africa and his brown and yellow brothers of Asia, South America and the Caribbean, the United States Negro is moving with a sense of great urgency toward the [promised land of racial justice.] If one recognizes this [vital urge that has engulfed the Negro community,] one should read-ily understand why public demonstrations are taking place. The Negro has many [pent-up resentments] and latent frustrations, and he must release them. So let him march; let him make prayer pilgrimages to the city hall; let him go on freedom rides—and try to

Not a threat

understand why he must do so. If his repressed emo-tions are not released in nonviolent ways, they will seek expression through violence; this is not a threat but a fact of history. So I have not said to my people:

"Get rid of your discontent." Rather, I have tried to say that this <u>normal and healthy discontent</u> can be [channeled into the <u>creative outlet of nonviolent direct action</u>.] And now <u>this approach is being termed extremist</u>.

9   But though I was initially disappointed at being categorized as an extremist, as I continued to think about the matter <u>I gradually gained a measure of satisfaction from the label</u>. Was not (Amos) an <u>extremist for justice</u>: "Let justice roll down like waters and righteousness like an ever-flowing stream." Was not (Paul) an <u>extremist for the Christian gospel</u>: "I bear in my body the marks of the Lord Jesus." Was not (Martin Luther) an <u>extremist</u>: "Here I stand; I cannot do otherwise, so help me God." And (John Bunyan:) "I will stay in jail to the end of my days before I make a butchery of my conscience." And (Abraham Lincoln:) "This nation cannot survive half slave and half free." And (Thomas Jefferson:) "We hold these truths to be self-evident, that all men are created equal...." (So the question is not whether we will be extremists, but what kind of extremists we will be.) <u>Will we be</u> extremists for hate or for love? <u>Will we be</u> extremists for the preservation of injustice or for the extension of justice? In that <u>dramatic scene on Calvary's hill</u> three men were crucified. We must never forget that all three were crucified for the same crime—the crime of extremism. <u>Two were extremists for immorality</u>, and <u>thus fell</u> below their environment. The other, (Jesus Christ,) was an <u>extremist for love, truth and goodness, and thereby rose</u> above his environment. Perhaps the South, the (nation and the world are in dire need of creative extremists.)

10   <u>I had hoped</u> that the white moderate would see this need. Perhaps <u>I was too optimistic</u>; perhaps <u>I expected too much</u>. I suppose I should have realized that few members of <u>the oppressor race</u> can understand the deep groans and passionate yearnings of the <u>oppressed race</u>, and still fewer have the vision to see that [injustice must be rooted out] by strong, persistent and determined <u>action</u>. I am thankful, however, that some of our white brothers in the South have

¶8. Discontent is normal, healthy, and historically inevitable, but it must be channeled.

¶9. Redefines "extremism," embraces "extremist" label.

(Hebrew prophet)

(Christian apostle)

(founder of Protestantism)

(English preacher)

Compares self to great "extremists" — including Jesus.

Disappointed in the white moderate

¶10. Praises whites who have supported movement.

(Who are they?)

(been left unaided)

Metaphor: segregation is a disease.

grasped the meaning of this <u>social revolution</u> and committed themselves to it. They are still all too few in quantity, but they are big in quality. Some—such as Ralph McGill, Lillian Smith, Harry Golden, James McBride Dabbs, Ann Braden and Sarah Patton Boyle— have <u>written</u> about our struggle in eloquent and prophetic terms. Others have <u>marched</u> with us down nameless streets of the South. They have (languished) in filthy, roach-infested jails, <u>suffering the abuse and brutality</u> of policemen who view them as "dirty niggerlovers." Unlike so many of their moderate brothers and sisters, they have <u>recognized the urgency of the moment and sensed the need</u> for [powerful "action" antidotes] to combat the [disease of segregation.]

CHECKLIST

Annotating

To annotate a reading,

1. Mark the text using notations.

   - Circle words to be defined in the margin.
   - Underline key words and phrases.
   - Bracket important sentences and passages.
   - Use lines or arrows to connect ideas or words.

2. Write marginal comments.

   - Number and summarize each paragraph.
   - Define unfamiliar words.
   - Note responses and questions.
   - Identify interesting writing strategies.
   - Point out patterns.

3. Layer additional markings in the text and comments in the margins as you reread for different purposes.

TAKING INVENTORY

Taking inventory helps you analyze your annotations for different purposes. When you take inventory, you make various kinds of lists to explore patterns of meaning you find in the text. For instance, in reading the annotated passage by Martin Luther King Jr., you might have noticed that certain similes and metaphors are used or that many famous people are named. By listing the names (Socrates, Jesus, Luther, Lincoln, and so on) and then grouping them into categories (people who died for their beliefs, leaders, teachers, and religious figures), you could better understand why the writer refers to these particular people. Taking inventory of your annotations can be helpful if you plan to write about a text you are reading.

CHECKLIST

Taking Inventory

To take inventory of a text,

1. Examine the annotations you made for patterns or repetitions, such as recurring images, stylistic features, repeated words and phrases, repeated examples or illustrations, and reliance on particular writing strategies.

2. List the items that make up a pattern.

3. Decide what the pattern might reveal about the reading.

OUTLINING

Outlining is an especially helpful reading strategy for understanding the content and structure of a reading. **Outlining**, which identifies the text's main ideas, may be part of the annotating process, or it may be done separately. Writing an outline in the margins of the text as you read and annotate makes it easier to find information later. Writing an outline on a separate piece of paper gives you more space to work with, and therefore such an outline usually includes more detail.

The key to outlining is distinguishing between the main ideas and the supporting material, such as examples, quotations, comparisons, and reasons. The main ideas form the backbone that holds the various parts of the text together. Outlining the main ideas helps you uncover this structure.

Making an outline, however, is not simple. The reader must exercise judgment in deciding which are the most important ideas. The words used in an outline reflect the reader's interpretation and emphasis. Readers also must decide when to use the writer's words, their own words, or a combination of the two.

You may make either a formal, multileveled outline or an informal scratch outline. A formal outline is harder to make and much more time-consuming than a scratch outline. You might choose to make a formal outline of a reading about which you are writing an in-depth analysis or evaluation. For example, here is a formal outline a student wrote for an essay evaluating the logic of the King excerpt.

Formal outline of "Letter from Birmingham Jail"

I. "[T]he Negro's great stumbling block in his stride toward freedom is . . . the white moderate . . . " (par. 1).
   A. White moderates are more devoted to "order" than to justice; however,
      1. law and order exist only to establish justice (par. 2).
      2. law and order *without* justice actually threaten social order ("dangerously structured dams" metaphor, par. 2).
   B. White moderates prefer "negative peace" (absence of tension) to "positive peace" (justice); however,
      1. tension already exists; it is not created by movement (par. 2).
      2. tension is a necessary phase in progress to a just society (par. 2).
      3. tension must be allowed outlet if society is to be healthy ("boil" simile, par. 2).
   C. White moderates disagree with methods of movement; however,
      1. nonviolent direct action can't be condemned for violent response to it (analogies: robbed man; Socrates; Jesus, par. 3).
      2. federal courts affirm that those who seek constitutional rights can't be held responsible for violent response (par. 3).
   D. White moderates paternalistically counsel patience, saying time will bring change; however,
      1. time is "neutral"— we are obligated to use it *actively* to achieve justice (par. 4).
      2. the time for action is now (par. 4).
II. Contrary to white moderates' claims, the movement is not "extremist" in the usual sense (par. 5ff.).
   A. It stands between extremes in black community: passivity, seen in the oppressed and the self-interested middle class; and violent radicalism, seen in Elijah Muhammad's followers (pars. 5–6).
   B. In its advocacy of love and nonviolent protest, the movement has forestalled bloodshed and kept more blacks from joining radicals (pars. 5–7).
   C. The movement helps blacks channel urge for freedom that's part of historical trend and the prevailing *Zeitgeist* (par. 8).
III. The movement can be defined as extremist if the term is redefined: "Creative extremism" is extremism in the service of love, truth, and goodness (examples of Amos, Paul, Luther, Bunyan, Lincoln, Jefferson, Jesus, par. 9).

IV. Some whites — "few in quantity, but . . . big in quality" — have recognized the truth of the arguments above and, unlike the white moderates, have committed themselves to the movement (par. 10).

A scratch outline will not record as much information as a formal outline, but it is sufficient for most reading purposes. To make a scratch outline, you first need to locate the topic of each paragraph in the reading. The topic is usually stated in a word or phrase, and it may be repeated or referred to throughout the paragraph. For example, the opening paragraph of the King excerpt (p. 509) makes clear that its topic is the white moderate.

After you have found the topic of the paragraph, figure out what is being said about it. To return to our example: King immediately establishes the white moderate as the topic of the opening paragraph and at the beginning of the second sentence announces the conclusion he has come to — namely, that the white moderate is "the Negro's great stumbling block in his stride toward freedom." The rest of the paragraph specifies the ways the white moderate blocks progress.

The annotations include a summary of each paragraph's topic. Here is a scratch outline that lists the topics:

Scratch outline of "Letter from Birmingham Jail"

¶1. White moderates block progress
¶2. What the moderates don't understand
¶3. Questions clergymen's logic
¶4. Time must be used to do right
¶5. Puts self in middle of two extremes: complacency and bitterness
¶6. Offers better choice: nonviolent protest
¶7. Says movement prevents racial violence
¶8. Discontent is normal, healthy, and historically inevitable, but it must be channeled
¶9. Redefines "extremism," embraces "extremist" label
¶10. Praises whites who have supported movement

CHECKLIST

Outlining

To make a scratch outline of a text,

1. Reread each paragraph, identifying the topic and the comments made about it. Do not include examples, specific details, quotations, or other explanatory and supporting material.

2. List the author's main ideas in the margin of the text or on a separate piece of paper.

SUMMARIZING

Summarizing is important because it helps you understand and remember what is most significant in a reading. Another advantage of summarizing is that it creates a condensed version of the reading's ideas and information, which you can refer to later or insert into your own writing. Along with quoting and paraphrasing, summarizing enables you to integrate other writers' ideas into your own writing.

A **summary** is a relatively brief restatement, primarily in the reader's own words, of the reading's main ideas. Summaries vary in length, depending on the reader's purpose. Some summaries are very brief — a sentence or even a subordinate clause. For example, if you were referring to the excerpt from "Letter from Birmingham Jail" and simply needed to indicate how it relates to your other sources, your summary might look something like this: "There have always been advocates of extremism in politics. Martin Luther King Jr., in 'Letter from Birmingham Jail,' for instance, defends nonviolent civil disobedience as an extreme but necessary means of bringing about racial justice." If, however, you were surveying the important texts of the civil rights movement, you might write a longer, more detailed summary that not only identifies the reading's main ideas but also shows how the ideas relate to one another.

Many writers find it useful to outline the reading as a preliminary to writing a summary. A paragraph-by-paragraph scratch outline (like the one on p. 517) lists the reading's main ideas in the sequence in which they appear in the original. But summarizing requires more than merely stringing together the entries in an outline; it must fill in the logical connections between the author's ideas. Notice also in the following example that the reader repeats selected words and phrases and refers to the author by name, indicating, with verbs like *expresses*, *acknowledges*, and *explains*, the writer's purpose and strategy at each point in the argument.

Summary

King expresses his disappointment with white moderates who, by opposing his program of nonviolent direct action, have become a barrier to progress toward racial justice. He acknowledges that his program has raised tension in the South, but he explains that tension is necessary to bring about change. Furthermore, he argues that tension already exists, but because it has been unexpressed, it is unhealthy and potentially dangerous.

He defends his actions against the clergy's criticisms, particularly their argument that he is in too much of a hurry. Responding to charges of extremism, King claims that he has actually prevented racial violence by channeling the natural frustrations of oppressed blacks into nonviolent protest. He asserts that extremism is precisely what is needed now — but it must be creative, rather than destructive, extremism. He concludes by again expressing disappointment with white moderates for not joining his effort as some other whites have.

A summary presents only ideas. Although it may use certain key terms from the source, it does not otherwise attempt to reflect the source's language, imagery, or tone; and it avoids even a hint of agreement or disagreement with the ideas it summarizes. Of course, a writer might summarize ideas in a source like "Letter from Birmingham Jail" to show readers that he or she has read it carefully and then proceed to use the summary to praise, question, or challenge King's argument. In doing so, the writer might quote specific language that reveals word choice, imagery, or tone.

CHECKLIST

Summarizing

To restate briefly the main ideas in a text,

1. Make a scratch outline.

2. Write a paragraph or more that presents the author's main ideas largely in your own words. Use the outline as a guide, but reread parts of the original text as necessary.

3. To make the summary coherent, fill in connections between the ideas you present.

PARAPHRASING

Paraphrasing is restating a text you have read by using mostly your own words. It can help you clarify the meaning of an obscure or ambiguous passage. It is one of the three ways of integrating other people's ideas and information into your own writing, along with **quoting** (reproducing exactly the language of the source text) and **summarizing** (distilling the main ideas or gist of the source text). You might choose to paraphrase rather than quote when the source's language is not especially arresting or memorable. You might paraphrase short passages but summarize longer ones.

Following are two passages. The first is from paragraph 2 of the excerpt from King's "Letter." The second passage is a paraphrase of the first:

Original

I had hoped that the white moderate would understand that law and order exist for the purpose of establishing justice and that when they fail in this purpose they become the dangerously structured dams that block the flow of social progress. I had hoped that the white moderate would understand that the present tension in the South is a necessary phase of the transition from an obnoxious negative peace, in which the Negro passively accepted his unjust plight, to a substantive and positive peace, in which all men will respect the dignity and worth of human personality.

Paraphrase

King writes that he had hoped for more understanding from white moderates — specifically that they would recognize that law and order are not ends in themselves but means to the greater end of establishing justice. When law and order do not serve this greater end, they stand in the way of progress. King expected the white moderate to recognize that the current tense situation in the South is part of a transition process that is necessary for progress. The current situation is bad because although there is peace, it is an "obnoxious" and "negative" kind of peace based on blacks passively accepting the injustice of the status quo. A better kind of peace — one that is "substantive," real and not imaginary, as well as "positive" — requires that all people, regardless of race, be valued.

When you compare the paraphrase to the original, you can see that the paraphrase contains all the important information and ideas of the original. Notice also that the paraphrase is somewhat longer than the original, refers to the writer by name, and encloses King's original words in quotation marks. The paraphrase tries to be neutral, to avoid inserting the reader's opinions or distorting the original writer's ideas.

CHECKLIST

Paraphrasing

To paraphrase information in a text,

1. Reread the passage, looking up unfamiliar words in a college dictionary.

2. Translate the passage into your own words and sentences, putting quotation marks around any words or phrases you quote from the original.

3. Revise to ensure coherence.

SYNTHESIZING

Synthesizing involves presenting ideas and information gleaned from different sources. It can help you see how different sources relate to one another. For example, one reading may provide information that fills out the information in another reading, or a reading could present arguments that challenge arguments in another reading.

When you synthesize material from different sources, you construct a conversation among your sources, a conversation in which you also participate. Synthesizing contributes most when writers use sources, not only to support their ideas but to challenge and extend them as well.

In the following example, the reader uses a variety of sources related to the King passage (pp. 509–14) and brings them together around a central idea. Notice how quotation, paraphrase, and summary are all used.

Synthesis

> When King defends his campaign of nonviolent direct action against the clergymen's criticism that "our actions, even though peaceful, must be condemned because they precipitate violence" (King excerpt, par. 3), he is using what Vinit Haksar calls Mohandas Gandhi's "safety-valve argument" ("Civil Disobedience and Non-Cooperation" 117). According to Haksar, Gandhi gave a "non-threatening warning of worse things to come" if his demands were not met. King similarly makes clear that advocates of actions more extreme than those he advocates are waiting in the wings: "The other force is one of bitterness and hatred, and it comes perilously close to advocating violence" (King excerpt, par. 5). King identifies this force with Elijah Muhammad, and although he does not name him, King's contemporary readers would have known that he was referring also to his disciple Malcolm X, who, according to Herbert J. Storing, "urged that Negroes take seriously the idea of revolution" ("The Case against Civil Disobedience" 90). In fact, Malcolm X accused King of being a modern-day Uncle Tom, trying "to keep us under control, to keep us passive and peaceful and nonviolent" (*Malcolm X Speaks* 12).

CHECKLIST

Synthesizing

To synthesize ideas and information,

1. Find and read a variety of sources on your topic, annotating the passages that give you ideas about the topic.

2. Look for patterns among your sources, possibly supporting or challenging your ideas or those of other sources.

3. Write a paragraph or more synthesizing your sources, using quotation, paraphrase, and summary to present what they say on the topic.

CONTEXTUALIZING

All texts reflect historical and cultural assumptions, values, and attitudes that may differ from your own. To read thoughtfully, you need to become aware of these differences. **Contextualizing** is a critical reading strategy that enables you to make inferences about a reading's historical and cultural context and to examine the differences between its context and your own.

The excerpt from King's "Letter from Birmingham Jail" is a good example of a text that benefits from being read contextually. If you knew little about the history of slavery and segregation in the United States, it would be difficult to understand the passion expressed in this passage. To understand the historical and cultural context in which King wrote his "Letter from Birmingham Jail," you could do some library or Internet research. Comparing the situation at the time to situations with which you are familiar would help you understand some of your own attitudes toward King and the civil rights movement.

Here is what one reader wrote to contextualize King's writing, following the guidelines below.

Notes from a contextualized reading

1. I have seen documentaries showing civil rights demonstrators being attacked by dogs, doused by fire hoses, beaten and dragged by helmeted police. Such images give me a sense of the violence, fear, and hatred that King was responding to.

The creative tension King refers to comes across in his writing. He uses his anger and frustration to inspire his critics. He also threatens them, although he denies it. I saw a film on Malcolm X, so I could see that King was giving white people a choice between his own nonviolent way and Malcolm's more confrontational way.

2. Things have certainly changed since the 1960s. For one: Barack Obama is president. When I read King's "Letter" today, I feel like I'm reading history. But then again, every once in a while there are reports of police brutality and hate crimes. Some people have also suggested that in recent elections there have been efforts to deprive African Americans and other minorities of the right to vote in some areas of the country.

CHECKLIST

Contextualizing

To contextualize,

1. Describe the historical and cultural situation as it is represented in the reading and in other sources with which you are familiar. Your knowledge may come from other reading, television or film, school,

or elsewhere. (If you know nothing about the historical and cultural context, you could do some library or Internet research.)

2. Compare the historical and cultural situation in which the text was written with your own historical and cultural situation. Consider how your understanding and judgment of the reading are affected by your own context.

EXPLORING THE SIGNIFICANCE OF FIGURATIVE LANGUAGE

Figurative language — metaphor, simile, and symbolism — enhances literal meaning by implying abstract ideas through vivid images and by evoking feelings and associations.

Metaphor implicitly compares two different things by identifying them with each other. For instance, when King calls the white moderate "the Negro's great stumbling block in his stride toward freedom" (par. 1), he does not mean that the white moderate literally trips the Negro who is attempting to walk toward freedom. The sentence makes sense only if understood figuratively: The white moderate trips up the Negro by frustrating every effort to achieve justice.

Simile, a more explicit form of comparison, uses the word *like* or *as* to signal the relationship of two seemingly unrelated things. King uses simile when he says that injustice is "[l]ike a boil that can never be cured so long as it is covered up" (par. 2). This simile makes several points of comparison between injustice and a boil. It suggests that injustice is a disease of society as a boil is a disease of the skin, and that injustice, like a boil, must be exposed or it will fester and infect the entire body.

Symbolism compares two things by making one stand for the other. King uses the white moderate as a symbol for supposed liberals and would-be supporters of civil rights who are actually frustrating the cause.

How these figures of speech are used in a text reveals something of the writer's feelings about the subject. Exploring possible meanings in a text's figurative language involves (1) annotating and then listing some of the metaphors, similes, and symbols you find in a reading; (2) grouping and labeling the figures of speech that appear to express related feelings or attitudes; and (3) writing to explore the meaning of the patterns you have found.

The following example shows the process of exploring figures of speech in the King excerpt.

Listing figures of speech

"stumbling block in his stride toward freedom" (par. 1)

"law and order . . . become the dangerously structured dams" (par. 2) "the flow of social progress" (par. 2)

"Like a boil that can never be cured" (par. 2)

"the light of human conscience and the air of national opinion" (par. 2)

"the quicksand of racial injustice" (par. 4)

Grouping and labeling figures of speech

Sickness: "like a boil" (par. 2); "the disease of segregation" (par. 10)

Underground: "hidden tension" (par. 2); "injustice must be exposed" (par. 2); "injustice must be rooted out" (par. 10)

Blockage: "dams," "block the flow" (par. 2); "Human progress never rolls in on wheels of inevitability" (par. 4); "pent-up resentments," "repressed emotions" (par. 8)

Writing to explore meaning

The patterns labeled *underground* and *blockage* suggest a feeling of frustration. Inertia is a problem; movement forward toward progress or upward toward the promised land is stalled. The strong need to break through the resistance may represent King's feelings about both his attempt to lead purposeful, effective demonstrations and his effort to write a convincing argument.

The simile of injustice being "like a boil" links the two patterns of underground and sickness, suggesting that something bad, a disease, is inside the people or the society. The cure is to expose or to root out the blocked hatred and injustice as well as to release the tension or emotion that has long been repressed. This implies that repression itself is the evil, not simply what is repressed. Therefore, writing and speaking out through political action may have curative power for individuals and society alike.

CHECKLIST

Exploring the Significance of Figurative Language

To understand how figurative language — metaphors, similes, and symbols — contributes to a reading's meaning,

1. Annotate and then list all the figures of speech you find.

2. Group the figures of speech that appear to express related feelings and attitudes, and label each group.

3. Write one or two paragraphs exploring the meaning of the patterns you have found.

LOOKING FOR PATTERNS OF OPPOSITION

All texts carry within themselves voices of opposition. These voices may echo the views and values of readers the writer anticipates or predecessors to whom the writer is responding in some way; they may even reflect the writer's own conflicting values. Careful readers look closely for such a dialogue of opposing voices within the text.

When we think of oppositions, we ordinarily think of polarities: *yes* and *no*, *up* and *down*, *black* and *white*, *new* and *old*. Some oppositions, however, may be more subtle. The excerpt from King's "Letter from Birmingham Jail" is rich in such oppositions: *moderate* versus *extremist*, *order* versus *justice*, *direct action* versus *passive acceptance*, *expression* versus *repression*. These oppositions are not accidental; they form a significant pattern that gives a reader important information about the essay.

A careful reading will show that King always values one of the two terms in an opposition over the other. In the passage, for example, *extremist* (par. 9) is valued over *moderate* (par. 10). This preference for extremism is surprising. The reader should ask why, when white extremists like members of the Ku Klux Klan have committed so many outrages against African Americans, King would prefer extremism. If King is trying to convince his readers to accept his point of view, why would he represent himself as an extremist? Moreover, why would a clergyman advocate extremism instead of moderation?

Studying the **patterns of opposition** in the text enables you to answer these questions. You will see that King sets up this opposition to force his readers to examine their own values and realize that they are in fact misplaced. Instead of working toward justice, he says, those who support law and order maintain the unjust status quo. By getting his readers to think of white moderates as blocking rather than facilitating peaceful change, King brings readers to align themselves with him and perhaps even embrace his strategy of nonviolent resistance.

Looking for patterns of opposition involves annotating words or phrases in the reading that indicate oppositions, listing the opposing terms in pairs, deciding which term in each pair is preferred by the writer, and reflecting on the meaning of the patterns. Here is a partial list of oppositions from the King excerpt, with the preferred terms marked by an asterisk:

Listing patterns of opposition

moderate	*extremist
order	*justice
negative peace	*positive peace
absence of justice	*presence of justice

goals   *methods

*direct action   passive acceptance

*exposed tension   hidden tension

CHECKLIST

Looking for Patterns of Opposition

To explore and analyze the patterns of opposition in a reading,

1. Annotate the selection to identify words or phrases indicating oppositions.

2. List the pairs of oppositions. (You may have to paraphrase or even supply the opposite word or phrase if it is not stated directly in the text.)

3. For each pair of oppositions, put an asterisk next to the term that the writer seems to value or prefer over the other.

4. Write to analyze and evaluate the opposing points of view, or, in a reading that does not take a position, the alternative systems of value.

REFLECTING ON CHALLENGES TO YOUR BELIEFS AND VALUES

To read thoughtfully, you need to scrutinize your own assumptions and attitudes as well as those expressed in the text you are reading. If you are like most readers, however, you will find that your assumptions and attitudes are so ingrained that you are not always fully aware of them. A good strategy for getting at these underlying beliefs and values is to identify and reflect on the ways the text challenges you and how it makes you feel — disturbed, threatened, ashamed, combative, pleased, exuberant, or some other way.

For example, here is what one student wrote about the King passage:

Reflections

In paragraph 1, Dr. King criticizes people who are "more devoted to 'order' than to justice." This criticism upsets me because today I think I would choose order over justice. When I reflect on my feelings and try to figure out where they come from, I realize that what I feel most is fear. I am terrified by the violence in society today. I'm afraid of sociopaths who don't respect the rule of law, much less the value of human life.

I know Dr. King was writing in a time when the law itself was unjust, when order was apparently used to keep people from protesting and changing the law. But things are different now. Today, justice seems to serve criminals more than it serves law-abiding citizens. That's why I'm for order over justice.

CHECKLIST

Reflecting on Challenges to Your Beliefs and Values

To reflect on challenges to your beliefs and values,

1. Identify challenges by marking where in the text you feel your beliefs and values are being opposed, criticized, or unfairly characterized.

2. Write a paragraph or two reflecting on the differences between the beliefs and values you and others hold.

COMPARING AND CONTRASTING RELATED READINGS

When you compare two reading selections, you look for similarities. When you contrast them, you look for differences. As critical reading strategies, comparing and contrasting enable you to see both texts more clearly.

Both strategies depend on how imaginative you are in preparing the grounds or basis for comparison. We often hear that it is fruitless, so to speak, to compare apples and oranges. It is true that you cannot add or multiply them, but you can put one against the other and come up with some interesting similarities and differences. For example, comparing apples and oranges in terms of their roles as symbols in Western culture (say, the apple of Adam and Eve compared to the symbol for Apple computers) could be quite productive. The grounds or basis for comparison, like a camera lens, brings some things into focus while blurring others.

To demonstrate how this strategy works, we compare and contrast the excerpt from "Letter from Birmingham Jail" (pp. 509–14) with the following selection by Lewis H. Van Dusen Jr.

Lewis H. Van Dusen Jr.

Legitimate Pressures and Illegitimate Results

A respected attorney and legal scholar, Lewis H. Van Dusen Jr. has served as chair of the American Bar Association Committee on Ethics and Professional Responsibility. This selection comes from the essay "Civil Disobedience: Destroyer of Democracy," which first appeared in the American Bar Association Journal *in 1969. As you read, notice the annotations we made comparing this essay with the one by King.*

There are many civil rights leaders who show impa- 1 tience with the process of democracy. They rely on the sit-in, boycott, or mass picketing to gain speedier solutions to the problems that face every citizen. But we must realize that the legitimate pressures that [won concessions in the past] can easily escalate into the illegitimate power plays that might (extort)

(to get something by force or intimidation)

demands in the future.] The victories of these civil rights leaders must not shake our confidence in the democratic procedures, as the pressures of demonstration are desirable only if they take place within the limits allowed by law. Civil rights gains should continue to be won by the persuasion of Congress and other legislative bodies and by the decision of courts. Any illegal entreaty for the [rights of some] can be an injury to the [rights of others,] for mass demonstrations often trigger violence.

Those who advocate [taking the law into their own 2 hands] should reflect that when they are disobeying what they consider to be an immoral law, they are deciding on a possibly immoral course. Their answer

King's concern with time

is that the process for democratic relief is too slow, that only mass confrontation can bring immediate action, and that any injuries are the inevitable cost of the pursuit of justice. Their answer is, simply put, that

Ends vs. means debate
Any form?

the end justifies the means. It is this justification of any form of demonstration as a form of dissent that threatens to destroy a society built on the rule of law.

We had already read and annotated the King excerpt, so we read the Van Dusen selection looking for a basis for comparison. We decided to base our contrast on the writers' different views of nonviolent direct action. We carefully reread the Van Dusen selection, annotating aspects of his argument against the use of nonviolent direct action. These annotations led directly to the first paragraph of our contrast, which summarizes Van Dusen's argument. Then we reread the King excerpt, looking for how he justifies nonviolent direct action. The second paragraph of our contrast presents King's defense, plus some of our own ideas on how he could have responded to Van Dusen.

> King and Van Dusen present radically different views of legal, nonviolent direct action, such as parades, demonstrations, boycotts, sit-ins, or pickets. Although Van Dusen acknowledges that direct action is legal, he nevertheless fears it; and he challenges it energetically in these paragraphs. He seems most concerned about the ways direct action disturbs the peace, infringes on others' rights, and threatens violence. He worries that, even though some groups make gains through direct action, the end result is that everyone else begins to doubt the validity of the usual democratic procedures of relying on legislation and the courts. He condemns advocates of direct action like King for believing that the end (in this case, racial justice) justifies the means (direct action). Van Dusen argues that demonstrations often end violently and that an organized movement like King's can in the beginning win concessions through direct action but then end up extorting demands through threats and illegal uses of power.

> In contrast, King argues that nonviolent direct action preserves the peace by bringing hidden tensions and prejudices to the surface where they can be acknowledged and addressed. Direct action enhances democracy by changing its unjust laws and thereby strengthening it. Since direct action is entirely legal, to forgo it as a strategy for change would be to turn one's back on a basic democratic principle. Although it may inconvenience people, its end (a more just social order) is entirely justified by its means (direct action). King would no doubt insist that the occasional violence that follows direct action results always from aggressive, unlawful interference with demonstrations — interference sometimes led by police officers. He might also argue that neither anarchy nor extortion followed from his group's actions.

Notice that these paragraphs address each writer's argument separately. An alternative plan would have been to compare and contrast the two writers' arguments point by point.

CHECKLIST

Comparing and Contrasting Related Readings

To compare and contrast two related readings,

1. Read them both to decide on a basis or grounds for comparison or contrast.

(continued)

2. Reread and annotate one selection to identify points of comparison or contrast.

3. Reread the second selection, annotating for the points you have already identified.

4. Write up your analyses of the two selections, revising your analysis of the first selection to reflect any new insights you have gained. Or write a point-by-point comparison or contrast of the two selections.

EVALUATING THE LOGIC OF AN ARGUMENT

An argument includes a thesis backed by reasons and support. The **thesis** asserts a position on a controversial issue or a solution to a problem that the writer wants readers to accept. The **reasons** tell readers why they should accept the thesis, and the **support** (such as examples, statistics, authorities, analogies, and textual evidence) gives readers grounds for accepting it. For an argument to be considered logically acceptable, it must meet the three conditions of what we call the ABC test:

The ABC test

A. The reasons and support must be appropriate to the thesis.
B. The reasons and support must be believable.
C. The reasons and support must be consistent with one another as well as complete.

Testing for Appropriateness

To evaluate the logic of an argument, you first decide whether the argument's reasons and support are appropriate. To test for appropriateness, ask these questions: How does each reason or piece of support relate to the thesis? Is the connection between reasons and support and the thesis clear and compelling?

Readers most often question the appropriateness of reasons and support when the writer argues by analogy or by invoking authority. For example, in paragraph 2, King argues that when law and order fail to establish justice, "they become the dangerously structured dams that block the flow of social progress." The analogy asserts the following logical relationship: Law and order are to progress toward justice what a dam is to water. If you do not accept this analogy, the argument fails the test of appropriateness.

King uses both analogy and authority in paragraph 3: "Isn't this like condemning Socrates because his unswerving commitment to truth and his philosophical inquiries precipitated the act by the misguided populace in which they made him drink hemlock?" Not only must you judge the appropriateness of the analogy comparing the Greeks' condemnation of Socrates to the white moderates' condemnation of King, but you must also judge whether it is appropriate to accept Socrates as an authority. Since Socrates is generally respected for his teachings on justice, his words and actions are likely to be considered appropriate to King's situation in Birmingham.

Testing for Believability

Believability is a measure of your willingness to accept as true the reasons and support the writer gives in defense of a thesis.

To test for believability, ask: On what basis am I being asked to believe this reason or support is true? If it cannot be proved true or false, how much weight does it carry?

In judging facts, examples and anecdotes, statistics, and authorities, consider the following points:

Facts are statements that can be proved objectively to be true. The believability of facts depends on their *accuracy* (they should not distort or misrepresent reality), their *completeness* (they should not omit important details), and the *trustworthiness* of their sources (sources should be qualified and unbiased). King, for instance, asserts as fact that the African American will not wait much longer for racial justice (par. 8). His critics might question the factuality of this assertion by asking: Is it true of all African Americans? How does King know what African Americans will and will not do?

Examples and **anecdotes** are particular instances that may or may not make you believe a general statement. The believability of examples depends on their *representativeness* (whether they are truly typical and thus generalizable) and their *specificity* (whether particular details make them seem true to life). Even if a vivid example or gripping anecdote does not convince readers, it usually strengthens argumentative writing by clarifying the meaning and dramatizing the point. In paragraph 5 of the King excerpt, for example, King supports his generalization that some African American extremists are motivated by bitterness and hatred by citing the specific example of Elijah Muhammad's Black Muslim movement. Conversely, in paragraph 9, he refers to Jesus, Paul, Luther, and others as examples of extremists motivated by justice, love, and Christianity. These examples support his assertion that extremism is not in itself wrong and that any judgment of extremism must be based on its motivation and cause.

Statistics are numerical data. The believability of statistics depends on the *comparability* of the data (the price of apples in 1985 cannot be compared with the price of apples in 2012 unless the figures are adjusted to account for inflation), the *precision* of the methods employed to gather and analyze data (representative samples should be used and variables accounted for), and the *trustworthiness* of the sources.

Authorities are people to whom the writer attributes expertise on a given subject. Not only must such authorities be appropriate, as mentioned earlier, but they must be *credible* as well — that is, the reader must accept them as experts on the topic at hand. King cites authorities repeatedly throughout his essay. He refers to religious leaders (Jesus and Luther) as well as to American political leaders (Lincoln and Jefferson). These figures are likely to have a high degree of credibility among King's readers.

Testing for Consistency and Completeness

In looking for consistency, you should be concerned that all the parts of the argument work together and that they are sufficient to convince readers to accept the thesis or at least take it seriously. To test for consistency and completeness, ask: Are any of the reasons and support contradictory? Do they provide sufficient grounds for accepting the thesis? Does the writer fail to acknowledge, concede, or refute any opposing arguments or important objections?

A thoughtful reader might regard as contradictory King's characterizing himself first as a moderate and later as an extremist opposed to the forces of violence. (King attempts to reconcile this apparent contradiction by explicitly redefining extremism in par. 9.) Similarly, the fact that King fails to examine and refute every legal recourse available to his cause might allow a critical reader to question the sufficiency of his argument.

CHECKLIST

Evaluating the Logic of an Argument

To use the ABC test to determine whether an argument makes sense,

A. *Test for appropriateness* by checking that the reasons and support are clearly and directly related to the thesis.

B. *Test for believability* by deciding whether you can accept the reasons and support as likely to be true.

C. *Test for consistency and completeness* by deciding whether the argument has any contradictions and whether any important objections or opposing views have been ignored.

RECOGNIZING LOGICAL FALLACIES

Fallacies are errors or flaws in reasoning. Although essentially unsound, fallacious arguments seem superficially plausible and often have great persuasive power. Fallacies are not necessarily deliberate efforts to deceive readers. Writers may introduce a fallacy accidentally by not examining their own reasons or underlying assumptions, by failing to establish solid support, or by using unclear or ambiguous words. Here are some of the most common logical fallacies.

Slippery Slope

A **slippery-slope fallacy** occurs when someone asserts that if one thing happens, then a series of bad related consequences will *necessarily* follow. The name comes from the idea that if a person takes one step down a slippery slope, he or she cannot help sliding all the way to the bottom. Here's an example of this type of faulty reasoning: Antidrug campaigns often claim that smoking marijuana inevitably leads to the use of other illegal drugs. This is a fallacy because it assumes inevitability.

Post Hoc, Ergo Propter Hoc

One of the most common fallacies has the Latin name *post hoc, ergo propter hoc*, which means "after this, therefore because of this." A **post hoc fallacy** wrongly assumes that an event that occurs *after* another event is *caused* by the first event. In many cases, there is no connection at all between the events; in others, a connection does exist, but it is more complicated than the person making it realizes or admits. This fallacy in causal analysis often occurs when writers try to attribute to one cause something that has several or many causes. When complex issues are made to seem simple, look for this fallacy. Here's an example: "Some people argue that depictions of violence on television and in films cause teenagers to act violently. But most teenagers do not become violent even if they watch a great deal of violence on the screen." To avoid the *post hoc* fallacy, someone making this argument would have to show a clear connection between the amount of violence teenagers watch and the likelihood that they will become violent themselves. The person would also need to consider other possible causes, such as membership in gangs, alienation at school, parental abuse, and so on.

False Dilemma (Either/Or Reasoning)

One of the most common fallacies, the false dilemma or either/or reasoning, puts readers in the position of having to choose one of two options as if there were no other choices — but rarely in life are options narrowed down to only two. Writers who employ the **false dilemma fallacy** are usually trying to make the reader choose an option they favor by making the reader believe there are only two choices. Their reasoning avoids the complexities of most issues. Here's an example: Martin Luther King Jr., in paragraph 5 of the excerpt from "Letter from Birmingham Jail" (p. 511–12), refutes an either/or argument made by others. Arguing that the choice between a "force of complacency" or a force "of bitterness and hatred" is a false dilemma, King points out that there are other alternatives, among them the option of nonviolent protest that he represents.

Mistaking the Part for the Whole (Nonrepresentative Sample)

The **nonrepresentative sample fallacy** occurs when a writer assumes that if something is true of a part of a larger whole, then it is true of the whole, or vice versa. Sometimes this is indeed the case, but often it is not because the part is not representative — it does not have the typical characteristics — of the whole. This fallacy often occurs in connection with public opinion polls, especially online polls, when no effort is made to ensure that respondents accurately represent the characteristics of the larger group whose opinion they are said to reflect. Here's an example: Suppose that your school has the best football team in its conference. That does not necessarily mean that the quarterback, the kicker, or the defensive line is the best in the conference, because putting the various members of the team together gives the team as a whole qualities that are different from those of the individuals involved.

Hasty Generalization

When someone makes a **hasty generalization**, he or she leaps to a conclusion without providing enough evidence to support the leap. Here's an example: "Crime in this city is getting worse and worse. Just yesterday, two people were held up at ATMs downtown." Two crimes, no matter how serious, do not indicate that the overall *rate* of crime is rising. This may indeed be the case, but proving it would require statistics, not just a couple of examples.

Bandwagon Appeal

This fallacy occurs when someone appeals to the notion that "since everyone else does it, you should too." **Bandwagon appeals** are probably most common in advertising and political rhetoric. Here's an example: "A powerful new political tide is surging through America. Want to come together with millions of your fellow citizens in a movement to change our nation's priorities? Volunteer for Americans for National Renewal."

Ad Hominem (or Ad Personam) Attack

These Latin names mean "to the man" or "to the person." An **ad hominem** or **ad personam attack** occurs when writers attack the person who propounds the ideas with which they disagree, rather than attacking the ideas themselves. Certainly the character and credibility of the writer making the argument affect how persuasive a reader finds it, but they do not affect the underlying soundness of the argument. Here are two examples: "My opponent, one of the richest men in the state, wants to cut taxes for himself and his rich friends." "Of course my opponent favors raising corporate taxes. He's just a political hack who's never had to meet a payroll."

Straw Man (or Straw Person)

In a **straw-man fallacy**, the writer portrays an opponent's position as more extreme than it actually is so that it can be refuted more easily, as one would be able to knock down a straw scarecrow more easily than a live human being. As with many other fallacies, however, the line between what is and is not a straw-man argument is not always clear. Sometimes the writer claims that the opponent's position is part of a plan to achieve a more extreme position — and this claim could be considered either a straw-man argument (which would be fallacious) or a slippery-slope argument (which might be fallacious or might not). Here's an example: If a political candidate supports partial privatization of Social Security, an opponent who simply claims that the candidate "proposes doing away with Social Security" is creating a straw-man fallacy. If the opponent simply claims that "partial privatization would be a first step toward doing away with Social Security," this would be a slippery-slope argument — which may or may not be fallacious in itself but is not a straw-man argument because it does not actually misrepresent the candidate's position. Finally, if the opponent argues that the candidate "supports partial privatization as a first step toward doing away with Social Security," the reader would have to consider other evidence (such as other positions the candidate has taken or his or her voting record) to judge whether this is a fallacious straw-man argument or a sound slippery-slope one.

Begging the Question (Circular Reasoning)

In **begging the question**, the writer makes an argument that assumes the truth of what is theoretically the point at issue. In other words, to believe what the argument is trying to prove, the reader has to already believe it. Here's an example: "God created the world in seven days; this has to be true because the Bible says so, and the Bible is the word of God." This example shows why this fallacy is often called *circular reasoning*: the reasoning simply circles back to the original underlying claim that God is all-powerful. If the reader already believes that the Bible is the word of God and therefore is sufficient evidence for God's creation of the world in seven days, then there is no need to make this claim. If not, then he or she will not be convinced by this argument for it.

Red Herring

You can remember the **red herring fallacy** by the picture it presents — that of a dead fish being dragged across a trail to distract dogs from pursuing the scent of their real target. In this case, writers use irrelevant arguments to distract readers from the real issue, perhaps because their own argument is weak and they don't want the reader to notice. Red herrings often occur in political debates when one debater does not really want to address an issue raised by the other debater. Here's an example: "My opponent tries to blame my administration for the high price of prescription drugs, but he supports a government takeover of health care." That the opponent supports a government takeover of health care (whether true or false) has nothing to do with whether the policies of the speaker's administration are responsible for the high price of prescription drugs.

CHECKLIST

Recognizing Logical Fallacies

To determine whether the writer succumbs to any logical fallacies,

1. Annotate places in the text where you stop to think "wait a minute — that doesn't make sense" or where you think the writer has "gone too far."

2. Analyze these places to see if they represent any of the fallacies discussed in this section.

3. Write a few sentences exploring what you discover.

RECOGNIZING EMOTIONAL MANIPULATION

Writers often try to arouse emotions in readers to excite their interest, make them care, or move them to take action. There is nothing wrong with appealing to readers' emotions. What is wrong is manipulating readers with false or exaggerated appeals. Therefore, you should be suspicious of writing that is overly sentimental, that cites alarming statistics and frightening anecdotes, that demonizes others and identifies itself with revered authorities, or that uses potent symbols (for example, the American flag) or emotionally loaded words (such as *racist*).

King, for example, uses the emotionally loaded word *paternalistically* to refer to the white moderate's belief that "he can set the timetable for another man's freedom" (par. 1). In the same paragraph, King uses symbolism to get an emotional reaction from readers when he compares the white moderate to the "Ku Klux Klanner." To get readers to accept his ideas, he also relies on authorities whose names evoke the greatest respect, such as Jesus and Lincoln. But some readers might object that comparing his own crusade to that of Jesus is pretentious and manipulative. A critical reader might also consider King's discussion of African American extremists in paragraph 7 to be a veiled threat designed to frighten readers into agreement.

> **CHECKLIST**
>
> ## Recognizing Emotional Manipulation
>
> To assess whether emotional appeals are unfair and manipulative,
>
> 1. Annotate places in the text where you sense emotional appeals are being used.
>
> 2. Analyze the emotional appeals, explaining why you think they are or are not manipulative.

JUDGING THE WRITER'S CREDIBILITY

Writers try to persuade readers by presenting an image of themselves in their writing that will gain their readers' confidence. This image must be created indirectly, through the arguments, language, and system of values and beliefs expressed or implied in the writing. Writers establish credibility in their writing in three ways:

- By showing their knowledge of the subject

- By building common ground with readers

- By responding fairly to objections and opposing arguments

Testing for Knowledge

Writers demonstrate their knowledge through the facts and statistics they marshal, the sources they rely on for information, and the scope and depth of their understanding. You may not be sufficiently expert on the subject yourself to know whether the facts are accurate, the sources are reliable, and the understanding is sufficient. You may need to do some research to see what others say about the subject. You can also check **credentials** — the writer's educational and professional qualifications, the respectability of the publication in which the selection first appeared, and reviews of the writer's work — to determine whether the writer is a respected authority in the field. For example, King brings with him the authority that comes from being a member of the clergy and a respected leader of the Southern Christian Leadership Conference.

Testing for Common Ground

One way writers can establish **common ground** with their readers is by basing their reasoning on shared values, beliefs, and attitudes. They use language that includes their readers (*we*) and qualify their assertions to keep them from being too extreme. Above all, they acknowledge differences of opinion. You want to notice such appeals.

King creates common ground with readers by using the inclusive pronoun *we*, suggesting shared concerns between himself and his audience. Notice, however, his use of masculine pronouns and other references ("the Negro . . . he," "our brothers"). Although King addressed his letter to male clergy, he intended it to be published in the local newspaper, where it would be read by an audience of both men and women. By using language that excludes women — a common practice at the time the selection was written — King may have missed the opportunity to build common ground with more than half of his readers.

Testing for Fairness

Writers reveal their character by how they handle opposing arguments and objections to their argument. As a critical reader, pay particular attention to how writers treat possible differences of opinion. Be suspicious of those who ignore differences and pretend that everyone agrees with their viewpoints. When objections or opposing views are represented, consider whether they have been distorted in any way; if they are refuted, be sure they are challenged fairly — with sound reasoning and solid support.

One way to gauge the author's credibility is to identify the tone of the argument, for it conveys the writer's attitude toward the subject and toward the reader. Is the text angry? Sarcastic? Evenhanded? Shrill? Condescending? Bullying? Do you feel as if the writer is treating the subject — and you, as a reader — with fairness? King's tone might be characterized in different passages as patient (he doesn't lose his temper), respectful (he refers to white moderates as "people of good will"), or pompous (comparing himself to Jesus and Socrates).

CHECKLIST

Judging the Writer's Credibility

To assess an author's credibility,

1. As you read and annotate, consider the writer's knowledge of the subject, how well common ground is established, and whether the writer deals fairly with objections and opposing arguments.

2. Decide what in the essay you find credible and what you question.

11

Strategies for Research and Documentation

As many of the essays in *Reading Critically, Writing Well* show, writers often rely on research to expand and test their own ideas about a topic. This chapter offers advice on conducting research, evaluating potential sources, integrating source material you decide to use with your own writing, and documenting this material in an acceptable way.

PLANNING A RESEARCH PROJECT

To research and write about a topic effectively at the college level requires a plan. A clear sense of your rhetorical situation, as well as the practical needs of your research task (such as the due date and the level of detail required), will help you create one. Figure 11.1 below lists common elements that you will need to consider as you plan your research project, and also as you continue to find and evaluate sources and draft your project.

Define your research task and set a schedule.

Analyze your rhetorical situation.

- Determine your purpose.
- Analyze your audience to understand the interest and background your readers bring to the project, and analyze your attitude to determine how you want your readers to think of you.
- Determine the genre, or type, of research project you are creating, such as a proposal or laboratory report, and the expectations for research, writing, and design associated with this genre.

FIGURE 11.1 **Overview of a Research Project** (*continues*)

Understand the assignment.

- Check your syllabus or consult your instructor about the number and types of resources required, the length of the project, and so forth.
- Determine the final due date, and assign interim due dates to keep your project on track.

Establish a research log.

- Create a list of key words.
- Create a working bibliography, and annotate entries.
- Take notes on your sources.

Choose a topic, get an overview, and narrow your topic.

Choose a topic that is appropriate to the assignment and of interest to you and your readers.

- Consult with your instructor.
- Review textbooks and other course materials.
- Explore research studies, current publications, and Internet sites.

Get an overview, and narrow your topic (if necessary).

- Consult subject guides or a librarian to determine the availability of sources on your topic.
- Get necessary background by consulting encyclopedias and other general reference sources.
- Start a working bibliography to keep track of the bibliographic information of potential sources. (See pp. 544–46.)
- Draft questions to guide your research.

Search for in-depth information on your topic.

Conduct a search for sources, using carefully selected search terms.

- Check the library's resources (such as the catalog, databases, or home page) for books, articles, and multimedia.
- Check Internet sites for relevant Web sites, blogs, and groups.
- Keep a list of search terms in a research log, and annotate your working bibliography to keep track of sources.
- Add relevant sources to your working bibliography, and annotate entries to record the sources' main points and how you would use each source.
- Refine your research questions, and draft a working thesis.

FIGURE 11.1 **Overview of a Research Project**   *(continues)*

REFINE YOUR SEARCH.

Ask yourself questions like these:

- Is this what I expected to find?
- Am I finding enough?
- Am I finding too much?
- Do I need to modify my key words?
- Do I need to recheck background sources?
- Do I need to revise my research questions?
- Do I need to modify my working thesis?

Continue searching for relevant and reliable sources in response to your answers.

Evaluate your sources.

Determine the relevance of potential sources.

- Does the source explain terms or concepts or provide background?
- Does the source provide evidence to support your claims?
- Does the source offer alternative viewpoints or lend authority?

Determine the reliability of potential sources.

- Who wrote it?
- When was it published?
- Who published it?
- Is the source scholarly or popular (or something else)?
- Is the source printed or online?
- What does the source say?

Continue to evaluate and refine your search strategy based on your research results.

Use your research to support your ideas.

Use evidence from sources to support and refine your ideas.

- Synthesize ideas from multiple sources.
- Support your ideas with summaries, paraphrases, and quotations as appropriate.

Avoid plagiarism.

- Paraphrase and quote accurately to avoid plagiarism.
- Carefully integrate source material into your text.
- Cite sources using an appropriate citation style.

FIGURE 11.1   Overview of a Research Project

ANALYZING YOUR RHETORICAL SITUATION AND SETTING A SCHEDULE

Making your research manageable begins with defining the project's scope and goals. Begin by analyzing your *rhetorical situation*:

- What is your *purpose*? Is it to explain a concept, argue for a position, or analyze the causes of an event or a behavior?

- Who is your *audience* and what will their interests, attitudes, and expectations for the project be? How many and what kinds of resources does your audience expect you to consult? (For college research projects, your audience will likely be your instructor.)

- What *genre* is the research project, and how will that affect the kinds of sources you use? A student report in the social sciences may demand mainly *primary sources*, such as observations, interviews, and surveys. A student history essay normally requires mainly *secondary sources* (from published historians), but it may also include primary sources (such as interviews and documents from the time).

Also be sure you consider the following practical issues before you begin your research project:

- How long should the research project be?

- When is it due?

- Are any interim assignments required (such as an outline or an annotated bibliography)?

If you're not sure of the answers to these questions, ask your instructor to clarify the assignment or define any confusing terms so that you can work most efficiently.

Finally, set a schedule. Be sure to take into consideration the projects you have due for other classes as well as other responsibilities (to work or family, for example) or activities.

Some library Web sites may offer an online scheduler to help you with this process. Look for a link on your library's Web site.

CHOOSING A TOPIC AND GETTING AN OVERVIEW

Often students will be assigned a topic for a research project. If you are free to choose your own topic, consult course materials such as textbooks and handouts to get ideas, and consult your instructor to make sure your topic is appropriate.

Sometimes conducting an Internet search may give you an idea for a topic. Once you've chosen an appropriate topic, an overview can help you determine the kinds of issues you should consider. Reference sources, like encyclopedias and subject guides, can provide such an overview.

Using General Encyclopedias

General encyclopedias, such as *Britannica Online* and the *Columbia Encyclopedia*, provide basic information about many topics. Your library will likely have one or more general encyclopedias, available either on the shelf or through the library's digital portal. Often, encyclopedias are part of an online reference package. *Wikipedia*, too, offers a wealth of information, and it is often the first stop for students who are accustomed to consulting the Internet for information. Be aware, though, that *Wikipedia* is user generated rather than traditionally published, and for this reason, the quality of information found there can be inconsistent. Many instructors do not consider *Wikipedia* a reliable source, so you should ask your teacher for advice on consulting it at this stage. Whichever general encyclopedia you consult, bear in mind that general encyclopedias should be used only for an overview of a topic; the information is not sufficiently in-depth to be an appropriate resource for college research.

Using Specialized Encyclopedias and Other Overview Resources

Specialized, or **subject-specific**, **encyclopedias** cover topics in more depth than general encyclopedias do. Here are some examples:

> *Encyclopedia of Addictions*
> *Encyclopedia of Computer Science and Technology*
> *Encyclopedia of Global Warming and Climate Change*
> *Encyclopedia of Human Rights*
> *The Encyclopedia of Punk*
> *Grove Dictionary of Art* or *Grove Art Online*

In addition to providing an overview of a topic, specialized encyclopedias often include an explanation of issues related to the topic, definitions of specialized terminology, and selective bibliographies of additional sources. As starting points, specialized encyclopedias have two distinct advantages:

1. They provide a comprehensive introduction to your topic, including the key terms you will need to find relevant material in catalogs and databases.

2. They present subtopics, enabling you to see many possibilities for focusing your research.

Frequently, libraries prepare **guides to a subject** — lists of reliable sources on popular topics. A guide can offer very useful suggested resources for research, so check your library to find out if such a guide is available. You may also find resources that provide good overviews of topics, such as *CQ Researcher*. A reference librarian can help point you in the right direction.

NARROWING YOUR TOPIC AND DRAFTING RESEARCH QUESTIONS

After you have gotten a sense of the kinds of sources available on your topic, you may be ready to narrow it. Focus on a topic that you can explore thoroughly in the number of pages assigned and the length of time available. Finding your own take on a subject can help you narrow it as well.

You may also want to write questions about your topic and then focus in on one or two that can be answered through research. These will become the research questions that will guide your search for information. You may need to add or revise these questions as you conduct your search. The answers you devise can form the basis for your working thesis statement.

ESTABLISHING A RESEARCH LOG

One of the best ways to keep track of your research is to keep all your notes in one place, in a **research log**. Your log may be digital — a folder on your computer with files for notes, lists of keywords, and your working bibliography — or analog — a notebook with pockets for copies of sources.

Finding useful sources depends on determining the right **keywords** — words or phrases that describe your topic — to use while searching catalogs, databases, and the Internet. Start your list of keywords by noting the main words from your research question or working thesis. Look for useful terms in your search results, and use these to expand your list. Then add synonyms (or words with a similar meaning) to further expand your list.

For example, a student might start with a term like *home schooling* and then add *home education* or *home study*. After reading an article in an encyclopedia about her subject, she might also add *student-paced education* or *autonomous learning* to expand her scope.

CREATING A WORKING BIBLIOGRAPHY

A **working bibliography** is an ongoing record of the sources you discover as you research your subject. In your final project, you will probably not end up citing all the sources you list in your working bibliography, but recording the information you will need to cite a source — *as you identify it* — will save you time later. (Just be sure to double-check that your entries are accurate!)

Your working bibliography should include the following for each source:

- **Author(s) name(s)**

- **Title and subtitle**

- **Publication information:** A book's edition number (for example, *revised edition, 3rd ed.*), the name and location of the book's publisher, and the page numbers of the section you consulted; a periodical's name, volume and issue number or date, and the article's page numbers

- **Access information:** The call number of a book; the name of the database through which you accessed the source; the URL of the article (if available without a subscription), the URL of the source's home page, or the **DOI** (digital object identifier — a permanent identifying code that won't change over time or from database to database); the date you last accessed the source (for a Web page or Web site)

- **Medium of publication:** *Print* for printed books and articles, *Web* for online books and articles accessed through a database or found online, *DVD* for a film you watched at home, *MP3* for a music file, and so on

You can store your working bibliography in a computer file, in specialized bibliography software, or even on note cards. Each method has its advantages:

- A **computer file** allows you to move citations into order and incorporate the bibliography into your research project easily using standard software (such as Word or Excel).

- **Specialized bibliography software** (such as RefWorks, Zotero, or the Bedford Bibliographer) designed for creating bibliographies helps you create the citation in the specific citation style (such as MLA or APA) required by your discipline. These software programs are not perfect, however; you still need to double-check your citations against the models in the style manual you are using or in the MLA and APA citation sections of this chapter (pp. 581–98 and 599–608).

- **Index cards** (one card per source) are easy to arrange and rearrange and allow you to include notes on the cards themselves.

- A **notebook** allows you to keep everything — working bibliography, annotations, notes, copies of chapters or articles — all in one place.

This chapter presents two common documentation styles — one created by the Modern Language Association (MLA) and widely used in the humanities, and the other advocated by the American Psychological Association (APA) and used in the social sciences. Other disciplines have their own preferred styles of documentation. Confirm with your instructor which documentation style is required for your assignment so that you can follow that style for all the sources you put in your working bibliography.

ANNOTATING YOUR WORKING BIBLIOGRAPHY

An **annotated bibliography** provides an overview of sources that you have considered for your research project. Instructors sometimes ask students to create an annotated bibliography as a separate assignment to demonstrate that each student has done some preparatory research and has considered the usefulness of the sources he or she has found. But researchers frequently create annotated bibliographies for their own use, to keep a record of sources and their thoughts about them, especially when their research occurs over a lengthy period of time. Researchers sometimes also publish annotated bibliographies to provide others with a useful tool for beginning research projects of their own.

What an annotated bibliography includes depends on the researcher's writing situation. If the annotated bibliography is intended for publication, the emphasis is on the source's main claims and major supporting evidence. If the annotated bibliography is for the researcher's use (or if it is for a class assignment), the annotation may also include information about how the source could be used in the research project.

Most annotated bibliographies created for publication or a class assignment also include an introduction that explains the subject, purpose, and scope of the annotated references and may describe how and why the author selected those sources. For instance, an annotated bibliography featuring works about computer animation might have the following introduction:

> Early animations of virtual people in computer games tended to be oblivious to their surroundings, reacting only when hit by moving objects, and then in ways that were not always appropriate — that is, a small object might generate a large effect. In the past few years, however, computer animators have turned their attention to designing virtual people who react appropriately to events around them. The sources below represent the last two years' worth of publications on the subject from the *IEEE Xplore* database.

To annotate your working bibliography, answer these three questions about each source:

- What kind of source is this?

- What does the source say?

- How can I use the source?

Here are two example annotations:

MLA Style	APA Style
Drennan, Tammy. "Freedom of Education in Hard Times." *Alliance for the Separation of School and State*. SchoolandState.org, 26 Mar. 2010. Web. 9 May 2012.	Castelvecchi, D. (2008, August 30). Carbon tubes leave nano behind. *Science News*, *174*(5), 9-9. Retrieved from http://www.sciencenews.org
This Web page discusses the benefits of brainstorming ideas and tapping the community as options for overcoming economic hardships faced by home-schoolers. I have concerns about the reliability of this source, since it does not identify its members or funding sources. (It seems to be a one-woman show, with all the documents on the site written by Tammy Drennan.) But it's interesting because it is written by a home-schooling parent herself. I might be able to use this as evidence of the limitations of home schooling—a lack of resources such as lab equipment and subject-matter experts.	This news article, which describes a new, flexible lightweight material 30 times stronger than Kevlar and possibly useful for better bulletproof vests, provides evidence of yet another upcoming technology that might be useful to law enforcement. I can focus on the ways in which lighter, stronger bulletproof materials might change SWAT tactics—for instance, enabling officers to carry more gear, protect police vehicles, or blend into crowds better.

TAKING NOTES ON YOUR SOURCES

The summaries that you include in a working bibliography or that you make on a printed or digital copy of a source are useful reminders, but you should also make notes that analyze the text, that synthesize what you are learning with ideas you have gleaned elsewhere or with your own ideas, and that evaluate the quality of the source.

You will mine your notes for language to use in your draft, so be careful to

- summarize accurately, using your own words and sentence structures;
- paraphrase without borrowing the language or sentence structure of the source;
- quote exactly and place all language from the source in quotation marks.

You can take notes on a photocopy of a printed text or use comments or highlighting to annotate a digital text. Whenever possible, download, print, photocopy, or scan useful sources, so that you can read and make notes at your leisure and so that you can double-check your summaries, paraphrases, and quotations of sources against the original. These strategies, along with those discussed later in this chapter in the section Using Sources to Support Your Ideas (pp. 569–80), will keep you from plagiarizing inadvertently.

FINDING SOURCES

Students today are surrounded by a wealth of information. This wealth can make finding the information you need to support your ideas exciting, but it also means you will have to sift through possible sources carefully. What you are writing about and who will read your writing project will help you decide what types of sources will be most appropriate.

SEARCHING LIBRARY CATALOGS AND DATABASES

For most college research projects, finding appropriate sources starts with your library's home page, where you can

- use your library's catalog to find books, reference sources (such as encyclopedias and dictionaries), reports, documents, multimedia resources (such as films and audio recordings), and much more;

- use your library's databases to find articles in newspapers, magazines, and scholarly journals.

Some libraries may allow you to search catalogs and databases at once, all from the library's home page. Your library's home page is also the place to find information about the brick-and-mortar library—its floor plan, its hours of operation, and the journals it has available in print. You might even be able to find research guides, find links to what you need in other libraries, or get online help from a librarian.

Using Appropriate Search Terms

Just as with a search engine like *Google*, you can search a library catalog or database by typing your search terms—an author's name, the title of a work, a subject term or keyword, even a call number—into the search box. To search successfully, put yourself in the position of the people writing about your topic to figure out what words they might have used. If your topic is "ecology," for example, you may find information under the keywords *ecosystem*, *environment*, *pollution*, and *endangered species*, as well as a number of other related keywords, depending on the focus of the research.

Narrowing (or Expanding) Your Results

When conducting a search, you may get too few hits and have to broaden your topic. To broaden your search, try the following:

Replace a specific term with a more general term	Replace *sister* or *brother* with *sibling*
Substitute a synonym for one of your keywords	Replace *home study* with *home schooling* or *student-paced education*
Combine terms with *or* to get results with either or both terms	Search *home study or home schooling* to get results that include both *home study* and *home schooling*
Add a wildcard character, usually an asterisk (*) or question mark (?) (Check the search tips to find out which wildcard character is in use.)	Search *home school** or *home school?* to retrieve results for *home school, home schooling,* and *home-schooler*

Most often, you'll get too many hits and need to narrow your search. To narrow a search, try the following:

Add a specific term	Search not just *home schooling* but *home schooling statistics*
Combine search terms into phrases or word strings	Search *Home schooling in California*

In many cases, using phrases or word strings will limit your results to items that include *all* the words you have specified. In a few cases, you may need to insert quotation marks around the terms or insert the word *and* between them to create a search phrase or word string. Check the search tips for the database, catalog, or search engine you are using.

Finding Books (and Other Sources) through Your Library's Catalog

Books housed in academic library collections offer two distinct advantages to the student researcher:

1. They provide in-depth coverage of topics.

2. They are more likely to be published by reputable presses that strive for standards of accuracy and reliability.

To find books (as well as reference works and multimedia resources) on your topic, turn to your library's catalog. You can generally search the online catalog by author's name, title, keyword, or subject heading, and narrow your search by using the catalog's advanced search options.

Though you can search by keywords, most college libraries' catalog sources use special subject headings devised by the Library of Congress (the national library of the United States). Finding and using the subject headings most relevant to your search will make your research more productive. You can locate the subject headings your library uses by pulling up the record of a relevant book you have already found and looking for the list of words under the heading "Subject" or "Subject headings." Including these terms in your search may help you find additional relevant resources. Ask a librarian for help if you cannot identify the headings.

Finding Articles in Periodicals Using Your Library's Databases

Much of the information you will use to write your research project will come from articles in **periodicals**, publications such as newspapers, newsletters, magazines, or scholarly journals that are published at regular intervals. To locate relevant articles on your topic, start your search with one of your library's databases. Why not just start with a *Google* search? There are two very good reasons:

1. *Google* will pull up articles from any publication it indexes, from freely available personal Web sites to scholarly journals. Results rise to the top of the list based on a number of factors but not necessarily the reliability of the source. A *Google* search will turn up helpful sources, but you will need to spend a good deal of time sifting through the numerous hits you get to find sources that are both relevant and reliable. (*Google Scholar* may help you locate more reliable sources than those you might find through a typical *Google* search.)

2. Sources you find through *Google* may ask you to pay for access to articles, or they may require a subscription. Your library probably already subscribes to these sources on your behalf. Also adding databases to your search strategy will round out and diversify your search, and provide you with access to resources not available through a search engine such as *Google*.

Most college libraries subscribe at least to **general databases** and **subject-specific databases** as well as databases that index newspapers. General databases (such as *Academic OneFile*, *Academic Search Premier* or *Elite* or *Complete*, and *ProQuest Central*) index articles from both scholarly journals and popular magazines.[1] Subject-specific databases (such as *ERIC — Education Resources Information Center*, *MLA International Bibliography*, *PsycINFO*, and *General Science Full Text*) index articles only in their discipline. Newspaper databases (such as *Alt-Press Watch*, *LexisNexis Academic*, *National Newspaper Index*, and *ProQuest Newspapers*) index newspaper articles. For college-level research projects, you may use all three types of databases to find appropriate articles. (Note that many libraries also offer ways to search multiple databases at once.)

If your database search returns too many unhelpful results, use the search strategies discussed on p. 549 or use the database's advanced search options to refine your search. Many databases allow users to restrict results to articles published in academic journals, for example, or to articles that were published only

---

[1]The names of these databases change over time and vary from library to library, so ask your instructor or a reference librarian if you need help identifying a general database.

after a certain date. Use the Help option or ask a librarian for guidance about how the databases at your school work.

Increasingly, databases provide access to full-text articles, either in HTML or PDF format. When you have the option, choose the PDF format, as this will provide you with photographs, graphs, and charts in context, and you will be able to include the page numbers in your citation. If you find a citation to an article that is not accessible through a database, however, do not ignore it. Check with a librarian to find out how you can get a copy of the article.

SEARCHING FOR GOVERNMENT DOCUMENTS AND STATISTICAL INFORMATION ONLINE

Federal, state, and local governments make many of their documents available directly through the Web. For example, you can access statistical data about the United States through the U.S. Census Bureau's Web site (www.census.gov), and you can learn a great deal about other countries through the Web sites of the U.S. State Department (travel.state.gov) and the CIA (www.cia.gov/library /publications/the-world-factbook/geos/xx.html).

The Library of Congress provides a useful portal for finding government documents (federal, state, local, and international) through its Web site (www .loc.gov), and the U.S. Government Printing Office provides free electronic access to documents produced by the federal government through its FDsys Web page (www.gpo.gov/fdsys).

Some libraries have collections of government publications and provide access to government documents through databases or catalogs. Your library may also offer statistical resources and data sets. See if your library has a guide to these resources, or ask a librarian for advice. You can also find government documents online using an advanced *Google* search (www.google.com/advanced_search) and specifying *.gov* as the type of site or domain you want to search (see Figure 11.2 on the following page).

SEARCHING FOR WEB SITES AND INTERACTIVE SOURCES

By now, you are likely quite familiar with searching the Web. This section introduces you to some tools and strategies to use it more efficiently. But first, a few cautions:

- *Your research project will be only as credible as the sources you use.* Because search engines index Web sources without evaluating them, not all the results a search engine like *Google* generates will be reliable and relevant to your purposes.

FIGURE 11.2   **An Advanced Google Search**
Use *Google*'s advanced search (www.google.com/advanced_search) to locate information within specific sites or domains (such as *.edu* or *.gov*) or to narrow results to sites that include or exclude specific words, that appear only in English or another language, etc.

- **Web sources may not be stable.** A Web site that existed last week may no longer be available today, or its content may have changed. Be sure to record the information you need to cite a source when you first find it, as well as the date you find it.

- **Web sources must be documented.** No matter what your source — a library book, a scholarly article, or a Web site or Web page — you will need to cite and document your source in your list of works cited or references. If you are publishing your report online, check also to determine whether you will need permission to reproduce an image or any other elements.

Using *Google Scholar* and *Google Book Search*

Although you may use search engines like *Google* with great rapidity and out of habit, as a college researcher you are likely to find it worthwhile to familiarize yourself with other parts of the *Google* search site. Of particular interest to the academic writer are *Google Scholar* and *Google Book Search*. *Google Scholar* retrieves articles from a number of scholarly databases and a wide range of general-interest and scholarly books. *Google Book Search* searches both popular and scholarly books. Both *Google Scholar* and *Google Book Search* offer overviews and, in some cases, the full text of a source.

Note: Whatever search engine you use, always click on the link called *Help*, *Hints*, or *Tips* on the search tool's home page to find out more about the commands and advanced-search techniques it offers to narrow (or expand) your search.

Using Other Search Options

No matter how precisely you search the Web with a standard search engine, you may not hit on the best available resources. Starting your search from a subject guide, such as those provided by the *Internet Public Library* (www.ipl.org/div /special), *Infomine* (www.infomine.ucr.edu), or the librarians at your school, can direct you to relevant and reliable sources of online information.

Using Interactive Sources

Interactive sources, including blogs, wikis, RSS feeds, social networking sites (like *Facebook* and *Twitter*), and discussion lists, can also be useful sources of information, especially if your research project focuses on a current event or late-breaking news.

- **Blogs** are Web sites that are updated regularly, often many times a day. They are usually organized chronologically, with the newest posts at the top, and may contain links or news stories, but generally focus on the opinions of the blog host and visitors. Blogs by experts in the field are likely to be more informative than blogs by amateurs or fans.

- **Wikis** — of which *Wikipedia* is the best-known example — offer content contributed and modified collaboratively by a community of users. Wikis can be very useful for gleaning background information, but because (in most cases) anyone can write or revise wiki entries, many instructors will not accept them as reliable sources for college-level research projects. Use wikis cautiously.

- **RSS (Really Simple Syndication) feeds** aggregate frequently updated sites, such as news sites and blogs, into links in a single Web page or e-mail. Most search engines provide this service, as do sites such as *NewzCrawler* (www .newzcrawler.com) and *FeedDemon* (www.feeddemon.com). RSS feeds can be useful if you are researching news stories or political campaigns.

- **Social networking sites**, like *Facebook* and *Twitter*, allow users to create groups or pages on topics of interest or to follow the thoughts and activities of newsmakers.

- **Discussion lists** are electronic mailing lists that allow members to post comments and get feedback from others interested in the same topic. The most reliable discussion lists are moderated and attract experts on the topic. Many online communities provide some kind of indexing or search mechanism so that you can look for "threads" (conversations) related to your topic.

Although you need to evaluate carefully the information you find in all sources, you must be especially careful with information from social networking sites and discussion lists. However, such sources can provide up-to-the-minute information. Also be aware that whereas most online communities welcome guests and newcomers, others may perceive your questions as intrusive or naive. It may be useful to "lurk" (that is, just to read posts) before making a contribution.

CONDUCTING FIELD RESEARCH

In universities, government agencies, and the business world, **field research** can be as important as library research. In some majors, like education or sociology, as well as in service-learning courses, primary research projects are common. Even in the writing projects covered in Chapters 2–9, observations, interviews, and surveys may be useful or even necessary. As you consider how you might use field research in your writing projects, ask your instructor whether your institution requires you to obtain approval, and check the documentation sections that appear later in this chapter to learn about citing interviews you conduct yourself.

CONDUCTING OBSERVATIONAL STUDIES

Observational studies are commonly assigned in college writing, psychology, and sociology courses. To conduct an observational study effectively, follow these guidelines:

Planning an Observational Study

To ensure that your observational visits are productive, plan them carefully:

- **Arrange access if necessary.** Visits to a private location (such as a day-care center or school) require special permission, so be sure to arrange your visit in advance. When making your request, state your intentions and goals for your study directly and fully. You may be surprised at how receptive people can be to a college student on assignment. But have a fallback plan in case your request is refused or the business or institution places constraints on you that hamper your research.

- **Develop a hypothesis.** In advance, write down a tentative assumption about what you expect to learn from your study — your **hypothesis**. This will guide your observations and notes, and you can adjust your expectations in response to what you observe if necessary. Consider, too, how your presence will affect those whom you are observing, so you can minimize your impact or take the effect of your presence into consideration.

- **Consider how best to conduct the observation.** Decide where to place yourself to make your observations most effectively. Should you move around to observe from multiple vantage points, or will a single perspective be more productive?

Making Observations

Strategies for conducting your observation include the following:

- **Description:** Describe in detail the setting and the people you are observing. Note the physical arrangement and functions of the space, and the number, activities, and appearance of the people. Record as many details as possible, draw diagrams or sketches if helpful, and take photographs or videos if allowed (and if those you are observing do not object).

- **Narration:** Narrate the activities going on around you. Try initially to be an innocent observer: Pretend that you have never seen anything like this activity or place before, and explain what you are seeing step by step, even if what you are writing seems obvious. Include interactions among people, and capture snippets of conversations (in quotation marks) if possible.

- **Analysis and classification:** Break the scene down into its component parts, identify common threads, and organize the details into categories.

Take careful notes during your visit if you can do so unobtrusively, or immediately afterward if you can't. You can use a notebook and pencil, a laptop or tablet, or even a smartphone to record your notes. Choose whatever is least disruptive to those around you. You may need to use abbreviations and symbols to capture your observations on-site, but be sure to convert such shorthand into words and phrases as soon as possible after the visit so that you don't forget its significance.

Writing Your Observational Study

Immediately after your visit, fill in any gaps in your notes, and review your notes to look for meaningful patterns. You might find mapping strategies, such as clustering or outlining, useful for discovering patterns in your notes. Take some time to reflect on what you saw. Asking yourself questions like these might help:

- How did what I observed fit my own or my readers' likely preconceptions of the place or activity? Did my observations upset any of my preconceptions? What, if anything, seemed contradictory or out of place?

- What interested me most about the activity or place? What are my readers likely to find interesting about it?

- What did I learn?

Your purpose in writing about your visit is to share your insights into the meaning and significance of your observations. Assume that your readers have never been to the place, and provide enough detail for it to come alive for them. Decide on the perspective you want to convey, and choose the details necessary to convey your insights.

CONDUCTING INTERVIEWS

A successful interview involves careful planning before the interview, but it also requires keen listening skills and the ability to ask appropriate follow-up questions while conducting the interview. Courtesy and consideration for your subject are crucial at all stages of the process.

Planning the Interview

Planning an interview involves the following:

- **Choosing an interview subject.** For a profile of an individual, your interview will primarily be with one person; for a profile of an organization, you might interview several people, all with different roles or points of view. Prepare a list of interview candidates, as busy people might turn you down.

- **Arranging the interview.** Give your prospective subject a brief description of your project, and show some sincere enthusiasm for your project. Keep in mind that the person you want to interview will be donating valuable time to you, so call ahead to arrange the interview, allow your subject to specify the amount of time she or he can spare, and come prepared.

Preparing for the Interview

In preparation for the interview, consider your objectives:

- Do you want details or a general orientation (the "big picture") from this interview?
- Do you want this interview to lead you to interviews with other key people?
- Do you want mainly facts or opinions?
- Do you need to clarify something you have observed or read? If so, what?

Making an observational visit and doing some background reading beforehand can be helpful. Find out as much as you can about the organization or company (size, location, purpose, etc.), as well as the key people.

Good questions are essential to a successful interview. You will likely want to ask a few **closed questions** (questions that request specific information) and a number of **open questions** (questions that give the respondent range and flexibility and encourage him or her to share anecdotes, personal revelations, and expressions of attitudes):

Open Questions

What do you think about .... ?

Describe your reaction when ....
happened.

Tell me about a time you were ....

Closed Questions

How do you do .... ?

What does .... mean?

How was .... developed?

The best questions encourage the subject to talk freely but stick to the point. You may need to ask a follow-up question to refocus the discussion or to clarify a point, so be prepared. If you are unsure about a subject's answer, follow up by rephrasing that answer, prefacing it by saying something like "Let me see if I have this right" or "Am I correct in saying that you feel .... ?" Avoid forced-choice questions ("Which do you think is the better approach: .... or .... ?") and leading questions ("How well do you think .... is doing?").

During the Interview

Another key to good interviewing is flexibility. Ask the questions you have prepared, but also be ready to shift gears to take full advantage of what your subject can offer.

- **Take notes.** Take notes during the interview, even if you are recording your discussion. You might find it useful to divide several pages of a notebook into two columns or to set up a word processing file in two columns. Use the left-hand column to note details about the scene and your subject or about your impressions overall; in the right-hand column, write several questions and record answers to your questions. Remember that how something is said is as important as what is said. Look for material that will give texture to your writing — gesture, verbal inflection, facial expression, body language, physical appearance, dress, hair, or anything else that makes the person an individual.

- **Listen carefully.** Avoid interrupting your subject or talking about yourself; rather, listen carefully and guide the discussion by asking follow-up questions and probing politely for more information.

- **Be considerate.** Do not stay longer than the time you were allotted unless your subject agrees to continue the discussion, and show your appreciation for the time you have been given by thanking your subject and offering her or him a copy of your finished project.

Following the Interview

After the interview, do the following:

- **Reflect on the interview.** As soon as you finish the interview, find a quiet place to reflect on it and to review and amplify your notes. Asking yourself questions like these might help: What did I learn? What seemed contradictory or surprising about the interview? How did what was said fit my own or my readers' likely expectations about the person, activity, or place? How can I summarize my impressions?

Also make a list of any questions that arise. You may want to follow up with your subject for more information, but limit yourself to one e-mail or phone call to avoid becoming a bother.

- **Thank your subject.** Send your interview subject a thank-you note or e-mail within twenty-four hours of the interview. Try to reference something specific from the interview, something you thought was surprising or thought-provoking. And send your subject a copy of your finished project with a note of appreciation.

CONDUCTING SURVEYS

Surveys let you gauge the opinions and knowledge of large numbers of people. You might conduct a survey to gauge opinion in a political science course or to assess familiarity with a television show for a media studies course. You might also conduct a survey to assess the seriousness of a problem for a service-learning class or in response to an assignment to propose a solution to a problem (Chapter 9). This section briefly outlines procedures you can follow to carry out an informal survey, and it highlights areas where caution is needed. Colleges and universities have restrictions about the use and distribution of questionnaires, so check your institution's policy or obtain permission before beginning the survey.

Designing Your Survey

Use the following tips to design an effective survey:

- **Conduct background research.** You may need to conduct background research on your topic. For example, to create a survey on scheduling appointments at the student health center, you may first need to contact the health center to determine its scheduling practices, and you may want to interview health center personnel.

- **Focus your study.** Before starting out, decide what you expect to learn (your hypothesis). Make sure your focus is limited — focus on one or two important issues — so you can craft a brief questionnaire that respondents can complete quickly and easily and so that you can organize and report on your results more easily.

- **Write questions.** Plan to use a number of closed questions (questions that request specific information), such as two-way questions, multiple-choice questions, ranking scale questions, and checklist questions (see Figure 11.3 on the following page). You will also likely want to include a few open questions

This is a survey about scheduling appointments at the student health center. Your participation will help determine how long students have to wait to use the clinic's services and how these services might be more conveniently scheduled. The survey should take only 3 to 4 minutes to complete. All responses are confidential.

Two-way question

1. Have you ever made an appointment at the clinic?

   ❑ Yes   ❑ No

Filter

If you answered "No" to question 1, skip to question 5.

Multiple-choice questions

2. How frequently have you had to wait more than 10 minutes at the clinic for a scheduled appointment?

   ❑ Always   ❑ Usually   ❑ Occasionally   ❑ Never

3. Have you ever had to wait more than 30 minutes at the clinic for a scheduled appointment?

   ❑ Yes   ❑ No   ❑ Uncertain

4. Based on your experience with the clinic, how would you rate its system for scheduling appointments?

   ❑ 1 (poor)   ❑ 2 (adequate)   ❑ 3 (good)   ❑ 4 (excellent)

Ranking questions

5. Given your present work and class schedule, which times during the day (Monday through Friday) would be the most and least convenient for you to schedule appointments at the clinic? (Rank your choices from 1 for most convenient time to 4 for least convenient time.)

	1	2	3	4
	(most convenient)	(more convenient)	(less convenient)	(least convenient)
morning (7 a.m.–noon)	❑	❑	❑	❑
afternoon (noon–5 p.m.)	❑	❑	❑	❑
dinnertime (5–7 p.m.)	❑	❑	❑	❑
evening (7–10 p.m.)	❑	❑	❑	❑

6. If you have had an appointment at the student health center within the last six months, please evaluate your experience.

7. If you have had an appointment at the student health center within the last six months, please indicate what you believe would most improve scheduling of appointments at the clinic.

Open questions

8. If you have never had an appointment at the student health center, please indicate why you have not made use of this service.

Thank you for your participation.

FIGURE 11.3   **Sample Questionnaire: Scheduling at the Student Health Center** (questions that give respondents the opportunity to write their answers in their own words). Closed questions are easier to tally, but open questions are likely to provide you with deeper insight and a fuller sense of respondents' opinions. Whatever questions you develop, be sure that you provide all the answer options your respondents are likely to want, and make sure your questions are clear and unambiguous.

- **Identify the population you are trying to reach.** Even for an informal study, you should try to get a reasonably representative group. For example, to study satisfaction with appointment scheduling at the student health center, you would need to include a representative sample of all the students at the school — not only those who have visited the health center. Determine the demographic makeup of your school, and arrange to reach out to a representative sample.

- **Design the questionnaire.** Begin your questionnaire with a brief, clear introduction stating the purpose of your survey and explaining how you intend to use the results. Give advice on answering the questions, estimate the amount of time needed to complete the questionnaire, and — unless you are administering the survey in person — indicate the date by which completed surveys must be returned. Organize your questions from least to most complicated or in any order that seems logical, and format your questionnaire so that it is easy to read and complete.

- **Test the questionnaire.** Ask at least three readers to complete your questionnaire before you distribute it. Time them as they respond, or ask them to keep track of how long they take to complete it. Discuss with them any confusion or problems they experience. Review their responses with them to be certain that each question is eliciting the information you want it to elicit. From what you learn, revise your questions and adjust the format of the questionnaire.

Administering the Survey

The more respondents you have, the better, but constraints of time and expense will almost certainly limit the number. As few as twenty-five could be adequate for an informal study, but to get twenty-five responses, you may need to solicit fifty or more participants.

You can conduct the survey in person or over the telephone; use an online service such as *SurveyMonkey* (surveymonkey.com) or *Zoomerang* (zoomerang .com); e-mail the questionnaires; or conduct the survey using a social media site such as *Facebook*. You may also distribute surveys to groups of people in class or around campus and wait to collect their responses.

Each method has its advantages and disadvantages. For example, face-to-face surveys allow you to get more in-depth responses, but participants may be unwilling to answer personal questions face to face. Though fewer than half the surveys you solicit using survey software are likely to be completed (your invitations may wind up in a spam folder), online software will tabulate responses automatically.

Writing the Report

When writing your report, include a summary of the results, as well as an interpretation of what the results mean.

- **Summarize the results.** Once you have the completed questionnaires, tally the results from the closed questions. (If you conducted the survey online, this will have already been done for you.) You can give the results from the closed questions as percentages, either within the text of your report or in one or more tables or graphs. Next, read all respondents' answers to each open question to determine the variety of responses they gave. Summarize the responses by classifying the answers. You might classify them as positive, negative, or neutral or by grouping them into more specific categories. Finally, identify quotations that express a range of responses succinctly and engagingly to use in your report.

- **Interpret the results.** Once you have tallied the responses and read answers to open questions, think about what the results mean. Does the information you gathered support your hypothesis? If so, how? If the results do not support your hypothesis, where did you go wrong? Was there a problem with the way you worded your questions or with the sample of the population you contacted? Or was your hypothesis in need of adjustment?

- **Write the report.** Reports in the social sciences use a standard format, with headings introducing the following categories of information:

  - **Abstract:** A brief summary of the report, usually including one sentence summarizing each section

  - **Introduction:** Includes context for the study (other similar studies, if any, and their results), the question or questions the researcher wanted to answer and why this question (or these questions) is important, and the limits of what the researcher expected the survey to reveal

  - **Methods:** Includes the questionnaire, identifies the number and type of participants, and describes the methods used for administering the questionnaire and recording data

  - **Results:** Includes the data from the survey, with limited commentary or interpretation

  - **Discussion:** Includes the researcher's interpretation of results, an explanation of how the data support the hypothesis (or not), and the conclusions the researcher has drawn from the research

EVALUATING SOURCES

As soon as you start your search for sources, you should begin evaluating what you find not only to decide whether they are relevant to your research project but also to determine how credible or reliable they are.

CHOOSING RELEVANT SOURCES

Sources are **relevant** when they help you achieve your aims with your readers. Relevant sources may

- explain terms or concepts;

- provide background information;

- provide evidence in support of your claims;

- provide alternative viewpoints or interpretations;

- lend authority to your point of view.

A search for sources may reveal many seemingly relevant books and articles — more than any researcher could ever actually consult. A search on the term *home schooling* in one database, for example, got 1,172 hits. Obviously, a glance at all the hits to determine which are most relevant would take far too much time. To speed up the process, resources, such as library catalogs, databases, and search engines, provide tools to narrow the results. For example, in one popular all-purpose database, you can limit results by publication date, language, and publication or source type, among other options. (Check the Help screen to learn how to use these tools.)

After you have identified a reasonable number of relevant sources, examine the sources themselves:

- Read the preface, introduction, or conclusion of books, or the first or last few paragraphs of articles, to determine which aspect of the topic is addressed or which approach to the topic is taken. To obtain a clear picture of a topic, researchers need to consider sources that address different aspects of the topic or take different approaches.

- Look at the headings or references in articles, or the table of contents and index in books, to see how much of the content relates specifically to your topic.

- Consider the way the source is written: Sources written for general readers may be accessible but may not analyze the subject in depth. Extremely specialized works may be too technical. Poorly written sources may be unreliable. (See Choosing Reliable Sources, below, for more on scholarly versus popular sources and for a discussion of why researchers should avoid sources that are poorly written or riddled with errors.)

If close scrutiny leaves you with too few sources — or too many sources from too few perspectives — conduct a search using additional or alternative keywords, or explore links to related articles, look at the references in a particularly useful article, or look for other sources by an author whose work you find useful.

CHOOSING RELIABLE SOURCES

Choosing relevant sources is crucial to assembling a useful working bibliography. Determining which of those relevant sources is also likely to be reliable is even more important. To determine reliability, ask yourself the questions below.

Who Wrote It?

Consider, first, whether the author is an expert in the field. The fact that someone has a PhD in astrophysics is no indication that he or she will be an expert in military history, for example, so be careful that the area of expertise is directly relevant to the topic.

To determine the author's area of expertise, look for the author's professional affiliation (where he or she works or teaches). This may be indicated at the bottom of the first page of an article or in an "About the Author" section in a book or on a Web site. Frequently, Googling the author will also reveal the author's affiliation, but double-check to make sure the affiliation is current and that you have located the right person. You may also consult a biographical reference source available through your library. Looking to see what other works the author has published, and with whom, can also help you ascertain his or her areas of expertise.

Contributors to blogs, wikis, and online discussion forums may or may not be experts in the field. Determine whether the site screens contributors, and double-check any information taken from sites for which you cannot determine the credentials of contributors.

Also consider the author's perspective. Most writing is not neutral or objective and does not claim to be. Knowledge of the author's perspective enables you to assess bias and determine whether the author's perspective affects the presentation of his or her argument. To determine the author's perspective, look for the main point and ask yourself questions like these:

- What evidence does the author provide to support this point? Is it from authoritative sources? Is it persuasive?

- Does the author make concessions to or refute opposing arguments?

- Does the author avoid fallacies, confrontational phrasing, and loaded words?

When Was It Published?

In general, especially when you are writing about science or technology, current events, or emerging trends, you should consult the most up-to-date sources available on your subject. The date of publication for articles you locate should be indicated in your search results. For a print book, look for the copyright date on the copyright page (usually on the back of the title page); for an e-book, look for the copyright date at the beginning or end of the electronic file. If your source is a Web site, consider when it, and the content within it, was last updated (often indicated at the bottom of the Web page or home page).

You may also need older, "classic" sources that establish the principles, theories, and data on which later work is based and may provide a useful perspective for evaluating other works. To determine which sources are classics, note the ones that are cited most often in encyclopedia articles, lists of works cited or references, and recent works on the subject. You may also want to consult your instructor or a librarian to help you determine which works are classics in your field.

Is the Source Scholarly, Popular, or for a Trade Group?

Scholarly sources (whether books or articles) are written by and for experts in a field of study, frequently professors or academic researchers. They can be challenging to read and understand because they use the language of the field and terminology that may be unfamiliar to those outside the discipline, but they are considered reliable because the contents are written by specialists and **peer-reviewed** (reviewed by specialists) before publication. Scholarly sources also tend to delve deeply into a subject, often a narrowly defined subject. Scholarly sources may be published by a university press, a scholarly organization, or a commercial publisher (such as Kluwer Academic or Blackwell). Though scholarly sources may provide an overview of the subject, they generally focus on a specific issue or argument and generally contain a great deal of original research.

In contrast, **popular sources** are written to entertain and educate the general public. For the most part, they are written by journalists who have conducted research and interviewed experts. They may include original research, especially on current events or emerging trends. Mainly, though, they report on and summarize original research and are written for interested, nonspecialist readers.

Of course, popular sources range widely along the reliability spectrum. Highly respected newspapers and magazines, such as the *New York Times*, the *Guardian*, the *Economist*, and *Harper's Magazine*, publish original research on news and culture. These newspapers and magazines check facts carefully and are often considered appropriate sources for research projects in entry-level courses (although you should check with your instructor to find out her or his expectations). Magazines that focus on celebrity gossip, such as *People* and *Us*

Weekly, are unlikely to be considered appropriate sources for a college-level research project. Table 11.1 summarizes some of the important differences between scholarly journals and popular magazines.

Trade publications—periodicals that report on news and technical advances in a specific industry—are written for those employed in the industry and include such titles as *Advertising Age, World Cement,* and *American Machinist.* Some trade publications may be appropriate for college research projects, especially in the sciences, but keep in mind that these publications are intended for a specialist audience and may focus on marketing products to professionals in the field.

TABLE 11.1   Scholarly Journals versus Popular Magazines

Scholarly Journals	Popular Magazines
Journals are usually published 4 to 6 times per year.	Magazines are usually published weekly or monthly.
Articles are usually written by scholars (with *PhD* or academic affiliations after their names).	Authors of articles are journalists but may quote experts.
Many articles have more than one author.	Most articles have a single author.
In print journals, the title page often appears on the cover, and the covers frequently lack artwork.	Photographs, usually in color, appear on the covers of most print magazines.
Articles may include charts, tables, figures, and quotations from other scholarly sources.	Articles frequently include color pictures and sidebars.
An abstract (summary) of the article may appear on the first page.	A headline or engaging description may precede the article.
Most articles are fairly long—5 to 20 pages.	Most articles are fairly short—1 to 5 pages.
Articles cite sources and provide a bibliography (a list of works cited or references).	Articles rarely include a list of works cited or references but may mention or quote experts.

Who Published It?

Determining who published or sponsored a source you are considering can help you gauge its reliability and ascertain the publication's slant (or point of view). Look to see whether the source was published by a commercial publisher (such as St. Martin's or Random House); a university press (such as the University of Nebraska Press); a corporation, an organization, or an interest group (such as the RAND Corporation, the World Wildlife Fund, or the National Restaurant Association); a government agency (such as the Internal Revenue Service or the U.S. Census Bureau); or the author on his or her own. Determining the publisher or sponsor is particularly important for material published on the Web.

If your source is a Web page, look at the URL (uniform resource locator) to find its top-level domain, which is indicated by a suffix. Some of the most useful ones are listed here:

.gov   U.S. federal government and some state or local government institutions

.org   nonprofit organizations

.edu   educational institutions

.com   businesses and commercial enterprises

.net   usually businesses or organizations associated with networks

.mil   the U.S. military

For the most part, *.gov* and *.edu* are the most likely to offer reliable sources of information for a college research project. However, sources with any of these domains may vary in reliability. For example, a file with a *.com* suffix may offer a highly reliable history of a corporation and be an appropriate source for someone writing a history of corporate America, whereas a file with an *.edu* suffix may have been posted by a student or by a faculty member outside his or her area of expertise. It is essential to look at Web sites carefully. Determine who sponsors the site: Is it a business, a professional group, a private organization, an educational institution, a government agency, or an individual? Look for a link, usually at the top or the bottom of the home page, called something like "Who We Are" or "About Us." If you cannot determine who sponsors a site, carefully double-check any information you find there.

Consider, too, checking how often the Web site has been linked to and the types of links provided by the Web site. That a site has been linked to repeatedly does not guarantee reliability, but the information may be helpful in conjunction with other recommendations in this chapter. To determine the number of times a Web page has been linked to, type *link:* plus the URL into a *Google* search box. To check the links provided, click on them and apply the criteria in this chapter.

If the source was published by a commercial publisher, check out the publisher's Web site, and ask yourself questions like these:

- Does the publisher offer works from a single perspective or from multiple perspectives?

- Do the works it publishes cover a wide variety of topics or focus on a particular topic?

- Does the publisher's Web site host links to a particular type of site?

The Web sites of book publishers may offer a link to a catalog. If so, look at the works it lists. Does the publisher seem to publish works on a particular topic or from a particular point of view? Does the publisher generally offer popular, academic, or professional works?

If your source is a periodical, consider whether it focuses on a particular topic or offers a single point of view. In addition to looking at the article you are considering, visit the publisher's Web site, which may help you determine this.

How Is the Source Written?

Most works that are published professionally (including popular newspapers and magazines, as well as scholarly journals and trade magazines) will have been edited carefully. These sources will generally avoid errors of grammar, punctuation, and spelling. Web sites sponsored by professional organizations, too, will generally avoid these kinds of errors. Personal Web sites, however, are unlikely to have been professionally edited and fact-checked. If a Web site is riddled with errors, be very careful to double-check any information you take from that site.

What Does the Source Say?

Finally, and perhaps most importantly, consider the source itself. Answering the following questions can help you determine whether the source is worth consideration:

- What is the intended audience of the source? Does the source address an audience of experts, or is it intended for a general audience?

- What is the purpose of the source? Does it review a number of different positions, or does it argue for a position of its own? If it makes its own argument, analyze the argument closely.

- What is the tone of the source? Is the tone reasonable? Does the source respond to alternative viewpoints, and are those responses logical and reasonable?

- What evidence is offered to support the argument? Is the evidence relevant and reliable? What kinds of citations or links does the source supply?

USING SOURCES TO SUPPORT YOUR IDEAS

Writing a college research project requires you to

- analyze sources to understand the arguments those sources are making, the information they are using to support their claims, and the ways those arguments and the supporting evidence they use relate to your topic;

- synthesize information from sources to support, extend, and challenge your own ideas;

- integrate information from sources with your own ideas to contribute something new to the "conversation" on your topic;

- document your sources using an appropriate documentation style.

SYNTHESIZING SOURCES

Synthesizing means making connections among ideas from texts and from your own experience. Once you have analyzed a number of sources on your topic, consider questions like the following to help you synthesize ideas and information:

- Do any of the sources you read use similar approaches or come to similar conclusions? What common themes do they explore? Do any of them use the same evidence (facts, statistics, research studies, examples) to support their claims?

- What differentiates the sources' various positions? Where do the writers disagree, and why? Does one writer seem to be responding to or challenging one or more of the others?

- Do you agree with some sources and disagree with others? What makes one source more convincing than the others? Do any of the sources you have read offer support for your claims? Do any of them challenge your conclusions? If so, can you refute the challenge or do you need to concede a point?

Sentence strategies like the following can help you clarify where you differ from or agree with the sources you have read:

- ▶ A study by X supports my position by demonstrating that ....
- ▶ X and Y think this issue is about .... But what is really at stake here is ....
- ▶ X claims that .... But I agree with Y, who argues that ....
- ▶ On this issue, X and Y say .... Although I understand and to some degree sympathize with their point of view, I agree with Z that this is ultimately a question of ....

To learn more about synthesizing, see Chapter 10, pp. 520–21.

The paragraph from Patrick O'Malley's paper on p. 572 shows how ideas and information from sources can be synthesized to support the writer's claim.

ACKNOWLEDGING SOURCES AND AVOIDING PLAGIARISM

In your college writing, you will be expected to use and acknowledge **secondary sources** — books, articles, published or recorded interviews, Web sites, computer bulletin boards, lectures, and other print and nonprint materials — in addition to your own ideas, insights, and field research. The following information will help you decide what does and does not need to be acknowledged and will enable you to avoid plagiarizing from sources inadvertently.

Determining What Does (and Does Not) Need to Be Acknowledged

For the most part, any ideas, information, or language you borrow from a source — whether the source is in print or online — must be acknowledged by including an in-text citation and an entry in your list of works cited (MLA style) or references (APA style). The only types of information that do not require acknowledgment are common knowledge (for example, John F. Kennedy was assassinated in Dallas), facts widely available in many sources (U.S. presidents used to be inaugurated on March 4 rather than January 20), well-known quotations ("To be or not to be / That is the question"), and material you created or gathered yourself, such as photographs that you took or data from surveys that you conducted.

Remember that you need to acknowledge the source of any **visual** (photograph, table, chart, graph, diagram, drawing, map, screen shot) that you did not create yourself as well as the source of any information that you used to create your own visual. (You should also request permission from the source of a visual if your essay is going to be posted online without password protection.) When in doubt about whether you need to acknowledge a source, do so.

The documentation guidelines later in this chapter present two styles for citing sources: MLA and APA. Whichever style you use, the most important thing is that your readers be able to tell where words or ideas that are not your own begin and end. You can accomplish this most readily by taking and transcribing notes carefully, by placing parenthetical source citations correctly, and by separating your words from those of the source with **signal phrases** such as "According to Smith," "Peters claims," and "As Olmos asserts." (When you cite a source for the first time in a signal phrase, use the author's full name; after that, use just the last name.)

Avoiding Plagiarism

When you use material from another source, you need to acknowledge the source, usually by citing the author and page or publication date in your text and including a list of works cited or references at the end of your essay. Failure to acknowledge sources — even by accident — constitutes **plagiarism**, a serious transgression. By citing sources correctly, you give appropriate credit to the originator of the words and ideas you are using, offer your readers the information they need to consult those sources directly, and build your own credibility.

Writers — students and professionals alike — occasionally fail to acknowledge sources properly. Students sometimes mistakenly assume that plagiarizing occurs only when another writer's exact words are used without acknowledgment. In fact, plagiarism can also apply to paraphrases as well as to such diverse forms of expression as musical compositions, visual images, ideas, and statistics. Therefore, keep in mind that you must indicate the source of any borrowed information, idea, language, or visual or audio material you use in your essay, whether you have paraphrased, summarized, or quoted directly from the source or have reproduced it or referred to it in some other way.

Remember especially the need to document electronic sources fully and accurately. Perhaps because it is so easy to access and distribute text and visuals online and to copy material from one electronic document and paste it into another, some students do not realize, or may forget, that information, ideas, and images from electronic sources require acknowledgment in even more detail than those from print sources. At the same time, the improper (unacknowledged) use of online sources is often very easy for readers to detect.

If you are confused about what is and what is not plagiarism, be sure to ask your instructor.

USING INFORMATION FROM SOURCES TO SUPPORT YOUR CLAIMS

When writing a research project, remember that the goal is to use the ideas and information you find in sources to support your own ideas. Make sure that each of your supporting paragraphs does three things:

1. States a claim that supports your thesis;

2. Provides evidence that supports your claim;

3. Explains to readers how the evidence supports your claim.

Consider this paragraph from Patrick O'Malley's proposal in Chapter 9, "More Testing, More Learning" (pp. 483–88):

States claim

> The main reason professors should give frequent exams is that when they do and when they provide feedback to students on how well they are doing, students learn more in the course and perform better on major exams, projects, and papers. It makes sense that in

Explains how evidence supports claim

> a challenging course containing a great deal of material, students will learn more of it and put it to better use if they have to apply or "practice" it frequently on exams, which also helps them find out how much they are learning and what they need to go over again.

Provides evidence

> A 2006 study reported in *Psychological Science* journal concluded that "taking repeated tests on material leads to better long-term retention than repeated studying," according to the study's coauthors, Henry L. Roediger and Jeffrey Karpicke (ScienceWatch .com, 2008). When asked what the impact of this breakthrough research would be, they responded: "We hope that this research may be picked up in educational circles as a way to improve educational practices, both for students in the classroom and as a study strategy outside of class." The new field of mind, brain, and education research advocates the use of "retrieval testing." For example, research by Karpicke and Blunt (2011) published in *Science* found that testing was more effective than other, more traditional methods of studying both for comprehension and for analysis. Why retrieval testing works is not known. A UCLA psychologist, Robert Bjork, speculates that it may be effective because "when we use our memories by retrieving things, we change our access" to that information. "What we recall," therefore, "becomes more recallable in the future" (qtd. in Belluck, 2011).

O'Malley connects this body paragraph to his thesis by beginning with the transition *The main reason* and by repeating the phrase *perform better* from his forecasting statement. He synthesizes information from a variety of sources. For example, he uses quotations from some sources and a summary of another to provide evidence. And he doesn't merely stitch quotations and summary together; rather, he explains how the evidence supports his claim by stating that it "makes sense" that students "apply or 'practice'" what they learn on frequent exams.

Deciding Whether to Quote, Paraphrase, or Summarize

As illustrated in O'Malley's paragraph above, writers integrate supporting evidence by quoting, paraphrasing, or summarizing information or ideas from sources. This section provides guidelines for deciding when to use each of these three methods and how to quote, paraphrase, and summarize effectively. Note that all examples in this section follow MLA style for in-text citations, which is explained in detail later in this chapter.

As a rule, quote only in these situations:

- When the wording of the source is particularly memorable or vivid or expresses a point so well that you cannot improve it;

- When the words of reliable and respected authorities would lend support to your position;

- When you wish to cite an author whose opinions challenge or vary greatly from those of other experts;

- When you are going to discuss the source's choice of words.

Paraphrase passages whose details you wish to use but whose language is not particularly striking. Summarize any long passages whose main points you wish to record as support for a point you are making.

Altering Quotations Using Italics, Ellipses, and Brackets

Quotations should duplicate the source exactly, even if they contain spelling errors. Add the notation *sic* (Latin for "thus") in brackets immediately after any such error to indicate that it is not your error but your source's. As long as you signal them appropriately, you may make changes to

- emphasize particular words;

- omit irrelevant information;

- insert information necessary for clarity;

- make the quotation conform grammatically to your sentence.

Using Italics for Emphasis. You may italicize any words in the quotation that you want to emphasize; add a semicolon and the words *emphasis added* (in regular type, not italicized or underlined) to the parenthetical citation:

> In her 2001 exposé of the struggles of the working class, Ehrenreich writes, "The wages Winn-Dixie is offering—$6 *and a couple of dimes to start with*—are not enough, I decide, to compensate for this indignity" (14; emphasis added).

Using Ellipsis Marks for Omissions. You may decide to omit words from a quotation because they are not relevant to the point you are making. When you omit words from within a quotation, use **ellipses**—three spaced periods (...)—in place of the missing words. When the omission occurs within a sentence, include a space before the first ellipsis mark and after the last mark:

Hermione Roddice is described in Lawrence's *Women in Love* as a "woman of the new school, full of intellectuality and . . . nerve-worn with consciousness" (17).

When the omission falls at the end of a sentence, place a period *directly after* the final word of the sentence, followed by a space and three spaced ellipsis marks:

But Grimaldi's commentary contends that for Aristotle rhetoric, like dialectic, had "no limited and unique subject matter upon which it must be exercised. . . . Instead, rhetoric as an art transcends all specific disciplines and may be brought into play in them" (6).

A period plus ellipses can indicate the omission not just of the rest of a sentence but also of whole sentences, paragraphs, or even pages.

When a parenthetical reference follows the ellipses at the end of a sentence, place the three spaced periods after the quotation, and place the sentence period after the final parenthesis:

But Grimaldi's commentary contends that for Aristotle rhetoric, like dialectic, had "no limited and unique subject matter upon which it must be exercised. . . . Instead, rhetoric as an art transcends all specific disciplines . . ." (6).

When you quote only single words or phrases, you do not need to use ellipses because it will be obvious that you have left out some of the original:

More specifically, Wharton's imagery of suffusing brightness transforms Undine before her glass into "some fabled creature whose home was in a beam of light" (21).

For the same reason, you need not use ellipses if you omit the beginning of a quoted sentence unless the rest of the sentence begins with a capitalized word and still appears to be a complete sentence.

Using Brackets for Insertions or Changes.   Use brackets around an insertion or a change needed to make a quotation conform grammatically to your sentence, such as a change in the form of a verb or pronoun or in the capitalization of the first word of the quotation. In this example from an essay on James Joyce's short story "Araby," the writer adapts Joyce's phrases "we played till our bodies glowed" and "shook music from the buckled harness" to fit the grammar of her sentences:

In the dark, cold streets during the "short days of winter," the boys must generate their own heat by "play[ing] till [their] bodies glowed." Music is "[shaken] from the buckled harness" as if it were unnatural, and the singers in the market chant nasally of "the troubles in our native land" (30).

You may also use brackets to add or substitute explanatory material in a quotation:

Guterson notes that among Native Americans in Florida, "education was in the home; learning by doing was reinforced by the myths and legends which repeated the basic value system of their [the Seminoles'] way of life" (159).

Some changes that make a quotation conform grammatically to another sentence may be made without any signal to readers:

- A period at the end of a quotation may be changed to a comma if you are using the quotation within your own sentence.

- Double quotation marks enclosing a quotation may be changed to single quotation marks when the quotation is enclosed within a longer quotation.

Adjusting the Punctuation within Quotations. Although punctuation within a quotation should reproduce the original, some adaptations may be necessary. Use single quotation marks for quotations within the quotation:

Original from David Guterson's **Family Matters** *(pp. 16–17)*

E. D. Hirsch also recognizes the connection between family and learning, suggesting in his discussion of family background and academic achievement "that the significant part of our children's education has been going on outside rather than inside the schools."

Quoted version

Guterson claims that E. D. Hirsch "also recognizes the connection between family and learning, suggesting in his discussion of family background and academic achievement 'that the significant part of our children's education has been going on outside rather than inside the schools'" (16–17).

If the quotation ends with a question mark or an exclamation point, retain the original punctuation:

"Did you think I loved you?" Edith later asks Dombey (566).

If a quotation ending with a question mark or an exclamation point concludes your sentence, retain the question mark or exclamation point, and put the parenthetical reference and sentence period outside the quotation marks:

Edith later asks Dombey, "Did you think I loved you?" (566).

Avoiding Grammatical Tangles. When you incorporate quotations into your writing, and especially when you omit words from quotations, you run the risk of creating ungrammatical sentences. Avoid these three common errors:

- verb incompatibility

- ungrammatical omissions

- sentence fragments

Verb incompatibility occurs when the verb form in the introductory statement is grammatically incompatible with the verb form in the quotation. When your quotation has a verb form that does not fit in with your text, it is usually possible to use just part of the quotation, thus avoiding verb incompatibility:

The narrator suggests his bitter disappointment when "~~I saw myself~~ as a creature [*he describes seeing himself "*] driven and derided by vanity" (35).

As this sentence illustrates, use the present tense when you refer to events in a literary work.

Ungrammatical omissions may occur when you delete text from a quotation. To avoid this problem, try adapting the quotation (with brackets) so that its parts fit together grammatically, or use only one part of the quotation:

> From the moment of the boy's arrival in Araby, the bazaar is presented as a commercial enterprise: "I could not find any sixpenny entrance and . . . ~~handing~~ [*hand[ed]*] a shilling to a weary-looking man" (34).

> From the moment of the boy's arrival in Araby, the bazaar is presented as a commercial enterprise: "I could not find any sixpenny entrance ~~and~~ [*He "*] [*"*] ~~. . . handing a shilling to a weary-looking man"~~ [*so had to pay a shilling to get in*] (34).

Sentence fragments sometimes result when writers forget to include a verb in the sentence introducing a quotation, especially when the quotation itself is a complete sentence. Make sure you introduce a quotation with a complete sentence:

The girl's interest in the bazaar ~~leading~~ [*leads*] the narrator to make what amounts to a sacred oath: "If I go . . . I will bring you something" (32).

Using In-Text or Block Quotations

Depending on its length, you may incorporate a **quotation** into your text by enclosing it in quotation marks or by setting it off from your text in a block without quotation marks. In either case, be sure to integrate the quotation into your essay using the strategies described here:

In-Text Quotations. Incorporate brief quotations (no more than four typed lines of prose or three lines of poetry) into your text. You may place a quotation virtually anywhere in your sentence:

At the Beginning

> "To live a life is not to cross a field," Sutherland, quoting Pasternak, writes at the beginning of her narrative (11).

In the Middle

Woolf begins and ends by speaking of the need of the woman writer to have "money and a room of her own" (4)—an idea that certainly spoke to Plath's condition.

At the End

In *The Second Sex*, Simone de Beauvoir describes such an experience as one in which the girl "becomes an object, and she sees herself as object" (378).

Divided by Your Own Words

"Science usually prefers the literal to the nonliteral term," Kinneavy writes, "—that is, figures of speech are often out of place in science" (177).

When you quote poetry within your text, use a slash (/) with spaces before and after to signal the end of each line of verse:

Alluding to St. Augustine's distinction between the City of God and the Earthly City, Lowell writes that "much against my will / I left the City of God where it belongs" (4-5).

Block Quotations.   In MLA style, use the **block form** for prose quotations of five or more typed lines and for poetry quotations of four or more lines. Indent the quotation an inch from the left margin, as shown in the following example:

In "A Literary Legacy from Dunbar to Baraka," Margaret Walker says of Paul Lawrence Dunbar's dialect poems:
> He realized that the white world in the United States tolerated his literary genius only because of his "jingles in a broken tongue," and they found the old "darky" tales and speech amusing and within the vein of folklore into which they wished to classify all Negro life. This troubled Dunbar because he realized that white America was denigrating him as a writer and as a man. (70)

In APA style, use block form for quotations of forty words or more. Indent the block quotation half an inch.

In a block quotation, double-space between lines just as you do in your text. Do not enclose the passage within quotation marks. Use a colon to introduce a block quotation unless the context calls for another punctuation mark or none at all. When quoting a single paragraph or part of one in MLA style, do not indent the first line of the quotation more than the rest. In quoting two or more paragraphs, indent the first line of each paragraph an extra quarter inch. If you are using APA style, indent the first line of subsequent paragraphs in the block quotation an additional half inch from the indentation of the block quotation.

Note that in MLA style the parenthetical page reference follows the period in block quotations.

Using Punctuation to Integrate Quotations

Statements that introduce in-text quotations take a range of punctuation marks and lead-in words. Here are some examples of ways writers typically introduce quotations:

Introducing a Quotation Using a Colon.   A colon usually follows an independent clause placed before the quotation:

> As George Williams notes, protection of white privilege is critical to patterns of discrimination: "Whenever a number of persons within a society have enjoyed for a considerable period of time certain opportunities for getting wealth, for exercising power and authority, and for successfully claiming prestige and social deference, there is a strong tendency for these people to feel that these benefits are theirs 'by right'" (727).

Introducing a Quotation Using a Comma.   A comma usually follows an introduction that incorporates the quotation in its sentence structure:

> Similarly, Duncan Turner asserts, "As matters now stand, it is unwise to talk about communication without some understanding of Burke" (259).

Introducing a Quotation Using *That*.   No punctuation is generally needed with *that*, and no capital letter is used to begin the quotation:

> Noting this failure, Alice Miller asserts that "the reason for her despair was not her suffering but the impossibility of communicating her suffering to another person" (255).

Paraphrasing Sources Carefully

In a **paraphrase**, the writer restates in his or her own words the relevant information from a passage, without any additional comments or any suggestion of agreement or disagreement with the source's ideas. A paraphrase is useful for recording details of the passage when the order of the details is important but the source's wording is not. Because all the details of the passage are included, a paraphrase is often about the same length as the original passage. It is better to paraphrase than to quote ordinary material in which the author's way of expressing things is not worth special attention.

Here is a passage from a book on home schooling and an example of an acceptable paraphrase of it:

Original source

Repeated words   Bruner and the discovery theorists have also illuminated conditions that apparently pave the way for learning. It is significant that these conditions are unique to each learner, so unique, in fact, that in many cases classrooms can't provide them. Bruner also contends that the more one discovers information in a great variety of circumstances, the more likely one is to develop the inner categories required to organize that information. Yet life at school, which is for the most part generic and predictable, daily keeps many children from the great variety of circumstances they need to learn well.

— DAVID GUTERSON, *Family Matters: Why Homeschooling Makes Sense*, p. 172

Acceptable paraphrase

According to Guterson, the "discovery theorists," particularly Bruner, have found that there seem to be certain conditions that help learning to take place. Because individuals require different conditions, many children are not able to learn in the classroom. According to Bruner, when people can explore information in many different situations, they learn to classify and order what they discover. The general routine of the school day, however, does not provide children with the diverse activities and situations that would allow them to learn these skills (172).

The highlighting shows that some words in the paraphrase were taken from the source. Indeed, it would be nearly impossible for paraphrasers to avoid using any key terms from the source, and it would be counterproductive to try to do so, because the original and the paraphrase necessarily share the same information and concepts. Notice, though, that of the total of eighty-five words in the paraphrase, the paraphraser uses only a name (*Bruner*) and a few other key nouns and verbs for which it would be awkward to substitute other words or phrases. If the paraphraser had wanted to use other, more distinctive language from the source — for example, the description of life at school as "generic and predictable" — these adjectives would need to be enclosed in quotation marks. In fact, the paraphraser puts quotation marks around only one of the terms from the source: "discovery theorists" — a technical term likely to be unfamiliar to readers.

Paraphrasers must, however, avoid borrowing too many words and repeating the sentence structures from a source. Here is an unacceptable paraphrase of the first sentence in the Guterson passage:

Unacceptable Paraphrase: Too Many Borrowed Words and Phrases

Repeated sentence
structure   Apparently, some conditions, which have been illuminated by
Repeated words   Bruner and other discovery theorists, pave the way for people to
                 learn.

Here, the paraphrase borrows almost all of its key language from the source sentence, including the entire phrase *pave the way for*. Even if you cite the source, this heavy borrowing would be considered plagiarism.

Here is another unacceptable paraphrase of the same sentence:

Unacceptable Paraphrase: Sentence Structure Repeated Too Closely

Repeated words	Bruner and other *researchers* have also *identified circumstances*
Synonyms	that *seem to ease the path* to learning.
Repeated sentence structure	

If you compare the source's first sentence and this paraphrase of it, you will see that the paraphraser has borrowed the phrases and clauses of the source and arranged them in an almost identical sequence, simply substituting synonyms for most of the key terms. This paraphrase would also be considered plagiarism.

Summarizing to Present the Source's Main Ideas in a Balanced and Readable Way

Unlike a paraphrase, a **summary** presents only the main ideas of a source, leaving out examples and details.

Here is one student's summary of five pages from David Guterson's book *Family Matters*. You can see at a glance how drastically summaries can condense information, in this case from five pages to five sentences. Depending on the summarizer's purpose, the five pages could be summarized in one sentence, the five sentences here, or two or three dozen sentences.

> In looking at different theories of learning that discuss individual-based programs (such as home schooling) versus the public school system, Guterson describes the disagreements among "cognitivist" theorists. One group, the "discovery theorists," believes that individual children learn by creating their own ways of sorting the information they take in from their experiences. Schools should help students develop better ways of organizing new material, not just present them with material that is already categorized, as traditional schools do. "Assimilationist theorists," by contrast, believe that children learn by linking what they don't know to information they already know. These theorists claim that traditional schools help students learn when they present information in ways that allow children to fit the new material into categories they have already developed (171-75).

Summaries like this one are more than a dry list of main ideas from a source. They are instead a coherent, readable new text composed of the source's main ideas. Summaries provide balanced coverage of a source, following the same sequence of ideas and avoiding any hint of agreement or disagreement with them.

CITING AND DOCUMENTING SOURCES IN MLA STYLE

The following guidelines are sufficient for most college research assignments in English and other humanities courses that call for MLA-style documentation. For additional information, see the *MLA Handbook for Writers of Research Papers*, Seventh Edition (2009), or check the MLA Web site (http://mla.org).

USING IN-TEXT CITATIONS TO SHOW WHERE YOU HAVE USED SOURCE MATERIAL

The MLA system requires parenthetical in-text citations that are keyed to a list of works cited in the paper. In-text citations generally include the author's last name and the page number of the passage being cited. There is no punctuation between author and page. The parenthetical citation should follow the quoted, para-phrased, or summarized material as closely as possible without disrupting the flow of the sentence. (Note that the parenthetical citation comes before the final period. With block quotations, however, the citation comes after the final period, preceded by a space; see p. 582 for an example.)

	author's last name	*appropriate verb*
SIGNAL PHRASE	Simon, a well-known figure in New York literary society, described the impression Dr. James made on her as a child in the Bronx: He was a "not-too-skeletal Ichabod Crane" (68).	
		page number
PARENTHETICAL CITATION	Dr. James is described as a "not-too-skeletal Ichabod Crane" (Simon 68).	
	author's last name + page number	
WORKS-CITED ENTRY	Simon, Kate. "Birthing." *Bronx Primitive: Portraits in a Childhood.* New York: Viking, 1982. 68-77. Print.	

In most cases, you will want to use a signal phrase because doing so lets you put your source in context. The signal-phrase-plus-page-reference combination also allows you to make crystal clear where the source information begins and ends. Use a parenthetical citation alone when you have already identified the author or when citing the source of an uncontroversial fact.

Directory to In-Text-Citation Models

One author 582
More than one author 583
Unknown author 583
Two or more works by the same
    author 583
Two or more authors with the same
    last name 583
Corporation, organization, or
    government agency as
    author 583
Literary work (novel, play,
    poem) 584

Work in an anthology 584
Religious work 584
Multivolume work (one volume,
    more than one volume) 585
Indirect citation (quotation from a
    secondary source) 585
Entire work 585
Work without page numbers or a
    one-page work (with / without
    other section numbers) 585
Two or more works cited in the
    same parentheses 585

One author   When citing most works with a single author, include the author's name (usually the last name is enough)* and the page number on which the cited material appears.

author's last name + appropriate verb   page number

SIGNAL PHRASE   Simon describes Dr. James as a "not-too-skeletal Ichabod Crane" (68).

PARENTHETICAL CITATION   Dr. James is described as a "not-too-skeletal Ichabod Crane" (Simon 68).

author's last name + page number

author's name

BLOCK QUOTATION   In Kate Simon's story "Birthing," the description of Dr. James captures both his physical appearance and his role in the community:

> He looked so much like a story character—the gentled Scrooge of a St. Nicholas Magazine Christmas issue, a not-too-skeletal Ichabod Crane. . . . Dr. James was, even when I knew him as a child, quite an old man, retired from a prestigious and lucrative practice in Boston. . . . His was a prosperous intellectual family, the famous New England Jameses that produced William and Henry, but to the older Bronx doctors, *the* James was the magnificent old driven scarecrow. (68)

page number

(A works-cited entry for "Birthing" appears on p. 581.)

*But see entries for "Two or More Works by the Same Author" and "Two or More Authors with the Same Last Name" on p. 583 and for "Work without Page Numbers or a One-Page Work" on p. 585.

More than one author   To cite a source by two or three authors, include all the authors' last names. To cite a source with four or more authors, model your in-text citation on the entry in your works-cited list: Use either all the authors' names or just the first author's name followed by *et al.* ("and others" in Latin, not italicized).

SIGNAL PHRASE   Dyal, Corning, and Willows (1975) identify several types of students, including the "Authority-Rebel" (4).

PARENTHETICAL CITATION   The Authority-Rebel "tends to see himself as superior to other students in the class" (Dyal, Corning, and Willows 4).

The drug AZT has been shown to reduce the risk of transmission from HIV-positive mothers to their infants by as much as two-thirds (Van de Perre et al. 4-5).

Unknown author   If the author's name is unknown, use a shortened version of the title, beginning with the word by which the title is alphabetized in the works-cited list.

An international pollution treaty still to be ratified would prohibit ships from dumping plastic at sea ("Plastic Is Found" 68).

The full title of the work is "Plastic Is Found in the Sargasso Sea; Pieces of Apparent Refuse Cover Wide Atlantic Region."

Two or more works by the same author   If you cite more than one work by the same author, include a shortened version of the title.

When old paint becomes transparent, it sometimes shows the artist's original plans: "a tree will show through a woman's dress" (Hellman, *Pentimento* 1).

Two or more authors with the same last name   When citing works by authors with the same last name, include each author's first initial in the citation. If the first initials are also the same, spell out the authors' first names.

Chaplin's *Modern Times* provides a good example of montage used to make an editorial statement (E. Roberts 246).

Corporation, organization, or government agency as author   In a signal phrase, use the full name of the corporation, organization, or government agency. In a parenthetical citation, use the full name if it is brief or a shortened version if it is long.

SIGNAL PHRASE   According to the Washington State Board for Community and Technical Colleges, a tuition increase . . . from Initiative 601 (4).

PARENTHETICAL CITATION   A tuition increase has been proposed for community and technical colleges to offset budget deficits from Initiative 601 (Washington State Board 4).

Literary work (novel, play, poem)   Provide information that will help readers find the passage you are citing no matter what edition of the novel, play, or poem they are using. For a novel or other prose work, provide the part or chapter number as well as the page numbers from the edition you used.

NOVEL OR
OTHER PROSE
WORK
In *Hard Times*, Tom reveals his utter narcissism by blaming Louisa for his own failure: "'You have regularly given me up. You never cared for me'" (Dickens 262; bk. 3, ch. 9).

For a play in verse, use act, scene, and line numbers instead of page numbers.

PLAY (IN VERSE)
At the beginning, Regan's fawning rhetoric hides her true attitude toward Lear: "I profess / myself an enemy to all other joys . . . / And find that I am alone felicitate / In your dear highness' love" (*King Lear* 1.1.74-75, 77-78).

For a poem, indicate the line numbers and stanzas or sections (if they are numbered) instead of page numbers.

POEM
In "Song of Myself," Whitman finds poetic details in busy urban settings, as when he describes "the blab of the pave, tires of carts . . . the driver with his interrogating thumb" (8.153-54).

If the source gives only line numbers, use the term *lines* in your first citation and use only the numbers in subsequent citations.

> In "Before you thought of spring," Dickinson at first identifies the spirit of spring with a bird, possibly a robin—"A fellow in the skies / Inspiriting habiliments / Of indigo and brown" (lines 4, 7-8)—but by the end of the poem, she has linked it with poetry and perhaps even the poet herself, as the bird, like Dickinson "shouts for joy to nobody / But his seraphic self!" (15-16)

Work in an anthology   Use the name of the author of the work, not the editor of the anthology, in your in-text citation.

SIGNAL PHRASE
In "Six Days: Some Rememberings," Grace Paley recalls that when she was in jail for protesting the Vietnam War, her pen and paper were taken away and she felt "a terrible pain in the area of my heart—a nausea" (191).

PARENTHETICAL
CITATION
Writers may have a visceral reaction—"a nausea" (Paley 191)— to being deprived of access to writing implements.

Religious work   In your first citation, include the element that begins your entry in the works-cited list, such as the edition name of the religious work you are citing, and include the book or section name (using standard abbreviations in parenthetical citations) and any chapter or verse numbers.

> She ignored the admonition "Pride goes before destruction, and a haughty spirit before a fall" (*New Oxford Annotated Bible*, Prov. 16.18).

Multivolume work (one volume, more than one volume)   If you cite only one volume of a multivolume work, treat the in-text citation as you would any other work, but include the volume number in the works-cited entry (see p. 589).

ONE VOLUME   Forster argued that modernist writers valued experimentation and gradually sought to blur the line between poetry and prose (150).

When you use two or more volumes of a multivolume work, include the volume number and the page number(s) in your in-text citation.

MORE THAN ONE VOLUME   Modernist writers valued experimentation and gradually sought to blur the line between poetry and prose (Forster 3: 150).

Indirect citation (quotation from a secondary source)   If possible, locate the original source and cite that. If not possible, name the original source but also include the secondary source in which you found the material you are citing, plus the abbreviation *qtd. in.* Include the secondary source in your list of works cited.

E. M. Forster says that "the collapse of all civilization, so realistic for us, sounded in Matthew Arnold's ears like a distant and harmonious cataract" (qtd. in Trilling 11).

Entire work   Include the reference in the text without any page numbers or parentheses.

In *The Structure of Scientific Revolutions*, Thomas Kuhn discusses how scientists change their thinking.

Work without page numbers or a one-page work (with / without other section numbers)   If a work (such as a Web page) has no page numbers or is only one page long, omit the page number. If it uses screen numbers or paragraph numbers, insert a comma after the author's name, an identifying term (such as *screen*) or abbreviation (*par.* or *pars.*), and the number.

WITHOUT PAGE OR OTHER NUMBERS   The average speed on Montana's interstate highways, for example, has risen by only 2 miles per hour since the repeal of the federal speed limit, with most drivers topping out at 75 (Schmid).

WITH OTHER SECTION NUMBERS   Whitman considered African American speech "a source of a native grand opera" (Ellison, par. 13).

Two or more works cited in the same parentheses   If you cite two or more sources for a piece of information, include them in the same parentheses, separated by semicolons.

A few studies have considered differences between oral and written discourse production (Scardamalia, Bereiter, and Goelman; Gould).

If the parenthetical citation is likely to prove disruptive for your reader, cite multiple sources in a footnote or an end note.

CREATING A LIST OF WORKS CITED

The MLA documentation system requires a works-cited list providing bibliographic information for every in-text citation in the text. The basic model is usually for printed texts, and other versions (such as online journals, newspapers, and magazines or e-books) are variations on that basic documentation model. Double-space the works-cited list and use a hanging indent (with the first line flush left and subsequent lines indented half an inch.) Alphabetize entries by the first main word in the citation.

Directory to Works-Cited-List Models

Author Listings
One author 587
Two or three authors 587
Four or more authors 587
Unknown author 587
Corporation, organization, or
   government agency as
   author 587
Two or more works by the same
   author 588

**Books (Print, Electronic,
   Database)**
Basic format 588
Anthology or edited collection 588
Work in an anthology or edited
   collection 588
Introduction, preface, foreword, or
   afterword 589
Translation 589
Graphic narrative 589
Religious work 589
Multivolume work 589
Later edition of a book 589
Republished book 589
Title within a title 590
Book in a series 590
Dictionary entry or article in
   another reference book 590

Government document 590
Published proceedings of a
   conference 591
Pamphlet or brochure 591
Doctoral dissertation 591

Articles (Print, Online, Database)
From a scholarly journal 591
From a newspaper 592
From a magazine 593
Editorial or letter to the editor 593
Review 593

**Multimedia Sources (Live, Print,
   Electronic, Database)**
Lecture or public address 594
Letter 594
Map or chart 594
Cartoon or comic strip 594
Advertisement 594
Work of art 595
Musical composition 595
Performance 595
Television or radio program 595
Film 596
Online video 596
Music recording 596
Interview 596

Other Electronic Sources
Web page or other document on a
    Web site 596
Entire Web site 597
Online scholarly project 597
Book or a short work in an online
    scholarly project 597

Blog 597
Wiki article 598
Discussion group or newsgroup
    posting 598
E-mail message 598

AUTHOR LISTINGS

One author   List the author last name first (followed by a comma), and insert a period at the end of the name.

> Isaacson, Walter.

Two or three authors   List the first author last name first (followed by a comma). List the other authors in the usual first-name / last-name order. Insert the word *and* before the last author's name, and follow the name with a period.

> Saba, Laura, and Julie Gattis.

> Wilmut, Ian, Keith Campbell, and Colin Tudge.

Four or more authors   Either list all the authors' names *or* just the first one followed by *et al.* (which means *and others* in Latin) in regular type (not italics). Whichever you do, use the same format in your in-text citation.

> Hunt, Lynn, Thomas R. Martin, Barbara H. Rosenwein, R. Po-chia Hsia, and
>   Bonnie G. Smith.

> Hunt, Lynn, et al.

Unknown author

> *Primary Colors: A Novel of Politics.*

> "Out of Sight."

Corporation, organization, or government agency as author   Use the name of the corporation, organization, or government agency as the author.

> RAND Corporation.

> United States. National Commission on Terrorist Attacks.

Two or more works by the same author　Replace the author's name in subsequent entries with three hyphens, and alphabetize the works by the first important word in the title:

> Eugenides, Jeffrey. *The Marriage Plot.*
>
> ---. *Middlesex.*
>
> ---. "Walkabout."

BOOKS (PRINT, ELECTRONIC, DATABASE)

Basic format

	Author, last name first	Title (and subtitle, if any), italicized	Publication info	Medium
PRINT	Eugenides, Jeffrey.	*The Marriage Plot.*	New York: Farrar, 2011.	Print.

> City of publication　Publisher (abbreviated)　Year of publication

E-BOOK

> Print publication info

> Eugenides, Jeffrey. *The Marriage Plot.* New York: Farrar, 2011.
> Kindle e-book file.

> Medium

DATABASE

> Print publication info

> Whitman, Walt. *Leaves of Grass.* Philadelphia: McKay, 1900.
> *Bartleby.com.* Web. 28 Nov. 2011.

> Database name, italicized　Medium　Access date

Anthology or edited collection　If you are referring to the anthology as a whole, put the editor's name first.

> Masri, Heather, ed. *Science Fiction: Stories and Contexts.* Boston: Bedford, 2009. Print.

Work in an anthology or edited collection　If you're referring to a selection in an anthology, begin the entry with the name of the selection's author.

> Hopkinson, Nalo. "Something to Hitch Meat To." *Science Fiction: Stories and Contexts.* Ed. Heather Masri. Boston: Bedford, 2009. 838-50. Print.

If you cite more than one selection from an anthology or collection, you may create an entry for the collection as a whole (see the model above) and then cross-reference individual selections to that entry.

Selection author   Selection title   Anthology editor

Hopkinson, Nalo. "Something to Hitch Meat To." Masri 838-50.

Selection pages in anthology

Introduction, preface, foreword, or afterword

Murfin, Ross C. Introduction. *Heart of Darkness*. By Joseph Conrad. 3rd ed.
Boston: Bedford, 2011. 3-16. Print.

Translation

Tolstoy, Leo. *War and Peace*. Trans. Richard Pevear and Larissa Volokhonsky.
New York: Vintage, 2009. Print.

Graphic narrative   If the graphic narrative was a collaboration between a writer and an illustrator, begin your entry with the name of the person on whose work your research project focuses. If the author also created the illustrations, then follow the basic model for a book with one author (p. 588).

Pekar, Harvey, and Joyce Brabner. *Our Cancer Year*. Illus. Frank Stack. New York:
Four Walls Eight Windows, 1994. Print.

Religious work   Give the title of the edition, the editor's and translator's names as available, publisher, and date.

The Qu'ran: English Translation and Parallel Arabic Text. Trans. M. A. S. Abdel
Haleem. New York: Oxford UP, 2010. Print.

Multivolume work   If you use only one volume from a multivolume work, indicate the volume number after the title. If you use more than one volume, indicate the total number of volumes after the title.

One volume cited

Sandburg, Carl. *Abraham Lincoln*. Vol. 2. New York: Scribner's, 1939. Print.

More than one volume cited

Sandburg, Carl. *Abraham Lincoln*. 6 vols. New York: Scribner's, 1939. Print.

Later edition of a book

Rottenberg, Annette T., and Donna Haisty Winchell. *The Structure of Argument*.
6th ed. Boston: Bedford, 2009. Print.

Republished book   Provide the original year of publication after the title of the book, followed by publication information for the edition you are using.

Original publication date

Alcott, Louisa May. *An Old-Fashioned Girl.* 1870. New York: Puffin, 1995. Print.

Republication information

Title within a title   When a title that is normally italicized appears within a book title, do not italicize it. If the title within the title would normally be enclosed in quotation marks, include the quotation marks and also set the title in italics.

> Hertenstein, Mike. *The Double Vision of* Star Trek*: Half-Humans, Evil Twins, and Science Fiction.* Chicago: Cornerstone, 1998. Print.

> Miller, Edwin Haviland. *Walt Whitman's "Song of Myself": A Mosaic of Interpretation.* Iowa City: U of Iowa P, 1989. Print.

Book in a series   Include the series title and number (if any) after the medium of publication. If the word *Series* is part of the name, include the abbreviation *Ser.* before the series number. (This information will appear on the title page or on the page facing the title page.) Abbreviate any commonly abbreviated words in the series title.

> Zigova, Tanya, et al. *Neural Stem Cells: Methods and Protocols.* Totowa: Humana, 2002. Print. Methods in Molecular Biology 198.

Dictionary entry or article in another reference book

PRINT   Trenear-Harvey, Glenmore S. "Farm Hall." *Historical Dictionary of Atomic Espionage.* Lanham: Scarecrow, 2011. Print.

Web site (italics)   *Site sponsor*

ONLINE   "Homeopathy." *Merriam-Webster.com.* Merriam-Webster, Inc., 2011. Web. 29 Nov. 2011.

Medium   Access date

DATABASE   Powell, Jason L. "Power Elite." *Blackwell Encyclopedia of Sociology.* Ed. George Ritzer. Wiley-Blackwell, 2007. *Blackwell Reference Online.* Web. 29 Nov. 2011.

Database (italics)   Medium   Access date

Government document

Issuing government   Issuing department

PRINT   United States. Dept. of Health and Human Services. *Trends in Underage Drinking in the United States, 1991-2007.* By Gabriella Newes-Adeyi et al. Washington: GPO, 2009. Print.

Authors

Issuing agency

ONLINE   United States. Centers for Disease Control. "Youth Risk Behavior
          Surveillance—United States, 2009." *Morbidity and Mortality*
          Weekly Report. Centers for Disease Control. Dept. of Health

Web site (italics)   *Site sponsor*

          and Human Services, 4 June 2010. Web. 30 Nov. 2011.

Publication date   Medium   Access date

Published proceedings of a conference   *Conference name included in title*

Duffett, John, ed. *Against the Crime of Silence: Proceedings of the International*
    War Crimes Tribunal. Nov. 1967, Stockholm. New York: Clarion-Simon, 1970.
    Print.

Pamphlet or brochure

U.S. Foundation for Boating Safety and Clean Water. *Hypothermia and Cold Water*
    Survival. Alexandria: U.S. Foundation for Boating, 2001. Print.

Doctoral dissertation

Title in italics

PUBLISHED   Jones, Anna Maria. *Problem Novels / Perverse Readers: Late-*
          Victorian Fiction and the Perilous Pleasures of Identification.
          Diss. U of Notre Dame, 2001. Ann Arbor: UMI, 2001. Print.

Dissertation information

Title in quotation marks

UNPUBLISHED   Bullock, Barbara. "Basic Needs Fulfillment among Less Developed
          Countries: Social Progress over Two Decades of Growth."
          Diss. Vanderbilt U, 1986. Print.

Dissertation information

ARTICLES (PRINT, ONLINE, DATABASE)

From a scholarly journal

Author, last name first   Title of article (in quotation marks)

PRINT   Garas-York, Keli. "Overlapping Student Environments: An
          Examination of the Homeschool Connection and Its Impact
          on Achievement." *Journal of College Admission* 42.4 (2010):
          430-49. Print.

                   Title of journal   Volume
Pages   Medium   *(italics)   Issue   Year*

ONLINE   Saho, Bala S. K. "The Appropriation of Islam in a Gambian Village:
Life and Times of Shaykh Mass Kay, 1827-1936. *African Studies
Quarterly* 12.4 (2011): n. pag. Web. 12 Dec. 2011.

> *No page numbers   Medium   Access date*

DATABASE   Garas-York, Keli. "Overlapping Student Environments: An
Examination of the Homeschool Connection and Its Impact
on Achievement." *Journal of College Admission* 42.4 (2010):
430-49. *Academic Search Complete.* Web. 13 Dec. 2011.

> *Database (italics)   Medium   Access date*

If a journal does not use volume numbers, provide the issue number only.

> *Author, last name first   Article in quotation marks*

PRINT   Haas, Heather A. "The Wisdom of Wizards—and Muggles
and Squibs: Proverb Use in the World of Harry Potter."
Journal of American Folklore 124.492 (2011): 29-54. Print.◄

> *Periodical title, italicized   Vol. and issue number   Date of publication (year)   Page numbers   Medium*

ONLINE   Markel, J. D. "Religious Allegory and Cultural Discomfort in Mike
Leigh's *Happy-Go-Lucky*: And Why *Larry Crowne* Is One of
the Best Films of 2011." *Bright Lights* 74 (2011): n. pag. Web.◄
29 Nov. 2011.

> *Access date   Issue number only   No page numbers   Medium*

DATABASE   Haas, Heather A. "The Wisdom of Wizards—and Muggles and
Squibs: Proverb Use in the World of *Harry Potter*." *Journal of
American Folklore* 124.492 (2011): 29-54. *Academic Search
Complete.* Web. 29 Nov. 2011.

> *Database (italics)*

Online journals may not include page numbers; if paragraph or other section numbers are provided, use them instead. Otherwise, insert *n. pag.* (for *no page numbers*). If the article is not on a continuous sequence of pages, give the first page number followed by a plus sign. (See entry below for a print version of a newspaper for an example.)

From a newspaper

PRINT   Stoll, John D., et al. "U.S. Squeezes Auto Creditors." *Wall Street
Journal* 10 Apr. 2009: A1+. Print.

> *Noncontinuous pages*

ONLINE   Medina, Jennifer, and Brian Stelter. "Police Clear Occupy
               Encampments in Two Cities." *New York Times.* New York Times,

                                            Web site (italics)   Site sponsor

            30 Nov. 2011. Web. 30 Nov. 2011.

            Publication date   Medium   Access date

DATABASE   Lopez, Steve. "Put Occupy L.A. on the Bus." *Los Angeles Times*
               30 Nov. 2011, Home ed.: n. pag. *LexisNexis Academic.* Web.
               30 Nov. 2011.
                                     Edition   No page   Database (italics)   Medium
               Access date   name   numbers

From a magazine

                                                    Publication date (weekly)

PRINT   Harrell, Eben. "A Flicker of Consciousness." *Time* 28 Nov. 2011:
               42-47. Print.

                                                         Publication date (monthly)

            Branch, Taylor. "The Shame of College Sports." *Atlantic* Oct. 2011:
               80-110. Print.

                                            Web site (italic)   Site sponsor

ONLINE   Harrell, Eben. "A Flicker of Consciousness." *Time.* Time, Inc.
               28 Nov. 2011. Web. 30 Nov. 2011.

                               Medium   Access date

DATABASE   Harrell, Eben. "A Flicker of Consciousness." *Time* 28 Nov. 2011:
               42-47. *Academic Search Complete.* Web. 7 Dec. 2011.

                               Database (italics)   Medium   Access date

Editorial or letter to the editor

"Stay Classy." Editorial. *New Republic* 1 Dec. 2011: 1. Print.

Wegeiser, Art. "How Does He Know?" Letter. *Pittsburgh Post-Gazette*
   30 Nov. 2011: B6. Print.

Review

Cassidy, John. "Master of Disaster." Rev. of *Globalization and Its Discontents,*
   by Joseph Stiglitz. *New Yorker* 12 July 2002: 82-86. Print.

MULTIMEDIA SOURCES (LIVE, PRINT, ELECTRONIC, DATABASE)

Lecture or public address

Title of lecture   *Conference title*

Birnbaum, Jack. "The Domestication of Computers." Conf. of the Usability
  Professionals Association. Hyatt Grand Cypress Resort, Orlando.
  10 July 2002. Lecture.
                                                   Location

Date of lecture   *Medium*

Letter If the letter has been published, treat it like a work in an anthology
(p. 588), but add the recipient, the date, and any identifying number after the
author's name. If the letter is unpublished, change the medium to *MS* ("manuscript") if written by hand or *TS* ("typescript") if typed.

Sender   *Recipient*   *Date*   *Medium*

DuHamel, Grace. Letter to the author. 22 Mar. 2008. TS.

Map or chart

PRINT   *Map of Afghanistan and Surrounding Territory*. Map. Burlington:
                   GiziMap, 2001. Print.

ONLINE   "North America, 1797." Map. *Perry-Castañeda Library Map
                   Collection*. U of Texas, 21 June 2011. Web. 1 Dec. 2011.

Cartoon or comic strip

PRINT   Cheney, Tom. Cartoon. *New Yorker* 10 Oct. 2005: 55. Print.

ONLINE   Hunt, Tarol. "Goblins." Comic strip. *Goblinscomic.com*. Tarol Hunt,
                   29 Sept. 2011. Web. 30 Nov. 2011.

Advertisement

PRINT   Hospital for Special Surgery. Advertisement. *New York Times* 13 Apr.
                   2009: A7. Print.

BROADCAST   Norwegian Cruise Line. Advertisement. *WNET.org*. PBS, 29 Apr.
                   2012. Television.

ONLINE   Volkswagen Passat. Advertisement. *Slate*. Slate Group, 1 Dec. 2011.
                   Web. 1 Dec. 2011.

Work of art

Date of composition   *Medium*

MUSEUM   Palmer Payne, Elsie. *Sheep Dipping Time.* c. 1930s. Oil on canvas. Nevada Museum of Art, Reno.

Location

PRINT   Chihuly, Dale. *Carmine and White Flower Set.* 1987. Glass. Tacoma Art Museum, Tacoma. New York: Abrams, 2011. 109. Print.

Print publication information

Location of original

WEB SITE   Sekaer, Peter. *A Sign Business Shop,* New York. 1935. International Center of Photography, New York. *International Center of Photography.* Web. 5 Dec. 2011.

Web site

Medium   *Access date*

Musical composition

Beethoven, Ludwig van. *Violin Concerto in D Major, Op. 61.* 1809. New York: Edwin F. Kalmus, n.d. Print.

Gershwin, George. *Porgy and Bess.* 1935. New York: Alfred, 1999. Print.

Performance

The Agony and the Ecstasy of Steve Jobs. Writ. and perf. Mike Daisey. Dir. Jean-Michele Gregory. Public Theater, New York. 25 Nov. 2011. Performance.

Television or radio program   Treat a show you streamed as you would a Web page, but include information about key contributors (host or performers, for example) as you would for a broadcast television or radio program. If you downloaded the program as a podcast, include the information as for a broadcast program, but change the medium to match the type of file you accessed (*MP3, JPEG file*).

Program   *Key contributor*   *Network*   *Location*

BROADCAST   *Frontline.* Prod. Greg Barker. PBS. WNET, New York, 22 Nov. 2011. Television.

Local station   *Broadcast date*

Medium

Episode

STREAMED   "A Perfect Terrorist." *Frontline.* Writ., prod., and dir. Thomas Jennings. *WNET.org.* PBS, 22 Nov. 2011. Web. 1 Dec. 2011.

Web site   *Sponsor*   *Post date*   *Medium*   *Access date*

DOWNLOADED   "Patient Zero." *Radio Lab.* Host. Jad Abumrad and Robert Krulwich. Natl. Public Radio. WNYC, New York, 14 Nov. 2011. MP3.

Medium

Film

THEATER   *Space Station*. Prod. and dir. Toni Myers. Narr. Tom Cruise. IMAX, 2002. Film.

DVD   *Casablanca*. Dir. Michael Curtiz. Perf. Humphrey Bogart, Ingrid Bergman, and Paul Henreid. 1942. Warner Home Video, 2003. DVD.

STREAMED   *The Social Network*. Dir. David Fincher. Writ. Aaron Sorkin. Perf. Jesse Eisenberg, Justin Timberlake, and Andrew Garfield. Columbia Pictures, 2010. iTunes. Web. 1 Dec. 2010.

Online video

Film School. "Sunny Day." *YouTube*. YouTube, 12 June 2010. Web. 1 Dec. 2010.

Music recording

Beethoven, Ludwig van. *Violin Concerto in D Major, Op. 61*. U.S.S.R. State Orchestra. Cond. Alexander Gauk. Perf. David Oistrakh. Allegro, 1980. CD.

Maroon 5. "Moves Like Jagger." *Hands All Over*. A&M/Octone Records, 2011. MP3.

Interview   If a personal interview takes place through e-mail, change "Personal interview" to "E-mail interview."

PRINT   Ashrawi, Hanan. "Tanks vs. Olive Branches." Interview by Rose Marie Berger. *Sojourners* Feb. 2005: 22-26. Print.

BROADCAST   Dobbs, Bill. "Occupy Wall Street." Interview by Brooke Gladstone. *On the Media*. Natl. Public Radio. WNYC, New York, 7 Oct. 2011. Web. 1 Dec. 2011.

PERSONAL   Ellis, Trey. Personal interview. 3 Sept. 2008.

OTHER ELECTRONIC SOURCES

Web page or other document on a Web site

Author / editor, last name first   Document title (in quotation marks)

McGann, Jerome J., ed. "Introduction to the Final Installment of the Rossetti

Title of site (italicized)

Archive." *The Complete Writings and Pictures of Dante Gabriel Rossetti:*

Sponsor

A Hypermedia Archive. Institute for Advanced Technology in the Humanities,

Publication date / last update   Access date

U of Virginia, 2008. Web. 16 Oct. 2012.

Entire Web site   For an untitled personal site, put a description such as *Home page* where the Web site's title would normally appear (but with no quotation marks or italics). If no site sponsor or publisher is named, insert *N.p.* (for *No publisher*).

> Gardner, James Alan. *A Seminar on Writing Prose*. N.p., 2001. Web. 1 Dec. 2011.
>
> *The Complete Writings and Pictures of Dante Gabriel Rossetti: A Hypermedia Archive*. Ed. Jerome J. McGann. Institute for Advanced Technology in the Humanities, U of Virginia, 2008. Web. 16 Oct. 2012.
>
> Chesson, Frederick W. Home page. N.p., 1 Apr. 2003. Web. 26 Apr. 2008.

Online scholarly project   Treat an online scholarly project as you would a Web site, but include the name of the editor, if given.

> *The Darwin Correspondence Project*. Ed. Janet Browne. American Council of Learned Societies and U Cambridge, 2011. Web. 1 Dec. 2011.

Book or a short work in an online scholarly project   Set the title in italics if the work is a book and in quotation marks if it is an article, essay, poem, or other short work, and include the print publication information (if any) following the title.

> Heims, Marjorie. "The Strange Case of Sarah Jones." *The Free Expression Policy Project*. FEPP, 2 Nov. 2011. Web. 1 Dec. 2011.

Original publication information

> Corelli, Marie. *The Treasure of Heaven*. London: Constable, 1906. *Victorian Women Writer's Project*. Ed. Percy Willett. Indiana U, 10 July 1999. Web. 10 Sept. 2008.

Blog   If the author of the blog post uses a pseudonym, begin with the pseudonym and put the blogger's real name in brackets. Cite an entire blog as you would an entire Web site (see above).

Blog title   *Sponsor*

> *Talking Points Memo*. Ed. Josh Marshall. TPM Media, 1 Dec. 2011. Web. 1 Dec. 2011.

Pseudonym   *Real name*

> Negative Camber [Todd McCandless]. *Formula1blog*. F1b., 2011. Web. 1 Dec. 2011.

Post author   *Post title*

> Marshall, Josh. "Coke and Grass at Amish Raid." *Talking Points Memo*. TPM Media, 1 Dec. 2011. Web. 1 Dec. 2011.

Wiki article Since wikis are written and edited collectively, start your entry with the title of the article you are citing.

> "John Lydon." *Wikipedia*. WikiMedia Foundation, 14 Nov. 2011. Web. 1 Dec. 2011.

Discussion group or newsgroup posting

Post author Subject line Group name Site sponsor

Martin, Francesca Alys. "Wait—Did Somebody Say 'Buffy'?" *Cultstud-L*. U of S Fl, 8 Mar. 2000. Web. 8 Mar. 2008.

Post date

E-mail message

Sender Subject line Recipient

Olson, Kate. "Update on State Legislative Grants." Message to the author. 5 Nov. 2008. E-mail.

Date sent Medium

CITING AND DOCUMENTING SOURCES IN APA STYLE

When using the APA system of documentation, include both an in-text citation and a list of references at the end of the research project. In-text citations tell your readers where the ideas or words you have borrowed come from, and the entries in the list of references allow readers to locate your sources so that they can read more about your topic.

The most common types of in-text citations follow. For other, less common citation types, consult the *Publication Manual of the American Psychological Association*, Sixth Edition (2010). Most libraries will own a copy.

USING IN-TEXT CITATIONS TO SHOW WHERE YOU HAVE USED SOURCE MATERIAL

When citing ideas, information, or words borrowed from a source, include the author's last name and the date of publication in the text of your research project. In most cases, you will want to use a signal phrase to introduce the works you are citing, since doing so gives you the opportunity to put the work and its author in context. A signal phrase includes the author's last name, the date of publication, and a verb that describes the author's attitude or stance:

Smith (2011) complains that . . .

Jones (2012) defends her position by . . .

Use a parenthetical citation — *(Jones, 2012)* — when you have already introduced the author or the work or when citing the source of an uncontroversial fact. When quoting from a source, also include the page number: *Smith (2011) complains that he "never gets a break" (p. 123).* When you are paraphrasing or summarizing, you may omit the page reference, although including it is not wrong.

Directory to In-Text-Citation Models

One author 600

More than one author 600

Unknown author 600

Two or more works by the same author in the same year 600

Two or more authors with the same last name 601

Corporation, organization, or government agency as author 601

Indirect citation (quotation from a secondary source) 601

Two or more works cited in the same parentheses 601

One author

SIGNAL PHRASE   Upton Sinclair (2005), a crusading journalist, wrote that workers
sometimes "fell into the vats; and when they were fished out, there
was never enough of them left to be worth exhibiting" (p. 134).

PARENTHETICAL   *The Jungle*, a naturalistic novel inspired by the French writer
CITATION   Zola, described in lurid detail the working conditions of the time,
including what became of unlucky workers who fell into the vats
while making sausage (Sinclair, 2005).

author's last name + date

REFERENCE-LIST   Sinclair, U. (2005). *The jungle*. New York, NY: Oxford University
ENTRY   Press. (Original work published 1906)

More than one author   In a signal phrase, use the word *and* between the authors'
names; in a parenthetical citation, use an ampersand (&). When citing a work by
three to seven authors, list all the authors in your first reference; in subsequent
references, just list the first and use *et al.* (Latin for *and others*).

SIGNAL PHRASE   As Jamison and Tyree (2001) have found, racial bias does not
diminish merely through exposure to individuals of other races.

PARENTHETICAL   Racial bias does not diminish through exposure (Jamison &
CITATION   Tyree, 2001).

FIRST CITATION   Rosenzweig, Breedlove, and Watson (2005) wrote that biological
psychology is an interdisciplinary field that includes scientists from
"quite different backgrounds" (p. 3).

LATER   Biological psychology is "the field that relates behavior to bodily
CITATIONS   processes, especially the workings of the brain" (Rosenzweig et al.,
2005, p. 3).

For a first reference to a work with more than seven authors, list the first six, an
ellipsis (. . .), and the last author.

Unknown author

An international pollution treaty still to be ratified would prohibit all plastic
garbage from being dumped at sea ("Plastic Is Found," 1972).

The full title of the article is "Plastic Is Found in the Sargasso Sea; Pieces of Apparent Refuse Cover Wide Atlantic Region."

Two or more works by the same author in the same year   Alphabetize the
works by title in your list of references, and add a lowercase letter after the date
(2005a, 2005b).

Middle-class unemployed workers are better off than their lower-class counterparts, because "the white collar unemployed are likely to have some assets to invest in their job search" (Ehrenreich, 2005b, p. 16).

Two or more authors with the same last name

F. Johnson (2010) conducted an intriguing study on teen smoking.

Corporation, organization, or government agency as author   Spell out the name of the organization the first time you use it, but abbreviate it in subsequent citations.

(National Institutes of Health, 2012)

(NIH, 2012)

Indirect citation (quotation from a secondary source)   Cite the secondary source in the reference list, and in your essay acknowledge the original source.

E. M. Forster said that "the collapse of all civilization, so realistic for us, sounded in Matthew Arnold's ears like a distant and harmonious cataract" (as cited in Trilling, 1955, p. 11).

Two or more works cited in the same parentheses   List sources in alphabetical order separated by semicolons.

(Johnson, 2010; NIH, 2012)

CREATING A LIST OF REFERENCES

The APA documentation system requires a list of references providing bibliographic information for every in-text citation in the text (except personal communications and entire Web sites). Double-space the reference list, and use a hanging indent (with the first line flush left and subsequent lines indented half an inch). Alphabetize entries by the first main word in the citation.

Directory to Reference-List Models

Author Listings
One author   602
More than one author   602
Unknown author   602

Corporation, organization, or government agency as author   603
Two or more works by the same author   603

(continued)

Books (Print, Electronic)
Basic format for a book 603
Author and editor 603
Edited collection 604
Work in an anthology or edited
     collection 604
Translation 604
Dictionary entry or article in
     another reference book 604
Introduction, preface, foreword, or
     afterword 604
Later edition of a book 604
Government document 604
Unpublished doctoral
     dissertation 604

Articles (Print, Electronic)
From a scholarly journal 605
From a newspaper 605
From a magazine 605

Editorial or letter to the editor 606
Review 606

**Multimedia Sources (Print,
     Electronic)**
Television program 606
Film, video, or DVD 606
Sound recording 606
Interview 606

Other Electronic Sources
Web site 607
Web page or document on a Web
     site 607
Discussion list and newsgroup
     postings 607
Blog post 607
Wiki entry 608
E-mail message 608

One author

> Ehrenreich, B. (2001). *Nickel and dimed: On (not) getting by in America.*
>   New York, NY: Metropolitan.

More than one author

> Saba, L., & Gattis, J. (2002). *The McGraw-Hill homeschooling companion.*
>   New York, NY: McGraw-Hill.

> Hunt, L., Po-Chia Hsia, R., Martin, T. R., Rosenwein, B. H., Rosenwein, H., &
>   Smith, B. G. (2001). *The making of the West: Peoples and cultures.* Boston,
>   MA: Bedford.

If there are more than seven authors, list only the first six, insert an ellipsis
(. . .), and add the last author's name.

Unknown author   If an author is designated as "Anonymous," include the word
Anonymous in place of the author, and alphabetize it as "Anonymous" in the reference list.

> Anonymous. (2006). *Primary colors.* New York, NY: Random House.

> Communities blowing whistle on street basketball. (2003). *USA Today,* p. 20A.

Corporation, organization, or government agency as author

American Medical Association. (2004). *Family medical guide*. Hoboken, NJ: Wiley.

Two or more works by the same author

When you cite two or more works by the same author, arrange them in chronological (time) order.

Pinker, S. (2005). So how does the mind work? *Mind and Language, 20*(1): 1-24. doi:10.1111/j.0268-1064.2005.00274.x

Pinker, S. (2011). *The better angels of our nature: Why violence has declined.* New York, NY: Viking.

When you cite two works by the same author in the same year, alphabetize entries by title and then add a lowercase letter following each year.

Pinker, S. (2005a). *Hotheads.* New York, NY: Pocket Penguins.

Pinker, S. (2005b). So how does the mind work? *Mind and Language, 20*(1), 1-24. doi:10.1111/j.0268-1064.2005.00274.x

BOOKS (PRINT, ELECTRONIC)

When citing a book, capitalize only the first word of the title and subtitle and any proper nouns (*Dallas, Darwin*). Book titles are italicized.

Basic format for a book

Author   Year   Title

PRINT   Pinker, S. (2011). *The better angels of our nature: Why violence has declined.* New York, NY: Viking.

City, State (abbr.)   Publisher

E-BOOK   Pinker, S. (2011). *The better angels of our nature: Why violence has declined.* New York, NY: Viking. [Nook Book Edition].

E-publication information

DATABASE   Darwin, C. (2001). *The origin of species.* Retrieved from http://bartleby.com (Original work published 1909-14)

Database information

If an e-book has been assigned a **digital object identifier** (or *doi*) — a combination of numbers and letters assigned by the publisher to identify the work — add that information at the end of the citation.

Author and editor

Arnold, M. (1994). *Culture and anarchy* (S. Lipman, Ed.). New Haven, CT: Yale University Press. (Original work published 1869)

Edited collection

> Waldman, D., & Walker, J. (Eds.). (1999). *Feminism and documentary*. Minneapolis, MN: University of Minnesota Press.

Work in an anthology or edited collection

> Fairbairn-Dunlop, P. (1993). Women and agriculture in western Samoa. In J. H. Momsen & V. Kinnaird (Eds.), *Different places, different voices* (pp. 211-226). London, England: Routledge.

Translation

> Tolstoy, L. (2002). *War and peace* (C. Garnett, Trans.). New York, NY: Modern Library. (Original work published 1869)

Dictionary entry or article in another reference book

> Rowland, R. P. (2001). Myasthenia gravis. In *Encyclopedia Americana* (Vol. 19, p. 683). Danbury, CT: Grolier.

Introduction, preface, foreword, or afterword

> Graff, G., & Phelan, J. Preface (2004). In M. Twain, *Adventures of Huckleberry Finn* (pp. iii-vii). Boston, MA: Bedford.

Later edition of a book

> Axelrod, R., & Cooper, C. (2013). *The St. Martin's guide to writing* (10th ed.). Boston, MA: Bedford.

Government document

> U.S. Department of Health and Human Services. (2009). *Trends in underage drinking in the United States, 1991-2007*. Washington, DC: Government Printing Office.

Note: When the author and publisher are the same, use the word *Author* (not italicized) as the name of the publisher.

Unpublished doctoral dissertation

> Bullock, B. (1986). *Basic needs fulfillment among less developed countries: Social progress over two decades of growth* (Unpublished doctoral dissertation). Vanderbilt University, Nashville, TN.

ARTICLES (PRINT, ELECTRONIC)

For articles, capitalize only the first word of the title, proper nouns (*Barclay, Berlin*), and the first word following a colon (if any). Omit quotation marks around the titles of articles, but capitalize all the important words of journal, newspaper, and magazine titles, and set them in italics. If you are accessing an article through a database, follow the model for a comparable source.

From a scholarly journal

PRINT

<small>Author   Year   Article title</small>

Tran, D. (2002). Personal income by state, second quarter 2002.
Current Business, 82(11), 55-73.

<small>Journal title   Volume (issue) Pages</small>

Shan, J. Z., Morris, A. G., & Sun, F. (2001). Financial development
and economic growth: A chicken and egg problem? *Review of
Economics, 9,* 443-454.

<small>Volume only   Pages</small>

Include the digital object identifier (or *doi*) when available. When a doi has not
been assigned, include the journal's URL.

ELECTRONIC

Tharp, R. G. (1989). Psychocultural variables and constants: Effects
on teaching and learning in schools. *American Psychologist,
44*(2), 349-359. doi:10.1037/0003-066X.44.2.349

<small>doi</small>

Houston, R. G., & Toma, F. (2003). Home schooling: An alternative
school choice. *Southern Economic Journal, 69*(4), 920-936.
Retrieved from http://www.southerneconomic.org

<small>URL</small>

From a newspaper

<small>Year Month Day</small>

PRINT

Peterson, A. (2003, May 20). Finding a cure for old age. *The Wall
Street Journal,* pp. D1, D5.

ELECTRONIC

Barboza, D., & LaFraniere, S. (2012, May 17). 'Princelings' in China
use family ties to gain riches. *The New York Times.* Retrieved
from http://www.nytimes.com

From a magazine

If a magazine is published weekly or biweekly (every other
week), include the full date following the author's name. If it is published monthly
or bimonthly, include just the year and month (or months).

<small>Weekly or biweekly</small>

PRINT

Gross, M. J. (2003, April 29). Family life during war time. *The
Advocate,* 42-48.

<small>Monthly or bimonthly</small>

Shelby, A. (2005, September/October). Good going: Alaska's glacier
crossroads. *Sierra, 90,* 23.

ELECTRONIC

Marche, S. (2012, May). Is Facebook making us lonely? *The Atlantic.*
Retrieved from http://theatlantic.com

Editorial or letter to the editor

> Kosinski, T. (2012, May 15). Who cares what she thinks? [Letter to the editor]. *The Chicago Sun-Times*. Retrieved from http:// www.suntimes.com/opinions /letters/12522890-474/who-cares-what-she-thinks.html

Review
"Review of" + item type + title of item reviewed

> Cassidy, J. (2002, July 12). Master of disaster [Review of the book *Globalization and its discontents*]. *The New Yorker*, 82-86.

If the review is untitled, use the bracketed information as the title, retaining the brackets.

MULTIMEDIA SOURCES (PRINT, ELECTRONIC)

Television program

> Charlsen, C. (Writer and producer). (2003, July 14). Murder of the century

Label

> [Television series episode]. In M. Samels (Executive producer), *American Experience*. Boston, MA: WGBH.

Film, video, or DVD
Label

> Nolan, C. (Writer and director). (2010). *Inception* [Motion picture]. Los Angeles, CA: Warner Bros.

Sound recording

PODCAST   Dubner, S. (2012, May 17). Retirement kills [Audio podcast]. *Freakonomics Radio*. Retrieved from http://www .freakonomics.com

Label

RECORDING   Maroon 5. (2010). Moves like Jagger. On *Hands all over* [CD]. New York, NY: A&M/Octone Records.

Interview   Do not list personal interviews in your reference list. Instead, cite the interviewee in your text (last name and initials), and in parentheses give the notation *personal communication* (in regular type, not italicized) followed by a comma and the date of the interview. For published interviews, use the appropriate format for an article.

OTHER ELECTRONIC SOURCES

A rule of thumb for citing electronic sources not covered in one of the preceding sections is to include enough information to allow readers to access and

retrieve the source. For most online sources, provide as much of the following
as you can:

- name of author

- date of publication or most recent update (in parentheses; if unavailable, use
  the abbreviation *n.d.*)

- title of document (such as a Web page)

- title of Web site

- any special retrieval information, such as a URL; include the date you last
  accessed the source only when the content is likely to change or be updated
  (as on a wiki, for example)

Web site   The APA does not require an entry in the list of references for entire
Web sites. Instead, give the name of the site in your text with its Web address in
parentheses.

Web page or document on a Web site

> American Cancer Society. (2011, Oct. 10). *Child and teen tobacco use.* Retrieved
> from http://www.cancer.org/Cancer/CancerCauses/TobaccoCancer
> /ChildandTeenTobaccoUse/child-and-teen-tobacco-use-what-to-do

> Heins, M. (2003, January 24). The strange case of Sarah Jones. *The Free Expression
> Policy Project.* Retrieved from http://www.fepproject.org/commentaries
> /sarahjones.html

Discussion list and newsgroup postings   Include online postings in your list of
references only if you can provide data that would allow others to retrieve the
source.

Label

> Paikeday, T. (2005, October 10). "Esquivalience" is out [Electronic mailing
> list message]. Retrieved from http://listserv.linguistlist.org/cgi-bin
> /wa?A15ind0510b&L5ads-1#1

Label

> Ditmire, S. (2005, February 10). NJ tea party [Newsgroup message]. Retrieved from
> http://groups.google.com/group/TeaParty

Blog post   Label

> Mestel, R. (2012, May 17). Fructose makes rats dumber [Web log post]. Retrieved
> from http://www.latimes.com/health/boostershots/la-fructose-makes-rats
> -stupid-brain-20120517,0,2305241.story?track5rss

Wiki entry   Start with the article title and include the post date, since wikis may be updated frequently (use *n.d.* if there is no date), as well as the retrieval date.

> Sleep. (2011, November 26). Retrieved May 21, 2011, from Wiki of Science: http://wikiofscience.wikidot.com/science:sleep

E-mail message   Personal correspondence, including e-mail, should not be included in your reference list. Instead, cite the person's name in your text, and in parentheses give the notation *personal communication* (in regular type, not italicized) and the date.

Strategies for Analyzing Visuals

We live in a highly visual world. Every day we are deluged with a seemingly endless stream of images from television, magazines, billboards, books, Web pages, newspapers, flyers, storefront signs, and more, all of them competing for our attention, and all of them loaded with information and ideas. Forms of communication that traditionally used only the written word (letters, books, term papers) or the spoken word (telephone conversations, lectures) are today increasingly enhanced with visual components (PowerPoint slides, cell-phone graphics, video, photos, illustrations, graphs, and the like) for greater impact. And most of us would agree that *visuals* do, indeed, have an impact: A picture, as the saying goes, is worth a thousand words.

In part because of their potentially powerful effect on us, visuals and visual texts* should be approached the way we approach written texts: analytically and critically. Whether their purpose is to sell us an idea or a car, to spur us to action or inspire us to dream, visuals invite analysis both of their key components and their *rhetorical context*. As we "read" a visual, therefore, we should ask ourselves a series of questions: Who created it? Where was it published? What *audience* is it addressing? What is it trying to get this audience to think and feel about the subject? How does it attempt to achieve this *purpose*?

Let's look, for example, at the visual text on the following page: a public service announcement (PSA) from the World Wildlife Fund (WWF).

The central image in this PSA is a photo of an attractive, smiling young couple. Most of us will immediately recognize the dress, posture, and facial expressions of the young man and woman as those of a newly married couple; the

---

*In this chapter, we use the word *image* to refer primarily to photographs. We use the word *visual* as a broader designation for visual elements of texts (including images, but also such components as diagrams, charts, and graphs), and *visual text* for documents such as ads, brochures, and the like, in which visuals are strongly featured, but which consist of more than a single image.

FIGURE 12.1 "Wedding," from the WWF's "Beautiful Day U.S." Series

photo-mounting corners make the image seem like a real wedding album photo, as opposed to an ad agency's creation (which would be easier to ignore). After noting these things, however, we are immediately struck by what is wrong with the picture: a hurricane rages in the background, blowing hair, clothing, and the bride's veil forcefully to one side while showering the bride's pure white dress with spots (of rain? mud?) and threatening to rip the bridal bouquet from her hand.

So what do we make of the disruption of the convention (the traditional wedding photo) on which the PSA image is based? In trying to decide, most of us will look next to the text below the image: "Ignoring global warming won't make it go away." The disjunction between the couple's blissful expression and the storm raging around them turns out to be the point of the PSA: Like the young couple in the picture, the PSA implies, we are all blithely ignoring the impending disaster that global warming represents. The reputable, nonprofit WWF's logo and URL, which constitute its "signature," are meant to be an assurance that this threat is real, and not just an idea a profit-seeking ad agency dreamt up to manipulate us.

People continue to argue about how urgent the problem of climate change is and what, if anything, we need to do about it. Not everyone will be convinced by this PSA to support the work of the WWF, and some viewers may feel manipulated by the visual image. They may disagree that the problem is as dire as the depiction implicitly claims it is. They may feel that our resources and energy would be better directed toward other problems facing the world. Nevertheless, most people would agree that with a single cleverly constructed image, a single line of text, and a logo, the PSA delivers its message clearly and forcefully.

CRITERIA FOR ANALYZING VISUALS

The primary purpose of this chapter is to help you analyze visuals and write about them. In your college courses, some of you will be asked to write entire papers in which you analyze one or more visuals (a painting or a photo, for example). Some of you will write papers in which you include analysis of one or more visual texts within the context of a larger written essay (say, by analyzing the brochures and ads authorized by a political candidate, in an argument about her campaign).

Of course, learning to analyze visuals effectively can also help you gain a more complete understanding of any document that *uses* visuals but that is not entirely or predominantly composed of them. Why did the author of a remembered event essay, for example, choose a particular photo of a person mentioned in the text — does it reinforce the written description, add to it, or contradict it in some way? If there is a caption under the photo, how does it affect the way we read it? In a concept explanation, why are illustrations of one process included but not those of another? How well do the charts and graphs work with the text to help us understand the author's explanation? Understanding what visuals can do for a text can also help you effectively integrate images, charts, graphs, and other visuals into your own essays, whatever your topic.

The chart below outlines key criteria for analyzing visuals and provides questions for you to ask about documents that include them.

CRITERIA FOR ANALYZING VISUALS

Key Components

Composition

- Of what elements is the visual composed?
- What is the focal point—that is, the place your eyes are drawn to?
- From what perspective do you view the focal point? Are you looking straight ahead at it, down at it, or up at it? If the visual is a photograph, what angle was the image shot from—straight ahead, looking down or up?
- What colors are used? Are there obvious special effects employed? Is there a frame, or are there any additional graphical elements? If so, what do these elements contribute to your "reading" of the visual?

People/Other Main Figures

- If people are depicted, how would you describe their age, gender, subculture, ethnicity, profession, and socioeconomic class? How stereotypical or surprising are the people?
- Who is looking at whom? Do the people represented seem conscious of the viewer's gaze?
- What do the facial expressions and body language tell you about power relationships (equal, subordinate, in charge) and attitudes (self-confident, vulnerable, anxious, subservient, angry, aggressive, sad)?

Scene

- If a recognizable scene is depicted, what is its setting? What is in the background and the foreground?
- What has happened just before the image was "shot"? What will happen in the next scene?
- What, if anything, is happening just outside of the visual frame?

(continued)

CRITERIA FOR ANALYZING VISUALS *(continued)*

Words

- If text is combined with the visual, what role does the text play? Is it a slogan? A famous quote? Lyrics from a well-known song?
- If the text helps you interpret the visual's overall meaning, what interpretive clues does it provide?

Tone

- What tone, or mood, does the visual convey? Is it lighthearted, somber, frightening, shocking, joyful? What elements in the visual (color, composition, words, people, setting) convey this tone?
- What is the tone of the text? Humorous? Elegiac? Ironic?

Context(s)

Rhetorical Context

- **What is the visual's main purpose?** Are we being asked to buy a product? Form an opinion or judgment about something? Support a political party's candidate? Take some other kind of action?
- **Who is its target audience?** Children? Men? Women? Some sub- or super-set of these groups (e.g., African American men, "tweens," seniors)?
- **Who is the author? Who sponsored its publication?** What background/ associations do the author and the sponsoring publication have? What other works have they produced?
- **Where was it published, and in what form?** Online? On television? In print? In a commercial publication (a sales brochure, billboard, ad) or an informational one (newspaper, magazine)?
- **If the visual is embedded within a document that is primarily written text, how do the written text and the visual relate to each other?** Do they convey the same message, or are they at odds in any way? What does the image contribute to the written text? Is it essential or just eye candy?
- *Social Context.* **What is the immediate social and cultural context within which the visual is operating?** If we are being asked to support a certain candidate, for example, how does the visual reinforce or counter what we already know about this candidate? What other social/cultural knowledge does the visual assume its audience already has?
- *Historical Context.* **What historical knowledge does it assume the audience already possesses?** Does the visual refer to other historical images, figures, events, or stories that the audience would recognize? How do these historical references relate to the visual's audience and purpose?
- *Intertextuality.* **How does the visual connect, relate to, or contrast with any other significant texts, visual or otherwise, that you are aware of?** How do such considerations inform your ideas about this particular visual?

A SAMPLE ANALYSIS

In a composition class, students were asked to do a short written analysis of a photograph. In looking for ideas, Paul Taylor came across the Library of Congress's *Documenting America,* an exhibit of photographs taken 1935–1945. Gordon Parks's photographs struck Paul as particularly interesting, especially those of Ella Watson, a poorly paid office cleaner employed by the federal government. (See Figure 12.2.)

After studying the photos, Paul read about Parks's first session with Watson:

> My first photograph of [Watson] was unsubtle. I overdid it and posed her, Grant Wood style, before the American flag, a broom in one hand, a mop in the other, staring straight into the camera.[1]

Paul didn't understand Parks's reference to Grant Wood in his description of the photo, so he did an Internet search and discovered that Parks was referring to a classic painting by Wood called *American Gothic* (Figure 12.3). Reading further about the connection, he discovered that Parks's photo of Watson is itself commonly titled *American Gothic* and discussed as a parody of Grant Wood's painting.

FIGURE 12.2 *American Gothic* (Gordon Parks), Washington, DC, 1942

FIGURE 12.3 *American Gothic,* Grant Wood (1930)

Source: The Art Institute of Chicago. © Figge Art Museum, successors to the estate of Nan Wood Graham/VAGA.

[1]Gordon Parks, *A Choice of Weapons* (New York: Harper & Row, 1966), 230–31.

After learning about the connection with *American Gothic*, Paul read more about the context of Parks's photos:

> Gordon Parks was born in Kansas in 1912. . . . During the Depression a variety of jobs . . . took him to various parts of the northern United States. He took up photography during his travels. . . . In 1942, an opportunity to work for the Farm Security Administration brought the photographer to the nation's capital; Parks later recalled that "discrimination and bigotry were worse there than any place I had yet seen."[2]

Intrigued by what he had learned so far, Paul decided to delve into Parks's later career. A 2006 obituary of Parks in the *New York Times* reproduced his 1952 photo *Emerging Man* (Figure 12.4), which Paul decided to analyze for his assignment. First he did additional research on the photo. Then he made notes on his responses to the photo using the criteria for analysis provided on pp. 611–12.

FIGURE 12.4 *Emerging Man* (Gordon Parks), Harlem, New York, 1952

[2]Martin H. Bush, "A Conversation with Gordon Parks," in *The Photographs of Gordon Parks* (Wichita, KS: Wichita State University, 1983), 36.

PAUL TAYLOR'S ANALYSIS OF *EMERGING MAN*

Key Components of the Visual

Composition

- **Of what elements is the visual composed?** It's a black-and-white photo showing the top three-quarters of a man's face and his hands (mostly fingers). He appears to be emerging out of the ground—out of a sewer? There's what looks like asphalt in the foreground, and buildings (out of focus) in the far background.
- **What is the focal point—that is, the place your eyes are drawn to?** The focal point is the face of the man staring directly into the camera's lens. There's a shaft of light angled (slightly from the right?) onto the lower-middle part of his face. His eyes appear to glisten slightly. The rest of his face, his hands, and the foreground are in shadow.
- **From what perspective do you view the focal point?** We appear to be looking at him at eye level—weird, since eye level for him is just a few inches from the ground. Was the photographer lying down? The shot is also a close-up—a foot or two from the man's face. Why so close?
- **What colors are used? Are there obvious special effects employed? Is there a frame, or are there any additional graphical elements?** There's no visible frame or any graphic elements. The image is in stark black and white, and there's a "graininess" to it: We can see the texture of the man's skin and the asphalt on the street.

People / Other Main Figures

- **If people are depicted, how would you describe their age, gender, subculture, ethnicity, profession, level of attractiveness, and socioeconomic class?** The man is African American and probably middle-aged (or at least not obviously very young or very old). We can't see his clothing or any other marker of class, profession, etc. The fact that he seems to be emerging from a sewer implies that he's not hugely rich or prominent, of course—a "man of the people"?
- **Who is looking at whom? Do the people represented seem conscious of the viewer's gaze?** The man seems to be looking directly into the camera and at the viewer (who's in the position of the photographer). I guess, yes, he seems to look straight at the viewer—perhaps in a challenging or questioning way.
- **What do the facial expressions and body language tell you about power relationships (equal, subordinate, in charge) and attitudes (self-confident, vulnerable, anxious, subservient, angry, aggressive, sad)?** We can only see his face from the nose up, and his fingertips. It looks like one eyebrow is slightly raised, which might mean he's questioning or skeptical. The expression in his eyes is definitely serious. The position of his fingers implies that he's clutching the rim of the manhole—that, and the title, indicate that he's pulling himself up out of the hole. But since we see only the fingers, not the whole hand, does his hold seem tenuous—he's "holding on by his fingertips"? Not sure.

(continued)

PAUL TAYLOR'S ANALYSIS OF
EMERGING MAN (continued)

Scene

- **If a recognizable scene is depicted, what is its setting? What is in the background and the foreground?** It looks like an urban setting (asphalt, manhole cover, buildings, and lights in the blurry distant background). Descriptions of the photo note that Parks shot the image in Harlem. Hazy buildings and objects are in the distance. Only the man's face and fingertips are in focus. The sky behind him is light gray, though—is it dawn?
- **What has happened just before the image was "shot"? What will happen in the next scene?** He appears to be coming up and out of the hole in the ground (the sewer).
- **What, if anything, is happening just outside of the visual frame?** It's not clear. There's no activity in the background at all. It's deserted, except for him.

Words

- **If text is combined with the visual, what role does the text play?** There's no text on or near the image. There is the title, though—*Emerging Man*.
- **If the text helps you interpret the visual's overall meaning, what interpretive clues does it provide?** The title is a literal description, but it might also refer to the civil rights movement—the gradual racial and economic integration—of African Americans into American society.

Tone

- **What tone, or mood, does the visual convey? What elements in the visual (color, composition, words, people, setting) convey this tone?** The tone is serious, even perhaps a bit spooky. The use of black and white and heavy shadows lends a somewhat ominous feel, though the ray of light on the man's face, the lightness of the sky, and the lights in the background counterbalance this to an extent. The man's expression is somber, though not obviously angry or grief-stricken.
- **What is the tone of the text?** Hard to say. I guess, assuming wordplay is involved, it's sort of witty (merging traffic?).

Context(s)

Rhetorical Context

- **What is the visual's main purpose?** Given Parks's interest in politics and social justice, it seems fair to assume that the image of the man emerging from underground—from the darkness into the light?—is a reference to social progress (civil rights movement) and suggests rebirth of a sort. The use of black and white, while certainly not unusual in photographs of the era, emphasizes the division between black and white that is in part the photo's subject.
- **Who is its target audience?** Because it appeared first in *Life* magazine, the target audience was mainstream—a broad cross-section of the magazine-reading U.S. population at mid-twentieth century. Were *Life* readers primarily white or various ethnicities?
- **Who is the author? Who sponsored its publication?** During this era, Gordon Parks was best known as a photographer whose works documented and commented on social conditions.

- **If the visual is embedded within a document that is primarily written text, how do the written text and the visual relate to each other?** The photo accompanied an article about Ellison's *Invisible Man*, a novel about a man who goes underground to escape racism and conflicts within the early civil rights movement. Now the man is reentering mainstream society?
- *Social Context.* **What is the immediate social and cultural context within which the visual is operating?** The civil rights movement was gaining ground in post–World War II society.
- *Historical Context.* **What historical knowledge does it assume the audience already possesses?** For a viewer in 1952, the image would call to mind the current and past situation of African Americans. Uncertainty about what the future would hold (Would the emergence be successful? What kind of man would eventually emerge?) would be a big part of the viewer's response. Viewers today obviously feel less suspense about what would happen in the immediate (post-1952) future. The "vintage" feel of the photo's style and even the man's hair, along with the use of black and white, probably have a "distancing" effect on the viewer today. At the same time, the subject continues to be relevant—most viewers will likely think about the progress we've made in race relations and where we're currently headed.
- *Intertextuality.* **How does the visual connect, relate to, or contrast with any other significant texts, visual or otherwise, that you are aware of?** *Invisible Man*, which I've already discussed, was a best-seller and won the National Book Award in 1953.

After writing and reviewing these notes and doing some further research to fill in gaps in his knowledge about Parks, Ellison, and the civil rights movement, Paul drafted his analysis. He submitted this draft to his peer group for comments, and then revised. His final draft follows.

Paul Taylor

Professor Stevens

Writing Seminar I

4 October 2012

The Rising

Gordon Parks's 1952 photograph *Emerging Man* (fig. 1) is as historically significant a reflection of the civil rights movement as are the speeches of Martin Luther King and Malcolm X, the music of Mahalia Jackson, and the books of Ralph Ellison and James Baldwin. Through striking use of black and white—a reflection of the racial divisions plaguing American cities and towns throughout much of the nineteenth and twentieth centuries—and a symbolically potent central subject—an African American man we see literally "emerging" from a city manhole—Parks's photo evokes the centuries of racial and economic marginalization of African Americans, at the same time as it projects a spirit of determination and optimism regarding the civil rights movement's eventual success.

In choosing the starkest of urban settings and giving the image a gritty feel, Parks alerts the viewer to the gravity of his subject and gives it a sense of immediacy. As with the documentary photographs Parks took of office cleaner Ella Watson for the Farm Security Administration

Fig. 1. Gordon Parks, *Emerging Man* (Harlem, New York, 1952)

Fig. 2. Gordon Parks, *American Gothic*
(Washington, DC, 1942)

in the 1940s—see fig. 2 for one example—the carefully chosen
setting and the spareness of the treatment ensure the viewer's focus on
the social statement the artist is making (*Documenting*). Whereas the
photos of Ella Watson document a particular woman and the actual
conditions of her life and work, however, *Emerging Man* strips away
any particulars, including any name for the man, with the result that
the photo enters the symbolic or even mythic realm.

The composition of *Emerging Man* makes it impossible for us
to focus on anything other than the unnamed subject rising from the
manhole—we are, for instance, unable to consider what the weather
might be, though we might surmise from the relatively light tone of
the sky and the emptiness of the street that it is dawn. Similarly, we
are not given any specifics of the setting, which is simply urban and,
apart from the central figure, unpopulated. Reducing the elements to
their outlines in this way keeps the viewer focused on the grand central
theme of the piece: the role of race in mid-twentieth-century America
and the future of race relations.

The fact that the man is looking directly at the camera, in a way
that's challenging but not hostile, speaks to the racial optimism of the

Taylor 3

period among many African Americans and whites alike. President Truman's creation of the President's Committee on Civil Rights in 1946 and his 1948 Executive Order for the integration of all armed services were significant steps toward the emergence of the full-blown civil rights movement, providing hope that African Americans would be able, for perhaps the first time in American history, to look directly into the eyes of their white counterparts and fearlessly emphasize their shared humanity (Leuchtenburg). The "emerging man" seems to be daring us to try to stop his rise from the manhole, his hands gripping its sides, his eyes focused intently on the viewer.

According to several sources, Parks planned and executed the photograph as a photographic counterpart to Ralph Ellison's 1952 *Invisible Man*, a breakthrough novel about race and society that was both a best-seller and a critical success. *Invisible Man* is narrated in the first person by an unnamed African American man who traces his experiences from boyhood. The climax of the novel shows the narrator hunted by policemen controlling a Harlem race riot; escaping down a manhole, the narrator is trapped at first but eventually decides to live permanently underground, hidden from society ("Ralph Ellison"). The correspondences between the photo and the book are apparent. In fact, according to the catalog accompanying an exhibit of Parks's photos selected by the photographer himself before his death in 2006, Ellison actually collaborated on the staging of the photo (*Bare Witness*).

More than just a photographic counterpart, however, it seems that Parks's *Emerging Man* can be read as a sequel to *Invisible Man*, with the emphasis radically shifted from resignation to optimism. The man who had decided to live underground now decides to emerge, and does so with determination. In this compelling photograph, Parks—himself an "emerging man," considering he was the first African American photographer to be hired full-time by the widely respected mainstream *Life* magazine—created a photograph that celebrated the changing racial landscape in American society.

Taylor 4

Works Cited

Bare Witness: Photographs by Gordon Parks. Catalog. Milan: Skira;
  Stanford, CA: Iris & B. Gerald Cantor Center for Visual Arts at
  Stanford University, 2006. Traditional Fine Arts Organization.
  Resource Library. Web. 29 Sept. 2012.

Documenting America: Photographers on Assignment. 15 Dec. 1998.
  *America from the Great Depression to World War II: Black-and-
  White Photographs from the FSA-OWI, 1935-1945.* Prints and
  Photographs Div., Lib. of Cong. Web. 27 Sept. 2012.

Leuchtenburg, William E. "The Conversion of Harry Truman." *American
  Heritage* 42.7 (1991): 55-68. *America: History & Life.* Web. 29
  Sept. 2012.

Parks, Gordon. *Ella Watson.* Aug. 1942. *America from the Great
  Depression to World War II: Black-and-White Photographs from
  the FSA-OWI, 1935-1945.* Prints and Photographs Div., Lib. of
  Cong. Web. 27 Sept. 2012.

---. *Emerging Man.* 1952. *PhotoMuse.* George Eastman House and
  ICP, n.d. Web. 26 Sept. 2012.

"Ralph Ellison: *Invisible Man.*" *Literature and Its Times: Profiles of 300
  Notable Literary Works and the Historical Events That Influenced
  Them.* Ed. Joyce Moss and George Wilson. Vol. 4. Gale Research,
  1997. *Literature Resource Center.* Web. 30 Sept. 2012.

ACKNOWLEDGMENTS

Text Credits

Beth Bailey. *Front Porch to Back Seat: Courtship in Twentieth-Century America* (pp. 25–56). Copyright © 1988 by the Johns Hopkins University Press. Reprinted with permission of the Johns Hopkins University Press.

David Bornstein. "Fighting Bullying with Babies" from the *New York Times*, November 8, 2010. Copyright © 2010 by the New York Times. All rights reserved. Used by permission and protected by the Copyright Laws of the United States. The printing, copying, redistribution, or retransmission of this Content without express written permission is prohibited. www.nytimes.com

Kelly D. Brownell and Thomas R. Frieden. "Ounces of Prevention — The Public Policy Case for Taxes on Sugared Beverages" from the *New England Journal of Medicine*, 360:1805–8, April 30, 2009. Copyright © 2009 by Massachusetts Medical Society. Reprinted with permission from Massachusetts Medical Society.

Susan Cain. "Shyness: Evolutionary Tactic?" from the *New York Times* Sunday Review; the Opinion Pages, June 25, 2011. Copyright © 2011 by the New York Times. All rights reserved. Used by permission and protected by the Copyright Laws of the United States. The printing, copying, redistribution, or retransmission of this Content without express written permission is prohibited. www.nytimes.com

Nicholas Carr. "Is Google Making Us Stupid?" from *Atlantic Monthly* (Ideas Issue), Summer 2008. Copyright © 2008 by Nicholas Carr. Reprinted by permission of the author.

Jenée Desmond-Harris. "Tupac and My Non-Thug Life" from *The Root*, September 13, 2011. Copyright © 2011 by the Slate Group. All rights reserved. Used by permission and protected by the Copyright Laws of the United States. The printing, copying, redistribution, or retransmission of the Material without express written permission is prohibited. www.theroot.com

Annie Dillard. Excerpt from *An American Childhood* (pp. 45–49) by Annie Dillard. Copyright © 1987 by Annie Dillard. Reprinted with permission of HarperCollins Publishers and Russell & Volkening as agents for the author.

John T. Edge. "I'm Not Leaving Until I Eat This Thing," originally published in *Oxford American* (September/October 1999). Copyright © 1999 by John T. Edge. Reprinted by permission of the author.

Amitai Etzioni. "Working at McDonald's," originally published in the *Miami Herald*, August 24, 1986. Copyright © 1986 by Amitai Etzioni. Author of *The Spirit of Community*; Director, George Washington University Center for Communication Policy Studies. Reprinted by permission of the author.

Malcolm Gladwell. "The Order of Things: What College Rankings Really Tell Us" by Malcolm Gladwell. Copyright © 2005 by Malcolm Gladwell. Originally published in the *New Yorker*. Reprinted by permission of the author.

Brian Greene. "Put a Little Science in Your Life" from the *New York Times*, June 1, 2008. Copyright © 2008 by the New York Times. All rights reserved. Used by permission and protected by the Copyright Laws of the United States. The printing, copying, redistribution, or retransmission of this Content without express written permission is prohibited. www.nytimes.com

Dan Hurley. "Can You Make Yourself Smarter?" from the *New York Times*, April 18, 2012. Copyright © 2012 by the New York Times. All rights reserved. Used by permission and protected by the Copyright Laws of the United States. The printing, copying, redistribution, or retransmission of this Content without express written permission is prohibited. www.nytimes.com

Dana Jennings. "Our Scars Tell the Stories of Our Lives" from the *New York Times*, July 21, 2009. Copyright © 2009 by the New York Times. All rights reserved. Used by permission and protected by the Copyright Laws of the United States. The printing, copying, redistribution, or retransmission of this Content without express written permission is prohibited. www.nytimes.com

Martin Luther King Jr. Excerpt from "Letter from Birmingham Jail." Copyright © 1963 by Dr. Martin Luther King, Jr.; copyright renewed 1991 by Coretta Scott King. Reprinted by arrangement with the Heirs to the Estate of Martin Luther King, Jr., c/o Writers House as agent for the proprietor, New York, NY.

Shankar Vedantam. Excerpt from "The Telescope Effect" from *The Hidden Brain: How Our Unconscious Minds Elect Presidents, Control Markets, Wage Wars, and Save Our Lives* by Shankar Vedantam. Copyright © 2010 by Shankar Vedantam. Used by permission of Spiegel & Grau, an imprint of the Random House Publishing Group, a division of Random House, Inc. Any third party use of this material, outside of this publication, is prohibited. Interested parties must apply directly to Random House, Inc. for permission. For online information about other Random House, Inc. books and authors, see the Web site at http://www.randomhouse.com.

Rob Walker. "Replacement Therapy" as first published in the *Atlantic Magazine.* Copyright © 2011 by the Atlantic Media Company. All rights reserved. Distributed by Tribune Media Services.

Claudia Wallis. "The Multitasking Generation" from *TIME Magazine*, March 27, 2006. Copyright © 2006 by TIME, INC. Reprinted by permission. TIME is a registered trademark of Time Inc. All rights reserved.

Dan Zevin. "Father Shops Best" from *Dan Gets a Minivan* by Dan Zevin. Copyright © 2012 by Dan Zevin. Reprinted with the permission of Scribner, a division of Simon & Schuster, Inc. All rights reserved.

Photo Credits

Page 44, courtesy of Jenée Desmond-Harris; **71,** Shannon Stapleton/Reuters/Landov; **82,** Shannon Brinkman Photo; **91,** © inga spence/Alamy, **105,** © Scott Ryan; **107,** Mario Anzuoni/Reuters/Landov; **152,** © Alisha Marie Ragland; **280,** © Universal/courtesy Everett Collection; **281,** (top and bottom) © Universal/courtesy Everett Collection; **283,** © Universal/courtesy Everett Collection; **401,** Ken Ige/Reuters/Landov; **409,** Tom Cheney/The New Yorker Collection/cartoonbank.com; **450,** (left and right) Melanie Gordon; **467,** data courtesy of Barry M. Popkin/Carolina Population Center; **468,** data from the US Bureau of Labor Statistics; **552,** Google and the Google logo are registered trademarks of Google Inc., used with permission; **566,** (left and right) © Bill Aron/PhotoEdit; **610,** courtesy of World Wildlife Fund/worldwildlife.org; **613,** (left) *American Gothic*, Washington, D.C., 1942. Copyright The Gordon Parks Foundation. Courtesy The Gordon Parks Foundation; (right) *American Gothic*, Grant Wood (1930) The Art Institute of Chicago. Art © Figge Art Museum, successors to the Estate of Nan Wood Graham/Licensed by VAGA, New York, NY; **614 & 618,** Copyright The Gordon Parks Foundation. Courtesy The Gordon Parks Foundation; **619,** *American Gothic*, Washington, D.C., 1942. Copyright The Gordon Parks Foundation. Courtesy The Gordon Parks Foundation.

Index to Methods of Development

This index lists the readings in the text according to the writing methods or strategies the authors used to develop their ideas. For readings relying predominantly on one method, we indicate the first page of the reading. If a method plays a minor role in a reading, we also provide the paragraph number(s) where the method is put to use. Readings designated with the ⓔ symbol appear in the Bedford Integrated Media and can be found at **www.bedfordstmartins.com/readingcritically**. A complete list of these selections, with an indication of the medium and type of each selection, appears at the end of this book.

Argument

Katherine Haines, "Whose Body Is This?" 161

Susan Cain, "Shyness: Evolutionary Tactic?" 181

Amitai Etzioni, "Working at McDonald's," 249 (pars. 11–13)

Malcolm Gladwell, "What College Rankings Really Tell Us," 260

Christine Rosen, "The Myth of Multitasking," 270

William Akana, "*Scott Pilgrim vs. the World*: A Hell of a Ride," 279

Christine Romano, "Jessica Statsky's 'Children Need to Play, Not Compete': An Evaluation," 287

Brian Greene, "Put a Little Science in Your Life," 315

Karen Stabiner, "Boys Here, Girls There: Sure, If Equality's the Goal," 325

Sherry Turkle, "The Flight from Conversation," 334

Daniel J. Solove, "Why Privacy Matters Even If You Have 'Nothing to Hide,' " 341

Jessica Statsky, "Children Need to Play, Not Compete," 349

Stephen King, "Why We Crave Horror Movies," 378

Claudia Wallis, "The Multitasking Generation," 385

Shankar Vedantam, "The Telescope Effect," 400

Nicholas Carr, "Is Google Making Us Stupid?" 408

Sheila McClain, "Fitness Culture: A Growing Trend in America," 418

David Bornstein, "Fighting Bullying with Babies," 447

William F. Shughart II, "Why Not a Football Degree?" 459

Kelly D. Brownell and Thomas R. Frieden, "Ounces of Prevention — The Public Policy Case for Taxes on Sugared Beverages," 466

Karen Kornbluh, "Win-Win Flexibility," 474

Patrick O'Malley, "More Testing, More Learning," 483

Francine Wheeler, "Sandy Hook Victim's Mother Delivers President Obama's Weekly Radio Address, April 13, 2013" ⓔ (ch. 4)

Justin Ton, "Hip-Hop You Don't Stop" ⓔ (ch. 5)

Linda Stone, "Continuous Partial Attention" ⓔ (ch. 5)

Brittany Lemus, "*Requiem for a Dream*: Fantasy versus Reality" ⓔ (ch. 6)

Marlon Bishop, "Gig Alert: Bright Eyes" ⓔ (ch. 6)

Tan-Li Hsu, "High on Caffeine: Regulating Energy Drinks" ⓔ (ch. 7)

Ad Council/Dept. of Transportation, "The 'It's Only Another Beer' Black and Tan" ⓔ (ch. 7)

Michele Cox, "The Truth about Lying" ⓔ (ch. 8)

On the Media, "The Reel Sounds of Violence" ⓔ (ch. 8)

Molly Coleman, "Missing the Fun" ⓔ (ch. 9)

Phoebe Sweet and Zach Wise, "The Problem with Lawns: The Transforming Landscape of Las Vegas" e (ch. 9)

Cause or Effect

Tom Ruprecht, "In Too Deep," 32 (pars. 1–2)

Brian Cable, "The Last Stop," 104 (pars. 22–23)

Gabriel Thompson, "A Gringo in the Lettuce Fields," 89 (pars. 5, 15–16)

Brent Staples, "Black Men and Public Space," 132 (pars. 2, 3, 6)

———, "From *Parallel Time*," 140 (pars. 2–6)

Rob Walker, "Replacement Therapy," 156

Katherine Haines, "Whose Body Is This?," 161

Deborah Tannen, "Marked Women," 192 (pars. 19–23)

Beth L. Bailey, "Dating," 201

Dan Hurley, "Can You Make Yourself Smarter?," 212

Amitai Etzioni, "Working at McDonald's," 249 (pars. 11–14)

Christine Rosen, "The Myth of Multitasking," 270 (pars. 7–16)

Brian Greene, "Put a Little Science in Your Life," 315 (pars. 7–20)

Karen Stabiner, "Boys Here, Girls There: Sure, If Equality's the Goal," 325 (pars. 6–7, 15)

Jessica Statsky, "Children Need to Play, Not Compete," 349 (pars. 3–10)

Stephen King, "Why We Crave Horror Movies," 378

Claudia Wallis, "The Multitasking Generation," 385

Shankar Vedantam, "The Telescope Effect," 400

Nicholas Carr, "Is Google Making Us Stupid?," 408

Sheila McClain, "Fitness Culture: A Growing Trend in America," 418

David Bornstein, "Fighting Bullying with Babies," 447

William F. Shughart II, "Why Not a Football Degree?," 459 (pars. 2, 13–14)

Kelly D. Brownell and Thomas R. Frieden, "Ounces of Prevention — The Public Policy Case for Taxes on Sugared Beverages," 466

Patrick O'Malley, "More Testing, More Learning," 483 (pars. 4–6)

Sarah Kate Kramer, "Niche Market: Fountain Pen Hospital" e (ch. 3, par. 2)

Wendy Lee, "Peeling Bananas" e (ch. 4, pars. 4, 6, 8)

Francine Wheeler, "Sandy Hook Victim's Mother Delivers President Obama's Weekly Radio Address, April 13, 2013" e (ch. 4)

Linda Stone, "Continuous Partial Attention" e (ch. 5)

Tan-Li Hsu, "High on Caffeine: Regulating Energy Drinks" e (ch. 7)

Ad Council/Dept. of Transportation, "The 'It's Only Another Beer' Black and Tan" e (ch. 7)

Michele Cox, "The Truth about Lying" e (ch. 8)

On the Media, "The Reel Sounds of Violence" e (ch. 8)

Phoebe Sweet and Zach Wise, "The Problem with Lawns: The Transforming Landscape of Las Vegas" e (ch. 9)

Comparison and Contrast

Saira Shah, "Longing to Belong," 37 (pars. 2, 5, 10)

The *New Yorker*, "Soup," 71 (par. 2)

John T. Edge, "I'm Not Leaving Until I Eat This Thing," 80 (par. 5)

Peggy Orenstein, "The Daily Grind: Lessons in the Hidden Curriculum," 96 (pars. 9, 19–20)

Brian Cable, "The Last Stop," 104 (par. 3)

Brent Staples, "From *Parallel Time*," 140 (pars. 3, 6)

Dan Zevin, "Father Shops Best," 149

Dana Jennings, "Our Scars Tell the Stories of Our Lives," 143

Susan Cain, "Shyness: Evolutionary Tactic?," 181 (pars. 1–3, 14–15, 18–19)

Beth L. Bailey, "Dating," 201

Linh Kieu Ngo, "Cannibalism: It Still Exists," 223 (par. 8)

Amitai Etzioni, "Working at McDonald's," 249 (pars. 4–7, 17, 18)

Malcolm Gladwell, "What College Rankings Really Tell Us," 260

Brian Greene, "Put a Little Science in Your Life," 315 (par. 11)

Daniel J. Solove, "Why Privacy Matters Even If You Have 'Nothing to Hide,'" 341 (pars. 6–10)

Stephen King, "Why We Crave Horror Movies," 378 (pars. 3, 4, 6, 12)

Claudia Wallis, "The Multitasking Generation," 385 (pars. 16, 20)

Nicholas Carr, "Is Google Making Us Stupid?," 408 (pars. 8–9, 11–12, 22)

William F. Shughart II, "Why Not a Football Degree?," 459 (pars. 4–5)

Karen Kornbluh, "Win-Win Flexibility," 474 (par. 7)

Shannon Lewis, "We Were Here" e (ch. 2)

Kate Beaton, "Treasure" e (ch. 2)

Justin Ton, "Hip-Hop You Don't Stop" e (ch. 5, par. 7)

Marlon Bishop, "Gig Alert: Bright Eyes" e (ch. 6)

Tan-Li Hsu, "High on Caffeine: Regulating Energy Drinks" e (ch. 7, pars. 4–5)

On the Media, "The Reel Sounds of Violence" e (ch. 8)

Phoebe Sweet and Zach Wise, "The Problem with Lawns: The Transforming Landscape of Las Vegas" e (ch. 9)

Definition

Annie Dillard, "An American Childhood," 22 (pars. 1, 6)

John T. Edge, "I'm Not Leaving Until I Eat This Thing," 80 (par. 5)

Dana Jennings, "Our Scars Tell the Stories of Our Lives," 143 (par. 8)

Rob Walker, "Replacement Therapy," 156

Susan Cain, "Shyness: Evolutionary Tactic?," 181

Deborah Tannen, "Marked Women," 192 (par. 9)

Beth L. Bailey, "Dating," 201 (pars. 1, 5, 6)

Dan Hurley, "Can You Make Yourself Smarter?," 212

Linh Kieu Ngo, "Cannibalism: It Still Exists," 223 (pars. 5, 6)

Malcolm Gladwell, "What College Rankings Really Tell Us," 260 (par. 2)

Christine Rosen, "The Myth of Multitasking," 270 (pars. 2, 7, 8)

Claudia Wallis, "The Multitasking Generation," 385 (par. 21)

Justin Ton, "Hip-Hop You Don't Stop" e (ch. 5, pars. 3, 7, 8)

Linda Stone, "Continuous Partial Attention" e (ch. 5)

Tan-Li Hsu, "High on Caffeine: Regulating Energy Drinks" e (ch. 7, par. 3)

Description

Annie Dillard, "An American Childhood," 22 (par. 16)

Tom Ruprecht, "In Too Deep," 32 (pars. 6–7)

Jenée Desmond-Harris, "Tupac and My Non-Thug Life," 42

Brad Benioff, "Rick," 49

The New Yorker, "Soup," 71

John T. Edge, "I'm Not Leaving Until I Eat This Thing," 80 (pars. 3–12)

Gabriel Thompson, "A Gringo in the Lettuce Fields," 89

Peggy Orenstein, "The Daily Grind: Lessons in the Hidden Curriculum," 96 (pars. 1–2, 9)

Brian Cable, "The Last Stop," 104 (pars. 2–4, 5, 15)

Brent Staples, "Black Men and Public Space," 132 (pars. 1, 3, 5)

---, "From Parallel Time," 140 (pars. 1, 4–5, 7, 9)

Dana Jennings, "Our Scars Tell the Stories of Our Lives," 143

Rob Walker, "Replacement Therapy," 156 (par. 1)

Deborah Tannen, "Marked Women," 192 (pars. 1–7)

Shannon Lewis, "We Were Here" e (ch. 2)

Kate Beaton, "Treasure" e (ch. 2)

Brianne O'Leary, "Fatty's Custom Tattooz and Body Piercing" e (ch. 3)

Sarah Kate Kramer, "Niche Market: Fountain Pen Hospital" e (ch. 3)

Brittany Lemus, "Requiem for a Dream: Fantasy versus Reality" e (ch. 6)

Division and Classification

Jenée Desmond-Harris, "Tupac and My Non-Thug Life," 42 (par. 10)

Dana Jennings, "Our Scars Tell the Stories of Our Lives," 143 (pars. 2, 7)

Susan Cain, "Shyness: Evolutionary Tactic?," 181

Linh Kieu Ngo, "Cannibalism: It Still Exists," 223 (pars. 6–14)

William Akana, "Scott Pilgrim vs. the World: A Hell of a Ride," 279

Brianne O'Leary, "Fatty's Custom Tattooz and Body Piercing" e (ch. 3, pars. 4, 9)

Michele Cox, "The Truth about Lying" e (ch. 8, pars. 2–6)

Example

The New Yorker, "Soup," 71 (par. 6)

Gabriel Thompson, "A Gringo in the Lettuce Fields," 89

Brent Staples, "Black Men and Public Space," 132 (pars. 1, 8, 9, 10)

Dana Jennings, "Our Scars Tell the Stories of Our Lives," 143

Rob Walker, "Replacement Therapy," 156 (pars. 2, 5–6)

Katherine Haines, "Whose Body Is This?," 161 (pars. 6–10)

Susan Cain, "Shyness: Evolutionary Tactic?," 181 (pars. 11–14, 20–21, 23)

Deborah Tannen, "Marked Women," 192

Dan Hurley, "Can You Make Yourself Smarter?," 212 (pars. 16–19)

Linh Kieu Ngo, "Cannibalism: It Still Exists," 223 (par. 7)

Malcolm Gladwell, "What College Rankings Really Tell Us," 260 (pars. 1, 3–4)

Christine Rosen, "The Myth of Multitasking," 270 (pars. 3–6, 13)

William Akana, "Scott Pilgrim vs. the World: A Hell of a Ride," 279 (pars. 3–8)

Christine Romano, "Jessica Statsky's 'Children Need to Play, Not Compete': An Evaluation," 287 (pars. 4–9)

Brian Greene, "Put a Little Science in Your Life," 315 (pars. 4–5, 8, 12–13)

Sherry Turkle, "The Flight from Conversation," 334 (pars. 2, 5–7, 18)

Daniel J. Solove, "Why Privacy Matters Even If You Have 'Nothing to Hide'" 341 (pars. 2, 5, 11–14)

Jessica Statsky, "Children Need to Play, Not Compete," 349 (par. 8)

Claudia Wallis, "The Multitasking Generation," 385 (pars. 1–9)

Nicholas Carr, "Is Google Making Us Stupid?," 408 (pars. 5–6, 13–14)

David Bornstein, "Fighting Bullying with Babies," 447 (pars. 2, 4)

William F. Shughart II, "Why Not a Football Degree?," 459 (par. 1)

Brianne O'Leary, "Fatty's Custom Tattooz and Body Piercing" [e] (ch. 3, pars. 4, 6)

Sarah Kate Kramer, "Niche Market: Fountain Pen Hospital" [e] (ch. 3)

Wendy Lee, "Peeling Bananas" [e] (ch. 4, par. 3)

Justin Ton, "Hip-Hop You Don't Stop" [e] (ch. 5, pars. 4–6, 9)

Linda Stone, "Continuous Partial Attention" [e] (ch. 5)

Brittany Lemus, "*Requiem for a Dream*: Fantasy versus Reality" [e] (ch. 6, pars. 2–6)

Marlon Bishop, "Gig Alert: Bright Eyes" [e] (ch. 6)

Tan-Li Hsu, "High on Caffeine: Regulating Energy Drinks" [e] (ch. 7, pars. 3, 5)

Michele Cox, "The Truth about Lying" [e] (ch. 8, pars. 2–4, 6)

On the Media, "The Reel Sounds of Violence" [e] (ch. 8)

Molly Coleman, "Missing the Fun" [e] (ch. 9, pars. 1, 6)

Phoebe Sweet and Zach Wise, "The Problem with Lawns: The Transforming Landscape of Las Vegas" [e] (ch. 9)

Narration

Annie Dillard, "An American Childhood," 22

Tom Ruprecht, "In Too Deep," 32

Saira Shah, "Longing to Belong," 37

Jenée Desmond-Harris, "Tupac and My Non-Thug Life," 42

Brad Benioff, "Rick," 49 (pars. 8–20)

The *New Yorker*, "Soup," 71 (pars. 7–11)

John T. Edge, "I'm Not Leaving Until I Eat This Thing," 80 (pars. 1, 2, 13–19)

Gabriel Thompson, "A Gringo in the Lettuce Fields," 89

Peggy Orenstein, "The Daily Grind: Lessons in the Hidden Curriculum," 96

Brian Cable, "The Last Stop," 104

Brent Staples, "Black Men and Public Space," 132

---, "From *Parallel Time*," 140

Dan Zevin, "Father Shops Best," 149

Katherine Haines, "Whose Body Is This?," 161 (pars. 1–4, 8, 10, 14–16)

Susan Cain, "Shyness: Evolutionary Tactic?," 181 (pars. 1, 14–15)

Dan Hurley, "Can You Make Yourself Smarter?," 212 (pars. 1–3)

Linh Kieu Ngo, "Cannibalism: It Still Exists," 223 (pars. 1–3)

Shankar Vedantam, "The Telescope Effect," 400 (pars. 1–5)

Shannon Lewis, "We Were Here" [e] (ch. 2)

Brianne O'Leary, "Fatty's Custom Tattooz and Body Piercing" [e] (ch. 3)

Kate Beaton, "Treasure" [e] (ch. 2)

Wendy Lee, "Peeling Bananas" [e] (ch. 4, pars. 7, 8)

Francine Wheeler, "Sandy Hook Victim's Mother Delivers President Obama's Weekly Radio Address, April 13, 2013" [e] (ch. 4)

Ad Council/Dept. of Transportation, "The 'It's Only Another Beer' Black and Tan" [e] (ch. 7)

Molly Coleman, "Missing the Fun" [e] (ch. 9, pars. 1, 6)

Process

Gabriel Thompson, "A Gringo in the Lettuce Fields," 89

Brian Cable, "The Last Stop," 104 (par. 6)

Dan Zevin, "Father Shops Best," 149

Susan Cain, "Shyness: Evolutionary Tactic?," 181 (par. 8)

Dan Hurley, "Can You Make Yourself Smarter?," 212 (pars. 12–13)

Malcolm Gladwell, "What College Rankings Really Tell Us," 260

Nicholas Carr, "Is Google Making Us Stupid?," 408 (par. 16)

David Bornstein, "Fighting Bullying with Babies," 447 (par. 5)

Karen Kornbluh, "Win-Win Flexibility," 474 (pars. 16–22)

On the Media, "The Reel Sounds of Violence" [e] (ch. 8)

Molly Coleman, "Missing the Fun" [e] (ch. 9, par. 9)

Phoebe Sweet and Zach Wise, "The Problem with Lawns: The Transforming Landscape of Las Vegas" [e] (ch. 9)

Index of Authors, Titles, and Terms

Entries followed by an ⓔ symbol may be found online at **bedfordstmartins.com/readingcritically**.

ABC test, 530
absolute phrases, 123
abstract, 562
academic conversation, 2–3
academic habits of mind, 1–13
    critical analysis/civility, 2, 9–13
    curiosity, 1, 3–8
    rhetorical sensitivity, 1, 8–9
Academic OneFile, 300, 363, 430, 495, 550
Academic Search Complete, 300, 363, 430, 496, 550
action verbs, 27–28, 57, 168–69
adages, 154
additional points, transitional words and phrases
    for, 293
ad hominem/ad personam attack, 534
adverbs, conjunctive, 373
advertisements, MLA citation, 594
afterword
    APA citation, 604
    MLA citation, 589
Akana, William, "*Scott Pilgrim vs. the World*: A Hell
    of a Ride," 279–83
alternative views
    of reader, anticipating/responding to, 383,
        434–35, 439, 441, 455, 472, 496–97, 502–4
    writers' response to. *See* concession; refutation
AltPress Watch, 550
American Psychological Association (APA) style.
        See APA style
analogies
    in concept explanation, 220
    for logical relationships, 531–32
    to support evidence, 323, 339

"An American Childhood" (Dillard), 22–26
anecdotes
    to present problem, 493–94
    in reflection, 154
    to support evidence, 256, 322, 339, 531
annotated bibliography, 546–47
annotating, 507, 508–14
    forms of, 508, 514
    and inventory taking, 515
    "Letter from Birmingham Jail" (King),
        509–14
anthology
    APA citation, 604
    MLA citation, 584, 588–89
APA style, 545, 570, 599–608
    annotated bibliography, 547
    block quotations, 577
    directory, 599, 601–2
    references list, 601–8
    in-text citations, 599–601
appeals, 323
appositives, 238–39, 244
appropriateness, testing for, 530–31
arguments. *See* evaluation; position arguments;
        speculative arguments
    logic of, testing for, 424, 508, 530–32
articles in periodicals
    APA citation, 604–6
    finding, 550
    MLA citation, 591–93
    in trade publications, 566
artworks, MLA citation, 595
assumptions, 3, 5–6, 101

audience and purpose
 analysis of readers, 232, 428–29, 494
 engaging readers, 139, 190, 237–38, 241, 244
authoritarian writer, 384
authoritative writer, 384
authority. *See also* credibility of writer
 to support evidence, 532
authors
 APA citation, 600–604
 MLA citation, 582–83, 587–88
autobiography, 20–67
 effective, elements of, 54
 genre, thinking about, 21–22
 guide to reading: comparing and contrasting
  readings, 41; dominant impression, 29, 31,
  40–41; dramatic arc, 27–28; intensifying
  strategies, 27–28, 35–36; people, presenting,
  30, 40–41, 53–54; places, describing, 29;
  significance, conveying, 31, 47, 55; visuals, 48
 guide to writing: critical reading of draft, 62–63;
  dominant impression, 59, 62; draft, troubleshooting, 64–65; dramatic arc, 56–57, 62, 64;
  editing and proofreading, 66; people and
  places, describing, 57–58, 64–65; revising,
  63–66; sentence strategies, 61; significance,
  conveying, 59–60, 63, 65; subject, choosing,
  55–56; visuals, using, 58; working thesis, 59–60
 readings: "An American Childhood" (Dillard),
  22–26; "Longing to Belong" (Shah), 37–39;
  "Rick" (Benioff), 49–51; "In Too Deep"
  (Ruprecht), 32–34; "Tupac and My
  Non-Thug Life" (Desmond-Harris), 42–45
 rhetorical situations for, 20–22

backstory, 56–57
backward planning, 114
Bailey, Beth L., "Dating," 201–9
bandwagon appeal, 534
Beaton, Kate, "Treasure" e
Bedford Bibliographer, 545
begging the question, 535
beliefs. *See* values and beliefs
believability, testing for, 531–32
Benioff, Brad, "Rick," 49–51
bibliography
 annotated, 546–47
 working, 544–46
bibliography software, 545
Bishop, Marlon, "Gig Alert: Bright Eyes" e
"Black Men and Public Space" (Staples), 132–35
block quotations, 577, 581
blogs
 APA citation, 607
 MLA citation, 597
 as reading source, 553

bookmarks, Internet sites, 233, 363, 431,
  496
books
 APA citation, 600–604
 library, finding, 549–50
 MLA citation, 582–85, 587–90, 597
Bornstein, David, "Fighting Bullying with Babies,"
  447–52
"Boys Here, Girls There: Sure, If Equality's the
  Goal" (Stabiner), 325–30
brackets, for insertions/changes in quotations,
  574–75
brainstorming, 15, 300
Britannica Online, 543
Brownell, Kelly D., "Ounces of Prevention — The
  Public Policy Case for Taxes on Sugared
  Beverages," 466–71
bulleted lists, 122, 293

Cable, Brian, "Last Stop, The," 104–9
Cain, Susan, "Shyness: Evolutionary Tactic?,"
  181–86
"Cannibalism: It Still Exists" (Ngo), 223–26
"Can You Make Yourself Smarter?" (Hurley),
  212–19
Carr, Nicholas, "Is Google Making Us Stupid?,"
  408–15
cartoons, MLA citation, 594
cause and effect, 3
 causes, types of, 429
 effect, consequences, 430
 as explanatory strategy, 235
 speculating about. *See* speculative arguments
 transitional words and phrases for, 293
charts, MLA citation, 594
checklist questions, 559
"Children Need to Play, Not Compete" (Statsky),
  349–54
chronological order
 in sentences, 383
 signal phrases for, 76, 159
circular reasoning, 535
civility, 2, 14
 developing, 9–13
classification, 235
clauses, essential and nonessential, 244
climax, in dramatic arc, 27–28, 57
closed questions, 557–58
coherence, strategies for, 138, 159, 173, 175
Coleman, Molly, "Missing the Fun" e
Columbia Encyclopedia, 543
commas, with quotations/quotation marks, 116,
  575
common ground, finding, 17, 365, 370, 426, 439,
  442, 538